FORSYTHIA

OTHER BOOKS BY PETER LONGLEY

Two Thousand Years Later
Love is Where Your Rosemary Grows
Legacy of a Star
A Star's Legacy
Beyond the Olive Grove
The Mist of God

Information on these novels can be found at
www.PeterLongleyBooks.com

FORSYTHIA

A Memoir of Lost Generations

PETER HOVENDEN LONGLEY

iUniverse, Inc.
Bloomington

FORSYTHIA
A Memoir of Lost Generations

I would like to express my gratitude and thanks to Christopher Sinclair-Stevenson, the agent for the estate of John Galsworthy for his personal permission to precis and reproduce chapters and contents from the text of *The Forsyte Saga* without which this work would make no sense.

iUniverse books may be ordered through booksellers or by contacting:

iUniverse
1663 Liberty Drive
Bloomington, IN 47403
www.iuniverse.com
1-800-Authors (1-800-288-4677)

ISBN: 978-1-4759-3352-9 (sc)
ISBN: 978-1-4759-3353-6 (e)
ISBN: 978-1-4759-3354-3 (dj)

Library of Congress Control Number: 2012942094

Printed in the United States of America

iUniverse rev. date: 1/14/2013

Dedicated to my parents,
my grandparents and my great-grandparents
of
the Longley, Hovenden,
Collings and Cuthbertson families

Four generations of the Longley family in 1942

My great-grandfather, Oliver Longley
My grandfather, Charles William Longley
My sister, Diane Patricia Longley
My father, Charles William Hovenden Longley

My father carried this photograph in his wallet from 1942 until he
died in 2008

PREFACE

Charles Dickens was one of those great reformers who defined his times with such vitality and eloquence that his reforming zeal became almost second to his masterful storytelling. He wrote for, and about, a great new class of society that dominated Victorian and Edwardian England, and although declining, flew its flag over English society during the 1920s and '30s, refusing to die until the Suez crisis of 1956 spelled the end of its sustaining force—The British Empire. Dickens undoubtedly did his best to awaken the conscience of Victorian England. His readers were this burgeoning, upper-middle class, who were reaping the rewards of running *'the Empire on which the sun never sets.'* Many of the reforms that he wanted to initiate in the society of his times were encouraged through the mouthpiece of his novels. *The Eminent Victorians,* to borrow from Lytton Strachey, did create a fairer and more just world, and they believed it their Christian and moral duty to take those reforms paternalistically around the world through the benign British Empire. That Charles Dickens himself meant his characters to give a true message of social reform in a fast moving world is indisputable, but whether his readership were ready to enact his vision is questionable. They lined their libraries with his works, and loved the eccentricities of his characters. They recognized themselves in his pages, but they fell under the spell of his descriptive genius more than his message. Like Dickens himself, they were self-made, having risen through the ranks of Victorian respectability from more humble beginnings. And so, we come to the Forsytes.

Shortly after the Suez Crisis, the BBC produced a long episodical radio version of John Galsworthy's *The Forsyte Saga.* We sat around the wireless every week to listen to the gripping story of an English family struggling with its times; the story of Soames, 'Young Jolyon', Jon and Fleur, and the wronged Irene. We saw the ghosts of our own great-aunts in Hester, Juley and Ann, and our great-grandparents in 'Old Jolyon', Uncle Timothy and the robust Uncle Swithin. And, didn't we all have an Aunt Emily? Emily was the wife of James, that stalwart founder of the family firm, Forsyte, Bustard and Forsyte. She tended to be a hypochondriac, often feeling poorly for no real reason. She reminded me of my great-aunts, Nellie and Allie, who were often poorly. 'Old Jolyon' Forsyte was a tea merchant, dealing in one of the most important commodities of the British Empire. Nicholas was in mines, property, and railways, the lifelines of the Empire. Timothy was a publisher, but played the burgeoning stock market that Galsworthy alludes to as "in Consols." These were men of property—the movers and shakers of that imperial world. They lived in grand houses, rode in fine carriages, but also had their rakish family members like 'Young Jolyon', Soames' cousin; Montague Dartie, Soames' brother-in-law; and their cousin, George Forsyte. I have always remembered an opening line, not actually found in Galsworthy's novels but heard when I was a child listening to the wireless after supper with my mother and father and my older sister—"Forsytes all over London were dressing for dinner." Actually, Soames Forsyte reminds us before his death in 1926 in the continuation of the Forsyte chronicles, his family came from more humble beginnings. Soames made a pilgrimage, shortly before he died, to the Dorset coast where the family tree had begun. There, he looked up the tombstones of his ancestors.

His grandfather, Jolyon Forsyte, more commonly remembered as 'Superior Dosset' was according to his headstone born in 1770. He was a successful builder and craftsman, who had married the daughter of a country solicitor. They were of yeoman stock, that great British phenomenon that perhaps saved England from the excesses of a French-style revolution. Born just nineteen years before the French Revolution and six years before the rebellion in America, 'Superior Dosset' Forsyte was an example of the rising squirearchy. Many of the great families of Victorian and Edwardian England did not, just like the Forsytes, have their origins in the aristocracy. They had risen from yeomanry to squirearchy in the peaceful growth of English rural society.

Great Britain avoided a major political social revolution because a middle class of free, landed people had developed on her islands three hundred years earlier than in the continental European nations. This had in part occurred because of the machinations of the English Reformation. A century of dynastic squabbling in the fifteenth century, popularly known to students of English history as the Wars of the Roses, had temporarily been abated by the victory of Owen Tudor over his Yorkist cousin, King Richard III, at the Battle of Bosworth Field. Right there, at the battlefield in 1483, Owen Tudor was crowned King Henry VII and became the founder of the Tudor dynasty. His eldest son and heir, Prince Arthur, died as a teenager shortly after his political marriage to Catherine of Aragon, a daughter of the rising power of the throne of Spain. To protect this new Spanish alliance, King Henry VII agreed, on the fair knowledge that the political union of Catherine to Prince Arthur had never been consummated, to the alliance being secured through the marriage of Catherine to his second son, Prince Henry. An annulment of the first marriage was easily obtained from the pope, and with great ceremony Prince Henry was married to his former elder brother's young widow. In 1507, when Henry VII died, Prince Henry and Catherine of Aragon were proclaimed king and queen. They were young and healthy, and their children would assuredly create a line of succession for the Tudor dynasty that would bring settled times for England after the bitter century of the Wars of the Roses. Catherine, however, bore only stillborn children to the vigorous king, apart from one girl, the Princess Mary Tudor, and as the years passed King Henry VIII became obsessed with the need for a strong male heir to stop the return to fifteenth-century chaos. A religious Renaissance prince as he was, and well-educated and schooled in the Roman Catholic faith, Henry VIII felt that maybe his marriage to Catherine of Aragon was cursed. He had broken the biblical laws of Leviticus that stated a man could not take in marriage his brother's wife. He, therefore, sought to divorce Catherine of Aragon, believing that God had cursed him despite the papal annulment. His wishes may well have been granted but for the fact that Queen Catherine's nephew, King Charles V of Spain, by 1527, held the pope captive in the Papal States. Papal permission for an annulment of Henry VIII's marriage was necessary, but the pope, as prisoner of the mighty Hapsburg Emperor, Charles V, could hardly grant an annulment against Catherine of Aragon. His Holiness' hands were tied despite numerous attempts between 1527 and 1532 to negotiate a deal through the agency of Campeggio, Henry VIII's papal legate. During this time of endless balked proceedings, a young courtier was presented to the king—Ann Boleyn of Hever Castle in Kent. The Boleyns had ambitions. Ann's elder sister was already a lady-in-waiting of the court. The timing was perfect. Henry was attracted to Ann and saw the young courtier as a way out of his problem. If the pope could not dissolve his marriage to Catherine, then the king would do it himself through act of parliament. This, in turn, would of course put him in breach with Rome, but he would marry Ann Boleyn.

Was this simple need to divorce the real reason for the English Reformation? The Roman Catholic scholar Philip Hughes certainly put a convincing case that this was so in his *History of the English Reformation*. Through parliament, the king successfully divorced Catherine of Aragon, pensioning her off relatively comfortably, and then married the young courtier. Soon, Ann was pregnant. The nation waited for the necessary Tudor male heir. The king was disappointed when the awaited heir proved to be another girl, the Princess Elizabeth Tudor. Meanwhile, the king had created a scenario whereby England was ex-communicated by the pope, who was still a prisoner of the Spanish throne and Holy Roman Emperor. Queen Ann Boleyn came under treasonable suspicion in these times of uncertain papal allegiance and paid for it with her life. Henry VIII's third marriage, to Jane Seymour, then gave him his male heir, the future King Edward VI, but at the expense of the queen's own life in childbirth. Despite these serious and sad domestic setbacks, the problem of papal excommunication had to be resolved, and with political genius, step by step, King Henry VIII passed through parliament a series of acts that established England's own church, separate from Rome. In 1533, this left the king in possession of vast church lands—the holdings of numerous monasteries, friaries, priories and convents that had been held by the second estate. Seeing this land as a valuable asset, in 1536, through a further act of parliament, the king dissolved the religious orders and their monastic property. This gave the crown these vast properties that the king could both gift and sell to his supporters, which in turn would help to pay for an inevitable clash with the Spanish Catholic Hapsburg alliance.

The premier properties went to some of the most powerful feudal families, but much of the land went for rewards to lesser persons, who in turn then sold and let further property to those who had served them. The squirearchy was born. These yeomen of England were free farmers, leading merchants, legal representatives, and they often married into the now non-celibate clergy of a nationally independent church. The yeomanry created the patterns of the English countryside and its villages that are inherent in the landscape to this day. Their homes were comfortable, and by the late eighteenth century, even grand. They were the Bennett's of Jane Austen's *Pride and Prejudice,* not of the aristocracy, even somewhat looked down upon by the great landed families, as Jane Austen readily shows in the attitudes of Mr. Bingley's sisters and of such characters as Lady Catherine de Burgh, but they were the backbone of England, the class of society that made the village and its cottage industries work. It was this free society that led Naploeon Bonaparte to describe England as a "nation of shopkeepers."

In *The Forsyte Saga,* 'Superior Dosset' Forsyte's father, Jolyon Forsyte, was a yeoman farmer of Hays, near Dencombe in Dorset. One of his sons was the mayor of the provincial town of Bosport. Another, was an officer in the merchant navy. His other son, Edgar, manufactured jute. Half a century later, descendants of such families became the unshakable bastions of the British Empire—the investors, planters, industrialists, engineers, and administrators that made it all work. They never considered themselves members of the aristocracy, although they went to the same schools and at times married into a coat of arms. They came into their own on the cusp of the industrial revolution and spread their wings as caretakers of the British Empire. My family was such a family.

In the early1960s, Wolf Mankowitz, composer Cyril Ornadel and lyricist Leslie Bricusse, created a musical version of Charles Dickens' *The Pickwick Papers.* Harry Secombe, one of 'the Goons' from a zany British radio comedy, was cast as Samuel Pickwick. He was perfect in the part—a goon with an operatic voice. The hit song of the musical *Pickwick* when it played at London's West End was *If I ruled the World.* It summed up this elite British upper-middle class to perfection. Here are Wolf Mankowitz's own words:

> *When Harry Secombe suggested, on a West Indian beach,*
> *deep into a hot morning and after several bowls of punch,*
> *that the character of 'Pickwick' might fit him well, it was*
> *immediately obvious that, even in a bathing costume, he was*
> *right. Being Secombe, it was, of course, impossible to pre-*
> *vent Pickwick singing. So the idea of this musical was born.*
> *Afterwards, I went back to writing my novel. Experience in*
> *the tropics teaches one that ideas that occur after the third*

rum punch are to be discounted. But Harry returned to Mr. Delfont, who warmed to the idea even in the cold of a London winter, and materialized it by commissioning my friends Bricusse and Ornadel to write the score and myself to put together a book.

Samuel Pickwick himself was an accident. Dickens was commissioned to write a story to go with a set of pictures a publisher had already bought. But so successful was the character he created that every Christmas more copies of The Pickwick Papers sell than any book other than The Bible. For, in Pickwick, Dickens created an image of British eccentricity at its best, an image which England is loathe to lose even when it has lost the Empire that sustained its Pickwickian past.

What is the magic of the buffoonish Pickwick? He is the Chairman of a Club convened for the purpose of pursuing good-fellowship and the most meaningless of pseudo-scientific pursuits. Though a wealthy retired businessman apparently accompanied by prosperous comrades in his picturesque rambles, Pickwick and the Pickwickians are unworldly to an impossible extreme. Their immovable good nature makes them unrealistic. It also, I think has made them immortal.

This essentially Dickensian quality which Pickwick embodies was, in fact, an ideal of the British upper-middle class at its zenith when Dickens created his image. Its members saw themselves as hearty good fellows, drinking their bottle of port to a man, hunting the fox, enlightening and guiding the lower classes, and pursuing gentlemanly activities such as Pickwick's observation of the tittle-bats on Hampstead Heath. Pickwick's class, that of the wealthy tradesmen or professionals, who having made their fortunes now wished to cultivate better things, had no aristocratic leanings, although they were impressed by aristocracy. They had no intention of being confused with the vast working class, but they didn't regard its members as enemies.

The England of 'Pickwick' is still merry, living is cheap. Though there are many who can't afford it, the Empire is in the ascendant, and to be an Englishman is in itself a qualification. Its Christmasses will forever afterwards be revived annually on seasonal cards, with turkey's impossibly huge, beer dreadfully strong, and characters bigger than they have ever been since.

From Philips Original London Cast Recording of
"Pickwick"

Samuel Pickwick is reincarnated in many of Charles Dickens' most beloved characters. He is partly present in Mr. Brownlow of *Oliver Twist*, in Mr. Jarndyce of *Bleak House*, and even in the transformed Ebeneezer Scrooge of *A Christmas Carol*. These benefactors of the Dickensian world express the solidity, hope and aspirations of the eminent Victorians. Their success was related to their times. The Empire of exports had become the Empire of imports.

The early British Empire had primarily centered on the Americas. The colonies were developed by the disestablished—the dissenters, debtors, the religiously persecuted, and the merchant adventurers. They sought peace in a new world, relatively remote from the strictures of the mother country. Much of this changed, however, after the Seven Years War in the middle of the eighteenth century. The English victories over France in Canada and India heralded the start of a new form of Empire. And so its heroes, General James Wolfe of Quebec and Sir Robert Clive of Plassey in India, became the schoolboy heroes of three to four generations of colonial administrators.

A splendid group of buildings stands in the area of Fort St. George in Madras, India, today known as Chennai. Gracious black columns support classic porticoes glimpsed through deep-set gateways in the original ramparts where canons are still mounted guarding India's tallest flagstaff. This was the headquarters of the most powerful trading company that once governed large areas of the world—The Honorable British East India Company, more popularly known as "John's Company." Here, can be found the oldest church building east of Suez—St. Mary's. The church walls are adorned with plaques and medallions that rival those found in any English country church, telling of eighteenth and early nineteenth-century persons, who lived and died serving in the honorable company's ranks. In the late eighteenth century, among those who served in the militia for the company in Fort St. George was Colonel, the Honorable Arthur Wellesley, a younger brother of Lord Wellesley, who at that time was Governor-General and secured South India for the British. There, in Madras, the young Wellesley met a subordinate named William Light. The two became friends and when

xv

Arthur Wellesley was transferred from Madras to lead British forces out from the Torres Vedras in Portugal as the first major counter-attack in the land campaign against Napoleon Bonaparte, he took William Light with him as an intelligence officer. They served together in the successful liberation of the Iberian peninsula that drove the French from Spain. Arthur Wellesley was rewarded for his efforts and given the title the Duke of Wellington, while his friend William Light, fell into temporary historical obscurity.

Ironically, not far from Madras, lies the area of Pondicherry, which was originally a French foothold in South India. Only just three decades before Arthur Wellesley walked the streets of Fort St. George, the French had finally been defeated by the British under Sir Robert Clive during the Seven Years' War. It was these events that had assured the future of The Honorable East India Company in Madras. It was during this same conflict, too, that General James Wolfe in North America, defeated the French at Quebec. However, it was not until the defeat of Napoleon Bonaparte that we see the hegemony of Great Britain in Europe. Of course, it is well known that in the aftermath of Wolfe's great victory at Quebec, and during the securing of India, that Great Britain lost thirteen of her North American colonies to an internal independence movement. How ironic it is that the loss of this old Empire was in so many ways sustained by the growth of the new. As Wellesley defeated Napoleon in Spain, so Napoleon saw fit to relinquish France's interest in the Americas. There were still large French holdings along the Mississippi and its delta that pinned the fledgling United States from westward expansion. Napoleon's dream, however, was not colonial, but a vision for a "United Europe." To consolidate this dream, he engineered the Louisiana Purchase, filling needy coffers and giving up all French claims to the Mississippi trading posts. The fledgling United States was now poised to grow, but, it would take a civil war and two world wars for the United States to eclipse the enormous power of the new rising British Empire.

In 1805, at the famous battle of Trafalgar, under Admiral Lord Nelson, the British navy defeated the French and became masters of the seas for the next one hundred and fifty years. The lifelines of Empire were secured. And in 1814, Napoleon was defeated on land and imprisoned by the European allies on the island of Elba off the Italian coast, not too far from his birthplace of Corsica. However, "the little corporal", as the British liked to call Emperor Napoleon, escaped from Elba and returned to Paris where he gathered up his 'Grand Armee' once again. As the Duke of Wellington, in 1815, Arthur Wellesley led the European allies to final victory over Napoleon at Waterloo. This time, the allies under the leadership of Great Britain, took no chances—they exiled "the little corporal" to St. Helena, a God-forsaken British possession isolated in the vast ocean area of the South Atlantic. There, some five years later, Napoleon died. The world was now Great Britain's oyster.

History is full of surprises, however. The story of Arthur Wellesley and William Light does not end at Waterloo. In the aftermath of Captain Cook's latter eighteenth-century voyages in the South Pacific, far distant lands were assured British sovereignty rather than French. Among them was the landmass of Australia. With the loss of the American colonies, Australia seemed a good new choice for the export of misfits from the mother country. Australia was founded as New South Wales, and established as a penal colony. Most its earliest British exports were convicts, many sent to this harsh place the other side of the world for crimes from murder to as little as stealing a loaf of bread. The original penal colony was at Botany Bay near Sydney cove. The city of Sydney was built by convict labor. Later, the main penal prison was at Port Arthur in Tasmania, and remained so through much of the first half of the nineteenth century. Once again, Charles Dickens was well aware of the Australian scenario. One of his finest novels is *Great Expectations*, the melodramatic story of a convict sent out to Australia, who became the benefactor of young Mr. Pip. So, where do William Light and Arthur Wellesley fit into this story?

As the Duke of Wellington, along with the deceased Admiral Lord Nelson, Arthur Wellesley was the savior of England. He embarked on a career in politics and he became, as "The Iron Duke", England's prime minister under King William IV. Dickens' *Great Expectations* is set around this time. Some of the early convicts in Australia had by the 1830s made a success of the harsh land "down under." Magwitch, as a New South Wales sheep farmer, is Dickens' incarnation of this success. In 1833, slavery and the slave trade had been abolished throughout the British Empire, and the philosophy of paternalistic rulership in a free enterprise world, rich with raw materials, became the new watchword of Empire. It was deemed important, therefore, to establish a totally free city in Australia to promote these aims. The city was Adelaide, named after King William IV's queen.

As prime minister, it was the Duke of Wellington who commissioned his old friend William Light to design and found the city of Adelaide on Australia's southern shores. To this day, a statue of Willam Light on a small hill points to the center of the city he founded for free Australians.

One can assume, although it is never a part of Galsworthy's narrative, that most Forsytes would have been possessors of that eminent Victorian staple—a family Bible. When I look at my family's Bible, I feel a little like Soames Forsyte when he motored down to Dorset to see the graves of his forebears. Like Jolyon Forsyte, born back in 1741, my family were yeoman farmers. They lived for the most part in the county of Kent. The Hovendens owned a rambling sixteenth and seventeenth-century farmhouse near Cranbrook, named Hocker Edge, and the Longleys lived in a series of similar Kentish yeoman houses in 'the Weald.' Originally weavers and clothiers, by the late eighteenth century some of the Hovendens had established themselves as medical doctors, and the more successful branch had moved to London, settling in Holland Park. By the middle of the nineteenth century, the Longleys, too, had mostly moved to London and become engaged in the business of marketing game. The fate of younger sons, however, always interests me. Julius Longley made his way out to Australia in the 1870s, the time of the Ballarat gold rush just outside Melbourne. He died and was buried there, no doubt attempting to make his fortune as a free Australian. Younger Hovendens made passage to America and settled in Peoria, Illinois. The majority, however, became 'Forsytes'—lords of their own enterprises within the Empire.

Galsworthy's Forsytes arrived in London at just about the same time as the Hovendens and the Longleys. They established themselves in similar addresses to the Holland Park of the Hovendens. There was 'Old Jolyon' at Stanhope Gate. There was James in Park Lane. Swithin lived in Hyde Park Mansions. Roger was in Princes Gardens. Timothy and the aunts kept a house in the Bayswater Road. Nicholas' home was in Ladbroke Grove. At this point, it is probable that the Hovendens were closer to 'Forsythia' than the Longleys. For the most part, they all lived in the better areas of the West End, with its tree-filled, Regency squares. The Longleys lived in the suburbs, in Bickley and Beckenham, on the very rural outskirts of London, but which in the later period of 'Forsythia' became the more desirable. Did not Soames himself decide on building the house at Robin Hill, and himself moving even further out to Mapledurham on the banks of the upper Thames?

"Forsytes all over London were dressing for dinner," and so begun the next radio broadcast of the saga that fascinated the British public as they looked back in an immediate post-Suez world at themselves. A decade later, the series was filmed by the BBC in a brilliant color production, one of the first in a great series of BBC period pieces. The Forsytes came alive to a generation like my own, which had seen just the tail end of their era. Then again, in 2002, a new version of the saga was brought out on DVD by Acorn Media. 'Old Jolyon', 'Young Jolyon', uncles Timothy, Nicholas, Swithin, and the aunts, Ann, Hester and Juley; Soames, June, Bosinney and Irene; Winifred, Montague Dartie and George; and the tragic younger Forsytes, Jon, Fleur, Val and Holly, all came alive again, beckoning us back in tragedy and nostalgia to a world where Britain believed in her duty as the paternalistic caretaker of the *Empire on which the sun never sets.*

I was born during World War II. The Empire stood fully behind the mother country, whether as Ghurkas fighting the Japanese in Burma or the Australians and New Zealanders in the Italian Campaign, or the Canadians supplementing the Royal Air Force. We fought against Hitler and Hirohito for our very existence. With the aid of our original colonies, the powerful United States of America, we won. We defeated "the nasty little bastard with a black moustache." The war was over, we licked our wounds, lost India, queued up with our ration books, drank endless cups of tea, and for ten years pretended that 'Forsythia' was still our world. And so it was until 1956, when with little beyond diplomatic sabre rattling, we lost the lifeline of the Empire to President Abner Gammel Nasser of Egypt, and bowed to diplomatic pressure from the United States to back down from defending our interests. The British no longer had sovereignty over the Suez Canal. The Empire started to collapse and we handed our mantle of paternalistic caretaker to our former colonies—the United States of America. 'Forsytes' became a dying breed.

In a way they had been dying since the first rattles of imperial sabres shook the Empire. Val Darte and Jolly Forsyte signed up to fight the rebellious Boers in South Africa. Some historians have considered the Boer War to be the first sign of the Empire's demise. It ended pretty much a stalemate, and South Africa remained a segregated crown jewel of our Empire in Africa for many years yet to come. At that time, however, the events of those early years of the twentieth century at the tip of Africa affected the thinking of a young Indian barrister-at-law living in Durban in the Natal. He left South Africa for India and became known to the world as the man who silently brought the British Empire to its knees. He was Mahatma Ghandi. It was on the home front, however, that the heaviest early cracks opened. In 1916, after nearly a century of strife, the Irish successfully rebelled in Dublin, capturing key points of the city in a demand for independence. This was negotiated after a bloody civil war, and the Irish Free State was formed by treaty in 1924. Ironically, events leading up to this are chronicled in part by another great saga, Anthony Trollope's *The Palliser Novels,* which like *The Forsyte Saga* was brilliantly filmed in a BBC TV series in the 1970s. Britain retained the six counties of Northern Ireland, and through continued troubles, the shackles of Empire are still being played out there to this day.

In the immediate aftermath of World War II, most of the British Empire was still intact. The great Dominions of Canada, South Africa, Australia and New Zealand were proud of their contribution, and despite bitter religious strife between moslems and hindus, the Indian Army, largely commanded by British officers, was also proud to have served. District commissioners, judges, engineers, and diverse merchants, along with tea, coffee, and sugar planters, returned to their staples. Rubber planters tapped from their trees in Malaya, and a semblance of the pre-war benign empire was manifest. Even with the division and loss of India, the last Viceroy, Lord Mountbatten, was still in an advisory capacity, and many British families were assisting the new Indian nations of Pakistan, East Pakistan, now Bangladesh, and Burma, now Myanmar, to their feet. My own great-uncle, Bert Cuthbertson, continued to supervise coolies building dams and railroads in the sub-continent. Teachers, doctors and lawyers, engineers and agricultural specialists, still took the long sea passage either south to the Cape, or east through Suez to India and the Far East. The Union Jack still flew from flagpoles in almost every time zone of the world. So, like our fathers before us, we 'Forsytes' were sent to our segregated boarding schools to become the new generation of imperial administrators. In fact, despite the Boers, Ireland, and the loss of almost a generation of youth in the trenches of World War I, and despite the devastating flu epidemic of 1918, 'Forsythia' remained stronger than ever. German colonies in Africa became British after the Treaty of Versailles in 1919. The well-oiled machine of the Empire required more Gilbert and

Sullivan singing, Latin quoting, Shakespeare spouting, young cricketers from the 'Public Schools' of England to run its affairs through the changing times of the 1920s and '30s than ever before. Despite 'Old Jolyon' and uncles James' and Timothy's bemoaning of changing times on Queen Victoria's death in 1901, or Soames' pleasure at knowing that in 1920 at least the Eton versus Harrow cricket match still required top hats in the enclosures, 'Forsythia' lived on until the stand off at Suez. Neither the abdication of the King Emperor Edward VIII in 1936, nor Adolf Hitler's relentless bombs, shook the belief of the British people that theirs was the kingdom. Blindly, we believed that after a good cup of strong, Indian tea, and a game of croquet on the lawn, 'Forsythia' would go on forever.

In these pages, I am going to take the reader through a precis of John Galsworthy's *The Forsyte Saga*. Passages from the novels are in italics and it is strongly recommended that readers should make themselves familiar with John Galsworthy's famous saga before attempting to understand *Forsythia*. I apply these passages as to how we saw our world, in my childhood, the last generation of 'Forsytes', in those final rays of sunlight that filtered across the Empire on which we thought the sun would never set.

Peter Longley
January, 2012

"But, though the impingement of Beauty, and the claims of Freedom, on a possessive world, are the main prepositions of the Forsyte Saga, it cannot be absolved from the charge of embalming the upper-middle class. As the old Egyptians placed around their mummies the necessaries of a future existence, so I have endeavoured to lay beside the figures of Aunts Ann and Juley and Hester, of Timothy and Swithin, of old Jolyon and James; and of their sons, that which shall guarantee them a little life hereafter, a little balm in the hurried Gilead of a dissolving 'Progress.'

"If the upper-middle class, with other classes, is destined to 'move on' into amorphism, here, pickled in these pages, it lies under glass for strollers in the wide and ill-arranged museum of Letters to gaze at. Here it rests, preserved in its own juice: The Sense of Property."

John Galsworthy

BOOK ONE
THE MAN OF PROPERTY

PART ONE

CHAPTER ONE

'AT HOME' AT OLD JOLYON'S

It is 1887, and Forsytes are gathered together at 'Old Jolyon's' house in Stanhope Gate—a fashionable address in the West End. The occasion is to celebrate the engagement of his granddaughter, June, to a young architect with the almost comic name, Bosinney. Is this really a celebration or an inspection? Forsytes were pretty closed when it came to opening their hearts to a new family member.

In my own childhood, I remember well my father always quoting his grandmother, Minnie Longley, a proud and formidable woman, as saying that new family members were only an 'it' until they had proved themselves. "What does *it* think she is?" my father would say with a smirk, as he quoted his grandmother. In the same way, these Forsytes were inspecting young Bosinney.

First, Bosinney had no money, or very little. James Forsyte made this plain when he sidled up to his sister, Ann.

"I wonder at Jolyon's allowing this engagement. They tell me there's no chance of their getting married for years. This young Bosinney has got nothing. When Winifred married Dartie, I made him bring every penny into settlement—lucky thing, too—they'd ha' had nothing by this time!"

'Forsytes', because they attended the same educational establishments as the aristocracy and landed gentry, spoke 'the King's English' with much the same accent that led to the occasional deliberate stutter. We used to call it "speaking with marbles in our mouths."

In John Galsworthy's *Forsyte Saga*, James Forsyte and his son Soames, ran the family's financial affairs locked up in their firm of solicitors, Forsyte, Bustard and Forsyte. Soames' sister, Winifred, married Montague Dartie in 1879. The Forsyte's had gathered then, to assess the young man. Dartie, for in 'Forsythia' gentlemen entering into a family's ranks were usually only referred to by their last name until they had proved themselves, was a risk. He had no solid profession— was a man about town, rather too fond of the horses, or even the two-legged fillies, to have yet earned the right to his first name, Montague, but at least he was dressed the part. Yes, dress codes were important to 'Forsytes'. My father won over my exceptional maternal grandmother when courting my mother by dressing immaculately down to spats and carrying a cane.

Aunt Ann Forsyte, rarely spoke, but in response to her brother James, her facial expression said it all. She only had to look at her nephew, Soames, as James expressed his fears, to remind him of his own folly in allowing Irene into the family.

"Well," James said, standing back from her gaze. "I couldn't help Irene's having no money. Soames was in such a hurry; he got quite thin dancing attendance on her."

My paternal grandmother was a Hovenden, and all Hovendens had this same gift displayed here in the saga by Aunt Ann Forsyte. Granny Longley could express in one look the Hovenden glare, and a subject would be dropped with no further words spoken.

So Bosinney had no money, not terribly favorable to this family of property, but architects in general are dependent on their patrons. Bosinney had yet to prove himself as an architect. The Forsytes were used to June picking up "lame ducks." It was part of her struggle with the establishment of her day. And, yet, she herself, was from that establishment. She was a 'Forsyte'. She almost did it to spite her family. Her father, 'Young Jolyon', had run off with her Austrian governess, Helene Hilmer, leaving her to be brought up by her mother, Frances, a crusty old colonel's daughter. Some of the family probably thought her choices to run in her blood. Her father, cut off at least temporarily by the family, was himself an artist, and not a great painter at that, eking out a living with his young second wife in a less salubrious part of north London near St. John's Wood.

Whether it was to stress his profession or an expression of his relative poverty, Bosinney dressed somewhat casually for this fashionable gathering.

Aunt Hester remarked on this as she spread the gossip with Ann. Apparently, June had brought Bosinney to meet her and her sister Juley earlier at their house in the Bayswater Road.

"He came in a soft, grey hat—not even a new one—a dusty thing with a shapeless crown. So extraordinary my dear, so odd!"

Whether ashamed of his hat or not, Bosinney did not hand it to the butler, but sat it on a chair in the hall.

"I tried to shoo it off the chair," Hester whispered, *"I took it for a strange, disreputable cat—Tommy had such disgraceful friends! Can you imagine, I was disturbed when it did not move."*

And so the story spread around the room. Had Bossinney given a soft, grey hat to the butler this day? Where was his top hat? George Forsyte, Roger's son, who was the one Forsyte to team up with Winifred's rakish husband, Dartie, and who liked a flutter himself, on hearing Aunt Hester's story, grinned.

"The hat must have been worn as a practical joke! Very haughty," he said, *"the wild Buccaneer!"*

And so it was that this name for Bosinney was whispered around the room. Bosinney was a misfit, so they called him "The Buccaneer."

Generally in 'Forsythia' we had to pass muster. If the family did not approve of a forthcoming marriage or relationship, it would be expressed after the inspection. I remember sitting with my parents to watch a school play—*Judgement Day* in Big School at Tonbridge in 1957. I was thirteen, and my mother's sister, my Aunt Eileen, had just become engaged to a fellow officer in the Royal Air Force. He was a Squadron Leader, which still had some magic to us boys who had been brought up on the glamour of Battle of Britain aces and Barnes Wallace's bouncing bomb with 617 Squadron and the *Dam Busters*. That was all to his credit, but the inspection had not gone that well. Being at boarding school, I had not been present at the introduction, but my mother filled me in.

"He seems very nice," she said somewhat condescendingly, "but he supports a football team."

Now, that just wasn't cricket! 'Forsytes' didn't play football—soccer was the game of the lower classes! We played rugger and cricket! Uncle Jim was never to live this down. I heard this same story from both my maternal grandparents, too. It cut to the core of 'Forsythia' just as surely as Bosinney's felt hat. Aunt Eileen forever knew that she had married beneath herself, and Uncle Jim forever had a chip on his shoulder, because he was made to feel that he wasn't quite good enough for us. He resentfully expressed this more than once by describing my mother and Eileen as "being born with silver spoons in their mouths." However, like Bosinney, Jim was able to prove himself. Bosinney built an amazing house for the Forsytes at Robin Hill. Uncle Jim became a Wing Commander in the Royal Air Force, and when he retired, provided my aunt with a beautiful home. However, nobody would ever forget that he was a football fan! It just excluded him from the club.

The uneasiness of the Forsyte family has been justified by the simple mention of the hat. How impossible and wrong would it have been for any family, with regard for appearances which should ever characterize the great upper-middle class, to feel otherwise than uneasy.

And then, there was Irene Forsyte. Who was her mother, or was it her step-mother? Her father, Professor Heron, had died young—an educator. Well, that was acceptable, but it seems he had left his widow no money. It also transpired that his widow was actually Irene's step-mother and she and Irene really didn't get along. Her mother ran some sort of boarding house in Bournemouth on the south coast. Irene played the piano rather well. Soames had met them at a concert in the seaside town. Rumor had it that he had made some sort of settlement on Mrs. Heron so as to buy her respectability. However, this was rumor. As Soames' father Timothy always said:

"Nobody ever tells me anything."

Irene was very beautiful.

"Yes," said Roger Forsyte, as he walked with his brother Nicholas to the station after leaving the reception, *"she's a good-lookin' woman, that wife of Soames'. I'm told they don't get on."*

Roger Forsyte was in property. *His light grey eyes measured the street frontage of houses by the way, and now and then he would level his umbrella and take a 'lunar,' as he expressed it, of the varying heights. "She's a pretty woman,"* and he waved aside a crossing sweeper. *"How did he get hold of her? She must cost him a pretty penny in dress."*

"Ann tells me," replied Nicholas, *"he was half cracked about her. She refused him five times, James, he's nervous about it, I can see."*

"Ah!" said Roger again, "I'm sorry for James; he had trouble with Dartie." His pleasant color was heightened by exercise, he swung his umbrella to the level of his eye more frequently than ever.

When they reached the station, Roger asked:

"What class are you going? I go second."

"No second for me," said Nicholas, "you never know what you may catch."

I do not remember my great-grandfather, Oliver Longley. He died at The Breach, our family home in Cranbrook, when I was only eight months old. As children, my sisters and I used to refer to him as the "Great Ski." Ski was short for 'Popski', which is what my father's generation called my grandfather. In keeping with most 'Forsytes', however, they referred to my great-grandfather in the Latin, as "The Pater", and my great-grandmother, Minnie Longley, as "The Mater." Sometimes, this was affectionately abbreviated to "The Pate and the Mate." Whether 'Popski' was supposed to have some Tzarist connotation, referring to my grandfather as the head of the family, I don't know, but like Roger Forsyte, "Grandpop", as we called our grandfather, always carried a furled umbrella that he gesticulated with in just the same way as Roger Forsyte. In fact, in 'Forsythia' it was necessary to carry a furled umbrella at all times, regardless of weather conditions. The main purpose of an umbrella was to hail a cab. This, Grandpop always did with great gusto. He would walk from Smithfield Market where he was the senior director of our family firm. He would raise his umbrella in Holborn to hail a cab, be driven to Charing Cross station, from whence he traveled in a first-class compartment from London to Staplehurst, before driving home to The Breach.

The umbrella as a status symbol was part of our privileged world. At school, when we became Praeposters, one of our privileges at my school, Tonbridge, along with wearing a waistcoat, was to carry a furled umbrella. Grandpop took this further. At home at The Breach he often carried his father's gold-topped cane as he walked around his beloved acres, a cane which I am now privileged to possess. Umbrellas and walking canes, therefore, became known in my family, among us, the last generation of 'Forsythia', as "Ski sticks", abbreviated from my parents' generation's affectionate name for my grandfather.

First-class was also an interesting status symbol. Local suburban trains were comprised of individual compartments in those days, and were all one class. Forsytes didn't like to share their compartments, as Galsworthy shows much later in his saga. When we traveled as a family from Beckenham to London, we always had to travel in an empty compartment, *"as you never know what you may catch"* or worse still, enter a compartment where some foreigner might be seated, especially if they were of color.

On longer journeys, we did travel first-class, even Pullman class. One of my greatest childhood memories is taking the elaborate Pullman train, *The Thanet Belle,* from London to Birchington on the Kent coast for our annual summer seaside holiday. These trains were the ultimate in luxury—steam trains of course. We sat in comfortable armchairs and were served a five-course lunch on the finest silver and china, but most of all, I remember the 1920s-style lamps with their cochineal balls on each individual table.

Did we have misfits in our family, too—'Forsytes' that did not quite fit in? Well, apart from Uncle Jim, there were others. In my childhood, I always wondered why many in my family expressed some sort of sympathy for my grandfather's niece and secretary in the family firm. I always thought she was a lot of fun. She used to tell jokes and had a hearty laugh. Her name was Audrie, but as I grew up I learned of her story. She had met her 'Dartie', a coffee planter in Kenya named Lewis. He ran off and left her penniless with a beautiful daughter, my cousin Sally Ann, on whom for many years I had quite a crush. Aunt Audrie was my father's cousin, but the scandal of her failed marriage and other things as I learned later, somehow made her a second class member of the family, and Sally Ann Lewis, well she went on the stage. While she was a student at the fashionable Hyde Park School of Ballet, everything was fine. I remember a large family outing when we went to see Sally Lewis performing in the corps de ballet in *The Nutcracker* at the Festival Hall. However, when she made a full career of it—well! Oh, remember the words of Noel Coward, "Don't put your daughter on the stage, Mrs. Worthington." It was almost as if a member of the family had set herself up in the red light district!

And then, there were distant stories of my great-aunt, Emily. Alcohol they said. They always referred to her as "Aunt Golly." I don't know if that was because her sobriety was often in question, or whether it was a play on her married name, Emily Oliphant. Perhaps it was for this reason that one of the major charities to which Great-grandfather Longley always donated was The Temperance Society.

Chapter Two

Old Jolyon Goes to the Opera

'Superior Dosset' Forsyte was the first to move from Dorset to London. A successful builder and stonemason, he was among many who realized the capital to be gained as Regency London moved west from the city. Between Hyde Park and the Thames, Westminster and Chiswick, fields were fast gobbled up by hungry developers. 'Superior Dosset' was building the very houses that his sons and their sons would occupy over the next century as if they had always been there. 'Forsytes' were on the move, those members of the rural yeomanry, who saw their future gold in the imports and exports of the new Empire.

'*Superior Dosset' Forsyte* after he moved to London in the early nineteenth century, carried on building until he died. He *was buried in Highgate. He left over thirty thousand pounds between his ten children*—a sum that a few years earlier Jane Austen would have measured as quite a fortune, comparable to the Bingleys of *Pride and Prejudice*. The year of his death was 1850. The true Victorian age with its somber respectability had replaced the more rakish opportunism of the Regency. The new generation of Forsytes surrounded by their comfortable security were a little reticent about their origins. 'Old Jolyon' alluded to 'Superior Dosset,' if at all, as "a hard, thick sort of man; not much refinement about him." The second generation of Forsytes felt indeed that he was not greatly to their credit. The only aristocratic trait they could find in his character was a habit of drinking Madeira.

Aunt Hester, an authority on family history, described him thus to Soames:

> *"I don't recollect that he ever did anything; at least not in my time. He was er—an owner of houses, my dear. His hair about your Uncle Swithin's color; rather a square build. Tall? No-ot very tall. A fresh-colored man. I remember he used to drink Madeira; but ask your Aunt Ann. What was his father? He— er—had to do with the land down in Dorsetshire, by the sea."* Old Jolyon, in whom a desperate honesty welled up at times, would allude to his ancestors as: *"Yeomen—I suppose very small beer."* Yet he would repeat the word 'yeomen' as if it afforded him consolation.

My family spoke of their roots in the same way. Our ancestors were yeomen. The interpretation of yeoman among the British upper-class depends on one's origins. The old aristocratic families tend to look down on a yeoman, in their dictionary, describing a yeoman within the hierarchy of land as one class above a serf or yokel peasant. The upper-middle class, who were mostly originally of yeoman stock, describe a yeoman as an independent farmer at the least, and as one class below the landed gentry at best. Both definitions point to the same truth—from the time of the enclosure of monastic lands in Tudor England, there had grown up this body of independent landowners. Some became very prosperous through inter-marriage of their small estates, others became leading independent craftsmen. In time, they found their way into the professions, and by the early nineteenth century had risen to be the local squires of their domains.

A quirk of 'Forsythia' can be found in this latter interpretation. It became common practice, especially after the introduction of the penny postage in 1840, for members of this class to give themselves the title, 'Esquire'. On envelopes, in beautiful Victorian copper plate script, this was usually abbreviated to Esq. following a gentleman's name. Esquire, from Middle English, simply means out of the squirearchy— the sqirearchy being that generally recognized class just below, and sometimes of, the landed gentry. This practice was one of the differences that marked the upper-middle class from the lower-middle and working classes. The addition of Esq. on the addressed envelope acknowledged that the recipient was a gentleman. When I was sent away to boarding school in 1952, every Sunday we had to write letters home to our parents. We were supervised in a letter writing class to do this. We were not allowed to use a fountain pen, and certainly not a ballpoint. Letters had to be written with nib pens, the successors of quills, and dipped into inkwells, our writing efforts then to be dried with blotting paper. Sometimes, we got more ink on our fingers than we did on the page, but convenient pumice stones were provided in the washrooms to help remove the stains. My headmaster was most insistent that the addressed envelope to any male person must give that gentleman the title Esq. Misunderstanding his instructions, I wrote a letter to my grandmother addressing her as Mrs. C.W. Longley, Esq. I'm sure she would have been flattered, but the error was spotted in inspection and I was properly indoctrinated into the right use of 'Esquire'. Another interesting quirk of our class that my headmaster tried to perpetuate, but not with great success, was that we should, like our grandparents had before us, address our parents in Latin in our letters home as 'Dear Mater and Pater.'

Yeomen did not keep such obvious records of their lives as the aristocracy, however, and their origins are best traced in their tombstones throughout England's country churchyards rather than in the annals of history.

Most members of 'Forsythia', this burgeoning Victorian, upper-middle class, had only a weak knowledge of their earlier origins—the name of the village or market town, perhaps even a house such as the Hocker Edge and Borden homes of my Hovenden ancestors. They had, however, a pride in knowing that they were of yeoman stock. They were not peasants. Yes, 'Old Jolyon' Forsyte would repeat the word "yeoman" as if it afforded him consolation.

My great-grandfather, Charles William Hovenden, had no son, just three daughters. Catherine Amy married Grandpop Longley, and like many a 'Forsyte' wife, was marrying into the family firm. Oliver Longley, my great-grandfather, was the head of the firm, a series of firms in fact, dealing in purveyance of the finest wholesale meat, poultry and game in the City of London. All his sons were directors, either in E. Weatherley and Company, R.F. Potter and Company, or Campbell, Key and Longley. Weatherley, Potter, Campbell and Key had long disappeared like Scrooge's partner Marley in Dicken's *A Christmas Carol*, but their names remained on the elaborate stationary and the quaint red and green signs that swung from wrought iron brackets in the intricate tracery of the grand avenues of Smithfield Market. Among those who sent game, poultry, beef and lambs from rural England to the market, along with the Royal family, giving us potential 'By appointment' status, was a yeoman farmer from Essex, Will Goodchild.

Will Goodchild lived at Great Hornden Hall, and the Goodchild family were also set up in Smithfield Market. He and his brother George married my grandmother Longley's two older Hovenden sisters, Flo and Hetty. When Will Goodchild died just after World War II, his obituary made quite a splash in the local press. He was described as "the last true yeoman of England." East Hornden was a relatively small village in the prosperous wool country of East Anglia. Ever since land in the area had become Goodchild property it had been intensely farmed. "Uncle Will," as my father called him, was reputed to have used wool spun from his own sheep to tailor his suits. His brother, George, like him, lived in a very old rambling house on the edge of the village of Great Yeldham. Shortly before World War II while they were engaged, my father took my mother to stay with his Uncle George Goodchild and Aunt Hetty at Great Yeldham Hall. He was on a tour of East Anglian estates in order to persuade gamekeepers to send to the family firm. My mother described the visit in glowing terms as a "real encounter with 'merrie olde Englande'." Although there was electricity in the home, Great-uncle George used it sparingly as he had a fear of fire in the old yeoman house and electricity in his mind seemed less safe than candles. In the evening as soon as he could, he turned all the electricity off by a master switch situated beside his bed. From then on, oil lamps or candles that my mother found quite quaint were required to guide one to bedrooms or the bathroom. Tudor beams erupted at all angles, and the floors, in magnificent random width boards, sloped precariously. The antique furniture spanned from Jacobean to Edwardian. At both Great Yeldham Hall and East Hornden Hall much of the table fare was shot, fished or trapped on the properties. Life at both Goodchild homes in 1938 was much as it had been for four hundred years.

I am glad my mother had that experience, for so many of us in 'Forsythia', like *The Forsyte Saga's* Aunt Ann, brush aside our earlier origins. We became established heirs of the kingdom in the post industrial revolution's imperial world. Our family Bibles don't tell us much about what happened before 1800, and we must like first James Forsyte, and later his son, Soames, go back to our roots in the country to find out in the peaceful shadows of the yew trees, long grass and wild flowers of those ancient village churchyards, the truth read on those tombstones.

June Forsyte was rarely at home at 'Old Jolyon's' now she was engaged. 'Old Jolyon' felt very lonely in that great mansion that was witness to his success and pride, but deathly quiet in his older age. He sat at dinner alone. *His dinner tasted flat. His pint of champagne was dry and bitter stuff, not like the Veuve Cliquot of the old days.*

Over his cup of coffee, he bethought him that he would go to the opera. In the Times, *therefore—he had a distrust of other papers—he read the announcement,* below the court circular, *for the evening. It was 'Fidelio'.*

Mercifully not one of those new-fangled German pantomimes by that fellow Wagner.

As he looked out from the hansom cab on his way to the opera, he noted the changing streetscape. *'The hotels must be doing a tremendous business,' he thought. A few years ago there had been none of these big hotels. He made a satisfactory reflection on some property he had in the neighborhood. 'It must be going up by leaps and bounds! What traffic!'*

But from that, an obvious Forsyte observation, *he began indulging in one of those strange impersonal speculations, so uncharacteristic of a Forsyte, wherein lay, in part, the secret of his supremacy amongst them. What atoms men were, and what a lot of them! And what would become of them all.*

They had all done so well for themselves, these Forsytes, that they were all what is called "of a certain position." *They had shares in all sorts of things, not as yet—with the exception of Timothy—in Consols, for they had no dread in life like that of 3 per cent. for their money. They collected pictures, too, and were supporters of such charitable institutions as might be beneficial to their sick domestics. Originally, perhaps, members of some primitive sect, they were now in the natural course of things members of the Church of England, and caused their wives and children to attend with some regularity the more fashionable churches of the Metropolis. To have doubted their Christianity would have caused them both pain and surprise. Some of them paid for pews, thus expressing in the most practical form their sympathy with the teachings of Christ.*

My great-grandfather, Oliver Longley, paid for the family pew in Christ Church, Beckenham. The prayer books in the pew were stamped with his name, and yet, like most 'Forsytes' he was not a man of great religious belief. The eminent Victorians lived through interesting times. Their faith was challenged as their 'Pickwickian' collections of fossils and rocks, pointed the scholars of the age into a Biblical morass. Charles Darwin, himself perhaps the greatest of the eminent Victorians to challenge the religious status quo, lived in Down House just south of Beckenham. Oliver Longley, as a young man of property in this leafy suburb, was certainly aware of his proximity to the man who had turned religion upside down. 'Forsytes' observed and read these findings with a keen interest, but for propriety continued to pay necessary lipservice to the established church.

In this lipservice to religion, mourning was strictly adhered to in 'Forsythia'. Even in my childhood, we were taught to raise our schoolboy cap if we should pass a house where the curtains were drawn. Every Christmas morning, the whole Longley family assembled at Hillside, Oliver Longley's Victorian mansion in the fashionable Avenue adjacent to Beckenham Place Park on whose estate, the Cator Estate, much of Victorian and Edwardian Beckenham was built. From there, in a series of splendid automobiles, they would drive to Elmers End Cemetary to pay their respects to "dear Agnes." Minnie Agnes Longley had died in 1905 at the age of seventeen. She was a promising pianist and a student of Francesca Berger at the Guildhall School of Music in the City of London, but on the threshold, she was cut down by a burst appendix, and the resulting peritonitis took her young and promising life. Flowers would be laid at her grave every Christmas morning, while at the same time the fleet of servants at Hillside were busy preparing the Christmas feast for the returning mourners.

Francesca Berger had great hopes for Agnes, and it was always thought that she had the potential to be a well-recognized concert pianist—maybe even a Myra Hess. Sadly, she was cut off before the world would know, but Francesca Berger might have mentioned her to the composer Gustav Host, who was probably a frequent visitor to the Guildhall School of Music due to his own lifelong position as the Director of Music at St. Paul's City of London School for Girls. Somehow, probably through this connection, both Francesca Berger and Gustav Holst became good friends of my great-grandfather, Oliver Longley. Francesca Berger assisted my great-grandfather in purchasing a rather fine violin for my grandfather, who was also at this time considered quite a promising musician. Great-grandfather Oliver Longley saw himself as quite a connoisseur of the arts and his friendship with Gustav Holst continued over many years. Oliver Longley had a terrific ear for music and he and Gustav spent many hours critically listening to the phonograph. Hillside became quite a musical salon. There was a full concert grand in the drawing room, an upright grand piano in the study, and a further Steinway grand somewhere else in the house—the piano that eventually my father inherited. My grandmother, Catherine Amy, was always terrified of the place as Great-grandfather insisted on her playing at musical soirees, and although capable, she simply was not in the same league as the late Agnes. Grandpop was quite an accomplished violinist and there were times when the two of them, along with Agnes' sister Bernice, had to perform in front of Gustav Holst. These kind of musical soirees were not uncommon in 'Forsythia'. My maternal grandfather's family was also quite musical. My great-aunts, Babs and Nellie, both sang well, complimented by Grandpa Jack Collings, who played popular piano pieces superbly by ear, and Great-grandfather John Collings, who loved to entertain, was reputed to sometimes get them out of bed to perform for late night guests. My great-great-grandfather on my mother's side, Joseph Hubert, died while working with Sir Arthur Sullivan on the Gilbert and Sullivan operas. He was an assistant to Arthur Sullivan as a music copyist.

'Old Jolyon' Forsyte, however, considered the opera to not be what it was. In the early days of 'Forsythia' the Italians still reigned supreme, but the creeping German influence, especially of Wagner, signified change, and 'Forsytes' didn't like change.

Folding his opera hat, he sat down, drew out his lavender gloves in the old way, and took up his glasses for a long look round the house. Dropping them at last on his folded hat, he fixed his eyes on the curtain. More poignantly than ever he thought it was all over and done with him. Where were all the women, the pretty women, the house used to be so full of? Where was that old feeling in the heart as he waited for one of those great singers? Where that sensation of the intoxication of life and of his own power to enjoy it all?

The greatest opera-goer of his day! There was no opera now! That fellow Wagner had ruined everything; no melody left, nor any voices to sing it.

Little did 'Old Jolyon' know that in the twilight of 'Forsythia', when the Empire stood alone against Adolf Hitler, prophetically, the music of Wagner would indeed become the triumphal motivation of the enemy.

Yes, 'Old Jolyon' was lonely. And as *he sat watching the old scenes* beneath the elaborate presinium arch, *a numb feeling* gnawed *at his heart.*

Frail little June would be leaving his mausoleum of a house. His thoughts turned to his estranged son, 'Young Jolyon'. After June's mother Frances had died, and he had taken June into his own household, 'Young Jolyon' had made an honest woman of the governess—he married Helene Hilmer. Their first child had been born out of wedlock the year before. 'Old Jolyon' had heard they had named him Jolly. In 1881, two years later, as 'Young Jolyon's' legitimate second wife, Helene had given birth to a daughter. They had named her, Holly. With his granddaughter June about to give herself to this unproven architect—Bosinney—where did he get that name—'Old Jolyon' felt curiously drawn to know his other grandchildren.

After the opera, he hailed a cab and headed to the Hotch Potch Club. Back in 1880, he had sent his son a check for five hundred pounds, in the hope of thawing their estrangement now that at least 'Young Jolyon' had married the foreigner. The check had been returned with a letter addressed from the club.

My Dearest Father,
Your generous gift was welcome as a sign that you might think worse of me. I return it, but should you think fit to invest it for the benefit of the little chap who bears our Christian and, by courtesy, our surname, I shall be very glad.
I hope with all my heart that your health is as good as ever.
Your loving son, 'Jo'

'Old Jolyon' had replied:

My Dear Jo,
The sum of 500 pounds stands in my books for the benefit of your boy, under the name of Jolyon Forsyte, and will be duly credited with interest at 5 per cent. I hope that you are doing well. My health remains good at present.
With love, I am,

Your affectionate Father,
Jolyon Forsyte

And every year on the 1st of January he had added a hundred
and the interest. The sum was mounting up—next New Years Day it
would be fifteen hundred and odd pounds! And it is difficult to say how
much satisfaction he had got out of that yearly transaction. But the
correspondence had ended.

'Old Jolyon' reflected on the past as the hansom cab clip-clopped
its way toward the Hotch-Potch. He had given his son the best that
he could—an education at Eton and Cambridge. *Old Jolyon's feeling*
towards our public schools and 'Varsities never wavered, and he
retained touchingly his attitude of admiration and mistrust towards
a system appropriate to the highest in the land, of which he had not
himself been privileged to partake.

The great English 'public schools', which ironically mean private,
are responsible for the education of little more than three percent of the
population. 'Forsythia' represented this three percent. I was privileged,
as had been my father, his brothers, and my grandfather and his brothers,
to be educated at one of the finest—Tonbridge in Kent. There was a
further division, however, within this system, between the great 'public
schools', most of which were four to five hundred years old, and the minor
'public schools', most of which had been founded just to accommodate
this burgeoning three percent. Galsworthy never reveals exactly where
'Old Jolyon' went to school, but I do know that my mother's father was
always envious of the fact that I went to Tonbridge. He was educated at
Wilson's Grammar School, which although not considered in 'Forsythia'
to be one of the great 'public schools' was a well-known school in the
South London of his day. I am in possession of a number of school
prizes—beautifully bound Edwardian volumes of poetry and other
works—that had been awarded to my grandfather, Charles William
Longley, when he was at Tonbridge from 1902 to 1907. I also have
an equally impressive volume awarded to John William Collings, my
mother's father, presented to him by Wilson's Grammar School. The
minor 'public schools' were private schools and basically did give every
bit as good an education as the great 'public schools'. However, within
'Forsythia' there was just the slightest class division between the two,
and a probably higher entry rate to Oxford and Cambridge Universities
from the greats than from the minors. Grandpa Jack, never really

thought of Wilson's Grammar School as a 'public school', and like 'Old Jolyon', who probably also went to a minor 'public school', he had that dual *attitude of admiration and mistrust towards a system appropriate to the highest in the land, of which he had not himself been privileged to partake.*

Before one entered one's 'public school', we 'Forsytes' had to attend a preparatory school where we boarded for five years. Mine was on the south coast, at Seaford in Sussex—a school named Newlands. In the dining room at Newlands, there was a large framed print of Haileybury College, one of the great 'public schools'. The title caption rather mysteriously read 'Haileybury and The Imperial Service College.' As my education progressed, I came to understood this title better. Whether we attended the great 'public schools' like Eton and Harrow, Tonbridge and Winchester, or the minors, we were being educated for imperial service. We, in 'Forsythia', were the generations schooled to run the British Empire.

Leaving the cab, 'Old Jolyon' entered the club.

"Mr. Jolyon Forsyte still a member here?" he asked the hall porter.

"Yes, sir; in the Club now, sir. What name?"

No doubt furnishing a card for the silver tray, *"His father,"* he said.

The practice of presenting one's card to the porter, footman or butler, had all but disappeared in the twilight of 'Forsythia'. I do remember, however, the silver tray, an almost obligatory wedding present in 'Forsythia' marriages, that was displayed on a small table close to the front door of my grandmother Granny Mabs' house. It was silver plate from Mappin and Webb and over many years it had been polished so many times that part of the silver was wearing thin. I never saw it hold a card, but society dictated that it should be there by the front door. In fact, while I was at Tonbridge, we had a visiting Sunday preacher who was the curate at Christchurch in Beckenham. I attended a discussion group with him that same evening. He asked where we were all from, and when I said Beckenham, he asked my address.

"Park Langley," I said, for at that time we lived on Wickham Way, a prestigious street in that part of Beckenham.

Actually, my grandparents, two aunts and my cousins all lived on Wickham Way. It was a very gracious area developed as a private estate in the 1920s and really represented the last period of 'Forsythia' development in Beckenham.

The curate looked at me almost in disbelief.

"We don't go in that area often," he said. "At the houses on Wickham Way you are greeted by a butler with a silver tray."

Personally, I knew nobody in the 1950s living on Wickham Way who still had a butler, but my grandmother's card tray was ready.

The meeting of 'Old Jolyon' *and his son was terrible after all those years, for nothing in the world was so terrible as a scene. They met and crossed hands without a word. Then with a quaver in his voice, the father said:*

"How are you, my boy?"

The son answered:

"How are you, Dad? You look well."

"Middling," Old Jolyon answered.

Middling must be a 'Forsythia' word. I have never really known what it meant, but when a member of my family would be asked how they were, more often than not we would reply, "Fair to middling." My guess has always been that if we were middling, we were coping, but deep down there was something that was bothering us.

A lot bothered 'Old Jolyon', because his loneliness somehow made it hard for him to communicate with his son, whom he had ostracized for so long. Sometimes, it was like that between me and my father, whom I always loved dearly, but barely knew. It was our lot to be separated from our families at an early age, first in the nursery, and then away at boarding school.

Rather begrudgingly, 'Young Jolyon' agreed to go back to his father's house with him and at least learn news of his sister, June. But 'Old Jolyon's' reserve and pain was probably fostered further by the loneliness of the great house. *It was peculiarly vast and dreary, decorated with the enormous pictures of still life that* 'Young Jolyon' *remembered as a boy—sleeping dogs with their noses resting on bunches of carrots, together with onions and grapes lying side by side in mild surprise. But, under the influence of a cup of tea, which he seemed to stir indefinitely, he began to speak at last.*

Yes, my father always stirred his cup of tea incessantly, too. All his life he had a passion for tea. When he died we were reminded of that by my Uncle Dennis, his youngest brother, who in a tribute to my father's childhood told this story:

"Even as a child he could turn a tricky situation to his advantage. There was a story that, on one occasion, probably before the rest of us were on the scene, he had upset our mother, who had sent him to bed after lunch as a punishment for his misbehavior. At some stage of the afternoon he got fed up with this and rang the bell and when the maid appeared, asked her for tea and toast! Such was his charm that it was duly delivered to him. I don't suppose his mother could resist a smile at that."

In fact, tea was one of the last real requests of my father's long life. Hospitalized with pneumonia, my sisters and I had kept a long vigil at his bedside. Early in the morning, his breathing, even with his oxygen mask, became extremely faint. We expected his imminent death. Then, all of a sudden, refusing to die, he opened his eyes wide, made a 'T' with his fingers and uttered the one word: "Tea!" A few sips from a teaspoon and he lived another three days!

For the most part in 'Forsythia' we drank our tea with sugar and milk. It needed to be stirred. It was strong, Indian tea, unless we were entertaining, when maybe we would weaken to taking tea with a lemon slice and no sugar or milk. Tea was drunk incessantly at home in my childhood. It was the most valuable commodity in our ration books in the post-war world of the 1940s and '50s. We were lucky because we kept chickens in our garden at home. We were often able to swap eggs for extra tea rations. I, however, was a rebel in the family. I never liked tea. Grandmother Longley gave me the Hovenden glare when I refused to drink tea preferring an orange squash. Tea was a part of our lives, just as it had been a part of 'Old Jolyon's' life, the chairman of Forsyte and Treffrey, purveyors in tea.

Refreshed by tea, in 'Old Jolyon's' world, the thaw began in the long separation of father and son.

CHAPTER THREE

DINNER AT SWITHIN'S

*A*mong Forsytes the custom of solemnizing engagements by feasts was religiously observed. The engagement of June Forsyte to Philip Bosinney was no exception. *In Swithin's orange and light-blue dining-room, facing the Park, the round table was laid for twelve. A cut-glass chandelier filled with lighted candles hung like a giant stalactite above its centre, radiating over large gilt-framed mirrors, slabs of marble on the tops of side-tables, and heavy gold chairs with crewel worked seats.*

This dinner in honour of June's engagement had seemed a bore at first, but the labours of sending invitations and ordering the repast over, Swithin *felt pleasantly stimulated.*

He watched his valet screw the necks of three champagne bottles deeper into ice-pails. He checked on his wines sizing up how much he believed each member of the family would drink. None of them quite had the connoisseur's taste in wines that he believed he had. *Swithin had indeed an impatience of simplicity, a love of ormolu, which had always stamped him amongst his associates as a man of great, if somewhat luxurious taste.*

I sometimes saw Granny Longley in this same light. She always had the best of everything—sterling silver rather than plate, the most expensive china, draperies from Sandersons, an interesting taste in hats and outer garments, although somewhat less attractive taste in dress,

21

partly because of her rather large figure. However, in my humble opinion as a child, she had appalling taste in wallpaper. I also found it very sad when she remodeled the drawing room at The Breach ripping out an old Victorian marble fireplace and replacing it with a brick monstrosity that could only have looked good in a 1930s semi-detached suburban villa, and hardly suited the Regency character of the room. In reality, my other grandmother, Granny Mabs, had far better taste for far less cost. Her taste in most things won her the title from my sisters and myself of the 'Exceptional'.

Like Granny Longley, Swithin Forsyte had a greater opinion of his good taste than he always readily manifested. However, of all the guests coming to the engagement dinner, the one who fascinated him most was Soames' wife—the beautiful, almost whimsical, Irene. Thinking of her, *an expression like that of a cat who is just going to purr stole over his old face: Mrs. Soames!* In reality, however, it was his nephew Soames who really had the connoisseurs' taste among the Forsytes. He collected beauty—a good investment, and to him, Irene was his best investment—his property.

Aunt Juley was the first guest to arrive. *She had quite a reputation for saying the wrong thing, and tenacious like all her breed, she would hold to it when she had said it, and add to it another wrong thing, and so on.*

Granny Mabs, 'The Exceptional', had the same trait, and it seemed to be passed down to her daughters, my own mother and my Aunt Eileen. All three of them held tenaciously to their viewpoints, each adding further wrongs thinking that they would make a right. It would start almost every day when my grandparents would call in at our house, for they lived on the same street, on their way back from their morning visit to the local shops. A fierce discussion over shares would ensue in the kitchen, Granny Mabs and my mother never giving an inch to each other as a matter of principle, and it was even worse if my Aunt Eileen was present. Grandpa Jack, however, just hummed his way through the period of argument, tapping his feet in his musical drift, until eventually Granny would say, "I can't stand here all day arguing, I've got to get Jack his lunch," and off they would go as if no argument had taken place. It was a routine punctuated with "Oh Dorothy!"—"Oh Eileen!"—"Oh Mother!"

Aunt Juley, when she piled argument on argument in self-justification, just retired to talk to her pets. *She owned three canaries, the cat Tommy, and half a parrot—in common with her sister Hester; and these poor creatures unlike human beings, recognising that she could not help being blighted, attached themselves to her passionately.*

Most 'Forstyes' kept pets. My family always had cats, and my parents' generation always had dogs, too. But it is half a parrot that interests me. Parrots and cockatoos were fashionable in 'Forsythia'. Great-grandfather Oliver Longley had a parrot. My father can never remember Hillside without the parrot. They live forever! During the Second World War, the parrot mysteriously disappeared, and our intimacy with this parrot, which bird didn't appear to have a name, is found only in my father's recollections. The parrot lived in a large birdcage that was sometimes in the drawing room where as a young boy my father often played with a wooden train set. Periodically, the parrot over many years would start to make the noises of my young father pulling his train around the room: "Choo choo! Choo choo! Choo choo choo!"

When the parrot became unbearable it was moved for peace and quiet to the large black and white tiled kitchen. Kate, Great-grandmother's long time cook, used to hold court in the kitchen and laud it over the domestic staff in the 1920s and '30s. The full-time gardener, for Hillside was a suburban mansion with extensive formal plantings as well as vegetable and fruit gardens, used to come into the kitchen for his morning 'elevenses', a peculiarly 'Forsyte' mini-break mostly for domestics and served between breakfast and lunch. His name was Sewell, a name that has been passed down to my generation primarily through the parrot. Kate and Sewell had their ups and downs that the parrot with his beady eyes observed during their 'elevenses' spats. After the servants all left the kitchen to return to their duties, Kate was wont to cuss Sewell out. It was not long before the parrot was regularly repeating: "Sewell, the silly old fool."

The parrots of 'Forsythia' had been downsized by my generation, but I do believe in my childhood, every Longley household, including our own, kept budgerigars or parakeets. Today, many of these parakeets have literally flown the coop, as the world of 'Forsythia' has disappeared, and many escaped and bred in the wild. Now, they fly through London's parks giving a strange tropical feeling to the cool, dank climate!

"Mr. and Mrs. Nicholas Forsyte!" Swithin's valet announced.

Nicholas was obviously pleased with himself. *He had succeeded during the day in bringing to fruition a scheme for the employment of a tribe from upper India in the gold-mines of Ceylon. A pet plan, carried at last in the teeth of great difficulties—he was justly pleased. It would double the output of his mines, and as he had often forcibly argued, all experience tended to show that a man must die; and whether he died of a miserable old age in his own country, or prematurely of damp in the bottom of a foreign mine, was surely of little consequence, provided that by a change in his mode of life he benefited the British Empire.* Nicholas Forsyte was in property, mines and railroads—he worked the Empire from his offices in Town. *"For want of a few hundred of these fellows we haven't paid a dividend in years."* Now, it would all be different. The Empire of exports, through his negotiations, along with countless others, was to become the Empire of imports.

He was buoyant and confident and to add to his health he had just returned from a short seaside holiday. His brother Timothy still held to the spas for revitalization. Like the early 'Forsytes' he would take himself off to Bath, but Bath was less fashionable now. There were the new spas of 'Forsythia', like Harrogate, and even the revived Tunbridge Wells. In the Regency, too, the Prince of Wales had favored the seawaters of Brighton, establishing his extravagant pavilion there, and sea bathing and salt air gradually took over as the fountain of good health. *"I've tried Harrogate,"* Nicholas had said to Timothy at 'Old Jolyon's' reception for Bosinney. *"That's no good. What I want is sea air. There's nothing like Yarmouth. Now, when I go there I sleep."*

Yes, places like Yarmouth were becoming the summer holiday preference for 'Forsytes'. Yarmouth, itself had received publicity from Charles Dickens, where his young David Copperfield walked the sands. However, all around the coast, long, cast-iron pleasure piers were being built out over the water from once quaint fishing villages. Victorian pavilions provided entertainment at their extremities, and merchants sold enticing seafood, pies, and oysters for these city invaders. It was at just such a pier, in Bournemouth, that Soames Forsyte courted Irene, heavily chaperoned by the ambitious Mrs. Heron. Great-grandfather Oliver Longley often went to Margate on the Kent coast for his sea air. I have many old photographs of Great-grandfather walking with his business partner Mr. Hudson above the ocean along Margate pier.

Nicholas *had been to Yarmouth, and had come back feeling that he had added at least ten years to his own life.*

"Mr. and Mrs. James Forsyte! Mr. and Mrs. Soames Forsyte!" the servant announced.

Like all Forsyte's in their gallantry, *Swithin drew his heels together, his deportment ever admirable. His hand enclosed Irene's, and his eyes swelled. She was a pretty woman—a little too pale, but her figure, her eyes, her teeth! Too good for that chap Soames!*

Punctuality was an important trait in 'Forsythia'. Among the aristocracy, there was a tendency to be fashionably late, a trait even set by royalty, but 'Forsytes', like Jules Verne's ultimate 'Forsyte', Phileas Fogg of *Around the World in Eighty Days*, were punctilious. *The hands of Swithin's watch, which he held open in his hand, had left eight behind; it was half an hour beyond his dinner time—he had had no lunch—and a strange primeval impatience surged up within him.*

"It's not like Jolyon to be late!" he said to Irene, with uncontrollable vexation, "I suppose it'll be June keeping him!" for he knew of her friendship with his niece.

"People in love are always late," she answered.

My mother was a stickler for being on time. It frustrated her enormously that my sister, Sally, developed a lifestyle that seemed to center around being late. My father was more bemused than anything else, expecting Sally to be late for almost every event or family gathering. At worst, he would simply smile and state that he was now "past the meal." His mother, my Granny Longley, in true 'Forsyte' form was also a believer in punctuality. There was a bell at The Breach that was rung outside so that any of us in the garden or down the farmyard would make sure we got back to the house in time for lunch. Once in the house and cleaned up for the meal, a gong was then rung to summon us to the dining room. Granny Mabs, being 'The Exceptional', also never wanted us to be late for anything

We were rigidly taught this in our schooldays. It was a punishable offence to show up late for an event. Extreme tardiness even led to corporal punishment with the cane. When we first arrived at Tonbridge, we were at the beck and call of any praeposter for odd jobs that they might need done—anything from cleaning their shoes, polishing their bicycle, or fetching them an ice cream cone from the 'Grubber', as the Tuck Shop was called. They simply shouted "Boy!" from the top of their lungs, and the last of us to get to the senior boy was given the job. It paid to be speedy, or you might spend the next ten minutes warming up a toilet seat for the senior in the cold of our outside latrines!

Didn't Passepartout, as Phileas Fogg's manservant in *Around the World in Eighty Days,* have to learn to master punctuality? Phileas Fogg lived by the clock. His London home was filled with timepieces. Indeed, clocks did abound in 'Forsythia'—large grandfather clocks in the halls; enormous onyx or gilded clocks with matching urns or candelabra on drawing room mantels; carriage clocks, encased in glass, above the fireplaces of 'Forsyte' bedrooms—yes, time was important. It was important to these movers and shakers of an Empire that encompassed every time zone of the world—and it all worked from Greenwich, the center of the Empire!

At last, *"Miss June Forsyte—Mr. Jolyon Forsyte!"* And then a stumbling pause before the baffled servant struggled with, *"Mr. Boswainy!"*

Rather like my mother, *Swithin moved his arm, and said in a rumbling voice:*

"Dinner now—dinner!"

The early dinner conversation of these assembled Forsytes centered, as it usually did, on exchanges about their various ailments. These included the ailment of Juley's cat.

"Tom's bad again; I can't tell what's the matter with him!"—*"I suppose Ann doesn't come down in the mornings!"*—*"What's the name of your doctor, Fanny? Stubbs? He's a quack!"*—*"Winifred? She's got too many children. Four isn't it? She's as thin as a lath!"*

How many times, especially at Christmas, did my sisters and I sit with the grown-ups at the vast, superbly decorated dinner table, and listen to this endless bickering, forced sympathy, and occasional genuine concern, about the other family members' ailments. We used to call this "The Nellie disease conversation." Grandpa Jack's sister, my Great-aunt Nellie, was rarely with us for these family gatherings, having a considerable family of her own, the Doggetts, who had rather set themselves up in rivalry to our side of the family. I believe the division was all over a family scandal involving Great-grandfather Collings, who was a truly 'Pickwickian' character, and whose second wife, Emma, the source of this scandal, was never really accepted, except by my mother's immediate family. Somehow, at the table, the conversation usually ended up about Great-aunt Nellie, who I presume was somewhat sickly during our childhood, rather like Emily Forsyte, although on the two or three occasions I did meet her, she always seemed robustly fit!

With the second glass of champagne, a kind of hum makes itself heard, which, when divested of casual accessories and resolved into its primal element, is found to be James telling a story, and this goes on for a long time, encroaching sometimes even upon what must universally be recognised as the crowning point of a Forsyte feast—the saddle of mutton.

No Forsyte has given a dinner without providing a saddle of mutton.

The Longleys were great believers in the saddle of mutton, too, or any great roast joint of meat. Game, meat, and poultry were our business, after all. The huge joint, whether mutton, pork, beef, or lamb, waited to be carved on the sideboard with great ceremony by the head of the family. Possibly, in the heyday of 'Forsythia', the head of the household may have delegated this task to the butler, but in my lifetime, it was either my grandparents, great-uncles, or my father, who performed this task. We were the last generation to use those huge service meat platters, about twice the size of a turkey plate, in which all the fine juices of the succulent roast were gathered for natural gravy.

Once served, it being our business, discussion would turn as to the source of the joint. Was it Scotch, Welsh, Irish or possibly even New Zealand? *Forsytes were the same, each branch of the family tenaciously held to a particular locality—old Jolyon swearing by Dartmoor, James by Welsh, Swithin by Southdown, Nicholas maintaining that people might sneer, but there was nothing like New Zealand. As for Roger, he had discovered a shop where they sold German; on being remonstrated with, he had proved his point by producing a butcher's bill, which showed that he paid more than any of the others. It was on this occasion that old Jolyon, turning to June, and in earshot of Bosinney, had said in one of his burst's of philosophy:*

"You may depend upon it, they're a cranky lot, the Forsytes—and you'll find it out as you grow older."

The great saddle-of-mutton controversy at an end, eyes turned to Bosinney, the reason for the dinner.

Soames was watching. He had a reason of his own connected with a pet building scheme, for observing Bosinney. The architect might do for his purpose; he looked clever, as he sat leaning back in his chair, moodily making little ramparts with breadcrumbs.

To play with your food was another 'Forsythia' anathema. It was one of the most common admonitions rendered to us, both in the nursery and at the dinner table. By the time we were sent to our boarding schools, it was hoped that this primeval instinct had been stamped out forever.

It would seem that the young architect was showing signs other than his felt hat for not quite being up to 'Forsythia'.

June took up the conversation:

"I stayed on the river on my way home, and saw a beautiful site for a house."

"What, you're not thinking of buying land?" James *ejaculated, dropping his fork.*

June was greatly encouraged by his interest. It had long been her pet plan that her uncles should benefit themselves and Bosinney by building country houses.

The aristocracy still owned large tracts of England in great parks with home farms around their country seats. In the latter eighteenth and early nineteenth century, perhaps a decade before the Forsytes, they, too, had moved to London. Owning one of the new town houses of London's Regency squares was almost an obligatory addition to their country seat. For 'Forsytes', the move was in reverse. As yeomen, they had moved from the country to becoming the shakers and movers of the Empire in the city, but by the latter nineteenth century, they started to acquire additional property in the country, not too far from the city, so that they could ape their peers.

Great-grandfather Oliver Longley rented Frame Farm for many years, a beautiful farmhouse near Iden Green in Kent—a weekend retreat from Hillside in Beckenham. In 1907, he bought The Breach, the fine old Regency house on fifty acres of land encompassing the small village of Wilsley Pound. The very name 'Pound' has echoes of a bygone era. The pound was a small grass area where country roads met and provided a common enclosure where stray animals could be penned awaiting collection from local farmers. In an area before telephone communication, there was no way of letting fellow farmers know a stray was out. Farmers would find their animals compounded in the pound and thus retrieve them. At the time my great-grandfather purchased The Breach, along with much of the village of Wilsley Pound, the old pen was still there. I remember seeing photographs of Grandpop and my great-uncles sitting on the fencing. The Breach, was ironically, just a mile away from Hocker Edge, the magnificent old yeoman house that had belonged to his daughter-in-law's family in pre-'Forsythia' days. The Breach was my grandparents' home throughout my childhood and left a great impression on me.

My maternal great-grandparents, the Cuthbertsons, had a magnificent Edwardian mansion on Duncombe Hill in South London—Frainsville. However, in keeping with this passion for a place in the country, they also had a small weekend home on the River Thames at Tag's Island, not far from the place where June Forsyte had first seen the land that had started this discussion at Swithin's.

"Why don't you go into the country?" repeated June: 'it would do you a lot of good!"

"Why?" began James in a fluster. "Buying land—what good d'you suppose I can do buying land, building houses?—I couldn't get four per cent. for my money!"

Soames, however, listened with interest. Soames knew, and personally deeply wrestled with the fact that *it was known on Forsyte 'Change that Irene regretted her marriage.* Soames was doing well, business was good, and this prospect of building a country house, where he could house Irene away from the gossip and give her something creative to play with, just might be the very solution he sought to win her heart.

June, indeed, with her habit of championing the unfortunate, had dragged from Irene a confession, and, in return, had preached the necessity of facing the evil, by separation, if need be. But in the face of these exhortations, Irene had kept a brooding silence, as though she found terrible the thought of this struggle carried through in cold blood. He would never give her up, she had said to June, as she sat there in the new diamond necklace that Soames had just given to her.

"Who cares?" June cried: "let him do what he likes—you've only to stick to it."

Eyebrows were raised.

When the ladies left the room so the gentlemen could enjoy their after-dinner port and cigars, a tradition 'Forsytes' inherited from the aristocracy, with whom they did not really want to associate, but whom they secretly admired, the conversation turned to one of Swithin's more recent acquisitions.

"I gave four hundred pounds for it," he was saying. "Of course it's a regular work of art."

"Four hundred! H'm! that's a lot of money!" chimed in Nicholas.

The object alluded to was an elaborate group of statuary in Italian marble, which, placed upon a lofty stand diffused an atmosphere of culture throughout the room. The subsidiary figures, of which there were six, female, nude, and of highly ornate workmanship, were all pointing towards the central figure, also nude, and female, who was pointing at herself; and all this gave the observer a very pleasant sense of her extreme value. Aunt Juley, nearly opposite, had had the greatest difficulty in not looking at it all the evening.

Displays of nudity were not common in 'Forsythia', although a period of Victorian sculpture favored the nymph and the female form. It was, however, by the 1880's somewhat passe.

As they discussed the value of Swithin's purchase, Bosinney, *the architect, was grinning behind the fumes of his cigarette. Now, indeed, he looked more like a buccaneer.*

"The poor foreign dey-vil that made it," went on Swithin, "asked me five hundred—I gave him four. It's worth eight. Looked half-starved, poor dey-vil."

"Ah!" chimed in Nicholas suddenly, "poor, seedy-lookin' chaps, these artists; it's a wonder to me how they live."

James shook his head. "Ah!" he said, "I don't know how they live!"

Great-grandfather Oliver Longley was somewhat of a patron of the arts. Apart from his love of music and friendship with Gustav Holst, he collected paintings—a connoisseur like Soames. He often tried to help out starving artists, if he felt their work might appreciate. He collected many paintings of early steamships, mostly the work of Charles Dixon, now a recognized master of maritime paintings, but his most supportive effort revolved around a young painter named Charles Spencelaugh. Spencelaugh borrowed the considerable sum of five hundred pounds from my great-grandfather, but when he was unable to pay him back, was commissioned by Oliver Longley to paint portraits of Oliver and Minnie. The portraits, painted in 1894, hung on either side of the great mahogany sideboard in the dining room at The Breach in my childhood. Now, they are in my possession. I, personally, have always loved these two portraits, and to some extent my great-grandfather was justified in supporting the young Charles Spencelaugh, as in the 1930s his works became recognized and made entry into the Royal Academy's Summer exhibitions.

Soames had an eye for good art, too, and he observed the architect Bosinney's reactions to the Forsyte discussion on Swithin's recent acquisition with interest. *'I wonder what he thinks of it?' thought Soames, who knew well enough that this sculptured group was hopelessly vieux jeu; hopelessly of the last generation. There was no longer any sale at Jobson's for such works of art.* Soames did not have to speak. James addressed Bosinney *still shrouded in smoke.*

"Now, what do you say, Mr. Bosinney? You're an architect; you ought to know all about statues and things!"

Bosinney replied cooly:

"The work is a remarkable one."

Soames, goaded, asked, *"Remarkable for what?"*

"For its naivete," replied 'The Buccaneer.'

Yes, this might be Soames' man to build his country house.

Chapter Four

Projection of the House

S oames *could not understand what* Irene *found wrong with him. It was not as if he drank! Did he run into debt* like his brother-in-law, Dartie, *or gamble, or swear: was he violent; were his friends rackety; did he stay out all night? On the contrary.*

The profound, subdued aversion which he felt in his wife was a mystery to him, and a source of the most terrible irritation. That she had made a mistake, and did not love him, had tried to love him and could not love him, was obviously no reason. He that could imagine so outlandish a cause for his wife's not getting along with him was certainly no Forsyte.

In 'Forsythia' marriages were made for life. A wife supervised the large Victorian and Edwardian household, bore children, and supported her husband as needed. If there was intimacy, well I'm sure it was appreciated, but it was not a requirement. Without intimacy, were there unhappy marriages?—assuredly yes, but they were not made public. Was this not the very problem that 'Young Jolyon' had brought on the family when he abandoned June's mother, Frances, for their girl's governess, Helene Hilmer? Was this not the reason why 'Young Jolyon' and Helene were not present either at 'Old Jolyon's' reception for June and Bosinney, or at Swithin's dinner party for the engaged couple?

I am not really sure if Great-grandfather John Collings ever actually divorced my great-grandmother, Harriet 'Penny', who was the daughter of a minor member of the Anglo-Irish aristocracy, a point that was much lauded by the estranged half of the family, seeing that his second partner, 'Great-grandmother' Emma, was only a seamstress in origins. This was, after all, a reason for the family rift. Divorce was not accepted in 'Forsythia'.

It is sad that after the demise of 'Forsythia', several members of my family became divorced, and in a world such as today, we are told marriages have less than a forty-per-cent chance of surviving without divorce. Of course, there are many social changes, both in the status of women and the workplace, that have made contribution to this dramatic social change. Having been divorced myself, I can relate to these changes. In my childhood, however, divorce was really not an option. It came as a great shock to my family when in the decades after 'Forsythia', my Uncle Dennis, my father's youngest brother, divorced from my Aunt Brigid. It was also sad, that in so doing, the family in essence, lost The Breach. During the difficult years when my family started to come to terms with this, it was often stated that if my grandmother, Catherine Amy Hovenden, had still been alive, this divorce would never have happened. Granny Longley would simply have said, "Don't be so silly, you must be balmy," given her Hovenden glare, and the matter would have been closed.

Soames, therefore, was determined to hold on to his marriage. Irene was his most prized possession.

On his way home from the City, *he had stopped to look in at a picture shop, for Soames was an 'amateur' of pictures, and had a little room* at his house, *No 62, Montpellier Square, full of canvases, stacked against the wall, which he had no room to hang.* He *would enter into this room on Sunday afternoons, to spend hours turning the pictures to the light, examining the marks on their backs, and occasionally making notes.*

They were nearly all landscapes with figures in the foreground, a sign of some mysterious revolt against London, its tall houses, its interminable streets, where his life and the lives of his breed and class were passed. Every now and then he would take one or two pictures away with him in a cab, and stop at Jobson's for evaluations *on his way into the City.*

Soames knew he was a man of property. *The times were good for building, money had not been so dear for years; and the site he had seen at Robin Hill,* southwest of London in Surrey—*what could be better?*

Within twelve miles of Hyde Park Corner, the value of land certain to go up, would always fetch more than he gave for it; so that house, if in really good style, would be *a first-class investment* in all his property, including his wife.

To get Irene out of London, away from opportunities of going about and seeing people, away from her friends and those who put ideas in her head! That was the thing! She was too thick with June! June disliked him. He returned the sentiment. They were of the same blood.

Irene *would enjoy messing about with the decoration, she was artistic*—an accomplished pianist. *The house must be in good style, something that would always be certain to command a price, something unique, like that last house of Parkes, which had a tower.*

Yes, all through the suburbs of late Victorian London, houses were being built with towers—was this fashioned after the Queen Empress' towered home at Osborne on the Isle of Wight? Why, even the new Government House in Melbourne, Australia, was modeled on Queen Victoria's home.

But Parkes had himself said that his architect was ruinous.

This was why Soames *had thought of Bosinney. 'One of the new school. Clever.' He had not been able to discover what houses Bosinney had built, nor what his charges were. It would be keeping the thing in the family, with Forsytes almost an instinct, and he would be able to get 'favoured-nation', if not nominal terms—only fair, considering the chance to Bosinney of displaying his talents, for this house must be no common edifice.*

Thus he fulfilled the inscrutable laws of his great class—of human nature itself—when he reflected, with a sense of comfort, that Bosinney would be easy to deal with in money matters.

After stepping into the cool of St. Paul's Cathedral, Soames reflected on his plan, *his gloved hands clasped in front over the handle of his furled umbrella. Some sacred inspiration perhaps had come to him.*

'Yes,' he thought, 'I must have room to hang my pictures.'

Was this yet one more motive for Great-grandfather Longley buying The Breach? Every inch of wall space at Hillside was laden with his collection of paintings both good and bad, elaborately framed in gilded splendor. The Breach would provide him with more wall space, and although I never knew Hillside, I remember the great, gilt frames ensconcing nineteenth-century landscapes that hung at The Breach.

Soames made his way to Bosinney's studio. *He refused a drink and came at once to the point.* *"If you've nothing better to do on Sunday, come down with me to Robin Hill, and give me your opinion on a building site."*

Soames was solicitor to this estate, and when they arrived at Robin Hill, *he spent nearly an hour in the agent's company.* *"Your people,"* he said, *"ought to come down in their price to me, considering I shall be the first to build."*

They came to a temporary agreement, and Soames looked at the site gesticulating with his umbrella like Nicholas, even though it was a warm August day without a cloud in the sky. "Where Is Bosinney?" he asked himself. Leaving the agent, he found Bosinney further up the hill.

"Hello, Forsyte," the architect *said, "I've found the very place for your house! Look here!"*

Soames stood and looked, then he said coldly:

"You may be very clever, but this site will cost me half as much again."

"Hang the cost, man. Look at the view!"

Soames hated to admit it, but as a connoisseur, he knew 'the Buccaneer' was right.

"I could build you a teaser here," said Bosinney. *"For about eight thousand I could build you a palace."*

Soames didn't want to admit Bosinney was making a good offer. He was a Forsyte—a damned good businessman. He *returned to the agent's cottage alone.* After *about half an hour* he re-joined *Bosinney,* and they *started for the station.*

"Well," Soames *said, hardly opening his lips.* *"I've taken that site of yours, after all."*

Bosinney was to build Soames his country house.

CHAPTER FIVE

A FORSYTE MENAGE

Like the enlightened thousands of his class and generation in this great City of London, who no longer believed in red velvet chairs, and know that groups of modern Italian marble are 'vieux jeu,' Soames Forsyte inhabited a house which did what it could. It owned a copper door knocker of individual design, windows which had been altered to open outwards, hanging flower-boxes filled with fuschias, and at the back a little court tiled with jade-green tiles, and surrounded by pink hydrangeas in peacock-blue tubs. Here, under a parchment-colored Japanese sunshade covering the whole end, inhabitants or visitors could be screened from the eyes of the curious while they drank tea and examined at their leisure the latest of Soames' little silver boxes.

This sense of privacy was very important in 'Forsythia'. My mother started to write a novel during the war years. She provisionally titled it *An Englishman's Castle*. Being a novel about 'Forsythia' in the years immediately prior to World War II, the title was very appropriate for the times. An Englishman's home was his private castle, and in the late Victorian and Edwardian suburbs of 'Forsythia' each home was a decided unit unto its own. Brick walls, tall hedges, or solid wooden slatted fences, hid all but the entry and exit driveways behind impressive gates hinged on capped pillars that for some reason in my childhood became known as "larders." Gardens were also separated by tall hedges, usually of privet or conifers, designed to keep the home place secret from neighbors, even in winter. This sense of privacy gave the leafy suburbs a great peace. My mother's novel was sadly never completed, but she started another work that was a biographical look at the family into which in 1940 she married—*Long live the Longleys*. The opening line described my great-grandfather, Oliver Longley, at The Breach— *Oliver Longley pulled down his cap and looked over his beloved acres*. An Englishman's home is his castle.

The inner decoration of Soames' house *favoured the First Empire and William Morris. For its size, the house was commodious; there were countless nooks resembling birds' nests, and little things made of silver were deposited like eggs.*

The influence of William Morris hung over 'Forsythia'. His school of design and furnishings, based on old crafts, but mass-produced for the new class of urban wealth, could be found in almost every latter 'Forsythia' home. This was in part because of a new phenomenon that had grown up in latter nineteenth-century London—the department store. Early 'Forsytes' had to rely on the cabinetmakers and exclusive boutiques that had served the aristocracy of Regency London. By the mid-century, however, and largely because of the mass-produced work of the William Morris school, and the textile and potteries industries of northern England, there developed a new market for these goods. The department store was a central focus of 'Forsythia' life right up to my own childhood. Now, however, few of these great emporiums are still around, replaced by supermarket chains, shopping malls, and a return to expensive boutiques more for London's visitors than her inhabitants. The department stores disappeared when 'Forsythia' died. They were spawned to serve the masters of the British Empire, and they died with the British Empire.

Both my grandmothers made regular trips up to London in my childhood to shop at these stores. There were the great stores of Oxford Street and Regent Street, of which only Selfridges retains its original feel. There were Goringes and The Army and Navy stores in Victoria that were amongst other things, the principal suppliers of all officers' kit, and sold uniforms for preparatory schools and 'public schools', as well as the armed forces. A visit to Goringes was essential every school holiday to renew the countless uniform and sporting garments in their own individual colors that all our preparatory schools required. And there were a lot, as they filled a whole, old-fashioned traveling trunk for every term. Then, there was Kensington. A string of famous department stores lined Kensington High Street—not just Harrods. One of my favorites was Derry and Toms, largely because of the beautiful roof garden that was a must visit for shoppers. It particularly attracted us children born in World War II, because up on the roof garden were the remains of a World War II bomb that had landed on Derry and Toms, but failed to explode. Defused, it remained as a witness of the department store's salvation and the defiance of the British Empire against Hitler. Derry and Toms, too, like almost all these department stores, had a wonderful restaurant and tearoom. I remember the restaurant was called the Rainbow Room on the floor below the roof garden, because of the multi-colored lighting in the shades of a rainbow that lit the great tray ceiling.

When we visited these department stores it was a whole day out. The lifts were still operated by men in smart commissionaire uniforms, who called out the wares on each level. Equally smart commissionaires, in top hats and livery, opened taxicab doors for 'Forsyte' ladies and their families on arrival, and hailed taxicabs for their departure.

Everything that could possibly be wanted in the 'Forsyte' home could be purchased in these emporiums, from pattern books for dressmakers and all the haberdashery that went with that, to fine furniture, china, porcelain, and glassware; the latest fashions in ready-made clothing for men, women, boys and girls; fabrics for personal tailoring in the tailors' department; fabrics for drapes, cushions, slip-covers or the re-covering of earlier antiques; wall hangings, wall papers, kitchen gadgets and kitchen ware; corsetry and hosiery that embraced ladies' underwear, the word 'lingerie' still considered in respectability to be a French frivolity; sporting goods—even fishing rods, shot guns, tennis rackets, cricket bats, and sets of Croquet and lawn bowls were available.

One of the most important departments, however, was the millinery—a word that has almost disappeared, but which was the ultimate place for 'Forsytes' to express their originality. Here, the female members of a 'Forsyte' family bought their accessories—hats, gloves and bags. Throughout 'Forsythia' these accessories were essential. There were accessories for morning, afternoon, and evening wear. The millinery department was full of mirrors. These accessories, especially the hats, had to be just right for "Madam." Perhaps, more than any other department, the millinery department epitomized a social change in the status of women. The accessories were very personal, and as such they needed sales ladies who could really understand their ladies' needs. There grew up, therefore, with the department stores, long before women were commonly found in the workplace, a certain class of female, usually widowed or single, who worked in these stores to accommodate this upper-middle class clientele. Some of them, as widows, might even have stepped from a less fortunate branch of 'Forsythia' themselves, and at one time furnished similar homes to their clientele—well versed in the patterns of William Morris. Many, came from the aspiring ranks of those just below 'Forsythia'—matrons of the lower-middle class, but definitely not working class. Some of these ladies unconsciously put on airs themselves through their constant dealings with their peers. They developed a somewhat over-refined version of the clipped upper-class English of the three percent. "Oh, Madam would look very fetching in that!" "Oh, Madam, it's perfect for you." " Oh, Madam, its just right for you." Or even the basic, "Oh, Madam, that's you!" They flattered their clientele.

Grandmother Longley just loved this, so much so that her own childrens' generation, within the family started to address Granny as, "Madam." Now, this might have been because of the very popular play in the West End during the 1950's, *Call me Madam,* but, in keeping with my perceived origins for this title, they actually pronounced it, "Modom." Modom sounded rather like the exaggerated lower-middle class attempt at being posh that was so obvious in many of these somewhat refined department store sales ladies.

The very word posh, however, is worthy of mention. The administrators and controllers of the Empire, had to travel out to India or the Far East on the great steamships of the era. The ships, however, were not air-conditioned, and it was, therefore, most comfortable to have a cabin on the port, or left side in the shadow of the ship, on the outward journey, and starboard on the homeward journey, the right side of the ship then being in shadow. This way, the hot tropical sun did not glare into their cabins all day. "Posh," therefore, came into the English language on the sea routes of the Empire—port outward, starboard homeward.

But, back in the department stores—unlike today, make-up and perfumery were not prominent. 'Forsytes' didn't wear much make-up, just face powder, and possibly a face night cream that could as easily be purchased at a local chemist as in a department store. In fact, I don't remember make-up ever really to be seen on either of my grandmothers' dressing tables or that of my mother. A powder compact was all that was required. Make-up was something that one only associated with the stage and painted ladies of the night, and to a 'Forsyte' mind, these two professions kind of went together. This is interesting, as the supermarket successors to these old department stores usually bombard you with a whole ground floor of perfumes and make-up today.

Fine perfumes were available, of course. And it is ironic that this was very much a part of the Hovenden empire. As yeomen, the Hovendens were weavers and clothiers as aforementioned, but like all yeomen with their own home and land, they grew herbs for the household. Interest in herbs took my Hovenden forebears into late eighteenth-century medicine. Arriving in London as doctors, they then reverted back to their interest in herbs. They established in the House of Hovenden one of the premier perfume companies of the Empire, herbs being the base of most perfumes. It was through this connection that they were able to establish themselves as liverymen in the Worshipful Company of Barbers in the City of London. Perfumery was considered a subsidiary of the barber's trade, but there were always more medical practitioners in the ancient medieval guild of barbers than hairdressers. High-class hairdressing and wig dressing was, after all, usually performed by valets and menservants in 'Forsythia'. In fact, I don't remember my mother, or her mother, ever going to a beauty salon, except perhaps when they were on holiday. A young hairdresser started to dress my mother's and my grandmother's hair just before World War II. She did so all her life, and became a close confidant and friend of the family— Mary Jackson. In the heyday of 'Forsythia', a ladies' maid would have performed this function. However, it is interesting today, that one of the few medieval trade symbols to have survived is the barber's pole. A red and white striped pole, or animated cylinder, is found in front of almost every barber's shop and beauty salon. The symbol goes back to the Middle ages, like the three balls of the pawnbroker or the boot of the cobbler. It stands for the blood and the bandages of the blood-letter, bleeding thought to be a major medical cure for medieval illness where disease was thought to be found mainly in the bloodstream. The sharp instrument used for making blood-letting incisions became both the scalpel and the razor, combining the principle tool of both a barber and a surgeon. Under King Henry VIII, in 1512, the Worshipful Company of Barbers and Surgeons were united, and practiced as such until 1745 when the Royal College of Surgeons was formed as an offshoot of the Barbers' Company to govern the nation's surgical practices. During those years, the company's property in Monkwell Square was called Barber-Surgeons' Hall and the present hall of the company is still Barber-Surgeons' Hall, although the original was burned in the Great Fire of London in 1666. The second hall was destroyed in the blitz in 1940. From its ashes, however, a new hall was built in 1967. Behind the Hall, stands part of London's original Roman wall that shelters a peaceful herb garden maintained by the company, reminding liverymen and their guests of the origins of both professions.

The Hovendens were great benefactors to the company, and my great-grandfather, Charles William Hovenden, and his brother, Robert Hovenden, were both masters of the company in the heyday of 'Forsythia'. All liverymen of the present company, including myself, are allowed one free dinner a year, usually the Ladies Livery Dinner. This is because of a bursary provided by the Hovenden family and still intact. As perfumers and barbers sundriesmen, the Hovendens established secret recipes, and their scents and perfumes were considered the finest of their era. In the family, it was commonly thought, however, that my great-grandfather's frequent visits to France, might not always have centered around the need to garner the necessary herbs of Provence!

On Charles William Hovenden's death, my great-grandfather having no male heir, the secret Hovenden recipes continued with Robert Hovenden and Sons, the last owner being Robert Hovenden, a cousin of my grandmother known as Uncle 'Bob' whom my father and his brothers and sister considered to be "very rich." On Robert Hovenden's death in the1930s the perfume House of Hovenden came to an end and my grandmother received a portion of the inheritance. In 1937, my grandmother had my father apprenticed to her cousin in the Worshipful Company of Barbers, Maurice Hovenden. Maurice Hovenden had been master of the company the year before. My father, before he died at ninety-three, was the oldest living member and past master of the guild, and in 1965, during the same year that my father was master of the Company, I was admitted to the livery through patrimony.

During the age of 'Forsythia', perfumes were marketed in exclusive shops rather than department stores, found in streets like Pall Mall or Old Bond street, but almost everything else that a 'Forsyte' lady or gentleman might require was found in those department stores. A young subaltern, sahib, civil engineer, lawyer, or district commissioner about to be posted to some far flung part of the Empire, was kitted out with pith helmet, khakis and tropical dress, at these department stores, just as we boys were fitted out for our preparatory and 'public schools.'

In Soames' well ordered home, *two kinds of fastidiousness were at war. There lived here a mistress who would have dwelt daintily on a desert island; a master whose daintiness was, as it were, an investment, cultivated by the owner for his advancement, in accordance with the laws of competition. This competitive daintiness had caused Soames in his Marlborough* school *days to be the first boy into white waistcoats in the summer, and corduroy waistcoats in the winter, had prevented him from ever appearing in public with his tie climbing up his collar, and induced him to dust his patent-leather boots before a great multitude assembled on Speech Day to hear him recite Moliere.*

Marlborough may have run to French recitation on Speech Day, but at Tonbridge, founded in 1553 by Sir Andrew Judde, who was master of one of those city livery companies, the Worshipful Company of Skinners, and left the trust of the school to that guild in which hands it is to this day, the head boy's speech to the governors was always spoken in Latin, we boys being schooled ahead of time to laugh in appropriate places!

The reference to clothing privileges at Marlborough reminds me of the steady progression of clothing privileges that we went through as boys at Tonbridge. Our basic uniform was a green lovat jacket worn with gray trousers. Our shirts were worn with stiff separate collars and the cuffs heavily starched to match the collars. This made it easier to insert the gold cufflinks that we proudly wore. Our first year, we wore one or the other of two school ties—a red cloth tie or a rather fine navy blue silk tie with yellow boar's heads throughout its design, the boar's head being the heraldic beast of the school. All was topped with a stiff straw boater that sported the colored ribbon of our house—in my case the black and magenta colors of Judde House. We were obligated to wear these straw boaters if we ever left the grounds of the school, and it was obligatory on Sundays, when we wore lovat green suits, that we must wear our boaters at all times. There were special racks in the Tonbridge School chapel pews to hold these boaters that we preferred to call barges because they floated well if they fell into the River Medway that passed through the town. In fact, the wetter our boaters got, the stiffer the straw became when it dried out, the resin having reset in the weave of the straw.

After a year, we might have been awarded a house tie for some sporting achievement. These were more flamboyant in wide stripes representing the colors of our house. Also, in our second year we were allowed to display a silk handkerchief in our jacket's pocket. If and when we became a House Praeposter, we could wear a felt or silk waistcoat or vest in any color we chose and on Sundays our lovat green suit could have a matching waistcoat. The biggest privilege that came with praepostership, however, was the right to carry a furled umbrella regardless of the weather.

Outside dress, the other issue of fastidiousness for Soames Forsyte was his bath. Soames *would not have gone without a bath for worlds—it was the fashion to take baths,* 'Forsytes' being the first generation to have the benefit of hot and cold running water in their new homes. The water was heated by big boilers fired and fueled like the kitchen range by endless sacks of the Empire's greatest resource—coal. *But Irene could be imagined, like some nymph, bathing in wayside streams, for the joy of the freshness and of seeing her own fair body.*

In this conflict throughout the house the woman had gone to the wall. As in the struggle between Saxon and Celt still going on within the nation. 'Forsytes' were indeed, well aware of the political rumblings in Celtic Ireland throughout their era—the first salvos to rock the Empire on which stood their security.

Soames and Irene sat *at a handsome rosewood table; they dined without a cloth—a distinguishing elegance* more associated with the aristocracy than 'Forsythia'. Their conversation was limited. *Could a man own anything prettier than this dining table,* possibly purchased at the department store of Maples, *with its deep tints, the starry soft-petalled roses, the ruby colored glass, and quaint silver furnishing; could a man own anything prettier than the woman who sat at it?* But *Soames only experienced a sense of exasperation amounting to pain, that he did not own her as it was his right to own her, that he could not, as by stretching out his hand to that rose, pluck her and sniff the very secrets of her heart.*

"Anybody been here this afternoon?" Soames asked.

"June."

"What did she want?"

An Englishman's home is his castle. *It was an axiom with the Forsytes that people did not go anywhere unless they wanted something.* For Soames, especially seeing it was June, this was an invasion.

My father and mother tended to react the same way whenever the doorbell rang, especially in the evening.

"Who can that be?" my mother would say, and on learning who was at the door, my father would chime in with, "What does she want?"

Such an interruption was considered an invasion into the mystical privilege of the castle home.

"You're a pretty wife!" Soames *said* to Irene. *"You're cracked about June! I can tell you one thing: now that she has the Buccaneer in tow, she doesn't care twopence about you and you'll find it out. But you won't see so much of her in the future; we're going to live in the country."*

June had already spilled the beans. Soames was surprised to hear that Irene already knew.

After dinner, Irene retired into the garden. *Soames went to the drawing-room, and peered at her through the window.*

Out in the shadow of the Japanese sunshade she was sitting very still, the lace on her white shoulders stirring with the soft rise and fall of her bosom.

But about this silent creature sitting there so motionless, in the dark, there seemed a warmth, a hidden fervour of feeling, as if the whole of her being had been stirred, and some change were taking place in its very depths.

CHAPTER SIX

JAMES AT LARGE

This business of building a country house puzzled Soames' father, James, a man wedded to London; and rumors that Soames and Irene were not getting along, even sleeping in separate rooms, was bothersome to him, too. He had gone through a difficult time with Dartie—what problems that man gave to his daughter Winifred *when his son-in-law had that financial crisis, due to speculation in Oil Shares.* James *made himself ill worrying over it; the knell of all prosperity seemed to have sounded. It took him three months and a visit to Baden-Baden to get better; there was something terrible,* and shameful to a Forsyte, *in the idea that but for his, James's money, Dartie's name might have appeared in the Bankruptcy List.*

Grandpa Jack Collings always carried a small brown suitcase with him whenever he left the house on a visitation. It was his portable safe in which he stored his important papers. I remember a sad truth being revealed on his death in 1970. Grandpa was such a mild man. Like his father, he was everybody's friend, but he was more secretive in his dealings than Great-grandpa Collings. There was a gambling streak in the Collings family. Great-grandfather had made three fortunes and lost two. He gambled in commodities, including American hops. When things were going well, he lived high off the hog, and he was lavish in his entertaining, but at other times his financial circumstances were dubious to say the least. There was a time, in between highs, when as a 'Forsyte' he found himself living above a tobacconist's shop in the Old Kent Road. In fact, it was there that his youngest daughter, my Great-aunt Dorrie, was born. It was not surprising, therefore, that it was Dorrie seeking social recognition more earnestly than Babs, Nellie, or my grandfather, who clung most rigidly to the belief that her mother was indeed a daughter of the Anglo-Irish Massey family, and a good reason why she would never accept Emma, the seamstress, as her stepmother. Fortunately, the latter part of his life was less volatile, and Great-grandpa lived with Emma, the somewhat dubious second Mrs. Collings, in a rather fine Regency house on the north Kent coast— Reculver Lodge. His personal business was in the Borough Market, but he played with stocks, and with the growth of Empire, all sorts of new ventures were coming up on the Exchange. His son, my Grandpa Jack, was Chief Accountant for Oxo, a well-established food company in Southwark, but Grandpa had a friend, simply known to us as Allan, who advised him to make some rather unwise investments. In that brown suitcase that we were forced to go through after his death, there were several certificates for considerable share investments in various imperial mining ventures, most of which had been bankrupt for many years. Granny Mabs was always very shrewd and invested her money extremely safely. Apparently, Grandpa lost almost everything shortly before World War II, largely due to his association with Allan, but Granny was able to cover for his misfortune, and Grandpa did have a fairly generous pension from Oxo, so nobody in the family ever really knew how close they had been to financial disaster. This does explain, however, Granny Mabs' obsession with her shares and good investments. Dartie's misadventures in *The Forsyte Saga* were rather more obvious than Grandpa Jack's. For one thing, he did not just follow bad advice in the stock market, but he openly gambled on racehorses, and at his London clubs. His cousin, George Forsyte, was no great help to him in this, and more than once, James had cause to bail Dartie out of his debts.

Now, it was Soames who worried old James Forsyte. He paternalistically felt there might be more to this country house nonsense than met the eye, but *nobody ever tells* him *anything. This idea of Soames's building a house, that would have to be looked into. As to the trouble with Irene, he didn't know what would become of that—anything might come of it!*

He pondered this as he walked steadily to Soames' house where he had invited himself to dinner. He held *his umbrella carefully by the wood, just below the crook of the handle, so as to keep the ferrule off the ground, and not fray the silk in the middle.* Oh, how important the humble umbrella had become.

Like many in 'Forsythia', *to have creatures who were parts of himself, to whom he might transmit the money he saved, was at the root of his saving; and at seventy-five, what was left that could give him pleasure, but—saving? The kernel of life was in this saving for his children.*

Great-grandfather Oliver Longley, like the aristocracy, believed in leaving his inheritance to his oldest son—primogenitor. My grandfather did not agree with this, following a more 'Forsyte' viewpoint. Great-grandfather had provided for all his children by making them directors in the family firms, but the residual of his considerable estate and his two properties, he was to leave to his eldest son, my grandfather, Grandpop Longley. Grandpop disputed this in his 'Forsythia' fairness, and insisted in a codicil to his father's will that divided the estate up between them all. At that time, there was plenty to go round, the riches of 'Forsythia' still intact, despite the hardships of war, but by the time Grandpop died in 1969, after the demise of 'Forsythia', he had applied the same principles to his own will. By then, there was not much for the benefit of anyone.

James Forsyte *entered 62, Montpellier Square with the fullest intentions of being miserable.* He was worried and concerned.

Irene, seated in the drawing room, *was wearing her gold-colored frock—for, having been displayed at a dinner-party, a soiree, and a dance, it was now to be worn at home—and she had adorned the bosom with a cascade of lace, on which James' eyes riveted themselves at once.*

"Where do you get these things?" he said in an aggravated voice. He could see *she was spending a pretty penny on dress.*

The Charles Spencelaugh portrait of Minnie Longley that my great-grandfather had commissioned in lieu of that five-hundred-pound debt, shows my great-grandmother in a similar dress. It was painted in 1894, just eight years later than this description of Irene's dress in *The Forsyte Saga.* Minnie's dress was pink, but *she had adorned the bosom with a cascade of lace.*

The gong sounded, and, putting her white arm within his, Irene took James *into the dining-room.*

After dinner, which truly had satisfied him, and when Soames had left them to look over his latest acquisitions in that special room at the top of the house, James challenged Irene again.

"What d'you do with yourself all day? You never come round to Park Lane!"

He thought he knew the answer and blurted it out after she made some pitiful excuses.

"You're always about with June. I expect you are useful to her with her young man, chaperoning, and one thing and another. They tell me she's never at home now; your Uncle Jolyon, he doesn't like it, I fancy, being left so much alone as he is. They tell me she's always hanging about for this young Bosinney; I suppose he comes here every day. Now, what do you think of him? D'you think he owns his own mind? He seems to me a poor thing. I should say the grey mare was the better horse!'

He realized he had ruffled her.

"Perhaps you don't understand Mr. Bosinney," she said

"Don't understand him!" James hurried out. *"Why not?—you can see he's one of these artistic chaps. They say he's clever—they all think they're clever. You know more about him than I do,"* he added; and again his suspicious glance rested on her.

"He is designing a house for Soames," she said softly, evidently trying to smooth things over.

"That brings me to what I was going to say," continued James; *"I don't know what Soames wants with a young man like that; why doesn't he go to a first-rate man?"*

Irene replied:

"Perhaps Mr. Bosinney is first-rate."

She had dared to challenge her father-in-law, but her motives were quite different to those of her husband, and James knew it.

"That's it, you young people all stick together; you think you know best! All I can say is, these artistic people, or whatever they call themselves, they're as unreliable as they can be; and my advice to you is, don't you have too much to do with him!" James capped his warning with a reminder of her duty. *"I tell you my opinion, it's a pity you haven't got a child to think about, and occupy you!"*

Like my Granny Mabs after her morning arguments with my mother, he stood and made himself ready to leave.

"Well, I must be going," he announced.

Irene, politely saw him out.

CHAPTER SEVEN

OLD JOLYON'S PECCADILLO

J une was hardly ever at home—*she had just that one idea now, Bosinney and his affairs—and she left* 'Old Jolyon' *stranded in his great house, with a parcel of servants, and not a soul to speak to from morning to night. His club was closed for cleaning; his* business *boards in recess; there was nothing, therefore, to take him to the City.* To amuse himself, he took himself off to Lord's cricket ground to watch whatever match was on. For many 'Forsytes,' membership of the Marylebone Cricket Club at Lord's was almost a social necessity. The pavilion was a fair substitute for "the club."

The match, some county game, did not greatly interest 'Old Jolyon' and he left the cricket ground before the tea recess in the afternoon, *with the intention of going home. Before he had reached Hamilton Terrace he changed his mind, and hailing a cab, gave the driver an address in Wisteria Avenue. He had taken a resolution.*

And so that afternoon he took his journey through St. John's Wood, in the golden light that sprinkled the rounded green bushes of the acacias before the little houses, in the summer sunshine that seemed holding a revel over the little gardens; and he looked about him with interest; for this was a district which no Forsyte entered without open disapproval and secret curiosity.

His cab stopped in front of a small house of that peculiar buff colour which implies a long immunity from paint. It had an outer gate and a rustic approach.

A small of stature and unkempt maid opened the door.

"Mrs. Jolyon Forsyte at home?" he asked.

Flustered in the presence of such a distinguished looking gentleman, the maid informed him, *"Oh, yes sir!—what name shall I say, if you please sir?"*

There was no silver tray for 'Old Jolyon's' card, but he gave his name.

He followed her through the dark hall, into a small, drawing-room where the furniture was covered in chintz, and the little maid placed him in a chair.

Even more flustered now that the maid knew that this grand gentleman, *his massive head, with its drooping moustache and wings of white hair, very upright, under an excessively large top hat* that she had not taken from him, was a Forsyte, *she informed him, "They're all in the garden, sir: if you'll kindly take a seat, I'll tell them."*

In the silence after she left, 'Old Jolyon' looked around. *The whole place seemed to him, as he would have expressed it, pokey; there was a certain—he could not tell exactly what—air of shabbiness, or rather of making two ends meet, about everything.*

I remember having that same feeling at a children's party to which I had been invited by a friend at my first school, St. Christopher's, The Hall. It was really a girls' private school in Beckenham, but, from the age of four to eight, boys were admitted. Some of these boys were 'Forsytes' like me, young boys waiting to be shipped off to boarding school at eight. Some, however, were not of 'Forsythia' waiting to move on to the state schools, using St. Christopher's as a sort of private pre-school. I remember this particular birthday party, which pretty much my whole form, as classes were called, attended. It was at a house very similar to that in which 'Old Jolyon' now found himself. Adjacent to Beckenham, were two less salubrious areas in a valley between the leafy suburb and Sydenham Hill on which had stood the famous Crystal Palace, a symbol of the mercantile Empire of early 'Forsythia'—the housing of the world's first international exhibition of industry in 1851. These areas were parts of Penge and Catford. Much of Penge was working class, a recruitment area for the army of domestics that 'Forsythia's' Beckenham required. Catford was lower-middle class—populated by artisans, clerks, and apprentices. It was at one of these Catford homes, without really knowing the shades of class, that I felt the discomfort that appeared to bother 'Old Jolyon.' But, 'Old Jolyon' knew that this was his son's home.

These little houses were all old, second rate concerns; he should hope the rent was under one hundred a year; it hurt him more than he could have said, to think of a 'Forsyte'—his own son—living in such a place.

It is interesting to note that in the days of 'Forsythia', although the lower-middle class did not run a household of domestics, one simple maid was often employed.

The maid returned. *"Would he please to go down into the garden?"*

Young Jolyon, his wife, his two children, and his dog Balthasar, were all out there under a pear tree.

Pear trees were popular in the London gardens of 'Forsythia'. They had a good shape, were usually healthy, and carried a lot of beautiful white blossom in the spring, not to mention the advantage of fresh fruit in the fall. There was an orchard of plums, apples, and pears at Chelston, and when we moved to Hockeredge in Wickham Way we were blessed with a beautiful pear tree in the back garden on a corner of the lawn closest to the house. Just like 'Young Jolyon' and his family, my parents and my sisters invariably had afternoon tea in the garden in the shade of the pear tree.

'Old Jolyon's' *walk towards* his estranged family all gathered under the pear tree *was the most courageous act of* his *life.*

The dog Balthasar sniffed round the edges of his trousers, then *walked round the three small flower beds, to show his extreme contempt for things at large.*

After an introduction, *Old Jolyon seated himself in a wicker chair, that creaked under his weight; the garden beds looked 'daverdy'; on the far side* of the garden *on a smut stained wall, cats had made a path.* 'Pokey,' he thought. *His two grandchildren,* whom he was seeing for the first time, stood *one on each side of his knees, looked at him silently, never having seen so old a man.*

The dog sat in front of him, *a mongrel—offspring of a liaison between a Russian poodle and a fox terrier, staring up with eyes that did not blink.*

Although during the years of 'Forsythia' most my family kept pet dogs, including Granny Mabs and Grandpa Jack during my mother's childhood, we never had a dog. Uncle Jim and Aunt Eileen had a beagle named Billy. When they would visit us the beagle came, too. Seeing that Granny Mabs and my mother had been around dogs most of their lives, it always struck me as odd how little they cared for Jim's dog. Was this something to do with Jim not quite fitting in? Sensibilities pass from humans to their dogs. Maybe the beagle felt slighted in the same way as Jim. Whatever, just as Balthasar sat staring at 'Old Jolyon', so Jim's and Eileen's dog, which also had a habit of letting off undesirable odors, added further tension to that already found.

While 'Old Jolyon' and his grandchildren thus regarded each other with the peculiar scrutiny, curious, yet trustful, that passes between the very young and the very old, young Jolyon watched his wife.

Helene Hilmer's whole world was about to be turned upside down. This man who had ostracized them, with typical 'Forsyte' contempt, had just walked in, unannounced, back into their lives. *Suddenly* she *got up and hurried indoors. A minute later her husband muttered an excuse, and followed. Old Jolyon was left alone* under the pear tree *with his grandchildren. And that tenderness for children, that passion for the beginnings of life which had once made him forsake his son and follow June, now worked in him to forsake June and follow these little things*—Jolly and Holly.

In 'Forsythia', there was little excuse for what 'Young Jolyon' had done—leave his wife to run off with the governess. This only happened in gothic novels—an affair perhaps, but a complete break with the family—no. How would, Jolly, too, ever live down the stigma of being born out of wedlock. At least Holly was legitimate, born after June's mother had died and 'Young Jolyon' had made an honest woman of the governess. I suppose it is understandable, therefore, that my great-aunts, Nellie and Dorrie, felt so strongly about their father deserting their aristocratic mother, or her memory, to run off with the seamstress. Grandpa Jack, however, perhaps because he was Great-grandfather John Collings' only son, never did completely break his ties with his father. I don't know that he was fond of "the second Mrs. Collings" as he called Emma, but I do know he managed to be there for my great-grandfather at his death. In true 'Pickwickian' form Great-grandfather clasped Grandpa's hand.

"Jack, my boy," he said. "I've had a damned good life, now you see you do the same."

Those were his last words.

Despite a strong difference of opinion over Emma, partly made the more significant when Emma left all her jewelry to my mother and Aunt Eileen, excluding the Doggetts, there was, like with the Hovendens and the Goodchilds, a close connection in marriage. Montague Doggett was a very good-looking and brilliant member of the imperial firm of civil engineers—Sturtevents. So was my Granny Mabs' younger brother, Bert Cuthbertson. Sturtevents built bridges, dams, roads and railways all over the Empire, and Uncle Bert, known in my mother's family as "Uncle Moley," because of his amusement over a poem Aunt Eileen recited to him as a little girl about "a mole in a hole," was posted out to far flung parts of the Empire most of his working life. From time to time he would write glowing letters to my grandmother describing the beauty and wonders of the Empire and always with a postscript inquiring after the "two squirts" as he always called my mother and Eileen.

Probably because of his adventurous life, Great-uncle Bert was slow to settle down. He was for a while engaged to Babs Collings after the Collings family moved to Brockley Rise adjacent to Duncombe Hill and Granny Mabs had met Granpa Jack, but for some reason Babs broke it off. It was not until a mature age that Great-uncle Bert eventually married a rather glamorous, English girl, serving the Empire in Bombay, India. Ruby was half his age, which raised a few eyebrows in our 'Forstyte' circles, although I have to admit as a young boy, my young, great-aunt's glamour, did attract me even if my father sometimes described her as "old mutton dressed up as lamb." It was always planned that their son, my cousin John Cuthbertson, who was born in India, would follow on into the firm; and I believe it was Sturtevents that paid for a part of his education at Rugby School and Oxford, where he was a scholar and also became a triple blue in cricket, raquets, and hockey. Unfortunately, his father did not live to see all John's sporting accomplishments, but they thrilled Grandpa Jack. And so it was that two members of my mother's family became part of the Sturtevent family, for apart from Great-uncle Bert Cuthbertson, Montague Doggett married my great-aunt, Nellie Collings. These kind of intricate, close, but sometimes difficult family relationships, were to become a major problem for the Forsytes of Galsworthy's *Forsyte Saga*.

In fact, my great-grandfather, John Cuthbertson, who was never very faithful to his wife, my great-grandmother, Eliza Louisa Hubert, who had been a designer of Royal Doulton china before they were married in 1884, shocked the family on her death by marrying his son Cecil's sister-in-law, Jeanne. I think this was one reason why Granny Mabs had such sympathy for "Poor Allie," Cecil's wife, and it made for a very strained relationship between her and her father in the latter part of his life. To Granny Mabs, her mother, Eliza Hubert, was a saint, but her father "a dreadful man—a rotter."

Among the Forsytes, despite their ostracism, 'Young Jolyon' and Helene Hillier had made some sort of a life for themselves. 'Old Jolyon' weakened when he found a painting by his son for sale at a small insignificant price in one of the lesser London galleries. He had quite a few now, but he locked them away. He did not want other members of the family to know he had them—not that he considered them great works of art, but because despite it all, blood runs deep. Was that not why, on impulse, in his loneliness he had ordered his cab to take this route to Wisteria Road in St. John's Wood?

In the absence of their parents, 'Old Jolyon' warmed to his newly found grandchildren. *And to those small creatures he became at once a place of pleasure, a place where they were secure, and could talk and laugh and play; till, like the sunshine, there radiated from old Jolyon's wicker chair the perfect gaiety of three hearts.*

When 'Young Jolyon' returned, leaving his distressed wife in their bedroom, *old Jolyon had little Holly on his knee; she had taken possession of his watch;* and what watches those were—heavy, gold, double hunters, which opened both back and front and made a loud tick that commanded the British Empire.

While Holly was playing with 'Old Jolyon's' watch, *Jolly, very red in the face, was trying to show that he could stand on his head. The dog Balthasar, as close as might be to the tea-table, had fixed his eyes on the cake.* Upset, 'Young Jolyon' *spoke sharply to the children. What business had his father to come and upset his wife like this? It was a shock after all these years! He ought to have given them warning; but when did a Forsyte ever imagine that his conduct could upset anybody,* as assuredly as God is an Englishman.

Greatly surprised, for they had never heard their father speak sharply before, they went off, hand in hand, little Holly looking back over her shoulder.

Young Jolyon poured the tea—tea, not only being his father's business, but the solution to all life's problems.

"My wife's not the thing today," 'Young Jolyon' said, without looking his father in the eye. Small talk was not going to come easily.

"You've got a nice little house here," 'Old Jolyon' said without conviction, *"I suppose you have a lease on it."*

Young Jolyon nodded.

"I don't like the neighborhood," said old Jolyon; *"a ramshackle lot."*

"Yes, we're a ramshackle lot."

They drank their tea in soothing silence while Balthasar scratched himself.

"I suppose I oughtn't to have come here, Jo: but I get so lonely." Tears were forming in his eyes. *Young Jolyon got up and put his hand on his father's shoulder.* They were, after all, despite their differences, unlike most the Forsytes, the Forsytes with heart.

There was a drowsy hum of very distant traffic; the creepered trellis round the garden shut out everything but sky, and house and pear tree, with its top branches still gilded by the sun.

Old Jolyon rose to go, and not a word was said about his coming again, but the ice was melting.

'Old Jolyon' *walked towards the Edgeware Road, between rows of little houses, all suggesting to him shady histories of one sort or kind. He stumped his umbrella on the ground, as if to drive it into the heart of that unfortunate body, which had dared to ostracize his son and his son's son in whom he could have lived again! He stumped his umbrella fiercely; yet he himself had followed Society's behaviour for fifteen years—had only today been false to it.*

Back at home, the loneliness descended.

The butler came to lay the table for dinner. This bearded man also wore a moustache, which had given rise to grave doubts in the minds of many members of the family—especially those who, like Soames, had been to Public Schools, and were accustomed to niceness in such matters. Could he really be considered a butler? Playful spirits alluded to him as: 'Uncle Jolyon's non-conformist;' George, the acknowledged wag, had named him: 'Sankey.'

Now, 'Old Jolyon' couldn't even trust his butler.

If Ireland and South Africa were the first clouds over the British Empire, assuredly the trenches of World War I were another. Grandpop

Longley served with the Honourable Artillery Company through most of World War I—in his day, the Great War. He won the Military Cross for bravery. After the war, in common with many other 'Forsytes', in an attempt to help shell-shocked enlisted men get back on their feet, Grandpop engaged his batman—enlisted military servant—as his butler. All went well, until in a burst of shell-shocked anger the butler was found chasing the cook with a carving knife in the kitchen! There, ended the experiment.

"Dinner is on the table, sir!" the bearded, moustached butler of Forsyte folly announced.

Slowly, old Jolyon got up out of his chair and sat alone *at his table to eat his dinner.*

CHAPTER EIGHT

PLANS OF THE HOUSE

Bosinney was the son of a Lincolnshire country doctor of Cornish extraction, who in his will had left him a private annuity of one hundred and fifty pounds a year. Otherwise, he was dependent on what architectural and consulting fees he could garner. However, he had for a while been taken under the wing of his *uncle by marriage, Baynes, of Baynes and Bildeboy, a Forsyte in instincts if not in name, who had little that was worthy to relate of his brother-in-law.*

"An odd fellow!" he would say: "always spoke of his three eldest boys as 'good creatures, but so dull;' they're all doing capitally in the Indian Civil."

During 'Forsythia', the Indian Civil Service had become a sort of hang out for upper-middle class family misfits, just as the army or the church had been for lesser sons of the aristocracy.

Philip was the only one of his nephews that Baynes *liked. "He's got a streak of his father's Byronism,"* he said on one of June's meetings with him, *"why look at the way he left my office; going off like that for six months with a knapsack, and all for what?—to study foreign architecture—foreign! What could he expect?"*

For most 'Forsytes', foreign meant European, or anywhere that was not part of the British Empire. 'Forsytes' never trusted Europe. At school as we were prepared for Imperial service, we gleefully learned that "all wogs begin at Calais." Wog actually was a colonial word for far eastern members of the Empire—successful and reliable Chinese or Malay persons—western Oriental gentlemen; but the word came into our schoolboy language as referring to Europeans, so as to make that clear distinction that Great Britain was assuredly not a part of Europe. When my father's brother, Uncle Gyles, married a French girl in 1948, my Aunt Ginette had to put up with much friendly ribbing that she was a "wog."

Bosinney undoubtedly gained much by studying 'foreign', or European architecture. He was able, in so doing, to break from many of the conventions of the post-Pugin English gothic school and could be perceived as a forerunner of such a great English architect and designer as Lutyens.

On one of June's visits to Mr. Baynes at his home in Lowndes Square, Baynes expressed his confidence in his nephew.

"This house of Mr. Soames's—what a capital man of business—is the very thing for Philip."

The Forsytes rarely referred to Bosinney as Philip—the young architect had not proved himself yet, but they were aware that was his name, as on a plate outside his studio home was clearly stated *'Philip Baynes Bosinney, Architect.'* By incorporating Baynes into his name, his family had acknowledged the 'Forsythian' influence of his successful uncle.

The continuance of family names as Christian or first names, was quite common in 'Forsythia'. Just as the aristocracy tended to merge family connection in titles and coats of arms, so in 'Forsythia' names of families that seemed a good marriage were also passed down. My father was christened Charles William Hovenden Longley. Both his father and his mother's father were Charles William, but the Hovenden honored my Grandmother Longley's rather successful family. The name was then passed down to me. I was christened Peter Hovenden Longley. According to my mother, they wanted to christen me Peter Charles Longley, perpetuating Charles, but my mother was shrewd enough to note that this might lead to difficulties for me at school where I would carry the initials P.C. Longley. P.C. in England stands for Police Constable!

Without a habitat a Forsyte is inconceivable, but Bosinney's *rooms in Sloane Street on the top floor were not those of a Forsyte.*

He had no sitting-room apart from his office, but a large recess had been screened off to conceal the necessaries of life—a couch, an easy

*chair, his pipes, spirit-case, novels and slippers. The business part of
the room had the usual furniture; an open cupboard with pigeon-holes,
a round oak table,* more likely picked up second-hand than from Maples
department store, *a folding washstand, some hard chairs, a standing
desk of large dimensions covered with drawings and designs.*

He was believed to have a bedroom at the back.

As I read Galsworthy's description of Bosinney's studio here, I am
reminded of the endless newspaper snipes in 1959, just as 'Forsythia'
began to crumble, when Her Royal Highness the Princess Margaret
became engaged to the royal family's 'buccaneer'—Anthony Armstrong-
Jones. There were many like descriptions of photographer Anthony
Armstrong-Jones' little studio in Pimlico. The parallels are striking,
and like Bosinney, Anthony Armstrong-Jones had yet to really prove
himself, something that in my opinion he did very successfully later in
his artistic and creative career as Lord Snowdon.

It was rare that Bosinney visited June at Stanhope Gate. On the
one occasion he did, *by one of those coincidences of which she was a
mistress,* Aunt Juley *arrived* just after him. *Thereon Bosinney rose and
hid himself, according to previous arrangement, in the little study, to
wait for her departure.*

"My dear," said Aunt Juley to June, *"how thin he is! You mustn't
let it get worse. There's extract of veal; it did your Uncle Swithin a lot
of good."*

Extracts of beef became an important home remedy in 'Forsythia',
enriching soups; they also made a palatable sandwich spread. The
company of which Grandpa Jack was chief accountant was just such
a company, as its name 'Oxo' showed. They manufactured a similar
beef extract, perhaps not quite as refined as Barlow's extract of veal,
but nutritious and tasty.

Aunt Juley gave June a hard time, pressing her on both Bosinney
and Irene.

"I'm very sorry, Auntie," she said as Aunt Juley prepared to leave,
"but I wish they'd let Irene alone."

After she was gone, *the tears sprang up in June's eyes; running into
the little study, where Bosinney was sitting at the table drawing birds on
the back of an envelope, she sat down by his side and cried:*

"Oh Phil! It's all so horrid!"

On the following Sunday, Bosinney called at Soames' to take him
to the studio to see the plans. Soames was pleased to see that Irene was

congenial in the presence of the architect, even played the piano for him while he was waiting.

The plans were spread on the oak table at the studio. Soames bent over them for a long time without speaking.

He said at last in a puzzled voice:

"It's an odd sort of house!"

A rectangular house of two storeys was designed in a quadrangle round a covered-in court. This court, encircled by a gallery on the upper floor, was roofed with a glass roof, supported by eight columns running up from the ground.

It was indeed, to Forsyte eyes an odd house, although one can see the influence of the 'foreign' Roman atrium.

"There's a lot of room cut to waste," pursued Soames.

"The principle of the house," said the architect, "was that you should have room to breathe—like a gentleman!"

The planned house was all about light, which Bosinney attempted to explain, obstinately standing his ground. Soames, with a view to his growing collection of pictures, secretly agreed. He did not want to give Bosinney too much credit, however, as he might then up the price.

"Won't it look like a barrack?" he enquired.

He did not at once receive a reply.

"I can see what it is," said Bosinney, "you want one of Littlemaster's houses—one of the pretty and commodious sort, where the servants will live in the garrets, and the front door be sunk so that you may come up again. By all means try Littlemaster, you'll find him a capital fellow. I've known him all my life."

Yes, the houses of the likes of Littlemaster, decorated in the William Morris style, could still be found all over the suburbs of late Victorian London, but Bosinney was a clever salesman, he used this common architecture as a take-away from his own masterpiece.

Soames was alarmed. He had really been struck by the plans, and the concealment of his satisfaction had been merely instinctive.

"It's—a big place," he said.

"Space, air, light," he heard Bosinney murmur, "you can't live like a gentleman in one of Littlemaster's—he builds for manufacturers."

Bosinney knew how to play a 'Forsyte'.

"It's all very well all this," Soames said, "but what's it going to cost."

"It'll cost you eight thousand five hundred." It was five hundred over. *"Can't be done for a penny less,"* replied Bosinney cooly. *"You must take it or leave it."*

Conscience told Soames *to throw the whole thing up. But the design was good, and he knew it—there was completeness about it, and dignity; the servants' apartments were excellent too. He,* Soames, *would gain credit by living in a house like that—with such individual features, yet perfectly arranged.*

When they returned to Montpelier Square, and as Irene poured them tea, Soames made one more plea, hoping that the fact that his wife and the architect appeared to approve of each other, even if it was only because he was June's fiancé:

"Can't you see your way to do it for eight thousand after all?" he asked.

Bosinney drank off his tea at a gulp, put down his cup, and answered:

"Not one!"

It was done. *A few minutes later Bosinney rose to go.*

"Well, what do you think of the 'Buccaneer'," he asked his wife after the architect had left.

He looked at the carpet while waiting for her answer, and he had to wait some time.

"I don't know," she said at last.

"Do you think he's good-looking?"

Irene smiled. And it seemed to Soames that she was mocking him.

"Yes," she answered: *"very."*

Chapter Nine

Death of Aunt Ann

In September 1886, the first of that older generation of Forsyte's born and bred in London, died. Aunt Ann passed on peacefully, but the shock of her death was hardly peaceful among Forsytes. It was as if an era had ended.

Aunts Juley and Hester were overwhelmed by the shock. Secretly they felt it unreasonable of Ann to have left them like this without a word, without even a struggle. Perhaps what really affected them so profoundly was the thought that a Forsyte should have let go her grasp of life. If one, then why not all!

Were they afraid of their own end?

In the drawing room *the blinds were drawn*.

There was in 'Forsythia' a ritual to mourning. The very funeral itself was an outward sign of this class, and the first function, not just at the home of the deceased, but at the homes of the deceased's closest relatives, was the drawing of drapes facing the street.

Peeking out, 'Forsytes' would then have the comfort of seeing total strangers pass by and raise their hats—more than just a comfort, but an acknowledgement of their 'Forsyte' status, too.

It was not until five o'clock on the day of Ann's death that *three of the brothers, Jolyon and James and Swithin arrived. Nicholas was at Yarmouth* again, *and Roger had an attack of the gout.*

"I knew how it would be;" muttered James, *"I told you she wouldn't last through the summer."*

Aunt Hester made no reply. She went up to tell her sister that the brothers were there. Aunt Juley, *came down at once. She looked severely at Swithin's trousers, for they were of light blue—he had come straight from the club, where the news had reached him.*

Through much of the era of 'Forsythia', mourning was strictly observed, and mode of dress was paramount in this. For years, the queen had worn black mourning dress after the loss of her beloved Albert, the Prince Consort, and the habit had permeated down through the upper classes. Among the working class, mourning was not nearly as strenuously observed, partly because it was costly, but also in part because the working class had less life expectancy and took death more in its stride. In fact, mourning in the working class was more of a celebration, a final glass of ale at the pub in honor of the deceased:

"Here's to Arthur, he was a good man."

These older Forsytes were schooled in mourning, and to outward appearances it was both an expression of their loss and their class, but 'Old Jolyon', he was different. In his loneliness he allowed some of his philosophy to brood. His heart told him that it was time to kick some of these conventions. They had robbed him of his son and his son's son.

He *stood at the bottom of* Ann's *bed* long after the others, *his hands folded in front of him. He alone of those in the room remembered the death of his mother, and though he looked at Ann, it was of that he was thinking—*'Superior Dosset' and Ann Pierce—yeoman stock who had made good. What were the pretensions of their children and their grandchildren? But death comes to all. *Ann was an old woman, but death had come to her at last! His face did not move, his gaze seemed traveling from very far.*

When the aunts started *moving about, doing 'what was necessary'* in the room. 'Old Jolyon' went downstairs. *In the hall,* he ran into *Smither,* the maid. *He began to ask her about the funeral, and, finding that she knew nothing, complained bitterly that if they didn't take care, everything would go wrong. She had better send for Mr. Soames—he knew all about that sort of thing.*

Then, lacking confidence in his sisters or old Timothy, he said *Smither might send to Park Lane any time she wanted advice. Of course, his carriage was at their service for the funeral. He supposed she hadn't such a thing as a glass of claret and a biscuit—he had had no lunch!*

Soames quickly organized things. The funeral was to be on October 1st. Aunt Ann would be buried in the family vault at Highgate Cemetery. Carriages would meet at The Bower, Bayswater Road, at 10:45 a.m.

The morning came, cold, with a high grey, London sky, and at half-past ten the first carriage, that of James, drove up. It contained James and his son-in-law Dartie.

In 'Forsythia', it was the usual practice for only the male members of the family to attend the actual funeral procession and burial—their ladies gathered in mourning at the family home for the reception after the funeral, and saw that the necessary food and beverages were prepared.

Soames, in his capacity of executor, received the guests.

As I lived in Ireland, and was also often in the United States, in the immediate post-'Forsythia' years of my family, I was not present at the funerals of either of my grandfathers. I did attend the cremation of Granny Mabs, and two years later read the scripture at the burial of Granny Longley. My Uncle Dennis was the executor for Granny Longley's funeral, and I well remember seeing him in a surprisingly 'Forsyte' light as he organized the procession and told us pretty much where we were to stand. There was to Granny's funeral something akin to that of Aunt Ann—it heralded the end of an era. Granny Longley died at The Breach and was buried in Sissinghurst churchyard, her grave very close to that of Sir Harold Nicholson, our aristocratic neighbor, who had been married to the famous member of the Bloomsbury set, Lady Victoria Sackville-West. The garden that Lady 'Vita' had created at their home, Sissinghurst Castle, was one of the most famous horticultural achievements of the twentieth century. As a keen gardener myself, I can certainly relate to that, but in my family, our associations with Sissinghurst Castle were more with the 'man of letters'—Harold Nicholson. Grandpop Longley and Sir Harold Nicholson were well acquainted and quite often took the train up to London from Staplehurst in the same first-class compartment. They were both presidents of the Sissinghurst Village Cricket Club—in a sense, the two squires of Sissinghurst. However, Sir Harold Nicholson was the aristocracy's squire, whereas Grandpop was the 'Forsyte' squire. Their social circles were engaged, but not the same. However, as a small tribute to 'Forsythia', my grandmother's tombstone reads Catherine Amy Longley, nee Hovenden. Both the Hovendens and the Longleys had moved full circle through three generations of 'Forsythia' back to their roots in the Weald of Kent.

Now, when Great-grandfather Oliver Longley died at The Breach in 1945, his funeral procession, despite the difficulties of petrol rationing, had to take him back to 'Forsythia', so that he could be buried with "dear Agnes" and other members of the family at Elmers End Cemetery in Beckenham—a slow procession over some thirty-five miles!

At Uncle Timothy's, *entering the scarlet and green drawing-room, whose apparel made so vivid a setting for their unaccustomed costumes, each* Forsyte *tried nervously to find a seat, desirous of hiding the emphatic blackness of his trousers. There seemed a sort of indecency in that blackness and in the color of their gloves—a sort of exaggeration of the feelings; and many cast shocked looks of secret envy at 'The Buccaneer', who had no gloves, and was wearing grey trousers. A subdued hum of conversation rose, no one speaking of the departed, but each asking after the other, as though thereby casting an indirect libation to this event, which they had come to honour.*

And presently James said:

"Well, I think we ought to be starting."

They went downstairs, and two by two, as they had been told off in strict precedence, mounted the carriages.

When all the male Forsytes were ready, the procession set off to follow Aunt Ann to her resting place. They numbered twenty-one persons—all the male members of the family—all except Timothy, who was poorly, and the ostracized 'Young Jolyon' and his son. One can imagine what thoughts went through 'Old Jolyon's' mind when he saw his great-nephews riding in the Forsyte carriages at a solemn pace behind the black-plumed hearse. Where were his son 'Jo' and little Jolly? But, no other Forsyte, least of all the executor himself, gave it a thought. That branch, simply, along with that wicked woman—the governess—had not been invited.

Upon arriving, the coffin was borne into the chapel, and, two by two, the mourners filed in behind it. This guard of men, all attached to the dead body by kinship, was an impressive and singular sight in the great city of London, with its overwhelming diversity of life, its innumerable vocations, pleasures, duties, its terrible hardness, its terrible call to individualism.

The family had gathered to triumph over all this, to give a show of tenacious unity, to illustrate gloriously that law of property underlying the growth of their tree, by which it had thriven and spread, trunk and branches, the sap flowing through all, the full growth reached at the appointed time. The spirit of the old woman lying in her last sleep had called them to this demonstration. It was her final appeal to that unity which had been their strength—it was her final triumph that she had died while the tree was yet whole.

'Pride comes before a fall!' In accordance with this, the greatest of nature's ironies, the Forsyte family had gathered for a last proud pageant before they fell. Their faces to right and left, in single lines, were turned for the most part impassively toward the ground, guardians of their thoughts; but here and there, one looking upward, with a line between his brows, seemed to see some sight on the chapel walls too much for him, to be listening to something that appalled. And the responses, low-muttered, in voices through which rose the same tone, the same unseizable family ring, sounded weird, as though murmured in hurried duplication by a single person.

Then, *the vault stood open, and, round it, men in black were waiting.*

From that high and sacred field, Highgate, *where thousands of upper-middle class lay in their last sleep, the eyes of the Forsytes traveled down across the flocks of graves*—the Elmers End of North London.

A few words, a sprinkle of earth, the trusting of the coffin home, and Aunt Ann had passed to her last rest.

Round the vault, trustees of that passing, the five brothers stood, with white heads bowed; they would see that Ann was comfortable where she was going. Her little property must stay behind, but otherwise, all that could be should be done.

There was to be a lunch at Timothy's. Swithin, followed by James and Roger, set off for the reception. *The others gradually melted away, old Jolyon taking three nephews to fill up his carriage; he had a want of those young faces.*

The reception at The Breach in 1969, following Granny Longley's funeral, was very much the end of an era in my family, too. Grandpop had died at The Breach in the spring, rather suddenly of a heart attack, and as is often the case, Granny followed him only a few months later. I was actually one of the last people to speak to her before she passed on. She had been fighting a bout of pneumonia. I visited her in her bedroom at the back of The Breach. She looked at me in between heavy breaths, then said:

"Peter, what I need now is a good, long, sea trip." There was a pause, then she continued: "But it wouldn't be any good; they don't build boats with proper funnels any more."

Not only were these words somewhat final, but they were prophetic. In 1969, the Cunard ocean liner *Queen Elizabeth 2* had just come into service. Granny Longley had kept most of her money in shipping, the lifeline of the British Empire, but she did not regard the single, slightly rakish, funnel of the *Queen Elizabeth 2* as proper to shipping. Nor did it follow the lines of the last of Great-grandfather's maritime painting collection in their gilt frames on the walls of The Breach—those *Titanic*-like 'four stackers'. Little did the old lady know, too, that exactly twenty years later I would be the cruise director of the *Queen Elizabeth 2,* and that the slim rakish final painted white rather than Cunard red, had been enlarged to a more acceptable size displaying the correct and proud livery of the Cunard Line!

Almost all the Longley family members were present at the reception in the old house after the funeral. It was the last great gathering at The Breach—the end of an era. It was sad, but cheerful; in fact the old lady had even left a supply of wine for the inevitable event. The Breach was very dear to us all, three generations of Longleys nurtured by the old house, with its peculiar odor, a strange mixture of furniture polish, roast beef, and generations of love. Even the slightly estranged members of the family were present: Great-aunt Bernice's son, Bill Haynes, and Aunt Audrie. Indeed, Granny's funeral was the last time, I believe, that I ever saw Audrie and her daughter, my beautiful cousin, Sally Ann Lewis, to whom a year or two before I had sent a dozen roses to be delivered to her dressing room when she opened in Scarborough with *The Black and White Minstrel Show.* Uncle Dennis was not yet divorced. Uncle Gyles was over from France with his vivacious wife, my Aunt Ginette. My father's sister, Aunt Biddy was down from Scotland, and of course, my mother and father, my sisters and all my Cranbrook cousins were gathered. Like Soames, with dignity, Uncle Dennis had marshaled us in our task. With dignity we had buried the old lady. And as she would have wished, we came back to the old house to celebrate this bastion of 'Forsythia' together for the last time. Like my sisters and I always said of The Breach:

"Whoosh and off comes the cork."

Things would never be the same again. That bell would never again call us in from the farmyard or the gardens. That gong would never summon us into the dining room for the traditional roast. The era was past, but we raised our glasses in salutation.

Soames took advantage of Aunt Anne Forsyte's funeral to talk over things with Bosinney. From the cemetery, *they strolled to Hampstead, lunched together at the Spaniard's Inn, and spent a long time in going into practical details connected with the building of the house.*

Soames was *in excellent spirits when he arrived home and confided to Irene at dinner that he had had a good talk with Bosinney, who really seemed a sensible fellow. If only it had not been for poor Aunt Ann he would have taken her to the theatre; as it was they must make the best of an evening at home.*

"The Buccaneer asked after you more than once," he said suddenly. And moved by some inexplicable desire to assert his proprietorship, he rose from his chair and planted a kiss on his wife's shoulder.

PART TWO

CHAPTER ONE

PROGRESS OF THE HOUSE

The shell of the house at Robin Hill was completed by the end of April. Soames had *an appointment with Bosinney to go over the accounts.*

"I can't make them out," he said at last; "they come to nearly seven hundred more than they ought!"

"I've told you a dozen times," Bosinney answered sharply, "that there'd be extras. I've pointed them out to you over and over again."

Both Soames and Bosinney were pig-headed in their stances— Bosinney as the artist, and Soames as a 'Forsyte', careful with his money. They argued profusely over the accounts, but there were more than just business practices in their mistrust of each other. There was Irene.

"I wish I'd never undertaken your house," said Bosinney suddenly. "You come down here worrying me out of your life. You want double the value for your money anybody else would and now that you've got a house that for its size is not to be beaten in the county, you don't want to pay for it. If you're anxious to be off your bargain, I daresay I can find the balance above the estimates myself, but I'm damned if I do another stroke of work for you!"

Yes, there was Irene to be thought of. Soames *really believed it was only because she had taken to Bosinney that she tolerated the idea of the house at all,* even if their friendship seemed to be a little out of hand.

"Look here," said Bosinney, and Soames was both annoyed and surprised by the shrewdness of his glance. *"You've got my services dirt cheap. For the kind of work I've put into this house, and the amount of time I've given to it, you'd have had to pay Littlemaster or some other fool four times as much. What you want, in fact, is a first-rate man at a fourth-rate fee, and that's what you've got!"*

Soames realized the consequences if he allowed their differences to continue. Bosinney held the trump card. Soames *saw his house unfinished, his wife rebellious, himself a laughing stock.* This whole project was meant to solve his problems with Irene, not aggravate them.

"Let's go over it" he said sulkily, *"and see how the money's gone."*

"Very well," assented Bosinney. *"But we'll hurry up, if you don't mind. I have to get back to take June to the theatre."*

Soames cast a stealthy look at him, and said, knowingly, *"Coming to our place, I suppose to meet her?"*

He was always coming to their place, and Irene seemed always too eager to receive him. Soames reflected on the times he had proposed to her—several. *Once, after they were married he asked her: "What made you refuse me so often?" She had answered by a strange silence. An enigma to him from the day that he first saw her still...*

As Bosinney hurried Soames through the house, he wore a smug look of almost blissful happiness, as if he knew he had won this round. He even was so brazen as to say of his suggestions, *"I would like Irene's opinion."* Soames noted they were on first name terms. *"You want to aim all through the decorations at what I call—charm,"* Bosinney added.

Soames, almost with deliberate attempt to correct the 'Buccaneer's' familiarity *said: "You mean that my wife has charm? I suppose you find Irene very artistic?"*

"Yes." The abrupt answer was as distinct a snub as saying: *'If you want to discuss her you can do it with someone else.'*

* * *

Back in London that evening, June met with them all for dinner before she was to go to the theatre with her fiancé. *The maid Bilson told her that Mr. Bosinney was in the drawing room; the mistress—*

she said—was dressing, and would be down in a minute. She would tell her that Miss June was here.

It was always said by my family in 'Forsythia' that the maids knew far more about what was going on in family affairs than members of the family. Gossip was always rife, and often exaggerated 'below stairs'.

June, forever impatient, did not wait in the hall for Irene to chaperone her. *She opened the drawing-room door softly, meaning to take 'Phil' Bosinney by surprise.*

She took a long breath of the perfume of azaleas, and heard Bosinney's voice, not in the room, but quite close, saying:

"Ah! There were heaps of things I wanted to talk about, and now we shan't have time!"

Irene's voice answered: "Why not at dinner?"

"How can one talk..."

June's first thought was to go away, but instead she crossed to the long window opening on the little court. It was from here that the scent of azaleas came, and, standing with their backs to her, their faces buried in the golden pink blossoms, stood her lover and Irene.

"Come Sunday by yourself—we can go over the house together..."

June saw Irene look up at him through her screen of blossoms. It was not the look of a coquette, but—far worse to the watching girl—of a woman fearful that look should say too much.

"I've promised to go for a drive with Uncle..."

"The big one! Make him bring you; it's only ten miles—the very thing for his horses."

June interrupted them, her anger visible, as she said with sarcasm:

"Were you talking about the house? I haven't seen it yet, you know—shall we all go on Sunday?"

"I am going for a drive that day with Uncle Swithin," Irene answered.

"Uncle Swithin! What does he matter? You can throw him over!"

"I am not in the habit of throwing people over!" Irene said haughtily to her one-time friend.

Soames entered and Irene quickly changed the subject.

"Well! If you are all ready, dinner is too!"

CHAPTER TWO

JUNE'S TREAT

It was more than evident that June's treat of going to the theatre with her fiancé was ruined, as dinner was served at Soames'.

She had looked forward to this evening with keen delight; it was stolen, chaperone-less.

There was a deathly silence around the table. June refused to eat, turning away each course and all the wines. Irene made small talk about the spring that Bosinney eagerly enhanced, only to have June flatly denounce. Soames, himself more than suspicious took it out on the dinner itself.

"The asparagus is very poor. Bosinney, glass of sherry with your sweet? June, you're drinking nothing!"

However, as a sample menu of a 'Forsythia' dinner table, Galsworthy's scene is very revealing. Soup was served first. Soup was always served at both Hillside and at Chelston—Grandpop's house in Beckenham. It was standard practice to have a stockpot forever cooking in a Longley kitchen, or most 'Forsythia' kitchens. The bones of every roast, cutlet, chop, or game bird, were constantly boiled up to make the stock for soups that were then enhanced with garden produce; for in latter 'Forsythia', in its leafy suburbs, most the great Victorian, Edwardian, and 'twenties homes had sizeable kitchen gardens. As Sewell lauded over the gardens at Hillside, so Spencer lauded over the gardens at Chelston. In childhood, the sense of smell is one of our strongest memories—the smell of tomatoes, an odor now almost unknown—of onions hanging in great sets, of plums, their juices oozing from the wasp holes, organic apples, real mushrooms grown in the valuable horse dung collected off the unpaved streets—these were the odors of that first playground for my sisters and myself, the kitchen garden at Chelston.

'Forsythia' was a world before the deep freeze, before mass-produced, forced vegetables and fruits purveyed by supermarkets in technicolor glory. Onions hung, herbs were wrapped, fruits were put up, and vegetables were grown in season. If the asparagus for the dinner at Soames' was poor, it was probably because it would have been early in the asparagus season—too thin to be truly succulent.

At Soames', fish was served after the soup, *a fine fresh sole from Dover.* Dover sole was always a favorite in my family, and although not often found today in private homes, was a favorite course in the days when Cook could sauté the whole fish in one skillet. 'Forsyte' cooks prepared these great dinners on wood or coal-fed ranges that took up the best part of one whole wall of the kitchen, allowing them to juggle the large utensils needed in preparation. The fish would have arrived fresh in a box of light straw and ice shavings, on the day of consumption. The fishmonger's boy would have delivered it, either by horse and dray, or in a large basket on the front of a bicycle. The World War II years, however, greatly reduced the number of domestics in the twilight of 'Forsythia', and many post-war households, such as ours, did not employ full-time cooks and butlers as in the pre-war years. A daily maid often called a charwoman, a title brought back from imperial India meaning 'Tea' woman, had taken the place of three to five servants of the past.

Granny Mabs and my mother shared a daily maid, one of the more formative persons of my earliest years—Mrs. Lloyd, or Lloydy as we called her. My first real memory is of Lloydy drawing butterflies for me on a sofa in the drawing room at Chelston. Charwomen in the 1950's did not wear cap and apron like the domestics of my grandparents' and great-grandparents' era, but rather wore large, all encompassing floral aprons, probably easily purchased as utility clothing after the Second World War. Lloydy cooked wonderful cakes for us. In fact, the odor of fresh cake permeated from the kitchen at least twice a week. There were three other tasks that I always remember fell to Lloydy. She regularly cleaned all the brass and silver. The brass included all the brass stair rods that kept the long Turkish runner carpet in place. Every day she was at our house she would scrub the kitchen table so that the boards were bleached in septic cleanliness. Her third task seemed to always be to scrub the stone step at the front door and polish the red tiles of the porch. I have vague recollections, too, of her turning the handle of the large two-roller mangle in the scullery to squeeze out the rinsing water from the laundry.

The bread, the milk, and the coal were still all delivered by horse and cart, although in the post-war world, we usually picked up our own fish and meat from local fishmongers and butchers, who in turn had stocked their windows and cold rooms with fresh produce from the Billingsgate and Smithfield markets early in the morning before opening for business.

There was, even by the 1950s, a subtle difference between the classes in the definition of trade. Many 'Forsytes', like my family as wholesale produce merchants, traded, but we were not like the butcher and the fishmonger "in trade." We were the directors of trades. Wholesale business was accepted at the level of a profession, but those we supplied, even though owners of their own small businesses, were regarded as "in trade." Herein, apart from education, lay a major division between the upper-middle class and the lower-middle class of 'Forsythia'. This manifested itself in an interesting way when I was at my preparatory boarding school, Newlands, at Seaford in Sussex. While preparing for the Common Entrance Examination for Entry into Public Schools, once again, meaning private schools like Tonbridge, we had to have French conversation classes. A standard question from the examiner was to ask us in French what our fathers did. At Newlands, most my contemporaries' families were in colonial administrative service, officers in the armed forces, members of the legal profession, stockbrokers, company directors, in property, or aspects of inherited landed agriculture. When asked in French what was my father's profession, I floundered for the right French words. I knew not how to say in French that he was the director of three family firms—wholesale produce merchants in fresh meat, game, and poultry in Smithfield Market. I said, in my best schoolboy French, in front of the whole class, "Mon pere est un bucheur," which translates, "My father is a butcher." I had to then explain to my chiding 'Forsyte' schoolmates what I really meant. It would be very unlikely that a butcher in the 1950s would have considered sending his son to a private and elitist school, not so much because he may not have been able to afford the fees, as because he would not have been of 'Forsyte' class.

After dry champagne was poured, the tense dinner party at Soames' moved on to its next course.

Lamb *cutlets were handed, each pink frilled about the legs. They were refused by June, and silence fell.*

There followed a salad—*Spring chicken* salad.

Then, June and Irene continued their spat about spring, Bosinney only championing Soames' beautiful wife.

An apple charlotte came upon a silver dish. Then, *olives from France, with Russian caviare, were placed on little plates. And Soames,* no doubt out of peeve that this pre-theatre dinner for June was causing her to be so rude to his wife Irene, even if for apparent good reason— nay, maybe peeved for that very reason himself, *remarked: "Why can't we have the Spanish?" But no one answered.*

The olives were removed. A silver tray was brought, with German plums. There was a lengthy pause. In perfect harmony all were eating them.

Bosinney counted up the stones: "This year—next year—sometime... dared he to look at Irene? This was a game that we 'Forsytes' all played as children. It was supposed to determine if we would get married. Whoever picked up the last stone had his or her answer according to which of four time periods were revealed by the pips.

Irene finished softly: "Never."

Egyptian cigarettes were handed in a silver box. Soames taking one, remarked: "What time's your play begin?"

Noting the time, Bosinney and June soon left.

June made her lover take her on the top of a bus, saying she wanted air, and there sat silent, with her face to the breeze.

The tradition of double-decker public transport stretched way back into 'Forsythia'. The horse drawn omnibuses of June's day attracted the more adventurous 'Forsytes' just as the big, red double-deckers of my childhood. Often, on those visits with Granny Mabs and my mother to Derry and Toms and other Kensington department stores, my sisters and I would ride from Victoria Station to Kensington on the top of a double-decker bus—number 52, which we always remembered as it was the same as the street number of Hockeredge, our house in Wickham Way. Sometimes, the treat was banned because we had smuggled our teddy bears onto the train in Beckenham, which always caused great wrath, not so much because my mother and Granny disapproved of the bears, but more because they were afraid we would leave the bears somewhere, especially on the top of a double-decker bus. 'Forsytes', if they allowed themselves this adventure in public transport, never rode in the bottom of the bus. We always tried to sit in the front seats on the upper deck, where we had a fantastic bird's eye view of the streets. It always fascinated me that from our seated position it looked as if the bus was actually driving along the sidewalk, but, best of all, when riding from Victoria to Kensington, we would skirt the garden wall of Buckingham Palace. We could look in to that great oasis of lake, lawns and borders spreading up to the terrace and garden façade of the royal residence.

'Forsytes' were not great royalists, although everything they did in their professional lives would be in the name of king and country. Close association with royalty and court presentations was more in the lifestyle of the aristocracy, and the monarchy as the opium of the people, lay among the lower-middle class. 'Forsytes', however, were brought up on the folklore of monarchy, and in Edwardian England this was epitomized in A.A. Milne's nursery rhyme of Christopher Robin and Alice.

"They're changing the guard at Buckingham Palace," said Alice.

Somehow, like Christopher Robin and Alice, we all expected to see the king or queen if we were within sight of Buckingham Palace.

Our teddy bears were part of this same comfortable nursery world epitomized by A. A. Milne, and one of my most loved heirlooms is a touched up photographic portrait of my mother when she was about five and clutching her teddy bear. In England, we were not party to any story of an American president named 'Teddy' Roosevelt sparing a brown bear out hunting—in twentieth century 'Forsythia', our childhood teddy bears were named after King Edward VII—'Teddy' being a popular nickname for Edward. Sometimes, this was also applied to one of our first great Saxon kings, starting the long unbroken line of British monarchy—King Egbert. It was not surprising, therefore, that the bears that Diane and I used to try to smuggle on our persons so they could ride the double-decker buses and look into Buckingham Palace, were named Winnie, after A. A. Milne's immortal Edwardian teddy, and Egbert. Now, my sister Sally, being four years my junior, barely knew 'Forsythia'. Her bear was one of the first of a new breed of post-'Forsythia' teddies. They had longer fur and later, much wider faces. Nonetheless, her bear was as precious to her in our childhood as were Winnie and Egbert. He was named Timmy.

From their seats on the top of an open omnibus, June and Bosinney would have enjoyed that same bird's eye view of London's streets. Just as spring had moved Irene and Bosinney, and as a result so infuriated June, it had got into the blood of the driver of the omnibus. *He felt the need for letting steam escape, and clucked his tongue* once June and Bosinney were seated, *flourishing his whip, wheeling his horses, and even they, poor things, had smelled the spring, and for a brief half-hour spurned the pavement with happy hooves.*

The whole town was alive; men in evening dress had thrown back overcoats, stepping jauntily up the steps of clubs; working folk loitered; and women—solitary and moving eastward in a stream—swung slowly along with expectation in their gait; dreaming of good wine and a good supper, or, for an unwonted minute, of kisses given for love.

As Bosinney drank in the spring fever, June withdrew further into her silence.

Leaving the omnibus, *they entered the theatre. And mounted to their seats in the upper boxes. From the age of fifteen* June *had habitually accompanied her grandfather to the stalls, and not common stalls, but the best seats in the house towards the centre of the third row, booked by old Jolyon, at Gregan and Boyne's, on his way home from the City, long before the day* of performance.

My father used to do the same. Every school holiday there would be a theatre treat. In the latter days of 'Forsythia', Gregan and Boyne's had been replaced by Keith Prowse. At home, we had the Keith Prowse book that showed a seating plan of every theatre in London. When my father brought the tickets home we would excitedly look in the book to see where we would be sitting. Often, our seats like 'Old Jolyon's', were in that select area in the stalls—but never the common stalls. If we were not in that small privileged area of the stalls, we had seats in the front row of the dress circle—not the common upper circle.

June *had expected reward for her subterfuge, planned for her lover's sake; she had expected it to break up the thick, chilly cloud, and make the relations between them—which had been so puzzling, so tormenting—sunny and simple again as they had been before the winter. She had come with the intention of saying something definite; and she looked at the stage with a furrow between her brows, seeing nothing, her hands squeezed together in her lap. A swarm of jealous suspicions stung and stung her.*

In the interval, she finally got up her courage, speaking to him.

"I want to say something to you Phil," she said.
"Yes?"
"You don't give me a chance to be nice to you; you haven't for ages now!"
Bosinney made no answer.
June cried passionately: "You know I want to do everything for you—that I want to be everything to you..."
She finally challenged him:
"Phil, take me to see the house on Sunday!"
With a smile quivering and breaking her lips, and trying, how hard! Not to show that she was watching she searched his face, saw it waver and hesitate, saw a troubled line come between his brows, the blood rush into his face. He answered: "Not Sunday, dear, some other day."
"Why not Sunday? I shouldn't be in the way on Sunday."
He made an evident effort and said: "I have an engagement."
"You are going to take..."
His eyes grew angry; he shrugged his shoulders, and answered: "An engagement that will prevent my taking you to see the house!"
The theater lights extinguished mercifully hiding *the tears of rage rolling down her face.*
Yet in this world of Forsytes let no man think himself immune from observation.
Three rows behind, sat *Euphemia, Nicholas' youngest daughter with her married sister, Mrs. Tweetyman.*
For 'that little June' this evening, that was to have been 'her treat' was the most miserable she had ever spent.

* * *

June's grandfather tried to console her after Bosinney returned her to Stanhope Gate. Shrewdly, 'Old Jolyon' asked if Irene was there—*and Bosinney?*
"Yes" was all that his granddaughter had to say.
June left to retire. *When the door was closed, old Jolyon dropped his paper, and stared long and anxiously in front of him.*
'The beggar!' he thought. 'I always knew she would have trouble with him.'

* * *

On 'Forsyte 'Change' the word soon got out at Timothy's, how Euphemia and Mrs.Tweetyman had seen June and her fiancé at the theater. *With tears of enjoyment in their eyes, they related how she had kicked a man's hat as she returned to her seat in the middle of an act, and how the man had looked.*

Aunt Juley repeated: *"My dear! Kicked a ha-at? Oh! I shall die."*

The word was out, *that engagement wouldn't last long.*

CHAPTER THREE

DRIVE WITH SWITHIN

Sunday *was as balmy as a day in June.* Swithin *had put on a blue frock-coat, dispensing with an overcoat, after sending* his coachman *Adolf down three times to make sure that there was not the least suspicion of east in the wind. Majestic on the pavement he fitted on a pair of dog-skin gloves; with his large bell-shaped top hat.*

"Adolf!"

"Sare!"

"The new plaid rug! The phaeton hood down; I am going—to—drive—a—lady!"

A pretty woman would want to show off her frock; and well—he was going to drive a lady! It was like a new beginning to the good old days.

Like all the Forsytes, he had fallen to the charms of Irene—'Mrs. Soames.'

Going up to his horses' heads, he examined their bits; not that he knew anything about bits—he didn't pay his coachman sixty pounds a year to do his work for him, that had never been his principle.

Someone at the club, after seeing him drive his greys up to the door—he always drove grey horses, you got more style for the money, some thought—had called him 'Four-in-hand Forsyte.' Swithin had ever after conceived it right to act up to it. The name had taken his fancy, not because he had ever driven four-in-hand, or was ever likely to, but because of something distinguished in the sound. Four-in-hand Forsyte! Not bad!

If Swithin Forsyte had come to London twenty years later than he did, he would have looked, and probably played the part of that new breed of city gentlemen—a stockbroker, but his profession had been as an auctioneer—an auctioneer of property. Like many of this new breed, to drive a fine pair, or quartet of horses, was a challenge that was accepted in 'Forsythia' as a hobby.

In my childhood, this tradition lived on in my own family. Uncle Dennis' first wife, my Aunt Brigid, was a driver—not exactly 'four-in hand,' but a keen member of the Driving Club patronized most of my life by His Royal Highness, The Prince Philip, Duke of Edinburgh. She had a trap that she would truss up for weddings in the Cranbrook area, and in the 1950s and '60s, was quite a well-recognized figure at local fairs and county events. As family members on our visits to The Breach, we were often treated to a round-trip ride through the Kentish lanes in the trap, taking in a traditional pub lunch en route. Grandpop, who had some knowledge of horses from his World War I experiences, along with Uncle Gyles and my father, would inspect the harness and tack in much the same way as Swithin, not really having much of a clue as to its purpose.

In the study at The Breach there were numerous photo albums and framed pictures of Grandpop's training and action with the Honorable Artillery Company. Not only were the officers mounted, but the guns were drawn by teams of horses. I must assume, therefore, that Grandpop was a reasonably competent horseman as a young man, although he showed no sign of equestrian skills later in life. Likewise, during army training with the Officers' Training Corps while at Tonbridge School, my father became a passable horseman by chance. He had never ridden as a young boy, beyond possible donkey rides, but when it came to training exercises on Salisbury Plain where the whole school Officers' Training Corps was camped at the end of each summer term, he was coaxed into becoming the dispatch rider. During the maneuvers there was only one dispatch rider for Tonbridge School, and when asked for a volunteer, a rather mean boy suggested my father, expecting to laugh at his lack of equestrian skills. My father surprised them all, becoming quickly competent enough. He never had to walk back to camp if his platoon was eliminated, as he was the only dispatch rider. He learned fast enough to enjoy five pleasant military summer camps riding his horse around Salisbury Plain!

My mother used to inspect the brasses that were sometimes hanging from the martingales of working horses. She collected horse brasses most of her life. She was most insistent as she went around country antique stores, to see that they were proper, hand-forged brasses that really had hung from the forward tack of brewery and colliers' teams— for the breweries and colliers of 'Forsythia' had the finest teams of Clydesdales to pull their heavy drays. This collection of horse brasses hung on an oak beam above the inglenook fireplace of the dining room at Hockeredge. My mother used to lovingly polish them herself—a task she never gave to Lloydy or her charwoman successors.

Aunt Brigid looked the part up on the driver's seat of her trap, and the locals waved and smiled as we would ride by. She sounded the part, too, as of all my relatives of that generation she had the most county or horsey accent—very upper crust, although in her personal life she had no pretensions. She was the daughter of Cranbrook's dentist, who was first generation over from Dublin and still spoke with a fine, but cultured, Irish brogue. In the latter days of her driving career, she drove oxen, and I remember a splash in the local paper on her skills that was somewhat reminiscent of that article on Great-uncle Will Goodchild as 'The last Yeoman of England.'

Adolf was already up behind; the cockaded groom at the horses' heads stood ready to let go; everything was prepared for the signal, and Swithin gave it. The equipage dashed forward, and before you could say Jack Robinson, with a rattle and flourish drew up at Soames's door. I don't know who Jack Robinson was, but in 'Forsythia' we all used that expression for something that happened fast.

Irene was ready and waiting. She stepped up and in the phaeton *as light as—er—Taglioni, no fuss about it, no wanting this or wanting that.* She wore a simple white veil.

"White veil—capital taste," Uncle Swithin remarked, *"Where to?"*

"Robin Hill."

Swithin opened his eyes at the mention of Robin Hill, it was a long way for his horses, and he always dined at half-past seven, before the rush at the club began; the new chef took more trouble with an early dinner—a lazy rascal!

He would like to have a look at the house, however. A house appealed to any Forsyte, and especially to one who had been an auctioneer.

A look of solemn pride came portentously on his shaven square old face, he rolled his head in his stand up collar, like a turkey-cock preening himself.

She was really a charming woman.

With a crack of the whip they were off.

At Robin Hill, *Bosinney came out to meet them, and all three entered the house together; Swithin in front making play with a stout gold-mounted Malacca cane, put into his hand by Adolf, for his knees were feeling the effects of their long stay in the same position.*

Bosinney showed Swithin and Irene over the house. Swithin had a few comments to make, some that amused Irene, such as his reaction to the spacious atrium.

"Ah! The billiard-room!"

When told it was to be a tiled court with plants in the centre, he turned to her.

"Waste this on plants? You take my advice and have a billiard table here!"

Irene *had lifted her veil, and the smile of her dark eyes seemed to Swithin more charming than ever.*

The wine cellar particularly impressed Swithin, but when Bosinney suggested they take a look at the elevation of *the house from the copse below, Swithin came to a stop.*

Bosinney provided him with a chair and then escorted Irene alone to the copse. Swithin admired the view and felt content as he watched them go down the hill. Dozing, he saw himself *a sentinel on the top of the rise, he appeared to rule over the prospect—remarkable—like some image blocked out by the special artist of primeval Forsytes in Pagan days, to record the domination of mind over matter.*

And all the unnumbered generations of his yeoman ancestors, wont of a Sunday to stand akimbo surveying their little plots of land, their grey unmoving eyes hiding their instinct with its hidden roots of violence, their instinct for possession to the exclusion of all the world—all these unnumbered generations seemed to sit there with him on the top of the rise.

And so it was as my mother conjured up her image of her young husband's grandfather as she put her pen to paper to start her tribute to this 'Forsyte' family into whom she had married—*'Oliver Longley pulled down his cap and looked over his beloved acres.'*

But in his deeper sleep, Swithin Forsyte's fantasy took him down to the copse. He visualized the beautiful Irene unchaperoned with 'The Buccaneer.' *His Forsyte spirit watched her balanced on a log, her pretty figure swaying, smiling down at that young man gazing up with such strange, shining eyes; slipping now—a-ah! Falling, o-oh! Sliding—down his breast; her soft, warm body clutched, her head bent back from his lips; his kiss, her recoil; his cry: "You must know—I love you!" Must know—indeed, a pretty—? Love! Hah!*

Swithin awoke. He knew he had dreamed, and he knew it troubled him. *Virtue had gone out of him. He had a taste in his mouth. He had dreamed something about a new soup, with a taste of mint in it. Or, perhaps…*

Those young people—where had they got to?

As he arose, Swithin then saw them. *Irene was in front; that young fellow—'The Buccaneer!'—looked precious hang-dog there behind her; had got a flea in his ear, he shouldn't wonder. Serve him right, taking her down all that way to look at the house! The proper place to look at a house from was the lawn.*

The lawn at The Breach was in front of the house, and extensive. To the left was a formal rose garden surrounded by beds of lavender from which emanated a strong perfume. A tall flagstaff stood sentinel in the corner of the rose garden, from which a 'victory' union jack had flown at the end of World War II and probably nearly three decades before on Armistice Day, November 11, 1918. The best view of the creeper-clad, old Regency house was from the lawn—and the lawn was the host for summer pleasures. There was a hammock and a tennis court—a 'Forsythia' essential of the 1920s and '30s, not so much because of the ardor of the game as the excuse for a social gathering. Grandpop's house Chelston, and Beulah, Granny and Grandpa Jack's house in Sydenham before they moved to Park Langley in Beckenham, both had tennis courts. In fact, in his tribute to my father at the memorial service in thanksgiving for his life, Uncle Dennis alluded to these tennis parties.

"Charles enjoyed life at home where the family entertained a wide circle of cousins and friends, who were always made welcome at Chelston. Impromptu tennis parties and games often took place and these were invariably followed by something to eat with everyone setting to and helping to prepare the meal and then doing the clearing up afterwards."

At The Breach, on the lawn sat substantial wooden garden furniture where 'Madam', and her mother-in-law before her, sat and lauded over formal afternoon teas, with real Jersey cream supplied by the farm's pedigree Jersey cow, Betty. The lawns were always cut in immaculate stripes, and the further back one walked the greater was the aspect of the old family home with its crooked chimney pot that no Longley saw fit to change and the big cedar tree beside the house. The building had character, as did the splendid automobiles from Great-grandfather's six cylinder Daraq to Grandpop's Rover and my father's Armstrong Siddley—the Star Sapphire—that over three generations had been parked in the gravel drive in front of its façade.

For Swithin Forsyte, however, somehow in his snooze his feelings for Bossiney's house had cooled. He had no doubt that Irene had told him what she thought, *and no wonder, over a house like that—a great ugly thing, not the sort of house he was accustomed to.*

He looked intently at their faces with his pale immovable stare. That young man looked very queer!

"You'll never make anything of this," he said tartly, pointing at the mansion; "too new-fangled!"

Swithin, however, brightened at the mention of tea—the cure-all for all 'Forsytes' throughout 'Forsythia', even though *he had a contempt for tea—his brother Jolyon had made a lot of money by it—but he was so thirsty, and had such a taste in his mouth, that he was prepared to drink anything.*

In 'Forsythia', it could truly be said that at four o'clock everything stopped for tea. Cricket matches stopped for tea. Tennis games stopped for tea. Shoppers stopped for tea. I believe, even debate in the Houses of Parliament stopped. All my family joined the ritual. Like Granny Longley with her Hovenden glare, Granny Mabs had a way of expressing her disapproval for my dislike of tea: "Don't like tea," she said, her face tilted on one side, "well, you are a funny boy." I still don't drink tea— but, the ceremony—of that I approve; the large silver tea pot and the even bigger silver hot water pot used for brewing and pouring; the silver tea strainer, the sugar cubes and tongs, which all help to make it taste better. In the winter, there were crumpets on a toasting fork, meringues bursting with cream, 'Battenberg' cake, gingerbread, and sandwiches of 'Patum Pepperum'—an anchovy paste known as the gentleman's relish.

Once in a while, too, there were scones with strawberry jam and thick jersey cream. In the summer, there were cucumber sandwiches, tomato sandwiches, even sardine sandwiches, shortbread, and fruitcake that my father always called "British Rail cake," and in season, strawberries and cream. Yes, tea was a ritual, and it was served with very much these same ingredients throughout the Empire.

At four o'clock, with the regularity of Big Ben at nine, from Victoria in Canadian British Columbia to Hong Kong and Penang in the Far East, everything stopped for tea. If I could substitute water or an orange squash for the cup of tea, I could certainly enjoy the rest.

I got to know Hong Kong pretty well during its last twenty years as a crown colony of the British Empire. There, I met Aileen Bridgewater, a radio host for the local English speaking broadcasting station. One time, when I was cruise director of the *Queen Elizabeth 2,* she interviewed me as King Neptune, having witnessed my antics in that role when she was on board and crossed the equatorial line in the Pacific. I remember blowing bubbles in a glass through a straw as my signature from the ocean depths before the interview commenced in her Hong Kong studio! Unfortunately, the ship's doctor, Nigel Roberts, was also waiting to be interviewed. He ruined my act by saying in a loud voice: "Peter why are you blowing bubbles through a straw in that glass?" Aileen Bridgewater had been born in Shortlands, a suburb of Bromley adjacent to Beckenham, so we immediately had something in common. In fact, before we moved to Chelston we lived in the same street in Shortlands as Aileen's family—Kingswood Road. Our little house there, Copthorne, was my parents' first home, and after I was born in Scotland while Copthorne awaited repairs from bomb damage, it was my first home. Several times I stayed with Aileen and her husband Ken in Hong Kong, and as late as the 1990s they were still serving traditional English afternoon tea in their little garden. If we splurged, we might even go to the terrace at the Repulse Bay Hotel, a recently restored colonial haunt where an excellent afternoon tea was served.

Likewise, in British Columbia, Canada, I have often enjoyed one of the best representations of true English afternoon tea at the grand old Empress Hotel on Victoria's waterfront, and of course, on the great Cunard ocean liner *Queen Elizabeth 2* everything stopped for afternoon tea. The tea was served in individual silver Cunard teapots and the sandwiches and scones rested on Royal Doulton china. The waiters delivered white glove service. On one occasion, the famous

Shakespearean actor Patrick Stewart, who is perhaps even more famous for playing Captain Kirk on *Startrek*, invited me for afternoon tea in his suite. As he stirred his teacup he looked at me and said: "Peter, one of the reasons I like to travel on the *Queen Elizabeth 2* is because it is one of the few places today where you can still get a proper cup of English tea."

Swithin Forsyte was rather like me. He enjoyed the accoutrements of English afternoon tea, but he supplemented his cup of tea with a glass of champagne just as I supplemented mine with a glass of orange squash.

On the drive back to London, Swithin could not help but notice *a half smile on Irene's face—a smile of hopeless surrender and of secret joy.* As if his dream had come back to him, he thought: *'I shouldn't wonder a bit if that architect chap were sweet on Mrs. Soames.'*

Even in the face of an accident, when Swithin's horses bolted, Irene retained that otherworldly look.

"I've never been in an accident before," she said.

"Don't you move!" Swithin commanded gallantly, noting, despite his nervousness, *she was smiling,* and *perfectly calm. "Sit still. Never fear, I'll get you home!"*

He was surprised to hear her answer:

"I don't care if I never get home!"

Later, *Swithin described* this incident *at Timothy's—"I pulled 'em up, there she was as cool as myself. God bless my soul! She behaved as if she didn't care whether she broke her neck or not! What was it she said: 'I don't care if I never get home!'" Leaning over the handle of his cane, he wheezed out to his sister Juley: "And I'm not altogether surprised, with a finickin' feller like young Soames for a husband!"*

CHAPTER FOUR

JAMES GOES TO SEE FOR HIMSELF

*A*fter Swithin had related at Timothy's the full story of his memorable *drive, the same, with the least suspicion of curiosity, the merest touch of malice, and a real desire to do good, was passed on to June* and generally made the rounds on *Forsyte 'Change.*

The proper construction was put on her reception of the news. She was upset. Something was therefore very wrong. Odd! She and Irene had been such friends.

Gossip was almost a protection of property in 'Forsythia'. *That great class to which they had risen, and now belonged, demanded a certain candour, a still more certain reticence. This combination guaranteed their membership.*

Only real wrongdoers would suffer in a protective game of one-upmanship. Forsytes had little brief for *George,* Roger's son, *when he lost all that money playing billiards:* or for Dartie, who had to be bailed out from the bailiffs. Small wonder that those two had kind of teamed up. Or *young Roger,* George's brother, *when he was so dreadfully near to marrying the girl to whom, it was whispered, he was already married by the laws of Nature; or again Irene, who was thought, rather than said, to be in danger,* but with whom almost every Forsyte felt sympathy because of their own secret feelings for her beauty—'too good for Soames.'

Timothy's was but one of hundreds of such homes in this City of London—the homes of neutral persons of the secure classes, who are out of the battle themselves, and must find their reason in the battles of others. To talk about them was as near as they could get to the possession of all those children and grandchildren after whom their soft hearts yearned.

Yes, in 'Forsythia' protective gossip placed one branch of a family against another, the more obvious because, in 'Forsythia', families were larger, most having at least five children. 'Old Jolyon's' generation of Forsytes numbered ten. The next generation twenty-three cousins, and the third generation twelve. So it was in my family.

According to the family bible, my great-great-grandfather, Giles Longley, born on October 23 in 1828, married Martha Anne Southon in 1854. Part yeoman farmer from Marden, near Cranbrook in Kent, and part businessman, he and Martha were the first Longleys to live in the style of 'Forsythia'. They had eleven children, including two sets of twins. Six of their children died before they were two years of age. Charles William Longley was the oldest son, but he died in France when he was twenty-five. This left his brother Oliver, my great-grandfather, as the primogenitor heir. Great-grandfather married Minnie Anna Rendall in 1887 and they had six children, who fared rather better than the previous generation, but for the tragic death of Agnes in 1905. In the last generation of 'Forsythia', the five remaining children, Grandpop, and of his brothers, Oliver, known as 'Tig,' and George, and a younger daughter, Bernice, all had children, scattering cousins throughout the metropolis. Only Grandpop's brother Douglas, had no children, but Douglas did have a stepson, Roy Follitt, who was killed in the Second World War at Salerno, in the Italian campaign. Roy's father, Reg Follitt, had been my Great-uncle Douglas' best friend, and they both served in the Royal Flying Corps in World War I. Reg was one of the unlucky ones and was killed in the latter part of the war. After the war, Great-uncle Douglas married Lillian, his best friend's widow—the former Mrs. Follitt—known in our family as 'Auntie Woggs.' Her son, Roy, was very close to my father's family and a great friend of his step-cousin, my Uncle Gyles. They attended Tonbridge together, Uncle Gyles at Judde House and Roy at Park House. Later, they served in the same theater in World War II before Roy was killed. It was somewhat ironic that Roy died in the same battle that rewarded my Uncle Gyles with his Military Cross for bravery. It is touching that Uncle Gyles in 2010 had hoped to join a battlefield tour to Monte Cassino, which included Salerno, when it was his intention to lay a poppy wreath on Roy's grave in the British Military Cemetery at Salerno. Unfortunately, due to health reasons, he was unable to go, but instead a friend layed the wreath on his behalf.

In those twilight 'Forsyte' years after they left Tonbridge and before war broke out in 1939, Roy spent much time with my uncle, along with my father and their other siblings. They both joined the Beckenham Hockey Club, The Bickley and Chiselhurst Squash Club, and the Park Langley Tennis Club, although I feel more for society than gamesmanship. As Uncle Gyles described those halcyon days: "They were great days of tennis parties at Chelston, dances and pub crawls, nightclubs and shows in London, falling in and out of love, and travel." In 1936 and 1937, Roy and Gyles went on Mediterranean cruises together. Then, Roy married Joan Brothers, who lived in Wickham Way, and possibly they met at the Park Langley Tennis Club. It was here, too, that my father first met the Collings sisters of Wickham Way, at first attracted to Eileen, the younger girl, and then to my mother Dorothy, whom he married in 1940. My mother introduced my father to Langley Park Golf Club and the start of a long courtship with the game that was more about my mother than his own sporting qualities.

Roy and Joan had a daughter, Pera, and Gyles was asked to be her godfather, just as later, in 1944, my parents asked Uncle Gyles to be my godfather. Roy worked for H.J. Searle and Sons, furniture manufacturers with a showroom in Lewisham. The firm was owned by the same family who lived in the Avenue across the street from my great-grandparents, Oliver and Minnie Longley. Great-uncle George had married Marjorie Searle, and Douglas Searle, her much younger brother, was at Park House, Tonbridge, with Roy Follitt. Uncle Gyles had thought of working in the Electric company showrooms in Beckenham, during these salad days, but by chance he got the opportunity to join Gestetner, auditing their subsidiaries, and found himself from 1938 to 1939 in Europe, including Berlin in the days approaching World War II.

Roy was the first to join up. He was commissioned into the Queen's Own Royal West Kent Regiment, later the same regiment that I was attached to as a sergeant in the Tonbridge School Combined Cadet Force in the 1950s. Gyles joined up in October 1939 after he left Paris on September 4—one day after war was declared on Germany. He became an infantryman in the Dorsetshire Regiment and was later commissioned as an officer in the Royal West Kent, but he was in a different battalion to Roy.

Eventually, Uncle Gyles joined the 44th Reconnaissance Regiment and went overseas with them to Egypt in May 1942. He was in North Africa until that campaign ended with the German surrender in Tunisia in July 1943. After that, it was training for the Italian Campaign, Winston Churchill's—"Soft underbelly of Europe." It was anything but soft, and produced some of the most ferocious fighting of World War II. It was at Salerno that Roy and Gyles found themselves in the same battle, and for Roy a tragic reenactment of his father's death some twenty-five years earlier.

The Hovendens and the Goodchilds were no less prolific, having nine children in the second generation and a raft of cousins in the third. I remember many of the third generation of Goodchilds coming to tea at Hockeredge and my being astounded that a family could have so many children. That was the one and only time I ever really remember encountering these Goodchild cousins, but there were some interesting link ups between us all in the second generation. John Goodchild trained as an artillery officer in World War II, and befriended in his unit the nephew of Lord Montefiore. After the war, Hugh Montefiore, a convert from that Jewish family, was ordained as a priest in the Church of England. While I was at Cambridge, Hugh Montefiore was the 'avant-garde' vicar of the University Church of Great St. Mary's, and one of my lecturers in New Testament studies. It so happened that his niece, Alice, daughter of his brother Lord Montefiore, married David Gestetner, who was chairman of the French Gestetner duplicating company at the time Uncle Gyles was their managing director. The connection led to my being invited to a formal afternoon tea at the Great St. Mary's vicarage while I was an undergraduate at St. Catherine's College, Cambridge.

On my mother's side, Great-grandpa Collings had one son and three daughters, Grandpa Jack and my great-aunts, Babs, Nellie, and Dorrie, and the Cuthbertsons, along with Granny Mabs had two surviving sons, my great-uncles, Cecil and Bert. Their other son, Frank, was a casualty of World War I. Their descendents were less prolific than the Longleys, but were still the cause of 'Forsyte' frictions when it came to scandal, each branch protecting its property, pedigree and pitch.

The subtle rivalry between the Doggetts and my mother has already been shown, and to some extent it was perpetuated in the second generation by my Great-aunt Nellie's two daughters, my aunts, Daphne and Betty, who were always promoting their offspring over our direct line. We all lived in Wickham Way in the last days of 'Forsythia', but we saw very little of our cousins even though they lived next door. They were considered smarter than us, just as their mothers had considered themselves smarter than my mother. None of this was really true, as we were all pretty intelligent and well educated, but in that 'Forsyte' game of one-upmanship the Doggetts were masters. Aunt Betty's son, my cousin Michael, lived in Cambridge, and many years after the demise of 'Forsythia', I found myself sitting next to him at a lunch party given by our Aunt Daphne at Worthing on the Sussex coast. I had hardly spoken to Michael since we were teenagers. When the conversation turned to Cambridge, he was astounded to see how much I knew about the city, and even more astounded when he found out that I was a graduate of the university! Nobody had ever revealed in his branch of the family that any of us Longleys had gone to the university, in reality, a feather in my cap as neither of my O'Callaghan cousins were alumni!

My mother, and Daphne and Betty, all went to Sydenham High School for Girls at about the same time. They befriended the daughter of an Italian painter—Emilio Tafani. Lola Tafani, although close to all three of them, chose my mother for a graduating trip to Paris, France. Her father then painted my mother's twenty-first birthday portrait, which in reality was one of the best portraits this accomplished artist, who exhibited at the Royal Academy's Summer exhibitions in the 1930s, ever painted—a lot better than subsequent portraits that he did of Daphne and Betty.

A certain rivalry also developed in the splintering generations of Oliver Longley's family. Audrie was Great-uncle 'Tig's' daughter, and as we have seen, made a hasty marriage to a ne'er-do-well planter in Kenya, who left her for another woman, penniless, and with a young daughter. 'Tig' died in 1942. My grandfather, and later my father, tried to take care of Audrie and her brother Chris, but at times there were tensions, especially after my father decided to sell out at Smithfield where Audrie had enjoyed a safe haven. There was also something that was not quite right in Great-aunt Bernice's marriage—almost as if she had married beneath herself, a little like the tension between Aunt Eileen's husband, Jim Sullings, and the Collings family, but more of that later.

Then, there was my Aunt Ginette. Everybody loved her—vivacious, always beautifully groomed and dressed, chic, and French. She was the Irene of my family. She was the one daughter-in-law who could get around my grandmother. For one thing, in 'Forsythia' it was chic to smoke, and Ginette and Granny Longley smoked incessantly. My mother could not stand their cigarettes, and could never find the same favor with her mother-in-law as Ginette. Ginette also enjoyed a Gin and Dubonnet, or maybe a Cinzanno Bianco that like Audrie she called a "chinky-binky." My mother hardly drank at all. It is ironic that despite these minor tensions, more between Granny Longley and my mother than between Ginette and my mother—for Ginette always admired the fact that my mother spoke rather good French—my sister painted a portrait of Granny that really captured the essence of this last matriarch of The Breach. It is not flattering, but it was Granny, with her stolid independence both of fortune and character. She is sitting at her card table in the drawing room, glass of gin and tonic on the table, cigarette dangling from her mouth, and a jig-saw puzzle underway, and the great lawn of the house stretching out through the Regency paned window behind her. If Ginette and my mother were there at one of those family get-togethers, Granny, with her apricot miniature poodle, Flap, perched on her lap, would be laughing and chatting with Ginette, while my mother would be sitting in stony silence waiting for my gentleman of a grandfather to cheer her up as he always did.

Aunt Brigid with her farm dogs, the collies Tessa and Phlip, breezed in and out of these gatherings, adding that county tone with her voice, but showing us that in post-'Forsythia' years the land had to be farmed by those who owned it, unlike in Great-grandfather's day when the foreman, Williams, and his assistant, Collard, took care of things. However, when the family heard of the divorce between Aunt Brigid and Uncle Dennis, it was considered a sad scandal and it was quite a while before the family accepted Dennis' new wife, my Aunt Pat. Now, she is much loved, just as Brigid was much loved.

James Forsyte feared that something was seriously wrong in the relationship of his daughter-in-law, Irene, and his son, Soames. *She didn't get on with Soames as well as she might, but she was a good little thing! It was long since young Jolyon's escapade*, running off with that governess, the foreigner from Austria—now that was a scandal. To 'Forsytes' it was accepted *that one could reckon on having love, like measles, once in due season, and getting over it comfortably for all time—as with measles, on a soothing mixture of butter and honey—in the arms of wedlock.*

Of all those whom this strange rumour about Bosinney and Mrs. Soames reached, James was the most affected.

He had long forgotten the small house in the purlieus of Mayfair, where he had spent the early days of his married life with Emily, yes, *Emily though pretty had nothing,* but passion had driven him then. Had history repeated itself with Soames? However, in 'Forsythia' the outward vow of the wedding ceremony was sacred, "till death do us part." Actually, James *had forgotten the early days, not the small house, a Forsyte never forgot a house—he had afterwards sold it at a clear profit of four hundred pounds. He had forgotten those days, with their hopes and fears and doubts about the prudence of the match, and that strange irresistible attraction that had drawn him on, till he felt he must die if he could not marry the girl.*

James had passed through the fire, but he had passed also through the river of years that washes out the fire; he had experienced the saddest experience of all—forgetfulness of what it was like to be in love.

He doubted it, but he hoped that the rumors would abate.

A scandal! A possible scandal!

To repeat this word to himself thus was the only way in which he could focus or make it thinkable. He had forgotten the sensations necessary for understanding the progress, fate, or meaning of any such business; he simply could no longer grasp the possibilities of people running any risk for the sake of passion.

Ah! But there was no truth in it—could not be. He was not afraid; she really was a good little thing.

James, like his brothers, admired Irene. She had brought elegance and glamour to the family, just like my aunt, Ginette. And in our minds, as the younger generation of the Longley family, it was a tough pick between Ginette and the equally vivacious, but rather more approachable, Brigid. Diane and I had stayed with Uncle Dennis and Aunt Brigid in their first small home, The Chip—ironically, literally a chip, or small end wing, of that rambling old seventeenth-century farmhouse, Hocker Edge, that had belonged to the Hovendens back in their yeoman days. It was a gloriously happy time. We played adventurous games in the woods behind the house, took long baths with all Aunt Brigid's collection of aquatic toys, and we accompanied Dennis and Brigid on trips to the seaside before we had grown wary of the cold ocean of the south coast. There is old silent film taken on Uncle Dennis' cine camera of all of us scampering in the waves. Ginette is there in a chic bathing suit, along with my robust cousins from Scotland, Aunt Biddy's sons, John and Gyles—John always known as 'Johnny' and Gyles then known as 'Jaykie.' These were happy times. We helped milk the cows, fed the ducks, watched the pigs eat swill, and walked those beloved acres with my grandfather at The Breach. Beyond a vague notion that Aunt Brigid suffered severe migraine headaches, we could see no end to this happy 'Forsythia' world. My cousins were born—Aunt Brigid's sons, Daniel and Robert. The great dining table at The Breach needed all its leaves to accommodate us. The happy days rolled on. "Whoosh, off came the cork." So, where were the winds of change? In 1958, we all assembled together at the Elizabethan Barn outside Tunbridge Wells for a black-tie dinner-dance to celebrate Uncle Gyles and Aunt Ginette's tenth wedding anniversary. Again, in 1964, we all attended a magnificent private dinner at the exclusive Mirabelle Restaurant in Mayfair, London—white tie and tails—to celebrate Granny and Grandpop's golden wedding. A year later, we were at The Mansion House in London, to attend the Livery Dinner of the Worshipful Company of Barbers when my father was master—again, white tie and tails.

In fact, before the war, every Friday, the Longleys all attended a family dinner at Hillside, for Grandpop and his brothers all lived in Beckenham in the heyday of 'Forsythia'. It was a tradition to celebrate the week's close of business at Smithfield. It was always white tie and tails. The huge joint, almost certainly furnished by R. F. Potter and Co., was wheeled in on the meat trolley, covered by one of those heavy silver domes with handles of entwined leaves and acorns, so hard to keep completely free of tarnish. And, here, on Fridays, would ensue the 'Forsyte 'Change' of the Longley family—those little concerns of patronizing gossip that were meant in the best interests of all and the preservation of property.

In a less pretentious way, Granny Mabs and Grandpa Jack celebrated their Golden Wedding in 1960. It was one of the most beautiful balmy July evenings in their 'exceptional' garden that I can remember—the same beautiful garden that had been the venue of my mother and father's wedding reception, and Aunt Eileen and Jim's reception. On those occasions as on this, the Longley and Collings families came together. We sat in the garden until midnight having enjoyed a very lovely catered finger buffet, and an appropriate amount of champagne, Grandpa Jack's favorite drink that he only got to enjoy on rare occasions.

Granny Longley and Granny Mabs never got along very well; Granny Mabs being practical and shrewd, Granny Longley being a spendthrift and extravagant. It was always difficult when they were at the same events. Like with the Forsytes, there was an undercurrent that was tangible if not spoken.

Oh, how James Forsyte felt this same undercurrent. How his sisters, Juley and Hester, rubbed it in. *What could he do?*

Talk it over with Soames? That would only make matters worse. And, after all, there was nothing in it, he felt sure.

It was all that house. He had mistrusted the idea from the first. What did Soames want to go into the country for? And if he must go spending a lot of money building himself a house, why not have a first-rate man, instead of this young Bosinney, whom nobody knew anything about? He had told them how it would be. And he had heard that the house was costing Soames a pretty penny beyond what he had reckoned on spending.

James decided he needed to see this house for himself.

Without saying a word, therefore, to anyone, he took a hansom to the station and proceeded by train to Robin Hill; thence—there being no 'flies,' in accordance with the custom of the neighborhood—he found himself obliged to walk.

He started slowly up the hill, his angular knees and high shoulders bent complainingly, his eyes fixed on his feet, yet neat for all that, in his high hat and his frock-coat, on which was the speckless gloss imparted by perfect superintendence. Emily saw to that; that is, she did not, of course, see to it—people of good position not seeing to each other's buttons, and Emily was of good position—but she saw that the butler saw to it.

My father did not take great care of his clothes much of his adult life. In fact, his trousers became so baggy and disheveled at one point that my sisters and I nicknamed him 'The Clown,' and the name stuck for the rest of his life. However, in his younger days he was immaculate in dress. My mother always said it was because at Chelston, before the war in those golden days of 'Forsythia', maids always prepared his clothes for him and automatically picked anything up off the floor. Granny Mabs was very impressed in the late 1930s when my father started courting my mother on a three-year engagement, for Father always looked like Fred Astaire, clothes pressed and carrying a cane and gloves. In the post-war years I remember him being very smart, too, leaving for work in a pressed suit with his bowler hat, his furled umbrella, gray gloves, and gray spats over highly polished shoes. Actually, he was always good at polishing his shoes, it was a task he rather enjoyed, and in the 1950s every week we had a pick-up service from the University Tailors cleaners and pressers, who took care of his clothes. In post-'Forsythia' this service disappeared, along with such luxuries as the knife sharpener, who regularly pedaled the streets of Beckenham with his grinding wheel that sharpened the blades of countless kitchen knives. Alas, without the props of 'Forsythia', my beloved father became 'The Clown.'

At length, James saw the house at Robin Hill, just a glimpse and then he was there. On such a beautiful day *even British workmen scarcely cared to do more than they were obliged, and moved about their business without the drone of talk that wiles away the pangs of labor.* I am reminded of a popular song about the British workman in the late 1950s when 'Forsythia' pride was crumbling—*'Right said Fred, let's have another cup of tea.'*

*Through spaces of the unfinished house, shirt-sleeved figures worked slowly, and sounds arose—spasmodic knockings, the scraping of metal, the sawing of wood, with the rumble of wheelbarrows along boards—*so much a part of my own childhood as the builders of Beckenham started to clear and rebuild after the devastation of war damage. The smell of sawdust, fresh plaster, and that sickly, clean odor of wallpaper glue, still permeate my nostrils. In fact, Chelston sustained some war damage. In 1946, when Granny and Grandpop moved down to The Breach, we moved from Kingswood Road, Shortlands, to the old house in Overbury Avenue. At Chelston, we lived in the whole house for two years and then had it divided into three flats, one on each floor. We lived in the middle flat. Throughout the alterations, we were in residence.

Bosinney found Soames' father poking around at Robin Hill.

"How do you do, Mr. Forsyte! Come down to see for yourself?"

It was exactly what James had come for, and he was made correspondingly uneasy. He held out his hand, however, saying:

"How are you" without looking at Bosinney.

As they walked around, James kept asking about costs. They argued about the big oak tree on the lawn, and finally on entering inside noted the inner court. *Like Swithin, James was* at first *impressed.*

"You must have spent a dooce of a lot of money here," he said, after staring at the columns and gallery for some time. *"Now, what did it cost to put up those columns?"*

"I can't tell you off-hand," thoughtfully answered Bosinney, "but I know it was a deuce of a lot!"

"I should think so," said James "I should..." He caught the architect's eye and broke off. Bossiney realized this clever young man was playing him.

He grew discouraged. The fellow was sharper than he had thought, and better looking than he had hoped. He reminded James of a hungry cat. He felt the mockery.

Then, looking sharply at Bosinney, he played his ace.

"I daresay you see a good deal of my daughter-in-law; now, what does she think of the house? But she hasn't seen it, I suppose?"

Bosinney did not fall for the trap. He calmly acknowledged her visits.

"Soames brought her down, I suppose?"

Bosinney smilingly replied, "Oh, no!"

"What, did she come down alone?"

"Oh, no!"

"Then—who brought her"

"I really don't know whether I ought to tell you who brought her."

James gave up. He had achieved nothing. The 'Buccaneer' was clever with his answers. James was no nearer to knowing the truth.

"Well," he said, "if you don't want to tell me, I suppose you won't! Nobody tells me anything."

He turned to leave.

"By the by," Bosinney said, having sized up 'Forsyte 'Change', "could you tell me if there are likely to be any more of you coming down? I should like to be on the spot!"

Very slowly, more bent than when he came, lean, hungry, and disheartened, James made his way back to the station.

The Buccaneer, watching him go so sadly, felt sorry perhaps for his behaviour to the old man.

CHAPTER FIVE

SOAMES AND BOSINNEY CORRESPOND

Nicholas' youngest daughter, Euphemia, stirred the pot again at Timothy's at a time when James was visiting *on a matter connected with a drainage scheme which was being forced by the sanitary authorities on Timothy.*

"I saw Irene yesterday at the Stores: she and Mr. Bosinney were having a nice little chat in the Groceries," she stated. She had observed them while busying herself purchasing *a box of Tunisian dates.*

Boxes of dates were traditional fare throughout 'Forsythia'and had always looked the same. Succulent crystalized dates, still on the stem, wrapped in lace-patterned paper, were packed tightly into boat-shaped boxes that had exotic Saharan scenes on the covers. They had looked as much the same in Great-grandfather's time at Hillside as they did in the post-war era of my childhood, when for some reason they were fairly easily obtainable despite rationing. At Christmas, these boxes of dates lay open, beside the Turkish Delight all covered in powdered sugar, and among the muscatels, tangerines, nuts, stem ginger, marzipan, and crystallized fruits that wove their way between candles and crackers on our Dickensian Christmas dinner tables. 'Forsytes' liked dates.

Both Granny Longley and my mother were very particular about their Christmas tables. My mother spent weeks making Christmas decorations for the table, selecting candles to match Christmas crackers, flowers and napkins, and wrapping table gifts to match the china.

And, apparently, according to a Christmas letter that I received from Aunt Biddy, Granny Longley always arranged her own table either on Christmas morning or on Boxing Day, for most Christmas Days in the 1920s and '30s, the Longley family celebrated at Hillside with my great-grandparents. In those days, there were plenty in domestic staff to lay up a holiday table as they did at Hillside, but apparently, Granny used to shut herself up in the dining room and not let anyone in until she had arranged her special table with annual surprises.

In the Groceries store, Bosinney *seemed to be pleading. Indeed, they talked so earnestly—or, rather, he talked so earnestly, for Mrs. Soames did not say much—that they caused inconsiderately, an eddy in the traffic. One nice old General, going towards Cigars, was obliged to step quite out of the way, and chancing to look up and see Mrs. Soames's face, he actually took off his hat, the old fool! So like a man!* Yes, every man took note of Irene. *But it was Mrs. Soames's eyes that worried Euphemia. She never once looked at Mr. Bosinney until he moved on, and then she looked after him. And oh, that look!*

James still was not convinced, wanting to isolate himself and his branch of the family from scandal.

"Oh," he said, *"they'd be after wallpapers no doubt."*

Euphemia smiled. *"In the Groceries!"*

Worried, but refusing to be drawn into this aspect of 'Forsyte 'Change', James left for the office, *Forsyte, Bustard and Forsyte.* He didn't always go to the office now, leaving most the business to Soames.

Soames was *sitting in his revolving chair.*

He produced a letter from Bosinney he had just received.

James read it, perhaps feeling a little guilty that he had to this point said little about his visit to Robin Hill.

'I had your father here yesterday afternoon, who made further valuable suggestions.

Yes, he was right, he must have upset Bosinney.

'Please make up your mind, therefore, whether you want me to decorate for you, or to retire, which on the whole I would prefer to do.

'But understand that, if I decorate, I decorate alone, without

interference of any sort.'

James asked him what he was going to say, but Soames seemed loath to discuss this with his father. Soames was now the trusted solicitor of the family firm. James only handled a few clients. Soames would handle this himself. He was entrenched in 'Forsyte' values. He was *safe. Tradition, habit, education inherited aptitude, native caution, all joined to form a solid professional honesty, superior to temptation from the very fact that it was built on an innate avoidance of risk.* Countless of his class trusted him. Avoidance of risk was a hallmark of good business in 'Forsythia'. It was also relatively easy as the Empire provided little risk, everything booming to the benefit of the mother country in exchange for good government, education and order.

After Great-grandfather died, when Grandpop was chairman of the family business and my father the most active director, my father was approached by a sender in Sussex, who was starting a chicken processing plant. These chickens would be factory bred and frozen for mass marketing—the first such venture in England. The company was to be named Buxted Chicken. My father was offered ground floor shares in the venture with the idea that he could provide the outlet in Smithfield for this excursion into factory farming. Grandpop was still the controlling director and advised my father against the offer. After all, my family's firms were among the oldest established wholesale purveyors of game, fresh poultry, and meat in Smithfield.

"The chicken will be tasteless, not of our quality," was Grandpop's viewpoint. "We should not deal in mass produced tasteless chickens."

Naturally, the chairman's advice was taken. My father declined the offer. Buxted Chicken became one of the most lucrative marketing ventures in the industry, leading to the mass marketing of almost all poultry and most meat products from the 1960s onward. My father would have made a fortune, and probably also caused a new impetus to Campbell, Key and Longley and E. Weatherley and Co. that would be desperately needed in the post-'Forsythia' world of frozen foods and the direct marketing of the same for the rise of supermarket chains. But alas, 'Forsythia' was *built* like Forsyte, Bustard and Forsyte *on an innate avoidance of risk.*

Soames believed that he should not rashly answer this letter without consulting with his Uncle Jolyon. There was more to Bosinney's reaction than he personally wanted to admit.

'Old Jolyon' was chairing a shareholders' meeting of The New Colliery Company that very afternoon, and Soames was to be there as their solicitor, *in case 'anything should arise.'* Shareholders rarely challenged 'Old Jolyon', who predictably as one of his class, was well able to govern in the name of the Board of Directors, giving an air of confidence that the shareholders were in safe hands, but on this particular occasion there was an issue on the table that could potentially cause trouble.

A telegram had come from Scorrier, the mining expert, on a private mission to the mines, informing them that Pippin, their Superintendent, had committed suicide.

Mining accidents were not uncommon and suicide, to the Board, was a mining accident. Whatever had led this man to suicide, was not their main concern, but the compensation to his family was their concern. Hemmings the clerk, the equivalent of a Dickensian Mr. Macawber to this Board, a groveling member of the lower-middle class with a Mr. Guppy of *Bleak House* sense of his rising importance, spoke to Soames.

"What our shareholders don't know about our affairs isn't worth knowing. You may take it from me, Mr. Soames."

It is interesting that these clerical assistants of 'Forsythia' had their mode of addressing their employers. The chairman would undoubtedly have been addressed as "Sir," or "Mr. Forsyte, Sir," but the junior partners, so often in 'Forsythia', as in my own family, were often less formally addressed by these company clerks. Some of these clerks had respectfully known the sons of the founder from boyhood, and almost as a confirmation of their being party to family business affairs, they often addressed the junior partners by their first names, but with the title, "Mr."—hence Hemmings' "Mr. Soames."

In a truly 'Pickwickian' sense, however, the employees of 'Forsythia', particularly in London where cockneys predominated, usually addressed their bosses as "Guv'nor." It was about 1954 when my father first took me to Smithfield Market, just so I could observe a little of what we were all about. I was between nine and ten years of age; and dressed in my best—short pants suit, a flannel shirt and school tie, polished shoes with long socks held up by invisible garters, and my gray preparatory school cap, with its red griffin crest—I followed my father down the great avenues of the market with all their elaborate iron tracery and glass, reminiscent of the great Crystal Palace, he dressed in his suit, bowler hat, and carrying that badge of 'Forsythia'—the furled umbrella. The porters, the salesmen, all alike would greet us with that splendid Dickensian call: "Mornin' Guv'nor!" and they addressed it to me as much as to him. In the office, however, with its archaic Dickensian ledger desks, it was "Mr. Charles" and "Mr. Peter."

* * *

At the Board Meeting, 'Old Jolyon' as chairman, stood up: *"I propose, then, that the report and accounts be adopted."*

He expected to almost immediately be able to close the meeting.

To his surprise, several of the shareholders following the initial query of *a tall, white-bearded man, with a gaunt, dissatisfied face,* expressed their views on the payment of 5,000 pounds *'To the widow and family of our late superintendent,' who ill advisedly committed suicide, at a time when his services were of utmost value.* Some thought it too much, some too little, like the superintendent's brother-in-law, and *The Rev, Mr. Boms* said, *"I should say that the fact of the—er—deceased having committed suicide should weigh very heavily—very heavily with our worthy chairman."*

Forsytes and particularly, 'Old Jolyon', who had his own philosophy of life, were not as involved with the moral ethics, particularly of the disestablished churches of the lower-middle class, as this worthy cleric. That suicide was a mortal sin did not weigh that heavily on 'Old Jolyon'.

The shareholders turned to Soames—yes, 'something had come up.'

"The point," he said, *"is by no means clear. As there is no possibility of future consideration being received, it is doubtful whether the payment is strictly legal. If it is desired, the opinion of the court could be taken."*

There was a huge growth in company law in the era of 'Forsythia'. And legal cases over property, inheritance and payments would sometimes take many years to settle, as witnessed in the long case of Jarndyce versus Jarndyce in Dickens' *Bleak House.* Soames, no doubt thought that his answer would deter the shareholders from entering into lengthy court proceedings.

The Superintendent's brother-in-law frowned and looked from Soames to old Jolyon in a pointed manner.

However, Soames felt victory, again on the principle of not taking risk. A court proceeding would be risking the company, and not to his surprise, a more stolid shareholder with 'Forsyte' interest in maintaining the profits and good name of the company, ended the matter.

"I deprecate the proposal altogether. We are expected to give charity to this man's wife and children, who, you tell us, were dependent on him. They may have been; I do not care whether they were or not. I object to the whole thing on principle. It is high time a stand was made against this sentimental humanitarianism. The country is eaten up with it. I object to my money being paid to these people of whom I know nothing, who have done nothing to earn it. I object in toto; it is not business. I now move that the report and accounts be put back, and amended by striking out the grant altogether.

The Board was relieved. The motion was carried.

Soames placed his attention once again on speaking with Uncle Jolyon about Bosinney and his letter. He did so as they walked from the meeting.

Old Jolyon ran his eyes unwillingly over the letter.

"What he says is clear enough," he said.

"He talks about 'a free hand'," replied Soames.

"Well if you don't trust him why do you employ him?"

"It's much to late to go into that," Soames answered, sensing where his uncle was coming from. *"I thought if you were to speak to him, it would carry more weight!"*

"Tell me," said old Jolyon; *"I don't know what you mean. You come worrying me about a thing like this. I don't want to hear about your affairs, you must manage them yourself!"*

Soames was useful as a solicitor to the Board, but in his family affairs 'Old Jolyon' didn't want to know. Besides, *in old Jolyon's mind there was always the secret ache that the son of James should be pursuing the paths of success, while his own son...!* That was what really bothered him. Forsytes were born to stand on their own two feet. And that is what he now so wished for his own son, whom he himself had ostracized. It gnawed at his heart.

* * *

Soames wrote to Bosinney.

He gave him his 'free hand' but stated:

*'I wish you to clearly understand that the total cost of the
house as handed over to me completely decorated, inclusive of
your fee, must not exceed twelve thousand pounds—12,000.'*

As an artist, Bosinney offered his resignation if he was to be pursued
to the exact sum for decorating.

Soames, fearful that there was a lot more to this than the house, but
ever fearing scandal, wrote back:

*'I did not mean to say that if you should exceed the sum
named in my letter to you by ten or twenty or even fifty pounds
there would be any difficulty between us. This being so, I
should like you to reconsider your answer.'*

Bosinney replied the next day:

'Dear Forsyte,
'Very well.
Ph. Bosinney'

CHAPTER SIX

OLD JOLYON AT THE ZOO

'**O**ld Jolyon's' relationship with his granddaughter, June, was becoming ever more soured by this Bosinney business—*she had been such a companion to him ever since she was three years old! Forces regardless of family or class or custom were beating down his guard; impending events over which he had no control threw their shadows on his head. The irritation of one accustomed to have his way was roused against he knew not what.*

His desire to see Jo's children, Jolly and Holly, ever increased in his loneliness. 'Old Jolyon' arranged to meet with them at the zoo. He arrived at the zoo door to find it was a 'shilling day'—the expensive day at the zoo. He paid for his ticket and entered.

From the stone terrace above the bear-pit his son and his two grandchildren came hastening down when they saw old Jolyon coming, and led him away toward the lion-house. They supported him on either side, holding one to each of his hands, whilst Jolly, perverse like his father, carried his grandfather's umbrella in such a way as to catch people's legs with the crutch of the handle. Young Jolyon followed, still mystified and suspicious of his father's change of Forsyte heart—a softening.

Thus they reached the lion-house.

I remember my sister Diane and I being taken to the London Zoo in Regent's Park, but I can not recall whether it was my parents or my grandparents who took us on the treat. Ironically, the only thing I really remember about the London Zoo was the lion-house, but in the late 1940s there was a lot of publicity surrounding the birth of a polar bear cub named Brumus at the zoo. Not surprisingly, therefore, a white teddy bear named Brumus, joined Winnie and Egbert in our nursery.

The British have an almost universal love of animals and the Empire took the menagerie far beyond the horses and hunting dogs of the eighteenth-century aristocracy. Apart from the parrots, cockatoos and budgerigars found in many a 'Forsyte' home, there were pet monkeys, very popular in the twenties and thirties, often brought back after a tropical tour of duty, and there was a fascination with the big cats of Africa and India.

For the most part, the London Zoo was patronized by the lower-middle class, many in 'Forsythia' having had that first-hand experience of exotic animals in the lands of the Empire. My mother was not particularly fond of the London Zoo in Regents Park. For one thing, it was laced with the strong, pungent odor of big cat dung due to the relatively small areas of caged captivity. Later in our childhood, my sisters and I went to Whipsnade Zoo, where the animals had safari park freedom, and we could enjoy a picnic at the zoo free of those pungent odors. Later in life, at least three times, I had the opportunity to visit the game parks on safari in Africa. Once you have seen giraffes, zebra, elephants, hippos, crocodiles, antelope, and the big cats in the wild, and even more so, once you have seen them under the vast African or Indian sky, the zoo almost disgusts.

However, for the lower-middle class and the working class, the zoo, was in 'Forsythia' a major attraction. Entry was cheap, except on 'shilling days'. It was the setting for many jokes and one of the most famous working class recitations of all time, *Albert and the lion,* which tells the macabre story of Albert, Mr. and Mrs. Ramsbottom's son, dressed all in his Sunday best, when taken to zoo, pokin' lion with stick with 'orses 'ead 'andle that led to lion eatin' poor Albert in front of Mr. and Mrs. Ramsbottom, too!

There had been a morning fete at the Botanical Gardens in Regent's Park on the day that 'Old Jolyon' had this rendez-vous with 'Young Jolyon' and his family. *A large number of Forsy—that is, of well-dressed people who kept carriages—had brought them on to the Zoo, so as to have more if possible for their money before going back to Rutland Gate or Bryanston Square.*

"Let's go to the Zoo," they had said to each other; "it will be great fun!" It was a shilling day; and there would not be all those horrid common people.

They lined up waiting to see the animals fed.

A well-fed man in a white waistcoat said slowly through his teeth: "It's all greed; they can't be hungry. Why, they take no exercise." At these words a tiger snatched a piece of bleeding liver, and the fat man laughed. His wife, in a Paris-model frock and gold nose-nippers, reproved him: "How can you laugh, Harry? Such a horrid sight!"

Young Jolyon frowned. He held a contempt for the shallow arrogance of his class. *To shut up a lion or tiger in confinement was surely a horrible barbarity,* but *the idea of its being barbarous to confine wild animals had probably never even occurred to his father.*

As they were leaving the zoo, *Old Jolyon found an opportunity of speaking to his son on the matter next to his heart. "I don't know what to make of it," he said; "if June's to go on as she's going now, I can't tell what's to come. I wanted her to see the doctor, but she won't. She's not a bit like me. She's your mother all over. Obstinate as a mule! And then, there's this Bosinney. I should like to punch the fellow's head, but I can't."*

It was impossible to discuss with his son the true nature and meaning of Bosinney's defection. Had not his son done the very same thing fifteen years ago?

But, 'Young Jolyon' got the message.

"I suppose he's fallen in love with some other woman?"

Old Jolyon gave him a dubious look. "I can't tell," he said; "they say so."

"Then it's probably true, and I suppose they on 'Forsyte 'Change' *have told you who she is?"*

"Yes," said Old Jolyon—"Soames's wife."

For a moment there was a heart rending spark of truth that flew between them. 'Young Jolyon' knew that his father knew that he would understand. There was that first glimmer of shared trust between them.

Surprisingly, however, *Old Jolyon came to a sudden halt.*

"I don't believe a word of it," he said, "it's some old woman's tale. Get me a cab, Jo, I'm tired to death!"

As they stood to hail a cab, endless carriages of 'Forsytes' were leaving the zoo. *Amongst these carriages was a barouche coming at a greater pace than the others, drawn by a pair of bright bay horses. The chariot attracted Young Jolyon's attention; and suddenly on the back seat he recognized his Uncle James.* Also with Uncle James, were his cousins, Rachel Forsyte and Winifred Dartie, and beside his uncle, Dartie himself.

Those in the carriage made eye contact with the group of kin awaiting a cab. *Young Jolyon saw that he had been recognized, even by Winifred, who* he had not seen since *he had forfeited the right to be considered a Forsyte. Old Jolyon did not see them pass; he was petting poor Holly who was tired.*

"Uncle James has just passed with his female folk," said young Jolyon.

His father looked black. "Did your uncle see us? Yes? Hmph! What's he want, coming down into these parts?"

The silent bonding between father and son climbed up another stair.

'Old Jolyon' hailed an empty cab. *"I shall see you again before long, my boy!" he said.*

CHAPTER SEVEN

AFTERNOON AT TIMOTHY'S

There was now a deep mistrust between 'Old Jolyon' and his brothers. In defense of June, 'Old Jolyon' *had made up his mind that Bosinney was maligned.* This was something brought on by James' family and Soames in particular. He decided to confront his brothers, knowing that on 'Forsyte 'Change' at Timothy's, the incident at the zoo was probably causing even more gossip.

'Old Jolyon's' hunch was right. *He saw James's carriage blocking the pavement in front of 'The Bower'. So they had got there before him—cackling about having seen him, he dared say! And farther on, Swithin's greys were turning their noses towards the noses of James's bays, as though in conclave over the family, while their coachmen were in conclave above.*

Yes, it was always said in 'Forsythia' that the servants knew more about the family's goings on than some of the family themselves.

'Old Jolyon' *found the front drawing-room full.* They were all there.

Of them all, it was Swithin who had greatest pride in the family. *If he had heard in dark, pessimistic moments the words 'yeoman' and 'very small beer' used in connection, with his origin did he believe them? No, he cherished the secret theory that there was something distinguished somewhere in his ancestry.*

"Must be," he once said to young Jolyon, before the latter went to the bad. *"Look at us, we've got on! There must be good blood in us somewhere."*

This claim to good blood somewhere in their ancestry was common among 'Forsytes'. A claim to ties with the aristocracy or the landed gentry, however dubious, was much prized. Although not directly participating in, or interfering with the lifestyle of the established aristocracy, 'Forsytes' liked to believe that some of that 'blue blood' had found its way into their veins. Early in life, I learned that belief that Grandpa Jack's mother was a Massey, a daughter of the lineage of Lord Massey of Tipperary. However, Grandpa was never sure that she was legitimate. The family did have a book that was inscribed from Lord Massey, but it was also quite well known that some members of the Massey family were notorious Irish absentee landlords, who liked to dally in London, staying at their clubs and possibly indulging in affairs. It seems that Great-grandmother Harriet 'Penny' Massey was brought up in London, and not Ireland, and was courted by my great-grandfather during one of his periods of prosperity. My grandfather's youngest sister was my Great-aunt Dorrie. She was born during one of Great-grandfather Collings' periods of misfortune, when the family was living in those rooms above the tobacconist's shop in Camberwell—a time when Grandpa Jack remembers actually playing football with "the ruddy-nosed kids" on Camberwell Green. Great-aunt Dorrie saw her father recover his fortunes, but no doubt because of the more humbler origins of her birth, she was the one for whom this aristocratic connection seemed most important.

Great-aunt Dorrie never married, but after serving as a nurse in World War I she divided her time between her sisters and my grandfather as the poor relation, until, to the relief of all, she met Douglas Stevens, a teacher of elocution. She became his housekeeper and companion and they stayed together for the rest of their lives, although they never married.

George Bernard Shaw wrote his play *Pygmalion* in the Edwardian era—a play about a professor of elocution who believed he could educate a cockney flower girl so that she could pass as a lady in 'Forsythia'. In the musical version of his play, *My Fair Lady*, that was a Lerner and Lowe smash hit in the 1950s, is the line *'an Englishman's way of speaking absolutely classifies him.'* A clipped upper-class accent was the hallmark of 'Forsythia' and was the most obvious difference between that class and the much larger lower-middle class. There was little difference between the way 'Forsytes' spoke and the accents of the aristocracy and landed gentry—an accent fostered at those private public schools and further developed in the refined world of the ancient universities of Oxford and Cambridge. It was the accent of the rich young rulers of the British Empire.

For those on the fringe of 'Forsythia', the elocution teacher, that professor of speech, who is epitomized in George Bernard Shaw's Professor Higgins, was an important person. He held the key to their success. If for some reason a 'Forsyte' child started to pick up any traits of a lower-middle class or working class accent, perhaps even from nursery staff, he or she would be sent to a professor of speech for elocution lessons. In Ireland, the Anglo-Irish aristocracy and 'Forsytes' used to call this de-bogging their children.

Mr. Douglas Stevens, especially after the merging of classes in the armed forces during World War II, still had enough pupils to keep him busy in the last decade of 'Forsythia'. In keeping with his profession, he also had a magnificent library of folio books, including many rare editions of Shakespeare and seventeenth and eighteenth-century poets and philosophers. On his death, his collection was bequeathed to the Municipal Library at Croydon, but when we as children would be taken over to Mr. Steven's house in Purley to visit our Great-aunt Dorrie, Mr. Stevens would allow us to look over some of his precious collection.

Swithin Forsyte *had been fond of* his nephew, *Young Jolyon; the boy had been in a good set at college, had known that old ruffian Sir Charles Fiste's sons—it was a thousand pities he had run off with that foreign girl—a governess, too!*

No doubt as he heard the recent gossip he reflected on 'Old Jolyon's' son's lost opportunity, although it was almost worse that he had run off with a foreigner than that she was just a governess.

Governesses often tended to be foreigners—particularly French, but sometimes, Swiss or Austrian. It was still considered chic in 'Forsythia' to be able to speak reasonable French, and prior to World War I, good German. A governess of such origins, helped 'Forsytes' to get a grounding in these languages from the nursery onward. Later, daughters of 'Forsytes' often went on to 'Finishing Schools' in Europe, something that replaced the eighteenth-century "grand tour" of the aristocracy. My grandmother, as Catherine Amy Hovenden, was sent to a 'Finishing School' in Germany. She always said that the main thing she learned there was to smoke cigarettes, which she did in excess all her life.

The last real governess in my family was Ellen Coath, who was not a foreigner, at least not from Europe, but my family nicknamed her "Pixie" because her family were celts from Cornwall. One of her sisters ended up living in Southport, Lancashire, and for 'Forsytes' almost anywhere that was north of the River Thames other than Cambridge was treated with 'foreign' suspicion. Although Miss Coath could mimic a Lancashire accent, she did spend most of her life in the south of England, and at the time she joined the Longley family as governess to Uncle Dennis, she was working as a receptionist at one of the spa hotels in Royal Tunbridge Wells. She prepared my father's youngest brother for entrance to Clare House Preparatory School and coached him a little until he went on to Tonbridge. She then stayed on with my family as my grandmother's companion until Granny Longley's death in 1969. She was my godmother, and was not beyond giving me advice in my childhood, especially on the subject of writing 'thank-you' letters! Sometimes, too, she would give little hints to my sisters and me at The Breach should we not have reacted to the Hovenden glare and be annoying Granny in some way! It never really occurred to my sisters and me that Miss Coath would ever not be a part of our family. Governesses lived 'en famille' and although we were aware that they were some form of family retainer, they were treated by us more like an aunt. In fact, although Grandpop always addressed Ellen Coath as Miss Coath, we all called her "Auntie Coathie." Granny just called her "Coath," and most our cousins and other family members called her "Cooch" or "Coochie."

On Granny's death, Miss Coath went to live for a year with my Aunt Biddy and Uncle Mark in Scotland. Her sister, Bertha, eventually persuaded her to come and live with her in Southport, Lancashire— perhaps an indication that the era of 'Forsythia' really had come to an end. Sadly, shortly before she died, Uncle Dennis and Aunt Pat went to visit her. She did not recognize them, partly because of her failing health, but she did smile and say to Dennis:

"You remind me of a little boy that I once used to teach."

In the post-war era, that last decade of 'Forsythia' saw a kind of merging of the roles of the nanny and the governess. Diane and I did have a formal starched English nanny for a short while, Nanny Needham, but later we were subjected to a series of foreign 'au pair' girls. The first was a French girl, whom we called "Auntie Morisette." These girls were from European families who wanted their daughters to learn better English than they had enjoyed in school, especially as many of them had been in European schools during the war years when English was probably not that popular in a Europe dominated by The Third Reich. My main memory of 'Auntie Morisette' was the fact that she always seemed to want to sneak out to meet boys. Our second 'au pair' was Swiss. She joined us shortly after we had moved from Chelston to Hockeredge on Wickham Way. She was engaged through the help of my Aunt Daphne and her husband Gordon Noble, who liked to go on ski trips to Switzerland. They brought Erica back with them, and I remember being introduced to Erica in the dining room. Diane and I were very curious to know what a Swiss girl would look like—probably very different from a French girl. My mother and Aunt Daphne were talking to Erica in French, although Erica could speak some English. These 'au pair' girls didn't really have to teach us as we were already in school and my mother had taught us to read, so they acted more as live-in baby-sitters, who helped 'Forsyte' ladies with some of the household chores like laundry and ironing. My younger sister, Sally, was not yet in school when Erica came into our lives, so Erica probably helped my mother quite a bit in the nursery with her. My main memories of Erica were of a house that I designed on a piece of paper for her to live in that would replace the rather poor garage that we had at Hockeredge, and the elaborate cut paper stars that she taught us to make for Christmas!

In those days, however, the presence of a live in 'au pair' at the house did give my mother some freedom to pursue her two sports—golf and badminton. She regularly played badminton at the Park Langley Tennis Club, and was a keen golfer in the ladies' section of Langley Park Golf Club, having herself been taught by one of England's greatest golfers of the late 1930s—Henry Cotton, who was Langley Park's professional.

Our third 'au pair' was Italian. Laura Tafani was the niece of Emilio Tafani, the artist who had painted my mother's portrait, and Emilio wanted her to stay in an English family for a while. Laura was primarily Sally's 'au pair,' Diane and I by this time now both attending boarding schools. However, I liked Laura, even had a slight crush on her. I used to write her letters from Newlands. On one such occasion, a mocking school friend wrote 'Longley loves Laura' on the blackboard during letter writing class. The second master saw this before it was erased and belittled me in front of the whole class.

"This sort of thing," he said, "is not befitting of a gentleman. It is the sort of thing that one would expect from Beckenham Grammar School."

To attend a state Grammar School would strip me of 'Forsyte' privilege. 'Forsytes' did not go to state schools. Ironically, tongue in cheek, my mother used to threaten me if I had done something wrong in the same way:

"You don't want to have to go to the 'Green Cap' school, do you?"

The 'Green Cap' school was the State primary school in Beckenham.

'What was he now?' Swithin Forsyte thought, as he continued to reflect on his disgraced nephew, 'Young Jolyon'. *'An underwriter at Lloyd's;'* potentially all right for a lesser 'Forsyte'.

Uncle Gordon, Aunt Daphne's husband, was an underwriter at Lloyd's, but Swithin dwelt more on the fact that a good part of his nephew's living apparently now came from painting pictures, and not pictures that he ever saw in the galleries.

Damme! He might have ended as Sir Jolyon Forsyte, Bart., with a seat in Parliament and a place in the country!

Swithin had pursued his ideas on his family origins further. He *went to the Heralds' Office, where they assured him that he was undoubtedly of the same family as the well-known Forsites with an 'i' whose arms were 'three dexter buckles on a sable ground gules,' hoping no doubt to get him to take them up.*

Heraldry was taught to us in class at Newlands. We were supposed to know how to read a coat of arms and understand the archaic medieval French terminology, which in Swithin's case, probably was too much.

But having ascertained that the crest was a 'pheasant proper,' and the motto 'For Forsite,' Swithin *had a pheasant proper placed upon his carriage and the buttons of his coachman, and both crest and motto on his writing paper. It strengthened his conviction that he was a gentleman. Imperceptibly the rest of the family absorbed the 'pheasant proper.'*

On the Longley side of my family, much was made in my formative years that His Grace, the Most Reverend Charles Thomas Longley, Archbishop of Canterbury and Primate of England, who started the Lambeth Conferences for Bishops of the Anglican Communion throughout the Empire in 1867, was a relative. Certainly Charles is a family name, but at best, the archbishop was a cousin and not of direct line until well before 'Forsythia'. My father, too, in his mischievous way, always reminded us, when regaled with our possible relationship to this important cleric, who has a simple, but commanding monument in Canterbury Cathedral's left aisle of the nave, that a distant relative of the Longleys had also been hung for stealing sheep!

Swithin, possibly secretly hoped on hearing the gossip that James and Winifred had seen 'Old Jolyon' at the zoo with 'Young Jolyon' and "the children that governess had given him," that there might now be some family reconciliation to bring 'Young Jolyon' back into the fold.

It was then that Euphemia dropped news on Irene.

Swithin detested Euphemia altogether, to whom he always alluded as "Nick's daughter, what's she called—the pale one?" He had just missed being her godfather—indeed, would have been, had he not taken a firm stand against her outlandish name. He hated becoming a godfather. Euphemia knew this and equally detested her uncle.

She *turned to Aunt Hester, and began telling her how she had seen Irene—Mrs. Soames—at* the Groceries, *the Church and Commercial Stores.*

"And Soames was with her?"

"Soames with her? Of course not!"

"But was she all alone in London?"

"Oh, no; there was Mr. Bosinney with her. She was perfectly dressed."

Swithin interrupted them. *"Dressed like a lady, I've no doubt. It's a pleasure to see her."*

At this moment James and his daughters were announced. Dartie was not with them, having said he had an appointment with his dentist, but in reality he was busy placing a bet at his club on the Lancashire Cup, the afternoon's four-thirty race.

Throughout most of 'Forsythia' sportsmen placed their bets discreetly through the agency of the porters at their clubs. Betting shops were frequented by the lower classes. Their proprietors, bookmakers or turf accountants, more often called 'bookies', were not considered of 'Forsyte' class.

Naturally, like in most casinos, 'bookies' tend to be the winners. The Collings' neighbor on Wickham Way during my childhood was a successful 'bookie'—Mr. Magrath. Their house was beautiful, and they spent a lot of money on their garden, but they were not really accepted in the Park Langley set. My grandmother would certainly speak to the

Magraths if she ran into them, but from a very early age I was aware that there was something about them being 'bookies' that set them outside our circle. They were almost quarantined in their beautiful house and garden.

In the meantime, old Jolyon had found the remaining chair in Timothy's commodious drawing-room. There was an awkward silence broken eventually by Aunt Juley.

"Yes, Jolyon," she said, *"we were just saying that you haven't been here for a long time; but we mustn't be surprised. You're busy of course? James was just saying what a busy time of year..."*

"Was he?" *said old Jolyon, looking hard at James.* "It wouldn't be half so busy if everybody minded their own business."

"And how is dear June?" asked Aunt Juley.

"Bad! London don't agree with her—too many people about, too much clatter and chatter by half." *He laid emphasis on the words, and again looked James in the face.*

Nobody spoke.

Swithin rose and left.

Juley offered 'Old Jolyon' tea.

Old Jolyon rose: "Thank you," *he said, looking straight at James,* "but I've no time for tea, and—scandal, and the rest of it! It's time I was home. Goodbye, Julia; good-bye, Hester; good-bye, Winifred," but there was no "good-bye" for James.

Meanwhile, Soames made, an unusual for him, visit to Dartie's club.

It would not do, as Dartie *kept repeating to himself. It absolutely would not do, with finances as low as his, and the 'old man' James, rusty ever since that business over the oil shares, which was no fault of his, to risk a row with Winifred.*

If Soames were to see him in the club it would be sure to come round to her that he wasn't at the dentist's at all. He never knew a family where things 'came round' so.

He hid in the card room *wondering where the deuce he was to get the money if 'Erotic' failed to win the Lancashire Cup.*

His thoughts turned gloomily to the Forsytes.

That fellow Soames would have a fit if you tried to borrow a tenner from him. And that wife of his, he had tried to be on good terms with her, as one naturally would with any pretty sister-in-law, but he would be cursed if the—would have anything to say to him—she looked at him, indeed, as if he were dirt—and yet she could go far enough, he wouldn't mind betting. He knew women; they weren't made with soft eyes and figures like that for nothing, as that fellow Soames would jolly soon find out, if there were anything in what he had heard about this Buccaneer Johnny.

CHAPTER EIGHT

DANCE AT ROGER'S

Roger's house in Prince's Gardens was brilliantly alight. Large numbers of wax candles had been collected and placed in cut-glass chandeliers, and the parquet floor of the long, double drawing-room reflected these constellations. An appearance of real spaciousness had been secured by moving out all the furniture in to the upper landings.

In a remote corner, embowered in palms, was a cottage piano, with a copy of the 'Kensington Coil' open on the music stand.

This particular dance tune was popular in the family and increasingly so among young 'Forsytes' in general. It had been composed by Roger's daughter, Francie, who was struggling with the older generation of Forsytes as to her desires to be a musician, composer, and poetess.

Her father was giving a dance for the young Forsytes—the new generation now in their late teens and twenties.

In the last days of the yeomanry, Jane Austen gives us a wonderful insight into English country life. Most her heroines were the approximate age of this current generation of young Forsytes. In her novels, she shows the intermingling, often forced by boredom and necessity, of these yeoman country families with the landed gentry and the aristocracy—balls, horses, and cards being their common amusement. This pattern, established in the late eighteenth and early nineteenth centuries and formalized in the social season at Bath, became the pattern later for

'Forsythia'. Balls and dances were the means of launching the 'young' in society. The aristocracy had court presentations and debutante balls to mark the coming of age of their daughters, but in 'Forsythia' where there was no great feeling for the formality of the court, the 'coming out dance'—a more homespun affair—became the norm. This ritual persisted one way and another right up to that last decade of the era—my childhood in the 1950s, before it disappeared in the social revolution of the 1960s. It is also interesting to note that the monarchy abolished court presentations at around the same time, although the traditional debutante balls of the London season continued for a year or two.

Debutante balls often took place at the aristocracy's country seats, they were also often staged in the grand ballrooms of London's premier hotels, or at exclusive private clubs. The coming out dances of 'Forsytes' were usually 'at home' affairs such as this dance at Roger Forsyte's home in Prince's Gardens.

'Forsyte' homes were spacious even in the twentieth century. They may not have had an historic set of rooms, sometimes rather inaccurately called 'state apartments' such as are found in many of England's aristocratic stately homes, but they did have double drawing-rooms such as Roger's at Princes Gate, or large reception rooms and halls that could double as ballrooms. Hillside, Great-grandfather Longley's Victorian home on The Avenue in Beckenham, like all the houses on The Avenue, had a very large drawing room. Great-grandfather Cuthbertson's Edwardian mansion, 'Frainsville', on Duncombe Hill in southeast London, had a vast hall with a 'Romeo and Juliet' gallery that was ideal for musicians. Grandpop's Chelston was a large, comfortable home that like so many of 'Forsythia' boasted a conservatory, so useful for sitting out at a dance. Granny Mabs' and Grandpa Jack's home, Redcroft, like our own house on the same street, had a spacious hall and sizeable drawing room and dining room. So did those of my mother's cousins, the Doggett girls, Daphne and Betty—four related families with houses within five hundred yards of each other and all part of Park Langley, 'Forsythia's' last development in Beckenham before the encroach of middle-class suburban sprawl.

When my sister Diane, and my cousins Michael and Hillary O'Callaghan—Aunt Betty's children—came of age, they all had dances 'at home'. So, too, did my parents give a dance for me. Sally came of age in the late sixties, by which time 'Forsythia' was in its last days, and although my parents gave her a party, it was not in the form of a traditional dance.

Our parents invited as many of their generation to these dances as our own age group. In the earlier days of 'Forsythia' they would have been the chaperones, by our day it was more for curiosity and moral support. Just as at Roger Forsyte's, furniture from the hall that became the ballroom was carried to upper landings to make space.

So it was, that Roger Forsyte and his wife Mary, gave that dance for the Forsyte young in 1887. In reality, Roger hated these events, but he was to pay the bill and he knew he would be expected to look the part of host. Mary, however, *whom Roger had long since reduced to chronic dyspepsia, went to bed on such occasions.* In reality, it was their daughter Francie, who arranged it all. *Thin but brilliant, in her maize-colored frock with much tulle about the shoulders, she went from place to place, fitting on her gloves, and casting her eye over it all.*

To the hired butler, she spoke about the wine.

Roger Forsyte did not keep a butler, only maids, but when the occasion needed it, a butler was hired. In the same way, in those last days of 'Forsythia', a good meaning fellow, known through trade connections, or the son of an associate or friend of the family, but not a relative, might be hired "to help with the drinks." So it was for us.

Francie knew that her father, *indeed, after making himself consistently disagreeable about the dance, would come down presently, with his fresh color and bumpy forehead, as though he had been its promoter; and he would smile, and probably take the prettiest woman into supper; and at two o'clock, just as they were getting into the swing, he would go up secretly to the musicians and tell them to play 'God save the Queen,' and go away.*

Francie devoutly hoped he might soon get tired, and slip off to bed.

Punctually on the stroke of nine Aunt Juley arrived.

Some of Francie's maiden friends were staying at the house and *came now from their rooms, each by magic arrangement in a differently colored frock, but all with the same liberal amount of tulle on the shoulders and at the bosom—for they were, by some fatality, lean to a girl. They were all taken up to* Aunt Juley. *None stayed with her more than a few seconds, but clustering together, talked and twisted their programmes, looking secretly at the door for the first appearance of a man.*

My mother thought it would be a novel idea for our dances to be 'Programme' dances, and we had great fun designing and making up the programmes, which we did by hand, my sister Diane by then being an accomplished calligrapher. In the 1950s, we did not engage musicians as had the generation before. There was plenty of dance music in strict tempo available on gramophone records that could be played on that post-war essential of 'Forsythia'—a radiogram—a fine piece of furniture that combined a gramophone and a wireless set in a cabinet. We picked out and listed an assortment of dances for the programme, mostly waltzes, foxtrots and quicksteps to the music of Victor Sylvester; Latin dances, apart from a possible cha-cha, being only on the fringe of becoming popular.

After the guests arrived, the men would busy themselves over cocktails or a fruit punch, that my father made very well, asking the girls for a dance on their programme sheet. However, to ensure that nobody would be left out, there was nearly always one 'Paul Jones', which was a mixer where the men walked around the girls in two opposite moving circles and when the music stopped the men danced with the partners to whom they found themselves facing. Three other mixers were the 'Gay Gordons', the 'Barn Dance' and the 'Valeta', all of which we had learned at our ballroom dance classes—an almost must in the education of a 'Forsyte'. Diane and I had been sent at the age of fourteen to the ballroom dance school of a local teacher, Daphne Hellier. Such ladies could be found in all the 'Forsythia' suburbs of London.

Back in 1887, as the carriages drew up, so all the younger Forsytes and their parents and chaperones arrived at Prince's Gardens.

Three or four of Francie's lovers now appeared, one after the other; she had made each promise to come early.

Men were scarce, and wallflowers wore their peculiar, pathetic expression, a patient, sourish smile which seemed to say: "Oh, no! don't mistake me, I know you are not coming up to me. I can hardly expect that!" And Francie would plead with one of her lovers: "Now, to please me, do let me introduce you to Miss Pink; such a nice girl really!" and she would bring him up, and say: "Miss Pink—Mr. Gathercole. Can you spare him a dance?" Then Miss Pink, smiling her forced smile, colouring a little, answered: "Oh! I think so!" and screening her empty card, wrote on it the name of Gathercole, spelling it passionately.

Thus, introductions were made.

As at Princes' Gate, so seventy years later in Beckenham, half of our guests were relatives, and others were schoolfriends and their brothers or sisters, acquaintances whom we only vaguely knew, some of whom, like Francie's maidens, stayed with us overnight. At our dance, one such girl was Hazel Strouts. Every schoolboy at Tonbridge knew Hazel as she had played Joan of Arc in our school production of Bernard Shaw's *St. Joan*. She attended Fosse Bank, a private girl's school at the south end of Tonbridge. She had been invited by our drama department to play the role in a joint school production. Naturally, Tonbridge being one of those all-male boarding schools of 'Forsythia', each and every one of us fell for this teenage beauty. After her performance in the play, I met Hazel at the Fosse Bank school dance, to which a few of us Tonbridge boys were invited to be dance partners for the senior girls, who were well chaperoned by their teachers. Like all school dances in 'Forsythia', it was a black tie affair, in fact at the Tonbridge School dance, our school masters and old Tonbridgians still dressed in white tie and tails. I liked to dress up and enjoyed these adventures outside our normal all-boys' routine. It was as much to my surprise as everyone else's that Hazel Strouts accepted an invitation from me to come to our dance in Beckenham that was really celebrating my sister Diane's coming of age.

In 'Forsythia', such events were always evening dress, although after World War II most were 'black tie' rather than 'white tie.' For these 'at home' dances, invitations were sent out in much the same way as they had been for a hundred years; they were formal on white card with a gold trim. They always announced the dress code, so we were schooled to know that 'Evening Dress' meant white tie and tails, 'Dinner Jacket' meant black tie, and 'Carriages' meant the anticipated time for the event to end.

We were also the last generation to formally RSVP these invitations with Edwardian wording:

Peter Hovenden Longley thanks Lady Sarah Parkinson for her kind invitation to attend a dance in honour of her daughter Jane, at The Mill House, Egglesford, on the occasion of her coming of age, at 7:00 p.m. on Saturday, January 16th, and has much pleasure in accepting.

I only remember in those last days of 'Forsythia' receiving one such invitation requesting 'Evening Dress.' It was the one and only true debutante ball that I attended, the coming of age of Lady Melissa Bligh, the daughter of Lord Cobham of Cobham Hall, a magnificent Elizabethan Manor House outside Rochester in Kent. My mother and father drove me up to London to attend the pre-ball dinner party to which I had been assigned at the United Hunts' Club on Park Lane, for at these large 'London Season' debutante balls, several aristocratic ladies played hostess to the young invites at different locations in the city before we all drove out to the country seat where the ball was to be held. At dinner, to my surprise, I actually found myself sitting beside a young debutante, Jane Lowther, who was a friend of my sister, Diane. They were both students at the rather exclusive Byam Shaw School of Drawing and Painting at Notting Hill Gate. This at least made me look as if I was a part of the 'London Season'. After dinner, Charles Keane and his roomate from Oxford, Charles Flower, who had introduced me to the Hon. Adam Bligh, Melissa's sister, when they were staying at Cappoquin House in Ireland, drove me down to Cobham Hall.

I had known Cobham Hall for a number of years having done a local history paper on the manor while in the History Sixth at Tonbridge. It was strange to be a guest in the magnificent house just two years later, but I felt the part among the aristocracy as I wandered through the impressive rooms in my white tie and tails, sipping on champagne served by footmen in powdered wigs. Swithin Forsyte would have enjoyed this feeling, too. There were occasions when the aristocracy and 'Forsythia' met; after all, we were all part of that small, three percent, even if living in two different circles. However, Granny Longley gave me her sound advice before I attended this event. Typical of her perceived grandeur, she said to me:

"Peter, if the *Tatler* (London's Society Magazine) comes up to you, just remember you are Peter Hovenden Longley (she put emphasis on the Hovenden) and not A. N. Other." But almost as soon as she said these words, to prove that like Swithin Forsyte, 'we were no small beer,' she continued: "And don't you ever be a snob."

At first, I was surprised, this coming from the grandmother whom many in my family addressed as "Madam," but she defined her statement further and I understood:

"Snobbery is not about who you are or what you do, but it is about how you treat other people in relationship to who you are and what you do."

Needless to say, my photo did not appear in the *Tatler* as one of London's eligible society bachelors.

At the dance at Roger's, *mothers, slowly fanning their faces, watched their daughters, and in their eyes could be read all the story of those daughters' fortunes. As for themselves, to sit hour after hour, dead tired, silent, or talking spasmodically—what did it matter, so long as the girls were having a good time! But to see them neglected and passed by! Ah! they smiled, their eyes stabbed like the eyes of an offended swan.*

And all the cruelties and hardness of life, its pathos and unequal chances, its conceit, self-forgetfulness and patience, were presented on the battlefield of this Kensington ballroom.

Is not this characteristic of Jane Austen's matrons, in particular the ambitious but somewhat simple and over-protective Mrs. Bennett in *Pride and Prejudice*? And, well do I remember my aunts, Daphne and Betty, my mother's best friend Zena Fielding, Granny Mabs and that ever-present family retainer, always ready for gossip, Mary Jackson the hairdresser, watching over us:

"Who is this Hazel Strouts? Where did she come from? Whose sister is she?" or even my father waiting for the unfortunate lady to prove herself, "Who does *it* think she is?"

At Roger's, *not a second before ten o'clock came the James's— Emily, Rachel, Winifred and Cicely the youngest, making her debut; behind them, following in a hansom from the paternal mansion where they had dined, Soames and Irene.*

All these ladies had shoulder straps and no tulle—thus showing at once, by a bolder exposure of flesh, that they came from the more fashionable side of the Park.

Evening dress for ladies in our post-World War II decade was much harder than that for men. We wore dinner jackets or tails, black tie or white tie, and we often inherited this dress from our parents or grandparents after they had put on a little middle-aged spread, requiring slightly broader models. My evening tails and morning suit had been Grandpop's, and my dinner jacket Grandpa Jack's. If not inherited, 'Forsytes' bought evening clothes at men's stores, inasmuch as their tailoring really had not changed for half a century and there was still plenty of stock around. In the era of liberty clothing, rationing, and a depressed economy following the war, evening gowns were rather limited. Ladies had to 'make do' with what they had worn in the 1930s—those slinky full-length gowns in taffeta and satin that we remember following the slightly shorter, ruffled dresses of the 'Charleston' era, and that were often depicted on those Trans-Atlantic liner posters. By the late 1950s, these dresses were in competition with the full petticoat, knee-length, gowns that had become fashionable as the country got back on its feet. I remember my mother offering my sister Diane one of her beautiful old 1930s gowns for her coming out, but Granny Longley then took Diane up to Marshall and Snelgrove, one of Granny's favorite department stores, and bought her two gowns of the new fashion.

She needed the two gowns because often, in these latter days of 'Forsythia', a coming of age was celebrated with two parties—an 'at home' dance, and a dinner and theatre party in town, usually all-in-one at a place like The Talk of the Town or the Café Royal—supper and cabaret clubs popular at the time with the Princess Margaret set. Both Diane and I were given cabaret dinners when we became twenty-one. Many of the same young folks, the cousins, and the sisters and brothers of school or college friends, were invited to both events.

Soames Forsyte was decidedly bored at these events, not himself being a dancer; in fact, *his sense of 'form' had never permitted him to dance with Irene since their marriage.* He sidled *back from the contact of the dancers,* and *took up a position against the wall. Guarding himself with his pale smile, he stood watching. Waltz after waltz began and ended, couple after couple brushed by with smiling lips, laughter, and snatches of talk; or with set lips, and eyes searching the throng; or again, with silent parted lips, and eyes on each other. And the scent of festivity, the odour of flowers, and hair, of essences that women love,* possibly originating from the House of Hovenden, *rose suffocatingly in the heat of the summer night.*

Eyes were on Irene. *She passed dancing with other men, her dress, iris-coloured, floating away from her feet. She danced well;* Soames *was tired of hearing women say with an acid smile: "How beautifully your wife dances, Mr. Forsyte—it's quite a pleasure to watch her!"*

My mother loved to dance, and she, too, was a good dancer, but my father was not keen, so she rarely got to dance. At these social gatherings, however, my father was always lively, coming out of his normal shyness, and everyone loved him. He was the host more than my mother was the hostess. I am glad to say, however, that many years later, after I had become an accomplished ballroom dancer through my career in entertainment and as a cruise director, I had the opportunity to dance with my mother before she became too old to enjoy it. My mother and father visited me at Sea Island in Georgia where I was well known in the Cloister Hotel clubrooms, and able to waltz with my mother on several nights. She almost cried with happiness. My family also cruised with me several times on both Royal Viking Line and the *Queen Elizabeth 2* where nightly ballroom dancing to superb orchestras was a feature.

Soames *heard Roger's voice behind, giving an order about supper to a servant.* Why didn't Uncle Roger employ a full time butler for this task? *Everything* to Soames *was very second-class! He wished that he had not come!*

Why had he come? For the last quarter of an hour he had not even seen Irene.

His cousin George, Roger's rakish son, approached him. *It was too late to get out of his way.*

"Have you seen 'The Bucaneer?'" said this licensed wag; *"he's on the warpath—hair cut and everything!"*

Soames did not want to be drawn into this and left George to look out over the balcony at the street below. *A carriage had driven up with late arrivals*—June and her grandfather, 'Old Jolyon'. *What had made them so late? They looked fagged. Fancy Uncle Jolyon turning out at this time of night. Why hadn't June come to Irene, as she usually did, and it occurred to him suddenly that he had seen nothing of June for a long time now.*

Watching her face with idle malice, he saw it change, grow so pale that he thought she would drop, then flame out crimson. Turning to see at what she was looking, he saw his wife on Bosinney's arm coming from the conservatory at the end of the room. Her eyes were raised to his, as though answering some question he had asked, and he was gazing at her intently.

The music started again. In moments, Irene and Bosinney swept past the balcony. Soames *caught the perfume of the gardenias that she wore, saw the rise and fall of her bosom, the languor of her eyes, her parted lips, and a look on her face that he did not know. To the slow, swinging measure they danced by, and it seemed to him that they clung to each other; he saw her raise her eyes, soft and dark, to Bosinney's and drop them again.*

Soames turned back to the street. He saw June and her grandfather enter their carriage and drive away. Little did he know that *deep down in her heart* June had *resolved that evening to win* Bosinney *back*. For the first time, he now felt as slighted as his niece.

CHAPTER NINE

EVENING AT RICHMOND

O ther eyes besides the eyes of June and of Soames had seen 'those two', as Euphemia had already begun to call them, coming from the conservatory; other eyes had noticed the look on Bosinney's face.

It supplied, however, the reason of June's coming to the dance at Roger's so late and disappearing again without dancing, without even shaking hands with her lover.

The gossip on 'Forsyte 'Change' centered on this for several days, and then came the news that June had gone to the seaside with Old Jolyon.

They had gone to Broadstairs, for which place there was just then a feeling, Yarmouth having lost caste, in spite of Nicholas. The air was considered more bracing. Charles Dickens had his home there in this heyday of 'Forsythia'. He called it Bleak House, the name of his famous novel. The Bleak House of Bleak House, however, was not a bleak place, but a rather happy place of hope. Could it be that Dickens named his home at Broadstairs, not after the novel, but because of its bleak setting on the cliff roads of Broadstairs, looking out over the bracing Straits of Dover? Certainly, in Dickens' time, Broadstairs became a fashionable place, along with the lesser Kent resorts of Margate and Ramsgate, all known for their bracing climate around the North Foreland.

A bracing sea breeze was considered in 'Forsythia' to be very good for the health. It was at these seaside towns, therefore, that in the later Victorian and Edwardian era numerous preparatory schools were built to prepare 'Forsytes' for their further education at the great public schools. My cousin, John Cuthbertson, Great-uncle Bert and Aunt Ruby's son, was sent to St Peter's Preparatory School in Broadstairs. Because the Christmas and Easter Holidays were too short to merit the sea trip back to India, my cousin spent those holidays with his Auntie Mabel, my Granny Mabs. John was a very good-looking boy, who made a success of everything he did. He was a better than average scholar, but most obviously excelled at every sport—especially cricket. Grandpa Jack loved this, and in some ways, our cousin John was to my grandparents the replacement son for John William, my mother's older brother, whom they had lost in infancy. There grew up, therefore, three sets of cousins on Wickham Way, all different branches of the Collings family. Aunt Betty supported by her sister Daphne, the Doggett girls, naturally favored the Doggett children, Michael and Hilary O'Callaghan, who in their eyes were so much more accomplished than us Longley children. My parents, naturally favored us over our cousins, although they had the difficulty of our talents being in less practical directions as we toyed with the arts. Cousin John was favored by my grandparents, his superiority over the Longleys and the O'Callaghans being found in his sporting achievements at St. Peter's, Broadstairs, and later at Rugby, his public school made so famous in 'Forsythia' as the setting for Thomas Hughes' *Tom Brown's Schooldays*. As cousins, we were all heading in very different directions despite our similar education.

I was sent to a preparatory school on the Sussex coast. Newlands was one of a dozen or more such schools in Seaford active in that last decade of 'Forsythia'. Later, both my sisters joined me at one of the three girls' boarding schools in the town—Micklefield. As for John at Broadstairs, so for us at Seaford, part of the 'Forsyte' attraction to educate us in these seaside towns was that need for 'Forsyte' young to be toughened up in a bracing environment after their nursery childhood. It was always ten degrees cooler than inland, the sea breezes whistling around the gables and tiles of these Edwardian mansions that were our educational prisons. Windows were always open to let in this bracing air, a practice enforced by matrons and their assistants in starched caps. Our mornings started with cold showers. We did not have running water in our dormitories, and so in the evening we fetched our water from the bathrooms in big pitchers and poured their contents into bowls supported by wooden stands. And the wind howled. Sometimes, in winter, there was a crusting of ice from residue in our washbasins by morning. Diane, Sally and I coined a phrase for any cold wind—"a Seaford wind," and we still use that expression to this day. A little further along, down the coast on the way to Brighton, was one of England's premier girl's schools for the more moneyed of 'Forsythia'—Roedean. It was a gaunt, gothic structure, standing on cliff tops with few trees—the model for caricaturist Ronald Searle's *St. Trinians*. The girls had it almost as bracing as we boys.

So June Forsyte and 'Old Jolyon' *went to the sea. The family awaited developments; there was nothing else to do.*

Soames' sister, Winifred Dartie, who had imbibed with the breezes of Mayfair more fashionable principles in regard to matrimonial behaviour than were current, laughed at the idea of there being anything in these rumors about Irene. *The 'little thing'—Irene was taller than herself, and it was real testimony to the solid worth of a Forsyte that she should always thus be a 'little thing'—the 'little thing' was bored. Why shouldn't she amuse herself? Soames was rather tiring; and as for Mr. Bosinney—she maintained that he was very chic.* However, Winifred had had to put up with a great deal in her own marriage and could sympathize with Irene with reference to certain men.

Winifred's "little thing" was very similar to my father's "it", which he in turn had inherited from an older generation of Longley and Hovenden 'Forsytes'. Until Irene could prove herself otherwise, she would remain to Winifred "the little thing" just as any female entering into the Longley family was an "it."

However, *this dictum—that Bosinney was chic—caused quite a sensation. It failed to convince on 'Forsyte 'Change'. That he was 'good-looking in a way' they were prepared to admit, but that anyone could call a man with soft felt hats chic was only another instance of Winifred's extravagant way of running after something new.* The incident of that felt hat in the hall at the 'Bucaneer's' engagement party had qualified him as a male 'it' forever. No doubt on 'Forsyte 'Change', Aunt Juley continued to say how she had thought it one of the cats and tried to shoo it off the chair.

The summer of this gossip, while June and Jolyon were in Broadstairs, was unusually hot. The sun *swung his brazen shield above the Park, and people did strange things, lunching and dining in the open air.*

'Forsytes' would prepare picnics, outings to Hyde Park or by the river. Perhaps they had some recollection of halcyon days in punts on the rivers Isis or the Cam when they had wiled away their salad days at Oxford or Cambridge. In fact, it is interesting to note that one of the last English musicals to celebrate 'Forsythia' in London's West End theatre was Julian Slade's *Salad Days*. The musical was in many ways a swan song to 'Forsythia' and as schoolboys of the 1950s we knew all the songs. Some aspects of *Salad Days* were still present in my undergraduate days at St. Catherine's College, Cambridge. We still had to wear academic gowns after dark or whenever we were in tutorials or supervisions—we did not have classes. During my undergraduate days, many of us wore suits: we always wore ties and polished shoes, and I don't believe I ever saw at Cambridge a student in blue-jeans or sneakers. College dinners were black tie; college balls were white tie and tails. Our rooms, off a staircase, were taken care of by a personal gyp or manservant. Male and female colleges were separated, and occasionally, should we get locked in the wrong college after midnight—the curfew hour—we would be forced to enact the old 'Forsyte' practice of 'climbing out' and 'climbing in'. If caught in this process by the proctor and his bulldogs, in their archaic top hats and frock coats parading the streets carrying a leather-strapped copy of the university's book of rules, we would be fined six shillings and eight pence. We were never referred to as students, but as gentlemen. These were our salad days in an unbelievable setting, amid unbelievable culture, and yet academically on the cutting edge of a new world that would bury 'Forsythia' forever. We were the last generation brought up to rule the great British Empire that by my salad days was fast dwindling.

I remember my mother and father taking us for picnics in Hyde Park and Kew Gardens. I used to love the beetroot rolls that my mother always made, and the patum peperum and sardine sandwiches that my father liked. There were usually banana sandwiches and tomato sandwiches, too. Sometimes, there were chicken legs, and there were always 'Thermos' flasks of tea, although I preferred lemonade. We also enjoyed numerous picnics on our summer holidays, which we spent first at Birchington on the Kent coast, then later at Cromer in Norfolk. Finally, we were considered old enough as teenagers to appreciate my mother's favorite summer holiday retreat, Thurlestone in South Devon.

On those warm summer evenings in London's fashionable West End, 'Forsytes' often walked in the enclosed gardens of their squares, *taking the cool after dinner in* these *precincts to which they alone had keys,* gardens that earlier in the day had been the preserve of nannies and their 'Forsyte' young.

In southeast London in Edwardian times there sprung up around Dulwich and Sydenham, the home of the great Crystal Palace, similar enclaves of private dwellings. The houses were not town houses as in the great squares of Belgravia, but large Edwardian mansions that backed onto common parks or squares. One of the best examples of this type of development was Duncombe Hill where Great-grandfather Cuthbertson had his home, Frainsville. It was here that Granny Mabs met Grandpa Jack.

Great-grandfather John Collings moved to Brockley Rise parallel to Duncombe Hill in one of his periods of prosperity, after the shame of living above that tobacconist's shop in Camberwell. The Collings' home was on the opposite side of the enclosed park to Frainsville. Like the 'Forsytes' and aristocrats of the London squares, the residents of Duncombe Hill and Brockley Rise had keys to admit them to this central park with its leafy trees at the end of their own spacious gardens. It was on balmy evenings in this enclosure that Jack Collings first courted Mabel Cuthbertson, and Bert Cuthbertson was able to introduce his young business associate, Montague Doggett, to Nellie Collings. Here, too, Great-uncle Bert had first put his sights on Nellie's sister, Babs.

Some vague sympathy evoked by the scent of limes in Hyde Park and these London squares, some sisterly desire to see for herself, some idea of demonstrating the soundness of her dictum that there was 'nothing in it;' or merely the craving to drive down to Richmond, irresistible that summer, moved Winifred *to write a note to her sister-in-law.*

> *'I hear that Soames is going to Henley tomorrow for the night. I thought it would be great fun if we made up a little party and drove down to Richmond. Will you ask Mr. Bosinney. Emily will lend us the carriage. I will call for you at seven o'clock.'*

Dartie was to go with them, and he *was in good feather.* After losing on the horse 'Erotic' in the Lancashire Cup, he had taken the advice of *that little Jew boy Nathans. Owing some hundreds, which by no possibility could he pay, he went into town and put them all on 'Concertina',* the Jew boy's tip *for the Saltown Handicap.*

It came up. 'Concertina' was squeezed home by her neck—a terrible squeak, but as Dartie said: "There was nothing like pluck!"

'Forsytes', so many being descendents of good yeoman stock, had an interesting relationship with Jews. Jews were never really accepted within their ranks, and 'Forsythia' was always mildly anti-semitic. Among the aristocracy, the great debates between Gladstone and Disraeli in the nineteenth century showed suspicion of this political Jew, who was so loved by the queen. However, Queen Victoria, like 'Forsytes' in general, accepted Disraeli because he advanced the British Empire—the prime minister who had negotiated that clever deal with the French in Egypt, allowing him to buy up a majority of shares in the Suez Canal company—now this was a financial deal of which all Forsytes approved—it had opened the lifeline of the Empire to British control. Yes, Jews were tolerated because they were clever and good for investment and trade, but like the aristocracy, 'Forsytes' did not accept Jews socially. Dartie would willingly take the little Jew boy Nathans' advice when it came to a good racing tip, but he would not dine at his table at the club. Two generations later, the real life story of the award winning film *Chariots of Fire* was played out in 1920s undergraduate life at Cambridge. Jews were denied much despite their financial and sporting accomplishments. In my own childhood, even in a post-holocaust world, Jews were still thought of with suspicion. We did business with them, but we also spoke of them as separate from us. There were Jews who were members of the Langley Park Golf Club in the 1950s, but my mother and father knew who they were and subtly passed the information on to us. I invited an attractive teenage girl to the Tonbridge School dance in 1959. Her name was Susan Noad, and although my parents drove her to the event, they certainly let me know that she was Jewish. It was not a relationship to go further than a school dance. However, Susan was a promising young golfer, and her sporting prowess was acknowledged for the glory of the club.

Dartie called Nathans *that little Jew boy* with that Forsyte approval of contempt. He would remain "a little Jew boy" until he had proved himself, much as Winifred's "little thing" or my father's "it."

At half-past five the Park Lane footman came round to say: "Mrs. Forsyte was very sorry, but one of the horses was coughing!

So, they went to Richmond in hansom cabs, Irene and Bosinney sharing a cab. They met up as planned for dinner at The Crown and

Sceptre at 7:45 p.m. Bosinney and Irene had got there first. Dartie set about ordering dinner.

The best of everything! No sounder principle on which a man can base his life, whose father-in-law has a very considerable income, and a partiality for his grandchildren. Four little Darties were now a sort of perpetual insurance.

At Winifred's *suggestion they went after dinner to the public terrace overlooking the river.* "I should like to see the common people making love," *she said,* "it's such fun."

They sat on a bench, *Dartie at the end, next to him Irene, then Bosinney, then Winifred. Dartie pressed himself against Irene. It must be confessed that the man of the world had drunk quite as much as was good for him. 'Ah! he's a poor hungry looking devil that Bosinney!' he* thought. *The man of the world was more than ever determined to see what* Irene *was made of. There was the long drive home. That hungry architect chap might drive with his wife. A smile had become fixed in his thick lips.*

When they left the terrace to get hansom cabs homeward, Dartie's plans were somewhat thwarted. Bosinney got to the cabs first, Dartie being a little unsteady on his legs. Irene did not enter the hansom, but stroked the horse's nose speaking to Bosinney. All Dartie heard was… "That man."

Winifred was already in her cab. Dartie reflected that Bosinney would have a poorish time in that cab if he didn't look sharp! Suddenly he received a push which nearly overturned him in the road. Bosinney's voice hissed in his ear: "I am taking Irene back; do you understand?" *He saw a face white with passion, and eyes that glared at him like a wild cat's.*

"Eh?" *he stammered.* "What? Not a bit! You take my wife!"

"Get away!" *hissed Bosinney—*"or I'll throw you into the road!"

Dartie recoiled.

Dartie stood dumbfounded as Bosinney got in the hansom cab with Irene. *"Go on!" he heard Bosinney cry.* The cab sped off for London.

Dartie climbed in the other cab with his wife. *"Drive on!" he shouted to the driver, "and don't lose sight of that fellow in front!"*

Winifred watched knowingly, as Dartie's *angry eyes never deserted the back of that cab, which, like a lost chance, haunted the darkness in front of him.*

The evening had been a disaster, but it had confirmed the rumors on 'Forsyte 'Change'. Winifred could no longer be in denial of the relationship of June's fiancé and her sister-in-law, and in her heart saw how Dartie also weakened to her charms like every Forsyte.

CHAPTER TEN

DIAGNOSIS OF A FORSYTE

'**Y**oung Jolyon' realized how much he was a Forsyte *after the decisive step that had made him an outcast; since then the knowledge had been with him continually. He felt it throughout his alliance, throughout all his dealings with his second wife, who was emphatically not a Forsyte.*

He knew that if he had not possessed in great measure the eye for what he wanted, the tenacity to hold on to it, the sense of the folly of wasting that for which he had given so big a price—in other words, the 'sense of property'—he could never have retained her with him through all the difficulties, financial and social, that this twist of Forsyte sense had created for him. The grass is not always greener on the other side of the fence when that sense of belonging overcomes the emotion of the moment.

He was conscious, too, of being a Forsyte in his work, that painting of water-colours to which he devoted so much energy, always with an eye on himself, as though he could not quite take so impractical a pursuit quite seriously, and always with a certain queer uneasiness that he did not make more money at it.

When his father wrote to him from Broadstairs, the Forsyte in his character became dominant. He recognized the handwriting for *the Dad's handwriting had altered very little in the thirty odd years that he remembered it.*

There was a tendency in 'Forsythia' for there to be something of a uniformity of script—styles of handwriting taught from earliest years that had something of their origins in the dip pens and inkwells of our school desks. At Newlands, the man who used to fill our inkwells every day had been a stoker in ships of Queen Victoria's navy. My mother's handwriting never varied all her life—a very distinctive and obvious cursive script. Aunt Eileen, just two years younger than my mother, may have even originally been taught written letters by the same nanny, for her handwriting was almost identical to my mother's, so much so, that at Newlands when letters addressed to us were put up on a webbed board each day, I never knew whether these letters were from my mother or my aunt.

My sister Diane kept up the tradition with a very similar script to my mother, except, being left-handed she had it sloping in the opposite direction. Great-grandfather Longley and Grandpop also had very similar handwriting that was of Dickensian 'Copper Plate' origin. My father and I did not follow the pattern, however, both having atrocious handwriting. Originally, my hand was probably fairly true to 'Forsythia' and just about lasted me out through school examinations and entry to Cambridge University, but post-'Forsythia' it deteriorated to a flowery scrawl sloping in all directions. Maybe it is prophetic to the ending of that era. In my father's case, it might have been influenced by a 1920s and '30s style at Tonbridge, which in my day was still called the Tonbridge script—a rather small handwriting that never really joined up letters and was fostered by the famous cricket playing old Tonbridgians, John and Charles Knott, and at Tonbridge, encouraged in my day by David Kemp, one of their students and a man who tried to teach me Greek. The unjoined letters of the script probably had their origins in the Greek that these gentlemen taught, and I feel the Tonbridge script might have also influenced my Uncle Gyles, whose handwriting is similar.

'Old Jolyon' Forsyte wrote to Jo, informing him of June's despair. She did not seem to be communicating with him at Broadstairs and was moody and self-willed.

'She says nothing,' he wrote, 'but it is clear that she is harping on this engagement, which is an engagement and no engagement, and—goodness knows what. The fact is someone ought to speak to Bosinney and ascertain what he means. I am afraid of this myself, for I should certainly rap him over

the knuckles, but I thought that you, knowing him at the club,
might put in a word, and get to ascertain what the fellow is
about. You will of course in no way commit June. I shall be
glad to hear in a few days whether you have succeeded in
gaining any information. The situation is very distressing to
me, I worry about it at night. With my love to Jolly and Holly.
'I am,
'Your affect. Father,
'JOLYON FORSYTE.'

'Young Jolyon's' wife Helene was highly suspicious of this letter and
Jo remained secretive of the content, but as a Forsyte and June's father,
he made his way to the club.

There, he found Bosinney. *He didn't know him very well, and*
studied him attentively; an unusual looking man, unlike in dress, face,
and manner to most of the other members of the club—Young Jolyon
himself, however different he had become in mood and temper, had
always retained the neat reticence of Forsyte appearance.

Something in his face and attitude touched Young Jolyon. He knew
what suffering was like, and this man looked like he was suffering.

Young Jolyon sat down.

"I haven't seen you for a long time," he said, "How are you getting
on with my cousin's house?"

"It'll be finished in about a week."

"I congratulate you!"

"Thanks—I don't know that it's much of a subject for
congratulation."

"No?" queried Young Jolyon; "I should have thought you'd be glad
to get a long job like that off your hands; but I suppose you feel it much
as I do when I part with a picture—a sort of child?"

Both Diane and I painted prolifically in our teens. Every time we
went down to The Breach we loaded up the car with our latest paintings
for Granny Longley's inspection. Some, she actually bought from us, but
there was always a critique. Our paintings were our children. We both
hated parting with them, unless they were purchased by Granny to hang
at The Breach. Our house on Wickham way, named after Hocker Edge at
Cranbrook, was becoming saturated with our work. At that time, I was
in the habit of painting large three-foot by two-foot landscapes. They
took up a lot of wall space. Is the painting a commodity or a possession?

Both are Forsyte approaches, and were as real to 'Young Jolyon' as to Diane and me.

Thus, started between the architect and the artist an interesting discussion on 'Forsyte' values.

"A Forsyte," said young Jolyon, "is not an uncommon animal. There are hundreds among the members of this club. Hundreds out there in the streets; you meet them wherever you go!"

"And how do you tell them, may I ask?" said Bosinney.

"By their sense of property. A Forsyte takes a practical—one might say a common sense—view of things, and a practical view of things is based fundamentally on a sense of property."

If I sold a painting in those last days of 'Forsythia' I tended to paint another right away, to replace it—to counteract that sense of loss, of possession, even if the sale was practical. 'Forsytes' often had libraries of books, but were not great readers, most their literary knowledge having come from their excellent education at those public schools. Most my life I have had a fine library and books remain one of my collecting weaknesses, but do I read them? Sometimes...but for the most part it is the possession that is paramount. "If you own the book, then you own the knowledge within the book,"—it is a 'Forsyte' principle.

"We are of course, all of us slaves of property," 'Young Jolyon' continued, "and I admit that it's a question of degree, but what I call a 'Forsyte' is a man who is decidedly more than less a slave of property. He knows a good thing, he knows a safe thing, and his grip on property—it doesn't matter whether it be wives, houses, money, or reputation—is his hallmark."

"Ah!" murmured Bosinney. "You should patent the word."

'Young Jolyon' had struck a chord.

"You talk of them," said Bosinney, "as if they were half England."

"They are," repeated Young Jolyon, "half England, and the better half, too, the safe half, the three per cent, the half that counts. It's their wealth and security that makes everything possible, makes literature, science, even religion, possible. Without Forsytes, who believe in none of these things, but turn them all to use, where should we be? My dear sir, Forsytes are the middlemen, the commercials, the pillars of society, the cornerstones of convention; everything that is admirable!"

'Forsytes' in my childhood were England. We were the masters of the British Empire, one quarter of the landmass of our planet. The Empire was our greatest possession and its commerce, management and law was our domain. That we were only three percent was barely realized in our upbringing. It was not until the Empire disintegrated and our suzerainty ended that we came to realize fully that there was another ninety-seven percent! My mother always taught us that we were ordinary people, but there is little that is ordinary about three percent, and the three percent included the aristocracy and landed gentry. When my mother said we were ordinary people, she was simply acknowledging that we were not part of that hereditary world above us. We were aware of a working class, especially after the commonality of class that had got us all through World War II, but we rarely saw their streets, didn't speak their dialect or play their sports. We lived in our leafy suburbs, almost unaware of their existence except through trade—A "little man" here or there that would help us with our plumbing, sweep our chimneys, carry in our coal sacks, remove our trash in a dustcart, and cheerfully deliver our milk and our bread. The British Broadcasting Corporation broadcast radio programs for us, not for them; and newsmen read in clipped upper-class accents for us, not for them. They reported on our world, not theirs. And, if the news did touch their world, it was told through our eyes. In fact, the radio newsreaders even sat in front of their microphones to read us news over the airwaves in dinner jackets—black tie—to give us a better ethos. The BBC was even affectionately known in 'Forsythia' as "Auntie Beeb."

However, when the Empire collapsed with Indian independence, Suez, Kenya and the Mau Mau, Singapore and Malayan independence, the media changed, too. Playwrights produced 'kitchen sink' dramas about life among the ninety-seven percent, authors wrote books about working-class life. 'Forsytes' ceased to be the center of England's world—soccer became more important than cricket. Television spread its tentacles over the land, uniting north and south in a strange commonality of class.

For 'Young Jolyon', however, despite his rejection, the three percent ruled as a majority. *"The great majority of architects, painters, or writers have no principles, like any other Forsytes. Art, literature, religion, survive by virtue of the few cranks who really believe in such things, and the many Forsytes who make a commercial use of them. At a low estimate, three fourths of our Royal Academicians are Forsytes, seven eighths of our novelists, a large proportion of the Press."*

Did Bernard Shaw or Oscar Wilde write plays about the lower orders? No…they wrote about and for 'Forsythia'. Did Trollope, Forster,

Evelyn Waugh or Ryder Haggard write about the working class in their novels? No...they wrote for 'Forsytes' about 'Forsythia'. Even the earlier writers, Dickens and the Brontes, reformers though they may have been, made their heroes and heroines 'Forsytes' from the bumbling Mr. Pickwick to the endearing Mr. Pip. In fact, Mr. Pip's rise into 'Forsythia' in *Great Expectations* almost traces the rise from yeomanry into society. Dickens takes us into the underworld of the lower classes to make his reforming points, with wonderful characters like Mr. Smallweed of *Bleak House*. Fagin and Nancy are plausible, if larger than life characters from that underworld in *Oliver Twist*, but who is the real hero of that novel—isn't it Mr. Brownlow, who rescues young Oliver from this underworld? Of course, it is true that these authors had to write for a reading public, and during 'Forsythia' not many in the working classes read.

"Of science I can't speak," 'Young Jolyon' continued. *"'Forsytes' are magnificently represented in religion; in the House of Commons perhaps more numerous than anywhere. But I'm not laughing,* Bosinney, *it is dangerous to go against the majority—and what a majority!"* 'Young Jolyon' fixed his eyes on Bosinney: *"It's dangerous to let anything carry you away—a house, a picture, a—woman!"*

He had said it all. Bosinney looked pale.

"Don't mistake me," 'Young Jolyon' said. *"It doesn't do to despise a Forsyte; it doesn't do to disregard them!"*

"You've done it yourself!" Bosinney pleaded.

"You forget," 'Young Jolyon' *said with a queer pride, "I can hold on, too—I'm a Forsyte myself."*

Bosinney rose and left, as if he was fleeing.

A man fled when he was in danger of destroying hearth and home, when there were children, when he felt himself trampling down ideals, breaking something.

'Young Jolyon' *himself had not fled. Yet he had gone further than Bosinney, had broken up his own unhappy home, not someone else's. And the old saying came back to him: 'A man's fate lies in his own heart.'*

In his own heart! The proof of the pudding was in the eating— Bosinney had still to eat his pudding.

'Young Jolyon' could see both sides. *Most people would consider such a marriage as that of Soames and Irene quite fairly successful; he had money, she had beauty; it was a case of compromise. There*

*was no reason why they should not jog along, even if they hated each
other. It would not matter if they went their own ways a little so long as
the decencies were observed—the sanctity of the marriage tie, of the
common home, respected. Half the marriages of the upper classes were
conducted on these lines. Do not offend the susceptibilities of Society;
do not offend the susceptibilities of the Church. To avoid offending these
is worth the sacrifice of any private feelings. The advantages of the
stable home are visible, tangible, so many pieces of property; there is
no risk in the status quo. To break up a home is at the best a dangerous
experiment, and selfish into the bargain.*

Young Jolyon sighed.

*'The core of it all,' he thought, 'is property, but there are many
people who would not like it put that way. To them it is "the sanctity of
the marriage tie"; but the sanctity of the marriage tie is dependent on
the sanctity of the family, and the sanctity of the family is dependent on
the sanctity of property. And yet I imagine all these people are followers
of One who never owned anything. It is curious!'*

Again, 'Young Jolyon' sighed. He left the club and walked home
to his less salubrious living in 'Forsythia'. *Before reaching Wisteria
Avenue he removed old Jolyon's letter from his pocket, and tearing it
into tiny pieces, scattered them in the dust of the road.*

CHAPTER ELEVEN

BOSINNEY ON PAROLE

Soames came home the day after the Richmond outing somewhat surprised to find Irene in.

"Are you expecting somebody?" he asked.

"Yes—that is, not particularly."

"Who?"

"Mr. Bosinney said he might come."

"Bosinney. He should be at work."

To this Irene *made no answer.*

"Well," said Soames. *"I want you to come out to the stores with me, and after that we will go to the Park."*

Seeing her reaction, he challenged her.

"I don't know what your idea of a wife's duty is. I never have known."

She reminded him that before they were married he had promised to let her go if the marriage was not a success. *"Is it a success?"* she asked.

"It would be a success if you behaved yourself properly!"

"I have tried," said Irene, *"Will you let me go?"*

"How can I let you go? We're married, aren't we? For God's sake don't let's have any of this sort of nonsense! Get your hat on and come and sit in the Park."

Such a succinct statement from a 'Forsyte' could have come from my own grandmother. This would have been a Hovenden statement to go with the Hovenden glare. "What are you talking about? Just get on with your life. You made your bed, now you lie in it." If Granny had been alive when Uncle Dennis sought to divorce my aunt, Brigid, I have no doubt that is what she would have said, barely looking up, but for a momentary glare, her cigarette dangling as she spoke, and her jigsaw puzzle continuing to occupy the foremost part of her concentration.

One time when Diane was staying at The Breach, she was preparing some mushrooms for supper. She noticed some maggots in the mushrooms and took them to Granny, thinking she should throw them out. Granny peered at them momentarily and then looked Diane in the eye in a forthright 'Forsyte' way:

"There's nothing wrong with that," she said, "they are full of protein."

The subject was closed and the mushrooms were cooked maggots and all!

"Let you go," Soames repeated. *"What on earth would you do with yourself if I did? You've got no money! Understand, once and for all, I won't have you say this sort of thing. Go and get your hat on!"*

Irene *did not move.*

"I suppose," said Soames, *"you don't want to miss Bosinney if he comes!"*

Irene got up slowly and left the room. She came down with her hat on.

In Hyde Park, Soames saw Bosinney walking fast. He needled his wife:

"Look at that ass! He must be mad to walk like that in this heat." He knew Irene would look up, as until then conversation was lacking between them. *"Hello! It's our friend the Buccaneer!"*

Soames called to Bosinney. *"What are you doing in the Park?"*

Bosinney did not seem to hear; he made his answer to Irene: "I've been round to your place; I hoped I should find you in."

Civilly, but with intentions, Soames invited 'the Buccaneer' back with them for dinner. *Into that invitation he put a strange bravado, a stranger pathos: 'You can't deceive me,' his look and voice seemed to be saying, 'but see—I trust you—I'm not afraid of you!'*

'Forsytes' were trained to keep that stiff upper lip in the face of danger—it was how they ruled the Empire. It was ingrained in us from our earliest years. We did not sneak on others, and if we were hurt it was not to show. 'Forsytes' suppressed their emotions. 'Forsythia' was the society of the stiff upper lip. Even on the playing fields of our schooldays, we were firmly taught: "It matters not whether you win or lose, but how you play the game." There was no rah-rah bravado in 'Forsythia', that was a trait of the lower classes and the natives of the Empire; we were to be the masters of the understatement, hiding our emotions so we could "get on with it." Perhaps that is why we played cricket, a game that officially takes five days to play, and merits only mild applause expressed in the clapping of hands to appreciate good play, while the lower classes played soccer and screamed in loud cheers for their teams.

Soames observed Bossiney and his wife through dinner.

After dinner when 'the Buccaneer' showed his eagerness to leave, Soames extended his hand to him. It was ice cold.

"You must come again soon:" he said, *"Irene likes to have you talk about the house!"*

Soames *went to bed with the certainty that Bosinney was in love with his wife.*

That warm night he reflected on how he had been captivated by Irene wishing to possess her just as Bosinney, now. Four years ago, the night but one before his marriage, *he had hurried on his clothes and gone down into the street, down past houses and squares, to the street where she was staying, and there had stood and looked at the front of the little house* where Irene lived. Was Bosinney doing the same?

*He stole across to the front of the house, stealthily drew aside a blind, and raised a window. The lamps were still alight, all pale, but not a soul stirred—no living thing in sight—*not even the *early water cart, cleansing the reek of the streets.*

Although 'Forsytes' did not show their emotions in public, they had emotions—even Soames. I am reminded of that last great musical of 'Forsythia' again, *My Fair Lady,* that played to packed houses in London and New York in the 1950s. Only in the darkness of night could a 'Forsyte' let down his stiff upper lip. Freddie Eynsford-Hill made his way to the house of Professor Henry Higgins to gaze upward in the wee hours at the window where he perceived Eliza Doolittle to be at rest. In the musical, he then sang one of the biggest hits of the show, *"I have often walked down this street before, but the pavement's always stayed beneath my feet before. Now, all at once am I, several stories high, knowing I'm on the street where you live."*

CHAPTER TWELVE

JUNE PAYS SOME CALLS

'**O**ld Jolyon' heard from his son while still at Broadstairs with June. It was *an unpractical letter, in which by rambling generalities the boy seemed trying to get out of answering a* plain question.

> *'I've seen Bosinney,' he wrote; 'he is not a criminal. The more I see of people the more I am convinced that they are never good or bad—merely comic or pathetic. You probably don't agree with me!'*

Old Jolyon did not; he considered it cynical to so express oneself. Perhaps he did not believe in 'Goodness' or 'Badness' any more than his son; but as he would have said: He didn't know—couldn't tell.

Many called my father a cynic, as once in a while he would let down his 'Forsyte' guard and give a mildly philosophical answer to a fragrant 'Forsyte' assumption—especially when it came to religion or morality.

Deep down, there was some comfort in 'Young Jolyon's' vague reply to his father's question, because it only affirmed 'Old Jolyon's' own philosophical leanings, although in public he was wont to admit it.

In writing to his son he did not really hope that anything would come of it. Since the ball at Roger's he had seen too clearly how the land lay—he could put two and two together quicker than most men—and with the example of his own son before his eyes, knew better than any Forsyte of them all that the pale flame singes men's wings whether they will or no.

He knew Irene cast a spell over men. *She was not a flirt, not even a coquette—words dear to the heart of his generation—but she was dangerous.*

He sighed and prepared his bag of papers to take to London for board meetings.

June requested to come with him. She wanted to visit Mrs. Smeech, one of her 'lame ducks'. In reality, her main purpose, however, not revealed to her grandfather, was her desire to meet with Bosinney's aunt, Mrs. Baynes.

Mrs. Baynes was in her kitchen organizing the cook when June was announced, for she was an excellent housewife. 'Forsytes' who did not retain a butler or housekeeper, still managed a variety of domestics of whom the cook was probably the most important. Many 'Forsyte' ladies managed their own households. Granny Mabs was such a 'Forsyte'. At Frainsville she had managed much of Great-grandmother Cuthbertson's household, and in her own married life, always was in charge of her own home. Such households were usually comprised of a cook, scullery maid, a houseparlor maid and a tweeny, who acted as an upstairs maid and ladies' maid. Great-grandmother Minnie Longley ran much of her household through Kate, the cook. At times, Grandpop had the luxury of a butler, and the Longleys always had a cook, although Granny Longley, like Granny Mabs, was a competent cook herself. The cook at The Breach in my childhood was Mrs. James, and Miss Coath, the governess, by then had pretty much taken over the management of the household. In all our households in the post-war years of my childhood, live-in maids were a thing of the past, although up to World War II they all had full staffs of maids. In the post-war period, daily charwomen took their place. It is, however, quite revealing to look back on our lifestyle in the 1950s, for at Wickham Way we at one time had three charwomen and an 'au pair', although they were not always all there at the same time. Outside, there was always a gardener, daily before World War II when he had assistants, too, and possibly twice a week after the war.

When my father died in May, 2008, among those who came to the memorial service in thanksgiving for his life, was a man about ten years my senior who had obviously dressed up for the occasion. My sisters knew fully well who he was, as in his latter years my father often visited with this man at a breakfast café in Beckenham High Street. They referred to him as "Bill the lizard," a name that had something to do with an earlier stage in Bill's life when he hung around snooker lounges. At the memorial service, he introduced himself to me.

"I used to be the gardener when you were a little boy," he informed me. "Actually, your father knew a lot more about gardening than I did."

"You grew the carnations, then," I replied, remembering that after we moved to Wickham Way, there was a special bed of carnations that were my father's pride and joy. Some of them had been moved from Chelston where the Longleys had always propagated carnations.

"Yes, your father knew a lot more about those carnations," Bill affirmed.

He had come to the memorial service with his friend, who had also regularly sat in the café with my father. We called him "the clock man." He had done some work servicing our old grandfather clock when it was moved from Wickham Way to Springpark Drive. The clock had been in the Longley family for four generations—almost the span of 'Forsythia'.

Mrs. Baynes' husband, Bosinney's uncle and mentor, was an architect *who built that remarkably fine row of tall crimson houses in Kensington which compete with so many others for the title of 'the ugliest in London.'*

This enclave of tall crimson houses is found between Kensington High Street, the squares of Belgravia, and Chelsea. I have to admit that after the majesty of Belgravia, where Granny Longley always said she would have liked to have lived, these red sandstone structures, hiding small bistros and endless flats, are somewhat of a let down until one emerges on the fringes of Kensington Gardens and Hyde Park. Marking the entrance to this warren of Baynes' style architecture, however, even though in the same red sandstone, are the formidable architectural structures of Harrods and the Royal Albert Hall.

Mrs. Louisa Baynes *had been hoping for this visit for some time past. Whispers had reached her that things were not all right between*

*her nephew and his fiancée. She had asked Phil to dinner many times;
his invariable answer had been 'too busy.'*

Her instinct was alarmed. She ought to have been a 'Forsyte' for
she was a very proper woman. *Her name was upon the committees of
numberless charities connected with the Church—dances, theatricals,
or bazaars—and she never lent her name unless sure beforehand that
everything had been thoroughly organised. Organisation was the only
thing, for by organisation alone could you feel sure that you were
getting a return for your money. The only thing against her was that
she did not have a double name. She was a power in upper-middle-class
society, with its hundred sets and circles.*

'Forsytes' expected to sit on charity boards and "do their bit." In
my childhood, it was the Doggett girls, my aunts, Betty and Daphne,
who led the family in this field. Daphne was a local organizer of 'Meals
on Wheels' delivering hot food to isolated and infirm old folks. Betty
was a leading light in the Park Langley Players, who often rehearsed in
Charles Darwin's old home at Down. The National Trust residence was
the leased home of the Knox-Johnstons in that last decade of 'Forsythia'.
Yes, a double name, usually created through the inter-marriage of two
well-to-do 'Forsyte' families, lent credence to these social and charitable
circles. The Knox-Johnstons had two sons more or less our age—one,
Robin, became famous as just the third solo yachtsman to sail around
the world. My sister, Diane, used to perform with the Park Langley
Players and recalls a party that the Knox-Johnstons gave, to which, as
a member of the players' circle, she was invited. It was given at a time
on Robin's journey when he was lost—out of radio contact. The Knox-
Johnstons gave the party in the good faith that their son was not lost,
and sure enough, a few days later his yacht emerged from an English
Channel fog off Plymouth Ho to celebrate the end of his successful
voyage. Robin's younger brother, Christopher, married my cousin Hilary
O'Callaghan—Aunt Betty's daughter. The Doggett superiority raised
its head again. Personally, however, I always felt that the double name
Hovenden Longley had far more panache than Knox-Johnston, for both
Knox and Johnston were fairly common names, whereas Hovenden and
Longley were rare surnames. We never officially hyphenated our name,
but both my father and I carried the union of Hovenden and Longley in
our names and there were times when it was useful. Remember Granny
Longley's advice before the Cobham Hall ball: "Now, Peter, if the *Tatler*

takes your picture, remember you are Peter Hovenden Longley and not
A.N. Other."

My father played his part "doing his bit," often controversially, on
the Parish Council of St. George's in Beckenham, and also took on
charity work for the Imperial Cancer Society. My mother was a leading
member of the Ladies' section at Langley Park Golf Club. Their efforts,
no less sincere, seemed to go less noticed than those of my mother's
cousins. In fact, my sisters and I coined our own phrase for something
that was well organized in terms of charity or society—"It was very
'Daphne'." Somehow, we never seemed to be quite as organized as
those Doggetts.

Although Mrs. Baynes moved in 'Forsyte' circles with her charitable
good works, she was well aware that June's father was *extremely well
off.* Phil Bosinney had told her so. She prepared herself to make the best
impression on June. *Today she felt the emotion with which we read a
novel describing a hero and an inheritance, nervously anxious lest, by
some frightful lapse of the novelist, the young man should be left without
it at the end.* She knew nothing of the 'Forsyte 'Change' rumors. *She
supposed June heard from Phil every day.*

"No," June said, *"he never writes!"*

Perhaps she had heard something of Irene from Bosinney himself.
Her guard went up. *"Why, my dear—he's quite the most harum-scarum
person; one never pays the slightest attention to what he does!"*

"Do you see him?" June challenged.

*"Oh yes! I don't remember when he was here last—indeed, we
haven't seen much of him lately. He's so busy with your cousin's house;
I'm told it will be finished directly. We must organize a little dinner to
celebrate the event; do come and stay the night with us!"*

June rose to go. *'I'm only wasting my time, this woman will tell me
nothing,'* she thought.

Mrs. Baynes rose, too, flustered. *Only that morning her husband had
said: "Old Mr. Forsyte must be worth well over one hundred thousand
pounds!"*

*The chance might be slipping away—she couldn't tell—the chance
of keeping* June *in the family, and yet she dared not speak.*

Her eyes followed June to the door.

It closed.

June decided to go to Phil and confront him herself—*ask him what
he meant. She had a right to know.*

She went to his apartment. *She rang the bell. The door did not open.* She rang again and again, then *sitting down at the top of the stairs, buried her face in her hands.*

Presently she stole down, out into the air. She *had no desire now but to get home as quick as she could.*

Suddenly—over on the opposite side, going towards his rooms from the direction of Soames' home, *she saw Bosinney himself.*

Their eyes met, and he raised his hat. An omnibus passed, obscuring her view; then, from the edge of the pavement, through a gap in the traffic, she saw him walking on.

And June stood motionless, looking after him.

CHAPTER THIRTEEN

PERFECTION OF THE HOUSE

"**O**ne mockturtle, clear; one oxtail; two glasses of port."
In a corner of the old poultry market at Smithfield was situated The Cock Tavern. Such an order, prior to a good plate of solid English food, was often called out there. 'Guv'nors,' salesmen, and even a few hungry porters would meet there for lunch. In particular, I remember this being the haunt of my Great-uncle George, Director of R.F. Potter in my childhood. He was Grandpop Longley's youngest brother and rather more egalitarian than my grandfather or even my father. He usually wore a white coat, like his salesmen, whereas I never saw my father or Grandpop in a white coat. He had a very pink face, less hair than my side of the family, and wore wire-rim glasses. He had married the girl across the street, Marjorie Searle, whom the family in a rather unflattering way always called "Podge." The Searle Family were in the furniture business, but also published *The Meat Trades Journal*. Occasionally, my father and his cousin Audrie Lewis, would drop in to The Cock and join their Uncle George for a whiskey. Audrie, in particular, liked her whisky, which she usually called "a whickie." It is highly probable, however, that in the height of 'Forsythia' when Great-grandfather was a young man in Smithfield, that he might well have called for port, as did James Forsyte in *the upper room of French's, where* like at The Cock, *a Forsyte could still get heavy English food.*

Of all eating-places James Forsyte *liked best to come* to French's; *there was something unpretentious, well-flavoured, and filling about it, and though he had been to a certain extent corrupted by the necessity for being fashionable, and the trend of habits keeping pace with an income that would increase, he still hankered in quiet City moments after the tasty flesh-pots of his earlier days. Here,* as at The Cock Tavern, *you were served by hairy English waiters in aprons; there was sawdust on the floor, and three round gilt looking-glasses hung just above the line of sight. They had only recently done away with the cubicles, too, in which you could have your chop, prime chump, with a floury potato, without seeing your neighbours, like a gentleman.*

My father always said that the best meat was served in these pub restaurants around the market, just as he also always assured us that The Great Western Railway bought the best meat on the market. Certainly, the dining cars of 'Forsythia's' railways, even in the 1950s, did serve wonderful lunches and dinners, not much less so than on those Pullman trains. The restaurant car manager would come through the train issuing tickets for first or second sitting and you knew you could wile away a pleasant hour on your journey through the English countryside, enjoying an excellent three-course meal featuring roast beef or roast lamb with all the trimmings, or maybe pork and apple sauce, or plaice, sole, or trout meuniere, all accompanied by an appropriate glass of wine poured from a convenient half bottle.

"How are you going to Robin Hill?" James asked his son at French's. *"You going to take Irene? You'd better take her. I should think there will be a lot that'll want seeing to."*

Without looking up from his soup, *Soames answered: "She won't go."*

"Won't go? What's the meaning of that? She's going to live in the house, isn't she?"

Soames remained introvert and secretive, not wishing to discuss his troubled marriage with his father.

The hairy *waiter brought the two glasses of port, but Soames stopped him.*

"That's not the way to serve port," he said.

Soames had benefited from his father's wealth and was perhaps a little less at home in this sawdust floored pub, despite the excellence of the English fare, than James, whose origins in 'Forsythia' had been just a little more humble. Port should be served in a decanter, and in gentlemanly circles the decanter should be passed around the table, one gentleman pouring the port for the other gentleman—a practice that had its origins in the desire among gentlemen to prove no suspicion of poison having been slipped into the heavy wine. On rare occasions, such as Christmas, my father would provide our table with after-dinner liqueurs and port. The port was always decanted and the heavy cut crystal container passed around from right to left.

James persisted. *"Your mother's in bed," he said; "you can have the carriage to take you down. I should think Irene'd like the drive. This young Bosinney'll be there, I suppose, to show you over?"*

Soames nodded.

"I should like to go and see for myself what sort of a job he's made finishing off," pursued James. "I'll just drive round and pick you both up."

Soames remained on the defensive. *"I am going down by train. If you like to drive round and see, Irene might go with you, I can't tell."*

James *could see that Soames wouldn't stand very much more of her goings on! It did not occur to him to define what he meant by her 'goings on'; the expression was wide, vague, and suited a Forsyte.* I think every member of my family used this expression, and it covered just about everything from giggling fits, to outings, or from larks, to adultery!

James was determined and he arrived with his barouche and groom to take Irene to Robin Hill.

"Your mother-in-law's in bed," he began, hoping at once to enlist her sympathy. "I've got the carriage here. Now be a good girl and put on your hat and come with me for a drive. It'll do you good!"

On the journey, James confronted his daughter-in-law.

"Soames is very fond of you—he won't have anything said against you; why don't you show him more affection?"

Irene flushed. "I can't show what I haven't got."

James felt in command. *"I can't think what you're about. He's a very good husband!"*

Irene's answer was so low as to be almost inaudible among the sounds of traffic. "You are not married to him!"

"What's that got to do with it? He's given you everything you want. He's always ready to take you anywhere, and now he's built you this house in the country. It's not as if you had anything of your own."

Again James looked at her.

"We're all very fond of you. If only you'd be more of a wife to him."

Irene did not answer.

James tried another tack to gain her reaction.

"I suppose that young Bosinney will be getting married to June now?"

"I don't know," she said, "you should ask her."

When they arrived at Robin Hill, James was at first impressed. *He could not restrain an exclamation of approval. Evidently, no pains had been spared. It was quite the house of a gentleman.* Inside, *he went on throwing open doors and peeping in. Everything was in apple-pie order, ready for immediate occupation.*

He turned round at last to speak to Irene, and saw her standing over in the garden entrance with Soames, who had already arrived by train, *and Bosinney* .

Getting Soames aside and noting *Irene was very close to the architect,* he asked, *"What's the matter? What's all this? Nobody tells me anything."*

"Our friend," Soames said sarcastically, *"has exceeded his instructions again, that's all. So much the worse for him this time."*

Later, when James took Irene home, *the sight of her face* made him feel *certain, quite certain,* she and Bosinney *had been making some appointment or other...*

On his way back up to London in the train, Soames mulled over the events of the afternoon. *Nothing in this world is more sure to upset a Forsyte than the discovery that something on which he has stipulated to spend a certain sum has cost more. If he cannot rely on definite values of property, his compass is amiss; he is adrift on bitter waters without a helm.*

On hearing from Bosinney that his limit of twelve thousand pounds would be exceeded by something like four hundred, Soames *had grown white with anger.* In his book, and on his suspicions concerning his wife, *over this last expenditure, Bosinney had put himself completely in the wrong. There could be no two opinions about it—the fellow had made himself liable for that extra four hundred, or, at all events, for three hundred and fifty of it, and he would have to make it good.*

Back in London he told Irene of his plan.

"Do you mean that you are going to make him pay that towards this hateful house?"

"Your friend the Bucaneer has made a fool of himself; he will have to pay for it," Soames said.

"And you know he's got nothing?"

"Yes"

"Then you are meaner than I thought."

Soames looked at her directly, twitching.

"Are you carrying on a flirtation with Bosinney?"

"No. I am not!"

"I believe you are made of stone." Soames gripped her arm. *"A good beating,"* he said, *"is the only thing that would bring you to your senses,"* but turning on his heel, he left the room.

CHAPTER FOURTEEN

SOAMES SITS ON THE STAIRS

S *oames went upstairs that night with the feeling that he had gone
too far. He was prepared to offer excuses for his words.*

Pausing, with his hand on the knob of Irene's bedroom *door,
he tried to shape his apology. But the door did not open.*

It dawned on him that he was barred out.

"Unlock the door, do you hear. Unlock the door!" he shouted. *"Do
you hear? Let me in at once—I insist on being let in."*

*In a rage he lifted his foot to kick in the panel; the thought of the
servants restrained him, and he felt suddenly that he was beaten.*

There was in 'Forsythia' a strange moral relationship between
'Forsytes' and their servants. The master and his family had a moral
duty to improve the lives of their servants. In part, this was to give them
a standard of living that they would not have enjoyed in their working
class environment. Did kitchen boys or scullery maids live better 'in
service' than they would have in Fagin's kitchen? Yes, for the raw
alternative for the millions of 'Forsyte' domestics was such a choice.
'In service' they had a chance to better themselves; even in marriage,
to raise themselves in the hierarchy of life below stairs. A housemaid,
who married a footman, or a cook, who married a butler, might well
raise themselves from working class to lower-middle class. The class
order was as strong below stairs as it was above. A 'Forsyte' master
and his lady also saw their role as a paternalistic example of how life

should be lived. The same principle applied to how the 'Forsyte' colonial administrators saw their paternalistic example for the natives of the Empire. "You rule by example," was the law of 'Forsythia'—however, that right to rule was a birthright—God given.

'Forsytes' cared for their servants. They nursed their servants in sickness. They provided for their servants in need. They advised them, when the opportunity arose, in their domestic squabbles. At Christmas, they gave them gifts, and Boxing Day was a special day off! Boxing Day is celebrated in England on St. Stephen's Day, the day after Christmas. In the early days of 'Forsythia' it was not celebrated. In *A Christmas Carol* Charles Dickens shows how Ebeneezer Scrooge expected his clerk, Bob Cratchit, to be back in the office, on time, the day after Christmas, but by the latter nineteenth century, this day after Christmas was one of the most celebrated days of the 'Forsyte' calendar, almost more so than Christmas Day. Dickens indicates this coming trend in the reality that after Scrooge's change of heart brought about by a restless night of nightmares in the form of apparitions, the old miser does give Bob Cratchit the day after Christmas off to celebrate with his family, and it is Scrooge who provides the family with their feast. So it was in Edwardian England and throughout 'Forsythia'. The old German Christmastide carol, *Good King Wenceslas,* tells the story of a king looking out from his castle on St. Stephen's Day and seeing a pauper at his gate. He immediately has pity on the pauper and provides for him. Servants of 'Forsythia' worked long, hard hours on Christmas Day, providing for their masters and families. There grew up, inspired by the example of King Wenceslas, the idea that the day after Christmas should be a holiday for the servants. The left over food from the family's Christmas feast was, therefore, boxed up for the servants to take home to their families—hence St. Stephen's Day became known as Boxing Day.

'Forsythia' households being without servants on Boxing Day, led to that day also becoming a sporting holiday for 'Forsytes'. Some, hunted the fox, others, attended the large number of race meetings around the country, and traditionally many visited their own relatives, as we always did. Boxing Day was a day to share with Granny Mabs and Grandpa Jack at their house, or to go down to The Breach for a day with Granny and Grandpop Longley.

In the 1950s, my father used to provide chickens, turkeys, or the occasional goose at Christmas for friends and neighbors, and for Lloydy and our other charwomen. I always remember him coming home just before Christmas with these hampers and sacks of succulent fresh birds already labeled for to whom they were designated. When I was about twelve, Lloydy, our so much loved domestic, fell ill with pneumonia just before Christmas. On Christmas Eve, I carried her chicken to her on my bicycle so she and her daughter, Doreen, who was married to a postman, Billy, would have their Christmas dinner. She lived in a small terrace house in Maple Road, Penge, that had been spared by just a few buildings from a devastating V2 rocket raid in the last weeks of the war. In those days, even in this rather undesirable neighborhood, I could safely ride my bicycle and leave it, unlocked, against the gate leading up to Lloydy's front door. Doreen took the chicken and I was shown into the little back room where Lloydy lay, looking very frail, in a brass bed that took up most the room. She had no teeth and could barely move. A small coal fire burned in the grate. I held her hand. I knew she was dying. I was the last member of my family to see Mrs. Lloyd. She died the next day, Christmas Day.

Of course, as masters, we in 'Forsythia' were expected to be an inspiration for our servants. It would not do for Soames Forsyte to be caught breaking the door down into Mrs. Soames' bedroom. It was bad enough that they should hear him raising his voice to the mistress. So, Soames *sat down on the stairs and buried his face in his hands.*

The whole meaning of his wife's *act of revolt came to him. She meant it to be for good. Since she had locked her doors she had no further claim as a wife and he would console himself with other women!* But *he had never had much, and he had lost the habit. He felt that he could never recover it. His hunger could only be appeased by his wife, inexorable and frightened, behind these shut doors. No other woman could help him.*

He became angry. *Her conduct was immoral, inexcusable, worthy of any punishment within his power. He desired no one but her and she refused him.*

She must really hate him, then!

Then he asked himself again if she were carrying on an intrigue with Bosinney. He did not believe that she was; he could not afford to believe such a reason for her conduct—the thought was not to be faced. It would be scandal and his failed marriage a bad example for society and servants alike. *It would be unbearable to contemplate the necessity of making his marital relations public property.*

But, *Bosinney was in love with* Irene! Soames *hated the fellow, and would not spare him now. He could and would refuse to pay a penny piece over twelve thousand and fifty pounds—the extreme limit fixed in the correspondence; or rather he would pay, he would pay and sue him for damages. He would go to Jobling and Boulter and put the matter in their hands. He would ruin the impecunious beggar! And suddenly— though what connection between the thoughts?—he reflected that Irene had no money either. They were both beggars. This gave him a strange satisfaction.* He now had a plan.

The next day, when Soames returned home to Montpelier Square from the City, a street lady was playing a barrel organ. As she turned the handle, *it was playing a waltz, and it went on and on, though nothing indeed but leaves danced to the tune. It was the waltz they had played at Roger's when Irene had danced with Bosinney; and the perfume of the gardenias she had worn came back to Soames, drifted by the malicious music, as it had been drifted to him then, when she passed, her hair glistening, her eyes so soft, drawing Bosinney on and on down an endless ballroom.*

The organ woman plied her handle slowly; she had been grinding her tune all day—grinding it in Sloane Street hard by, grinding it perhaps to Bosinney himself.

I probably come from the last generation to remember the organ grinder. They were a rarity in Beckenham during my childhood, but could still be found outside tube and railway stations in London, seeking pennies from passers by—pennies by the way that were then large respectable looking coins featuring a relief of Britannia seated on her shield of royal arms and ruling the waves. Decimalization later changed these coins to insigificance.

Soames lit a cigarette and looking from the window, he saw Irene, *her sunshade furled, hastening homewards down the Square, in a soft, rose-coloured blouse with drooping sleeves that he did not know. She stopped before the organ, took out her purse, and gave the woman money.*

She came in, put down her sunshade, and stood looking at herself in the glass. Her cheeks were flushed as if the sun had burned them; her lips were parted in a smile. She stretched her arms out as though to embrace herself, with a laugh that for all the world was like a sob.

Soames surprised her in the hall, *"Very—pretty!"* he said sarcastically.

As though shot she spun round, and would have passed him up the stairs. He barred the way.

"Why such a hurry?" he said.

He hardly recognised her. She seemed on fire, so deep and rich the colour of her cheeks, her eyes, her lips, and of the unusual blouse she wore.

"I don't like that blouse," he said slowly, "it's a soft, shapeless thing!"

He lifted his finger towards her breast, but she dashed his hand aside.

"Don't touch me," she cried.

"Where have you been?" he asked.

"In heaven—out of this house!" With those words she fled upstairs.

Outside—in thanksgiving—at the very door, the organ grinder was playing the waltz.

Soames knew Irene had spent the day with Bosinney.

PART THREE

CHAPTER ONE

MRS. MACANDER'S EVIDENCE

Active brutality is not popular with Forsytes; they are too circumspect, and, on the whole, too soft-hearted. And in Soames there was some common pride, not sufficient to make him do a really generous action, but enough to prevent him from indulging in an extremely mean one. Short of actually beating his wife, he perceived nothing to be done; he therefore accepted the situation without another word.

Throughout the summer and autumn he continued to go to the office, to sort his pictures and ask his friends to dinner. He did not leave town; and as *was a habit with him,* he continued *to tell* Irene *the doings of his day,* except perhaps concerning the case he was bringing against Bosinney.

Soames had brought a suit against the Buccaneer, in which he claimed from him the sum of three hundred and fifty pounds. A firm of solicitors, Messrs. Freak and Able, had put in a defence on Bosinney's behalf.

Irene, unlike all the other Forsytes, *refused to go away* on a summer holiday.

Soames was more than suspicious her reasoning had something to do with Bosinney. *Irene still met him, he was certain; where, or how, he neither knew, nor asked. Sometimes when he questioned his wife as to where she had been, which he still made a point of doing, as every

Forsyte should, she looked very strange. She went out on her own altogether too much. Sea air would have taken her away from the source of Soames' suspicions.

'Forsytes' always went away for a couple of weeks in August or September, and almost always to the seaside. After all, nowhere in England is more than seventy-five miles from the sea and that bracing air. In the early 1950s, my father did not have a car. In Beckenham, we all rode bicycles, but when it came to the summer holiday, my father used to rent a Rover, a Vauxhall, or an Armstrong Siddeley from Godfrey Davis. Sometimes, he would rent cars on other occasions, prior to one of his tours to sender's estates where he could procure business from gamekeepers, or some of the game fairs at which Campbell, Key and Longley and E. Weatherley gave prizes. One of the most exciting of these was an annual fair at Ditchley Park in Oxfordshire. When the car would arrive in our drive in the evening before such a trip, Diane and I would spot it from our nursery window. We always called them "the suspicious cars."

For our summer holiday, my mother spent many days packing two great trunks full of clothes, the trunks we used for school. Great care was taken to also pack an elaborate medicine chest for all emergencies. Then, there were shrimping nets, bathing shoes, buckets and spades, and those model yachts on a string like a kite that we would sail on long voyages in tidal pools. There were toys for rainy days, board games, and huge beach towels. Last, but not least, was the picnic hamper, complete with the paraffin kettle to boil water for the tea. When everything was packed it was all piled up onto the top of the 'suspicious car' and then covered in a vast tarpaulin strapped to the car, but that still flapped in the breeze.

We always left very early in the morning, when it was still dark. This was to avoid the worst of the traffic, but it made the venture all the more exciting. First, we would stop at Granny Mabs' and Grandpa Jack's house so they could wave us 'goodbye.' Granny and Grandpa received last minute instructions about the daily feeding of our cat, fish, and budgerigars, and then we were on our way.

My mother was a stickler for a motoring superstition over white horses. If we saw a white horse we had to cross our fingers until we saw another one. Sometimes, my mother's fingers would be crossed for an hour. Whether we were going to Kent, Norfolk, Sussex or Devon, we could always spot who was 'going away.' Their cars were piled up with luggage on the roof just like ours. If they were heading back to London, my father always said, "Going home," which added to the excitement that we were 'going away.'

A 'Forsyte' touch to these journeys that I always liked was breakfast. We had probably been on the road for about three hours after that four in the morning start, so we would stop for a full English breakfast at one of those lovely old coaching inns along the way. In the 1950s, they were nearly all owned and run by Trust Houses. I always remember the headwaiters in these inns greeting us as we entered those old timbered dining rooms with floors that creaked—reminiscent of Great Yeldham Hall or Hocker Edge. The headwaiter always wore a black tailcoat, striped trousers and a stiff, winged collared shirt.

The headwaiter's uniform fascinated me. In its way it contributed to my life's plans. I had three ambitions as a boy—to be the headwaiter on one of the two iconic ocean liners of my childhood, Cunard's *Queen Mary* and *Queen Elizabeth,* and little did I know at that time that later in my life fate would lead me to a position as the cruise director and third senior hotel officer on board their successor, Cunard's *Queen Elizabeth 2.* The headwaiter's tailcoat also might have spurred my imagination to be the conductor of a great orchestra. I showed little prowess as a musician, but I loved the uniform—white tie and tails! As a cruise director, however, I was in the entertainment business… for twenty-five years! My third ambition was to be a bishop, but it was not theology that guided this, even though that is what I came to read at Cambridge University, but the frock coat and gaiters that were still worn in the 1950s by most senior clerics of the Church of England. In fact, as students at the Cambridge Divinity School, we theologians referred to 'Gaiters' almost like receiving our colors for some sport in school. One day in the future, after we had served as curates and vicars, we would get promoted to 'Gaiters', meaning the standard dress of Archdeacons, Deans, Bishops and Archbishops. I never became a bishop, but by a strange set of circumstances I did find myself in 1973 in the role of acting dean of an Anglican Cathedral in Ireland! I did not wear frock coat and gaiters, not actually being ordained, but I do remember meeting over tea in the drawing room of the Shelbourne Hotel, His Grace, The Most Reverend George Simms, the Archbishop of Dublin, dressed in such Trollopian ecclesiastical splendor. For my part, however, when conducting Sunday services I always wore my tabs, those starched linen neck pieces that were the academic badge of the clergy and the legal profession. Returning to our annual summer vacations, however...

Our seaside holidays always saw all kinds of weather; rainy or overcast days, other days when we got sunburned and had to dab on lots of pink calamine lotion from the medicine chest, and cool windy days when we were forced to go inland for comfort. We visited cathedrals, teashops, amusement parks, and wild countryside, but whenever possible we braved the beach. In those days, my sisters and I didn't mind the cold ocean and could never understand why our father was "not keen." At four o'clock, on the beach, just as everywhere else, everything stopped for tea. There was the smell of paraffin as my father fired up the kettle for his and my mother's cups of tea. My mother handed us out beakers of orange squash, along with banana sandwiches and bread and butter with strawberry jam that always attracted grits of blowing sand.

We built sandcastles, sand bridges, and sand railway stations, collected seaweed and shells, and always hung the bladderack seaweed in the windows of our rooms at the hotel so we could forecast the weather—in the morning if the seaweed was dry and brittle it would be a sunny day, if oily and smooth it was likely to rain.

At home, we had high tea, a 'Forsyte' nursery tradition. We would have baked beans on toast, sardines on toast, or boiled eggs with soldiers—toast fingers that we could dip in the soft yoke. This would be served about six o'clock just before we went to bed. On our summer holiday, however, we ate later with my mother and father in the hotel dining room. We had to actually get dressed again after having our baths! We wore grown-up clothes. Then, we enjoyed such treats as melon or grapefruit as a first course, and ice creams for dessert.

While most the Forsytes were enjoying their summer holidays at the seaside, Soames was mulling over the bad news that Messrs. Freak and Able had raised a point that challenged the ease of his case against Bosinney.

Disturbed, Soames Forsyte entered Irene's room, *for she did not lock her doors till bed-time—she had the decency, he found, to save the feelings of the servants. She was brushing her hair, and turned to him with strange fierceness.*

"What do you want?" she said. "Please leave my room!"

He answered, "I want to know how long this state of things between us is going to last? I have put up with it long enough."

"Will you please leave my room?"

"Will you treat me as your husband?"

"No."

"Then I shall take steps to make you."

"Do!"

He stared, amazed at the calmness of her answer. He knew very well that he had no intention of taking steps, and he saw that she knew, too—knew he was afraid to.

He turned round and went sulkily out.

'Why did she hate him?' Even now he could not altogether believe it. It was strange to be hated!—the emotion was too extreme; yet he hated Bosinney, that Buccaneer, that prowling vagabond, that night-wanderer.

The end of September began to witness the return of the Forsytes from their seaside summer holidays. *In rude health and small omnibuses, with considerable colour in their cheeks, they arrived daily from the various termini. The following morning saw them back at their vocations.*

On the next Sunday Timothy's was thronged from lunch till dinner.

Amongst other gossip, Aunt Juley *mentioned that Soames and Irene had not been away.*

During September, *Mrs. MacAnder, Winifred Dartie's greatest friend, taking a constitutional with young Augustus Flippard, passed Irene and Bosinney walking from the bracken towards the Sheen Gate* down at Richmond.

It was about the middle of dinner at Timothy's, *just, in fact, as the saddle of mutton had been brought in by Smither, that Mrs. MacAnder, looking airily around, said:*

"Oh! Whom do you think I passed in Richmond Park? You'll never guess—Mrs. Soames and—Mr. Bosinney. They must have been down to look at the house!"

Winifred Dartie coughed, and no one said a word. It was the piece of evidence they had all unconsciously been waiting for.

To do Mrs. MacAnder justice, she had been to Switzerland and the Italian lakes with a party of three, and had not heard of Soames's rupture with his architect.

Afterwards in the drawing-room she sat down by Aunt Juley, realizing she had committed a faux pas. *And she began:*

"What a charming woman, Mrs. Soames; such a sympathetic temperament! Soames is a really lucky man!"

Her anxiety for information had not made sufficient allowance for that inner Forsyte skin which refuses to share its troubles with outsiders; Aunt Juley, *drawing herself up with a creak and rustle of her whole person, said, shivering in her dignity:*

"My dear, it is a subject we do not talk about!"

CHAPTER TWO

NIGHT IN THE PARK

"I *can't tell,"* James would say to Emily; *"it worries me out of my life. There'll be a scandal, and that'll do him no good."*

My father often used that same expression—"I can't tell, but it worries me out of my life." What was it that really worried 'Forsytes'? It was the reality that their property, physical, or their position in society, stood to be threatened by outside sources. My father was a very gentle man, but he worried like James, all his life—worried that the life that he inherited he might not be able to pass on to his children. However, unlike James, he lived through the demise of 'Forsythia'. My grandparents were able to live out their lives before the end really came, but I have no doubt that my father saw the end coming. After the demise, I remember my father often saying of this country or that country, of Malaya, India, Kenya, Rhodesia, and South Africa, "how much better off they all seemed to be when we ran them." And, how much better off were we, when those same countries sustained our world—'Forsythia'—the world of the three percent.

Within a week of Mrs. MacAnder's encounter in Richmond Park, to all of them—save Timothy, from whom it was carefully kept, was it known that 'those two'—Irene and Bosinney—had gone to extremes. Without an open scandal, which they could not see their way to recommending, it was difficult to see what steps could be taken.

Every 'Forsyte' saw grandchildren as the interest on their investment. James was no different. *"Well, I don't know; I expect the worst. This is what comes of having no children. I knew how it would be from the first. They never told me that they didn't mean to have any children—nobody tells me anything!"*

His great comfort, therefore, *was to go to* his daughter *Winifred's, and take the little Darties,* Imogen and Publius, *in his carriage over to Kensington Gardens, and there, by the Round Pond, he could often be seen walking with his eyes fixed anxiously on little Publius Dartie's sailing boat*—no doubt the same sailing boat attached to that long string that had recently come back with the Dartie entourage from the seaside.

In Victorian and Edwardian 'Forsythia', the Round Pond at Kensington Gardens was a focal point during daylight hours for grandparents and grandchildren to wile away happy hours together, away from the prying eyes of parents and nannies. In the evening, however, Hyde Park, including the enclave of Kensington Gardens, opened its gates to all London—not just 'Forsytes'. *Forsytes and tramps, children and lovers, rested and wandered seeking one and all some freedom from labour, from the reek and turmoil of the streets.*

On Saturday, October 5, the sky that had been blue all day deepened after sunset to the bloom of purple grapes. There was no moon, and a clear dark, like some velvety garment, was wrapped around the trees, whose thinned branches, resembling plumes, stirred not in the still warm air. All London had poured into the Park, draining the cup of summer to its dregs. This is a perfect description of what my sisters and I always described as a "brewing stormy petrol," that quiet before the first clap of thunder on a summer evening.

The instincts of self-forgetfulness, of passion, and of love, hiding under the trees, away from the trustees of their remorseless enemy, the 'sense of property', were holding a stealthy revel, and Soames, returning from Bayswater—for he had been alone to dine at Timothy's—walking home along the water, with his mind upon that coming lawsuit had the blood driven from his heart by a low laugh and the sound of kisses. He thought of writing to the Times *the next morning, to draw the attention of the editor to the condition of our parks* with so many of the lower classes soiling their solace and beauty.

Letters to the *Times* were often the mouthpiece of 'Forsythia' right up to that last decade in the 1950s—indeed right up to the very symbol of change, when after one hundred years, the traditional layout of the front page of the *Times* changed its format. I remember the day at Newlands when the change occurred. The newspapers were circulated to us boys during the half-hour before 'lights out' so that we could cut out any article that we felt fitting for a scrapbook. I used to cut out all articles that featured the Archbishop of Canterbury, because at that time, as aforementioned, I thought it might be fitting for me to hold that office that some in the family still felt an ancestor of ours had held before. Spurred by a visionary experience at Newlands, I considered ordination as a priest in the Church of England to possibly be a part of my 'Forsyte' future. The only photographs featured in the *Times* were in a block on the back page of the paper. But, on the day of change, when the classified announcements were taken from the front page to be replaced by headline news, photographs started to appear on the front page of the *Times*. This was a sad day—the end of a tradition that had separated the *Times* from all other newspapers.

The second master at Newlands, Captain T. D. Manning, R.N.V.R., often wrote letters to the *Times* and also kept us informed of any 'old boy,' a past pupil from Newlands, who had a letter published in the *Times*. We were expected to read such letters, many of which in my childhood were comments on some aspect of the recent World War II. To write a letter to the *Times* that was published was tantamount to saying one had intellectually arrived in 'Forsythia'.

Soames *stood still on the rise overlooking the Serpentine, where in full lamp-light, black against the silver water, sat a couple who never moved, the woman's face buried on the man's neck—a single form, like a carved emblem of passion, silent and unashamed.*

And, stung by the sight, Soames hurried on deeper into the shadow of the trees.

In this search, who knows what he thought and what he sought? For, again, who knew but that each dark couple, unnamed, unnamable, might not be he and she—Irene and Bosinney?

But it could not be such knowledge as this that he was seeking—the wife of Soames Forsyte sitting in the Park like a common wench! Such thoughts were unconceivable; but such thoughts had been formed. He watched until the couple moved.

But it was only a poor thin slip of a shop girl in her draggled blouse that passed him, clinging to her lover's arm.

Shaking himself with sudden disgust, Soames returned to the path, and left that seeking for he knew not what.

Rumbles of thunder accompanied the first drops of rain.

Although tempted for status, Soames *did not* write his letter to the *Times* the next morning, for with scandal looming, *he had a horror of seeing his name in print.*

Chapter Three

Meeting at the Botanical

Young Jolyon, whose circumstances were not those of a Forsyte, found at times a difficulty in sparing the money needful for those country jaunts and researches into Nature, without having prosecuted which no water-colour artist ever puts brush to paper.

He compromised by painting scenes in the Botanical Gardens at Regent's Park, close to the house in Wisteria Avenue—in bricks and mortar definitely a lower-middle-class home.

He had them critiqued.

"If you'd taken a definite subject," the art critic suggested, *"such as 'London by Night', or 'The Crystal Palace in the Spring', and made a regular series, the public would have known at once what they were looking at. I can't lay too much stress upon that."* For the art critic, however, the buying public meant 'Forsytes'—the three percent. *"And this stands to reason, for if a man's a collector, he doesn't want people to smell at the canvas to find out whom his pictures are by; he wants them to be able to say at once: 'A capital Forsyte!'*

'Young Jolyon' was loathe to agree with the conventional views of 'Forsythia', but he took up the critic's idea of making a series of water-colour drawings of London, *discovering in his own achievement another proof that he was a Forsyte. He decided to commence with the Botanical Gardens, where he had already made so many studies.*

He was musing over the leaves that had escaped the habits of 'Forsythia' falling from the autumnal trees to land in a little pond. The pond was free from the rakes of the gardeners. *On that little pond the leaves floated in peace, and praised heaven with their hues, the sunlight haunting over them.*

I remember a series of oil paintings executed by my sister Diane, while she was a student at the Byam Shaw School of Art and later at The Royal Academy—a series that showed sunlight catching the sanctuary tiles of various city churches. In that same vein, too, I recall, two of her greatest paintings from that era—Roman mosaics featuring sea monsters and tritons from a floor in ancient Ostia, Italy. The mosaics were pierced by vivid wild flowers such as we witnessed when we toured Italy together. Those two paintings are amongst my most prized possessions to this day.

I have no doubt that had the Crystal Palace not burned to the ground in 1936, my sister would have caught the sunbeams in the tracery of glass that made up this amazing exhibition hall. Originally designed by Joseph Paxton to house The Great Exhibition in Hyde Park in 1851, it was moved a year or two later to the then outskirts of south London— to Sydenham Hill close to the village of Dulwich. It stood there as a symbol of 'Forsythia', the home of the world's first International Trade Fair and a tribute to the hegemony of our British Empire leading 'Forsythia's' world. As such, it remained dear in the hearts of 'Forsytes' for three generations until that fateful fire, and in keeping with its architect's original plan, seeing Paxton was the head gardener of the Duke of Devonshire's estate at Chatsworth in Derbyshire where he had built a greenhouse to house the huge Victoria lilies discovered in the Amazon basin, it could well have been described as the world's largest greenhouse. Joseph Paxton, incidentally, received a knighthood for his architectural masterpiece—not bad for a head gardener in 'Forsythia'.

Around Sydenham Hill grew up an area of palatial 'Forsyte' villas in the 1860s, and to the southeast as the London Chatham Dover railway cut its way out of the metropolis, the Crystal Palace drew attention to the leafy parks of the Cator Estates around the little Kentish village of Beckenham, close by the market town of Bromley. 'Forsytes' like my great-grandparents moved into this area in the 1870s.

'Forsytes' of Beckenham continued that love affair with the Crystal Palace that could easily be seen on Sydenham Hill from many parts of the Cator Estates. My father always recalls the wonderful weekly firework displays that lit up all South London for two generations of 'Forsythia'. Others remember the beautiful gardens and the Dinosaur statues in the park. Today, the site of the palace and its grounds is mostly known for South London's television tower and numerous soccer fields—for 'Forsytes', the proletariat game.

Instead, Diane used her skill at painting glass tracery in several oils featuring London's railway termini, and also of the grand avenues in Smithfield Market. One such painting along with an impression of the 'The River Thames and Tower Bridge', won her the prestigious Landseer Prize at the Royal Academy of Art in Burlington House.

Yes, my sister had been given similar advice to 'Young Jolyon'—paint a series, about London.

'Young Jolyon' observed the leaves on that little pond blown by the autumn breeze, but his concentration was distracted. Twenty paces from his stand was a bench on which was sitting *a lady in a velvet jacket. He found himself looking furtively at this unknown dame. Who was she? And what doing there, alone? For what or whom was she waiting, in the silence, with the trees dropping here and there a leaf, and the thrushes strutting close on grass touched with the sparkle of the autumn rime?*

Then her charming face grew eager, and, glancing round, with almost a lover's jealousy, young Jolyon saw Bosinney striding across the grass.

Curiously he watched the meeting.

He had rowed in the galley himself! He knew the long hours of waiting and the lean minutes of a half-public meeting; the tortures of suspense that haunt the unhallowed lover. This was the real thing! This is what had happened to himself!

He could hear, yes, it had to be Irene, *he could hear her saying:* "But darling, it would ruin you!"

'And where does Soames come in?' young Jolyon thought. 'People think she is concerned about the sin of deceiving her husband! Little they know of women! She's eating, after starvation—taking her revenge! And heaven help her—for he'll take his.'

* * *

Meanwhile, June had returned from Europe with her grandfather. She immediately sought news of Bosinney. At Timothy's, she met her aunts, who informed her Uncle *Timothy was very poorly, he had had a lot of trouble with the chimney sweep in his bedroom; the stupid man had let the soot down the chimney! It had quite upset her uncle.*

In the last decade of 'Forsythia', our homes were still heated by coal fires—a fireplace in every room of the house. The annual visit of the chimney sweep was a major affair. Every piece of furniture and every carpet throughout the house had to be covered in dustsheets. My mother spent a whole day preparing for the chimney sweep, who always arrived early in the morning. Of course, the day before, no fires had been lit. The grates were all emptied and waiting for the man and his brushes. We children were confined to the nursery.

There was something slightly sinister about the chimney sweep. The chimney sweep, with his blackened face, was almost a representative of the underworld. He was a necessity, but also an imp. My mother was always very pleased when the chimneys had been swept and the house could return to normal again.

The sweep was not the only sinister character that visited our home, however. The window cleaner was another character, who appeared about once every two months, and unlike the sweep, was quite unannounced. We would be playing in the nursery when all of a sudden we would hear a thump outside the window. Then, our privacy would be invaded as the window cleaner climbed his ladder and his head loomed up and he peered into our world—usually make-belief adventure games with our large collection of ceremonial toy soldiers, all, of course, in those days painted in brilliant lead paint. We fled the nursery until such time as he was done. It was the fashion in latter 'Forsythia' for our houses to have many leaded panes in each window. It took the window cleaner some time to complete his task.

Having learned of Timothy's irritation with the sweep, June got little further information from either of her aunts. *Oh yes,* Soames and Irene *were in town, they had not been away at all. There was some little difficulty about the house* they believed.

Indeed, Aunt Juley was more concerned to know if June had needed to wear night-socks in those hotels so high up in the mountains.

So, June took herself off to Mrs. Baynes' house in Lowndes Square.

Soames was bringing an action against Bosinney over the decoration of the house, she learned. *There seemed little or no prospect of Bosinney's success.*

* * *

'Old Jolyon' made his way to the offices of Forsyte, Bustard and Forsyte. He sought out his brother, James Forsyte. Learning of the current case of Forsyte v. Bosinney, he said:

"I don't know what Soames is about to make a fuss over a few hundred pounds. I thought he was a man of property."

*"It's not the money—*James began.

'Old Jolyon' cut him short. He was not there to gossip.

"I've come in for my will."

"You going to make some alterations?"

Old Jolyon put the will in his breast pocket. With a cold handshake he was gone.

In the Board Room at the New Colliery Company, he perused the contents, *eye-glasses perched on the bridge of his nose, his gold pencil moving down the clauses of his will.*

Then, immediately, he took a cab *and drove to the offices of Paramor and Herring in Lincoln's Inn Fields. Jack Herring was dead, but his nephew was still in the firm, and old Jolyon was closeted with him for half an hour.*

He kept the hansom, and on coming out, gave the driver the address—3, Wisteria Avenue.

He felt a strange, slow satisfaction, as though he had scored a victory over James and the man of property. They should not poke their noses into his affairs any more; he had just cancelled their trusteeships of his will; he would take the whole of his business out of their hands and put it into the hands of young Herring, and he would move the business of his companies, too.

He had made a restitution to young Jolyon—revenge against time, sorrow, and interference, against all that incalculable sum of disapproval that had been bestowed by the world for fifteen years on his only son. It was sweet to think that at last he was going to make the boy a richer man by far than that son of James, that 'man of property.' And it was sweet to give Jo, for he loved his son.

Neither Jo nor his wife was home when he arrived, but the maid showed 'Old Jolyon' into the shabby drawing room.

'He's always at 'ome to tea, sir, to play with the children,' she said.

Indeed, 'Young Jolyon' was on his way home from the Botanical Gardens in Regent's Park, knowing he had witnessed the secret longings of Bosinney and Irene.

'Old Jolyon' *amused himself by thinking how with two strokes of his pen he was going to restore the look of caste so conspicuously absent from everything in that little house; how he could fill these rooms, or others in some larger mansion, with triumphs of art; how he could send little Jolly to Harrow and Oxford; how he could procure little Holly the best musical instruction, the child had a remarkable aptitude.*

When 'Young Jolyon' arrived *with characteristic decision old Jolyon came at once to the point. "I've been altering my arrangements, Jo,"* he said. *"You can cut your coat a bit longer in the future—I'm settling a thousand a year on you at once. June will have fifty thousand at my death, and you the rest. Yours won't come short of a hundred thousand, my boy. I thought you'd better know. I haven't much longer to live at my age. I shan't allude to it again. How's your wife? And—give her my love."*

Without any further discussion, 'Old Jolyon' left.

Jo *tried to realise all that this meant to him, and, Forsyte that he was, vistas of property were opened out in his brain. But in the midst of all he thought, too, of Bosinney and his mistress, and the broken song of the thrush. Joy—tragedy! Which? Which?*

When his wife came in he went straight up to her and took her in his arms; and for a long time he stood without speaking, his eyes closed, pressing her to him, while she looked at him with a wondering, adoring, doubting look in her eyes.

CHAPTER FOUR

VOYAGE INTO THE INFERNO

*T*he morning after a certain night on which Soames at last asserted *his rights and acted like a man, he breakfasted alone,* but *he was still haunted by the odd, intolerable feeling of remorse and shame he had felt, as he stood looking at her by the flame of the single candle, before silently slinking away.* Had he raped her? No, she was his property—but he felt the remorse.

It was Mrs. MacAnder who had made him do it. *Two nights before, at Winifred Dartie's, she had said to him, looking in his face with her sharp, greenish eyes: "And so your wife is a great friend of that Mr. Bosinney's?"*

Her words *had roused in him a fierce jealousy, which with the peculiar perversion of this instinct, had turned to fiercer desire.*

Now, Irene was still sobbing. He could hear her sobbing.

Soames went out into the fog. *The fog of late November wrapping the town as in some monstrous blanket till the trees of the Square were barely visible.*

Ironically, the last decade of 'Forsythia' was in essence also the last decade of those 'pea soup' fogs that not only does Galsworthy describe, but that permeate the London of Jack the Ripper, Edward Hyde, and Sherlock Holmes. I remember them, even in leafy Beckenham, for in late fall when we all started to burn those coal fires in the principal rooms of our homes, the smoke rose to mingle with the natural mists

181

of that season, to quote John Keats, *'of mellow mists and fruitfulness, close bosom friend of the fast maturing sun.'*

Personally, I associated the foggy, fading sun, with the football field at school, as did my sisters with the lacrosse pitch at their schools. We all hated this season that Keats loved so much in his *'Ode to Autumn'*. It made us think of standing around on those cold games fields, watching that fading orange sun while doing everything we could to avoid getting anywhere near the action of the sport, because none of us Longleys were keen on these ball games, but Keats was writing in the earliest days of 'Forsythia' when the air was less polluted. By the 1950s, 'Forsythia's' pollution had reached its height. Huge coal-fired power stations were adding their daily belch into the atmosphere above London, and the unseen pollution of countless automobiles and public transport, unknown to us, was adding to the 'pea soup' of the swirling fogs.

Every year on November the fifth, England celebrates Guy Fawkes' Night. That was one night that we prayed was clear of fog, so we could enjoy the fireworks that illuminated the skies over London in celebration of the capture of the Roman Catholic rebel, Guy Fawkes, in the cellars of the Palace of Westminster back in 1605, where he had aimed in the Gun Powder plot to blow up parliament. This popish plot failed, and the failure has been celebrated ever since, although Guy Fawkes himself was, as Swithin Forsyte would have said, *"small beer."* The real perpetrators of the plot escaped. Before we went away to our boarding schools, my father used to light fireworks for us in the garden at Chelston and in Wickham Way at Hockeredge. Granny Mabs and Grandpa Jack would come to watch, too, along with our 'au pair' girls, Erica and Laura, who probably had no idea what we were celebrating and were themselves Roman Catholics. In fact, in my childhood we always referred to the Roman Catholic church in Beckenham as the 'au pair' church. I remember one Guy Fawkes Night at Chelston my father building a huge bonfire using some of the old furniture from Chelston that we no longer needed. Diane and I felt very sad over this, wanting to save the old furniture, most of which in reality was worthless and broken having been damaged in the war. Big bonfires were also set for us at our schools, around which us boys were allowed to stay up an extra half-hour for the fireworks. Afterwards, we were fed mugs of cocoa that I hated. I never have liked chocolate products, except creamy milk chocolate, another factor that made Granny Mabs comment:

"Not like chocolate? You are a funny boy."

Grandpa Jack, however, knew that I did like 'Smarties', color sugar-coated chocolate beans that he kept in a large tube in the bookcase in the morning room at Redcroft, and that he secretly gave to my sisters and me when Granny was busy elsewhere in the house.

'Pea Soup' fogs were rare on the bracing Sussex coast with its 'Seaford' winds, but they often put a damper on November the fifth for the fireworks of London.

In his corner of the first-class compartment on the underground tube train *filled with City men, the smothered sobbing* of Irene *still haunted* Soames, *so he opened the* Times *with the rich crackle that drowns all lesser sounds, and, barricaded behind it.*

'Forsytes' tend not to speak to strangers. It is not in our nature. We were brought up that way. The open newspaper acts as a wall around us, keeping the mass of humanity at bay. We could hear the gossip of others, but as the three percent we were not engaged.

I remember sitting in the first-class lounge on a cross ferry steamer from Calais back to Dover after that holiday in Italy with my sister, Diane. There was an old 'Forsyte' couple sitting near us. He was surrounded by the *Times.* His wife kept asking him questions in a rather horsy upper crust accent, to which without a flicker of the paper he replied:

"Yes, Darling."

Finally, the barrage of conversational questions became too much. Without the slightest change in tone, the elderly gentleman answered with:

"Shut up, Darling."

And still, for Soames immersed in his paper, *inseparable from his reading, was the memory of Irene's tear-stained face, and the sounds from her broken heart.* He didn't want whomever he might have been sharing that first-class compartment with that day, to see his emotions stirred. A 'Forsyte' can not wear his emotions on his sleeve.

The case of Forsyte v. Bosinney was expected to be reached on the morrow, before Mr. Justice Bentham. Throughout the day, Soames reassured himself that he was surrounded by the best representatives of the legal profession.

Soames used the Underground again in going home.

The fog was worse than ever at Sloane Square Station.

The figure of a man, waited at the station door. Soames briefly observed him—a pathetic looking man of no consequence.

On night's like this, *shadowy figures, wrapped each in his own little shroud of fog, took no notice of each other. Their kind hearts beat a stroke faster for that poor, waiting, anxious lover in the fog; but they hurried by, well knowing that they had neither time nor money to spare for any suffering but their own.*

When Soames reached his home, *his wife was not in. She had gone out a quarter of an hour before. Out at such a time of night, into this terrible fog! What was the meaning of that?*

Irene knew, however, as she made her way to Sloane Square.

It was nearly seven when Soames *heard her come in.* She went straight up to her room, not heeding her husband's call.

Bilson came to lay dinner, and told him that Mrs. Forsyte was not coming down; she was having the soup in her room.

For once Soames did not 'change'; it was, perhaps, the first time in his life that he had sat down to dinner with soiled cuffs, and, not even noticing them, he brooded long over his wine

* * *

George Forsyte, the wittiest and most sportsmanlike of the Forsytes had passed the day reading a novel in the paternal mansion at Prince's Gardens. Since a recent crisis in his financial affairs he had been kept on parole by Roger, and compelled to reside 'at home'.

At five o'clock, he also *went out into the fog.* He took the underground from South Kensington Station and got out at Charing Cross, *choosing it in preference to his more usual St. James's Park, that he might reach Jermyn Street by better lighted ways.* There, he was to meet Montague Dartie for dinner and an *evening playing billiards at the Red Pottle.*

On the platform his eyes were attracted by a man who, leaping from a first-class compartment, staggered rather than walked towards the exit. George recognized the man; *"Why, it's 'The Buccaneer!'"*

Bosinney, obviously drunk, saw him and bolted back to the train. *He was too late. The train was already moving on.*

George's practised glance caught sight of the face of a lady clad in a grey fur coat at the carriage window. It was Mrs. Soames—and George felt that this was interesting.

George followed Bosinney out of the station and through the fog filled streets. He heard Bosinney muttering in his drunkenness. *George understood from those mutterings that Soames had exercised his rights over an estranged and unwilling wife in the greatest—the supreme act of property.*

And he thought: 'Yes, it's a bit thick! I don't wonder the poor fellow is half cracked!'

Bosinney's mutterings turned to anger. *And following a sudden impulse George touched him on the shoulder.*

Bosinney spun round.

"Who are you? What do you want?" Then, Bosinney ran from him. George followed. It seemed 'The Buccaneer' was heading for Soames'.

A cab rolled out of blackness, and into blackness disappeared. And suddenly George perceived that he had lost Bosinney.

At The Red Pottle George confided to Dartie. *"I lost him,"* he said.

"And who was she" Dartie asked as if he didn't know. *"A love lady?"*

"I made sure it was our friend Soa..."

"Did you?" and Dartie missed his shot

"I can't help thinking of that poor Buccaneer," George *said. "He may be wandering out there now in that fog. If he's not a corpse."*

"Corpse!" said Dartie, in whom the recollection of his defeat at Richmond flared up. "He's all right. Ten to one if he wasn't tight!"

George turned on him. "Dry up!" he said. "Don't I tell you he's 'taken the knock'!"

CHAPTER FIVE

THE TRIAL

S oames had to be in court the morning before his hearing on another case. *The court delivered judgement just before the luncheon interval. Soames went out to get something to eat. He met James standing at the little luncheon–bar, like a pelican in the wilderness of galleries, bent over a sandwich with a glass of sherry before him.*

Sherry was rapidly taking the place of Madeira as an aperitif before all events. It was the first real drink that we were allowed as young adults in that last decade of 'Forsythia'. It was used to fortify one for what was to come. When I went up to Cambridge University for interviews in 1962, the professors poured us a glass of sherry before we began. It was supposed to quiet our nerves and overcome our fears.

"When's your case coming on?" James asked. *"I shouldn't wonder if this Bosinney'd say anything; I should think he'd have to. He'll go bankrupt if it goes against him."* He took a large bite at his sandwich and a mouthful of sherry. *"Your mother,"* he said, *"wants you and Irene to come and dine to-night."*

The look that Soames gave his father said it all. James was still afraid to acknowledge any scandal, but his son's look... *James finished his sherry at a draught.*

Soames entered court to sit beside his solicitor on the front bench. James took his seat *on the end of the bench immediately behind counsel, his hands clasped over the handle of his umbrella.*

Mr. Justice Bentham, the judge, entered—*a thin, rather hen-like man, with a little stoop, clean-shaven under his snowy wig.* The court rose, but *James rose but slightly; he was already comfortable, and had no opinion of Bentham, having sat next but one to him at dinner twice at the Bumley Tomms'.* Forsytes knew their way around the law. The law upheld their class—the three percent. This was the law that had been exported to all corners of the Empire—British justice. It manifests itself in the pages of most of Dickens' novels. It was the glue that held the Empire together. It was administered for the three percent by the three percent. The great wig of the judge was almost symbolic of the system. We encountered the judge in his wig and tabs in early drama—we saw him peering through gold rimmed spectacles at puppet shows. He was a feature in our school plays, and a larger than life character in many Gilbert and Sullivan operettas—the most loved music of 'Forsythia' in as much as it was this great class ribbing itself.

To the underworld among Dickensian characters, however, the judge was an awesome administrator, "the beak," who held their lives in his hands, and what power these judges wielded beneath their wigs, tabs, and furrowed brows.

The case having been called on, Waterbuck, Q.C., pushing back his papers, hitched his gown on his shoulder, and, with a semi-circular look around him, like a man who is going to bat in a game of cricket, *arose and addressed the court.*

The facts, he said were not in dispute, and all that his lordship would be asked was to interpret the correspondence which had taken place between his client and the defendant, an architect, with reference to the decoration of the house. "My client, Mr. Soames Forsyte, is a gentleman, a man of property. It is as a matter of principle—and this I can not too strongly emphasize—as a matter of principle, and in the interests of others, he has felt himself compelled to bring this action."

He then read the correspondence.

Soames went into the box. His whole appearance was striking in its composure. He answered questions simply and to the point with the confidence of knowing that for sure the law was on his side.

James sat with his hand behind his ear, his eyes fixed upon his son. He was proud of him!

When it came to the turn of young Chankery, Bosinney's Counsel, to address the judge, James redoubled his attention. Bosinney was not in court.

Chankerry was placed by Bossiney's absence in an awkward position. He could not but fear—he said—that his client had met with an accident. He knew how anxious Mr. Bossiney had been to give his evidence.

His client not being a rich man, the matter was a serious one for him; he was a very talented architect, whose professional reputation was undoubtedly somewhat at stake. "What," he said, "will be the position of the artistic professions, if men of property like this Mr. Forsyte refuse, and are allowed to refuse, to carry out the obligations of the commissions which they have given."

One more time ushers of the court called for his client. There was no sign of Bosinney.

Mr. Justice Bentham gave his judgement.

Behind the wooden plateau by which he was fenced from more ordinary mortals, the learned judge leaned forward. The electric light, just turned on above his head, fell on his face, and mellowed it to an orange hue beneath the snowy crown of his wig; the amplitude of his robes grew before the eye; his whole figure, facing the comparative dusk of the court, radiated like some majestic and sacred body. He cleared his throat, took a sip of water, broke the nib of a quill against the desk, and folding his bony hands before him, began.

It was the majesty of the law; and a person endowed with a nature far less matter-of-fact than that of James might have been excused for failing to pierce this halo, and disinter therefrom the somewhat ordinary 'Forsyte' who walked and talked in everyday life under the name of Sir Walter Bentham. But this majesty was the Empire's glue. At times it became tangled, even challenged, as by E.M Forster in *A Passage to India*, but it was the body politick of 'Forsythia'.

"The question for me to decide," the judge said, "is whether or no the defendant is liable to refund to the plaintiff this sum. In my judgment he is so liable. He has accepted liability, and fallen back upon his rights against the defendant under the terms of the latter's engagement. It is manifest to me by his letter of May 20 he assented to a very clear proposition, by the terms of which he must be held to be bound. In my judgment the plaintiff is entitled to recover this sum from the defendant. For these reasons there will be judgment for the plaintiff for the amount claimed with costs.

James left and drove straight to Timothy's. At least, this scandal had been averted. *"Soames did very well,"* he announced. *"He's got his head screwed on the right way. This won't please Jolyon. It's a bad business for that young Bosinney; he'll go bankrupt, I shouldn't wonder."* Then, almost as an after-thought, he added, *"He wasn't there—now why?"*

CHAPTER SIX

SOAMES BREAKS THE NEWS

Soames, too, made his way to Timothy's after the verdict. He arrived just after his father left. The aunts already knew the verdict, but were more than anxious to fish for news on Irene. *They had never forgotten old Jolyon's visit, since when he had not once been to see them; they had never forgotten the feeling it gave all who were present, that the family was no longer what it had been—that the family was breaking up.* Soames, however, only spoke to them of his new interest in the Barbizon school of painters. *He had his eye on two pictures by a man called Corot, charming things; if he could get them at a reasonable price he was going to buy them—they would, he thought, fetch a big price some day.*

Soames' collection of paintings was first and foremost an investment, but it was also his escapism. This was why he spent his evenings up in that little room at the top of his house in Montpelier Square where he could lose himself in his treasures.

As we have seen, Great-grandfather Longley, was, like Soames, a connoisseur of paintings, although perhaps with a less fastidious eye for profit. My mother's cousin, John Hoby, son of my Great-aunt Babs, likewise was a fastidious collector of collectibles, including paintings that he also kept in a back room of his early Victorian terrace house in Chatham. We usually addressed him as "Uncle John", but amongst ourselves we always called him "Jong." Now, this was not an infantile mispronunciation of "John" carried on into life, but referred to several beautiful Mahjong sets that he had. Although a very unassuming man, who lived alone and never married, he had some great treasures that he loved to share with my sisters and me—his nieces and nephew. To us, among his greatest treasures were these Mahjong sets. Not only did we enjoy visiting him for this reason, but he also opened our eyes to the world of Dickens. Dickens set so much in his novels around the Chatham Naval Dockyards where his father had worked, and in Rochester, where still can be seen the inspiration for Miss Havisham's Satis House in *Great Expectations.*

Mahjong, however, was a game brought back to England from the great Chinese emporiums of Shanghai and Hong Kong. Hong Kong had fallen to the British Empire after the opium wars with imperial China in the 1840's. The harbor lay at the entrance of the Canton river that commanded the opium trade. By aiding the opium pirates, Great Britain was rewarded with the island of Hong Kong. Queen Victoria was "not amused," considering the island a useless barren rock. However, the island, along with other territories on the mainland leased from China in the late nineteenth century, became one of the British Empire's most successful commercial hubs.

Shanghai was carved up by Western powers in the last days of imperial China after the 'Boxer' rebellion, the British section of the city being the largest. It, too, grew to be in the 1920s and '30s a huge commercial hub for the export of Chinese goods into 'Forsythia's' world. Hong Kong and Shanghai were a direct reason for the enormous interest in Chinoiserie in the 1920s, and almost every respectable 'Forsyte' family came to possess a Mahjong set. Diane and I were fascinated by the wooden tiles with their birds of paradise, winds, dragons, pungs, and kongs. When we were young, we often took the box of tiles from its place in the dining room sideboard to play with them, building beautiful walls. My mother didn't like this, however, for fear of us losing a precious tile. They were so beautiful, and many of the sets, such as those of Granny Mabs and Uncle John, were made out of smooth shiny bamboo and ivory. In time, we learned to play the game as had so many 'Forsyte' families throughout the 1920s and '30s. In a pre-television world, and my father refused to bow to television until well into the 1960s, we played board and card games en famille when not listening to the wireless. From Snakes and Ladders, Snap and Pelminism, we graduated to Mahjong. It was a joy to handle these beautiful tiles even if my father somewhat cynically used to murder their names, calling the birds of paradise "Cockyollybirds" and the white dragons "Bars of soap."

I remember however that one of my father's better antique purchases was to buy a Mahjong set. The tiles were kept in drawers in a magnificently carved box mounted by Buddahs. You could only open the box in order to pull out the tile drawers by pressing a secret place that collapsed the front side revealing the drawers. My sister still has that beautiful set.

Soames' aunts, however, didn't want to know about his paintings or treasures, but wanted to know *what was his plan now that he had won his case; was he going to leave London at once and live in the country, or what was he going to do?*

Soames answered that he did not know, he thought they should be moving soon. He rose and kissed his aunts.

Aunt Juley rose to the full extent of her more than medium height and said: "I think you ought to know dear, that Mrs. MacAnder saw Irene walking in Richmond Park with Mr. Bossiney."

Lifting his hand, and as it were, selecting a finger, Soames bit a nail delicately; then drawing it out between set lips, he said: "Mrs. MacAnder is a cat!"

Without waiting for any reply, he left the room.

At first, he had hoped that now he had won his case on Forsyte principle, he could be reconciled to Irene, actually not pressing Bosinney and moving with her to Robin Hill right away, but now, *when he came out of Timothy's the smouldering jealousy and suspicion of months blazed up within him. He would put an end to that sort of thing once and for all; he would not have her drag his name in the dirt! If she could not or would not love him, as was her duty and his right—she should not play him tricks with anyone else! He would threaten to divorce her! That would make her behave; she would never face that. But—but—what if she did?*

A Divorce!

This jettisoning of his property with his own hand seemed uncanny to Soames. It would injure him in his profession. He would have to get rid of the house at Robin Hill, on which he had spent so much money. And she! She would no longer belong to him, not even in name! She would pass out of his life, and he—he should never see her again!

Soames was confused. *When his cab drew up at his door, he had decided nothing.*

"Where is your mistress?" Soames asked the maid Bilson as he went inside.

Bilson *told him that Mrs. Forsyte had left the house at noon, taking with her a trunk and a bag.*

Had Irene beaten him to it? He couldn't show emotion, however. *"What message did she leave?"* he asked.

A 'Forsyte', as we have observed, could not show emotion in front of a domestic. It was this stiff upper lip ability that kept them masters of the Empire.

"Mrs. Forsyte left no message, sir."

"No message; very well, thank you, that will do. I shall be dining out."

The words 'no message—a trunk, and a bag', played hide-and-seek in his brain.

Soames checked Irene's room, everything seemed in order. What had she taken? He then took a cab to Bosinney's. She was not there. And so, on to James' at Park Lane.

The butler asked whether Mrs. Soames was in the cab, the master had told him they were both expected for dinner.

Soames answered: "No, Mrs. Forsyte has a cold."

Upstairs, he joined his father and mother.

James, quick to take alarm, began: "You don't look well. I expect you've taken a chill—it's liver, I shouldn't wonder. Your mother'll give you..."

'Forsyte' mothers always up-held their position as matron in their families. My mother did. Long after our childhood, if my sisters or I so much as sneezed on a family visit, she would run straight to the medicine cabinet to procure a Beechams' powder. Beechams, incidentally, being one of the companies in which her mother, Granny Mabs, had shares that ultimately she inherited!

But Emily's response was different on this occasion. She *broke in quietly:*

"Have you brought Irene?"

Soames shook his head.

"No," he stammered, *"she—she's left me!*

Soames felt his mother pressing his hand. James, however, fought off emotion as a 'Forsyte'.

"There'll be a scandal; I always said so. And there you stand, you and your mother."

Emily spoke out courageously.

"Soames will do all he can to get her back. We won't talk of it. It'll all come right, I dare say."

And James: "Well, I can't see how it can come right. And if she hasn't gone off with that young Bosinney, my advice to you is not to listen to her, but to follow her and get her back."

At dinner with them were Winifred, her two daughters and Dartie; had Irene been present, the family circle would have been complete. James' advice: 'Don't you listen to her, follow her and get her back!' would, with here and there an exception, have been regarded as sound, not only in Park Lane, but amongst the Nicholases, the Rogers, and at Timothy's. Just as it would surely have been endorsed by that wider body of 'Forsytes' all over London, who were merely excluded from judgment by ignorance of the story.

James, Soames, and Dartie remained silent. Emily alone, a woman of cool courage, maintained a conversation with Winifred on trivial subjects, alleviating the suspicions of the servants. She was never more composed in her manner and conversation than that evening.

After dinner, Soames hastened home, his hands trembled as he took the late letters from the gilt wire cage into which they had been thrust through the slit in the door.

None from Irene.

He went up to her room. Everything still seemed in place. He checked her jewel-box. It was far from empty. Divided, in little green velvet compartments, were all the things he had given her, even her watch, and stuck into the recess that contained the watch was a three cornered note addressed 'Soames Forsyte' in Irene's handwriting. Soames read:

'I think I have taken nothing that you or your people have
given me.'

And that was all.

Nothing that she could have done, nothing that she had done, brought home to him like this the inner significance of her act. He understood that she loathed him, that she had loathed him for years, that for all intents and purposes they were like people living in different worlds, that there was no hope for him, never had been; even that she had suffered—that she was to be pitied.

In that moment of emotion he betrayed the Forsyte in him—forgot himself, his interests, his property—was capable of almost anything; was lifted in the pure ether of the selfless and unpractical.

Such moments pass quickly.

And as though with tears he had purged himself of weakness, he got up, locked the box, and slowly, almost trembling, carried it with him into his dressing room.

Chapter Seven

June's Victory

June had also attended the court hearing. She was not surprised that Phil Bosinney had not appeared or was surprised by the verdict; it was predictable in their world. Immediately, she made haste to Bosinney's architects' studio and apartment. She let herself in with the key under the mat.

It is an interesting reflection on 'Forsythia' that keys could be left in such obvious places. In our childhood, keys were left under front door mats as if there was no necessity to ever lock the house, at least by day. At night, doors were bolted, but by day in the leafy suburbs of 'Forsythia' and in those squares of the West End, numerous keys were left in obvious hiding places; perhaps because in a world where domestics were loyal to their masters, they became the police force of the neighborhood. Even in Dickens' *Great Expectations* Mr. Pip and Mr. Pocket keep the key to their rooms in a niche in the wall, although for melodramatic contrast it must be noted that the main gate to Miss Havisham's Satis House was kept locked, no doubt primarily to keep tradesmen out, something that somewhat irked the pompous Mr. Pumblechook!

June Forsyte *let herself in* to Bossiney's rooms *and left the door open that anyone who came might see she was there on business.*

She noticed the absence of all the little things he had set store by, not least the piece of Japanese pottery she herself had given him.

It was while looking at the spot where the piece of Japanese pottery had stood that she felt a strange certainty of being watched, and, turning, saw Irene in the open doorway.

Their exchange was far from harmonious—two one-time friends torn apart by this man in whose apartment they both now stood.

"You have no right here!" June cried defiantly.

Irene answered: "I have no right anywhere...'

"What do you mean?"

"I have left Soames. You always wanted me to!"

"Don't! I don't want to hear anything—I don't want to know anything. It's impossible to fight with you! What makes you stand like that, like stone? *Why don't you go?"*

Irene's lips moved: she seemed to be saying: "Where should I go?"

"How could you come? You have been a false friend to me! Why have you come? You've ruined my life and now you want to ruin his!"

Mournfully, Irene left.

June ran to the door. She called out: "Come back, Irene! Come back!"

Bewildered and torn, the girl stood at the top of the stairs. Why had Irene gone, leaving her mistress of the field? What did it mean? Had she really given him up to her? Or had she—? And she was the prey of a gnawing uncertainty... Bosinney did not come...

Shortly after June returned to Stanhope Gate, her grandfather came back from Wisteria Avenue, *where now almost every day he spent some hours.*

'Old Jolyon' *had made up his mind to tell June that he was reconciled with her father. He would no longer live alone, in this great house; he was going to give it up, and take one in the country for his son, where they could all go and live together. If June did not like this, she could have an allowance and live by herself.*

June listened as if the injured bird seeking comfort from her grandfather.

"You'll like your father," he said—"an amiable chap. Never was much push about him, but easy to get on with. You'll find him artistic and all that. As to your—your stepmother. I call her a refined woman— very fond of Jo. And the children," indeed, this sentence ran like music through all his solemn self-justification—"are sweet little things."

June made him nervous. She said nothing, *but presently he felt her warm cheek against his own, and knew that, at all events, there was nothing very alarming in her attitude towards his news.*

June was thinking on her own path, however. If *he was going to buy a house in the country, would he not—to please her—buy that splendid house of Soames's at Robin Hill? It was finished, it was perfectly beautiful, and no one would live in it now. They would be so happy there.*

Old Jolyon was on the alert at once. Wasn't the 'man of property' going to live in his new house, then?

"No"—June said—"he was not; she knew that he was not!" Irene's words still rang in her head: 'I have left Soames! Where should I go?'

If her grandfather would only buy it and settle that wretched claim that ought never to have been made on Phil! It would be the very best thing for everybody, and everything—everything might come straight!

June had planted a seed—an awkward one, but a seed. *Secretly the idea of wresting the house from James and his son had begun to take hold of him. To take from* Soames, *the 'man of property' that on which he had set his heart would be a crowning triumph over James, practical proof that he was going to make a man of property of Jo, to put him back in his proper position, and there to keep him secure. Justice once for all on those who had chosen to regard his son as a poor, penniless outcast.*

And still more secretly he knew that he could not refuse her.

But he did not commit himself. He would think it over—he said to June.

CHAPTER EIGHT

BOSINNEY'S DEPARTURE

June reminded her grandfather of her proposition at breakfast the next day. She was determined. *She asked him what time he should order the carriage.*

"Carriage!" 'Old Jolyon' *said, with some appearance of innocence;* *"What for? I'm not going out!"*

She answered: "If you don't go early, you won't catch Uncle James before he goes into the City."

"James! What about your Uncle James?"

"The house," she replied, in such a voice that he no longer pretended ignorance.

"I've not made up my mind," he said.

"You must! You must! Oh! Gran—think of me!"

Within the hour 'Old Jolyon' was at James' on Park Lane.

"How's Emily?" he asked; and waiting for no reply, went on: "I've come to see you about this affair of young Bosinney's. I'm told that new house of his is a white elephant."

"I don't know anything about a white elephant," said James, "I know he's lost his case, and I should say he'll go bankrupt."

'Old Jolyon' then pursued his intent. *"Now, what I was thinking was this: If* Soames *is not going to live there, I'm thinking of a house in the country myself, not too far from London, and if it suited me I don't say that I mightn't look at it, at a price."*

199

James peeked interest, although still suspicious of his brother. 'What had he heard? Did he know of possible divorce? How far had the scandal spread?'

Then, he turned 'Forsyte 'change' on his older brother. He divulged his suspicions. 'Old Jolyon' had removed his will from the family firm. He had been seen at the zoo with his son and grandchildren.

"They tell me you're altering your will in favour of your son."

"Who told you that?"

"I'm sure I don't know," said James; "I can't remember names... Soames spent a lot of money on this house; he's not likely to part with it except at a good price."

"It's not everyone's house, I hear!"

James, who was secretly of the same opinion, answered: "It's a gentleman's house. Soames is here now if you'd like to see him."

The door opened and Soames came in.

"There's a policeman out here," he said with his half smile, "for Uncle Jolyon."

Seeing the police as an extension of the Law, 'Forsytes' in 'Forsythia' saw them as defenders of the three percent. Police were always to be treated with courtesy. This was made plain to us in our earliest schooldays. The policeman was our friend, not someone to be feared.

My sister Diane's first success in the world of art was while a pupil at St. Christopher's, The Hall, in Beckenham. I was a very junior boy in the school at the time, but I remember the Beckenham Constabulary coming to the school to give us some road safety instruction. In the aftermath of this visit, a school art competition was held to show the friendly relationship that we should all have with the police. Diane won the competition with her representation of a Beckenham policeman, for which she was rewarded with a school prize and her first ever Premium Bond.

Police were still on the beat in the last decade of 'Forsythia'. They paraded the streets of Beckenham, or any town or borough, in pairs, immortalized in an early 1960s song, *Bobbies on bicycles two by two.* They were unarmed in those days, and paraded those leafy suburbs, not so much for crime prevention as to be available to lend a helping hand—helping the elderly to cross the street, controlling traffic at fetes, or to give directions to strangers.

When I was eleven years old I lost the upper dental plate with my braces on Wimbledon Common while visiting there with a school friend. My father immediately took me to Putney police station so we could report the loss so that should the friendly police find the plate it could be returned. That may have been, and was, wishful thinking, but compared with other nations, 'Forsytes' of Britain definitely saw the police as a helping hand rather than as the upholders of the law. Now, whether the working class saw the police in this same light, may be questionable, although it was the image still prevailing in the early post-'Forsythia' television series *Dixon of Dock Green*—but the first decades of television programming were also aimed at a 'Forsythia' audience—the three percent.

As 'Old Jolyon' Forsyte met with the policeman, Soames asked his father what Jolyon had come about.

"Your uncle's been here about the house!"

'Old Jolyon' returned. *He walked up to the table* where James and Soames sat. He *stood there perfectly silent pulling at his long white moustaches. James gazed up at him with opening mouth: he had never seen his brother look like this.*

Old Jolyon raised his hand and said slowly:

"Young Bosinney has been run over in the fog and killed."

Then standing above his brother and his nephew, and looking down at them with his deep eyes: "There's—some—talk—of—suicide," he said.

James's jaw dropped. "Suicide! What should he do that for?"

Old Jolyon answered sternly: "God knows, if you and your son don't!"

As James, paranoid, considered the scandal for he and his son, 'Old Jolyon' continued, *"Death was instantaneous. He lay all yesterday at the hospital. There was nothing to tell them who he was. I am going there now; you and your son had better come too."*

They rode with the police officer in 'Old Jolyon's' carriage, closed despite the pleasant day, because *it was not right that Forsytes should be seen driving with an inspector of police.* No wonder Bosinney had not appeared in court.

The inspector informed them, *"It appears that he was very hard up, we found several pawn tickets at his rooms, his account at the bank is overdrawn, and there's this case in today's papers."*

At the inspector's words, indeed, all James's doubts and fears revived. Hard—up—pawn—tickets—an overdrawn account! These words that had all his life been a far off nightmare to him, seemed to make uncannily real that suspicion of suicide which must on no account be entertained.

Accumulation of any debt was anathema to most members of 'Forsythia' and was a major contribution to James' mistrust and loathing of his son-in-law Montague Dartie. If a family member accumulated debts, other family members were expected to bail them out to protect the good name of the family. Indeed, throughout the first decades of 'Forsythia' the thought of the debtors' prison was very real, an experience to which its mouthpiece, Charles Dickens, was well aware through his own father's impecunity. There was in my family a mistrust of those family members who accumulated debt. Something was never quite right between my great-uncle, Arthur Douglas, and other members of my family. It was not a subject ever discussed even as late as my childhood, but there was an undercurrent that lasted through two generations. In reality, Douglas was not very successful in life. My great-grandfather bailed him out a few times rather like James Forsyte with Montague Dartie. After Douglas had failed in independent business, including a real estate firm in Lyminge, Kent, Great-grandfather set him up as a salesman in the family business, but that, too, was not a success. Ultimately, he ended up at his sister's house, my Great-aunt Bernice's, as a lodger. There was also a slight cloud over Bernice's family. Bernice had married Cecil Haynes, a 'man about town' somewhat like Dartie. He was secretary of the Frinton Golf Club at which fashionable Essex seaside town Great-grandfather had bought them a home. Sadly, Cecil Haynes was caught embezzling Golf Club funds and served a jail sentence. The house in Frinton was sold and the Haynes family went like Douglas into somewhat sinister isolation. Their, son, Bill Haynes, however, was rescued, and given a clerk's position in the family business at Smithfield where I remember him in my childhood. And he has remained a very loyal member of the family.

'Old Jolyon' Forsyte was also a little nervous. He did not want his granddaughter June's name to be brought into the looming awkwardness of a suicide scandal. On arrival at the mortuary, he dispatched his carriage to the Hotch Potch Club with instructions that *if Mr. Jolyon Forsyte were there to give him a card and bring him at once* to the morgue.

In the bare, white-walled room, empty of all but a streak of sunshine smeared along the dustless floor, lay a form covered by a sheet. With a huge steady hand the inspector took the hem and turned it back. A sightless face gazed up at them, and on either side of that sightless defiant face the three Forsytes gazed down.

Jo arrived. Soames and his father sheepishly left. 'Old Jolyon' lingered a little longer, *his eyes fixed on the body. Who shall tell of what he was thinking? Of himself, with his battle just beginning, the long, long battle he had loved; the battle that was over for this young man almost before it had begun? Of his grand-daughter, with her broken hopes? Of that other woman? Of the strangeness and the pity of it? And the irony, inscrutable and bitter, of that end? Justice! There was no justice for men, for they were ever in the dark!*

Or perhaps in his philosophy he thought: 'Better to be out of it all! Better to have done with it as this poor youth...'

A tear started up and wetted his eyelash. "Well," he said, "I'm no good here. I'd better be going." He looked at his son, "You'll come to me as soon as you can, Jo," and with his head bowed he went away.

The inspector then filled Jo in as to the details and added: *"There's more here, sir, however, than meets the eye. I don't believe in suicide, nor in pure accident, myself. It's more likely I think that he was suffering under great stress of mind, and took no notice of things about him. Perhaps you can throw some light on these."*

He took from his pocket a little packet. Carefully undoing it, he revealed a lady's handkerchief, pinned through the folds with a pin of discoloured Venetian gold, the stone of which had fallen from the socket. A scent of dried violets rose to young Jolyon's nostrils.

"Found in his pocket," said the inspector; *"the name has been cut away!"*

Young Jolyon with difficulty answered: "I'm afraid I can not help you." But vividly there rose before him the face he had seen light up, so tremulous and glad, at Bosinney's coming! *Of her he thought more than of his own daughter, more than of them all—of her with the dark, soft glance, the delicate passive face, waiting for the dead man, waiting even at that moment, perhaps, still and patient in the sunlight.*

Concerning the cause of this death—his family would doubtless reject with vigour the suspicion of suicide, which was so compromising! They would take it as an accident, a stroke of fate, and the law would support them. *In their hearts they would even feel it an intervention of Providence, a retribution—had not Bosinney endangered their two most priceless possessions, the pocket and the hearth? And they would talk of 'that unfortunate accident of young Bosinney's', but perhaps they would not talk—silence would be better.*

CHAPTER NINE

IRENE'S RETURN

For Soames Forsyte *the tragic event of Bosinney's death altered the complexion of everything. There was no longer the feeling that to lose a minute would be fatal, nor would he now risk communicating the fact of his wife's flight to anyone till the inquest was over.*

He informed the maid, Bilson, *that her mistress was at the sea; he would probably, he said, be going down himself from Saturday to Monday. This had given him time to breathe, time to leave no stone unturned to find her.*

He wandered aimlessly in the streets, looking.

On the way home, passing the steps of Jobson's about half-past four, he met George Forsyte, who held out an evening paper to Soames, saying:

"Here! Have you seen this about the poor Buccaneer?"

Soames answered stonily: "Yes."

"They talk of suicide here," George said.

Soames shook his head. "An accident," he muttered.

"H'mm! All flourishing at home? Any little Soameses yet?" George needled.

Soames brushed past him and was gone.

On reaching home, Soames was surprised to find Irene's *gold mounted umbrella lying on the rug chest* in his hall. *Flinging off his fur coat, he hurried to the drawing-room.*

"So you've come back?" he said. "Why are you sitting here in the dark?"

The supple erectness of her figure was gone, as though she had been broken by cruel exercise; as though there were no longer any reason for being beautiful, and supple, and erect.

"So you've come back," he repeated.

She had come back like an animal wounded to death, not knowing where to turn, not knowing what she was doing. The sight of her figure, huddled in fur, was enough.

Soames knew now *for certain that Bosinney had been her lover; knew that she had seen the report of his death—perhaps, like himself, had bought a paper at the draughty corner of a street and read it.*

They sat in silence either side of the cedar-burning fireplace. Not a word was spoken. When he could stand it no more, Soames got up and went outside for a breath of fresh air. *If only he could burst out of himself, out of this web that for the first time in his life he felt around him. If only he could surrender to the thought: 'Divorce her—turn her out! She has forgotten you. Forget her!'*

If only he could surrender to the thought: 'Let her go—she has suffered enough!'

If only he could surrender to the desire: 'Make a slave of her—she is in your power!'

If only even he could surrender to the sudden vision: 'What does it all matter?' Forget himself for a minute, forget that it mattered what he did, forget that whatever he did he must sacrifice something.

As we sat having high-tea, listening to the *Forsyte Saga* over the wireless in the 1950s, I remember how often my father shook his head and said sadly, "Poor Soames." My father was a man, too, who made many sacrifices in his life as 'Forsythia' collapsed around him—sacrifices of ideas in business, for family in life, and in the depths of marriage, but like Soames, he carried on. Soames is the epitome of 'Forsyte' success, he is the hero and most stable influence of this saga, but he is also the tragic hero, who suffered much, often through the circumstances of his times rather than his own excesses or weakness.

Soames saw he had left his front door open on his return, and black against the light from the hall a man standing with his back turned.

And sharply Soames *asked: "What is it you want, sir?"*

The visitor turned. It was young Jolyon.

"The door was open," he said. "Might I see your wife for a minute, I have a message for her?"

"My wife can see no one," he muttered doggedly.

Young Jolyon's glance shot past him into the hall, and Soames turned. There in the drawing-room doorway stood Irene, her eyes were wild and eager, her lips were parted, her hands outstretched. In the sight of both men that light vanished from her face; her hands dropped to her side; she stood like stone.

Soames spun round and met his visitor's eyes.

"This is my house," he said: "I manage my own affairs. I've told you once—I tell you again; we are not at home."

And in young Jolyon's face he slammed the door.

INTERLUDE

INDIAN SUMMER OF A FORSYTE

'**O**ld Jolyon' *bought his nephew Soames' ill-starred house and settled into it at Robin Hill*—he and his children and grandchildren.

It was as if he had been getting younger every spring, living in the country out of the racket of London and the cackle of Forsyte 'Change, free from his Boards, in a delicious atmosphere of no work and all play, with plenty of occupation in the perfecting and mellowing of the house and its twenty acres, and in ministering to the whims of Holly and Jolly.

Jo and Helene had taken June with them to Spain and left Holly in his care along with her French governess, Mam'zelle Beauce. Jolly had started his first term at boarding school.

Every one of these calm, bright, lengthening days, with Holly's hand in his, and the dog Balthasar in front looking studiously for what he never found, he would stroll, watching the roses open, fruit budding on the walls, sunlight brightening the oak leaves and saplings in the coppice, watching the water-lily leaves unfold and glisten and the silvery young corn of the one wheat-field; listening to the starlings and skylarks, and the Alderney cows chewing the cud, flicking slow their tufted tails; and every one of these fine days he ached a little from shear love of it all, feeling perhaps, deep down, that he had not much longer to enjoy it.

*The blackbirds and the sunsets never tired him, only gave him an
uneasy feeling that he could not get enough of them.*

Great-grandfather Oliver Longley spent his twilight years at The
Breach, and as my mother had written, loved 'his beloved acres.' He
would walk his guests and family members through the gardens that in
those days extended beyond the great lawn, with its herbaceous border,
to an azalea walk, before a country path took them further, over little
streams traversed by planking and on into the orchards, fields and woods
of his estate. In my childhood, Grandpop would take us on similar
perambles, although the azalea walk had fallen somewhat into decline.
In the spring, bluebells abounded and primroses raised their yellow
faces from clusters of leaves in the banks. Apple blossom broke from
all the original old trees, mostly Bramleys, that Great-grandfather had
planted. And, always, there was the sound of the rooks. We associated
these birds with The Breach—even called them "Brookian birds," which
was our childlike way of saying 'Cranbrook birds.' We were about
Holly's age at that time.

As 'Old Jolyon' Forsyte reflected on this peaceful pastoral scene,
a sudden recollection came into his mind—a face he had seen at the
*opera three weeks ago—Irene, the wife of his nephew Soames, that man
of property!*

He had not personally seen her since that 'at home' to celebrate
his grand-daughter, June's engagement. He had just missed seeing her
at that dance at Nicholas' that had so upset June, but *he had always
admired her—a very pretty creature.* He had heard that she had left
Soames at once, but he had no idea where she might be living now. In
some ways, it had relieved him. *It had been shocking to think of her a
prisoner in that house to which she must have wandered back, when
Jo saw her, wandered back for a moment—like a wounded animal to
its hole after seeing that news, 'Tragic Death of an Architect', in the
street.*

'Old Jolyon' had crossed the lawn with its daisies waiting to be
mowed, and made his way through the farm building and passed the
pond where he observed the water lilies. Holly was not with him. She
had a slight stomach upset from something she had eaten. He walked
on down the hill to the copse. *Balthasar, preceding him, uttered a
low growl. Old Jolyon stirred him with his foot, but the dog remained
motionless just where there was no room to pass, and the hair rose
slowly on his wooly back. Whether from the growl and the look of the*

dog's stivered hair, or from the sensation which a man feels in a wood, old Jolyon also felt something move along his spine. And then, the path turned, and there was an old mossy log, and on it a woman sitting.

'Forsytes' don't like trespassers, and 'Old Jolyon' as a Forsyte was no exception.

'She's trespassing—I must have a board put up!' he thought. And besides, she had upset his dog.

'Forsytes' were almost more concerned if their animals, particularly their horses, dogs, or cats were upset than over their own inner torments.

The woman turned, and 'Old Jolyon' recognized her face. *The face he had seen at the opera—the very woman he had just been thinking of! How pretty she is!*

"Don't let that dog touch your frock," he said: *"he's got wet feet."* He called the dog to him, but *Balthasar went on towards the visitor, who put her hand down and stroked his head.*

'Forsytes' hearts could be won by such kindness to their pets. It was in part, my mother's downfall in her relationship with her brother-in-law, Jim Sullings, when she failed to show unnecessary kindness to his dog, Billy. The dog was certainly spoiled—a fact that my mother pointed out on more than one occasion, but a simple act of kindness extended to this dog might have done much to improve her relationship with Jim and her sister Eileen.

"I saw you at the opera the other night, you didn't notice me," Old Jolyon said.

"Oh yes! I did."

She was here no doubt because of some past memory, he thought. "They're all in Spain. I'm alone: I drove up for the opera." Then, he beckoned to her and like my great-grandfather at The Breach played mine host. *"Have you seen the cow houses?"*

He found out she was living in a little flat in Chelsea—alone.

"All Alderneys," 'Old Jolyon' said pointing at the cows proudly—the chairman of city boards turned farmer. *"They give the best milk. This one's a pretty creature. Woa, Myrtle!"*

Alderneys are Channel Islands dairy cows along with Jerseys and Guernseys. Great-grandfather kept a Jersey cow for its rich table milk. Her name was Betty, and no tour of *his beloved acres* was complete without showing off Betty. Betty was still around in my childhood but the Jersey herd at The Breach had increased, producing commercial cream and milk under the 'Travelers' brand. Later, Uncle Dennis went into partnership with other Jersey, Guernsey, and Alderney cream producers of the Kentish Weald forming a company centered at Pluckley called Quality Dairy Products.

The pride and joy in Great-grandfather's time, when it came to the farmyard, were the wooden pigsties. A strong childhood memory for me at The Breach is that sickly-sweet smell of the pigswill. Grandpop would stand pointing out the great pink sows with his walking stick, before we would all return to the house after our constitutional walk around the estate.

"You must come up to the house *and have some dinner with me,"* 'Old Jolyon' Forsyte continued. "I'll send you home in the carriage."

"Thank you, Uncle Jolyon," Irene answered. *"I should like to."*

'Old Jolyon', as smitten in her presence as his brother Swithin had been, found out that she now taught music, and also *tried to help women who've come to grief.* She worked *assisting the Magdalenes of London.*

'Forsytes' embraced the church tradition that Mary Magdalene was a prostitute, despite the fact that there is very little scriptural evidence to support the claim. The tradition arises over the confusion of the name Mary, associated with the woman who anointed Jesus with the contents of an alabaster jar, and Mary, a sinner, translated from the Greek in the sixteenth century as a prostitute from whom Jesus cast out devils. Mary, or Miriam in Aramaic, was a very common name in the first-century Jewish world, including being the name of the Blessed Virgin, the mother of Jesus. Women in the first century, just as in 'Forsythia', did not in public have a place, however much they might have been the power wagging the tail behind closed doors. From its earliest days, the Christian Church tried to denigrate the role of Mary Magdalene, not wanting her to have been too close to Jesus. This was in order to reduce the problem that arises when she is found at the foot of the cross in all the gospel accounts and quoted to be the first at the empty tomb. Very soon, she became the outcast, the fallen woman, the prostitute, and the sinner. For the most part, she is still cast this way in the minds of most Christians, and certainly was seen so by traditional 'Forsytes'. Modern scholars in a post-'Forsyte' world have done much to try to show the virtues of this enigmatic Biblical figure. I myself wrote an entire trilogy on a plausible life and times of Mary Magdalene in which I tread a path of compromise, still acknowledging the prostitute role, but allowing for her spiritual renewal found in a close relationship with Jesus. It is interesting that the sexual revolution of the 1960s followed on the fall of 'Forsythia', and paved the way for a more acceptable role in the formation of the early Christian Church for Mary Magdalene— the centuries' old outcast—even allowing some to believe that Mary Magdalene and Jesus were lovers!

'Old Jolyon' Forsyte showed Irene around the house, but then remembered that she had been here before. *She nodded.* They looked in on Holly who was sleeping.

In the corridor an eccentric notion attacked him. To think that children should come to that which Irene had told him she was helping— The Magdalenes! *Women who were all, once, little things like this one sleeping there! 'I must give her a cheque!' he mused; 'can't bear to think of them!'*

After dinner, Irene played the piano—mostly Chopin. Then, 'Old Jolyon' requested music from the opera they had seen—'Orfeo.'

All of a sudden, he was conscious of something. *Like Orpheus, she of course—she, too, was looking for her lost one in the hall of memory!* He placed his hand on her shoulder and as he would to Holly, he said, "There, there—there, there. He let her cry. *It would do her good.* He gave her an affectionate kiss.

When the crunch of the carriage wheels was heard at last, he said: "You must come again: you must come to lunch, then I can show you things *by daylight.* And like so many 'Forsytes' he made his dog a spokesman for himself. *"This dog seems to have taken a fancy to you."*

As she got in the carriage, he slipped her a check for fifty pounds. *That meant one or two poor* Magdalene *creatures helped a little, and it meant that she would come again.*

'Old Jolyon' was fascinated by Irene, however, and made an excuse of buying boots to go to town and visit her. *"Just drive me to where you took that lady the other night,"* he instructed his coachman on reaching town.

"The lady in grey, sir?'

"Yes, the lady in grey."

On arrival, he noted her doorplate read *'Mrs. Irene Heron'. Ah! She had taken her maiden name again.*

He was led into a very small drawing-room. There was a mirror above the fireplace, and he saw himself reflected. An odd-looking chap!

He heard a rustle, and turned round. She was so close; his moustache almost brushed her forehead.

"I was driving up," he said. *"Thought I'd look in on you and ask how you got up the other night."*

And, seeing her smile, he felt suddenly relieved.

After a day together in Kensington Gardens, the scene was set for further visits to Robin Hill.

On the next Sunday, she came by train, and in anticipation set down the path to the copse to meet her half way up from the station. She had taken an earlier train and was already seated on the log. *Two hours of her society—missed!* he mused. *What memory could make that log so dear to her? His face showed what he was thinking, for she said at once:*

"Forgive me, Uncle Jolyon; it was here that I first knew."

'Phil Bosinney', he acknowledged to himself.

"Yes yes; there it is for you whenever you like. You're looking a little Londony; you're giving too many lessons. Where do you go to give them?" he asked

During 'Forsythia' almost all young girls were taught to play the piano. It was part of the expected education of a young lady. It was not so essential for boys. In fact, in my own case, my parents almost took the argument of many in 'Forsythia' that it would send the wrong signal for sons to learn to play the piano—effeminate. My sisters, however, were both given piano lessons at home and later at their boarding schools. A very prim lady with an exceptionally round face and no great sense of humor came to the house. She was quite a disciplinarian. Her name was Miss Cain.

As a result, we always called the Steinway Grand in our lounge "the cain," the one my father inherited from Hillside. The piano lessons were "cain lessons" and later, we referred to concert halls as "cain halls," and still do to this day.

"They're mostly Jewish families, luckily," Irene explained.

Old Jolyon stared; to all Forsytes Jews seem strange and doubtful— that undercurrent of anti-semitism that ran throughout the life of 'Forsythia'. As I have suggested, no 'Forsyte' would intentionally harm a Jew, but they separated themselves from Jews, at clubs, in their schools, and even in sports.

"They love music," she pleaded, *"and they're very kind."*

"They had better be, by George!" He took her arm—*his side always hurt him a little going uphill*—and said, changing the subject from the merits of Jews:

"Did you ever see anything like those buttercups? They came like that by night."

When Holly came back from church, 'Old Jolyon' introduced Irene as *'the lady in grey.'* The introduction went well, although Mam'zelle Beauce seemed a little put out.

Lunch and a lazy afternoon passed. At length, and at an appropriate moment when a special little friend of Holly's came by to play, 'Old Jolyon' plucked up courage to ask Irene:

"Does Soames never trouble you?" She shook her head. Her face had closed up suddenly. 'Were they divorced?' He asked himself. 'She likes to be addressed as Mrs. Irene Heron.'

Irene played piano for them—a waltz. The two little girls danced much to the chagrin of Mam'zelle Beauce, who did not believe they should be dancing on a Sunday. *But the children came close to old Jolyon, knowing that he would save them* from the wrath of Holly's governess.

"Better the day, better the deed, Mam'zelle. It's all my doing," he said before dispatching them off for their tea.

Now, having Irene alone again, he said:

"Well, there we are! Aren't they sweet? Have you any little ones among your pupils?"

"Yes, three—two of them darlings."

"Pretty?"

"Lovely!"

The moment he had been waiting for had come.

"My little sweet is devoted to music; she'll be a musician some day. You wouldn't give me your opinion of her playing, I suppose?"

"Of course I will."

"You wouldn't like..." but he stifled the words *'to give her lessons.'* That way he would see her regularly.

"I would like, very much; but there is—June. When are they coming back?"

Old Jolyon frowned. *"Not till the middle of next month. What does that matter?"*

"You said June had forgiven me; but she could never forget, Uncle Jolyon."

"Well, we shall see."

Weekly music lessons started with 'the lady in grey.' Everyone was happy except Mam'zelle.

Then, 'Old Jolyon' took his plans further. He instructed his new solicitor, Herring, to draw a codicil to his will leaving Irene Forsyte, born Irene Heron, *fifteen thousand pounds free of legacy duty.*

He took the train into town, so he could sign the codicil. He wanted to visit Irene in Chelsea, and take her to the opera. Either way he did not feel it any business of the servants—hence the train. *He would not have that fat chap Beacon,* the coachman, *grinning behind his back. He would see her as often as he wished.*

Servants were such fools; and, as likely as not, they had known all the past history of Irene and young Bosinney—servants knew everything, and suspected the rest.

The journey and the visit to his lawyer's, tired him. It was hot, too, and after dressing for dinner, for he had invited Irene to join him for dinner before the opera, *he lay down on the sofa in his bedroom to rest. He must have had a sort of fainting fit.*

He *was not conscious of how Irene came to be standing beside him, holding smelling salts to his nose, and pushing a pillow up behind his head.*

"Dear Uncle Jolyon, what is it? You mustn't come down, Uncle; you must rest."

"Fiddlesticks! A glass of champagne'll soon get me to rights. I can't have you missing the opera."

After dinner they did not make it to the opera, however. The dizziness returned. *When he parted from her, having paid the cabman to drive her to Chelsea, he sat down again for a moment to enjoy the memory of her words: 'You are such a darling to me, Uncle Jolyon.'*

Back at Robin Hill, 'Old Jolyon' thought he saw her in his study— was it hallucination or was it real? He smelled violets. *Opening his eyes he saw her, dressed in grey, standing by the fireplace, holding out her arms. The odd thing was that, though those arms seemed to hold nothing, they were curved as if round someone's neck, and her own neck was bent back, her lips open, her eyes closed. She vanished at once, and there were the mantelpiece and his bronzes. But those bronzes and the mantelpiece had not been there when she was, only the fireplace and the wall.* He knew she was in young Bosinney's arms, sometime, in this very room.

'I must take medicine', he thought. 'I can't be well.'

Music lessons continued on Wednesdays and Saturdays. *The servants perhaps wondered, but they were, naturally, dumb. Mam'zelle Beauce was too concerned with her own digestion, and too 'well-brrred' to make personal allusions.* As the date for June's return drew near, Irene began to back away. On the last Sunday, she did not come. A letter followed...

> *'I feel I can't come down and give Holly any more lessons,*
> *now that June is coming back. Thank you a million times for*
> *all your sweetness to me.'*

So there it was! Still, 'Old Jolyon' pleaded with a letter one more time.

To his surprise, the return post brought this message:

> *'Your letter received coming down this afternoon will be with*
> *you at four-thirty. Irene.'*

A little formal, but coming down! After all!

He meant to go down and meet her in the coppice, but felt at once he could not manage that in this heat. He sat down instead under the oak tree by the swing, and the dog Balthasar, who also felt the heat, lay down beside him. He sat there smiling. What a reverie of bright minutes. What a hum of insects, and cooing of pigeons! It was the quintessense of a summer day. She was coming; she had not given him up.

He smelled the scent of limes, and lavender. Ah! that was why there was such a racket of bees. They were excited and busy—as his heart was busy and excited.

The stable clock struck four; in half an hour she would be here. He would just have one tiny nap. A humble-bee alighted and strolled on the crown of his Panama hat. And the delicious surge of slumber reached the brain beneath that hat, and the head swayed forward and rested on his breast. Summer—summer! So went the hum.

The stable clock struck the quarter past. The dog Balthasar stretched and looked up at his master. The dog placed its chin over his master's *foot. It did not stir. The dog withdrew his chin quickly, rose, and leaped on old Jolyon's lap, looked in his face, whined: then, leaping down, sat on his haunches, gazing up. And suddenly he uttered a long, long howl.*

I do not know the circumstances around my great-grandfather's death at The Breach, but he did live out his twilight years on his beloved acres. Like 'Old Jolyon', in the country he wore a floppy Panama hat, always carried a walking cane and tended to wear one of those easily crumpled, light-weight linen summer coats that seemed to be a hallmark of the older generation in 'Forsyte' twilight years. A photograph that my father carried with him in his wallet from 1942 until his death in 2008, features four generations of Longleys sitting in garden chairs on the lawn at The Breach. It shows Great-grandfather Oliver in his Panama hat, but still wearing a stiff Edwardian collar and a tweed suit. He is smoking his pipe seated beside his eldest son, my beloved Grandpop. Grandpop is holding his first granddaughter, my sister Diane, and in the next lawn chair sits his eldest son, our proud father. These twilight years were a comfort for my great-grandfather just as for 'Old Jolyon'. His first great-grandchild, Diane, was born in Hawkhurst. My mother and father were staying in the old oast house that was part of the small village of Wilsley Pound, almost literally at the bottom of The Breach gardens. Most the village of Wilsley Pound was still owned by my great-grandfather—all except the pub that was owned by the brewery. Some of the cottages Great-grandfather had built for his own laborers earlier in the century. My grandparents were staying with him up in the old house that most of his time had been lit by oil lamps. All his immediate family felt safe here from the bombs that were falling on London and had damaged their suburban Beckenham homes; and throughout those war years, English summers seemed especially golden. They lingered on through September and into October. During Oliver Longley's last summer at The Breach—the very summer that I was myself born into this old 'Forsyte' family—1944—I have no doubt that like 'Old Jolyon', Great-grandfather spent many hours sitting on his lawn, smelling the lavender, listening to the buzzing of the bees, the cooing of doves, and the caw of the rooks. Eventually, he, too, fell asleep for the last time, and with him an era closed.

Book Two
In Chancery

Part One

CHAPTER ONE

AT TIMOTHY'S

The historian of the English 'eighties and 'nineties will, in his good time, depict the somewhat rapid progression from self-contented and contained provincialism to still more self-contented and contained imperialism—in other words, the 'possessive' instinct of the nation was on the move. And so, as if in conformity, was it with the Forsyte family.

In 1895, Susan Hayman, the married Forsyte sister and mother of 'the Dromios'—her sons Giles and Jesse—passed away in Campden. She was cremated, no doubt her wish, but not the convention in 'Forsythia'. However, *it made strangely little stir among the six old Forsytes left.*

Cremation was well known in 'Forsythia' as an Oriental funeral rite. Most 'Forsytes' were aware of the Hindu and Buddhist practice of cremation in India and the outposts of Empire beyond. They also associated with this, the barbaric practice of widows being burned with their husbands on the cremation pyre—the practice of suttee, something Jules Verne brought to our attention in *Around the World in Eighty Days,* where Phileas Fogg allows his manservant to rescue a doomed Indian princess from her husband's funeral pyre. Fogg, the eccentric Englishman, after educating the princess to play whist, brings her home to be his future bride! However, on the home front, among good Christian English people, the practice of cremation was shunned, at least by the three percent. Maybe the practice could be seen as a novel way of hygienically dispensing the dead bodies of the masses, but for 'Forsytes' funeral practices had status that went hand in hand with dignity.

Ann Forsyte had been buried in Highgate cemetery in the family vault. In 1891, Swithin Forsyte had joined her with an *entirely proper funeral.* One year later, with the passing of 'Old Jolyon' the pattern changed. He had defied them all by wishing to be buried at Robin Hill. *That burial had occasioned a great deal of talk on Forsyte 'Change.* Not only had the burial broken with sacred tradition, but also the subsequent reading of the will had named Irene the benefactor of fifteen thousand pounds! *Irene! That runaway wife of Soames; Irene, a woman who had almost disgraced the family, and—still more amazing—was to him no blood relation.* Forsytes did not like to see money, the ultimate property, passing out of the family. *Old Jolyon's claim to be the perfect Forsyte was ended once for all.*

When Aunt Juley had expressed her opinion on this burial of 'Old Jolyon' outside Highgate, Francie, Roger's poetess daughter of a somewhat Bohemian disposition, spoke up for the growing generation of younger Forsytes:

'It's a jolly good thing to stop all that stuffy Highgate business.'

All of this made it less stressful when Susan Hayman dropped the bombshell of her cremation.

However, sixty years on, those of us who lived in the last decade of 'Forsythia' were still skeptical about cremation. It was not quite the Church of England thing to do. There were even outmoded theological connotations that within the Christian belief system, bodies were still expected to be buried, not burned. They would only burn if they were condemned to Hell. Maybe by the 1950s it had become a fairly acceptable alternative means of disposal for the lower-middle class, many of who belonged to other denominations than the established church, but among the three percent it was still a rarity. We were also, still reeling from the revelation of Nazi death camps and their crematoria with tall chimneys belching forth the last gaseous remains of six million Jews.

Burial land was, however, becoming a premium, and little by little the more sanitary and practical solution of cremation spread even into our ranks.

The second reason for a surprising acceptance of this wish of Susan Hayman was *more expansive and Imperial.*

Besides the house on Campden Hill, Susan had a place left her by Hayman when he died just over the border in Hants, where the Dromios *had learned to be such good shots and riders, as it was believed. The fact of owning something countrified seemed somehow to excuse the dispersion of her remains—though what could have put cremation into her head they could not think! The usual invitations, however, had been issued, and Soames had gone down with young Nicholas, and the will had been quite satisfactory so far as it went.*

'Young Nicholas's' sister, Euphemia, daringly supported her aunt's cremation instructions.

"Well, I think people have a right to their own bodies, even when they're dead."

This remark, *making all allowances, did undoubtedly show expansion of the principle of liberty, decentralisation and shift in the central point of possession from others to oneself.*

When Nicholas heard his daughter's remark from Aunt Hester he had rapped out: "Wives and daughters! There's no end to their liberty in these days."

There was no denying the revolt among the younger Forsytes against being owned by others: that, as it were, Colonial disposition to own oneself, which is the paradoxical forerunner of Imperialism, was making progress all the time.

Still very much influenced by king, empire, and duty, in that last decade of 'Forsythia' we were part of a society almost in disbelief that after all we had gone through our world was about to collapse. Duty was the watchword of the royal family, had been the watchword of our armed forces through World War II, and was our expectation as we were educated to run our benign British Empire upon which the sun never set.

That link between, sovereign, empire, and duty permeated us in 'Forsythia'. 'Forsytes' were not much into the aristocratic social link with monarchy—court presentations and the like—but they were very much into royal duty. I remember the great pride that my family had when my Aunt Eileen, as a Squadron Officer in the WRAF, was chosen to be on duty at Buckingham Palace for a royal garden party. I remember taking photographs of her in her uniform in Granny Mabs' garden before she went to the palace. In the same way, I am reminded of my own emotions and feelings in 1990 when I was cruise director of *Queen Elizabeth 2* during the visit of Her Majesty the Queen for the 150th anniversary celebrations of the Cunard Line. Among my duties, I was to lead the cheer for Her Majesty during the Spithead review and to be toastmaster to the queen at the official luncheon on board. I was to spend much of the day in close proximity to Her Majesty and Prince Philip. On this very special voyage, my mother and father along with Uncle Gyles and Aunt Ginette were passengers. After our final officers' briefing for the royal visit the night before the great day, I remember inviting my family to the cruise director's suite. I poured them sherry and then almost broke down with emotion as I explained my duties. "This is a great honor for me," I croaked. "I will spend almost the whole day just a few paces from my sovereign. I will do my duty." I shed emotional tears as I hugged my family. However, those born just a few years after us saw a new world opening up in their childhood, where stuffy 'duty' was not the watchword, but where individual freedoms would blossom again, more assertively than they ever did in the 1890s and 1920s. We listened to Prime Minister Harold MacMillan speak of those "Winds of Change."

Thus, of the ten old Forsytes twenty-one young Forsytes had been born. This younger generation, *sooner than own children, preferred to concentrate on the ownership of themselves, conforming to the growing tendency—'fin de siecle,' as it was called. In this way little risk was run, and one would be able to have a motor-car. Indeed, Eustace,* Francie's brother, *already had one, but it had shaken him horribly, and broken one of his eye teeth; so that it would be better to wait till they were a little safer.*

By the turn of the century, Great-grandfather Oliver Longley had invested in his first motor vehicle and within seven years my grandfather also had his first car. These were very elegant, open automobiles, colorful, ornate, and adventuresome. They were not like the cars of 1920s 'Forsythia' designed to be driven by chauffeurs. They were the toys of their generation, driven by their owners in a swirl of dust and a sense of achievement. Apart from showing off the vehicle, they were not a means of traveling from one place to another. Trains were plentiful, branch lines worming their way out to every village and hamlet, and carriages with coachmen and livery were still the preferred mode of travel.

In the 1950s, because my preparatory school was not far from Brighton, for several years I was able to witness the traditional autumnal London to Brighton run for old cars. Still, in those days, motors of the

1890s and early 1900s made the traditional journey, most of their proud owners dressing for the occasion in Edwardian clothing. For some, at that time, these antique vehicles had never been out of their family ownership. I would love to have seen Great-grandfather Oliver and Minnie, my great-grandmother, driving down to Brighton in their 1906 Daraq—he with his great moustache, and she in her large Edwardian hat held tightly under the chin by a scarf, but by the 1950s they were gone, and the Daraq long gone. I could only watch other 'Forsyte' heirs drive into Brighton in their treasured toys.

In 1899, it was Roger Forsyte's turn to die—*his funeral at Highgate, in the old tradition, had been perfect.* Afterwards, the family assembled at Timothy's as usual.

Soames, still not divorced, but fully separated from Irene, had also moved to the country. Robbed of living in the house at Robin Hill—a house of which at best he was suspicious—he had bought a riverside home, The Shelter, at Mapledurham. There, *he had a gallery, beautifully hung and lighted, to which few London dealers were strangers. It served, too, as a Sunday afternoon attraction in those weekend parties which his sisters, Winifred or Rachel, occasionally organised for him.*

He was worth today well over a hundred thousand pounds and had no-one to leave it to. Money made money, and he felt that he would have a hundred and fifty thousand before he knew where he was.

A French girl, Annette, working on accounts for her mother at a Soho restaurant had caught his fancy. She was very beautiful, young and in his opinion, *not likely to lose her head, or accept any unlegalised position.*

He wanted no hole and corner liaison. A marriage at the Embassy in Paris, a few months' travel, and he could bring Annette back quite separated from a past which in truth was not too distinguished: he could bring her back as something very new and chic with her French taste and self-possession to reign at 'The Shelter' near Mapledurham. On Forsyte 'Change and among his riverside friends it would be current that he had met a charming French girl on his travels and married her. There would be the flavour of romance, and a certain cachet about a French wife.

So it had been in the latter 1940s when my father's brother, Uncle Gyles, working in Paris for the French division of Gestetner, the British duplicating company, met a beautiful French girl at a drama group associated with the British Embassy. I remember my mother and father leaving for Paris on the Night Ferry, a train that left Victoria Station in London to be cleverly shunted onto the cross-channel ferry taking its passengers undisturbed overnight to the French capital. There, my mother and father attended the wedding of Gyles and Ginette in 1948. My mother had on a green dress and wore a striking hat. Yes, in that last decade of 'Forsythia' one expected to dress up to travel, and ladies' hats, even gloves, were almost essential accoutrements of the wardrobe. My family was always slightly in awe of Ginette. We all described my French aunt as "chic" and there was a certain cachet in the reality that my good-looking Uncle Gyles had a French wife. They were married in the Embassy Church.

For Soames, it was not quite so easy. There was *this cursed undivorced condition of his and—and the question whether Annette would take him, which he dared not put to the touch until he had a clear and even dazzling future to offer her.*

This was paramount on Soames' mind as he entered the drawing room at Timothy's. And then, he was regaled with questions and gossip just as it had always been at Timothy's.

'How was his dear father?' as if they cared. *'Would Soames be sure to tell him that Hester had found boiled holly leaves most comforting for that pain in her side; a poultice every three hours?'*

Poultices were a common cure for us in the 1950s when we caught a cold. A big square of layered gauze covered in some thick, boiled mixture with the texture of porridge, was strapped on our chests. After a while, it tickled around the edges, and it was very painful when my mother would rip it off to remove it. Later, penicillin injections and a really bitter pill with the trade name of 'M and B' replaced the poultice, but back on Forsyte 'Change…

'Oh! And about the Darties—had Soames heard that dear Winifred was having a most distressful time with Montague? He had given some of Winifred's jewellery to a dreadful dancer. It was such a bad example for their son dear Val just as he was going to college.'

'And did he think these Boers were really going to resist! The price of Consols was so high, and Timothy *had such a lot of money in them. Did Soames think they must go down if there was a war?'*

Soames nodded.

Aunt Juley said, "I *would like to see that old Kruger sent to St. Helena. I can remember so well the news of Napoleon's death, and what a relief it had been to* your *grandfather."*

Soames was balancing a cup of tea, the perreniel post-funeral pick me up.

Aunt Juley continued, "Do you—do you *ever hear anything of Irene nowadays? They say dear Jolyon first left her that fifteen thousand out and out; then of course he saw it would not be right, and made it for her life only.*"

Soames nodded

"Your cousin Jolyon is a widower now. He is her trustee; you know that of course?"

Would that branch of the family that had stolen his house, given Irene money, now perhaps, steal her, too?

Soames shook his head. Young Jolyon and he had not met since the day of Bosinney's death.

'He must be quite middle-aged by now, He was born in December, '47, just before the Commune. He's over fifty! Fancy that! Such a pretty baby, and we were all so proud of him; the very first of you all.'

Soames put down his cup of tea and *rose, he was experiencing a curious piece of self-discovery. That old wound to his pride and self esteem was not yet closed.*

"Goodbye. Remember me to Uncle Timothy."

And in the street he instantly forgot them, repossessed by the image of Annette and the thought of the cursed coil around him. Why had he not pushed the thing through and obtained divorce when that wretched Bosinney was run over, and there was evidence galore for the asking! And he turned toward his sister Winifred Dartie's residence in Green Street, Mayfair.

CHAPTER TWO

EXIT A MAN OF THE WORLD

*A*t that roving age of forty-five, trying to Forsytes—and, though perhaps less distinguishable from any other age, trying even to Darties—Montague had fixed his current fancy on a dancer. It was no mean passion, but without money, and a good deal of it, likely to remain a love as airy as her skirts; and Dartie never had any money, subsisting miserably on what he could beg or borrow from Winifred—a woman of character, who kept him because he was the father of her children, and from a lingering admiration for those now dying good looks which in their youth had fascinated her.

Dartie had *acquired a half share in a filly of George Forsyte's. There was something delicious about Montague Dartie. He was as George Forsyte said, a 'daisy.'*

The filly ran at Newmarket. Dartie's winnings would go some way to advancing his relationship with the dancer. The filly fell, and *Dartie's shirt was lost.*

That night Dartie returned home without a care in the world. Under normal conditions, Winifred would have merely locked her door and let him sleep it off, but torturing suspense about her missing *pearls had caused her to wait up for him.*

Dartie, when challenged by his wife, took a small revolver from his pocket and aimed it at his chest.

"Don't be a clown, Monty. Have you been to Scotland Yard about the pearls?"

If he hadn't the right to take the pearls he had given her himself, who had? "That Spanish filly *has got'm. If* you *have any 'jection* I will cut—your—*throat."*

"Spanish filly! Do you mean that girl we saw dancing in the Pandemonium Ballet? Well, you are a thief and a blackguard. You are the limit, Monty."

Dartie seized his wife's arm and twisted it. *She wrenched it free* and left him in his stupor, locking her bedroom door.

When Dartie sobered up, he realized he had reached the limit. He realized there could be no reconciliation this time. Within half an hour he gathered a few things, including a framed photograph of his daughters, Maud and Imogen. He had four hundred pounds in fives and tens, the proceeds from the sale of his half of the filly back to George.

The ballet was going to Buenos Aires the day after tomorrow, and he was going too.

It was hard—hard to be thus compelled to leave his home! "D—n it!" *he muttered,* "I never thought it would come to this." *Noises above warned him that the maids were beginning to get up. Putting on his hat and overcoat, he took two others, his best malacca cane, an umbrella, and* carrying his two valises *opened the front door.*

Thus had passed Montague Dartie in the forty-fifth year of his age from the house, which he had called his own.

For the sake of the children Winifred suggested their father had gone to Newmarket, but when she noted the framed photo of Maud and Imogen was missing, she knew he had gone further, somewhere with that Spanish filly—*disgusting,* like Brighton!

Weekends with paramours in Brighton had been a part of English society ever since the small fishing village beside chalk cliffs on the south coast had become fashionable. Was it not Brighton that Jane Austen made the place of elopement for Lydia Bennett and the reckless Mr. Wickham in *Pride and Prejudice*? A little later, did not this growing seaside town become the love nest of George Frederick, Prince of Wales and his mistress Mrs. Fitzherbert. In the rakish period of the Regency, however, much was forgiven. Not so much, in the heyday of 'Forsythia'. Brighton was still frequented by those seeking illicit relationships, but it's reputation was no longer regal, but sordid. In the heyday of 'Forsythia' that class favored Eastbourne on the Sussex coast rather than racy Brighton. Brighton became the seaside resort of the lower-middle class, although it had its upper-class enclaves such as had attracted Soames after Irene left him, but Eastbourne became the more noted resort of 'Forsythia'.

Indeed, as late as the 1950s, Granny and Grandpop Longley frequently spent a week at one of the hotels on the front at Eastbourne. My parents used to stay at the Grand Hotel, Eastbourne, when they came to visit me at school—Newlands, at Seaford, being only a few miles west of Eastbourne, the other end of the Seven Sisters of chalk cliffs that terminate in the massive height of Beachy Head at the end of the Eastbourne promenade. The Grand Hotel at Eastbourne was one of only three five-star hotels outside London in those days—the others being the Majestic in Harrogate and the Imperial in Torquay. The Grand Hotel at Eastbourne left a great impression on me from its fluted columns in the entrance foyer to those potted ferns around Max Jaffa's orchestra, which played as one enjoyed rich afternoon teas with silver and white glove service. It was always very quiet, too, conversations hushed by the ceilings that seemed so high. This hotel, almost more than anything else, made me aware in the 1950s that I was a 'Forsyte'. Indeed, a childhood passion that I had at that time was drawing imaginary floor plans of grand hotels inspired by this Eastbourne landmark.

However, genteel Eastbourne was not without scandal in that last decade of 'Forsythia'. A series of wealthy, retired 'Forsyte' widows mysteriously died while in the care of an Eastbourne physician, Dr. Bodkin Adams. It seemed that the good doctor had murdered them with overdoses of drugs while collecting exhorbitant fees and even bequests. The scandal broke in 1955 at a time shortly after my sister Diane had been seriously ill with peritonitis at a nursing home in Eastbourne. Her surgeon was Mr. Snowball, a medical partner of Dr. Bodkin Adams!

The division of the medical profession into surgeons and doctors reflected the subtle shades of class even within the structure of 'Forsythia' and the three percent. Surgeons were never referred to as doctors and although the more highly trained branch of the medical profession, they dropped the title and were always referred to as "Mister." Doctors were considered members of the great upper-middle class, but not quite with the same respect as surgeons. This was well illustrated in the recent 2010 television mini-series *Downton Abbey.* This entailed estate of the fictitious Crawley family in late Edwardian England is to pass into the hands of a second cousin of Lord Grantham, whose father was a mere doctor…not a surgeon. As Lady Mary Crawley stated: "He is not one of us." 'Forsytes', however, never did claim to be aristocracy even if occasionally they would marry up into the aristocracy. They liked to call themselves upper-middle class, and within this division were those subtle shades of further class division such as illustrated in the medical profession. This subtle division also showed up in the legal profession where there is a little more prestige given to the barrister than to the solicitor—a barrister arguing legal cases in court and privileged to wear wig and gown like a judge, and a solicitor working the drudgery of legal paperwork in a lawyer's office without wig and gown.

For Winifred Dartie, musing over her husband's departure, what did that missing photograph really mean? Had Dartie left for good—gone to Brighton or the like? *As that conclusion hardened,* Winifred *stood quite still in the middle of his dressing-room, with all the drawers pulled out, to try and release what she was feeling. Though he was 'the limit' he was yet her property, and for the life of her she could not but feel the poorer. To be widowed yet not widowed at forty-two; with four children, made conspicuous, an object of commiseration! Gone to the arms of a Spanish jade! Mechanically she closed drawer after drawer, went to her bed, lay on it, and buried her face in the pillows.*

Winifred could only think of one thing. She needed to have her eldest son, Val, with her at this time. Val was at Littlehampton *taking his final gallops with his trainer for Smalls.* He would be going up to Oxford the next month at James's expense. She needed him now. *She caused a telegram to be sent to him.*

"I must see about his clothes," she said in excuse *to Imogen: "I can't have him going up to Oxford anyhow. Those boys are so particular."*

'Forsytes' who went to Oxford and Cambridge always went 'up' to the University.

Imogen did not really believe this was her mother's motive. *It was father, of course!* But *Val did come like a shot at six o'clock.*

Val's full name was Publius Valerius Dartie—a name that had caused him some problems. He *returned home from his first term at school complaining that life was a burden to him—they called him Pubby. Winifred—a woman of real decision—promptly changed his* preparatory *school and his name to Val, the Publius being dropped even as an initial.*

I am reminded of how my mother, with Winifred's insight, had insisted that my middle name should not be Charles as planned, because at school I might be ribbed as PC Longley—Police Constable—so I was christened Peter Hovenden Longley.

After kissing his mother and pinching Imogen, Val *ran upstairs three at a time, and came down four, dressed for dinner. He was awfully sorry, but his 'trainer', who had come up* to London, *too, had asked him to dine at the Oxford and Cambridge; it wouldn't do to miss—the old chap would be hurt. Winifred let him go with an unhappy pride. She had wanted him at home, but it was very nice to know that his tutor was so fond of him.*

The old chap was in reality only one year Val's senior. *He had missed being expelled from school a year before Val, had spent that year at Oxford, and Val could almost see a halo round his head. His name was Crum and no one could get through money quicker.*

After they had dined at the Oxford and Cambridge, *Crum said: "It's half an hour before they close; let's go on to the Pandemonium."*

There, amid the scents of promiscuity and decadence on this last night of the ballet, they heard a scuffling. *Three men, unsteady, emerged, walking arm in arm. The one in the centre wore a pink carnation, a white waistcoat, a dark moustache; he reeled a little as he walked. Crum's voice said slow and level: "Look at that bounder, he's screwed!"* Val turned to look. *"He seems to know you!"*

The 'bounder' spoke:

"H'llo! You f'llows look! There's my young rascal of a son!"

Val saw. It was his father.

To be ashamed of his own father is perhaps the bitterest experience a young man can go through. Val hurried away from the Pandemonium. *How could he go up to Oxford now amongst all those chaps, those splendid friends of Crum's, who would know that his father was a 'bounder'! And suddenly he hated Crum. He remembered how, at school, when some parent came down who did not pass the standard, it just clung to the fellow afterwards.* Would this now happen to him? Besides, *why had his mother married his father, if he was a 'bounder'?* However, *the worst of it was that now Crum had spoken the word, he realised that he had long known subconsciously that his father was not 'the clean potato.'*

When Val returned home, Winifred heard him on the landing: *'The dear boy's in. Thank goodness! If he takes after his father I don't know what I shall do! But he won't—he's like me. Dear Val!'*

My parents were very particular as to how they represented themselves when they visited our 'Forsyte' schools. My mother nearly always wore a hat and a garden party black coat that my father used to call her "Lady Mayoress outfit." My father had by the time I went to boarding school purchased his first Armstrong Siddeley—a car that definitely rubbed shoulders with Rolls Royces and Bentleys. Indeed, Armstrong Siddeleys, Daimlers, and Jaguars in the 1950s were often referred to as poor men's Bentleys. They were splendid cars, and when my parents rolled up the drive at Newlands on visiting weekends, there was an audible gasp of admiration at the sleek black car. On the hood was mounted a shining chrome sphinx; the interior gleamed with polished walnut wood, and vast, black leather bucket seats. My parents passed muster. Indeed, when dining with an old school friend from Newlands when we were up at Cambridge, I remember him saying: "I will always remember your father and that magnificent car."

However, if Montague Dartie was a bounder failing muster, it is probably true to say that most 'Forsyte' families had their bounders or lesser bounders. Audrie Longley's husband—the coffee planter from Kenya—obviously was something of a cad and a bounder, but some in my family considered her brother Chris to be a bounder. I'm not sure if he were truly a bounder, but like Montague Dartie he had a way of whittling through money. He never worked, somehow believing that it was his birthright not to have to work. This was not a 'Forsyte' trait. Money was important to 'Forsytes' and making money even more important, but having a good position in which to accomplish this was paramount. Not having a position caused one to be ostracized from the club. Members of the aristocracy were allowed to be the idle rich, often living off their land rather than their money, but not 'Forsytes'. As Great-uncle 'Tig's' heirs, Chris and Audrie came into a moderate sum of money on my great-grandfather's death, but as aforementioned, Great-uncle 'Tig' having passed away three years before his father, my grandfather, as executor, felt it better for the money apportioned to 'Tig's' heirs to be held in trust by him as 'Tig's' oldest brother. Somehow, Chris managed to break the trust, at least sufficiently to live a lifetime without working. In 'Forsyte' eyes, the mere fact of him not working was enough to consider him a bounder. Did Montague Dartie work? Galsworthy never alludes to his position as anything other than a "man of the world."

As noted, Audrie Lewis worked in the family firm, but also probably used a portioned part of her grandfather's inheritance towards sending her daughter, Sally Ann, to that fashionable ballet school at Hyde Park Gate. This was considered commendable as fashionable private education was important to 'Forsytes'.

Val Dartie's grandfather, James Forsyte, was to pay for Val's forthcoming education at Oxford, and somewhat like Grandpop Longley, so, too, had James put some restrictions on Montague Dartie. Suspicious of Dartie, this "man about town," James, even at the time of his engagement to his daughter, Winifred, had made sure that there were restrictions on Dartie's use of Forsyte funds, refusing to make a settlement on his daughter inclusive of Montague Dartie. Dartie had always had to beg funds from his wife, knowing that he would get short change from his father-in-law. As he said, *it was hard to get a 'tenner' or even a 'fiver' out of a Forsyte,* that was except for George, Uncle Nicholas' son, with whom he shared the delights of the turf and other impecunious adventures. However, even George had his limits, and like his Great-uncle Jolyon was still at heart a Forsyte—a man of property, unlike Dartie, the "man about town."

Great-grandfather Oliver Longley had made sure that all his sons had that fashionable private education so necessary for membership of their great class. First, they were sent to the new preparatory school for gentlemen that had opened in Beckenham—The Abbey School. Later, each of them in turn went on to Tonbridge School in Kent. In the next generation, Grandpop saw that his three sons also went to Tonbridge, and like he and his brothers, they were all enrolled in Judde House. Judde House was always also considered to be the country club house of the school, the most 'Forsyte', just as Christchurch College, known as 'The House' at Oxford, and Trinity College, at Cambridge, were considered the most 'Forsyte' university colleges. One's house or college at these privileged educational establishments was the place where one lived, and most importantly socialized, Houses had little to do with the actual education of the classroom, which was universal among house and college members. My father in the next generation saw that I, too, was enrolled in Judde House at Tonbridge School. One's name for these prestigious public schools and their houses was submitted at birth to ensure thirteen years later, one's place.

Not trusting Dartie to ever save for this important facet of the 'Forsyte' education of his children, James Forsyte, put Val's name down for Eton and paid for his education there and a forthcoming three years at Christchurch, Oxford. There was much speculation in my family as to whether my cousins, Daniel and Robert Longley, the children of Uncle Dennis and Aunt Brigid, would follow on in the family's Tonbridge tradition. Their names were put down for Judde House, but it became fairly obvious that Uncle Dennis' farming ventures at The Breach might not sustain the necessary income, Tonbridge rapidly becoming one of England's most expensive schools. Would my grandmother step in and pay the fees? That was widely assumed, but when it came to it, Dennis and Brigid chose to send them to Cranbrook School, one of the minor public schools that they could attend as dayboys at considerably less expense.

I was the last of the Longleys to attend Tonbridge School. My Scottish cousins, Aunt Biddy's sons, Johnny and Gyles Thompson, attended Strathallan, a prestigious Scottish public school at Forgandenny. I was also the last member of my family to attend Oxford or Cambridge. My cousin John Cuthbertson was up at Oxford just two years before I was up at Cambridge.

Not all 'Forsytes' went to university, but almost all took a strong loyalty to either Oxford or Cambridge in life. Nowhere was this more obvious than at the annual Oxford and Cambridge boat race. The grueling row on the Thames caught the imagination of all light blues and dark blues. The light blues supported Cambridge, and included almost all my family other than my cousin John Cuthbertson. The dark blues supported Oxford. Whether one had attended these learned schools or not, 'Forsytes' on boat race day took their sides. Grandpop Longley and his brothers were considered for Cambridge University, but instead, found themselves in the trenches of World War I. Grandpop had already applied for Gonville and Caius College, Cambridge. However, many 'Forsytes' if following into family businesses, did not take the higher education of Oxford and Cambridge, and in the case of my father this was his reality. His brothers did not attend either, finding themselves in the early 1940s, like their uncles before, drawn into active military service after the outbreak of World War II.

On leaving Tonbridge, like leavers of all the great public schools, an old boy was offered membership in the Oxford and Cambridge Club. It is not surprising, therefore, that we find Crum inviting Val Dartie to dine with him at this establishment that was usually a 'Forsyte's' first introduction to a London club. In 'Forsythia' school leavers were never called graduates. One only graduated from Oxford and Cambridge.

The Cambridge that I attended as the last generation of 'Forsythia' was not greatly different from that which Grandpop would have attended if he had gone to Gonville and Caius College. Perhaps, academics were taken a little more seriously than for earlier 'Forsytes', as I think in particular of Eveleyn Waugh's picture of Oxford in *Brideshead Revisited*, but our social life was much the same. There were a lot of formal dinners, representing different societies and sports, of which the most renowned were Boat Club dinners. Served in college halls, these were always black tie affairs. We were treated to the best college wines, and enjoyed famed ports and madeiras that circulated in fine crystal decanters in the glow of orange candlelight reflecting from the silver candelabra that had graced our college refectory tables for generations. The portraits of past masters of our colleges—portraits painted by Holbein, Lely, Reynolds, Gainsborough, and Lawrence—looked down on us from paneled walls of ancient English oak. Cigars were passed from huge silver boxes and later caused rings of smoke to make spirals upward to the hammer beams of medieval ceilings, or the decorative plaster of sixteenth and seventeenth-century craftsmen, colored by age and the soot of centuries of candles.

By day, we attended supervision by tutors in their private rooms, lined by mahogany bookcases and lit by brass or crystal chandeliers. The mullioned windows looked out on quadrangles of immaculate lawns and ancient college walls supporting roses, honeysuckle, wisteria, and figs. Clock towers chimed the hours. Tutors were tweedy—formally shabby, and we were rarely to be seen without a suit and tie. Some of us, including myself for a while, wore the stiff collars of our school uniforms, and for eccentricity even those wing collars that schools like Charterhouse still wore. Our suits were three-piece, or if not, included flamboyant waistcoats. Our sports jackets, still often worn with waistcoats or short sleeved sweaters were those tweedy ones with patches at the elbows, aping those of our tutors. I do not believe that in that last decade of 'Forsythia' I ever saw a student in bluejeans.

The social clubs we belonged to, or were lucky enough to be invited to, were run like London clubs with porters and servants or old retainers, from The Union to the exclusive Pitt Club, named after Britain's famous family of eighteenth-century prime ministers. We had our own beagling hunt pack, complete with stirrup cups at appropriate local country houses prior to each meet, and of course, an annual hunt ball. There were many balls during my time up at Cambridge and most still encouraged students to dress in white tie and tails, but the most prestigious was the annual college May Ball. The ball lasted all night and it was a tradition in the morning to punt up the river Cam to Grantchester for a Champagne breakfast, the more romantic of us also paying our respects to Rupert Brooke.

Punting along the 'Backs' was a common pastime, where ancient college buildings, gardens, and bridges made their way down to, and over the Cam, and you could enjoy the best views of Henry VII's Kings College chapel or Trinity's Christopher Wren library. On certain special occasions the river became crammed with punts, such as early on May morning when we gathered in mystical silence to await the choristers of Magdalene singing madrigals to Elizabethan lutes.

This was, however, all for a purpose—the 'Forsyte' purpose. Our education was first and foremost to place us in a position to achieve our inherited role—to be the guardians of the British Empire. Despite these eccentricities of our social life, academically Oxford and Cambridge gave us access to the greatest minds of our times and the best courses of study to equip us for our future role. As district commissioners, judges, administrators, engineers, and the future planters and businessmen of the Empire, we needed this balance of high academics, decision and sharpness of mind, along with a rare twilight sampling of that quintessential British culture, which we believed would civilize our subject peoples. Just as our forebears had quoted Latin and Shakespeare in the jungles of Malaya, sung Gilbert and Sullivan operas in their tropical clubs, so we expected we would do the same, but it was past 'Suez' and it was the twilight of our world.

Like the "man of the world"—Montague Dartie—'Forsythia' was about to make its exit.

CHAPTER THREE

SOAMES PREPARES TO TAKE STEPS

Soames called on his sister to find her sitting in her Louis-Quinz drawing room at her Buhl bureau with a letter in her hand. At first, Winifred *crumpled the letter, but seemed to change her mind and held it out to him. He was her lawyer as well as her brother.*

From the first Soames had nosed out Dartie's nature from underneath the plausibility, savoir faire, and good looks which had dazzled Winifred, their mother, and even James.

He read:

> 'You will not get chance to insult in my own again. I am
> leaving country tomorrow. It's played out. I'm tired of being
> insulted by you. You've brought on yourself. No self-respect-
> ing man can stand it I shall not ask you for anything again.
> Goodbye. I took the photograph of the two girls. Give them
> my love. I don't care what your family say. It's all their doing.
> I'm going to live new life. M.D.'

It occurred to Soames *that with this letter* Winifred *was entering that very state which he himself so earnestly desired to quit—the state of a Forsyte who was not divorced. He had come to her to talk of his own position, and get sympathy, and here was she in the same position, wanting of course to talk of it, and get sympathy from him.*

"Do you think he's really gone, Soames? You see the state he was in when he wrote that."

Soames made his way to the Iseeum Club.

There, finding his cousin George Forsyte, he enquired.

"Flitted, made a bolt to Buenos Aires with the fair Lola. Good for Winifred and the little Darties. He's a treat," George informed him, looking at Soames disdainfully.

Soames nodded. He did not want to converse with his cousin further, but George rattled on with snide remarks about his Uncle James and what he had had to put up with, even alluding to Irene.

"We may have to take steps," Soames said, *"I suppose there's no mistake?"*

"He was drunk as a lord last night; but he went off all right this morning. His ship's the Tuscarora;*"* and fishing out a card, he read mockingly:

"'Mr. Montague Dartie, Poste Restante, Buenos Aires.' I should hurry up with the steps if I were you. You'll enter Winifred *for the divorce stakes straight off if you ask me."*

"I must be getting back to her."

Soames stared vacantly at his cousin as George sat down dismissing him. *And the face of Annette rose before him, her brown hair and her blue eyes with their dark lashes, her fresh lips and cheeks, dewy and blooming in spite of London, her perfect French figure. 'Take steps!' he thought.*

In 'Forsythia' separation was a lot more common than divorce, and even separation was rare and treated with extreme suspicion. In fact, when I was away at boarding school during that last decade of 'Forsythia', I knew of only one boy whose parents were separated or divorced. 'Forsytes' made marriage vows for life, and for better or worse. This is not to say that members of 'Forsythia' did not stray from each other, have affairs or even a mistress, but marriage was sacred. Despite Darwin, evolution and its challenges to traditional Christianity—the great debate of the latter nineteenth century—most 'Forsytes' still believed in some superhuman God with whom they had a contract. Marriage, when it was performed in the established Church of England, was part of that contract. This belief was strong enough in 1936 to rock the British Empire—the king emperor, Edward VIII, gave up his throne because of his desire to marry a divorced person, Wallis Simpson, for as king he was also Supreme Head of the Church of England. Divorce was heavy stuff. Soames now wanted a divorce so he could be free to marry Annette. Would Irene, herself a member of this great class, agree to allow such an extreme measure? Soames needed to find out.

He hatched an ingenious plan. This is how he would 'take steps.'

His cousin Jolyon was Irene's trustee, the first step would be to go down and see him at Robin Hill—the house Bosinney had built for him and Irene—the house they had never lived in—the fatal house that he had sold to Uncle Jolyon. It belonged to his cousin 'Young Jolyon' now. *'They say he's got a boy at Oxford!' he thought. 'Why not take young Val down and introduce them!'*

Soames, on returning to his sister's house, spoke to Val. *"I should like to take you down with me tomorrow to where he lives. You'll find it useful. I'll call you after lunch. It's in the country—not far; you'll enjoy it."*

He then confirmed to Irene what George Forsyte had said. *"He's gone to Buenos Aires."*

They discussed what steps they should take, hopefully to avoid scandal or divorce.

"Of course, there's legal separation—we can get that."

"What does it mean?" asked Winifred desolately.

"That he can't touch you or you him; you're both of you married and unmarried." Soames grunted. *What was it in fact, but his own accursed position, legalised! No, he would not put her into that.*

"It must be divorce," he said decisively.

Winifred shook her head. "It's so beastly."

"Don't say anything to anybody, and don't pay any of his debts," Soames advised.

Winifred's reticence, even remorse—her sense of loss—seemed bereavement at the finality of divorce. Not to pay his debts? *Some richness seemed to have gone out of her life. Without her husband, without her pearls, without that intimate sense that she made a brave show above the domestic whirlpool, she would now have to face the world.*

'Forsytes' put up with much in life so long as they could put on that brave show—the stiff upper lip. At the end of that last decade of 'Forsythia' my sisters and I even worried about the stability of my parents' own marriage. They often argued, and my mother constantly got onto my father about his cigarette smoking. Frequently, my mother called my father "the limit," just like Winifred described Monty. This was also the time when the dapper young man, so smartly dressed, who had so impressed Granny Mabs, became 'The Clown'—that reference to his less cared for appearance and his rather baggy trousers. Then, there was Walter Hitchcock, the golf professional at Langley Park. We felt sure there was something between him and Mother. I remember about that time my father saying to me, "If I were to live my life again I would not get married." Apart from these suspicions, my mother had a way of nagging at him. Despite it all, however, their later years together were extremely happy and it was very obvious at their Golden and Diamond weddings that they and their friends looked back with great love and affection on this marriage as a good one. After my mother passed away, my father missed her very much. However, on several occasions after my mother had gone, my father expressed the opinion that my mother had been involved in some sort of illicit affair in the middle of their marriage. Naturally, we thought he was referring to the golf professional, but it was not Walter Hitchcock to whom he alluded, but a bridge-playing partner of my mother and father, who used to take my mother on golfing weekends. No more was ever said—'Forsytes' keep that stiff upper lip and do not discuss their private lives, unless scandal breaks.

As Soames took leave of his sister, with *a kiss he placed on her forehead* of *more than his usual warmth,* he brought up the first steps of his own plan.

"I have to go down to Robin Hill to-morrow to see young Jolyon on business. He's got a boy at Oxford. I'd like to take Val with me and introduce him. Come down to 'The Shelter' for the week-end and bring the children. Oh! By the way, no, that won't do: I've got some other people coming."

So saying, he left Winifred *and turned toward Soho* and the matter most pressing in his emotional life.

CHAPTER FOUR

SOHO

Soho is perhaps least suited to the Forsyte spirit. It was not a place 'Forsytes' frequented, except perhaps to dine at a restaurant. Being adjacent to the theatre district, 'Forsytes' would venture into Soho for a pre-show supper or a late dinner after the performance. Actually, my first teenage venture on my own, without my family, was to the theater with a friend from Tonbridge when we were just sixteen. His name was Michael de St. Croix and in some ways he was the Crum in my life at that time. His parents were in colonial service, and we were both chapel servers—acolytes at Tonbridge School—but Michael carried the cross at sung Eucharists, whereas I just carried a large taper candle. We had an early theater dinner at Kettners Restaurant in Soho before the show, but Soho was not a place to walk around. 'Forsytes' only ventured in by cab. It was *untidy, full of Greeks, Ishmaelites, cats, Italians, tomatoes, restaurants, organs, coloured stuffs, queer names, people looking out of upper windows.* However, on the western fringe, on Wardour Street, there were antique shops where Soames had picked up a treasure or two.

After Irene left him, Soames had sold his house on Montpelier Square. That is when like others with something to hide—the shame of his wife's desertion—he moved down to Brighton. For seven years he lived in Brighton, taking the train of Pullman cars on his commute up and down Monday through Friday, as he centered his life on the law and making money. *Forsyte, Bustard and Forsyte had become solicitors to more limited companies than they could properly attend to. Saturday to Monday was spent at his club in town. The Sunday visit to his family in Park Lane, to Timothy's, and to* Winifred's remained important to Soames. Then, he invested his financial gains in the house at Mapledurham—somewhere where he could actually display his treasures—his paintings and all those collectibles.

After buying a bit of Wedgewood one evening in April, he had dropped into Malta Street in Soho *to look at a house of his father's which had been turned into a restaurant—a risky proceeding, and one not quite in accordance with the terms of the lease.* The place looked trim with little bay trees in a recessed doorway and the name 'Restaurant Bretagne' above in gold letters. Soames was *rather favourably impressed.* There, in a back room he met the proprietor, Madame Lamotte and her daughter, who kept the books—Annette.

Annette's slim figure, pretty face and gracious moves impressed Soames. The legal matters paled in comparison. *Soames decided that the lease had not been violated: though to himself and his father he based the decision on the efficiency of those illicit adaptations in the building, on the signs of the prosperity, and the obvious business capacity of Madame Lamotte. He did not, however, neglect to leave certain matters to future consideration,* of which Annette was paramount. Thus started a series of visits, *which had gradually made him so definitely conscious that he desired to alter his condition from that of the unmarried man to that of the married man remarried.*

Turning into Malta Street on this evening of early October, 1899, he bought a paper to see if there were any after-development of the Dreyfus case—a question which he had always found useful in making closer acquaintanceship with Madame Lamotte and her daughter, who were Catholic and anti-Dreyfusard.

Dreyfus was a framed French army officer who happened to be a Jew. Almost obviously innocent of charges against him, he was sentenced to life imprisonment on the French imperial prison island off French Guyana—the infamous Devil's Island. Yes, without direct involvement, Jews were dispensable to 'Forsytes'. They were not members of the club. The last generation of 'Forsytes' were even somewhat indifferent to the holocaust, its horrors taking a back seat in the Second World War's recent history, to Prisoner of War camps like Colditz, where British prisoners had been kept in comparative luxury. It was enough

for us schoolboys to refer to our boarding preparatory school as Colditz,
however, and Colditz was the subject matter of adventurous war books
for boys on escapes. There was even a somewhat cynical schoolboy
lyric in the 1950s that was the closest I came to even knowing about
the holocaust: 'How odd of God to choose a Jew when he could have
had a purer Furhrer.' In 1964, as a theological student at Cambridge, I
spent the summer working as a *kibbutznik* in Israel with friends from
the university who wanted to visit the Holy Land. My family treated
this trip in a rather low-key way, as they would probably have all rather
I had visited archeological sights in Italy, Greece, or even Turkey, rather
than Israel—the new Jewish state.

Likewise, for Soames Forsyte, matters that rocked the Third French
Republic, especially involving a Jew, were not nearly as significant
as matters that might rock the British Empire, like these 'goings on'
in South Africa. There was an ominous leader in the paper about the
Transvaal and those Boers again. *'War's a certainty,'* he thought, *'the
stock exchange has taken a general fall. I shall sell my Consols.'*

*A look, as he passed the doorways of the restaurant, assured him that
business was good as ever, and this now gave him a certain uneasiness.
If the steps which he had to take ended in his marrying Annette, he
would rather see her mother safely back in France.*

While alone with Annette, after complimenting her, Soames asked
her directly if she was happy in England or whether she would rather
go back to France.

*"Oh, I like London. Paris of course. But London is better than
Orleans, and the English country is so beautiful. I have been to
Richmond last Sunday."*

*Soames went through a moment of calculating struggle.
Mapledurham! Dared he? After all, dared he go so far as that, and
show her what there was to look forward to.*

*"I want you and your mother to come for the afternoon next Sunday.
My house is on the river, it's not too late in this weather; and I can show
you some good pictures. What do you say?"*

"It will be lovelee. The river is so beautiful."

"That's understood, then. I'll ask Madame."

But *did one ask restaurant proprietors with pretty daughters down
to one's country house without design?*

Madame Lamotte's profession was not 'Forsyte'. Her daughter,
although beautiful, was not of that great class. However, within

'Forsythia' foreigners could be accepted on good looks as their accent disguised the rules of class. An English restaurant proprietor or her daughter would almost certainly not pass muster. Their lower-middle-class accents would give them away. Soames, also did not need the scandal or embarrassment of having a restaurant proprietor from Soho, albeit French, as a mother-in-law. *If the steps which he had to take ended in his marrying Annette, he would rather see her mother safely back in France, a move to which the prosperity of the Restaurant Bretagne might become an obstacle. He would have to buy them out, of course, for French people only came to England to make money; and it would mean a higher price.*

Walking home towards Park Lane—for he was staying at his father's, Soames considered his options. *Take steps! What steps! How? Dirty linen washed in public? Pah! With his reputation for sagacity, for far sightedness and the clever extrication of others, he, who stood for proprietory interests, to become the plaything of that law of which he was the pillar!*

Perhaps a liaison would be better and he could independently adopt a son and heir. *But I do want her,* he thought, *and I want a son.*

Throughout the era of 'Forsythia' despite the advance of women through the suffragette movement and two world wars, primogenitor was still the favored way of passing on property. 'Forsytes' accumulated wealth and possessions, property and prestige, in order to pass it all on to their eldest son.

At length, Soames concluded the only really practical solution: *'There's nothing for it but divorce—somehow—anyhow—divorce!'*

He thought of Irene. *'What could she be like now?—How had she passed the years, twelve years in all, seven already since Uncle Jolyon left her that money! Was she still beautiful? Would he know her if he saw her? Yes, she had made him suffer* but *divorce! It seemed ridiculous after all these years of separation! But it would have to be. No other way! 'The question',* he thought with sudden realism, *is—which of us? She or me? She deserted me. She ought to pay for it. There'll be someone, I suppose.'*

When Aunt Brigid and Uncle Dennis separated there was speculation among our family members as to whether this would just remain a legal separation. Longleys did not believe in divorce, and almost all sympathy was with my Aunt Brigid, but like Soames, the period of separation begged the question that during those months or even years, there must be someone else. There was—my very loving Aunt Pat, but it took a year or two for most members of my family to embrace the change, even after the grounds for divorce were established.

Soames had to face the same, even if he could show that in separation Irene could have found someone else. It would simply make the scandal less.

CHAPTER FIVE

JAMES SEES VISIONS

J ames Forsyte *was sitting* in the dining room *by the fire, in a big armchair, with a camel-hair shawl, very light and warm, over his frock-coated shoulders, on to which his long white whiskers drooped.* For James, 'Forsythia' felt like it was coming to an end. *At eighty-eight he was still organically sound, but suffering terribly from the thought that no one ever told him anything. It is, indeed, doubtful how he had become aware that Roger was being buried that day, for Emily had kept it from him,* but he had seen Soames' mourning trousers and soused it out.

Roger, his brother—he recalled how they had come back to London from boarding school in the West country in 1824 on the 'Slowflyer'. *Roger had got into the 'boot' and gone to sleep. James uttered a thin cackle.*

Emily *was always keeping things from him. Emily was only seventy! She would live fifteen or twenty years after he was gone, and might spend a lot of money; she had always had extravagant tastes. For all he knew, she might want to buy one of these motor cars.*

And now Roger was gone. The family was breaking up. Soames would know how much his uncle had left. Curiously, he thought of Roger as Soames's uncle, not now *as his own brother. Soames! It was more and more the one solid spot in a vanishing world.*

Where was Soames? He had gone to the funeral of course, which they had tried to keep from him. Roger! Roger in his coffin.

I remember, rather sadly, Grandpa Jack Collings, who was ninety when my grandmother died. He was not with her at the time, but staying with my mother, Granny Mabs having suggested he stay with us as she just needed a rest from taking care of him—or did she instinctively know that she would pass away that night. Grandpa was somewhat in dementia at the time. His mind rattled on rather like that of James. He did not go to Granny's funeral, but stayed in our house. I don't know if he was ever told we were at the funeral and he may well have not remembered if he had. He called for Mabs often after she was gone, sometimes knowing she was gone and believing it must have been his fault, and sometimes having no recollection that she had passed on.

James continued in his ramblings.

There was Val going to the university; he never came to see him now even though he was paying for his education. *He would cost a pretty penny up there. It was an extravagant age. And all the pretty pennies that his grandchildren could cost him danced before James's eyes. He did not grudge them the money, but he grudged terribly the risk which the spending of that money might bring on them; he grudged the diminution of security.*

A motor-car went past the window. Ugly great lumbering thing, making all that racket! But there it was, the country was rattling to the dogs!

And now there was this old Kruger! They had tried to keep old Kruger from him. But he knew better; there would be a pretty kettle of fish out there with those Boers in South Africa. *He shouldn't wonder if the Empire split up and went to pot. And this vision of the Empire going to pot* struck right at his 'Forsyte' core.

He had been dozing when he became aware of voices—low voices. Ah! They never told him anything! Winifred's and Emily's voices. He heard *'Monty!' That fellow Dartie—always that fellow Dartie!*

The voices receded. And an awful thought concreted again in his brain. Dartie had gone bankrupt—fraudulently bankrupt, and to save Winifred and the children, he—James—would have to pay! He saw Dartie in the dock, his grandchildren in the gutter, and himself in bed.

Looking up, he saw his Turner on the wall in its great gilt frame. Was it really a Turner? Why it might be a forgery! *He saw the doubted*

Turner being sold at Jobson's, and all the majestic edifice of property in rags.

Granny Mabs had two magnificent Alfred de Brianski landscapes in gilt frames gracing her dining room at Redcroft on Wickham Way. Diane, Sally, and I just loved those paintings, but how sad it was that on Granny's death, my mother and Aunt Eileen sold them off for a pittance to a dealer in the West End who doubted their authenticity.

Emily came in.

"Have you had a nice nap, James?"

Nap! He was in torment, and she asked him that!

"What's this about Dartie?" he said, and his eyes glared at her.

"What's this about Dartie?" repeated James. *"He's gone bankrupt. You never tell me anything. He's gone bankrupt."*

There was huge shame in 'Forsythia' over bankruptcy. It showed incompetence in managing 'Forsytes's' most prized possession and absorption—property. One of my family's Goodchild cousins went bankrupt. It was rarely spoken of. Incompetent firms in Smithfield Market had gone bankrupt, but their obsession with wasting their profits were swiftly pointed out by the directors of E. Weatherley and Co, Campbell, Key and Longley, and R.F. Potter.

"He has not," Emily *answered firmly. "He's gone to Buenos Aires."*

"What's he gone there for? He's got no money. What did he take?"

"He took Winifred's pearls and a dancer."

"What! I paid for them," James *said tremblingly; "he's a thief! I—I knew how it would be. He'll be the death of me; he—"* and as James' words failed him Emily feared it might be. She poured James some sal volatile. *She could* no longer *see the tenacious Forsyte spirit working in that thin, tremulous shape against the extravagance of the emotion called up by this outrage on Forsyte principles—the Forsyte spirit deep in there, saying: 'You mustn't get into a fantod, it'll never do. You won't digest your lunch. You'll have a fit!'*

James waived the medicine aside. 'Forsytes' did not like to consider themselves invalids, at least, not the males of that class. They liked to feel that they had that same stiff upper lip control over their bodies that they had over their emotional minds.

"What was Winifred about to let him take her pearls?"

"She can have mine," Emily offered, playing the matter down. *"I never wear them."* Then added almost nonchalantly, *"She'd better get a divorce."*

"There you go!" said James. *"Divorce! We've never had a divorce in the family. Where's Soames?"*

Emily left after calming him down.

But James sat there seeing visions—of Winifred in the Divorce Court, and the family name in the papers; of the earth falling on Roger's coffin; of Val taking after his father, of the pearls he had paid for and would never see again; of money back at four per cent—those confounded Boers—*and the country going to the dogs.*

Where was Soames? Why didn't he come in?

At length, Soames entered the dining room having returned from Soho, ready to take steps.

"There you are! Dartie's gone to Buenos Aires!" James shouted.

Soames nodded. "That's all right," he said; "good riddance."

A wave of assuagement passed over James's brain. Soames knew. Soames was the only one of them all who had sense.

"I wish you were more at home, my boy," he said.

"They sent their love to you at Timothy's," Soames *said. "It went off all right. I've been to see Winifred. I'm going to take steps."* Secretly, Soames did not want his elderly father to know of the steps he was planning for himself—another divorce.

'Forsytes' never wanted to burden their families with anything that might reflect failure or incompetence. We were trained for success, to be the leaders and rulers of that British Empire. That success was reflected in the pride felt of father for son. I will never forget the pinnacle of my own success when my parents came down to Southampton to have lunch with me after I had taken up my position as cruise director of the world's then most prestigious ocean liner—Cunard's *Queen Elizabeth 2*. At sailing time, they were standing in the visitors' gallery on the pier as I stood with the captain on the great ship's bridge. It was a 'Forsyte' moment.

"I've been poorly all day," James said. *"They never tell me anything."*

Soames helped his father upstairs.

"Good-night, my boy," said James at his bedroom door.

"Good-night, father."

Turning away from the light in his father's *open doorway*, he went to his own room.

'I want a son,' he thought, sitting on the edge of his bed; 'I want a son.'

Chapter Six

No-longer-young Jolyon at home

Bosinney had sat under the large oak tree at Robin Hill and suggested to Soames that this was where he should build his house. 'Old Jolyon' had sat under this tree—it was his favorite spot in the garden of the house that he had grown to love. He died under that tree. 'Young Jolyon' often painted under the same tree.

Bosinney had put his heart into the house. That was obvious to 'Young Jolyon'. Now, twelve years on, *Wisteria was already about its walls—the new look had gone.*

One whole side and corner of our house, Hockeredge on Wickham Way, was covered in wisteria. The feathery leaves of the wisteria vine are attractive all summer, the light purple blooms in May a feast for the eye, and the gnarled growth, devoid of leaves, pleasant through the winter months. Wisteria gives that cottage informality and sense of timelessness to the walls of even the grandest house. As we grew up at 52, Wickham Way, we all admired this wall of wisteria, and as long as my father lived in the house, it was sacred. Sadly, after he sold the house it was pulled from the wall to make way for an additional 'Granny' apartment and double garage. Hockeredge lost its wisteria and that new look, for years disguised, was renewed.

For 'Young Jolyon' at Robin Hill *there was the smack of reverence and ancestor worship, if only for one ancestor,* his father 'Old Jolyon', *in* the son's *desire to hand* the house *down to his son and his son's son.*

His father had loved the house, had loved the view, the grounds, that tree; his last years had been happy there, and no one had lived there before him.

'Young Jolyon', *if anything* looked *younger,* and *these last eleven years at Robin Hill had formed in Jolyon's life, as a painter, the important period of success. His drawings fetched high prices.*

He lost his wife, Helene, *in 1894. She had become increasingly jealous of her step-daughter June, jealous even of her own little daughter Holly.* Considered herself ill and *'useless to everyone, and better dead.'* Maybe she brought early death upon herself, but *it was one of those domestic tragedies, which turn out in the end for the good of all.*

Jolyon *had mourned her sincerely,* but without Helene, June spent most of her time now at Robin Hill. She became a motherly influence on Holly. Jolly was at Harrow. Jolyon was free to travel and paint, and spent several months in Paris.

I remember when my sister Diane showed such promise as an artist that Granny Longley, maybe tongue in cheek, often suggested Diane should have a flat in Paris. Granny loved Paris herself, which was one reason why she got on so well with her daughter-in-law, my Aunt Ginette. However, she also had the fixation of 'Forsythia' that a painter was not a true artist unless he or she had spent time in Paris.

With his youthful look, sporting a *short fair beard,* Jolyon saw himself more as an elder brother to his son Jolly, treating him and Holly *with a sort of whimsical equality.* This sometimes manifested itself this way in 'Forsythia' when children were not really brought up by their parents, but by their boarding schools. Parents had to win their children back during school visits and holidays, especially fathers, often doing so by acting in a big brotherly way. *When* Jolyon *went down to Harrow to see Jolly, he never quite knew which of them was the elder.*

Rather awkwardly, his only real fatherly advice on visiting his son when he went to Harrow was: *'Look here, old man, don't forget you're a gentleman.'*

It is interesting that 'Forsytes' tended to refer to their schools as places to go down to, but when it came to the university—Oxford or Cambridge, they were places you went up to. This is particularly quaint when it comes to Harrow. This great rival of Jolyon's own old school, Eton, was set on the top of a hill on the fringe of north London—Harrow on the hill.

The fact that Jolyon was himself an old Etonian became a sort of rivalry with his son at Harrow. This would come to a head at the great annual cricket match at Lords between Eton and Harrow. Only six schools had the privilege of playing annual cricket matches at Lords. Tonbridge was one of them, with an annual match against the west country school of Clifton.

The match always took place on the first two days of the summer holidays. It was compulsory, however, to attend. We were expected to show up at Lords Cricket Ground in London with our parents appropriately dressed in a garden party atmosphere. The strawberries and cream in the tea tent were as important as the game. In cricket, there is no raucous applause—just polite clapping and odd comments of a sporting nature: "Well played, sir," or as with Jolyon and his son, *"Hooray! Oh! Hard luck, old man!" or "hooray! Oh! Bad luck, Dad!"*

Jolyon would wear a grey top hat, instead of his usual soft hat, *to save his son's feelings, for a black top hat he could not stomach,* but top hats were the garden party dress of the day. In the last days of 'Forsythia', such formality was only reserved for the Buckingham Palace royal garden parties, two of which my father was privileged to attend. He was invited to this annual invitation from the sovereign to reward citizen subjects, in appreciation of his roles as master of both the Barbers' and Poulters' Companies. In fact, these were the last times I remember my father wearing a top hat. Although for weddings, in the last days of 'Forsythia' and lingering on for a decade or two, morning dress was usually worn, top hats were the first part of the formal Edwardian style dress to go.

Apart from my wedding day in 1993, I wore a top hat quite often when I lived in Ireland. I had four top hats, and still do—a gray for weddings, two black, one that I had purchased in London in the 1960s and one that had belonged to Great-grandfather John Cuthbertson, also a collapsible opera hat that had belonged to Grandpa Jack Collings. In Ireland in the 1960s and '70s, they were part of my dress for weddings, funerals, and hunt balls, and I wore my black top hat with clerical dress when I was acting Dean of Cashel Cathedral. I also had four bowler hats or derbies in Ireland—a steel rimmed black one for the hunting field, for I rode to hounds for ten years with the West Waterford Foxhounds and the Tipperary Foxhounds, and black, brown, and white bowlers to wear with appropriately colored suits or great coats. These, along with the top hats, became useful props during my subsequent years in entertainment as a cruise director, especially the white bowler, but apart from theatrical wardrobe, since the early 1970s, I have only worn a top hat with white tie and tails for livery dinners at Barber-Surgeons Hall, The Guildhall, or The Mansion House.

For Tonbridgians of my father's generation, top hats were no longer worn at Lords. In the aftermath of World War I, the day after the Lords cricket match, the whole school went to Officers' Training Corps camp. In my day at Tonbridge, the Officers' Training Corps had become the Combined Cadet Force in the aftermath of World War II, and annual camp was not compulsory, although strongly recommended. Between the wars, Father's training was always at Tidworth Park on Salisbury Plain, where he had found that comfortable role of dispatch rider; ours was usually at the army training area at Thetford in Norfolk.

The train for Thetford left from Kings Cross in the afternoon, so I would often go with a couple of friends to Smithfield beforehand, hoping that Grandpop or my father would take us out to lunch. Of course, we were dressed in our uniforms, fresh blanco on our webbed belts and gaiters, and brass buckles gleaming. The cockney porters and salesmen on the floor at Smithfield would whistle and shout out comments to us like, "We're in the army, now, we used to milk a cow" or "Here comes the army, Mrs. Brown." It was very much still in their recent memory that they had been conscripted into the army to fight in the Second World War or in the years of compulsory national service after the war.

The cockney British 'Tommy' had been the backbone of humor and camaraderie in army ranks throughout the generations of 'Forsythia'. Although they were not educated like us 'Forsytes' to run the British Empire, they were posted all over the Empire to support us 'Forsytes' in our administrative and commercial lives. For the most part, the Empire was benign—a great civilizing commercial venture, but not without that 'Forsyte' profit motive. Somehow, my sisters and I were very aware of all this as we played with our toy soldiers on the big nursery table—our favorite pastime. Our soldiers were posted to all corners of the Empire, mostly tropical. We created the imaginary backdrop for their activities by converting our teddy bears into rock formations with exciting caves and hiding places, and Diane skillfully painted jungle scenes with snakes, monkeys and exotic birds as scenic backdrops. When our soldiers spoke, they had cockney accents, as we mimicked the working class accents of our servants—cockney being the lower-class-accent of Londoners. They played cards a lot, and like the young Pip when he played cards at

Miss Havisham's with the pretty Estella in Dickens' *Great Expectations,* called the knaves "Jacks." We instinctively knew, as the young Estella knew, that the lower-classes called the knaves 'Jacks.' Our soldiers were adventurers and explorers, like many in the British army had been in the heyday of 'Forsythia' before the two World Wars. We were no doubt influenced in this interpretation by the imperial writings of Rudyard Kipling and Ryder Haggard in a world of sahibs, memsahibs and the adventures of *King Solomon's Mines* and *Alan Quartermain.* Weapons were only used in hunting the tiger and the lion or protecting oneself from fierce snakes. Our soldiers would speak of leave at home, back in England where nearly all their wives, daughters or girlfriends had the name Daphne. In fact, we incorporated the name Daphne into our childhood language, not just because our aunt of that name was well organized. Something imperial and toughly feminine we always said was very "Daphne," too. In part, this was because we saw our aunt who lived next door in this same light—Great-aunt Nellie's daughter. Daphne Noble was an imperialist—always right, strong, did not suffer fools gladly and very much into 'doing her bit' for society, working at charities and in other volunteer institutions of good works—the memsahib 'at home'.

These recreations of an imaginary imperial life on our nursery table occupied us for hours, unless interrupted by the window cleaner! But, regardless of our childhood influences, it was true that the postings of the cockney British 'Tommy' to all parts of the Empire was a binding emotional link between the classes—those who ruled the Empire and those who experienced the Empire.

After the lunch furlough at Smithfield, however, it was on to King's Cross and a week of army rations and maneuvers in the Norfolk countryside for us soldier boys of that last decade of 'Forsythia'.

When Jolly Forsyte *went up to Oxford, Jolyon went up with him,* the almost sibling rivalry continuing between them—Jolyon had gone to Cambridge, the other place.

At Oxford, where Jolly attended 'The House', Christchurch College, Jolyon gave his other piece of fatherly advice, which showed him to be a Forsyte at heart, even if a lifetime rebel.

"Look here, old man," he said to his young son, *"you're bound to get into debt; mind you come to see me at once. Of course, I will always pay them. But you might remember that one respects oneself more*

afterwards if one pays one's own way. And don't ever borrow, except from me, will you?"

My father could well have said the same thing. Debt was not something 'Forsytes' believed in, and should it occur, it needed to be dealt with immediately, and in the family. Outside the family, debt in 'Forsythia' became a *scandal*.

At Robin Hill, Jolly's sister, Holly, now eighteen and finally free of her French governess, Mademoiselle Beauce, after a period as a teenage ugly duckling, was growing into a beauty, a *rather dark one, always a shy one, but an authentic swan.* Jolyon was attempting to paint her portrait. He was on his fourth sketch when a maid entered presenting Soames' card. He had not seen Soames since that day that Soames had shut his front door in his face.

"Show him into the study, please, and say I'll be there in a minute," he said.

Instinctively, as Irene's trustee, even though he rarely saw her, he knew this had to be something to do with Soames' wife.

He looked at Holly and asked:

"Do you remember 'the lady in grey', who used to give you music-lessons?"

"Oh yes, why? Has she come?"

Jolyon shook his head and left to change before going to his study.

Standing by the french window, looking out across the terrace, were two figures, middle-aged and young, and Jolyon *thought: 'Who's that boy? Surely they never had a child?'*

Soames turned.

The meeting of those two Forsytes of the second generation, so much more sophisticated than the first, in the house built for the one and owned and occupied by the other, was marked by subtle defensiveness beneath distinct attempt at cordiality.

"This is Val Dartie," said Soames, *"my sister's son."* The mystery was solved. *"He's just going up to Oxford. I thought I'd like him to know your boy."*

"Ah! I'm sorry Jolly's away. What college?"

"B.N.C," replied Val.

"Jolly's at 'The House', but he'll be delighted to look you up."

"Thanks awfully."

'Forsytes' loved the word 'awfully' and applied it as an adjective simply as a superlative and not as a negative. A chap could be awfully decent. This way of speech was indicative of their class.

"Holly's in—if you could put up with a female relation, she'd show you round. You'll find her in the hall if you go through the curtains. I was just painting her."

With another "Thanks awfully!" Val vanished.

Soames and no-longer-young Jolyon faced each other.

"I haven't seen you for a long time," Jolyon said.

"No, not since—as a matter of fact, it's about that I've come. You're her trustee, I'm told."

Jolyon nodded.

"Twelve years is a long time," said Soames rapidly: *"I—I'm tired of it. I wish to be free."*

"I don't see her," murmured Jolyon. *"What exactly do you want?"*

"She deserted me. I want a divorce."

"Rather late in the day, isn't it? I don't know much about these things—at least I've forgotten," said Jolyon with a wry smile. He himself had had to wait for death to grant him a divorce from the first Mrs. Jolyon. *"Do you wish me to see her about it?"*

"I suppose there's someone?" Soames said, fishing.

"I don't know at all. I imagine you may have both lived as if the other were dead. It's usual in these cases." No doubt he was thinking of the ostracized years in which he had lived 'in sin' with Helene Hillier, and when Jolly had been born out of wedlock. He turned away from Soames and looked out of the window.

He *saw the figures of Holly and Val Dartie moving across the lawn to the stables. And for a swift moment he seemed to see his father's figure in the old arm-chair, just beyond Soames, sitting with knees crossed, the* Times *in his hand,* and looking out at the old oak tree. The vision *vanished.*

"My father was fond of her," he said quietly.

"Why he should have been, I don't know," Soames answered without looking round. *"She brought trouble to your daughter June; she brought trouble to everyone. I gave her all she wanted. I would have given her even—forgiveness—but she chose to leave me."*

"I can go and see her, if you like," Jolyon offered. *Compassion was checked by Soames' tone of voice. What was there in the fellow that*

made it so difficult to be sorry for him. "*I suppose she might be glad of a divorce, but I know nothing.*"

"*Yes, please go. I've no wish to see her.*"

The exchange over, Jolyon offered his cousin tea.

Chapter Seven

The colt and the filly

Holly's world was Robin Hill. Like many young ladies of her class, she had never been to school, all her education having been in the hands of Mademoiselle Beauce and those few piano lessons from 'the lady in grey'. She remembered her grandfather from those days with great affection. He had liked 'the lady in grey', too. In many ways—her adventures with him in the farmyard, the kitchen garden, and her memory of 'Old Jolyon' pushing her swing close to the big oak tree with its magnificent view—it was her grandfather who had made her love her home so much. Like most girls of her class growing up in the country, she loved horses, and although her grandfather had died before she had become an accomplished rider, she spent much of her time with her horse, Fairy, appropriately so named in her somewhat unreal world.

The outside world made some inroads into her life after her mother died, as her stepsister, June, spent more time supervising her, and the governess' influence waned. June was a young woman who knew the real world and frequently brought her 'lame ducks' to Robin Hill for recuperation. Much of her moral upbringing had come from June, although she did not always agree with her stepsister's opinions. For one, she liked to follow the hounds at foxhunting meets, but June told her it was cruel.

Holly had not encountered any young men in her life other than her older brother, Jolly, who was another mentor and who had protected her ever since she could remember, way back in those distant days when they had lived in that shabby little house in north London. However, much of the time since then, he had been away at boarding school and now he was up at Oxford. Still, she looked up to him with awe.

She extended a hand to Val Dartie as he introduced himself in the hall, a practice no doubt engrained in her from childhood by Mademoiselle, who considered it "well brrred."

'I wonder what this filly is like? She is *pretty,'* Val thought. *'What luck?'*

Holly did not withdraw her hand. She felt awkward and didn't really know what to do beyond the initial offering of it.

"I'm afraid you don't know me," Val *said. "My name's Val Dartie— I'm once removed, second cousin, something like that, you know. My mother's name was Forsyte."*

"I don't know many of my relations. Are there many?"

"Tons. They're awful—most of them. At least, I don't know—some of them. One's relations always are, aren't they?"

"I expect they think one awful, too," said Holly.

Holly, now having withdrawn her hand from his, *looked at him—the wistful candour of those grey eyes gave young Val a sudden feeling that he must protect her. "I don't know why they should. No one would think you awful,"* he said. *"I mean, there are people and people. Your Dad looks awfully decent, for instance."*

"Oh yes!" said Holly *fervently; "he is."*

When school friends of mine or my sisters' met my father, they always said the same thing. Everybody liked my father, for in the artificial world of 'Forsythia' with all its social conventions, stiff upper lip guardedness—all traits that my mother had, at least to the outer world—my father was genuine. In his rather shy, unpretentious and slightly downtrodden way, he always made people comfortable—really feel 'at home'. It was fitting on his death that so many alluded to this. His wry wit, challenging advice, keen mind, and the twinkle in his eye were missed by many, especially his fellow members of the Worshipful Company of Barbers. Peter Durrant, the clerk of the company at the time of his passing, wrote:

'It's just not going to be the same not having your father with

*us for Court meetings and social functions—he always was
so lively, so alert, so determined to enjoy himself, but at the
same time always willing to do his bit to make certain everything went well here at the Hall. Right to the very end he was
always prepared to act as host for external guests and they
always wrote to say what a perfect host he had been, firing
on all cylinders and with that marvelous twinkle in his eye for
which he is famous.'*

Most of my adult life I have been away from my family. I lived in
Ireland for sixteen years and have spent nearly forty years in the United
States of America. Often, I find myself answering questions about my
family to persons who will never be likely to meet them. Almost any
time I speak of my father, or my beloved sisters, a lump forms in my
throat and tears well in my eyes. There is to me, as there was to Holly,
something very special about Father, who like 'Young Jolyon', was not
a typical 'Forsyte' although very much of 'Forsythia'. Some people are
remembered as captains of commerce; for bravery in the armed forces;
or for public service in local and national politics. My father was not
one of them—somewhat downtrodden for a 'Forsyte' stepped upon by
more aggressive 'Forsytes'—but he was remembered, for he touched
people's lives for who he was.

Val reflected on his own father and that pathetic scene in the
Pandemonium with Crum. He then proceeded to vent his feelings about
his relatives—*how fearfully careful they were; not sportsmen a bit*—too
guarded; too rigid in their conventions; too sure of themselves.

Val resisted a desire to run his arm through Holly's.

"Show me around? *What's your brother like?"* he asked.

*Holly led the way on to the terrace and down to the lawn without
answering. How describe Jolly, who, ever since she remembered
anything, had been her lord, master, and ideal?*

"Does he sit on you?" *said Val shrewdly. "I shall be knowing him
at Oxford."* There was little response. He changed the subject. *"Have
you any horses?"*

Holly nodded. "Would you like to see the stables?"

"Rather! Horses are ripping, aren't they? My dad—" he stopped.

"Yes?" said Holly.

"Oh! I don't know—he's often gone a mucker over them. I'm jolly keen on them too—riding and hunting. I like racing awfully, as well. I should like to be a gentleman rider."

At the stables, he plucked up courage to ask her to ride with him in Richmond Park the following day.

Holly clasped her hands. "Oh yes! I simply love riding."

In my family it was my sister Sally who loved riding, at least as a teenager in those very last days of 'Forsythia'. Diane never wanted to ride much, although she had sat a horse in Scotland with my cousins. At the time most 'Forsyte' girls get this urge, she was suffering from those two bouts of peritonitis and rather withdrew from conventional teenage curiosity. Sally, however, was a member of 'The Pony Club' and learned to ride under the guidance of horsy, upper-class-women at a riding school in Keston, Kent. I remember one summer holiday we all went with her to settle her in to a Pony Club camp at Edenbridge. However, of the three of us, it was I who eventually became the horseman, and more by accident, like my father at those officers' training camps, than through 'Forsyte' training.

Apart from donkey rides in childhood one summer when my cousins from Scotland were at The Breach and Grandpop hired two donkeys for us all, I first sat a horse in Northern Ireland. I was staying with a school friend from Tonbridge and his sister had her own horse. I was quite keen on the girl, and she let me ride Stormy. There followed a vacation with another school friend on the Isle of Wight. We rode horses there on the downs under the watchful eye of a Colonel Tremble. However, I really learned to ride when I was the estate manager of Tullamaine Castle in Ireland, after I came down from Cambridge. Yes, seeing 'Forsytes' went up to Oxford or Cambridge, on graduation they came down! I exercised hunters and after riding to hounds for ten years, eventually in Missouri, I owned a saddlebred—Amadeus.

At the Robin Hill stables, Val Dartie was introduced to the aging dog, Balthasar. He rather slowly followed them back up over the lawn to that old oak tree.

"Balthasar's so old," Holly said, *"awfully old, nearly as old as I am. Poor old boy! He's devoted to dad. When grandfather died, he wouldn't eat for two days. He saw him die, you know—right here."*

"Was that Uncle Jolyon? Mother always said he was a topper."

"He was," said Holly simply.

After Val suggested they might ride out together, he learned that Holly rode Fairy in Richmond Park most days.

In the house, Soames and no-longer-young Jolyon were having tea. They were trying to be polite to each other, but it was hard to let past prejudice go.

"And how's Uncle James?" Jolyon asked.

"Thanks, very shaky."

"We're a wonderful family. Aren't we? The other day I was calculating the average age of the ten old Forsytes from my father's family bible. I make it eighty-four already, and five still living. They ought to beat the record?"

Family bibles seemed to end when 'Forsythia' ended. Our family bibles belonged to our grandparents and great-grandparents, who religiously filled in all deaths, births, marriages and christenings on their appropriate pages in beautiful copper plate script. After Suez, in 1956, nobody seemed to bother any more. If it were not for our family bibles I would not have known that Granny Mabs lost her son, John Collings, within days of birth, and my mother the brother who would have been my uncle. The loss was never spoken of. I would not have known that two of my great-great-uncles went out to Australia in the Ballarat gold rush, or that there had been a series of Longley twins.

"We aren't the men they were, you know," Jolyon *added.* *"We may live to their age, perhaps, but self consciousness is a handicap, you know, and that's the difference between us. We've lost conviction. How and when self consciousness was born I never can make out. My father had a little, but I don't believe any other of the old Forsytes ever had a scrap. Never to see yourself as others see you, it's a wonderful preservative. The whole history of the last century is in the difference between us. And between us and you."*

Jolyon looked at his daughter and young Val Dartie. *"There'll be— another difference. I wonder what."*

Soames smiled. 'Do you really think I shall admit that I'm not their equal, or that I've got to give up anything, especially life,' and like my Granny Mabs, he said, *"We must go, if we're to catch our train."*

At the front door Val *gave Holly's slim brown hand a long and surreptitious squeeze.* *"Look out for me to-morrow,"* he whispered; *"three o'clock. I'll wait for you in the road; it'll save time. We'll have a ripping ride."*

He gazed back at her from the Lodge gate, and, but for the principles of a man about town, would have waved his hand.

Soames looked back just once. *'What an age ago!'* he thought. *'I don't want to see* Irene, I *said to Jolyon. Was that true? I may have to.'*

CHAPTER EIGHT

JOLYON PROSECUTES TRUSTEESHIP

Jolyon decided to see Irene, but rather in the hope that she would not co-operate. *'I dislike* Soames,' he thought. *'I dislike him to the very roots of me. And that's lucky, it'll make it easier for me to back his wife.'* Half artist and half Forsyte, a little smile became settled in his beard. *'Ironical that Soames should come down* to Robin Hill—*to this house, built for himself! How he had gazed and gaped at this ruin of his past intention; furtively nosing at the walls and stairway, appraising everything! I believe the fellow even now would like to be living here. He could never leave off longing for what he once owned! Well, I must act somehow or other; but it's a bore—a great bore.'*

In London, he disliked the new motor cars and cabs. *'They've come to stay,'* he thought, *'Just so much more rattling round of wheels and general stink.'* Jolyon *was one of those rather rare liberals who object to anything new when it takes a material form.* My father was the same. He had philosophical and religious views that were liberal in the extreme. He held views on social justice that belonged more to our generation than his, but when it came to technical and material progress he had caution and doubt, like his father before him. My father waited until new technology was proven and tested before he accepted it. Although many ventured into television in that last decade of 'Forsythia', especially to see the coronation of Her Majesty Queen Elizabeth the Second in 1953, my father did not. In fact, as aforementioned, he did not purchase a television until well into the 1960s. There was no television at home throughout my childhood. We listened, as a family, to the radio, which throughout his life my father refused to call by any other name than the wireless—something that I then inherited from him. Again, too, he waited several years after color television became the rage to advance into that technology.

On my father's death, Past Master Chris Sprague of the Worshipful Company of Barbers noticed these traits. He wrote:

> 'Charles had an extremely sharp mind with well-informed
> and sometimes quite liberal views on many matters. He often
> hankered after the standards of behaviour in times past, as do
> many of us, but made an impassioned appeal to the Court of
> the Barber's Company in favour of the admission of women to
> the Livery. The Court obviously heeded his words.'

With some discomfort, now not so young Jolyon Forsyte could sense the changing times despite his liberal views. *The old century which had seen the plant of individualism flower so wonderfully was setting in a sky orange with coming storms. Rumours of war added to the briskness of a London turbulent at the close of the summer holidays. He instructed his driver to get down to the river quickly, out of the traffic, desiring to look at the water through the mellowing screen of plane trees. At the little block of flats which stood back some fifty yards from the Embankment, he told the cabman to wait, and went up to the first floor.*

Yes, Mrs. Heron was at home!

Irene *appeared to him not a day older, with* her *soft dark eyes and dark gold hair, with outstretched hand and a little smile.* They complimented each other on their retained youth.

"That's one thing about painting," Jolyon said. *"It keeps you young. Titian lived to ninety-nine, and had to have plague to kill him off. Do you know the first time I ever saw you I thought of a picture by him?"*

"When did you see me for the first time?"

"In the Botanical Gardens."

"How did you know me if you'd never seen me before?"

"By someone who came up to you."

Thoughts of Bosinney raced between them, *but her face did not change; and she said quietly: "Yes; many lives ago."*

"You remember my cousin Soames?"

He saw her smile faintly at that whimsicality, and at once went on:
"He came to see me the day before yesterday! He wants a divorce. Do
you?"

"After twelve years? It's rather late. Won't it be difficult?"

Jolyon looked hard into her face. "Unless..." he said.

"Unless I have a lover now. But I have never had one since."

Thoughts of Bosinney flashed between them again.

"But if you were to love again?"

"I should love." In that simple answer she seemed to sum up the
whole philosophy of one on whom the world had turned its back.

"Well, is there anything that you would like me to say to him?"

"Only that I'm sorry he is not free. He had his chance once. I don't
know why he didn't take it."

"Because he was a Forsyte; we never part with things, you know,
unless we want something in their place."

Irene smiled. "Don't you, Cousin Jolyon?—I think you do."

"Of course, I'm a bit of a mongrel—not quite a pure Forsyte. I never
take the halfpennies off my cheques, I put them on."

"Well, what does Soames want in place of me now?"

"I don't know; perhaps children."

She was silent for a little, looking down.

"Yes," she murmured; "it's hard. I would help him to be free if I
could."

After his visit, Jolyon immediately told his cab driver to head to
the Poultry, to the offices of Forsyte, Bustard and Forsyte. *In front of*
the Houses of Parliament and in Whitehall, newsvendors were calling:
"Grave situation in the Transvaal! Read all 'bout it."

In the 1950s, newsvendors still called out the headlines as they sold
their evening papers, mostly *The Evening Standard*, to businessmen
pouring out of their city offices for the homeward commute on the
tube—the London Underground—or from the great railway termini.
Like my father in those days, there were still many 'Forsytes' who did
not have television, and these evening papers were every bit as important
as the *Times* and the *Telegraph* in the morning. In their cockney voices,
the vendors always stated the obvious after shouting out the evening's
drama—"Read all 'bout it!"

Soames Forsyte was now the only partner in the firm that had
absorbed the offices of 'Tooting and Bowles'; his father, James, had
retired six years ago and never came into the office these days, and old

Bustard *dropped off, worn out, as many believed, by the suit of 'Fryer versus Forsyte', more in Chancery than ever and less likely to benefit its beneficiaries.* As mentioned, Dickens made mention of these cases in Chancery on several occasions, of which his most famous was that of 'Jondyce versus Jondyce' in *Bleak House.* This aspect of the law bothered him with his reformer's zeal. Smithfield Market was close to the Poultry, which was named after the medieval market, and close by, was another narrow street I remember well from my childhood, running from the market area to Holborn—Chancery Lane, no doubt named after these long legal proceedings.

Like Soames, who now was the sole practitioner of the law at Forsyte, Bustard and Forsyte, the Longley family had long had exclusive ownership of their three venerable old firms along the ornate avenues of the poultry and meat markets of Smithfield. The names of earlier ownership and partnership survived, however, throughout our family's time, Campbell, Key, Weatherley and Potter being mere names from the past.

At his office in the Poultry, Soames *was drawing out a list of holdings in Consols, which in view of the rumours of war* in Africa *he was going to advise his companies to put on the market at once, before other companies did the same. He looked round sidelong* when Jolyon entered.

"How are you? Just one minute. Sit down, won't you?"

"I have seen her," Jolyon explained.

Soames frowned.

"Well?"

"I was to tell you she is sorry you are not free. Twelve years is a long time. You know your law a lot better than I do, and what chance it gives you."

The ball was back in Soames' court. To legally get the divorce he needed his honor would be brought into scandal.

Suddenly Soames said: "I can't go on like this. I tell you, I can't go on like this."

"Surely," Jolyon said, *"it lies within yourself. A man can always put these things through if he'll take it on himself."* No doubt he thought again of how scandal had ostracized him while he lived with Helene 'in sin' until such time as Frances, June's mother, had died.

Soames sensed a lack of sympathy from his cousin.

"*Your father took an interest in her—why, goodness knows! And I suppose you do too? It seems to me that one only has to do another person a wrong to get all the sympathy. I don't know in what way I was to blame—I've never known. I always treated her well. I gave her everything she could wish for. I wanted her. After all,*" he *said with a sort of glum fierceness, "she was my wife.*"

'*There it is!*' thought Jolyon. '*Ownerships! Well, we all own things, But—human beings! Pah!*'

Jolyon got up.

"*Good-bye,*" he *said curtly.*

"*Good-bye,*" returned *Soames.*

Sensitive as he was, Jolyon did not feel comfortable having played his part as their go-between. From *Waterloo Station, all the way down in the train he thought of Irene in her lonely flat, and of Soames in his lonely office, and of the strange paralysis of life that lay on them both.* '*In chancery!*' he thought. '*Both their necks in chancery—and hers so pretty!*'

CHAPTER NINE

VAL HEARS THE NEWS

Val was experiencing *the stirrings* of poetry, *which he was feeling for the first time in his nineteen years. The liberty* with the forward *Cynthia Dark,* his first girlfriend *that almost mythical embodiment of rapture; the Pandemonium,* despite his recent memory of his father, *with the women of uncertain age—both seemed to Val completely 'off', fresh* now *from communion with this new, shy, dark-haired young cousin of his.* His ride with Holly had been a complete success, even to the point of cowing him somewhat as if in comparison *only his boots had shone throughout their two-hour companionship.*

He took out his new gold 'hunter'—present from James—and looked not at the time, but at sections of his face in the glittering back of its opened case. He had a temporary spot over one eyebrow, and it displeased him, for it must have displeased her.

During that last decade of 'Forsythia', on Grandpop's death, I inherited a double 'hunter' pocket watch on a gold chain with my grandfather's seal on the other end— CWL engraved backwards so as to make an impression in the red wax with which late Victorian and Edwardian envelopes were sealed. It had been given to him by my great-grandfather, Oliver Longley, probably as a gift on his leaving Tonbridge School in July 1907. I treasured this watch. Like Val, I could open the back casing and use it as a mirror in fine gold, at the same time one could open the front cover of pure gold to reveal the inner gold face of the watch. It was heavy—double 'hunters' were heavy—the crown jewels of gold pocket watches. Very sadly, I lost this precious watch in 1981. At the time, I was a cruise director with Royal Viking Line, based in San Francisco. A passenger had given me a prestigious 'Concorde' bag. The watch, with some other jewelry and some last minute clothing items was in this bag after a brief vacation at Big Sur with my Japanese girlfriend, Kazumi Masuda, on completion of a cruising tour of duty. The bag was supposed to be hand baggage, but at San Francisco airport they asked me to check it in as I already had two other pieces of hand baggage. I was flying from San Francisco to New York. The 'Concorde' bag never arrived in New York and was never traced.

'Concorde' is also significant as a 'Forsythia' dream. In the last decade of 'Forsythia', and in particular after the loss of British control over the Suez canal, jet travel was seen as the future lifeline of the Empire, expected to replace the great ocean liners. British engineers had developed the first long haul jet plane—the Comet. I remember cut away drawings of a Comet in the only periodical comic we were allowed at Newlands—the *Eagle*. The jet was designed to fly from London to India and on from India to Singapore and Australia. It became real for me when my cousin, John Cuthbertson, flew out by Comet jet to Bombay for his summer vacation with his parents, my Great-uncle Bert and Aunt Ruby, in the mid-1950s. Right after developing the Comet, however, British and French Engineers worked on an even more impressive supersonic jet—the Concorde. The technology was late 1950s, but way ahead of its time—probably to this day the most impressive passenger airplane ever built. However, just as it was developed, its purpose collapsed. The Concorde was a 'Forsythia' dream to link Empire and burgeoning Commonwealth peoples. The dream died with the Empire, as did 'Forsythia'. Concorde aircraft flew until the end of the century, but they were never commercially successful, especially as Britain took second place to the United States in a post-'Forsythia' world. The Americans never purchased Concordes and Britain and France kept the prestigious jets flying for no other reason than pride. They were a financial disaster, but that late 'Forsythia' technology remained, for four decades, ahead of its time. Neither the Russians nor the Americans, the two post-imperial powers, ever built a supersonic airliner to compare with this Anglo-French achievement.

Americans, however, liked the prestige of being Concorde passengers—flights were very expensive. A 'Concorde' bag, even if a gift to me from a Royal Viking passenger, smelled of money. Thus, I lost both the bag and my grandfather's double 'hunter' gold pocket watch.

A year or two later, I did acquire another 'Concorde' bag when I myself flew Concorde from New York to London on a surprise Christmas visit to my family. I actually called my family on the day before Christmas in the early afternoon, London time, from the Concorde Lounge at Kennedy International Airport in New York, and wished them a "Happy Christmas." I did not tell them I was flying Concorde or even coming to England for Christmas. Four and a half hours later, I rang the front door bell in Beckenham after a quick, just under three-hour, flight!

As for the loss of my double 'hunter' gold pocket watch—I replaced it with a nice new gold Wartham that I bought in New York, but it was no double hunter. At the end of its chain, I replaced Grandpop's seal with a gold cigar cutter that I had been given in Ireland and a fob on the center chain that was an heirloom of my Japanese girlfriend—a really interesting little miniature compass in a square gold case. The ensemble graces waistcoats of my formal dress to this day and on one occasion proved to be quite useful. *Queen Elizabeth 2* was a large ship and still structured somewhat as if it was divided into classes that were rigid at the time it was built. Although, by 1989 when I became her cruise director, the class structure had virtually been eliminated on board the great liner, there were anomalies harking back to that past such as stairwells and elevators that only connected first-class areas, and others that only connected tourist-class areas. A rather disgruntled passenger came through the receiving line for the Captain's Welcome Aboard Cocktail party. After shaking the captain's hand he came up to me and said: "I hate this ship, you need a bloody compass to get around." I pulled up the Japanese fob on my watch chain and said playfully: "I've got one, sir, right here." The gentleman laughed, and from then on came to like the ship!

In 2008, when my own father passed away, I found among his possessions a gold pocket watch—not a double 'hunter' but a ladies' pocket watch. It was not as heavy as my grandfathers' watch, but it was quite a bit older. Engraved on the back were the intertwined initials MS—Martha Southon—my great-great-grandmother, Oliver Longley's mother and Grandpop's grandmother.

Val Darte closed the gold cover of his 'hunter'. He knew it would be difficult for him to see Holly again before Oxford. He had to *go back* to Littlehampton on the morrow, and to Oxford on the twelfth—'to that beastly exam, too.'

He should write to her, however, and she had promised to answer. Did Val have a signet seal on the end of his 'hunter' watch chain with which to impressively seal those envelopes?

'At least,' Val thought, 'there is a chance she will visit Oxford to see her brother Jolly.'

With that thought in mind, he was surprised *when he came down, speckless after his bath,* to find *his mother scrupulous in a low evening dress, and, to his annoyance, his Uncle Soames. They stopped talking when he came in* the drawing room; *then his uncle said:*

"He'd better be told."

"Your father," his mother said, *"your father, my dear boy, has—is not at Newmarket; he's on his way to South America. He—he's left us."*

Val thought of the good times with his father. *There were precious memories of tailors' shops and horses, tips at school, and general lavish kindness, when in luck.* He had not *always been the bounder of the Pandemonium promenade.*

"But why?"

The mask of his mother's face was all disturbed.

"All right, Mother, don't tell me! Only, what does it mean?"

"A divorce, Val, I'm afraid."

Val's thoughts raced. He recollected *his own eyes glued to the unsavoury details of many a divorce suit in the public Press. Himself, the girls, their name tarnished in the sight of his schoolfellows and of Crum, of the men at Oxford, of—Holly! Unbearable.*

"It won't be public, will it? Can't it be done quietly somehow? It's so disgusting for—for mother, and—and everybody."

"Everything will be done as quietly as it can, you may be sure," Soames reassured his nephew.

"Yes—but why is it necessary at all? Mother doesn't want to marry again."

Soames glanced at Winifred. *"Shall I tell him?"*

Clenching her lips, she nodded.

"Your father has always been a burden around your mother's neck. She has paid his debts over and over again; he has often been drunk, abused and threatened her; and now he is gone to Buenos Aires with a dancer. He took your mother's pearls to give to her."

In Val, *the Dartie and the Forsyte were struggling. For debts, drinks, dancers, he had a certain sympathy; but the pearls—no! That was too much.*

"You see," he heard Soames say, "we can't have it all begin over again. There's a limit."

"But—you're never going to bring out that about the pearls! I couldn't stand that—I simply couldn't!"

Winifred intervened as his mother:

No, no, Val—oh no! That's only to show you how impossible your father is!"

Val reached for a thin curved cigarette case that was concealed in his hip pocket. It was a silver gift from his father, who probably thought it would be 'chic' for his son at Oxford. These thin curved silver cigarette cases were the latest thing.

I inherited one from my Uncle John—John Hoby—my mother's unmarried cousin, the one who lived in Chatham and had shared Dickens' world with me. The uncle who had that terrace house full of antiques and little treasures, so much so that some in my family, especially seeing John had never married, considered pointers to his being 'precious', not helped by his rather high, unmanly voice.

The curved silver case was designed to mould the contour of the body in the pocket. The one I inherited was engraved with the initials H J H—Harry John Hoby. It had belonged to John's father, my Great-uncle Harry. Harry Hoby had married Grandpa Jack Collings' sister Babs after she had broken off her engagement to my great-uncle, Bert Cuthbertson. Harry and Babs were themselves very fastidious and I remember Granny Mabs once describing how Babs had made her maids polish the brass nail heads in the floorboards of their home. As John was their only child, this almost 'precious' love of beauty might have been passed on in the genes.

If so, I was certainly in part a beneficiary of John's taste. Not only did I inherit this interesting curved silver cigarette case that had belonged to his father, but also a magnificent nineteenth-century silver salt cellar, an unusual silver marrow spoon, a beautiful nineteenth-century set of Dickens' novels, and a priceless 1576 Geneva Bible.

My mother spent a lot of time with her cousin John on summer seaside holidays on the Kent coast in the 1920s and '30s, and our side of the Collings family remained in close touch with the Hoby family over the years. As we have seen, in 'Forsythia' divorce was a major scandal, and even a second marriage was treated with suspicion. After, my Great-aunt Babs died when I was quite young, Harry Hoby, who was a medical doctor, married again—a nurse named Iris. Other members of the Collings family, the Doggetts and my Great-aunt Dorrie, rarely if ever accepted Iris Hoby, and even John, very much his mother's boy, was somewhat skeptical about his stepmother. My mother and father always treated Iris with respect, however, and Dr. John Hoby and Iris were always welcome at our house.

In a way, this was history repeating itself in the Collings family. John Collings' second wife, 'Great-grandmother' Emma, to most of the family was suspect—the seamstress— in comparison with Harriet 'Penny' Massey—the aristocrat. Although, my family all liked Aunt Daphne's husband, Gordon Noble, I do remember hearing about marriages in registry offices in my childhood with reference to this being Uncle Gordon's second marriage. There was also always something slightly sinister about the fact that Aunt Daphne had stepchildren, Barry and Carol. Although they lived next door, I do not remember us ever entertaining Barry and Carol. It was almost as if they were ostracized, albeit very politely. In a way this was a subtle prejudice enhanced by the folklore of children's fairy tales and Christmas pantomimes—the nursery literature of 'Forsythia'— where stepmothers were always wicked and stepsisters ugly and unkind.

When Soames insisted that there should be no delay in his mother's divorce, Val became aware that his Uncle Soames had been married himself—*yes—he remembered now—there had been an Aunt Irene, and something had happened—something which people kept dark.*

Val knew he really couldn't sway his uncle and mother, but he expressed concern on their determination to proceed as soon as possible. *"I'd like to know when it'll be. It's my first term* at Oxford, *you know. I don't want to be up there when it comes off."*

"Can't tell," Soames said, *"not for months. We must get restitution first."*

'What the deuce is that?' thought Val. 'What silly brutes lawyers are! Not for months! I know one thing: I'm not going to dine in.'

Looking to escape, he boldly said: *"Awfully sorry, Mother, I've got to go out to dinner now."*

Short of funds with only *eighteen-pence* in his pocket, he realized he could not dine out, but he made his way to *his grandfather's in Park Lane.* It would be better than Uncle Timothy's. *At his grandfather's he would probably get* a good *dinner on the spur of the moment. At Timothy's they gave you a jolly good feed when they expected you, not otherwise.* Besides, he got on very well with his Granny Emily and he needed to confide in her.

Dropping in on ones relatives was not generally favored in 'Forsythia', but with tested ground, it was possible, especially with grandparents. While I was at Tonbridge, on Sunday afternoons I often rode my bicycle the eighteen odd miles to The Breach. Like Val Dartie, I knew that I would get a good spur of the moment high tea—ham and eggs, and strawberries and cream in season. I also knew that Grandpop would drive me back to Tonbridge in time for Sunday evening chapel. My mother was a stickler about dropping in on people, however, and liked visits to relatives to be arranged many days in advance. Uncle Gyles was the same way, or so I found out, when I was in Paris with an earlier Irish girlfriend, and we dropped in on him at his flat. Aunt Ginette was not there and Uncle Gyles apparently was not pleased to have to entertain us, although he did so generously. For many weeks, however, it rumbled around the family how I had dropped in on Gyles in Paris, Aunt Ginette seeming to be the one who was most upset.

Val *rang the bell.*

The butler let him in.

"Any dinner for me, d'you think?"

"They're just going in Master Val. Mr. Forsyte will be very glad to see you. He was saying at lunch he never saw you nowadays."

At the great dining-table, shortened to its utmost, under which so many fashionable legs had rested, James sat at one end, Emily at the other. Val sat *halfway between them.*

"Why didn't you let us know? There's only saddle of mutton. Champagne, Warmson," said Emily.

Lowering his voice while his grandfather and Warmson were in discussion about sugar in the soup, Val *said to Emily:*

"It's pretty brutal at home, Granny. I suppose you know."

"Yes, dear boy, but *hush, we're keeping it from your grandfather."*

James' voice sounded from the other end.

"What's that? What are you talking about?"

"About Val's college," returned Emily.

"Well," said James, and the soup in his spoon dribbled over, "you'll have a good allowance but you must keep within it."

"How much will it be, Grandfather?"

"*Three hundred and fifty; it's too much.*"

Val sighed.

" *I had next to nothing at your age. I don't know what your young cousin has,*" continued *James;* "*he's up there. His father's a rich man.*"

"*Aren't you?*" *asked Val hardily.*

"*I've got so many expenses. Your father*"— *and he was silent.*

Val changed the subject and they discussed Robin Hill.

"*Was that house built for Uncle Soames?*" Val asked at length.

"*I wish you'd tell me about him, Granny. What became of Aunt Irene? Is she still going?* Uncle Soames *seems awfully worked up about something to-night.*"

The word Irene caught James' ear.

"*Who's been seeing her? I knew we hadn't heard the last of that. Is Soames getting a divorce?*"

"*Nonsense,*" *said Emily.*

With that the conversation died as Warmson served.

James gave Val an extra twenty pounds.

In the hall as Val prepared to leave, he asked his mother about Uncle Soames again, and why he was so keen on his mother getting a divorce.

"*Your Uncle Soames is a lawyer, my dear boy. He's sure to know best.*"

"*Is he,*" *muttered Val.* "*But what did become of Aunt Irene? I remember she was jolly good-looking.*"

"*She—er*"— *said Emily,* "*behaved very badly. We don't talk about it.*"

"*Well, I don't want everybody at Oxford to know about our affairs; it's a brutal idea. Why couldn't father be prevented without it being made public?*"

"*Your mother,*" *she said,* "*will be happier if she is quite free, Val. Good-night, my dear boy; and don't wear loud waistcoats up at Oxford, they're not the thing just now. Here's a little present.*"

With another five pounds in his hands, and a little warmth in his heart, for he was fond of his grandmother, Val *went out into Park Lane.*

With all that money in his pocket an impulse to 'see life' beset him; but he had not gone forty yards in the direction of Picadilly when Holly's shy face, and her eyes with an imp dancing in their gravity, came up before him. 'No, dash it!' he thought. 'I'm going home!'

Chapter Ten

Soames Entertains the Future

On Sunday, Annette and her mother, Madame Lamotte, came down on the train to Mapledurham to visit Soames at his country house. *The weather was lovely, and summer lingered below the yellowing leaves.* Soames had made certain that everything was perfect—every little detail. *This visit had been planned to induce in Annette and her mother a due sense of his possessions, so that they should be ready to receive with respect any overture he might later be disposed to make.*

With his own hands he put flowers around his little houseboat, and equipped the punt, placing those Chinese-looking cushions, popular at the turn of the century in the early days of Edwardian 'Forsythia'. I remember photographs of similar cushions surrounding my grandmother, Catherine Amy Longley, as she lay back in the hammock at The Breach in the latter days of Edwardian 'Forsythia'.

Looking at those cushions, Soames had a desire to take Annette out in the punt alone, but it would not be proper. *He dressed with great care, making himself neither too young nor too old, very thankful that his hair was still thick and smooth and had no grey in it. Three times he went up to his picture gallery. If they had any knowledge at all,* his guests *must see at once that his collection alone was worth at least thirty thousand pounds.* He inspected the bedroom that he hoped one day would be hers.

His wife! If only the whole thing could be settled out of hand, and there was not the nightmare of this divorce to be gone through first. They did not even know that he was married.

At the station, his guests were impeccably dressed. *What taste Frenchwomen had!* The 'Forsyte' love-hate relationship with all things French welled within Soames. *Madame Lamotte was in black with touches of lilac color, Annette in greyish lilac linen, with cream coloured gloves and hat.*

Soames *had ordered the lunch with intense consideration; the wine was a special sauterne, the whole appointments of the meal perfect, the coffee served on the veranda super-excellent.*

'Forsytes' were not coffee drinkers, indeed the English in general were not coffee drinkers in that era, but the French—Soames needed to impress his French guests. One compliment that Granny Longley always gave to my mother, however, was on her coffee—Coffee Anglaise with lots of sugar and milk—hardly French. However, I suspect this was probably a back handed compliment meant more to express that self-imposed difference between English and continental tastes.

After coffee, *Madame Lamotte accepted crème de menthe; Annette refused. Madame was in sedate French raptures. "Adorable! Le soleil est si bon! How everything is chic, is it not, Annette? Monsieur is a real Monte Cristo."*

Soames then took them on the river, *a short way towards Pangbourne, drifting slowly back, with every now and then an autumn leaf dropping on Annette or on her mother's black amptitude. And Soames was not happy, worried by the thought: 'How—when—where—can I say— what?' To tell them that he was married might jeapordise his every chance; yet, if he did not definitely make them understand that he wished for Annette's hand, it would be dropping into some other clutch before he was free to claim it.*

Pangbourne and Mapledurham are on that wonderful stretch of the River Thames not too far from Henley, home of England's most prestigious rowing regatta, and to this day somewhat of a fossil from 'Forsythia'. The river here was immortalized in Jerome K Jerome's *Three Men in a Boat*, written just a decade before, in 1889. In my childhood, Pangbourne also took on special meaning. As mentioned, the second master at Newlands and the man who really ran the school, was Captain T.D. Manning of the Royal Naval Voluntary Reserve. He was well connected with many prominent World War II naval officers whose sons were at Newlands. There was a strong naval bent to the school, and the Royal Naval Training School at Pangbourne, in its guise as a minor public school for cadets expected to take up naval commissions, was to be the home for further education of many of my contemporaries at Newlands. The Royal Navy had become, since Admiral Nelson defeated the French at Trafalgar in 1805, the senior service—something engrained in us in our childhood by a brand of cigarettes of the same name. This slight hegemony of the Royal Navy within 'Forsythia', over the army and newly won heroism of the Royal Air Force, was largely because the Royal Navy, in a pre-missile world, was the protector of the sea lanes of the Empire—'Forsythia's' precious lines of commerce.

At tea, which his French guests *took with lemon, Soames spoke of the Transvaal.*

"There'll be war," he said.

"Ces pauvres gens bergers!" Could they not be left to themselves?

Soames smiled—the question seemed to him absurd. Surely as a woman of business she understood that the British could not abandon their legitimate commercial interests.

But Madame Lamotte found the English, even Soames, *were a little hypocrite. They were talking of justice and the Uitlanders, not of business.*

"The Boers are only half civilised," remarked Soames; "they stand in the way of progress. It will never do to let our suzerainty go."

"What does that mean to say? Suzerainty! What a strange word!"

Soames became eloquent, roused by these threats to the principle of possession, and stimulated by Annette's eyes fixed on him.

"I think Monsieur is right. They should be taught a lesson."

Annette *was sensible!* Soames then moderated. He knew he had to capture them both, even if it was in his plan that he would make Madame an offer on the restaurant that she could not refuse in order to clear the way for the mother's return to Paris and Annette's graduation into the ranks of England's 'Forsythia'.

He showed them his picture gallery. *He waited with awe to see how they would view the jewel of his collection—an Israels whose price he had watched ascending till he was now almost certain it had reached top value, and would be better on the market again,* but *they did not view it at all.*

At the end of the gallery was a Meissonier of which Soames *was rather ashamed—Meissonier was so steadily going down. Madame Lamotte stopped before it.* The French artist registered with her.

"Meissonier! Ah! What a jewel!" she cried out delightfully.

Soames took advantage of that moment. Very gently touching Annette's arm, he said:

"How do you like my place, Annette?"

"Who would not like it? It is so beautiful!"

"Perhaps some day"— Soames said, but checked himself. *'If I hold off,' he thought, 'it will tantalise her'* and there was still the matter of the divorce.

Madame Lamotte was still in front of the Meissonier. Despite her pro-Boer French revolutionary politics, he had won her over. He felt he had won them both over.

He drove to the station with them, and saw them into the train. To the tightened pressure of his hand it seemed that Annette's fingers responded just a little; her face smiled at him. "Bon soir, monsieur."

Soames sent the carriage home and walked. *The poplars sighed in the darkness; an owl hooted. Shadows deepened in the waters. To know what was in her mind! The French—they were like cats—one could tell nothing! But—how pretty! What a mother for his heir! And he thought, with a smile, of his family and their surprise at a French wife, and their curiosity, and of the way he would play with it and buffet it—confound them!*

For most of their lives my parents remained in their 'Forsyte' world even though it was vanishing all around them. Did I confound them when, first I introduced them to my Japanese partner, Kazumi, and then my German fiancée and later wife, Bettine; and after my divorce, my father met my American partner, Nicole? In my parents' minds, after two world wars, was I introducing them to 'Boers'—the enemies of the Empire! However, the world had changed.

Soames thought out loud, *'I must be free. I won't hang about any longer. I'll go and see Irene. If you want things done, do them yourself. I must live again—live and move and have my being.'* And in echo to that *queer biblicality* that so many 'Forsytes' could almost set their watch by in their church pews, *church-bells chimed the call* in Mapledurham *to* Sunday *evening prayer.*

CHAPTER ELEVEN

AND VISITS THE PAST

Soames *left his hansom* cab *on the Embankment uncertain of the block of flats where he knew* Irene *lived. He found it hiding behind a much larger mansion; and having read the name, 'Mrs. Irene Heron'—Heron, forsooth! Her maiden name: so she used that again, did she? —he stepped back into the road to look up at the windows of the first floor. Light was coming through in the corner flat, and he could hear a piano being played.*

Shivers of anticipation ran through him. Then, *the lawyer stirred within him. Was he doing a foolish thing? Ought he not to have arranged a formal meeting in the presence of her trustee? No! Not before that fellow Jolyon, who sympathised with her! Never!*

When the door was opened to him his sensations were regulated by the scent which came—that perfume—from away back in the past, bringing muffled remembrance: fragrance of a drawing-room he used to enter, of a house he used to own.

"Say, Mr. Forsyte," he said to the maid. *"Your mistress will see me, I know." He had thought this out; she would think it was Jolyon.*

The music ceased, the maid said from the doorway:

"Will you walk in, sir?"

"You!" he heard her whisper.

Suddenly, *a kind of defensive irony welled up in* Soames.

"You have not changed," he said.

It is a natural opening gambit of humanity to make this flattering remark regardless of change. My mother was a mistress of it. "Oh, you haven't changed a bit," was a nervous 'Forsyte' gesture for establishing reunion. Usually it breaks the ice and renders the recipient somewhat coyly 'at home'. This was not the case with Irene, who exuded a new confidence.

"No! What have you come for?"

"To discuss things."

"I have heard what you want from your cousin."

"Well?"

"I am willing. I have always been."

"Perhaps you will be good enough, then, to give me information on which I can act. The law must be complied with."

Mutual incompatibility was not in 'Forsythia' a real ground for legal divorce. That inherited Christian ethic that marriage is made for life, demanded some infidelity or cruelty to give legality to any such proceedings—a third party—a breach of vows that had been made before God.

Irene, stabbed by her memory of Bosinney, firmly replied:

"I have none to give you that you don't know of."

"Twelve years! Do you suppose I can believe that?" Soames was desperate, because he knew twelve years without his pursuance of divorce rendered his case against Irene and Bosinney a hard one to get through the courts without bringing in his real motive—Annette.

"I don't suppose you'll believe anything I say," said Irene, *"but it's the truth."*

Soames looked at her hard. She had changed spiritually. There was more of her, as it were, something of activity and daring, where there had been sheer passive resistance. 'Ah!' Soames thought, 'that's her independent income! Confound Uncle Jolyon!'

"Why didn't you let me provide for you? I would have in spite of everything. You are still my wife."

The effect of this last statement *was startling.*

Almost in anger, Soames repeated:

"You had better tell me. It's to your advantage to be free as well as mine. That old matter is too old."

"I have told you."

"Do you mean to tell me there has been nothing—nobody?"

"Nobody. You must go to your own life."

It was almost as if she knew.

"That won't do." Soames asserted. *"You deserted me. In common justice it's for you"*—

Coldly she replied, knowing she had the upper hand:

"Yes. Why didn't you divorce me then? Should I have cared?"

Hurt by wounded pride and her unbridled beauty, the trap to his possessiveness, Soames pleaded:

"Why couldn't you have made me a good wife?"

"Yes;" Irene replied. *"it was a crime to marry you. I have paid for it. You will find some way perhaps. You needn't mind my name, I have none to lose. Now I think you had better go."*

In a 'Forsyte' attempt to still show, despite his emotions, that he was a gentleman, educated at Marlborough to keep that stiff upper lip and 'play the game' by the rules of his class, he asked if they could shake hands.

A faint smile curved her lips. She held out her hand. It was cold to his rather feverish touch. 'She's made of ice,' he thought—'she was always made of ice.'

After he left, *memory, flown back to the first years of his marriage, played him torturing tricks. She had not deserved to keep her beauty— the beauty he had owned and known so well.*

She had spoiled his life, wounded his pride to death, defrauded him of a son. And yet the mere sight of her, cold and resisting as ever, had this power to upset him utterly! It was some damned magnetism that she had! So Bosinney—cursed be his memory!—had lived on all this time with her! Soames could not tell whether he was glad of that knowledge or no.

He stopped to buy a paper. A headline ran: 'Boers reported to repudiate suzerainty!' Suzerainty! 'Just like her!' he thought: 'she always did. Suzerainty! I still have it by rights. She must be awfully lonely in that wretched little flat.'

CHAPTER TWELVE

ON FORSYTE 'CHANGE

O n his way home Soames dropped into the Remove to check the
tape and see where his shares stood in these uncertain times.
Uncle Nicholas had put him up for this club and they ran into
each other there.

Nicholas passed a comment on Roger's funeral in that conversational
way of 'Forsytes'—*Went off all right. The thing was very well done.*
Then, quickly the subject turned to the Boers.

"*That fellow Chamberlain's driving the country into war. What do
you think?*"

"*Bound to come,*" *murmured Soames.*

"*House property will go down if there's war. You'll have trouble
with Roger's estate. I often told him he ought to get out of some of his
houses. He was an opinionated beggar.*"

Soames was amused at their unpreparedness as he *noted that
Consols were down seven-sixteenths since the morning.*

If there was, however, *a subject on which the Forsytes really agreed,
it was the character of Montague Dartie.*

"*They tell me at Timothy's,*" *said Nicholas, lowering his voice,* "*that
Dartie has gone off at last. That'll be a relief to your father. He was
a rotten egg. Winifred should have the tooth out, I should say. No use
preserving what's gone bad.*"

Soames, exacerbated by the interview he had just come through with Irene, replied shortly: *"I'm advising her."*

"Well," said Nicholas, *"the brougham's waiting. I must get home."*

Soames reflected on Irene. He even considered taking her back. *'What age was she? Nearly thirty-seven—not too old to have a child— not at all!* It would be easier than divorce, if what she had said was true— nobody in twelve years, only her memory of the wretched Bosinney.' He remembered how he had always treated her well on her birthday—given her things—*his gifts had meant a semblance of gratitude, a certain attempt at warmth,* a self-justification for his attempt to buy favor with his property. *'I could send her a present for her birthday. After all, we're Christians! Couldn't I—couldn't we join up again!'*

He uttered a deep sigh. Annette! Ah! but between him and Annette was the need for that wretched divorce suit. Why should he take the scandal on himself with his whole career as a pillar of the law at stake? Nothing but fresh misconduct on her part would avoid that scandal—*but she had denied it.* Why hadn't he taken action twelve years before? It would have been a lesser scandal.

As he walked toward Park Lane he encountered a commotion in Trafalgar Square. Newspaper men were shouting so loud it was hard to understand them, especially with their cockney accents.

"Payper! Special! Ultimatum by Krooger! Declaration of war!"

Soames bought a *paper.*

'The Boers are committing suicide' he thought. *'Is there anything still I ought to sell?'* If so, he had missed the chance—there would certainly be a slump in the city tomorrow, but he was better prepared than most the Forsytes.

"What do you think of it?" he said to Warmson when he got to his father's house.

The butler ceased passing a hat-brush over the silk top *hat Soames had taken off.*

"Well, sir, they 'aven't a chance, of course; but I'm told they're very good shots. I've got a son in the Inniskillings."

"You, Warmson, why I didn't know you were married."

"No, sir. I don't talk of it. I expect he'll be going out."

The butler in a 'Forsyte' household was head of the servants 'below stairs'. He was looked up to and respected by his staff, whom he sometimes ruled with an iron rod. He knew almost everything about his master, mistress, and their family, but he was never to reveal it. The greatest asset of the perfect butler was his loyalty. For this reason discretion was the tool of his trade. Lesser servants, ladies' maids in particular, discussed much of their private lives with their mistress, and even in the latter days of 'Forsythia' when domestics were a lot less numerous, charwomen and cooks chattered away to their mistress about almost every facet of their family life. I sometimes thought that our own domestics in that last decade of 'Forsythia' were as much employed by my mother as companions than as housekeepers. They would sit over cups of tea together, stirring spoons in the liquid for half the morning as they revealed their lives to my mother. Then, there was Mrs. Jackson, my mother's weekly hairdresser, who was the fount of gossip.

Good butlers, however, were discreet. They discussed nothing with others about 'their' employers, and revealed nothing to either their employers or the household staff about their personal lives. It was an unwritten code of conduct that was magnificently portrayed in the BBC television series of nostalgia that made such an impact at about the same time as *The Forsyte Saga—Upstairs, Downstairs*—portraying the lives of the fictitious Bellamy family and their staff in the Edwardian heyday of 'Forsythia'.

Butlers never went by their first names. The other servants, as in *Upstairs, Downstairs* referred to the butler as Mr. 'udson. The Bellamys always referred to him as Hudson. And then, of course, there was P.G. Woodhouse's quintessential Jeeves. Recently, the PBS Masterpiece Theater mini-series *Downton Abbey* expresses the same hierarchy with reference to Carson, who keeps things close to his chest as butler, but can also be a fount of sound advice.

Warmson had been the butler to James Forsyte and his family and household for many years, but still Soames was unaware that Warmson was a married man and had a son who was old enough to be sent to war, in the Inniskillings—an Irish regiment.

Indeed, *the slighter shock Soames had felt on discovering that he knew so little of one whom he felt he knew so well was lost in the slight shock of discovering that the war might touch one personally.*

Two of the Haymans, his Aunt Susan's offspring, *he had heard were in some Yeomanry or other. And Archibald, he remembered, had once on a time joined the Militia, but had given it up because his father, Nicholas, had made such a fuss about his 'wasting his time peacocking about in a uniform.' Recently he had heard that young Nicholas's eldest, very young Nicholas, had become a volunteer.* Forsytes might go to war. His nephew Val might even go to war.

He thought of falling shares and house prices, too. *Opening the landing window* on his way up to his father's room he heard the rumble from Piccadilly—the new sound of those motor cars. *'If these motor-cars increase, it'll affect house property, too,'* he thought.

When Soames reached his father's room he broke the news:

"All the noise, *it's not a fire. The Boers have declared war—that's all.*"

"*H'm!*" James muttered, "*I shan't live to see the end of this.*"

"*Nonsense, James! It'll be over by Christmas,*" Emily reassured him.

"*What do you know about it?*"

Both Soames and Emily *noted something beyond the usual in* James' *voice, something of real anxiety. It was as if he had said: 'I shall never see the old country peaceful and safe again. I shall have to die before I know she's won.'*

"*Mark my word,*" James continued, "*Consols will go to par. For all I know, Val may go and enlist.*"

This was where it hurt.

A whole generation of 'Forsytes' had grown up in the 'Pax Brittanica', the benign rule of the Empire of commerce. Soames and his generation were born during the time of the Crimean War and the Indian Mutiny, but had no recollection during their ensuing lives of war. Oh, there were rumblings in Ireland from time to time, but that was just the Irish— "Those paddies always like to scrap." There was that awful misjudgement at Rourke's Drift with the Zulus. At the other end of Africa there had been that business with the Mardi, but the great success of 'Forsythia' to both Soames' and James' generations was the blessed peace of the British Empire and the advance of commercial gain that it gave. The next generation, however, were threatened, first by the Boers and later by the Huns—those upstart Germans, who had only been a united nation since 1866—younger than the Americans! The threats became complete reality for twentieth-century 'Forsytes' in the debacle not only of the Boer War in South Africa, but of the Great War from 1914 to 1918, and a generation later in the Second World War. My grandfathers and my great-uncles were just too young to volunteer in the Boer War, but most of them found themselves in the trenches fourteen years later. Then, the children of those who survived, found themselves either as civilians, or soldiers, sailors, and airmen serving and suffering through the Second World War from 1939 to 1945. They fought for the king, the British Empire, and 'Forsythia'.

The afternoon following the news of the declaration of war by the Boers *witnessed the greatest crowd Timothy's had known for many a year.* Even Aunt Juley had her opinion about the war—an opinion based on the prejudices of most older 'Forsytes', whose parents had lived through the Napoleonic wars.

She supposed that her nephews in the Yeomanry *would be very busy now guarding the coast, though of course, the Boers had no ships. But one never knew what the French might do if they had the chance.*

Invasion across the English Channel had been the great fear of the British in the Napoleonic War at the beginning of the century now about to close. Great Britain had not been invaded since 1066, but the fear of a conquest from Normandy was never more real than to Juley's parents' generation. At that time, the last series of castles were built to defend the south coast—designed by an architect and engineer of Italian origin—Martello. These circular gun emplacement 'Martello' towers were built at regular intervals along the south coast from Dover to Southampton. There was one at Seaford when I was at school, still standing on the waterfront promenade buffeted by those 'Seaford' winds. As boys we wanted to play in the tower, but sinister signs and chains forbade us, announcing 'Danger—Keep out.' Throughout the nineteenth century, 'Forsytes', indeed, almost all British people, remained suspicious of the French—a suspicion that was also almost instinctive within the British peoples over the centuries where France had been the traditional foe for almost one thousand years.

"Miss June Forsyte," was announced.

June had not been at Timothy's in years—the forgotten member of the Forsyte family.

Aunts Juley and Hester were on their feet at once. Dear June—after all these years! And how well she was looking!

"We've just been saying, dear, how dreadful it is about these Boers! And what an impudent thing of that old Kruger!" Aunt Juley informed June.

"Impudent!" said June. *"I think he's quite right. What business have we to meddle with them? If he turned out all those wretched* profiteering *Uitlanders it would serve them right. They're only after money."*

The silence of sensation was broken by the composer and poetess, Roger's daughter, Francie.

"What? Are you a pro-Boer?"

Thus came into the language of that great class the expression "Pro-Boer" that was used throughout the remaining decades of 'Forsythia' to describe anyone who held an opposite viewpoint to that of the establishment.

At this precise moment, Soames was the next to arrive at Timothy's.

Gathered Forsytes became silent and curious, *for it was shrewdly suspected, if not quite known, that* Soames and June *had not met since that old and lamentable affair of her fiancé Bosinney with Soames's wife.*

"Dear June is so original," Aunt Juley said, thinking she was breaking the tension. *"Fancy, Soames, she thinks the Boers are not to blame."*

"They only want their independence," said June; "and why shouldn't they have it?"

"Because," answered Soames, "they happen to have agreed to our suzerainty."

"Suzerainty!" repeated June scornfully; "we shouldn't like anyone's suzerainty over us."

"They got advantages in payment," replied Soames; "a contract is a contract."

"Contracts are not always just," flamed June, "and when they're not, they ought to be broken. The Boers are much the weaker. We could afford to be generous."

This pro-Boer sentiment was not held by any other members of the assembled family, so this time, Aunt Hester tried to shift the subject:

"What lovely weather it has been for the time of the year."

But June was not to be diverted.

Aunt Juley then turned to Soames:

"Have you bought any pictures lately."

"One or two," he muttered.

Pro-Boer or not, June was a Forsyte and *the Forsyte within her was seeing its chance. Why should not Soames buy some of the pictures of Eric Cobbley—her latest lame duck? And she promptly opened her attack: Did Soames know his work? It was so wonderful. He was the coming man.*

Oh yes, Soames knew his work. It was in his view 'splashy', and would never get hold of the public.

June blazed up.

"Of course it won't; that's the last thing one would wish for. I thought you were a connoisseur, not a picture-dealer."

"Of course Soames is a connoisseur," Aunt Juley said hastily; "he has wonderful taste—he can always tell beforehand what's going to be successful."

"Oh!" gasped June, "I hate that standard of success. Why can't people buy things because they like them?"

And in typical 'Forsyte' form, just like Granny Mabs on her daily morning visits to my mother, June got up and said, only addressing her Great-aunt Juley:

"Well, good-bye, Auntie. I must get on."

No sooner had June left and to the surprise of them all, James arrived. He had not been at Timothy's for over two years. His eyes searched for his son's face.

"Soames, I thought I'd come and see for myself. What have they answered Kruger?"

Soames took out an evening paper and read the headline.

"'Instant action by our government—state of war existing!'"

"Ah!" said James. "I was afraid they would cut and run like old Gladstone. We shall finish with them this time. Where's Timothy? He ought to pay attention to this."

All stared at him. James! Always fussy, nervous, anxious! James with his continual, 'I told you how it would be!' and his pessimism, and his cautious investments. There was something uncanny about such resolution in this oldest living Forsyte.

When my own father was dying from pneumonia and other complications at the age of ninety-three in early May, 2008, there was an important election for the Mayor of 'Greater' London. My father, along with most 'Forsytes' detested the incumbant, Ken Livingston, and had been determined to vote for his opponent, Boris Johnson. Hospitalized, he could not vote, but almost the last cognitive thing he said before passing was a very determined quizzing of my sister Diane's assessment of the day's activity at the polling booth. He died knowing that Ken Livingston had been defeated.

"The Boers are a hard nut to crack, Uncle James," remarked Francie.

"H'm!" muttered James. "Where do you get your information? Nobody tells me."

Young Nicholas remarked in his mild voice that Nick, his eldest, was now going to drill regularly.

James' thoughts were on his grandson, Val.

"He's got to look after his mother," he said, "he's got no time for drilling and that, with that father of his." He had passed June leaving as he came in, and changed the subject: "What did June want here? Her father's a rich man now."

Suddenly, they all wanted to know about the other 'lost' Forsyte— 'Young Jolyon'.

"He's going grey," Soames said.

Indeed, had Soames seen him? Soames nodded.

Aunt Hester, who had been looking for Timothy returned.

"Timothy," she said in a low voice, "Timothy has bought a map, and he's put in—he's put in three flags."

Flags on the map indicated reported successes. It was the second day of the war. If Timothy had indeed put in three flags already, well!—it showed what the nation could do when it was roused, and the advantages of the telegraph. The war was as good as over.

CHAPTER THIRTEEN

JOLYON FINDS OUT WHERE HE IS

Jolyon *had been restless for a week, since his attempt to prosecute trusteeship, uneasy in his conscience which was ever acute, disturbed in his sense of compassion which was easily excited, and with a queer sensation as if his feeling for beauty had received some definite embodiment.* He found it hard to concentrate on his painting.

The autumn days also frustrated him. Looking out from his studio—Holly's old nursery with such a view—he could only see the signs of autumnal decay. *Autumn was getting hold of the old oak tree, its leaves were browning. Sunshine had been plentiful and hot this summer. As with trees so with men's lives! 'I'm getting mildewed for want of heat.'*

For some people, because of its vibrant colors, autumn is their favorite season, but John Keats' 'Season of mellow mists and fruitfulness, close bosom friend of the fast maturing sun,' was not the favorite of most 'Forsytes'. It is the season of just that—close bosom friend of the fast maturing sun. My mother found autumn a sad time of the year, and my sisters and I felt very much the same way at our private boarding schools. We associated that 'fast fading sun' with compulsory games—lacrosse for my sisters, and football and rugger for me. How we hated those ball games. This may not have been the autumnal association of most our contemporaries, but the British do love their all too brief summers that grow such beautiful gardens, and they tend to dread those all too long dark winters. Many 'Forsytes', too, served the Empire in the tropics and adapted to those warmer climates away from dank, depressing English winters.

I myself spent many years in the tropics when I was a cruise director, and during those years, when I was on leave I made my home on the Georgia coast in the USA. St. Simons Island is a sub-tropical isle where humidity is high, sharing a Florida climate that meanders up the coasts of Georgia and the Carolinas in the low country known as the 'Tidewater'. I grew to love tropical heat along with its humidity. I often have tried to analyze this, as most Americans do not enjoy high humidity. My conclusion is that as an Englishman I became so delighted to be wet and warm rather than wet and cold that I embraced tropical humidity. This may well account for the ease with which so many British colonial administrators adapted to their tropical postings.

For my mother, and other 'Forsyte' families, a high point of the year was that annual summer seaside holiday. Usually, this was taken in August or even early September to fit in with school holidays, catching the last of the English summer. My mother so looked forward to these two weeks every year, and when they were over, there was that let down of evenings drawing in and autumn coming, heralding that raw, cold damp winter.

As Jolyon stared at Autumn out of the studio window, *memory of Paris gave no pleasure. Besides how could he go? He must stay and see what Soames was going to do. 'I'm* Irene's *trustee. I can't leave her unprotected,' he thought.*

He heard *the noise of hoofs. Holly was riding into the yard. She looked up* at the window *and he waved to her. She had been rather silent lately; getting* older *he supposed, beginning to want her future, as they all did—youngsters!*

He took up his brush. But it was no use; he could not concentrate his eye—besides with autumn coming *the light was going. 'I'll go up to town,' he thought.*

In the hall a servant met him.

"A lady to see you, sir; Mrs. Heron."

Extraordinary coincidence! Passing into the picture gallery, as it was still called, he saw Irene standing over by the window.

She came towards him, saying:

"I've been trespassing; I came up through the coppice and garden. I always used to come that way to see Uncle Jolyon."

"I was just thinking of you. You couldn't trespass here."

Irene smiled. And it was as if something shone through; not merely spirituality—serener, completer, more alluring.

"I once told Uncle Jolyon that love was for ever. Well, it isn't. Only aversion lasts."

Had she got over Bosinney at last?

"I came to tell you that Soames has been to see me. He said a thing that frightened me. He said: 'You are still my wife!'"

"What!" ejaculated Jolyon. "You ought not to live alone. What more?"

"He asked me to shake hands."

"Did you?"

"Yes. When he came in I'm sure he didn't want to; he changed while he was there."

"Ah! you certainly ought not to go on living there alone."

"I know no woman I could ask; and I can't take a lover to order, Cousin Jolyon."

"Heaven forbid!" said Jolyon. "What a damnable position!"

He offered her dinner, but she declined. She was lost. In propriety he could not ask her to stay, so he offered to go back to town with her. He had planned on going anyway.

In the train he put her through a sort of catechism as to what she did with her days.

Made her dresses, shopped, visited a hospital, played her piano, translated from French. She had regular work from a publisher, it seemed, which supplemented her income a little. She seldom went out in the evening. "I've been living alone so long, you see, that I don't mind it a bit. I believe I'm naturally solitary."

"I don't believe that," said Jolyon. "Do you know many people?"

"Very few."

After the train arrived at Waterloo, Jolyon hailed a hansom cab, *and he drove with her to the door of her mansions. Squeezing her hand at parting, he said:*

"You know, you could always come to us at Robin Hill; you must let me know everything that happens. Good-bye, Irene."

"Good-bye," she answered softly.

Jolyon climbed back into his cab. "Hotch Potch Club," he said through the trap-door.

They passed a man in a top hat and overcoat, *walking quickly, so close to the wall that he seemed to be scraping it.*

'*By Jove! It's Soames himself,*' *thought Jolyon. 'What's he up to now?*'

He stopped the cab and followed Soames. Soames halted in front of Irene's mansions, *and was looking up at the light in her windows.*

'*If he goes in, what shall I do,*' *Jolyon thought. 'What have I the right to do?*' What Soames *had said was true. She was still his wife, absolutely without protection from annoyance!* '*Well, if he goes in, I follow,*' *he concluded.*

Soames did not go in, however, he turned and started to walk away.

Jolyon retraced his steps back to his cab.

As he drove off, Soames called out to the cabby:

"Hansom! Engaged?"

"*Hallo!*" *said Jolyon. "You. I can give you a lift if you're going West.*"

"*Thanks,*" *answered Soames, and got in.*

"*I've been seeing Irene,*" *said Jolyon when the cab had started.*

"*Indeed!*"

"*You went to see her yesterday yourself, I understand.*"

"*I did, she's my wife, you know.*"

"*You ought to know best,*" *Jolyon said, "but if you want a divorce it's not very wise to go seeing her, is it? You can't run with the hare and hunt with the hounds.*"

"*You are very good to warn me,*" *said Soames* sarcastically, "*but I have not made up my mind.*"

"*She has,*" *said Jolyon. "She's in a damnable position, and I am the only person with any legal say in her affairs.*"

"*Except myself,*" *retorted Soames, "who am also in a damnable position. Hers is what she made for herself; mine what she made for me. I am not at all sure that in her own interests I shan't require her to return to me.*"

"*What!*" *exclaimed Jolyon.*

"*I don't know what you mean by 'what',*" *answered Soames coldly; "your say in her affairs is confined to paying out her income; please bear that in mind. In choosing not to disgrace her by a divorce* twelve years ago, *I retained my rights, and, as I say, I am not at all sure that I shan't require to exercise them. It would be the best thing that could happen to her in many ways.*"

'The sight of her has reawakened something. Beauty!' Jolyon thought.

"As I say," said Soames, "I have not made up my mind. I shall be obliged if you will kindly leave her quite alone."

Jolyon bit his lips.

"I can give you no such promise," he said shortly.

"Very well," said Soames, "then we know where we are."

He stopped the cab and alighted *without a word or sign of farewell.*

Jolyon traveled on to his club.

He had a disturbed heart.

CHAPTER FOURTEEN

SOAMES DISCOVERS WHAT HE WANTS

Soames *had got out of the cab in a state of anger—with himself for not having seen Irene, with Jolyon for having seen her; and now with his inability to tell exactly what he wanted.*

Indecision in desire was to him a new feeling. He was like a child between a promised toy and an old one which had been taken away from him. Only last Sunday at Mapledurham *desire seemed simple—just his freedom and Annette. 'I'll go and dine there,' he thought.* To see her *might bring back his singleness of intention, calm his exasperation, clear his mind.*

The restaurant was fairly full—a good many foreigners and folk whom, from appearance, he took to be literary or artistic. What he picked up of their conversations seemed very pro-Boer.

After dinner, he sought out Annette and her mother in the back office.

When Madame Lamotte went out to order a Grand Marnier for Soames, he was alone with Annette.

"Well, Annette?" was all he said.

The girl blushed. And yet—it was strange—but there seemed another face and form in the room too; and the itch in Soames' *nerves, was it for that, or for this? He jerked his head towards the restaurant and said:* "You have some queer customers. Do you like this life?"

"No," she said.

'I've got her', thought Soames, *'if I want her.'*

As he looked at the dingy little room, he saw Irene in a room with silvery walls and a satinwood piano—*a woman with white shoulders that he knew, and dark eyes that he sought to know. And as an artist who strives for the unrealisable and is ever thirsty, so there rose in him at that moment the thirst of the old passion he had never satisfied.*

"Well," he said calmly, *"you're young. There's everything before you."*

"I think sometimes there is nothing before me but hard work. I am not so in love with work as my mother." Annette sighed. *"It must be wonderful to be rich."*

Madame Lamotte returned with the liqueur.

After only a sip, Soames left.

'If only Irene had given him a son, he wouldn't now be squirming after women!' he mused. *'A son—something to look forward to, something to make the rest of life worthwhile, something to leave himself to, some perpetuity of self.'*

He was trying to think Annette the same as that other in this regard, *but she was not, she had not the lure of that old passion. 'And Irene's my wife,'* he thought, *'my legal wife. Why shouldn't she come back to me? It'd be the right thing, the lawful thing. It makes no scandal, no disturbance.' Why should he put to the shifts and sordid disgraces and the lurking defeats of the Divorce Court, when there she was like an empty house only waiting to be retaken into use and possessed by him who legally owned her?*

'No,' he mused, *'I'm glad I went to see that girl. I know now what I want most. If only Irene will come back I'll be as considerate as she wishes; she could live her own life; but perhaps—perhaps she would come round to me.'*

PART TWO

CHAPTER ONE

THE THIRD GENERATION

Jolly Forsyte was strolling down High Street, Oxford, on a November afternoon; Val Dartie was strolling up. Jolly had just changed out of boating flannels and was on his way to the 'Frying-pan', to which he had recently been elected. Val had just changed out of riding clothes and was on his way to the fire—a bookmaker's in Cornmarket.

The cousins had met but twice.

"Come into the Frying-pan and have tea," said Jolly, and they went in.

The Frying-pan was one of those social clubs that by rigid entry marked the difference between the "wealthies," their class associates, and lesser 'Forsytes'. The Cambridge equivalent was the Pitt Club for which I could have been sponsored by an old preparatory school friend, Philip Gwynn, who entertained me to tea there in a similar way to Jolly entertaining Val Dartie at the Frying-pan. I never, however, did join the Pitt Club as my Tonbridge friend and roommate at St. Catherines College talked me out of it as beyond our means. I did, however, attend the annual Hunt Ball of the Cambridge University Foot Beagles there. I was, for one season, a member of the hunt, and enjoyed our meets at country houses around Cambridge where after fortifying glasses of port with the local gentry, we followed the beagles chasing hares on winter afternoons.

Val and Jolly discussed their differences on gaming, Jolly only enjoying racing from a social perspective whereas Val had inherited some of the gambling traits of his father.

"You met my people, didn't you?" said Jolly. "They're coming up tomorrow."

Val grew a little red wondering if Holly had said anything to her brother.

"What do you do with yourself?" Jolly continued. "Row?"

"No—ride, and drive about. I'm going to play polo next term, if I can get my granddad to stump up."

"That's old Uncle James, isn't it. What's he like?"

"Older than forty hills," said Val, "and always thinking he's going to be ruined."

"I suppose my granddad and he were brothers."

"I don't believe any of that old lot were sportsmen," said Val; "they must have worshipped money. Money's only fit to spend. I wish the deuce I had more."

Jolly gave him that direct upward look of judgment which he had inherited from Old Jolyon: One didn't talk about money!

Certainly, this was ingrained in us by Granny Longley. We were never supposed to ask the price of anything. If our parents could afford it they could purchase it, if not, then they were not expected to buy it. They taught us the same. On one occasion, when Granny and Grandpop took us and our Scottish cousins, Johnny and 'Jaykie', to lunch at the Trocadero before a matinee pantomime in London's West End, Johnny commented on the price of a bowl of pea soup—"Two shillings!" He was firmly reprimanded right there at the table with more than just a Hovenden glare.

There was no financial credit in 'Forsyte' philosophy. Besides, something bought on credit would not be owned—would not truly be property! 'Hire purchase' as credit was called in the last days of 'Forsythia'—today's equivalent of layaway and before credit cards— was something for the lower-middle class, a means of allowing them to taste the delights of 'Forsythia' and hopefully better themselves.

Thus, it was a standard rule of the class—a rule of the club—you did not discuss price or money. However, one can allow for Val a little, for although in the eyes of his cousin this discussion was a betrayal of their class, young men going up to Oxford or Cambridge were often in charge of their spending for the first time in their sheltered lives. They had to get used to the reality of monetary values, and thus the subject invariably was discussed.

"Where are your people going to stay?" asked Val, partly to correct his error, but mostly with his thoughts on Holly.

"'Rainbow', What do you think of the war?"

"Rotten, so far. The Boers aren't sports a bit. Why don't they come out into the open?"

"Why should they? They've got everything against them except their way of fighting. I rather admire them."

"They can ride and shoot," admitted Val, "but they're a lousy lot."

Then, still wanting to impress his cousin, Val asked him if he knew Crum.

"Of Merton? Only by sight. He's in that fast set too, isn't he? Rather La-di-da and Brummagen."

Val said very fixedly, "He's a friend of mine."

"Oh! Sorry!" And they sat awkwardly staring past each other, having pitched on their pet points of snobbery.

Val finished *his* buttered *bun.*

"I suppose you'll be meeting your people?" he said, getting up. "I wish you'd tell them I should like to show them over B.N.C.—not that there's anything much there—if they'd care to come."

"Thanks, I'll ask them."

"Would they lunch? I've got rather a decent scout."

An Oxford scout was the undergraduate's manservant, who took care of the gentleman's rooms, acted as butler and waiter when the undergraduate wished to entertain, and was a 'Jeeves' type confidante in his young master's advance from adolescence to manhood. At Cambridge, the equivalent was one's 'Gyp'.

When my family came to visit me at Cambridge, George—my gyp—served a magnificent dinner in my rooms for them. Granny and Grandpop Longley came up with my mother and father and Miss Coath. We all sat at the beautiful Georgian dinner table that belonged to my roommate, Sebastian Jones. His family had loaned the antique to us while we were up. With silver candelabra, Waterford crystal, and a beautiful table arrangement of sweet smelling freesias, we were served smoked salmon with caviar, buttery asparagas soup, roast teal with all the game trimmings, and lemon meringue pie. George served wines to match from the magnificent St. Catherine's cellar.

Jolly doubted if they would have time for lunch. *"Very good of you,"* he said, *fully meaning that they should not go, but, instinctively polite, he added: "You had better come and have dinner with us tomorrow."*

"Rather. What time?"

"Seven-thirty."

"Dress?"

"No" And they parted, a subtle antagonism alive within them.

Holly and her father arrived the next day *by a midday train. It was* Holly's *first visit to the city of spires and dreams, and she was very silent, looking almost shyly at the brother who was part of this wonderful place.*

There was great rivalry between Oxford and Cambridge, which for me was best summed up by one of my tutors, Henry St. John Hart, of Queens College, Cambridge. St. John, as I learned at that time, when incorporated into a 'Forsyte' surname was always pronounced "Singent". Henry "Singent" Hart was my Hebrew professor. He also taught a course on the rise and fall of ancient empires in which he allowed us to handle his rare and extremely valuable collection of coins.

"Gentlemen and Lady," he said (for there were few female theological students in that last decade of 'Forsythia'), "Many hundreds of years ago in Ancient Greece, a certain philosopher gathered up his students in his garden in Athens where they discussed all manner of things from cabbages to kings. The name of that philosopher, Gentlemen and Lady, was Academus. So, Gentlemen and Lady, those gatherings in that garden were the first Academy. And that, Gentlemen and Lady, is the difference between Cambridge and the 'other' place."

Both cities have incredible buildings and dreaming spires, but Oxford is a city despite the university—also an industrial center. Cambridge is nothing but its university, set in a beautiful natural garden, with its college backs along the banks of the river Cam. Students' rooms in the older buildings of both universities were surprisingly grand.

Jolly's sitting-room, like mine on 'B' Staircase in Main Court at St. Catherines College, Cambridge, *was panelled.*

Holly and her father, suitably impressed by Jolly's rooms, were then taken to the river, for *Jolly was anxious that they should see him rowing. Slight in build—for of all the Forsytes only old Swithin and George were beefy—Jolly was rowing 'Two' in a trial eight.*

Rowing was also my sport at Cambridge. I rowed 'Bow', the man in front of 'Two' because I, too, was slight of build. The heavy men rowed

in the middle of the boat—the power house. My family were subjected
to the same routine and watched me row, and it was during the Lent
Bumping races that my eight was rather successful and we bumped
and over-bumped five other crews thus winning our oars. To this day I
have that oar.

In fact, had I taken the advantage of pulling an oar at Tonbridge, I
might have not just won my oar, but possibly the pink socks, too. These
are the prestigious colors of the famed Leander Club, in which selected
membership is really only second to an Oxford or Cambridge 'Blue'.
There were very few 'rowing' schools, as obviously such schools had
to be close to a suitable river. Tonbridge was on the River Medway,
and, because of the proximity of Kent's river, both sailing and rowing
were taught. I did not volunteer for either during my Tonbridge days,
but four to five years of rowing experience at one's public school gave
a 'gentleman' a great advantage when pursuing the sport at Oxford or
Cambridge. My roommate, Sebastian Jones, was an old Tonbridgian,
who had rowed five years on the Medway. He went straight into the St.
Catherine's First VIII, whereas I rowed in the Third VIII. He gained his
pink socks and membership of the elite Leander Club that provided in
the social calendar a rather nice Thames-side tent on Henley Reach for
the Henley Royal Regatta.

I was quite keen on Sebastian's sister Tina while we were up at
Cambridge, and like Holly, Tina was subjected to watching us row in the
college bumping races wearing a long skirt and large-brimmed hat.

*After they had watched Jolly's eight pass a second time, spurting
home along the barges, they returned across the river* from the tow path
and waited for him.

*"Oh!" said Jolly in the Christ Church meadows, "I had to ask that
chap Val Dartie to dine with us tonight. He wanted to give you lunch
and show you B.N.C., so I thought I'd better; then you needn't go. I don't
like him much."*

Holly's rather sallow face had become fused with pink.

"Why not?"

*"Oh! I don't know. He seems to me rather showy and bad form.
What are his people like, Dad? He's only a second cousin, isn't he?"*

Within the context of schools and colleges, 'Forsytes' nearly always
referred to their families as their "people." Grandpop always talked
about his "people."

"Ask Holly," Jolyon said; "she saw his uncle."

"I liked Val," Holly answered, staring at the ground before her; *"his uncle looked awfully different."*

Jolyon then proceeded to tell them both something of their family history and as to how Val and Jolly were cousins.

"It's quite a fairy-tale."

He told of their yeoman origins, and quoted old Swithin—"very small beer"—despite the fact that their great-aunt insisted they were agriculturalists in Dorset. He explained how the second Jolyon Forsyte, known as 'Superior Dosset' Forsyte—*built houses, begat ten children, and migrated to London town. The eldest of his six sons was the third Jolyon,* their grandfather—*tea merchant and chairman of companies.* Jolyon spoke of him with affection, never referring to the period he had been ostracized by 'Old Jolyon'. *"He was just and tenacious, tender and young at heart. You remember him, and I remember him. Pass to the others! Your Great-uncle James, that's young Val's grandfather, had a son called Soames—whereby hangs a tale of no love lost, and I don't think I'll tell it you. James and the other eight children of 'Superior Dosset', of whom there are still five alive, may be said to have represented Victorian England, with its principles of trade and individualism at five per cent and your money back—if you know what that means. At all events, they've turned thirty thousand pounds into a cool million between them in the course of their long lives. Their day is passing, and their type, not altogether for the advantage of the country. They were pedestrian, but they, too, were sound. I am the fourth Jolyon Forsyte, a poor specimen, representing, I'm afraid, nothing but the end of the century, unearned income, amateurism, and individual liberty."* He looked at his son, Jolly. *"That's a different thing from individualism, Jolly. You are the fifth Jolyon Forsyte and you, old man, open the ball of the new century."*

As he spoke they turned in through the college gates, and Holly said: "It's fascinating, Dad."

My college at Cambridge had rather spectacular gates, partly because the main court of St. Catherine's was not a quadrangle. The seventeenth-century buildings were built on three sides, the chapel and hall on the right and college rooms center and left, including 'B' staircase where my rooms were located. The gates and wrought iron fence formed the street side, separating the court with its immaculate lawn from a cobbled plaza, shaded by spreading chestnut trees, facing Trumpington Street.

Most college main courts, being quadrangles, had entry from the street through a porter's lodge with heavy double doors.

The oldest 'quad' at Cambridge was in Corpus Christi College across the street from St. Catherine's. Many of the older courts dating back to the thirteenth and fourteenth centuries boasted fine sundials— the only reliable time piece when the buildings were constructed, and as reliable today looking down from those ancient walls as they were then, if you do not allow for daylight savings time.

My tutor in old testament studies had rooms in the old court at Corpus Christi just above rooms once occupied by Christopher Marlowe.

There were no bathrooms in the rooms of these ancient buildings, and 'Forsytes' were used to chamber pots, until in the latter days of 'Forsythia', just as at our public schools, bathrooms were added in the basements and cellars, often requiring one to make a nocturnal dash across the 'quad'.

The Rainbow Inn, like these ancient colleges, *distinguished, as only an Oxford* or Cambridge *hostel can be, for lack of modernity, provided one small oak-panelled private sitting-room, in which Holly sat to receive, white-frocked, shy, and alone, when* their *only dinner guest arrived.*

Val Dartie *removed a gardenia from his coat.* He thought *it would look ripping in her hair.*

"Oh! No, I couldn't!" But she pinned it at her neck, having suddenly remembered that word 'showy'! Val's buttonhole would give offence; and she so much wanted Jolly to like him.

She confided in him that she had never said anything to her family about their ride in Richmond Park.

"Rather not! It's just between us."

"Do tell me about Oxford," Holly said, *"it must be ever so lovely."*

Val admitted that it was frightfully decent to do what you liked; the lectures were nothing, at least not compulsory for attendance, all one's work being done one on one in tutorials, *and there were some very good chaps* in college. *"Only,"* he added, *"of course I wish I was in town, and could come down and see you."*

At this moment Jolyon and Jolly came in; and romance fled into Val's patent leather and Holly's white satin toes, where it itched and tingled during an evening not conspicuous for open-heartedness

Sensitive to atmosphere, Jolyon soon felt the latent antagonism between the boys. Also, *a letter handed to him after dinner, reduced him to a silence hardly broken till Jolly and Val rose to go. He went out with them, smoking his cigar, and walked his son to the gates of Christchurch.*

He, then, read the letter beneath a lamp.

'Dear Jolyon,
'Soames came again tonight—my thirty-seventh birthday. You were right. I mustn't stay here. I'm going tomorrow to the Piedmont Hotel, but I won't go abroad without seeing you. I feel lonely and downhearted.
'Yours affectionately,
'Irene.'

Jolyon *turned into High Street, down the Turl, and on among a maze of spires and domes and long college fronts and walls, bright or dark-shadowed in the strong moonlight. In this very heart of England's gentility it was difficult to realise that a lonely woman could be importuned or hunted, but what else could her letter mean.*

Soames must have been pressing her to go back to him again, with public opinion and the law on his side, too! 'Eighteen-ninety-nine!' Jolyon *thought, 'but when it comes to property we're still a heathen people! I'll go up tomorrow morning. I daresay it'll be best for her to go abroad.' Yet the thought displeased him. Why should Soames hunt her out of England! Besides, he might follow.*

His thoughts turned to his daughter June. Could she help? Once on a time Irene had been her greatest friend, and now she was a 'lame duck', such as must appeal to June's nature.

Retracing his steps towards the Rainbow he questioned his own sensations. Would he be upsetting himself over every woman in like case? No! he would not.

He found Holly had gone to bed, but he could not sleep, and sat for a long time at his window, huddled in an overcoat, watching the moonlight on the roofs of the city of dreaming spires.

Holly, too, was awake, thinking what she could do to make Jolly like Val *better. The scent of the gardenia was strong in her little bedroom, and pleasant to her.*

Val, leaning out of his first-floor window in B.N.C., was gazing at a moonlit quadrangle without seeing it at all, seeing instead Holly, slim and white-frocked, as she sat beside the fire when he first went in.

Much of my time at Cambridge, I continued to court my roommate's sister, Tina. She came up for several parties and balls that we attended together in the romance of those moonlit quadrangles in the other city of spires and dreams. The Cambridge equivalent for hostelry to the Rainbow Inn was the Blue Boar or the Garden House.

Jolly, however, dreamed he was with Val in one boat, rowing a race against him, while his father was calling from the towpath: "Two! Get your hands away there, bless you!"

CHAPTER TWO

SOAMES PUTS IT TO THE TOUCH

Winifred's divorce case seemed straightforward enough. A judge *had advised that they should go forward and obtain restitution of conjugal rights, a point which to Soames had* never been in doubt. *When they had obtained a decree to that effect they must wait to see if it was obeyed. If not, it would constitute legal desertion, and they should obtain evidence of misconduct and file their petition for divorce.*

The simplicity in his sister's case only made him the more desperate about the difficulty in his own. Everything, in fact, was driving toward the simple solution of Irene's return. He, at least, had never injured her. He could offer her so much more than she had now. He would be prepared to make a liberal settlement on her which would not be upset. If he could only give tangible proof enough of his determination to let bygones be bygones, and to do all in his power to please her, why should she not come back to him.

Soames entered the fashionable jewelers Gaves and Cortegals his attention fixed on *a certain diamond brooch. He still knew a diamond when he saw one.*

"If the lady doesn't like it, sir, happy to exchange it any time. But there's no fear of that," the salesman said as Soames walked out with *the flat green morocco case in his breast pocket. If only there were not!*

Like an excited schoolboy in anticipation, he looked at the brooch several times while working at his office. Then, good news came in by cable from Buenos Aires. They had *the name and address of a stewardess who would be prepared to swear what was necessary.* Things looked good for Winifred.

He dined at Park Lane—*the homing instinct of all true Forsytes in anxiety or trouble, the corporate tendency* of family, which *kept them strong and solid,* just like the dear old Breach.

His father, *James, was in lugubrious mood, for the fire which the impudence of Kruger's ultimatum had lit in him had been cold-watered by the poor success of the last month, and the exhortations to effort in the* Times. *He didn't know where it would end.*

Winifred had also *heard from Val that there had been a 'rag' and a bonfire on Guy Fawkes Day at Oxford, and that he had escaped detection by blacking his face.* Although rags were an Oxford and Cambridge tradition, James might well question such activity seeing he was paying the boy's bills.

University rags were still a feature of Guy Fawkes Day at Oxford and Cambridge in the last decade of 'Forsythia'. Guy Fawkes Day just happened to be a good time in the Michaelmas Term for such activity— far enough away from academic pressures and sporting events to allow for a day of frivolities. The principle of official rag days was to raise money for charities. Climbing spires had always been a favorite rag. In 1899, fastening chamber pots to ancient spires, gables, or roof pinnacles was considered quite the thing. By the 1950s, in a post-suffragette world, the chamber pot routine had been replaced by high-masting certain articles of ladies' underwear. The ultimate, however, was achieved in a summer, post-exam rag at Cambridge in June, 1958.

Early risers strolling down King's Parade were astonished to see an Austin Seven van perched on the venerable Senate House's roof. Students on the ground had maneuvered the van into position for lifting and warded off the attentions of curious passers-by. Others crossed a plank bridge seventy feet above Senate House Passage, erected a derrick designed by their leader, a certain Peter Davey, an engineering student from Caius College, and hauled the van up on steel rope borrowed from the gliding club.

The Dean of Caius at the time was none other than The Very Reverend Hugh Montefiore, the same who during the war had teamed up with my father's cousin John Goodchild, which had brought for me that formal invitation to tea at the Montefiore home in Cambridge six years later when I was an undergraduate and he was Vicar of the University Church, Great St. Mary's. As Dean of Caius, he insisted that no-one knew the identity of the miscreants who had succeeded in conquering the Senate roof in this way, but nonetheless seemed to know to which Caius College staircase to send congratulatory champagne!

Thinking of his grandson Val spending too much of his allowance up at Oxford, made James Forsyte look *wistfully at his son* and murmur *that Soames had never had a boy. He would have liked a grandson of his own name. And now—well, there it was! There were Roger, Nicholas and Jolyon; they all had grandsons.*

Soames excused himself directly after dinner. Feeling the morocco case flat against his heart, he sallied forth. He moved slowly down the Row towards Knightsbridge, timing himself to get to Chelsea at nine-fifteen.

How mysterious women were! One lived alongside and knew nothing of them. What could she have seen in that fellow Bosinney to send her mad? For there was madness, after all, in what she had done—crazy moonstruck madness in which all sense of values had been lost, and her life and his life, ruined! And for a moment he was filled with a sort of exaltation, as though he were a man read of in a story who, possessed by the Christian spirit, would restore to her all the prizes of existence, forgiving and forgetting, and becoming the good fairy of her future.

'I would treat her well,' he thought incoherently, 'I would be very careful.'

And all that capacity for home life of which a mocking fate seemed forever to have deprived him swelled suddenly in Soames.

He watched a drunk. *What asses people were!*

'To have ruffians like that about, with women out alone!'

Then, he saw Irene, walking alone toward her building.

To make sure of her now, he followed.

At the door he said, breathless, *"Don't be alarmed. I happened to see you. Let me come in a minute."*

Her face was colorless, her eyes widened by alarm, but she said: *"Very well."*

Once in the silvery sitting room, she challenged him:

"Why have you come again? Didn't you understand that I would rather you did not?"

"It's your birthday. I brought you this," and he held out to her the green morocco case.

"Oh! No—no!"

"Why not?" he said, opening the case and exposing the diamonds. "Just as a sign that you don't bear me ill feeling any longer."

"I couldn't." She shrank back.

"Irene," he said, "let bygones be bygones. If I can, surely you might. Let's begin again, as if nothing had been. Won't you? Can you really want to live all your days half-dead in this little hole? Come back to me, and I'll give you all you want. You shall live your own life; I swear it."

He saw her face quiver.

"Yes," he repeated, "but I mean it this time. I'll only ask one thing. I just want—I just want a son. Don't look like that! I want one. It's hard."

Then the sight of her eyes fixed on him, dark with a sort of fascinated fright, which pulled him together and changed that painful incoherence to anger.

"Is it so unnatural? Is it unnatural to want a child from one's own wife? I still want you for my wife. Speak, for goodness sake! Do speak."

And almost with surprise he heard her say:

"You can't have a reasonable answer. Reason has nothing to do with it. You can only have the brutal truth: I would rather die."

Soames stared at her.

"Oh!" he said. And there intervened in him a sort of paralysis of speech and movement.

"Oh!" he said again, "as bad as that? Indeed! You would rather die. That's pretty!"

"I am sorry. You wanted me to answer. I can't help the truth, can I?"

Soames snapped the jewelry case closed.

"I don't believe a word of it," he shouted. "You have a lover. If you hadn't, you wouldn't be such a—such a little idiot."

He turned away to the door. But he could not go out. Something within him—that most deep and secret Forsyte quality, the impossibility of letting go, the impossibility of seeing the fantastic and forlorn nature of his own tenacity—prevented him.

"When I came here to-night I was—I hoped—I meant everything that I could do away with the past and start fair again. And you meet me with 'nerves' and silence, and sighs. There's nothing tangible. It's like—it's like a spider's web."

"Yes."

That whispered answer *maddened Soames afresh.*

"Well, I don't choose to be in a spider's web. I'll cut it. Now!"

He tried to kiss her, force himself on her. She pushed him away. *Shame, compunction, sense of futility flooded his whole being, he turned on his heel and went straight out.*

The next day, Irene booked herself into the Piedmont Hotel.

CHAPTER THREE

VISIT TO IRENE

Jolyon left Oxford, after breakfast at the Rainbow, saying he would be back in the evening. Holly could spend the day with Jolly even though her thoughts might have been with Val. June was waiting at Paddington Station having received his telegram while having breakfast in her studio in *a St. John's Wood garden*. She used the studio to promote some of her lame duck artists and came *to Paddington Station heated in her soul by a visit to Eric Cobbley. A miserable Gallery had refused to let that straight-haired genius have his one-man show after all. Its impudent manager, after visiting his studio, had expressed the opinion that it would only be a 'one-horse show from the selling point of view.' This crowning example of commercial cowardice towards her favourite lame duck* had set her thinking. Maybe, her father could help?

Before Jolyon had the opportunity to mention Irene, June assailed him.

"Dad, is it true that I absolutely can't get at any of my money?"

"Only the income, fortunately, my love."

June told him she wanted to buy a small gallery for ten thousand pounds.

"A small Gallery seems a modest desire. But your grandfather forsaw it."

"I think," cried June vigorously, *"that all this care about money is awful, when there's so much genius in the world simply crushed for*

want of a little. I shall never marry and have children; why shouldn't I be able to do some good instead of having it all tied up in case of things that will never come off?"

"Our name is Forsyte, my dear," replied Jolyon, "and Forsytes, you know, are people who so settle their property that their grandchildren, in case they should die before their parents, have to make wills leaving the property that will only come to themselves when their parents die. Do you follow that? Nor do I, but it's a fact anyway; we live by the principle that so long as there is a possibility of keeping wealth in the family it must not go out; if you die unmarried, your money goes to Jolly and Holly and their children if they marry. Isn't it pleasant to know that whatever you do you can none of you be destitute?"

I wonder if my grandfather, Grandpop Longley, ever had a similar conversation with Chris and Audrie, his deceased brother 'Tig's' children, who were so concerned that he held such a hold on their money as trustee of their inheritance from my great-grandfather, Oliver Longley.

"But can't I borrow the money," pleaded June.

Jolyon shook his head. "You can rent a Gallery, no doubt, if you could manage it out of your income," but Jolyon was well aware how much her lame ducks sucked from her income.

"I could buy for ten thousand; that would only be four hundred a year. But I should have to pay a thousand a year rent, and that would only leave me five hundred. If I had that Gallery, Dad, think what I could do. I could make Eric Cobbley's name in no time, and ever so many others."

"Did you ever know anybody living, my dear, improved by having his name made?"

"Yes, you," said June, pressing his arm.

Jolyon started. This was partly true. He had been rescued.

"Darling," she said, "you buy the Gallery, and I'll pay you four hundred a year for it. Then neither of us will be any the worse off. Besides, it's a splendid investment."

Jolyon wriggled. "Don't you think," he said, "that for an artist to buy a Gallery is a bit dubious? Besides, ten thousand pounds is a lump, and I'm not a commercial character. So, *where is this desirable Gallery?"*

"Just off Cork Street."

'Ah!' thought Jolyon, 'I knew it was just off somewhere. Now, for what I want out of her.'

"Well, I'll think about it, but not just now. You remember Irene? I want you to come with me and see her. Soames is after her again. She might be safer if we could give her asylum somewhere."

'Asylum' was a word that rang true for June. Could Irene be one of her lame ducks?

"Irene! I haven't seen her since—! Of course! I'd love to help her. I can't bear Soames, he sneers at everything that isn't successful."

They found Irene in the Ladies' drawing room of the Piedmont Hotel. Even in the last decade of 'Forsythia' many hotels had a Ladies' drawing room—a place where unchaperoned ladies could feel safe. There were Ladies' waiting rooms at railway stations, too. By the 1950s, half a century after woman suffrage, the connotation might have changed a little. These havens were not so much by then for unchaperoned safety, but were equally seen by some more progressive women as an expression of their growing equality, allowing them a certain status on their own. They were also for the most part for 'Forsytes' and not the working class.

When my mother and Granny Mabs would take us up to London for those shopping sprees at Goringes and Derry and Toms, we would wait in the ladies' waiting room at Beckenham Junction where it was warm. It was always open to children of either sex. But it was also convenient, so we did not have to be on the platform with persons who were not our class, or worse still, our color.

For Irene, in 1899, however, the Ladies' drawing room at the Piedmont gave her just a little more security from Soames or his potential spies.

June went right up to her former friend, kissed her cheek, and the two settled down on a sofa. Jolyon could see that Irene was deeply affected by this simple forgiveness.

"So Soames has been worrying you?" Jolyon said.

"I had a visit from him last night; he wants me to go back to him."

"You're not, of course," cried June.

Irene smiled faintly and shook her head. "But his position is horrible," she murmured.

"It's his own fault. He ought to have divorced you when he could."

Jolyon remembered how fervently in the old days June had hoped that no divorce would smirch her dead and faithless lover's name.

"Let us hear what Irene is going to do," he said.

Irene's lips quivered. "I had better give him fresh excuse to get rid of me. What else can I do?"

"Out of the question," said Jolyon very quietly, *"sans amour."*

June expressed her feelings strongly.

"I shall go to Soames and tell him he must leave you alone. What does he want at his age?"

"A child. It's not unnatural," Irene replied almost philosophically.

"A child!" cried June scornfully. "Of course! To leave his money to. If he wants one badly enough, let him take somebody and have one; then you can divorce him, and he can marry her."

Jolyon, who was being pulled in another emotional direction, suggested to Irene that maybe she would like to stay with them in safety at Robin Hill, at least until they could all see *how things shape up.*

Irene looked full at Jolyon—in all his many attempts afterwards to analyse that glance he never could succeed.

"No! I should only bring trouble on you all. I will go abroad."

"Don't you think you would be more helpless abroad, in case he followed?"

"I don't know. I can but try."

June ranted and raved about people being *tortured and kept miserable and helpless year after year by this disgusting sanctimonious law,* until someone else entered the Ladies' drawing room.

Jolyon asked Irene if she needed money, which she did not, and offered as her trustee to let out her flat.

"When shall you be going?" he asked.

"Tomorrow."

As they prepared to leave, Jolyon asked Irene to be sure to send him her address abroad.

June flung her arms around Irene.

"Don't think of him," she said under her breath; *"enjoy yourself, and bless you!"*

Outside, opposite the National Gallery, June lambasted the law again.

Jolyon did not respond. He had something of his father's balance. Irene was right; Soames's position was as bad or worse than her own. Hailing a cab, he told June he must catch his train back to Oxford, but he promised her *he would think over that Gallery* proposition.

In reality, *he thought over Irene. Pity they said, was akin to love! If so, he was certainly in danger of loving her, for he pitied her profoundly.*

Chapter Four

Where Forsytes fear to tread

The more Soames *brooded, the more certain he became that* Irene *had a lover—her words, 'I would sooner die!' were ridiculous if she had not.*

'*I'll take steps to know where I am*,' he thought; '*I'll go to Polteed's the first thing tomorrow morning.*'

Polteed's was the firm of private detectives that Soames used *in the routine of his profession*. He was currently using them *over Dartie's case, but he had never thought it possible to employ them to watch over his own wife,* but then, he remembered *she called herself by her maiden name of Heron. Polteed would not know, at first at all events, whose wife she was. She would just be the wife of one of* Forsyte, Bustard and Forsyte's *clients*. Nonetheless, feeling somewhat uncomfortable, rather than have Polteed come around to the office in the Poultry, *he walked rapidly to the agency.*

Without hesitation, Soames informed the secretary that he wanted to see Mr. Claud Polteed himself.

Mr. Claud Polteed—so different from Mr. Lewis Polteed—was one of those men with dark hair, slightly curved noses, and quick brown eyes, who might be taken for Jews but are really Phoenicians.

'Forsytes', when it came to needing some sort of undercover business, gravitated to these "big noses" as they called Jews or suspect Jews. They respected Jewish efficiency, but they knew that they did not have

320

to socialize with them—as aforementioned, Jews were not considered 'Forsytes'—were not members of the club. In fact, literally, most the gentlemen's clubs of 'Forsythia', including some golf clubs, did not accept non-gentile clientele. Jews were accepted in the latter days of 'Forsythia' at our golf club, Langley Park, but they were somewhat ostracized—the butt of social comment, and kept themselves to themselves.

This separation made it easier to use Jews, or Jewish types, for 'Forsyte' dirty work. They could be trusted to do a good job, even had pride in their somewhat sleazy occupations as Charles Dickens made plain in his various interpretations of London's underworld, but there was little danger of other 'Forsytes' knowing of their involvement in your affairs, which is why Soames chose to visit Claud Polteed at his offices rather than at his own.

That Jews ran the slightly shady side of London's business was probably also close to Soames. As a connoisseur, somewhat like my own great-grandfather, Oliver Longley, Soames was used to dealing with them in the world of art and 'objets d'art'. In this field, they were enormously successful and usually the winners. 'Forsytes', unless they were particularly shrewd, and Soames was pretty shrewd, rarely got the better of the deal. It was to one of these Jewish dealers in the more fashionable part of London's West End that on my grandparents' deaths, my mother and Aunt Eileen took those two Brianski landscapes that hung in the dining room at Redcroft. Sadly, not being as shrewd as Soames, they sold them to the dealer for a song, and then no doubt the Jew sold them off from his gallery at a handsome profit.

My sisters and I deeply resented this hasty loss of these two paintings that we had admired for years and we promptly gathered up whatever other ancestral items, as we called relics of 'Forsythia', that we could find about the house. Several of these—Chinoisserie vases, that silver card tray on that little table by the front door, and the silver plated meat covers that sat on tables beneath the Brianskis that Lloydy had polished until there was little silver left on them—I now have in my own home.

Great-grandfather Oliver Longley also had an Alfred de Brianski painting at Hillside. When Uncle Mark and Aunt Biddy were at Hillside announcing their engagement, Oliver Longley asked Mark what he thought of his paintings. Being a Scot, Mark particularly admired the Brianski landscape painted on the Isle of Skye. On Oliver Longley's death he willed the Brianski painting to Mark and Biddy. It hung for many years on reinforced hooks at their home in East Loathian—

Pathhead. Uncle Mark ended up selling it at a Christie's picture sale where it made a considerable sum of money. This corroborates my sister Diane's feeling that Granny Mabs' Brianski paintings were worth a lot more than the West End dealer gave for them when my mother and Aunt Eileen so hastily settled up Granny's estate.

Mr. Claud Polteed *received Soames in a room hushed by thickness of carpet and curtains. It was, in fact, confidentially furnished, without trace of document anywhere to be seen. Greeting Soames deferentially, he turned the key in the only door with a certain ostentation.*

"Now, sir, what can I do for you?"

"I've come to you early like this because there's not an hour to lose. Have you a really trustworthy woman free?"

Mr. Polteed unlocked a drawer, produced a memorandum, ran his eyes over it, and locked the drawer up again.

"Yes," he said; "the very woman."

"Send her off at once, then, to watch a Mrs. Irene Heron of Flat D, Truro Mansions, Chelsea, till further notice."

"Precisely," said Mr. Polteed; "divorce, I presume?"

"Deal with any reports yourself," resumed Soames, "and send them to me personally, marked confidential, sealed and registered. My client exacts the utmost secrecy."

The Jew, or Phoenician, gave Soames a knowing look, *as though saying: 'You are teaching your grandmother, my dear sir.'*

"No," said Soames, "understand me: Nothing may come of this. If a name gets out or the watching is suspected, it may have very serious consequences."

Mr. Polteed nodded. "I can put it into the cipher category. Under that system a name is never mentioned; we work by numbers."

Mr. Polteed wrote down the codes, locked away his copy and gave Soames the other. *"Keep that, sir; it's your key. Any hint or instruction while we're about it?"*

"No."

"Expense?"

Soames shrugged. *"In reason,"* he answered curtly, and got up. *"Keep it entirely in your hands."*

"Entirely," said Mr. Polteed.

Out in the street Soames *swore deeply, quietly, to himself. A spider's web, and to cut it he must use this spidery, secret, unclean method, so utterly repugnant to one who regarded his private life as his most sacred piece of property. But the die was cast, he could not go back.*

Back at his office he waited for Winifred. He had arranged a conference at the Temple law courts with Dreamer, Q.C., for them. He looked over the note Dartie had written from the Iseeum Club, obviously while drunk, and then at the letter Winifred had written—or rather the copy she had made as he leaned over her while she copied what he had pencilled—pleading for Dartie to return home. Winifred had been nervous. Would this trickery work?

'I am prepared to let bygones be bygones if you will return to me at once.'

"Suppose he comes, Soames" Winifred had said, *as if she did not know her own mind.*

"He won't come," Soames *had answered, "till he's spent his money. That's why we must act at once."*

Annexed to these documents, *was* Dartie's *cabled answer: 'Impossible return. Dartie.'*

Soames shook his head. If the whole thing were not disposed of within the next few months the fellow would turn up again like a bad penny. It saved a thousand a year to get rid of him, besides all the worry to Winifred and his father.

Winifred arrived in James's barouche drawn by James's pair. It looked quaint, almost old-fashioned with the rise in motorized transport. *'Times are changing,'* Soames *thought, 'one doesn't know what will go next.'* Top hats even were scarcer, being replaced by bowler hats, and the young wore those casual boaters that really should only be worn on the river, or by a fishmonger or butcher as a symbol of his trade, or worse still a singing barbers' quartet!

Each generation of 'Forsythia' saw these fashion changes, and it is interesting that the casual boater that became a young person's fashion at the end of the nineteenth century, became a hallmark of distinction for many 'Forsyte' public schools. Tonbridge was no exception. In Grandpop's day, the dress was still Eton collar, short black coat, often called a "bum-freezer," and striped trousers, but headed by the traditional black top hat resting lugubriously on the young schoolboy's ears. By the 1920s, the top hat had been replaced by the boater that as schoolboys we still wore in the last decade of 'Forsythia'. At Tonbridge, we called the straw hats "barges," because they had the capacity to float like a boat if wind should lift them from the head and they fell into the River

Medway. It was a punishable offence to visit the town at Tonbridge without wearing one's 'barge'—the symbol of the difference between Tonbridge School and the town—the young gentlemen of 'Forsythia' and the common folk. In the late 1950s, only Eton schoolboys still wore 'bum-freezers', Eton collars, and top hats. Harrow remained in traditional dress, but exchanged the top hat for a boater. At Tonbridge in my father's time, blue suits had replaced the traditional nineteenth-century dress, and in my day, lovat gray-green suits, but the stiff straw boater remained.

The evolution of the schoolboy's collar was interesting, too. For dispensing with the wide Eton collar did not bring any comfort to us. By my day, Tonbridge boys, as noted, still wore separate collars with studs and cuff links, and those collars and cuffs were starched just as stiff as an Eton collar.

Winifred Dartie, wanting tradition for her son, let it slip that Val wanted to play polo at Oxford next term. She knew their father would have to pay the expense, but as she said *she thought he was in a very good set. She added with fashionably disguised anxiety: "Will there be much publicity about my affair, Soames? Must it be in the papers? It's so bad for* Val *and the girls."*

Soames dismissed the papers, but acknowledged that *it's very difficult to keep things out.*

"You must seem genuinely anxious to get Dartie back—you might practice that attitude to-day."

Winifred sighed.

"Oh! What a clown Monty's been!" she said.

Soames gave her a sharp look. To save a little scandal now would only bring on his sister and her children real disgrace and perhaps ruin later on if Dartie were allowed to hang on to them, going downhill and spending the money James would leave his daughter. Though it was all tied up, that fellow would milk the settlements somehow, and make his family pay through the nose to keep him out of bankruptcy or even perhaps gaol!

Dreamer Q.C.'s Chambers were in Crown Office Row.

"Mr. Bellby is here, sir," said the clerk; "Mr. Dreamer will be ten minutes."

While they waited, Mr. Bellby and Winifred *spoke of the war. Soames interjected suddenly,* wanting Bellby in his wig and gown to stiffen Dreamer.

"If he doesn't comply we can't bring proceedings for six months. I want to get on with the matter Bellby."

"The Law's delays, Mrs. Dartie," Bellby murmured.

"Six months!" repeated Soames. *"We must put the screw on, Bellby."*

Before Dreamer Q.C., his junior Mr. Bellby breezily recapitulated the facts.

"I know all that;" and coming at Winifred smothering his words the Barrister said:

"We want to get him back, don't we, Mrs. Dartie?"

Soames interposed sharply:

"My sister's position, of course, is intolerable."

Dreamer growled. "Exactly. Now, can we rely on the cabled refusal, or must we wait till after Christmas to give him a chance to have written—that's the point, isn't it? What do you say, Bellby?"

"We won't be on till the middle of December. We've no need to give um more rope than that."

"I agree. We can go forward. Is there anything more?"

"Nothing at present," said Soames. *"I wanted you to see my sister."*

Dreamer growled softly: "Delighted. Good-evening!"

On their way out, Soames said to Mr. Bellby:

"The evidence is all right, I think. Between ourselves, if we don't get the thing through quick, we never may. Do you think he understands that?"

"I'll make um," said Bellby. *"Good man though—good man."*

Back in the carriage where Winifred cowed, Soames assured her:

"The evidence of the stewardess will be very complete."

All through that silent drive back to Green Street, the souls of both of them revolved in a single thought: 'Why, oh! Why should I have to expose my misfortune to the public like this? Why have to employ spies to peer into my private troubles? They were not of my making.'

CHAPTER FIVE

JOLLY SITS IN JUDGMENT

*T*he possessive instinct, which, so determinedly balked, was *animating two members of the Forsyte family towards riddance of what they could no longer possess, was hardening daily in the British body politic.* Even Nicholas, *originally so doubtful concerning a war which must affect property, had been heard to say that these Boers were a pig-headed lot.*

'Forsytes' in general were conservatives. And the possessive instinct was at the root of conservatism—laissez-faire. That conservatism included, when threatened, the nation and the Empire. Things were not going well in this war against the Boers down in South Africa. *One—two—three, came those ominous repulses at Stormberg, Magersfontein, Colenso.* 'Forsytes' called this Black Week. Some 'Forsytes' including Nicholas' grandson, 'very young Nicholas' who had joined the Devil's Own found themselves drilling for real. *The boy had only just eaten his dinners and* thus *been called to the Bar*—a lawyer in the making—barrister, or maybe even a judge. Throughout 'Forsythia' the process of graduating through the law schools at the Inns of Court in London was measured through a series of compulsory dinners. Now, Nicholas, with mixed feelings, realized that his grandson might end up fighting these Boers in South Africa.

Even at Oxford, among the young where rebellious liberalism spawned, there was a move toward patriotism in desperation. 'Pro-

Boers' were less obvious than the year before and Val, in his rather elitist circle, was all for a fight to the finish. There were still those in the liberal ranks who argued *for stopping the war and giving the Boers autonomy. Until Black Week, however, the groups were amorphous, without sharp edges, and argument remained but academic.*

Val still considered his cousin Jolly to be 'pro-Boer.'

In reality, *Jolly knew not where he stood.* 'Forsyte' conservatism was stirring within him, but *a streak of his grandfather old Jolyon's love of justice prevented him from seeing one side only.*

On the last Sunday of term, *Jolly was bidden to wine with 'one of the best'. After the second toast, 'Buller and damnation to the Boers',* despite the fact that Buller was not proving a very successful commander, *he noticed that Val Dartie was also a guest,* and *was looking at him with a grin and saying something to his neighbour. He was sure it was disparaging. The queer hostility he had always felt towards his second-cousin was strongly and suddenly reinforced.*

After the event and *more wine than was good for him,* he touched Val *on the arm.*

"What did you say about me in there?"

"Mayn't I say what I like?"

"No."

"Well, I said you were a pro-Boer—and so you are!"

"You're a liar!"

"D'you want a fight?"

"Of course, but not here; in the garden."

"All right. Come on."

All of us in 'Forsythia' had been taught to box in self-defense at school, some of us had also been taught the old-fashioned self-defense of fencing. At Newlands, we boxed, and at Tonbridge we fenced. This was in part a hangover from the gallant chivalry of resolving problems by fair fight—a duel. Charles Dickens expressed how eagerly 'Forsytes' of his day put this into practice in the fight between Herbert Pocket and Pip in the garden of Miss Havisham's Satis House. After the fight, the challenger having been defeated, Herbert Pocket and Mr. Pip became the best of friends.

Jolly and Val *climbed the garden railings.* These private gardens at Oxford and Cambridge colleges were often reserved for fellows—members of the teaching body. When I was at Newlands, I was impressed by a beautiful garden that ran alongside the east wing of the school.

Large wrought iron gates allowed one to peak in at an immaculate lawn and borders of old English flowers, including old-fashioned lavenders and tall hollyhocks that throughout the summer term rose ever higher unfurling their blooms so that we could see them from our classroom windows. Above the gates were the words, 'Fellows' Garden'. The only time we boys were ever allowed in this garden was in the two or three 'lame duck' weeks of our last term after we had sat for our Common Entrance exams for entry to our public schools. I suppose in a quaint way we were then considered graduates from Newlands and thus on a more equal footing with our teachers.

Climbing railings was a skill that was essential to Oxford and Cambridge 'Forsytes'. The art of successfully climbing in, or out, was the undergraduates' answer to the midnight curfew when college porters locked the gates. There was status and bravado associated with success in climbing out or climbing in, especially as the feat was nearly always after a bout of drinking.

"You're not screwed, are you?" said Jolly suddenly. *"I can't fight you if you're screwed."*

"No more than you."

"All right then."

They fought.

"Your names, young gentlemen?" a voice called out in the darkness.

Surely, it was the voice of the Proctors—the old fashioned university police, who paraded Oxford and Cambridge colleges and streets after dark, carrying the ancient rule books of the universities—the proctor in his academic dress, and his two henchmen, the bulldogs, in tail coats and top hats. They were still parading the streets of Cambridge in my own time, and still primarily administering a fine of six shillings and eight pence to any seeming undergraduate who was not wearing his academic gown after dark. If one was adept at climbing in or out, it was unlikely that these antiquated representatives of university law would be able to follow one to administer retribution.

Breaking the fight, Jolly and Val ran to *the railings, shinned up them* and *walked ten paces apart to the college gate. Val going towards the Broad along the Brewery, Jolly down the lane towards the High.*

Jolly's mind *strayed on to an imagined combat, infinitely unlike that which he had just been through, infinitely gallant, with sash and sword, with thrust and parry, as if he were in the pages of his beloved*

Dumas. He fancied himself La Mole, and Aramis, Bussy, Chicot, and D'Artagnan rolled into one.

Alexandre Dumas was one of those authors who appealed to us young 'Forsytes' through at least two generations, and not only for *The Three Musketeers*. Personally, I was heavily influenced at Newlands by *The Black Tulip*, which novel inspired me to write my first really exciting fiction in a writing competition that Newlands encouraged us to enter. I based much of my so-called fiction on the prisoner's tower where De Witt was held in the early chapters of *The Black Tulip*. No doubt because of the rather obvious plagiarism, I did not win a prize, but did get an honorable mention. Maybe this was the start of my literary career. *The Black Tulip* also might have influenced my on-going interest in horticulture—love of gardens both at home and in the exotica of the Empire, being a shared interest of most 'Forsytes' throughout the duration of 'Forsythia'.

Back to Jolly, however, Val could never be *Coconnas, Brissac or Rochefort. The fellow was just a confounded cousin who didn't come up to Cocker. Never mind, he had* punched his nose. *'Pro-Boer!' The word still rankled, and thoughts of enlisting jostled his aching head; of riding over the Veldt, firing gallantly, while the Boers rolled over like rabbits. And turning up his smarting eyes, he saw the stars shining between the housetops of the High, and himself lying out on the Karoo rolled in a blanket, with his rifle ready and his gaze fixed on a glittering heaven*—the patriotic romance of war—the beauty and the beast.

He had a fearful head the next morning which he doctored.

The next day he went 'down', and travelled through to Robin Hill. Nobody was there but June and Holly, for his father had gone to Paris. June, indeed, was occupied with lame ducks, whom, as a rule, Jolly could not stand, especially that Eric Cobbley and his family, 'hopeless outsiders', who were always littering up the house in the vacation. And between Holly and himself there was a strange division.

As the boring vacation ensued, so he thought more of enlisting. *They were appealing for Yeomanry recruits. Ought he to go?*

And then one day he saw that which moved him to uneasy wrath. He saw Holly riding in Richmond Park with that cousin of his, Val Dartie.

June had left for London and his father was still in Paris. He would have to deal with this on his own. *He felt that this was emphatically one of those moments for which he had trained himself, assiduously, at school, where he and a boy called Brent had frequently set fire to newspapers and placed them in the centre of their studies to accustom them to coolness in moments of danger.*

Ironically, within a week or two of my arrival at Tonbridge, we had an impromptu fire drill. I had been used to these drills at Newlands and knew there was no danger—just a roll call at the assembly point—but the hall was full of real smoke and there was an orange glow. The housemaster had placed burning newspapers in a galvanized dustbin lid on the tiled floor at the bottom of the house stairs. Like Jolly, we were being trained to overcome our fears. If we were to stand in the 'Forsyte' tradition and rule the British Empire, we had to overcome fear—never panic and keep that stiff upper lip at all times.

When Holly came in *flushed and ever so much prettier than she had any right to look,* Jolly escorted her to his grandfather's old study—a room dominated by the old man's chair, where they had sat on his lap as children, and a frayed Turkish rug.

A frayed Turkish rug had also graced the hall at Hockeredge, always at a jaunty angle to the square floor of stained boards. The Turkish rug in the hall or study, or even as a stair runner kept in place by brass rods, was a feature of late nineteenth-century 'Forsythia' that survived throughout the remaining decades.

Here—where the Waverley novels and Byron's works and Gibbon's 'Roman Empire' and Humbolt's 'Cosmos', and the bronzes on the mantlepiece, and that masterpiece of the oily school, 'Dutch fishing boats at sunset', were fixed as fate, and for all sign of change old Jolyon might have been sitting there still, with legs crossed in the armchair, and domed forehead and deep eyes grave above the Times—*here they came, those two grandchildren. And Jolly said:*

"I saw you and that fellow in the Park."

"Well?" she said.

"Do you know that he called me a pro-Boer last term. And I had to fight him."

"Who won?"

Jolly wished to answer: 'I should have,' but it seemed beneath him.

"Look here! What's the meaning of it? Without telling anybody!"

"Why should I? Dad isn't here; why shouldn't I ride with him?"

"I think he's an awful young rotter."

Holly went pale with anger.

"He isn't. It's your own fault for not liking him."

Holly stormed out.

Jolly mused as to why he didn't like Val Dartie. *He could not tell. Ignorant of family history, barely aware of that vague feud which had started thirteen years before with Bosinney's defection from June in favour of Soames's wife, knowing really almost nothing about Val, he was at sea.*

What was to be done? Tell Dad he must come home? Confide in June? Do nothing and trust to luck? Go up and see Val and warn him off? But how get his address? Holly wouldn't give it him!

He lit a cigarette. When he had smoked it halfway through his brow relaxed, almost as if his grandfather's *thin old hand had been passed gently over it; and in his ear something seemed to whisper: 'Do nothing; be nice to Holly, be nice to her, my dear!'*

But up in her room, divested of her habit, Holly was still frowning. 'He is not—he is not an awful young rotter!' *were the words which kept forming on her lips.*

CHAPTER SIX

JOLYON IN TWO MINDS

A little private hotel over a well-known restaurant near the Gare St. Lazare was Jolyon's haunt in Paris.

No 'Forsytes' came near this haunt, where he had a wood fire in his bedroom and the coffee was excellent.

Jolyon *spoke French well, had some friends, knew little places where pleasant dishes could be met with, queer types observed. He felt philosophical in Paris.*

On the surface, when he decided to go to Paris, *he was far from admitting that Irene's presence was influencing him.* Underneath, it was turning him inside out.

He wrote to her, asking to see her.

He received an answer which procured him a pleasurable shiver of nerves:

'My Dear Jolyon. It will be a happiness for me to see you.'

He took his way to her hotel on a bright day with a feeling such as he had often had going to visit an adored picture. No woman, so far as he remembered, had ever inspired him this special sensuous and yet impersonal sensation.

He was shown in to her in *the tarnished and ornate little lounge of a quiet hotel near the river.*

"Well," he said, "what news, poor exile?"

"None."

"Nothing from Soames?"

"Nothing."

"I have let the flat for you, and like a good steward I bring you some money. How do you like Paris?"

She owned that to be alone in Paris was a little difficult; and yet, Paris was so full of its own life that it was often, she confessed, as innocuous as a desert. Besides, the English were not liked just now!

France, the traditional foe, was pro-Boer. Their sentiments gravitated to their neighbors, the Dutch.

Having dispensed with those surface reasons for needing to see Irene, Jolyon allowed his deeper feelings to surface.

"Well, you must let me take you about while I'm here. We'll start tomorrow. Come and dine at my pet restaurant; and we'll go to the Opera-Comique."

So far as they could tell, no one knew her address except himself; she was unknown in Paris, and he but little known, so that discretion seemed unnecessary in those walks, talks, visits to concerts, picture-galleries, theatres, little dinners, expeditions to Versailles, St. Cloud, even Fontainbleau.

Irene's philosophy of life seemed to march in admirable step with his own, conditioned by emotion more than reason.

Jolyon made plans to renew this time in places still more delightful, where the sun was hot and there were strange things to see and paint.

However, this idyll, with no thought of Robin Hill, Jolly or Holly, came abruptly to an end *on the 20th of January with a telegram:*

'Have enlisted in Imperial Yeomanry.—Jolly.'

Jolyon received it just as he was setting out to meet Irene *at the Louvre. He felt disturbed to the soul, realising suddenly how Irene had twisted herself round the roots of his being.*

The 'Forsyte' rose within him. He had neglected his biggest asset and greatest property—his son and daughter, while dallying in an impractical romance brought on by the mystery of Paris. *He saw his feeling as it was, in the nature of an infatuation.*

His thoughts were of Jolly, and the prospect of him being sent out to South Africa. Pro-Boer though he had been, after Black Week those same 'Forsyte' principles that were gripping almost all his class, and the lower orders, too—patriotic fervor to preserve the Empire, the nation's possession—rose in Jolyon.

He was proud of this enlistment; proud for his boy for going off to fight for the country.

"Look!" he said to Irene on finding her in the Gallery.

She read the telegram, and he heard her sigh.

She knew as well as he. For Jolyon *to be loyal to his son he must shake her hand and go.*

"Of course you must go," she said.

"Well!" said Jolyon, holding out his hand. "Such is life! Take care of yourself, my dear!"

Passion had flown out of the window, but *from the doorway he saw her lift her hand and touch its finger with her lips. He raised his hat solemnly, and did not look back.*

* * *

'Forsythia' for me lingered on an extra decade. For most 'Forsytes' it ended in the late 1950s in that post-Suez world. For me it lingered on through the late 1960s.

This happened through a time warp in my life. By chance, on leaving Tonbridge in 1962, with the assistance of my headmaster The Reverend Canon Lawrence Waddy, DD., I became the private tutor to the son of a wealthy American Old Tonbridgian, at that time living at Twin Farms, near Woodstock in Vermont. Twin Farms was the home that Sinclair Lewis had shared with Dorothy Thompson. The Albertini family, although Americans, met me in Windsor, England. We immediately took a liking to each other and within three months I was with them in Ireland where they rented property.

Ireland in the 1960s was more like England had been in my grandparents' youth—simply put, behind the times. Introduced to a world of foxhunting, game fishing, shoots, and dinner parties where we all still dressed for dinner, the 'winds of change', the Beatles and the swinging sixties, passed me by. We lived on the estate of the Duke of Devonshire in Lismore, in a dower house across the river from the castle, a castle which was used by the BBC as Northanger Abbey in their early twenty-first-century Masterpiece Theatre production of Jane Austen's novel by the same name. Then, while I was at Cambridge, Mr. Albertini rented Carton House, in County Kildare. This is one of the largest eighteenth-century mansions in Ireland and was the home of Lord Brocket. Immediately before Mr. Albertini took the house, it had been rented out to Princess Grace of Monaco. There, during my spring vacation from Cambridge in 1964, I slept in a magnificent Louis Seize four-poster bed complete with carved cherubs blowing trumpets from the canopy and a headboard featuring carved eighteenth-century musical instruments. We sat in drawing rooms festooned with Lely, Reynolds, and Gainsborough portraits. In fact, the white and gilt drawing room with a full sized organ above the mahogany double doors leading to the dining room was featured as a substitute for the king's drawing room at Buckingham Palace in the 2010 film *The King's Speech.* The dining table could seat fifty, making even Uncle Timothy Forsyte's table small. And yet, there were only six of us, outside of the staff, living in this mansion.

Finally, just before I came down from Cambridge, Mr. Albertini purchased Tullamaine Castle in County Tipperary to make this his permanent residence. I became, at the young age of twenty-three, the estate manager of Tullamaine Castle. I was responsible for a domestic staff of twelve, two hundred and sixty acres of mixed farming, twenty-five acres of gardens, including two self-sustaining acres of kitchen gardens, and, of course, there were horse stables and dog kennels. For me, 'Forsythia' lived on, mingled with the archaic Anglo-Irish aristocracy of whom my great-grandmother, Harriet 'Penny' Massey, had been a daughter.

It was the world described in Somerville and Ross' well-known tales, *The Irish R.M. and his Experiences,* and one of the suspected models for the eccentric families of those tales was from Castletownshend in County Cork, the Salter-Townsends, who were acquainted with us in the 1960s. Sometimes, I think back on that world as an anachronism most, when I consider the telephone. We still had to ring a handle on the handset to contact the postmistress in Fethard, Mary Goldsmith, some four miles away, so we could be plugged in manually into her switchboard. Our telephone number was Fethard 2.

In 1969, a governess was engaged at Tullamaine Castle. June Kennedy was an attractive local girl from Fethard. She was young like me, and quite beautiful. In the small Tipperary town, they called her "Fethard's Golden girl." It was inevitable that we would take a liking to each other, but she was a Roman Catholic and I was a Protestant. In the Ireland of the 1960s these denominations did not mix. This was as much a division in society as religious. The Anglo-Irish were the three percent, a mixture of aristocracy and 'Forsytes', descendents of 'The Ascendancy', the protestant members of the Church of Ireland; the rest of the country were Roman Catholics. My relationship with June caused something of a rift between me and the Albertini family. They tended to take this out on June.

When not in Ireland, the family lived in a plantation house on St. Simons Island in Georgia, famous as the Black Banks Plantation of the Gould family in Eugenia Price's novels about the old south on St. Simons Island. Here, life was also somewhat of an anachronism. On my first visit to Georgia, I knew that I had arrived in the old south when we got off the *Silver Meteor* train from New York at Thalman. Two 'colored' Sea Island chauffeurs, for that was the accepted description of African Americans in the old south of the 1960s, met us. Their names were Mighty Fine and Forty-Five!

On June's only visit to St. Simons, I remained behind in Ireland to take care of the estate. We had a full spring of calving and foaling to contend with and the idea of separating June Kennedy from me also came into play. June was extremely unhappy on St. Simons Island where she was virtually kept prisoner at Black Banks, the family forbidding her any social life on an island that teamed with exciting social activities. She wrote bitterly to me of her situation, and she had my sympathy. Eventually, she snapped and left to be taken in by some sympathetic and friendly neighbors. Naturally, this outraged Mr. Albertini and he dismissed her and ensured that she be returned to Ireland, a matter in which in all fairness he had little choice for immigration reasons.

I had experienced the wrong side of the Albertini family at times and I felt the injustice. Our lives as appendages of such families constituted virtual ownership—the 'Forsyte' principle of property. To this end, I might compare myself with Jolyon. Jolyon had experienced the wrong side of Soames Forsyte as had his father. Both had taken sides with Irene in her stormy relationship with Soames, largely about this principle of ownership, as I did with June Kennedy. Although, 'Forsytes', both 'Old Jolyon' and 'Young Jolyon' tended to support the underdog, even if not to the extreme of June Forsyte. They were liberals in a conservative 'Forsyte' world. That summer, while the Albertini family remained in the United States, I fostered my friendship with June Kennedy. I started looking for other jobs knowing that my position as estate manager at Tullamaine Castle would be in jeopardy when the family returned. I would be ostracized just as 'Young Jolyon' had been ostracized, and in part because I had taken up with the governess just as 'Young Jolyon' had done with Helene Hilmer.

Ultimately, June and I found ourselves in Paris.

Ours was *a little private hotel over a well-known restaurant near the Gare Saint-Lazare.* We did not have a wood fireplace in the bedroom, actually we had separate bedrooms for June was from a very conservative Roman Catholic background, but *the coffee was excellent.* June had been staying with a friend on a stud farm in Normandy and took the train from Caen to Paris. My grandfather, Grandpa Jack Collings, had been taken ill at ninety and gave me the excuse to leave Tullamaine Castle to visit with him, but it also afforded me the opportunity to visit with June Kennedy in Paris. Our rendez-vous was the Gare Saint-Lazare. *No-one knew* our *address; we were unknown in Paris, so that discretion seemed unnecessary in* our *walks, talks, visits to concerts, picture-galleries, little dinners and* an expedition *to Versailles.* This was thanks to our somewhat ill-fated, but nonetheless well-used time with my Uncle Gyles—that unforgiveable moment when we dropped in.

June's *philosophy of life seemed to march in admirable step with* my *own, conditioned by emotion more than reason.* And, as with Jolyon, Paris ran away with our emotions. *Paris* is *at once the first and last place in which to be friendly with a pretty woman. Revelation was like a bird in* my *heart, singing: 'Elle est ton reve! Elle est ton reve!' Sometimes this seemed natural, sometimes ludicrous—a bad case of rapture.*

These feelings were shared by Jolyon and me, his in *The Forsyte Saga* and mine in real life. And just as for Jolyon, so for me, they ended abruptly. I proposed marriage at a sidewalk café—the first time I ever proposed to a young lady. June turned me down. What do you do in Paris after a whirlwind romance when the tint of the glass changes? She hastened back to Caen, and I returned to Ireland and Tullamaine Castle. The romance was over. June Kennedy became a nun, and I settled back in loyalty to my job as estate manager and to the Albertini family.

•

CHAPTER SEVEN

DARTIE VERSUS DARTIE

The suit—*Dartie versus Dartie*—for restitution of those conjugal rights concerning which Winifred was at heart so deeply undecided, was not reached before the courts rose for Christmas, but the case was third on the list when they sat again.

They celebrated Christmas at James'. Her father was relieved at the approaching dissolution of her marriage. *The disappearance of Dartie made the fall in Consols a comparatively small matter. What worried him as a lawyer and a parent was the fear that Dartie might suddenly turn up and obey the order of the court when made.* This *fear preyed on him so much that* he presented *Winifred with a large Christmas cheque* for her to send to *that chap out there to keep him from coming back.* It was in *the nature of insurance against that bankruptcy which would no longer hang over him if only the divorce went through.*

Winifred sent it. *Poor woman!—it cost her many a pang to send what must find its way into the vanity-bag of 'that creature'!*

Soames, hearing of it, shook his head. Still it would look well with the court.

Winifred put on a brave front with *her children at home gaping like young birds for news of their father—Imogen just on the point of coming out and Val very restive about the whole thing.*

Val made Soames nervous and he *was very careful to keep the proximity of the proceedings from his nephew's ears.* Then, *he asked*

338

him to dine at the Remove Club, *and over Val's cigar introduced the subject which he knew to be nearest to his heart.*

"I hear," he said, "that you want to play polo up at Oxford."

"Rather!"

"Well," continued Soames, "that's a very expensive business. Your grandfather isn't likely to consent to it unless he can make sure that he's not got any other drain on him."

Val grimaced awkwardly. "I suppose you mean my Dad!"

"Yes," said Soames; "I'm afraid it depends on whether he continues to be a drag or not:" and said no more, letting the boy dream it over.

Val's dreaming, however, centered on Holly. *All he cared for was to dress in his last-created riding togs, and steal away to Robin Hood Gate,* Richmond Park, *where presently the silver roan would come demurely sidling with its slim, dark-haired rider, and in the glades bare of leaves they would go off side by side, not talking very much, riding races sometimes, and sometimes holding hands.*

He kept this all to himself, for, as yet, the time was not right. *He would have to go through with college, and she would have to 'come out' before they could be married.*

Then, *one day in the middle of January the silver-roan palfrey and its rider were missing at the tryst.*

The next day the court hearing was up. Winifred dressed in her best, *after breakfast said to him, "Come in here, Val," and led the way to the drawing-room.* Val *was at once beset by qualms. 'Has she found out about Holly?'*

"Will you come with me this morning—I have to go to court this morning."

"You don't mean—," Val said, *noticing that his mother's lips were all awry.* "All right, mother; I'll come. The brutes! I suppose I'd better change."

They rode in James' carriage to the Courts of Justice, *his mother in furs* and a new hat, *with the appearance of one going to a Mansion House Assembly.*

The Mansion House, the Lord Mayor of London's official residence, had something of the status of a royal palace in 'Forsythia'. In fact, in some ways the Lord Mayor actually represented royalty in his city. For centuries the City of London has been independent, governing itself outside Westminster, so much so that royal family members traditionally have to request permission from the Lord Mayor to enter his city. The government of 'The City' where most 'Forsytes' did their business, is not elected by universal suffrage, but the electorate is formed from the liverymen of those ancient medieval trade guilds, such as the Barbers' Company of which the Hovenden family had been past masters, and in the very last days of 'Forsythia', my father master. The seat of the government of 'The City' is it's medieval Guildhall that suffered severe damage during the Great Fire of London in 1666 and further damage during the 1940 'Blitz' of World War II, but is still the oldest standing medieval gothic building in the City of London. Every fall, the Lord Mayor of London entertains the crown's government to dinner at the Guildhall. The occasion is a formal platform for the sovereign's prime minister to report to the Lord Mayor and the dignitaries of the City of London on the state of the government in the rest of the realm. The prime minister's speech to the Lord Mayor becomes in essence Great Britain's 'State of the Realm' address. It is also an occasion for the Lord Mayor, as elected head of the 'The City'—the financial hub of the British Empire in 'Forsythia' days, and still one of the most important financial centers of the world—to inform the prime minister of developments in 'The City'. However, 'The City' of London, throughout history has always been very loyal to the crown, one reason being that its electorate, the liverymen of those trade guilds, swear allegiance to the crown when they are admitted to their livery. Indeed, many companies' treasures in silver and gold, paintings and furnishings, have been donated to their halls by members of the royal family, past and present. Some members of the royal family are liverymen or honorary freemen of these companies, too. The late Queen Elizabeth, the Queen Mother was a member of the Barber's Company and also in my own time, H.R.H. Princess Ann, the Princess Royal, was Centenary Master of the Guild of Freemen of the City of London. I attended banquets graced by both royal personages. 'The City' is never in rebellion, but it is independent.

The Mansion House and the Guildhall are the focal points of this ancient pageantry of government and trade, where old medieval streets with quaint names like Threadneedle Street, Poultry, and Pudding Lane meet. Every year, these streets witness the pageant of the Lord Mayor's Show, with a procession of floats, mostly representing the livery companies, and the procession of the newly elected Lord Mayor riding in his gilt carriage of equal extravagance to the coronation coach of the monarch. He is surrounded, like the monarch, by the only private standing army outside the royal 'Beefeaters', the Tower Guard, allowed on British soil—The Honourable Company of Pikemen.

Invitations to City events at either the Mansion House or the Guildhall were much prized in the 'Forsyte' calendar, and still are. Visiting Heads of State are usually invited to a formal banquet by the Lord Mayor after they have attended the royal round at Windsor Castle or Buckingham Palace. On such occasions, they are often also given the prestigious Freedom of the City of London.

When my father hosted the Barbers' Company's formal Ladies' Livery Dinner at the Mansion House in 1965, it was because the Lord Mayor, Sir Lionel Denny, was a past master of the Barbers' Company. Because of that association, that same year, my father and mother were also present at the Guildhall banquet for Her Majesty's Government. My mother was seated on that occasion between the Archbishop of Canterbury and James Callaghan, then Chancellor of the Exchequer in Prime Minister Harold Wilson's cabinet. Later, James Callaghan succeeded Harold Wilson as prime minister.

Val Dartie looked at his mother in her 'Lady Mayoress' furs *and made but one allusion to the business in hand. "There'll be nothing about those pearls, will there?"*

The little tufted white tails of Winifred's muff began to shiver.

"Oh no," she said. "It'll be quite harmless today. Your grandmother wanted to come too, but I wouldn't let her. I thought you could take care of me. You look so nice, Val. Just pull your coat-collar up a little more at the back—that's right"

My mother often tried to correct our dress when we went out or if company was coming. I think she got it from her mother, 'The Exceptional', my Granny Mabs. Granny, who had so admired the way my father used to dress when he came courting my mother at Redcroft, was merciless on my sisters as to how they were dressed.

Winifred and Val arrived at The Law Courts *soon after ten.*

It was Val's first visit, and the building struck him at once.

"By Jove!" he said as they passed into the hall where Soames was waiting for them, *"this'd make four or five jolly good racket courts."*

Rackets was very much a 'Forsyte' game. It was the forerunner of Squash, but played on a larger back-walled court and with a harder and even faster ball. There are not that many true rackets' courts in England these days, but in my time at Tonbridge there was a very active Rackets Club and a fine old Victorian court built beside the gymnasium and the chapel—rackets, fencing, and the established Church of England—some of the staples of a 'Forsyte' education.

Val was roused from his musings.

"It's Happerly Browne, Court 1," Soames said. *"We shall be on first."*

Val cringed at the thought and observed that *people seemed to be lurking everywhere, and he plucked Soames by the sleeve.*

"I say, Uncle, you're not going to let those beastly papers in, are you?"

Soames led them to their place in the courtroom in high backed pews all packed together. *Val had a feeling that they might all slip down into the well.*

There was *mahogany, and* there were *black gowns, white blobs of wigs and faces and papers, all rather secret and whispery.*

Then an 'old Johnny' in a gown and long wig, came through a door into the high pew opposite. They all stood.

"Dartie versus Dartie!"

It seemed to Val unspeakably disgusting to have one's name called out like this in public!

Most 'Forsytes' lived within the law and had rare need to visit law courts unless they were of the profession—a profession favored in respectability upholding the law of the Empire, especially in far-flung possessions. 'Forsytes' administered the law, but rarely were cited by the law.

The only occasion I know of in my life that found my immediate family in court was unfortunate to say the least, and carried with it an awesome feeling of shame mingled with injury. I was about eleven and at Newlands at the time. My father was involved in a road accident while driving down to Seaford on one of our visiting weekends. He passed a stationary bus in the village of Uckfield and a man stepped out from in front of the bus right into his path. The Armstrong Siddeley hit the man, who died almost instantaneously before hospital aid could come to him. The man was an Indian prince. Naturally, the fact that he was an exotic prince of the Empire made this sad accident a story. Fortunately, in court, my father was totally exempted from blame, but there was no way of keeping the story out of the press. I remember feeling a little like Val, disgusted to see our family name in this court report in the newspaper, although relieved to know that the Sussex coroner had completely exonerated my father of blame.

Val heard someone behind him speaking of his family. *He screwed his face round to see an old be-wigged buffer, who spoke as if he were eating his own words—queer-looking old cuss, the sort of man he had seen once or twice at his grandfather's dining at Park Lane and punishing the port; he knew now where they 'dug them up.'*

It was this old buffer who spoke to the judge. His voice droned on from behind:

"Differences about money matters—extravagance of the respondent—strained situation—frequent absences on the part of Mr. Dartie. My client, very rightly, your Ludship will agree, was anxious to check a course—but lead to ruin—remonstrated—gambling at cards and on the race-course. Crisis early in October, when the respondent wrote her this letter from his club.

Val sat up and his ears burned.

"I propose to read it with the emendations necessary to the epistle of a gentleman who has been—shall we say dining, my Lud?"

The be-wigged lawyer read Dartie's note.

Val glanced sideways at his mother's impassive face; it had a hunted look in the eyes.

"'I am tired of being insulted by you,'" the voice droned on. "' am going to live a new life.—M.D.'"

'Poor mother,' Val thought and touched her arm with his own.

"And next day, me Lud, the respondent left by the steamship Tuscarora *for Buenos Aires. Since then we have nothing from him but a cabled refusal in answer to the letter which my client wrote the following day in great distress, begging him to return to her. With your Ludship's permission, I shall now put Mrs. Dartie in the box."*

Val followed with a certain glee the questions framed so as to give the impression that she really wanted his father back. It seemed to him that they were 'foxing Old Bagwigs finely.' And he had a most unpleasant jar when the Judge said suddenly:

"Now, why did your husband leave you—not because you called him 'the limit', you know?"

Val heard a shuffle of papers behind him; and instinct told him that the issue was in peril.

"No, my Lord," Winifred answered, her clipped 'Forsyte' accent correcting the barrister's professional 'me Lud', *"but it had gone on a long time."*

"What had gone on?"

"Our differences about money."

"But you supplied the money. Do you suggest that he left you to better his position?"

"No, my Lord, but you see, I had refused to give him any more money. It took him a long time to believe that, but he did at last—and when he did..."

"I see, you had refused. But you've sent him some since."

"My Lord, I wanted him back."

"And you thought that would bring him?"

"I don't know, my Lord, I acted on my father's advice."

Val could sense by the faces in court that his mother had made the right answer.

"Just one more question, Mrs. Dartie," said the Judge. "Are you still fond of your husband?"

His mother answered, rather low: "Yes, my Lord."

The Judge nodded.

Witnesses to his father's departure and continued absence followed— one of their own maids even, which struck Val as particularly beastly. Servants should not be involved in such intimate family matters was a rule of 'Forsythia', even though servants probably knew it all. However, the law was ruthless if a servant could be a good witness.

The Judge pronounced the decree for restitution, and they all *got up to go.*

"You behaved beautifully, dear," his mother said. *"It was such a comfort to have you. Your uncle and I are going to lunch."*

"All right," said Val, *and parting from them he bolted into a hansom and drove to the Goat's Club,* where he kept riding togs. *His thoughts were on Holly and what he must do before her brother showed her this thing in tomorrow's paper.*

* * *

Soames and Winifred made their way to The Cheshire Cheese, a pub frequented by lawyers. Soames *had suggested it as a meeting-place with Mr. Bellby.*

Mr. Bellby seemed pleased. *They had got the decree of restitution, and what was the matter with that?* There would be a divorce trial in about six months.

"Quite," said Soames in a suitably low voice, "but we shall have to begin again to get evidence. It will look fishy if it comes out that we knew of misconduct from the start."

Mr. Belby continued confidently.

"The Judge is *bound by precedent to give ye your divorce if the evidence is satisfactory. We won't let him know that Mrs. Dartie had knowledge of the facts. Dreamer did it very nicely—he's got a fatherly touch."*

Soames nodded.

"And I compliment ye, Mrs. Dartie," went on Mr. Bellby; "ye've a natural gift for giving evidence. Steady as a rock."

Their light lunch arrived—Lark pudding. These song birds were more of a working man's dish, favored in pubs, than the food of 'Forsytes', who usually ate out at their clubs, but Soames and Winifred put on a brave front encouraged by a glass of port apiece.

A well-known nursery rhyme of 'Forsythia' described twenty-four blackbirds being baked in a pie, but as children we were never served any such dish. The nearest I ever came to the experience was being dressed as a blackbird in a headpiece lovingly sewn by my mother for the re-enactment of this nursery rhyme under the great tulip tree in the garden of St. Christopher's, The Hall, that we created as our kindergarten contribution to the Beckenham Centenary pageant.

Conversation turned on the war, Soames thought Ladysmith would fall, and it might last a year. Bellby thought it would be over by the summer. Both agreed that they wanted more men. There was nothing for it but complete victory, since it was now a question of national prestige—the face of the British Empire in the world.

Winifred brought things back to more solid ground by saying that she did not want the divorce suit to come on till after the summer holidays had begun at Oxford, then the boys would have forgotten about it before Val had to go up again; the London season, too, in which Imogen would be coming out, *would be over.*

The lawyers reassured her.

They then *parted—Soames to the city, Bellby to his chambers—*in 'Forsythia' lawyers' offices were always referred to as chambers—and *Winifred took a hansom to Park Lane* to report to her mother, Emily.

They decided to tell James.

He received the report grudgingly and *gave Winifred a cheque,* after noting her dress, *saying:*

"*I expect you'll have a lot of expense. That's a new hat you've got on,*" *and as he thought of expenses he added,* "*Why doesn't Val come and see us?*"

Winifred promised to bring him to dinner soon.

CHAPTER EIGHT

THE CHALLENGE

Val was jogging toward the Roehampton Gate, whence he would canter on to their usual tryst. His spirits were rising rapidly. There had been nothing so very terrible in the morning's proceedings beyond the general disgrace of violated privacy. 'If we were engaged!' he thought, 'what happens wouldn't matter.' He felt, indeed, like human society, which kicks and clamours at the results of matrimony, and hastens to get married. But again, he was alone at the trysting spot, and this second defection on the part of Holly upset him dreadfully. He could not go back without seeing her today! He proceeded towards Robin Hill. Suppose her father were back or her sister or brother were in!

"Only Miss Holly is in, sir," the servant said.

"Oh! Thanks. Might I take my horse round to the stables? And would you say—her cousin, Mr. Val Dartie."

When he returned Holly was in the hall.

"I've been awfully anxious," said Val in a low voice. "What's the matter?"

"Jolly knows about our riding."

"Is he in?"

"No; but I expect he will be soon."

Holding her hand, he said: "I want to tell you something about my family. My Dad, you know, isn't altogether—I mean, he's left my mother *and they're trying to divorce him; so they've ordered him to come back, you see. You'll see that in the paper tomorrow."*

Her hand squeezed his.

"Of course, there's nothing very much at present," he continued, *"but there will be, I expect, before it's over; divorce suits are beastly, you know. I wanted to tell you, because—because—you ought to know—if—if you're going to be a darling and love me, Holly. I love you—ever so; and I want to be engaged." Dropping on his knees, he tried to get nearer to that soft, troubled face. "You do love me—don't you? If you don't, I..."*

There was a moment of silence and suspense, so awful that he could hear the sound of a mowing machine far out on the lawn pretending there was grass to cut.

All over the Empire, from Kuala Lumpur to Nairobi, from Calcutta to Simla, from Vancouver to Christchurch, New Zealand, or at home in Dorking, Surrey, 'Forsytes' cultivated their lawns. This obsession with neatly mown grass lasted throughout 'Forsythia's' decades and certainly was rampant in my own childhood. My first drawings as a child were of butterflies and lawn mowers. Lawns had to be cut in immaculate stripes made by rollers that bent the freshly mown grass in the trail of the machine. In 1899, such a lawn mower was probably drawn by a horse or pony wearing big flat shoes so as not to leave hoof imprints, at least on larger expanses of lawn such as that between the house and the copse at Robin Hill. Smaller lawns were cut by burly gardeners pushing a heavy cast iron mower with a cylinder of blades that turned against a plate cutting the grass to uniform height and followed by a roller that flattened the grass into those precious stripes. A decade or two later mowers were petrol driven, but followed the same principle. Two companies, Ransomme and Atco, monopolized these motor-mowing machines on 'Forsyte' lawns throughout the Empire. The striped lawn was almost a symbol of the mother country. In the 1950s, my greatest joy on visiting my grandparents at The Breach was after lunch when Grandpop would allow me to cut the grass in immaculate English stripes on that vast lawn. Ironically, at about the time of the Suez crisis and the beginning of the end of 'Forsythia', my grandfather bought a new lawn mower. It was silver rather than the traditional green of Ransomme and Atco machines, and it did not have cylinder blades or a roller—but was a rotary mower. I immediately disliked this mower. My sisters called it a 'Hoover sack' mower, as it sucked up the cut grass into a sack rather than throwing it out into a bin. All vacuum cleaners in the latter decades of 'Forsythia' were called 'Hoovers' after the principle firm that made vacuum cleaners. To this day, Diane and Sally still refer to rotary mowers as 'Hoover sack' mowers, with some disdain, regretting the days of good old Ransomme or Atco machines with their distinctive striped lawns. Today, rotary mowers are the norm, cylinder mowers almost only found on golf course greens or making those stripes on the Wimbledon tennis courts, but cylinder mowers were one reason why in 'Forsythia' lawns all looked like golf course greens! Could the rise of the rotary mower and the fall of the British Empire have something in common? The rotary mower destroyed one of the very symbols of the mother country—the striped English lawn!

To the whir of that distant machine, Holly *swayed forward; her free hand touched* Val's *hair, and he gasped; "Oh, Holly!"*

Her answer was very soft; "Oh, Val!"

So tremulous was she in his grasp, with her eyelids closed and his lips nearing them. Her eyes opened, seemed to swim a little; he pressed his lips to hers. Suddenly he sprang up, there had been footsteps, a sort of startled grunt. Val looked round. No one! But the long curtains which barred off the outer hall were quivering.

The sound of curtains being drawn is associated in my childhood with those that hung between the outer hall and the inner hall at Hockeredge. Whenever company rang the front door bell it was necessary to draw these curtains to let them in from the small ante-hall into our spacious beamed inner hall.

"My God! Who was that?" whispered Val.

"Jolly, I expect," Holly *whispered* back.

"All right!" Val said, *"I don't care a bit now we're engaged,"* and *striding towards the curtains he drew them aside. There at the fireplace in the hall stood Jolly.*

"I beg your pardon for hearing," Jolly said with dignity.

"Well!" Val said abruptly, "it's nothing to you."

"Oh!" said Jolly; "you come this way," and he crossed the hall. Val followed. At the study door he felt a touch on his arm; Holly's voice said:

"I'm coming too."

"No," said Jolly.

"Yes," said Holly.

In the study, *they stood in a sort of triangle on three corners of the worn Turkey carpet.*

Breaking silence, Val said:

"Holly and I are engaged."

Jolly stepped back.

"This is our house," he said; *"I'm not going to insult you in it. But my father's away. I'm in charge of my sister. You've taken advantage of me."*

"I didn't mean to," said Val hotly.

I think you did," said Jolly. *"If you hadn't meant to, you'd have spoken to me, or waited for my father to come back."*

Certainly, throughout 'Forsythia' it was generally the custom to ask a father or guardian for one's hoped for fiancée's hand in marriage before confirming the status.

"There were reasons," said Val.

"What reasons?"

"About my family—I've just told her. I wanted her to know before things happen."

"You're kids," Jolly *said, "and you know you are."*

"I am not a kid," said Val.

"You are—you're not twenty."

"Well, what are you?"

"I am twenty," said Jolly.

"Only just; anyway, I'm as good a man as you."

"We'll see that," Jolly *said. "I dare you to do what I'm going to do."*

"Dare me?"

Jolly smiled. "Yes," he said, *"dare you, and I know very well you won't. I haven't forgotten you called me a pro-Boer."*

Holly gasped as if she knew what was coming.

"Yes," went on Jolly, *with a sort of smile, "we shall soon see. I'm going to join the Imperial Yeomanry, and I dare you to do the same, Mr. Val Dartie."*

It was like a blow between the eyes, so utterly unthought of, so extreme and ugly in the midst of Val's *dreaming.*

"Sit down," said Jolly. *"Take your time! Think it over well."* And he *himself sat down on the arm of his grandfather's chair.*

If Val *did not take that 'dare' he would be disgraced in Holly's eyes, and in the eyes of that young enemy, her brute of a brother. Yet if he took it, ah! then all would vanish—her face, her eyes, her hair, her kisses just begun!*

"Take your time," said Jolly again; "I don't want to be unfair."

They both looked at Holly. She would be proud of her brother—that enemy! She would be ashamed of him!

"All right!" he said. "Done!"

Holly's face shone *with wistful admiration. Jolly stood up.*

"Tomorrow, then," he said, "we'll go together. We'll meet at the main recruiting office at twelve o'clock."

Jolly left them.

The confusion in the mind of Val thus left alone with her for whom he had paid this sudden price was extreme. The 'Forsyte' need to show a stiff upper lip, even of 'showing off' was still, however, uppermost.

"We shall get plenty of riding and shooting, anyway," he said, "that's one comfort. Oh! The war'll soon be over, perhaps we shan't even have to go out. I don't care, except for you." He would be out of the way of that beastly divorce. He felt her warm hand slip into his. Jolly had thought he had stopped their loving each other, did he? He held her tightly round the waist, looking at her softly through his lashes, smiling to cheer her up, promising to come down and see her soon, feeling somehow six inches taller and much more in command of her than he had ever dared feel before. So, swiftly, on the least provocation, does the possessive instinct flourish and grow.

CHAPTER NINE

DINNER AT JAMES'S

Dinner parties were not now given at James's in Park Lane—to every house the moment comes when master or mistress is no longer 'up to it'; no more can nine courses be served to twenty mouths above twenty fine white expanses; nor does the household cat any longer wonder why she is suddenly shut up.

Emily, being considerably younger than James, missed the old days and saw in a dinner party for Val an opportunity to do things in the old style one more time. Imogen was coming out, too. She needed the grand dining experience. *She ordered dinner for six instead of two, herself wrote a number of foreign words on cards, and arranged the flowers—mimosa from the Riviera, and white Roman hyacinths, not from Rome. There would only be, of course, James and herself, Soames, Winifred, Val and Imogen.*

My mother also liked to dress her own table—something I inherited and still try to do in the style of 'Forsythia'. My sister Diane and I were both influenced by my mother in setting an elegant table, and both of us pride ourselves in our ability to arrange table flowers. A few years after the demise of 'Forsythia', our Great-aunt Dorrie, gave my mother an epergne for Christmas, probably an old one that might have belonged to my great-grandmother, the first Mrs. Collings, or maybe even to Mr. Stevens' family. Diane and I did our best to arrange a table around this ornamental silver and glass stand for holding a cornucopia of fruit and flowers, but epergnes really require those dining tables that seat twenty. Such eperngnes graced the tables of many Victorian and Edwardian 'Forsyte' households and might well have held the mimosa and hyacinths that Emily had arranged.

Emily dressed for dinner in the grand manner of the 'good old days'.

"What are you putting on that thing for?" James remarked. *"You'll catch cold."*

Emily was unperturbed. *"Let me put you on one of those dickies I got you, James; then you'll only have to change your trousers and put on your velvet coat, and there you'll be. Val likes you to look nice."*

"Dicky!" said James. *"You're always wasting your money on something."*

Dickies were becoming the fashion among those just entering the ranks of 'Forsythia' at the turn of the nineteenth century to the twentieth. However, to old established 'Forsytes' like James, the idea of wearing an all-in-one shirtfront that included necktie, collar, shirt and waistcoat was nouveau riche. Emily would have purchased such an item at one of the department stores out of genuine concern that it would be easier for James dressing in his dotage. Her motives were without question, but the concept of anything new-fangled was of suspicion to one like James. The concept of old 'Forsyte' standards and new, were well illustrated in L.P. Hartley's novel, *The Go-Between,* in which a ready-made cravat is a cause of some concern in the snobbish rivalry between two Edwardian boys— Marcus Maudesley and Leo Colston—another expression of those shades of divide even within the three percent. It was always a great pride of mine when dressed in black tie or white tie that I always tied my own tie and never used a ready-made bow tie. In fact, I remember proving the fact in Ireland on the way to a hunt ball when dressed in white tie and tails. I undid and re-tied my white bow tie with dexterity and no mirror, to prove the point, or was it to impress the young lady I was taking to the ball! The skill to tie one's own bow tie, which in fact is just as easy as tying one's shoe laces, was a fact of pride in those latter days of 'Forsythia' in the 1950s and '60s, no doubt, in part, because we no longer had valets to do it for us. The choice had become, 'know the skill' or succumb to the shame of 'wearing a ready-made dicky bow.'

"I've made it a proper dinner-party," Emily said comfortably; "I thought it would be good practice for Imogen—she must get used to it now she's coming out."

"She'll be pretty, I shouldn't wonder," James muttered.

"She is pretty," said Emily. "She should make a good match."

"There you go," murmured James, now noting the convenience of the dicky and rising above his pride. "She'd much better stay at home and look after her mother." A second Dartie carrying off his grand-daughter would finish him!

"Where's Warmson?" he said suddenly, "I should like a glass of Madeira tonight."

"There's champagne, James."

James shook his head. "No body," he said; "I can't get any good out of it."

He instructed Warmson to fetch the last of a collection of fine Madeiras from his cellar. In the wine from that cellar was written the history of the forty-odd years since he had come to the Park Lane house with his young bride, and of the many generations of friends and acquaintances who had passed into the unknown; its depleted bins preserved the record of family festivity—all the marriages, births, deaths of kith and kin.

From that deep reverie the entrance of his son dragged him, followed very soon by that of Winifred and her two eldest.

Val could see that this was to be a proper full 'blow-out' with 'fizz' and port! And he felt in need of it, after what he had done that day—signed up with his cousin in the Imperial Yeomanry. As they sat through the courses, Val waited for his moment to divulge his action.

His grandfather's voice travelled to him thinly.

"Val, try a little of the Madeira with your ice. You won't get that up at college."

Val watched the slow liquid filling his glass, the essential oil of the old wine glazing the surface; inhaled its aroma, and thought: 'Now for it! This bombshell up his sleeve, this piece of sensational patriotism, or example, rather, of personal daring, to display—for his pleasure in what he had done for his Queen and Country was so far entirely personal. He was now a 'blood', indissolubly connected with guns and horses; he had a right to swagger—not, of course, that he was going to. He sipped; and a gentle glow spread in his veins, already heated. With a rapid look *round, he said: "I joined the Imperial Yeomanry to-day, Granny," and emptied his glass as though drinking the health of his own act.*

"What!" It was his mother's desolate little word.

"Young Jolly Forsyte and I went down there together."

"You didn't sign!" said his Uncle Soames.

"Rather! We go into camp on Monday."

"I say!" cried Imogen.

All looked at James. He was leaning forward with his hand behind his ear.

"What's that?" he said. "What's he saying, I can't hear."

Emily reached forward to pat Val's hand.

"It's only that Val has joined the Yeomanry, James; it's very nice of him. He'll look his best in uniform."

"Joined the—rubbish!" came from James, "you can't see two yards before your nose. He—he'll have to go out there. Why! He'll be fighting before he knows where he is."

Val saw Imogen's eyes admiring him.

Suddenly his uncle spoke.

"You're under age."

"I thought of that," smiled Val; "I gave my age as twenty-one."

He heard his grandmother's admiring: "Well, Val, that was plucky of you."

Fortifying himself with a sip of champagne, Val continued, *"It's all right, you know; we shall soon have them on the run. I only hope I shall come in for something."*

He felt elated, tremendously important all at once. This would show Uncle Soames, and all the Forsytes, how to be sportsmen. He had certainly done something heroic and exceptional in giving his age as twenty-one.

Emily chastised James as Warmson attempted to pour him a second glass of Madeira. *"You mustn't have a second glass, James."*

Granny Mabs used to do the same thing to Grandpa Jack, who would have liked his second glass—whether Madeira or Champagne. I remember Grandpa telling me once, at my Aunt Eileen's wedding, that Champagne was the finest drink in the world. Grandpa also used to hum little jingles while my grandmother and my mother were arguing about their shares—one of his favorites was: "Have some Madeira, my dear."

"Won't they be astonished at Timothy's!" burst out Imogen. *"I'd give anything to see their faces. Do you have a sword Val, or only a pop gun?"*

"What made you?" asked Soames. *"What had young Jolly Forsyte to do with it? Why did you go together? I thought you weren't friendly with him?"*

"I'm not," mumbled Val, *"but I wasn't going to be beaten by him."*

They all approved of him not being beaten by that cousin of his. There must be a reason!

"What's his father doing?" Soames asked in pursuit.

"He's away in Paris," Val said, staring at the very queer expression on his uncle's face.

"Artists!" said James.

The dinner party ended.

* * *

His mother sat opposite Val in the cab going home and *only said, indeed, that he must go to his tailor's at once and have his uniform properly made, and not just put up with what they gave him. But* Val *could feel that she was very much upset. He felt aggreived that she did not seem more proud of him.*

At home, before going to bed he said: *"I'm awfully sorry to have to leave you, Mother."*

"Well, I must make the best of it. We must try and get you a commission as soon as we can; then you won't have to rough it so. Do you know any drill, Val?"

"Not a scrap."

"I hope they won't worry you much. I must take you about to get the things to-morrow. Good-night; kiss me."

* * *

Soon, only one of the diners at James's was awake—Soames, in his bedroom above his father's.

So that fellow Jolyon was in Paris—what was he doing there? Hanging around Irene! The last report from Polteed had hinted that there might be something soon. Could it be this? 'I'll see Polteed to-morrow,' *he thought.* 'By God! I'm mad, I think, to want her still. That fellow! If—? Um! No!'

Chapter Ten

Death of the dog Balthasar

Jolyon who had crossed from Calais by night, arrived at Robin Hill on Sunday morning. He had sent no word beforehand, so walked up from the station, entering his domain by the coppice gate. Coming to the log seat fashioned out of an old fallen trunk, he sat down. And suddenly Irene seemed very near, just as she had been that day of rambling at Fontainbleau when they sat on a log to eat their lunch.

Fontainbleau was the royal palace that had been favored by the French monarchy prior to the expansion and creation of Louis XIV's Versailles. It had also been selected by Napoleon Bonaparte for his imperial palace just outside Paris, as for "The Emperor born of the 'Revolution'," to have resided at Versailles would have been hypocritical. Today, visitors to Fontainbleau remember most the table in the grand entrance foyer where is displayed Napoleon's famed cocked hat. I remember touring the palace with my friend from Tonbridge, John Bovenizer, when I stayed with John's family in Normandy and Paris in 1959. We were in a party of French tourists and we were trying to understand the French guide. It was difficult, not so much because of our schoolboy understanding of their language, but more because of the awful odor of garlic emanating from the gentleman who stood in front of us most of the tour.

In that last decade of 'Forsythia' and almost symbolic of its demise, Aunt Eileen's husband, my uncle, Wing Commander Jim Sullings, found himself posted to a branch of NATO, which had offices at that time in

Fontainbleau—a symbol of the post-World War II growing influence of the new superpower, the United States of America.

Fontainbleau is surrounded by ancient and very beautiful forests and was favored by the Barbizon painting school of French artists, especially Jean-Francois Millet, who pioneered natural landscape scenes in an 'avant-garde' but realistic form, no doubt one of the reasons why Jolyon had taken Irene there.

Odour drawn out of fallen leaves in the coppice *soaked* Jolyon's nostrils and reminded him even more of that time with Irene. *'I'm glad it isn't spring,' he thought. With the scent of sap, and the song of birds, and the bursting of the blossoms it would have been unbearable! 'I hope I shall be over it by then, old fool that I am.'*

My sister, Diane, visited with Uncle Jim and Aunt Eileen at Fontainbleau during their tour of duty there. While there, she made a series of watercolors of the forest, whose same ancient beauty had stirred the romantic peace of Jolyon and Irene and those Barbizon painters—even the post-impressionist Paul Cezanne with his *Winter in the Forest of Fontainbleau.*

At Robin Hill *up on the lawn above* the copse and *fernery, Jolyon could see his old dog Balthasar. Jolyon gave his special whistle. The old dog got off his haunches, and his tail, close-curled over his back, began a feeble, excited fluttering; he came waddling forward, gathered momentum, and disappeared over the edge of the fernery. Jolyon expected to meet him at the wicket gate, but Balthasar was not there, and, rather alarmed he turned into the fernery. On his fat side, looking up with eyes already glazing, the old dog lay.*

"What is it, my poor old man?" cried Jolyon. Balthasar's curled and fluffy tail just moved; his filming eyes seemed saying: 'I can't get up, master, but I'm glad to see you.'

Jolyon knelt down. "What is it, dear man? Where are you hurt?" The tail fluttered once; the eyes lost the look of life. Balthasar died. *His heart had simply failed in that obese body from the emotion of his master's return.*

Jolyon *stayed for some minutes kneeling, with his hand beneath the stiffening head. The body was very heavy when he bore it to the top of the field. 'I'll bury him myself,' he thought.*

During my time in Ireland, I became very close to Mrs. Albertini's standard poodle, a most loving dog, very similar in character to my Great Pyrenee, 'Orbit'. During the family's absences in Georgia,

'Wooly' was my constant companion and confidant in Ireland. During my later days at Tullamaine Castle, 'Wooly' became seriously ill with leptospira and a veterinary decision was made to put him down. It had been my responsibilty all those years to take care of veterinary matters. I had been the one to witness one of Mr. Albertini's hunters being put down. In my capacity as the Estate manager, I led the lethargic, limping 'Wooly', from the house to take him out into the stable yard where the vet would bring his life to a close. Tears welled in my eyes. To my surprise, Mr. Albertini, with whom I had a particularly cold relationship at that time, came running after me. He took the dog from me and said to me in a very kindly way, "Peter, you should not have to do this. He loved you? Let me take 'Wooly'." To this day, I have two beautiful portrait sketches I made of 'Wooly' with which I will never part.

When Jolyon reached the house, he found *June was at home; she had come down hot-foot on hearing the news of Jolly's enlistment. His patriotism had conquered her feeling for the Boers.* Jolyon gave the news of Balthasar's death to June and Jolly.

A link with the past had snapped—the dog Balthasar! Two of them could remember nothing before his day; to June he represented the last years of her grandfather; to Jolyon that life of domestic stress and aesthetic struggle at the house in St. John's Wood where Jolly was born out of wedlock. All before he came again into the kingdom of his father's love and wealth! And he was gone!

In the afternoon he and Jolly chose a spot, so they need not carry him far, and, carefully cutting off the surface turf, began to dig.

When they rested, Jolyon finally said to his son: *"Well, old man, so you thought you ought?"*

"Yes," answered Jolly; "I don't want to a bit, of course."

"I admire you for it, old boy. I don't believe I should have done it at your age—too much of a Forsyte I'm afraid. But I suppose the type gets thinner with each generation. Your son, if you have one, may be a pure altruist; who knows?"

"He won't be like me, then, Dad; I'm beastly selfish."

"No, my dear, that you clearly are not."

They started to dig again.

"Strange life, a dog's," said Jolyon suddenly; "the only four footer with rudiments of altruism and a sense of God!"

Jolly looked at his father.

"Do you believe in God, Dad? I've never known."

"What do you mean by God?" his father said philosophically. *"There are two irreconcilable ideas of God. There's the Unknowable Creative Principle—one believes in That. And there's the Sum of altruism in man—naturally one believes in That."*

"I see. That leaves out Christ, doesn't it?"

They both went back to their college days, Jolyon to Cambridge and Jolly to Oxford. *Jolyon stared. Christ, the link between these two ideas! Out of the mouths of babes! Here was orthodoxy scientifically explained at last! The sublime poem of the Christ life was man's attempt to join those two irreconcilable conceptions of God. And since the sum of human altruism was as much a part of the Unknowable Creative Principle as anything else in Nature and the Universe, a worse link might have been chosen after all.*

"What do you think, old man," Jolyon *said.*

Jolly frowned. "Of course, my first year we talked a good bit about that sort of thing. But in the second year one gives it up; I don't know why—it's awfully interesting."

Jolyon remembered that he also had talked a good deal about it in his first year at Cambridge, and given it up in his second.

Neither Jolyon or his son were theologians. Ironically, I read theology at Cambridge. At Oxford and Cambridge you do not study or take a subject, but you 'read' it. This is probably because in the tutorial system as opposed to classroom study, all teaching is conducted one on one. In between these tutorial sessions, we read appointed books. For stimulation, we attended lectures voluntarily, and like Jolyon and Jolly became involved in much discussion among ourselves.

Because my subject was theology, I was involved in such discussions beyond that natural first year curiosity about definitions of God and the Divine. I had the greatest difficulty in accepting the Christ story literally as a Biblical truth. I even, at times, questioned the reality that any of it was historic. We were encouraged to think this way— to let no stone remain unturned. A Cambridge New Testament scholar of the time, then the Bishop of Woolwich, The Right Reverend John A. T. Robinson, had recently published an extremely challenging book, *Honest to God.* I was very much a part of the 'Honest to God' debate. Most of those with whom I discussed these matters were fellow theologians, who were anticipating ordination as clergy within the Episcopal or Anglican Church of England. I had originally chosen the same path, but by the time I was up at Cambridge was wavering somewhat, partly because the Church of England had deferred my ordination. They considered me too much of a 'Forsyte'. There was a social liberalism exploding in the Church of England at the time of which the 'Honest to God debate' was an academic counterpart. As a 'Forsyte', the Church Advisory Council for the Ministry had deferred my application for ordination on the grounds that they felt that 'I came from too privileged and sheltered a background and that I should work in industry for a while.'

At Cambridge, however, I pursued academic liberalism in theology with great zeal, beyond the credibility of most my contemporaries. At one discussion, however, I remember a highly intelligent working-class student, with whom I had almost nothing socially in common, calmly saying after listening in on our little group: "Peter is the only one of you who is talking any sense." Today, Professor Steve Mennell is a well-respected university academic!

I had not read John Galsworthy's *Forsyte Saga* at the time, but only listened to the radio adaptation of the 1950s. In the radio adaptation, this gem of philosophy expressed by Jolyon, as he and Jolly were burying the old dog Balthasar, was not recorded. The expression 'The sublime poem of the Christ life' is truly in keeping with the philosophical thoughts that I developed on the gospels while studying them in Greek at Cambridge. That God is 'the Unknowable Creative Principle' with whom in the light of Darwin there is nothing that singles out man was right from the pages of *Honest to God*. There can, under such circumstances, be no human dialogue with such an 'Unknowable Creative Principle' unless we create a lesser super-human God. Did we do that in creating the mystical life of Christ as the son of such a god? Maybe? If so, could that pattern of the Christ life, be the key to man understanding, through his own terms, that altruism that shows the divine spark within all that is a part of the creation of the 'Unknowable Creative Principle'—selfless love. As Jolly said, *"It's awfully interesting."*

"I suppose," said Jolly, "it's the second God you mean, that old Balthasar had a sense of."

"Yes, or he would never have burst his poor old heart because of something outside himself."

"But wasn't that just selfish emotion, really?"

Jolyon shook his head. "No, dogs are not pure Forsytes, they love something outside themselves."

Jolly smiled.

"Well, I think I'm one," he said. "You know, I only enlisted because I dared Val Dartie to."

"But why?"

"We bar each other," said Jolly shortly.

"Ah!" muttered Jolyon. So the feud went on unto the third generation—this modern feud which had no overt expression!

'Shall I tell, the boy about it?' he thought. But to what end if he had to stop short at his own part?

And Jolly thought: 'It's for Holly to let him know about that chap. If she doesn't, it means she doesn't want him told, and I should be sneaking.'

It was not in the 'Forsyte' code to sneak. I remember in 1953 being very upset at Newlands when a boy stole my coronation transfer book. Transfers were like reversible stamps that you could peel onto the pages of a book to illustrate it. They were very popular in latter 'Forsythia' and my coronation transfer book was a prize possession. I knew Bayliss, the boy thief's last name, had taken my book and refused to give it back. I sneaked on him to the headmaster. I got the book back, but Bayliss was not severely punished and I was lectured by the headmaster on not sneaking on others. 'Forsytes' were to uphold that stiff upper lip, or settle things among themselves.

They dug on in silence.

"I can't bear this part of it," said Jolyon suddenly.

"Let me do it, Dad. He never cared much for me."

In that act, Jolly showed altruism, just as Mr. Albertini had showed selfless love to me. In all of us there is that moment, whatever our conditioned prejudices, when the Divine shows through.

With extreme care they raised the old dog's body. They laid it, heavy, cold and unresponsive, in the grave.

There went the past! If only there were a joyful future to look forward to! It was like stamping down earth on one's own life.

They returned to the house arm in arm, each, somehow, the richer for the experience.

My father had not expressed much interest in religion until I went up to Cambridge. From then on, throughout his life he had many interesting discussions with me that grew into a philosophy very similar to that which Jolyon formulates. He died, believing in that altruistic spirit of the Divine that he thought was the life force of the Universe, present as much in his beloved cat, Shon-Shon, whom he called "Pudsey," as in his fellow humans. It mattered not to him if the life of Christ was historic or a human allegory, its significance only being in a man's interpretation of the altruistic spirit—Divine love—selfless love. At times, my father loved to play the devil's advocate—he stirred the pot to make people think, but as was very manifest in the tributes that we received after his death on May 3, 2008, he was remembered for his altruistic spirit.

CHAPTER ELEVEN

TIMOTHY STAYS THE ROT

O*n Forsyte 'Change news of the enlistment spread fast, together with the report that June, not to be outdone, was going to become a Red Cross nurse.*

My Great-aunt Dorrie became a Red Cross nurse during the First World War and always made much of it, although according to Grandpa Jack, who could never stand his younger 'titch' of a sister, all she did was roll bandages.

A major change in 'Forsythia' was on the threshold—the role of women. The Boer War and the First World War played a major part in this change, while the suffragette movement assured political status to go with these changes. The new generation of 'Forsytes' wanted "to do their bit," as my Aunt Daphne always said, whether it was in the workplace or in physical charity work.

Timothy's was thronged next Sunday afternoon by members of the family *trying to find out what they thought about it all. Giles and Jesse Hayman,* the Dromios, *would no longer defend the coast, but go to South Africa quite soon; Jolly and Val would be following in April; as to June—well, you never knew what she would really do.*

Timothy, the youngest of the old Forsytes—scarcely eighty, in fact— had been invisible for so many years that he was almost mythical. After he sold his publishing business, he had made a living by careful investment. *He had doubled his capital in forty years. He was now putting aside some two thousand a year,* and according to *Aunt Hester, to double his capital again before he died.* Never married, it was not surprising that his nephews and nieces, especially those *free spirits such as Francie, Euphemia, or young Nicholas's second, Christopher, whose spirit was so free that he had actually said he was going on the stage,* were curious to know what would become of their uncle's fortune. *All admitted, however, that this was best known to Timothy himself, and possibly to Soames, who never divulged a secret.*

It was known that he had taken a surprising interest in the war, sticking flags into a map ever since it began. Aunt Hester was always declaring that he was very upset—the English were being driven into the sea. This Sunday, Timothy graced 'Forsyte 'Change' like the chair in person.

Francie was present, and Eustace had come in his car; Winifred had brought Imogen. and Marion Tweetyman arrived with the last news of Giles and Jesse. These, with Aunts Juley and Hester, young Nicholas, Euphemia, and—of all people!—George, who had come with Eustace in the car. There was not one chair vacant in the whole of the little drawing-room.

George made a mockery of all their endeavors—*asked Aunt Juley when she was going out with the Red Cross—Young Nick's a warrior bold, isn't he? The Dromios are off, I hear. We shall all be there soon. En Avant, the Forsytes! Roll, bowl, or pitch! Who's for a cooler?*

Aunt Juley gurgled. George was so droll. Should Hester get Timothy's map? Then he could show them all where they were.

There was relief when George *got up, offered his arm to Aunt Juley, marched up to Timothy, saluted him, kissed his aunt with mock* passion, called for Eustace *and walked out.*

"*Fancy not waiting for the map! You mustn't mind him,*" Juley said to Timothy.

"*I don't know what things are comin' to,*" her brother answered. "*What's this about goin' out there? That's not the way to beat those Boers.*"

"*What is, then, Uncle Timothy?*" asked Francie.

"*All this new-fangled volunteerin' and expense—lettin' money out of the country.*"

Hester came back with the map and placed it on the piano. Timothy *walked over and stood looking at his map as they all gathered round.*

"There you are," he said, *"that's the position up to date, and very poor it is. H'm!"*

"Yes," said Francie, greatly daring, *"but how are you going to alter it, Uncle Timothy, without more men?"*

"Men!" said Timothy; *"you don't want men—wastin' the country's money. You want a Napoleon, he'd settle it in a month."*

"But if you haven't got him, Uncle Timothy?"

"That's their business," replied Timothy. *"What have we kept the Army up for? They ought to be ashamed of themselves, comin' on the country to help them like this! Let every man stick to his business, and we shall get on. Volunteerin', indeed! Throwin' good money after bad! We must save! Conserve energy—that's the only way."*

With that he left the room, leaving a faint scent of barley-sugar behind him.

Young Nicholas then also took his leave.

"Really, I think Uncle Timothy's *right, you know,"* Francie said after Nicholas had gone. *"After all, what is the army for? They ought to have known. It's only encouraging them."*

"My dear," cried Aunt Juley, *"but they've been so progressive. Think of their giving up their scarlet. They were always so proud of it. And now they all look like convicts. Fancy what the Iron Duke would have said."*

Those scarlet uniforms had been a very symbol of the Empire, but the nature of hitherto minor imperial struggles, outside the mutiny of course—the Indian Mutiny that had ultimately been crushed and opened the way to Queen Victoria becoming the Empress of India—had now dramatically changed. The Boers didn't fight in formations and could not be put down by formations; their methods were hit and run, ambush and sniper fire. The world had moved on from uniforms, swords and muskets. The Zulu wars had seen to that.

"The new color's very smart," said Winifred. *"Val looks quite nice in his."*

Aunt Juley sighed.

"I do so wonder what Jolyon's boy is like. To think we've never seen him! His father must be so proud of him."

"His father's in Paris," said Winifred.

Aunt Juley prattled on with thoughts of Paris.

"We had dear little Mrs. MacAnder here yesterday, just back from Paris. And whom d'you think she saw there in the street? You'll never guess."

Hester bristled.

"Irene! Imagine!" Juley revealed. *"After all this time; walking with a fair bearded gentleman. And not a day older; she was always so pretty,"* she added, *with a sort of lingering apology.*

"Oh! Tell us about her, Auntie," cried Imogen; *"I can just remember her. She's the skeleton in the family cupboard, isn't she? And they're such fun."*

The skeleton in our family cupboard was Aunt 'Golly'—Emily Oliphant, Great-grandfather Longley's sister. She was an alcoholic and as aforementioned was the cause for my great-grandfather's lifelong financial support of the Temperance Society!

"She wasn't much of a skeleton as I remember her," murmured Euphemia, *"extremely well-covered."*

"What was she like?" persisted Imogen.

"I'll tell you, my child," said Francie, *"a kind of modern Venus, very well dressed."*

Euphemia said sharply, *"Venus was never dressed, and she had blue eyes of melting sapphire."*

"Was Uncle Soames awfully fond of her?" pursued the inexorable Imogen. *"I suppose she ran off with someone?"*

"No, certainly not;" Juley affirmed, catching Hester's eye, *"Not precisely."*

"What did she do, then, Auntie?"

Like Granny Mabs knowing the argument was played as far as it could, Winifred intervened:

"Come along, Imogen, we must be getting back."

But Aunt Juley interjected resolutely; "She—she didn't behave very well."

"Oh, bother!" cried Imogen; *"that's as far as I ever get."*

"Well, my dear," said Francie, *"she had a love affair which ended with the young man's death; and then she left your uncle. I always rather liked her."*

"I can't think what we are about," said Aunt Juley, raising her hands, *"talking of such things!"*

"Was she divorced?" asked Imogen from the door.

"Certainly not," cried Aunt Juley; *"that is—certainly not."*

Timothy re-entered. *"I've come for my map,"* he said. *"Who's been divorced?"*

"No one, Uncle," replied Francie with perfect truth.

Timothy took his map off the piano.

"Don't let's have anything of that sort in the family," he said. *"All this enlistin's bad enough. The country's breaking up; I don't know what we're comin' to."* He shook a finger at the room: *"Too many women nowadays, and they don't know what they want."*

He left again.

The seven women whom he had addressed broke into a subdued murmur, out of which emerged Francie's, "Really, the Forsytes—!" and Aunt Juley's: "He must have his feet in mustard and hot water tonight, Hester; will you tell Jane? The blood has gone to his head again, I'm afraid."

That evening when she and Hester were sitting alone she said: "Hester, I can't think where I've heard that dear Soames wants Irene to come back to him again. Hester, I have had such a dreadful thought."

"Then, don't tell me," said Aunt Hester quickly.

"Oh! But I must. You can't think how dreadful!" Her voice sank to a whisper.

"Jolyon—Jolyon, they say, has a—has a fair beard, now?"

Chapter Twelve

Progress of the Chase

Mr. Polteed summed up what he knew so far.

"A gentleman, 47, has been paying marked attention to 17 during the last month in Paris. But at present there seems to have been nothing very conclusive. The meetings have all been in public places—restaurants, the Opera, the Comique, the Louvre, Luxembourg Gardens, lounge of the hotel, and so forth. She has not been traced in his rooms, nor vice versa. They went to Fontainbleau—but nothing of value. In short, the situation is promising, but requires patience."

Then, Polteed dropped his bombshell:

"47 has the same name as—er—31!"

31—according to the code, that was Soames' number.

'*The fellow knows* or has an idea that *I'm her husband.*'

"Christian name—an odd one—Jolyon," continued Mr. Polteed. *"We know his address in Paris and his residence here."* He added with knowing caution, *"We didn't wish of course to be running a wrong hare."*

"Go on with it, but be careful," said Soames doggedly.

"Let me *see if there is anything fresh in."*

Polteed *returned with some letters. Re-locking the door he glanced at the envelopes.*

"Yes, here's a personal one from 19 to myself."

'19, the female spy,' Soames recalled from his code key.

"Um!" said Mr. Polteed, "she says: '47 left for England to-day. Address on his baggage: Robin Hill. Parted from 17 in Louvre Gallery at 3.30; nothing very striking. Thought it best to stay and continue observation of 17. You will deal with 47 in England if you think desirable, no doubt.'"

Mr. Polteed looked up at Soames:

"Very intelligent woman, 19, and a wonderful make-up. Not cheap, but earns her money well. There's no suspicion of being shadowed so far. I should rather advise letting up on 17, and keeping an eye on 47."

Slightly sarcastically, Polteed continued:

"You can tell your client that it's looking up very well."

"No," said Soames suddenly, *"I prefer that you should keep the watch going discreetly in Paris, and not concern yourself with this end."*

"Very well," replied Mr. Polteed, *"we can do it."*

As he set out for 'The City', Soames reflected on the revelation. *What was that fellow hanging round Irene for? Was it really as Polteed suggested? Or was Jolyon but taking compassion on her loneliness, as he would call it—sentimental radical chap that he had always been! If it were, indeed, as Polteed hinted! Soames stood still. It could not be! The fellow was seven years older than himself, no better looking! No richer! What attraction had he?*

'Besides, he's come back,' he thought; *'that doesn't look—I'll see him!'* and taking out a card he wrote:

'If you can spare half an hour some afternoon this week, I shall be at the Connoisseurs' any day between 5.30 and 6, or I could come to the Hotch Potch if you would prefer it. I want to see you.—S.F.'

He confided it to the porter at the Hotch Potch and took one of the new motor cabs into the City.

Jolyon received that card the same afternoon, and turned his face towards the Connoisseurs'. What did Soames want now? Had he got wind of Paris?

He was conducted to where Soames was drinking tea.

After formal greeting and a pause, Soames said: *"You've been in Paris, I hear."*

"Yes; just back."

"Young Val told me; he and your boy are going off, then?"

Jolyon nodded.

"You didn't happen to see Irene, I suppose. It appears she is abroad somewhere."

"Yes, I saw her," Jolyon replied uncomfortably.

"How was she?"

"Very well."

"When I saw you last, I was in two minds. We talked, and you expressed your opinion. I don't wish to re-open that discussion. I only wanted to say this: 'My position with her is extremely difficult. I don't want you to go using your influence against me. What happened is a very long time ago. I'm going to ask her to let bygones be bygones.'"

"You have asked her, you know," murmured Jolyon.

"The idea was new to her then, it came as a shock. But the more she thinks of it, the more she must see that it's the only way out for both of us."

"That's not my impression of her state of mind," said Jolyon. *"And forgive my saying, you misconceive the matter if you think reason comes into it at all."*

He had repeated her own words.

"I'm bound to use my influence *in the direction of what I think is her happiness,"* Jolyon continued. *"I am what they call a 'feminist', I believe."*

"Feminist!" repeated Soames. "Does that mean that you're against me?"

"Bluntly," said Jolyon, "I'm against any woman living with any man whom she definitely dislikes. It appears to me rotten."

"And I suppose each time you see her you put your opinions into her mind."

"I am not likely to be seeing her."

"Not going back to Paris?"

"Not so far as I know," said Jolyon, conscious of the intent watchfulness in Soames's face.

"Well that's all I had to say. Anyone who comes between man and wife, you know, incurs heavy responsibility."

Jolyon rose and made a slight bow.

Raising one's hat, shaking hands and making that slight bow, even bringing one's heels together, so exaggerated by the military, was practiced by 'Forsytes' throughout 'Forsythia'. It was ingrained into me, especially by Grandpa Jack, but also by both my headmasters, and as late as 1978, I was described by a young American girl, whose fancy I had taken, as "odd—he bows and clicks his heels." Her mother, however, found it charming. To most Americans, this was being quaintly English, but in reality it was being a 'Forsyte'. The English lower-middle class and vast working class never took on such habits among themselves.

Among my grandparents, it was Grandpa Jack who taught me most about such 'Forsyte' manners, even though of my four grandparents he was, in character, the least 'Forsyte'. He taught me to always walk on the outside when escorting a lady on the sidewalk. He gave as the reason the very practical and decent consideration that this protected the lady from the swirling dust and spattered mud that he remembered in his childhood was thrown up by passing carriages; others, also taught me in folklore that to be on the outside was more practical for drawing one's sword to protect the lady. Grandpa Jack also was a stickler for table manners, harassing me many times for the way I held my knife. I had a habit of letting the handle lazily rest between my thumb and forefinger instead of extending my forefinger along the top of the knife's handle. Nobody else in the family ever really picked up on this, so I can thank Grandpa for the correction. The practical reason for this particular piece of 'Forsyte' etiquette was presumably to allow for greater pressure in cutting one's meat—something that did not seem to be of particular benefit to the mass of lower-middle and working class folk, who held their knives in whatever way they liked.

'We Forsytes,' thought Jolyon, after leaving Soames and *hailing a cab, 'are very civilised, with simpler folk that might have come to a row. If it weren't for my boy going to the war...' The war! A gust of his old doubt swept over him. A precious war! Domination of peoples or of women! Attempts to master and possess those who did not want you! The negation of gentle decency! Possession, vested rights; and anyone 'agin' 'em—outcast! 'Thank Heaven!' he thought, 'I always felt "agin" 'em anyway! Yes! Even before his first disastrous marriage* to Frances, the Colonel's daughter, *he could remember fuming over the bludgeoning of Ireland, or the matrimonial suits of women trying to be free*—both matters still raising their heads in caring quarters and likely to lead to a challenge of the status quo as they did in the Irish proclamation of 1916 followed by 'the troubles', as the Irish refer to their civil war against the British; and also in the full flowering of the suffragettes. *Parsons*

*would have it that freedom of soul and body were quite different things!
Pernicious doctrine, that! Body and soul could not thus be separated.*

*Was there anything, indeed, more tragic in the world than a man
enslaved by his possessive instinct, who couldn't see the sky for it, or
even enter fully into what another person felt! 'I must write and warn
her,' he thought; 'he's going to have another try.' And all the way home
to Robin Hill he rebelled at the strength of that duty to his son which
prevented him from posting back to Paris.*

* * *

At the Connoisseurs', *Soames sat long in his chair.*

*'Does that mean that you're against me?' he had got nothing out of
that disingenuous question. Feminist! Phrasey fellow! 'I mustn't rush
things,' he thought. 'I have some breathing space; he's not going back
to Paris, unless he was lying. I'll let the spring come!'*

*Gazing into the street, where figures were passing from pool to
pool of light from the* new *high lamps, he thought: 'Nothing seems any
good—nothing seems worth while. I'm lonely—that's the trouble.'*

The new high lamps bothered my sister Diane, whose bedroom
at Hockeredge in Wickham Way was in the front of the house. In our
'Forsyte' childhood the street lamps along Wickham Way were quaint
lanterns on wooden posts that gave a subdued yellow light. Later, they
were replaced by taller, white pillar lights that threw much larger pools.
The light from one shone into the windows of both Diane's and Sally's
bedrooms and caused much concern. Diane called them "Speenyan
lights," which was undoubtedly an unfavorable description, although
where the word 'Speenyan' came from, I do not know. The high lamps,
however, were almost symbolic of the changing times and the demise
of 'Forsythia' in the 1960s.

CHAPTER THIRTEEN

'HERE WE ARE AGAIN!'

I*mogen's frocks for her first season exercised the judgment of her mother and the purse of her grandfather all through the month of March.*

Most 'Forsytes' aspired to be debutantes—as such they had arrived, but in reality only the wealthiest 'Forsytes' actually were debutantes. All 'Forsytes' came out, an expression for being launched into society, but to be a debutante meant to join with the aristocracy on the most important day of their London season—their court presentation.

Court presentation started in the eighteenth century in 1780 when King George III gave a birthday ball for Queen Charlotte. London society and the marriageable daughters of the aristocracy were invited to the ball at St. James' Palace. The idea was to introduce these young ladies to the eligible bachelors from among the aristocracy of the day. On the occasion of Queen Charlotte's Ball, each young lady was formally presented to Her Majesty, and so successful was the event that it was continued annually. With the birth of 'Forsythia', new nineteenth-century wealth joined with the aristocracy to celebrate this event and a protocol of lesser events built up around it to create the London Season. They included: Henley's Royal Regatta, the Eton and Harrow cricket match at Lords, the Royal Ascot race meeting, the 'Glorious' Goodwood Races, and an assortment of balls and dinners both in London and her surrounding country seats.

Queen Elizabeth II, however, realizing even at the start of her reign that hers was an era of change—not crowned Empress of India like her father, grandfather and great-grandmother, India having become a republic, and with other old imperial colonies rapidly taking on similar independence—abolished the court presentation. My predecessor as private tutor or governess to Mr. Albertini's son, Sally Keane, daughter of the playwright Molly Keane of *Harvest Moon* fame, was one of the last debutantes to actually be presented at court. So, in the 1950s, along with the Suez crisis and the demise of 'Forsythia', this focal point of the London season came to an end. The dinner parties and balls, however, continued, even a form of Queen Charlotte's Ball, but without the royal presence.

'Forsytes' attended many of these events—one reason why even I was able to attend Lady Melissa Bligh's coming-out party at Cobham Hall in 1963. Few of us, however, made the full round of the season without the prestige of that court presentation, unless from very wealthy families or lingering aristocracy. Most of us just attended each other's twenty-first birthday parties that had somewhat replaced the coming-out party.

With Forsyte tenacity Winifred quested for perfection. It took her mind off her boy and his fast approaching departure from which the news remained disquieting. She and Imogen *hovered in the shops of Regent Street, the establishments of Hanover Square and of Bond Street, lost in consideration and the feel of fabrics.*

Those dresses that Granny Longley purchased for my sister at Marshall and Snelgrove, however, were explicitly for her twenty-first birthday. Granny Longley bought the dresses, but it was Granny Mabs, who was the perfectionist and adjusted and fitted the dresses.

Dozens of young women of striking deportment and peculiar gait paraded before Winifred and Imogen, draped in 'creations'. The models—'Very new, modom; quite the latest thing...' as those aspiring middle-class shop ladies' would say, and *which those two turned down, would have filled a museum;* nonetheless, *the models* 'Modom' purchased, *nearly emptied James's bank.*

My mother's cousin, Jeanne Cuthbertson, had a flat in Hanover Square, the heart of this fashionable shopping district. Jeanne was considered quite 'chic' and was always beautifully dressed when she came to visit us. I remember her purchasing one of Diane's paintings—a still life—that she hung in that flat. She managed a rather fashionable patisserie and used to invite Diane there from time to time to enjoy Danish pastries. She married late in life—a man named Arthur Edny, who seemed pleasant enough, but came from the north—Newcastle on the Tyne—not 'Forsyte' territory. At that point, Jeanne kind of slipped out of our lives, our only contact being her name on the Christmas card list.

Returning to Green Street from one of these shopping expeditions, *on the afternoon of the 20th of March*, Winifred, Imogen no doubt carrying boxes, opened her front door—*freshly painted a light olive-green; nothing neglected that year to give Imogen a good send off. Winifred passed towards the silver basket to see if anyone had called, and suddenly her nostrils twitched. What was that scent? A male scent! A faint reek of cigars and lavender-water not smelt since that early autumn night six months ago when she called* Monty *'the limit.'*

She sent Imogen upstairs.

She looked round her. Nothing—not a thing, no tiniest disturbance of her hall, nor of her dining-room. A little daydream of a scent—illusory, saddening, silly! 'I must be tired,' she thought, 'I'll go and lie down.'

Upstairs the drawing-room was darkened. She passed on up to her bedroom. This, too, was half-curtained and dim, for it was six o'clock. Winifred threw off her coat—that scent again!—then stood, as if shot, transfixed against the bedrail. Something dark had risen from the sofa in the far corner. A word of—horror—in her family escaped her: "God!"

"It's I—Monty," said a voice.

Winifred reached up and turned the switch of the light hanging above her dressing-table. He looked dreadful—thin and aged, *no pin in his tie*, boots *split at the toecap.*

"Well," he said, "I got the letter. I'm back."

The nostalgia for her husband which had rushed up with that scent was struggling with a deeper jealousy than any she had felt yet. What force had done this to him—squeezed him like an orange to its dry rind! That woman!

"I'm back," he said again. "I've had a beastly time. By God! I came steerage. I've got nothing but what I stand up in, and that bag."

"And who has the rest?" cried Winifred, suddenly alive. "How dared you come? You knew it was just for divorce that you got that letter to come back. Don't touch me!"

Many times, yes—many times she had wanted him back. But now that he had come she was filled with this cold and deadly resentment.

"Gad!" he said: "If you knew the time I've had!"

"I'm glad I don't."

"Are the kids all right?"

Winifred nodded. "How did you get in?"

"With my key."

"Then the maids don't know. You can't stay here, Monty."

He uttered a sardonic laugh.

"Where then?"

"Anywhere."

"Well, look at me! That—damned..."

"If you mention her," cried Winifred, "I go straight out to Park Lane and I don't come back."

He shut his eyes. It was as if he had said: 'All right! I'm dead to the world!'

Winifred weakened.

"You can have a room for the night," she said: "your things are still here. Only Imogen is at home."

He leaned back against the bed-rail. "Well, it's in your hands. I've been through it. You needn't hit too hard—it isn't worth while. I've been frightened: I've been frightened, Freddie."

That old pet name, disused for years and years, sent a shiver through Winifred.

'What am I to do with him?' she thought. 'What in God's name am I to do with him?'

"Go and have a hot bath. I'll put some clothes out for you in the dressing-room. We can talk later."

While he was bathing, she slipped out and made her way to Park Lane. Soames would be home. *Back! Soames had always feared it—she had sometimes hoped it. Back! So like him—clown that he was—with this: 'Here we are again!' to make fools of them all—of the Law, of Soames, of herself! Yet, to have done with the Law, not to have that murky cloud hanging over her and her children! What a relief! Ah! but how to accept his return? That 'woman' had ravaged him, taken from him passion such as he had never bestowed on herself, such as she had not thought him capable of. There was the sting! Not right, not decent to take him back! And yet she had asked for him; the Law perhaps would make her now! He was as much her husband as ever—she had put herself out of court!*

She neared her father's house, driven this way and that, while all the time the Forsyte undertow was drawing her to deep conclusion that after all he was her property, to be held against a robbing world. And so she came to James's.

Her brother was dressing.

"Hullo!" he said, contemplating her in the glass; "what's wrong?"

"Monty!" said Winifred stonily.

Soames spun round. "What!"

"Back! What shall I do?—Well?"

"What has he to say for himself?"

"Nothing. One of his boots is split across the toe."

Soames stared at her.

"Ah!" he said, "of course! On his beam ends. So—it begins again! This'll about finish father."

"Can't we keep it from him?"

"Impossible. He has an uncanny flair for anything that's worrying."

"There ought to be some way in Law," Soames muttered, "to make him safe."

"No," cried Winifred. "I won't be made a fool of again; I'd sooner put up with him."

The two stared at each other. Their hearts were full of feeling, but they could give it no expression—Forsytes that they were.

"Where did you leave him?"

"In the bath."

"I'll go back with you," Soames suggested.

"What's the use?"

"We ought to make terms with him."

"Terms! It'll always be the same. When he recovers—cards and betting, drink and...!"

"Recovers?" replied Soames. "Is he ill?"

"No, burnt out, that's all."

Soames *threaded his watch chain,* and Winifred reflected that Monty no longer had a watch chain. *"We haven't any luck,"* he said.

And in the midst of her own trouble Winifred was sorry for him, as if in that little saying he had revealed deep trouble of his own.

Winifred asked for her mother, who came down with Soames and met her in the little dark study James no longer ever used.

"Oh! My poor dear!" said Emily. "How miserable you look in here! This is too bad of him, really!"

As a family they had so guarded themselves from the expression of all unfashionable emotion that it was impossible to go up and give her daughter a good hug. I really do not remember ever having my mother hug me. It simply wasn't done. In that practical 'Forsyte' way, Winifred did not encourage such emotion either.

"It's all right, Mother; no good fussing," she said

"I don't see," said Emily, looking at Soames, "why Winifred shouldn't tell him that she'll prosecute him if he doesn't keep off the premises. He took her pearls, and he's not brought them back, that's quite enough."

Winifred smiled. They would all plunge about with suggestions of this or that, but she knew already what she would be doing, and that was—nothing. The feeling that, after all, she had won a sort of victory, retained her property, was every moment gaining ground in her. No! if she wanted to punish him, she could do it at home without the world knowing.

"Well," said Emily after inviting Winifred to stay for dinner, *"leave it to me to tell your father."*

They were too late. James, curious to note light coming from his old study, was at the door.

"What's all this?" he said. "Tell your father! You never tell me anything."

It was Winifred who went up to him, and, laying one hand on each of his arms, said:

"Monty's not gone bankrupt, Father. He's only come back."

James replied *with a sort of dignity: "He'll be the death of me. I knew how it would be."*

"You mustn't worry, Father," said Winifred calmly, "I mean to make him behave."

James *turned, and walked firmly to the dining-room.*

"I don't want any soup," he said to Warmson, and sat down in his chair. They all sat down and Warmson laid the extra place. When he was gone, *James said: "What's he brought back?"*

"Nothing, Father."

"Divorce!" James *muttered; "rubbish! What was I about! I ought to have paid him an allowance to stay out of England. Soames! You go and propose it to him."*

It seemed so right and simple a suggestion that even Winifred surprised herself *when she said: "No, I'll keep him now he's back; he must behave—that's all."*

"You look for his revolver!" said James elliptically. *"Don't go to bed without. You ought to have Warmson to sleep in the house. I'll see him myself to-morrow."*

The advent of Warmson with fish diverted the conversation. Directly after dinner, Winifred went over to kiss her father goodnight.

"It's all right, Daddy dear; don't worry. I shan't need anyone— he's quite bland. I shall only be upset if you worry. Good-night, bless you!"

James repeated the words, "Bless you!"

It was a quaint fact of 'Forsythia', even an English trait, that throughout their lives, most upper-class families retained the mode of address to their parents as the nursery "Mummy" and "Daddy." Even His Royal Highness, the Prince Charles, heir to the throne, is known to address the queen as "Mummy" at home.

When Winifred reached home *Dartie was lying on the bed in the dressing-room, fully re-dressed.*

He said, sympathetically: "I suppose you've been to Park Lane. How's the old man?"

Winifred could not help the bitter answer: "Not dead."

He winced.

"Understand, Monty," she said. *"I will not have him worried. If you aren't going to behave yourself, you may go back, you may go anywhere. Have you had dinner?"*

"No."

"Would you like some?"

He shrugged his shoulders.

"Imogen offered me some. I didn't want any."

Imogen! In the plentitude of emotion Winifred had forgotten her.

"So you've seen her? What did she say?"

"She gave me a kiss. Does she know about me?"

It flashed through Winifred that here was the weapon she needed. He minded their knowing!

"No. Val knows. The others don't; they only know you went away."

She heard him sigh with relief.

"But they shall know," she said firmly, "if you give me cause."

"All right!" he muttered, "hit me! I'm down!"

Winifred went up to the bed. "Look here, Monty! I don't want to hit you. I don't want to hurt you. I shan't allude to anything. I'm not going to worry. What's the use?" She was silent a moment. "I can't stand anymore, though, and I won't! You'd better know. You've made me suffer. But I used to be fond of you. For the sake of that..." She met the heavy lidded gaze of his brown eyes with the downward stare of her grey-green eyes, touched his hand, then, turned her back, and went into her room.

Chapter Fourteen

Outlandish Night

Soames *doggedly let the spring come. Mr. Polteed reported nothing, except that his watch went on—costing a lot of money. Val and his cousin were gone to the war, whence came news* now *more favourable; Dartie was behaving himself so far; James had retained his health* through the winter.

Soames *did not exactly avoid Soho. But he had to be so restrained and cautious that he would often pass the door of the Restaurant Bretagne without going in.*

This particular night he had done just that—passed the door, but not entered, curious about Annette and her mother, but not as yet prepared to give up on Irene.

Leaving Soho, he wandered out *into Regent Street and the most amazing crowd he had ever seen: a shrieking, whistling, dancing, grotesque and formidably jovial crowd, with false noses and mouth-organs, penny whistles and long feathers, every appanage of idiocy, as it seemed to him. Mafeking! Of course it had been relieved! Good!* Whoever in 'Forsythia' ever really doubted we would eventually rout those Boers? But this…

Who were these people, what were they, where had they come from into the West End? Soames' face was tickled, his ears whistled into. Girls cried: "Keep your hat on stucco!" A youth then *so knocked off his top hat that he recovered it with difficulty. Fire-crackers were exploding beneath his nose, between his feet. He was bewildered, exasperated, offended. This stream of people came from every quarter, as if impulse had unlocked the flood-gates, let flow waters of whose existence he had heard, perhaps, but believed in never. This then was the populace, the innumerable living negation of gentility and Forsyteism. This was— egad!—Democracy! It stank, yelled, was hideous! In the East End or* the bad parts of *Soho, perhaps—but here in Regent Street, in Piccadilly! What were the police about!*

In 1900, Soames with his Forsyte thousands, had never seen the cauldron with the lid off; and now looking into it, could hardly believe his scorching eyes.

My grandmother, Granny Mabs, used to speak of "Mafeking Night." She was only a girl of about ten at the time, but probably observed the reaction of her parents, Great-grandpa and Great-grandmother Cuthbertson. She told us of the unruly mob completely out of control that invaded the streets, although I doubt she personally saw too much along the leafy confines of Duncombe Hill. Great-grandfather Cuthbertson was director of a firm of stevedores in the docklands, however, and probably encountered the mob in force on his way home that evening.

These people had no restraint, they seemed to think 'Forsytes' funny; swarms of them, rude, coarse, laughing—and what laughter!

From their club windows, 'Forsytes', Soames' own kind, were looking out on the mob with regulated amusement, but Soames, in the thick of it, felt innate fear. *Why this was serious—might come to anything! The crowd was cheerful, but some day they would come in different mood! He remembered there had been a mob in the late 'eighties when he was at Brighton; they had smashed things and made speeches. But, more than dread, he felt a deep surprise.*

They were hysterical—it wasn't English! And all about the relief of a little town as big as—Watford, six thousand miles away. Restraint, reserve! Those qualities to him more dear almost than life, those indispensable attributes of property and culture, where were they? It wasn't English! No, it wasn't English! It was like discovering that nine-tenths of the people of England were foreigners. And if that were so—then anything might happen!

At Hyde Park Corner he ran into George Forsyte.

"I say," his cousin George said, *"one of these days we shall have to fight these chaps, they're getting so damn cheeky—all radicals and*

socialists. They want our goods. You tell Uncle James that, it'll make him sleep."

There was but a trickle of roysterers in Park Lane, not very noisy. And looking up at the houses, Soames *thought: 'After all, we're the backbone of the country. They won't upset us easily. Possession's nine points of the law.'*

In 1957, I first encountered the mob, not to the extreme of Soames on 'Mafeking Night', but enough to open my eyes to the reality that our comfortable 'Forsyte' world was not the only England. Brought up in almost Edwardian nursery conditions, away at boarding school on the south coast in a town that hosted at least a dozen other boarding schools educating young 'Forsytes', and finally arriving at Tonbridge, the school of my father and grandfather, uncles and great-uncles, I first innocently met the outside world. It happened twice within one week of my arrival. The first occasion was when out on an afternoon run with a small group of fellow 'Novi'—the Tonbridge speak, or Latin to be correct, for 'new boys', we were suddenly surrounded by a crowd of town "yobbos," as we called them—lower-class boys who whistled at us, poked fun at us and let us know that there was a divide between town and college. They referred to us as "the college toffs" and jeered at us. On the second occasion, I was walking on the outskirts of Tonbridge with two other boys. When out walking, we were supposed to wear our straw boaters. We were proud of them—those clean, solid, straw hats decorated with the ribbon of our house, in my case the black and magenta of Judde House. Again, we ran into some 'yobbos', who knocked off our hats and threw them into the River Medway. When we retrieved them, we found out why the rest of the school referred to these straw boaters as "barges." They floated well and were easy to retrieve and the muddy water of the Medway added to the platina of the straw and hardened the glue that held those hats in shape.

Like Soames, we were not really aware that we were only the privileged three percent, and that over nine-tenths of the people of England were not of our background and class.

Back in the safety, security and peace of his father's mansion, Soames walked *into the centre of the great empty drawing-room. He stood still.* He had not had the courage to visit with Annette and her mother, but he wanted *a wife! Somebody to talk things over with. One had a right! Damn it! One had a right!*

PART THREE

CHAPTER ONE

SOAMES IN PARIS

Soames had traveled little, but decided to seek Irene out in Paris. Like most Forsytes, he was skeptical of the French on their own territory, and on his only previous visit to Paris felt *surrounded by people so strongly self-centered and 'foreign.'* Like my father always said, and conferred throughout our 'Forsyte' childhoods: "All wogs begin at Calais." Soames' *knowledge of their language,* like ours, was *derived from* our *public* schools, we *did not understand* the French *when they spoke.* At Tonbridge, like Eton, Harrow, or Soames' Marlborough, we were all taught to read and write good French; we studied the language for at least eight years, but we were never really taught to speak it. I can read French to this day, but I am lost in conversation. Even Uncle Gyles, who commands excellent grammatical French having lived in Paris most his life and was married to Ginette, to my mind speaks the language somewhat with that dogged English accent that we used in school.

Soames only *went* to Paris, *indeed, because things were getting past a joke. The watch* by Polteed's agent *went on and on, and—nothing— nothing! Jolyon had never returned to Paris, and no one else was 'suspect'!* Also, *since Mafeking night he had become aware that a 'young fool of a doctor' was hanging round Annette.* If Irene would not take him back, he needed his divorce—he needed to confront Irene.

There had to be somebody, even if not his cousin Jolyon, who was paying attention to her.

He went to a hotel in the Rue Caumartin, highly recommended to Forsytes, where everyone spoke English and *practically nobody spoke French. He had formed no plan.*

Next morning he set out.

Paris had an air of gaiety. He came on the 'Cours la Reine', where Irene's hotel was situated. He shouldn't wonder if Irene quite enjoyed this foreign life, she had never been properly English—even to look at! And he began considering which of those windows could be hers under the green sun-blinds.

Then, he saw her leaving the building *in a cream-coloured frock under a fawn-coloured parasol.*

For half an hour at least he kept his distance on the far side of the way till she had passed into the Bois de Boulogne. Following winding paths, he was reminded of how he had followed her and Bosinney in Hyde Park all those years ago. He encountered her in front of *a little green bronze Niobe veiled in hair to her slender hips, gazing at the pool she had wept.*

Irene *did not start up. She had always had great self command.*

As Soames spoke to her, *a lady, strolling by, paused to look at the fountain and passed on.*

Noting the lady, Irene remarked: *"One has always one's shadow."*

"Well, it's your own fault. You can be free of it any moment. Irene, come back to me and be free."

"You may hunt me to the grave. I will not come. God made me as I am," she said; *"wicked if you like—but not so wicked that I'll give myself again to a man I hate."*

That word 'hate'—so extreme, so primitive—made all the Forsyte in him tremble.

Irene moved on: Soames turned and left.

Sitting lunchless in the hall of his hotel he was visited by black dejection. In irons! His whole life, with every natural instinct and every decent yearning gagged and fettered, and all because fate had driven him seventeen years ago to set his heart upon this woman—so utterly that even now he had no real heart to set on any other! However, he was driven, he needed a son—a Forsyte heir.

He prepared a note and decided to deliver it to Irene by dining at her hotel. *He dressed carefully, and wrote as follows:*

'Your idyll with that fellow Jolyon Forsyte is known to me at
all events. If you pursue it, understand that I will leave no
stone unturned to make things unbearable for him. 'S.F.'

She was not at dinner. *He went over to the key-board and examined
the names. Number twelve on the first floor!*

*The door was locked. It fitted very closely to the floor; the note
would not go under. He thrust it back into his pocket.*

Back in the foyer, *he stopped at the bureau and said:*

"Will you kindly see that Mrs. Heron has this note?"

"Madame Heron left today, Monsieur—suddenly, about three
o'clock. There was illness in her family."

Soames compressed his lips. "Oh!" he said: "do you know her
address?"

"Non Monsieur. England, I think."

In a daze, Soames left the hotel; and taking a cab aimlessly rode
around the city.

'Like my life,' thought Soames, 'without object, on and on!'

Chapter Two

In the Web

Soames returned to England the following day. Within three days, he received a visit from Mr. Polteed.

Mr. Polteed leaned forward, smiled, opened his hand, looked into it, and said softly:

"I think we've done your business for you at last."

He then proceeded to describe to Soames his agent's report on what was obviously his own visit to Irene's hotel in Paris and how he had been seen coming from her bedroom in the hotel about ten o'clock in the evening.

"With a little care in the giving of the evidence that will be enough, especially as 17 has left Paris—no doubt with the party in question."

Soames stood there in sardonic fury. Congenital idiot—spidery congenital idiot! Seven months at fifteen pounds a week—to be tracked down as his own wife's lover!

He threw the window open in his internal fury.

"I doubt if that is quite enough," he said, drawling the words, "with no name or address, I think you may let that lady investigator have a rest, and take up our friend 47 at this end."

She must have run to Jolyon.

There was an image in 'Forsythia' that private investigators were bumbling fools, although their dirty work was sometimes needed. Arthur Conan Doyle shows this image in Sherlock Holmes' partner, the bumbling Dr. Watson, and the famous Inspector Fix of Jules Verne's *Around the World in Eighty Days* is seen in a similar light. However, both Arthur Conan Doyle and Jules Verne were writing at the Edwardian height of 'Forsythia' for a 'Forsyte' reading public as members themselves of that 'Forsyte' class.

That afternoon Soames left work early and made his way to the Restaurant Bretagne. Only Madame Lamotte was in. Would Monsieur have tea with her? A true 'Forsyte', and not a French import of the lower-middle class, would have asked him to "take tea" with her.

Soames bowed.

When they were seated he said abruptly:

"I want a talk with you, madame. I have to ask you something first: That young doctor—what's his name? Is there anything between him and Annette?"

"Annette is young," she said: "so is monsieur le docteur. Between young people things move quickly; but Annette is a good daughter. Ah! what a jewel of a nature!"

"Nothing definite, then?"

"But definite, no, indeed! The young man is veree nice, but—what would you? There is no money at present."

She raised her willow-patterned tea-cup. Soames did the same. Their eyes met.

Willow-pattern china in pseudo blue delph was the lower-middle classes' symbol of moderate prosperity in 'Forsythia' from Edwardian times right through to the 1960s. Upper-middle class 'Forsyte' families did not festoon their kitchen dressers with this attractive, but symbolic china, although it was a perfect gift for their senior retainers at Christmas. Soames, however, knew that Madame Lamotte was a social climber, shrewd and sharp, who knew the 'Forsyte' value of money. They could make a deal even over the willow-patterned delph.

"I am a married man," he said, "living apart from my wife for many years. I am seeking to divorce her."

Madame Lamotte put down her cup. Indeed! What tragic things there were! The entire absence of sentiment in her inspired a queer species of contempt in Soames, but he knew they could do business.

"I am a rich man," he added, fully conscious that the remark was not in good taste. "It is useless to say more at present, but I think you understand."

Madame's eyes, so open that the whites showed above them, looked at him very straight.

"Ah! ca—mais nous avons le temps!" was all she said. "Another little cup?" Soames refused and, taking his leave, walked westward.

In Chelsea, he observed Irene's old flat. *He arrived at the little Mansions at the dinner-hour. No need to enquire! A grey-haired lady was watering the flower boxes in* what had been Irene's window. The place *was evidently let.*

'Jolyon, number 47,' he thought.

CHAPTER THREE

RICHMOND PARK

While Soames was in Paris, his cousin Jolyon had personal news from South Africa.

'Your son down with enteric no immediate danger will cable again.'

Jolly was sick—sick enough for them to send a cable. *It reached* Robin Hill *to find a household* already agitated by the imminent departure of June, whose berth was booked for the following day. The resolution to become a Red Cross nurse, taken under stimulus of Jolly's enlistment, had been loyally fulfilled with the irritation and regret which all Forsytes feel at what curtails their individual liberties. Enthusiastic at first about the 'wonderfulness' of the work, June had begun after a month to feel that she could train herself so much better than others could train her.

Those who trained 'Forsytes' in these good works were either of the aristocracy, who sponsored schools of nursing and added their own maternal instinct over a world that was once shared only with the church, to whom they were also patrons, over their tenants, and the village poor; or they were trained by working-class girls or even lower-middle-class women, who flocked to such patriotic duty, and were also the very supporters of the new movement of rights for women—a movement that seemingly threatened 'Forsythia'.

In my family, to my knowledge nobody served as a Red Cross nurse in the Boer War. Granny Mabs was too young at the time, as were Grandpa Jack's sisters, Nellie and Babs. Great-aunt Dorrie was an infant—the baby that Grandpa Jack sometimes called "the mistake." Agnes Longley was too promising as a musician and Bernice just a very young girl. Granny Longley was a child, too, and her elder sisters, Charlotte and Hetty, were barely teenagers. During the Great War fifteen years later, followed by the Spanish flu epidemic in 1919, we find most of them married and having their families, all except Great-aunt Dorrie, who was always proud to say she joined the Red Cross. However, some of the spirit of the Great War female volunteers along with the new rights established by Emily Pankhurst and her suffragettes, did show in members of my family. My Aunt Daphne became very much a believer in female good works, and was firmly of the 'Forsyte' opinion, too, that she could train herself in such things so much better than others could train her. Remember, if volunteer work was done well in my childhood, our family often said that it was "very Daphne."

June Fosyte now had cold feet about her venture, *and if her step-sister, Holly, had not insisted on following her example and being trained, too, she must inevitably have cried off. The departure of Jolly and Val with their troop in April had further stiffened her failing resolve. But now, on the point of departure, the reading of that cablegram, clinched the matter. She saw herself already nursing Jolly—for, of course, they would let her nurse her own brother!*

Poor June! Jolyon reflected. *Could any Forsyte of her generation grasp how rude and brutal life was?* However, that *cablegram, grave though it was, was almost a relief.* Jolly *was now safe from bullets, anyway. And yet—this enteric was a virulent disease!* The Times *was full of deaths therefrom.*

Late that afternoon Holly seated herself in the swing, close to where Jolyon was drawing under the oak tree. She was *very silent and still.*

"I want to tell you something, Dad," she said. *"It was through me that Jolly enlisted and went out."*

"How's that?"

"When you were away in Paris, Val Dartie and I fell in love. We used to ride in Richmond Park; we got engaged. Jolly found it out, and thought he ought to stop it; so he dared Val to enlist. It was all my fault,

*Dad; and I want to go out too. Because if anything happens to either of
them I should feel awful. Besides, I'm just as much trained as June.*

*Jolyon gazed at her. So this was the answer to the riddle he had been
asking himself. Engaged! So this was why he had so lost touch with her!
And to young Val Dartie—nephew of Soames—in the other camp!*

He closed his easel and set his drawing against the tree.

"Have you told June?"

*"Yes; she says she'll get me into her cabin somehow. It's a single
cabin; but one of us could sleep on the floor. If you consent she'll go up
now and get permission."*

"You're too young, my dear; they won't let you."

*"June knows some people that she helped to go to Cape Town. If
they won't let me nurse yet, I could stay with them and go on training
there. Let me go, Dad!"*

Jolyon smiled because he could have cried.

"I never stop anyone from doing anything," he said.

Holly flung her arms round his neck.

"Oh! Dad, you are the best in the world."

*'That means the worst,' thought Jolyon. If he had ever doubted his
creed of tolerance he did so then.*

*"I'm not friendly with Val's family," he said, "and I don't know Val,
but Jolly didn't like him."*

Holly looked at the distance and said:

"I love him."

"That settles it," said Jolyon dryly.

*Unless he actually forbade her going it was obvious that he must
make the best of it, so he went up to town with June. Whether due to
her persistence, or the fact that the official they saw was an old school
friend of Jolyon's, they obtained permission for Holly to share the single
cabin.*

The 'old boy' network was rife throughout 'Forsythia', for all the
positions of authority in government, law, church, and banking were
filled by members of that establishment. They were from the three
percent. They had all been to the same schools—those private 'public'
schools. Many had been to the elite of those same schools—Eton, Harrow,
Winchester, Marlborough, Rugby, Repton, Radley, Stowe, Sherbourne,
Charterhouse, and Tonbridge. It was not hard to have connections to
run the Empire. Many had played each other on the cricket and rugby
pitches of their youth, sung the new Gilbert and Sullivan operettas

together in colonial postings, and served as liverymen together in the select guilds of the City of London. They found themselves staying with their families at the same seaside resorts for their summer holidays, and they shopped at the same department stores in Kensington and Oxford Street.

After Great-uncle Bert Cuthbertson died, which was not long after he and Aunt Ruby returned home from India, we lost contact with the good-looking cousin whom Diane, Sally and I called "Shon, the wonderboy." He no longer spent his winter and spring school holidays with his "Auntie Mabel"—our Granny Mabs. However, true to 'Forsythia', some five years later, when we were staying at Thurlestone on Devon's south coast for our annual summer holiday, who should we run into at the Golf Club—the widow Ruby, still blonde, sun-tanned and beautiful, and wearing shorts no less, and our cousin John Cuthbertson.

Likewise, one summer at Thurlestone, whom should we find renting a house on the cliffs just below the Links Hotel, but Richard Bradley, my favorite history and English teacher from Tonbridge.

Places like Thurlestone, a quaint little Devon village set in beautiful farmland sloping down to ragged cliffs, coves, and beaches, had become the summer playground of 'Forsytes' on holiday. Two family hotels had established themselves there, one on the edge of the village and the other atop the cliffs, both with superb views across Thurlestone Bay, looking out to a natural arch rock—the Thurl Stone. In the 1920s and '30s, Granny and Grandpa Jack often took my mother and Aunt Eileen there for their annual summer holiday. They saw the Thurlestone Hotel grow from a smugglers' Inn to a 'Forsyte' resort and all the time in the hands of the same caring family—the Grosse family. Granny Mabs always called it "the Grosse expansion." She would be surprised to know that still today the Thurlestone Hotel is owned by this same family, but caters now to the nouveau riche rather than vanished 'Forsythia'. During latter 'Forsythia', throughout the short season of July, August, and September, the clipped upper-middle-class accents of countless London 'Forsytes' could be heard beneath the cry of the gulls separating them from the earthy Devon accents of the villagers and local farmers. The golf course along the cliffs, and the bank of tennis courts were busy, the clubhouse reminiscent of those clubs found throughout the British Empire as home to the young white rulers of the Raj. There were other seaside bastions—Frinton in Essex, Cromer in Norfolk, also popular with my family, Shanklin on the Isle of White, Budleigh Salterton, also in Devon, and those quaint fishing ports of Cornwall and the North Devon and Somerset coasts. 'Forsytes' met 'Forsytes'. Much of the British Empire was tied together by that old school tie.

After he saw his daughters off the next day, Jolyon returned alone to Robin Hill. He had dinner and went out on the terrace and smoked a cigar. He listened to the night sounds. *A multitude of stars up there—bright and silent, so far off! No moon as yet! Just enough light to show him the dark flags and swords of the iris flowers along the terrace edge—his favorite flower that had the night's own colour on its curving crumpled petals. He turned round to the house. Stark loneliness! He could not go on living here alone. The night, maddeningly lovely, with bloom of grapes on it in starshine, and the breath of grass and honey coming from it, he could not enjoy while she who was to him the life of beauty, its embodiment and essence, was cut off from him, utterly cut off now, he felt, by honourable decency.*

Two days later, Jolyon *made up his mind to move to London and see if he could not get permission to follow his daughters to South Africa. He had just begun to pack the following morning when he received this letter:*

'GREEN HOTEL,
RICHMOND.
'June 13.

MY DEAR JOLYON,
   'You will be surprised to see how near I am to you. Paris became impossible—and I have come here to be within reach of your advice. I would so love to see you again. Since you left Paris I don't think I have met anyone I could really talk to. Is all well with you and with your boy? No one knows, I think, that I am here at present.

'Always your friend,
'IRENE.'

   Irene within three miles of him!
   About noon he set off across Richmond Park. 'Richmond Park! By Jove, it suits us Forsytes!' Not that Forsytes lived there—nobody lived there save royalty, rangers, and the deer.

A royal preserve, Richmond Park has two crown residences, one near its entrance and one right in the middle of the park. Thatched House

Lodge near the entrance was a home of the Duke of Kent's family, and at the demise of 'Forsythia' was the home of Princess Alexandria and her husband The Honourable Angus Ogilvy. The house in the center of the park is a large palladian-style mansion named White Lodge. At the time Galsworthy had Jolyon living at Robin Hill, White Lodge was the home of the Grand Duke of Teck, whose daughter, Princess 'May' of Teck was to become The Princess of Wales and later the formidable Queen Mary, wife of King George V. In the last decades of 'Forsythia', however, and during my childhood, by a strange coincidence the house was leased by the crown to a wealthy American, the son of Count Diaz-Albertini, whose wife, Nora, was from an English 'Forsyte' family named Denny. Her brother was the famous English Hollywood movie star Reginald Denny, and her sister, Mona, was married to a member of the English Ford family, whose name was embedded in the sheets of blotting paper that were placed on our school desks at Newlands every morning—Ford, the blotting paper king! Although they had left White Lodge by the time I joined the household of their eldest son, William Diaz-Albertini, this *was* the same family for whom I worked at Tullamaine Castle in Ireland and who brought me to the United States. After the Albertini family left White Lodge, the mansion became the home of The Royal Ballet School and has remained so to this day.

The Green Hotel, across the park, which Jolyon entered at one-o'clock, stood nearly opposite that more famous hostelry, the Crown and Sceptre, a name that acknowledged the royalty of Richmond. The Green Hotel *was modest, highly respectable, never out of cold beef, gooseberry tart, and a dowager or two, so that a carriage and pair was almost always standing before the door.*

Galsworthy's description of The Crown and Sceptre reminds me of another hotel not far from Richmond, but closer to Windsor. The place was called The Lodge and was situated at Englefield Green, just above Runnymede where the Magna Carta was signed in 1215. It was there in 1962 that I first joined the Albertini family. Throughout the 1920s and '30s this family had lived at crown properties on the fringe of Windsor Park and in the little Thameside village of Datchet before moving to White Lodge in Richmond Park. It was for this reason that William Diaz-Albertini was educated in England at Tonbridge at the same time that my father attended the school, although they were in different houses and did not know each other very well. It was not surprising, therefore, that on visits to England from America in the 1950s and

'60s, the Albertini family chose to stay in that genteel area southwest of London. The Lodge Hotel was run by a red-headed lady straight out of the 1920s, whom some said had been a madam at the Wheatsheaf before the Second World War—a notorious hang out for the well-to-do's of this unique area under the shadow of Windsor Castle including the Prince of Wales set. Hilda Downie reminded me of the *Duchess of Duke Street,* the semi-fictitious heroine of a great TV series that was based on the cockney girl and ex-mistress of King Edward VII, who became the delight of London Society and in real life founded the fashionable Connaught Hotel. Hilda ran the Lodge Hotel like a small country house, before country house hotels became fashionable. Like the Green Hotel at Richmond, *the place was modest, highly respectable, never out of* great food and wines, and definitely had amongst its guests *a dowager or two,* not to mention a bevy of old colonial administrators on leave from far flung parts of the Empire. The *carriage and pair* by 1962 had been replaced by Hilda Downie's private London taxicab, driven by her chauffeur, Mr. Bracy.

Every Thursday, Mr. Bracy drove Hilda Downie up to London where she shopped in the food markets at Harrods and Fortnum and Mason's for provisions for the Lodge Hotel. My grandmother, Granny Longley, used to also take a chauffered car up to London once a week in the 1920s and '30s to shop at the department stores. She used to hire a car from Bartlett, who was still running his chauffeur service on Bromley Road in the Beckenham of my childhood.

At the Green Hotel, Richmond, i*n a room draped in chintz, Irene was sitting on a piano stool covered with crewel work, playing 'Hansel and Gretel' out of an old score. Above her, on a wall not yet Morris-papered, was a print of* Queen Victoria *on a pony, amongst deer-hounds, Scotch caps, and slain stags. The Victorianism of the room almost talked; and in her clinging frock Irene seemed to Jolyon like Venus emerging from the shell of the past century.*

During the nineteenth century, partly through the romantic novels of Sir Walter Scott and Waverley, and partly because of Queen Victoria's personal love of the highlands at her retreat of Balmoral, 'Forsytes' slowly gravitated to appreciation of the hostile north. At the beginning of 'Forsythia', most adventurers from the more populous south of England traveled no further north than Derbyshire, an example being the Derbyshire tour of Mr. and Mrs. Gardiner in Jane Austen's *Pride and Prejudice*—a tour that in the novel was the cause of the happy, but coincidental reunion of Mr. Darcy and Elizabeth Bennett. This was partly because of transport, it being hard to post-chaise further north over the bleak moors of Yorkshire, still to be made famous by the Bronte sisters, and on up to the hostile land further north that was barely a generation out of the Jacobite rebellions and looked skeptically on "Sassenachs."

The massive growth of rail travel in the latter nineteenth century, however, opened up Scotland and the north. By the end of the nineteenth century, landscapes of the highlands found in many 'Forsyte' homes, such as the Brianski paintings in Granny Mabs' dining room, beckoned 'Forsytes' to follow the queen and travel north. The railways had crossed the Firths of Forth and Tay—the highlands beckoned.

In the last decades of 'Forsythia', the highlands were added to that list of fashionable 'Forsyte' vacation spots. The center of this was in a beautiful glen named Pitlochery. Here, in the short season that was bearable, upper-middle-class 'Forsytes' gathered just as they did in Thurlestone, Cromer, and Frinton. They took the train north—the sleeper to Edinburgh—and then further north to Pitlochery from where they explored the beauty of the highlands, enjoyed the health of the spa waters and the matchmaking of families on holiday within their class. My mother remembered several Pitlochery holidays and Grandpa Jack always said it was his favorite place. Granny Mabs and Grandpa Jack even hired a maid from Scotland through these connections in the late 1930s, but she only lasted a day or two, having used them to get her train fare south to meet her boyfriend. As Grandpa explained: "For two days all she did was paint her nails in the kitchen."

At the Green Hotel, Irene and Jolyon ate *cold beef, pickled walnut, gooseberry tart, and drunk stone-bottle ginger-beer.*

Ginger-beer was always a popular 'Forsyte' drink, and in my childhood was delivered to our house by the 'Carona' man—a company that purveyed in soft fizzy drinks that were capped with porcelain stoppers intriguingly held in place by a lever and springs. In our schooldays, too, both at Newlands, and for Diane and Sally at Micklefield, we cultured ginger beer in jars in our lockers. Ginger-beer plants, as these jars were called, could be sold off to other students as host plants and were a minor source of income.

At the demise of 'Forsythia', ginger-beer fell to the rise of American style fizzy drinks, led by Coca-Cola, and the stone jars and porcelain stoppers gave way to glass bottles and metal caps, and later, cans.

Ginger-beer today, still found in cans in England, does not remotely resemble the pleasant drink of 'Forsythia', anymore than does the cider of the west country of Somerset and Devon, that like ginger-beer of 'Forsythia' was once always found in stone jars.

When Jolyon and Irene walked out into Richmond Park, Jolyon asked the burning question:

"You haven't told me about Paris?"

"No. I've been shadowed for a long time;" Irene explained. *"You get used to that. But then Soames came. By the little Niobe—the same story; would I go back to him?"*

"Incredible!"

She had spoken without raising her eyes, but she looked up now. Those dark eyes clinging to his said as no words could have: 'I have come to an end; if you want me, here I am.'

The words: 'Irene, I adore you!' almost escaped Jolyon, but he thought of Jolly and his plans for South Africa.

"My boy is very ill out there," he said quietly.

Irene slipped her arm through his.

"Let's walk on; I understand."

No miserable explanation to attempt! She had understood! And they walked on among the bracken, knee-high already, between the rabbit holes and the oak trees, talking of Jolly. He left her two hours later at the Richmond Hill Gate, and turned towards home.

'She knows my feeling for her, then,' he thought. Of course! One could not keep knowledge of that from such a woman!

CHAPTER FOUR

OVER THE RIVER

Jolly was tired of dreams, just able to turn his eyes and gaze through the window near his cot to the trickle of river running by in the sands, at the straggling milk-bush of the Karoo beyond.

He knew what the Karoo was now, even if he had not seen a Boer roll over like a rabbit, or heard the whiffle of flying bullets. This pestilence had sneaked on him before he had smelled powder. A thirsty day and a rash drink, or perhaps a tainted fruit—who knew? Not he, who had not even strength left to grudge the evil thing its victory.

The sun was nearly down. It would be cooler soon. He would have liked to know the time—to feel his old watch, so buttersmooth, to hear the repeater strike. It would have been friendly, home-like.

Those things he used to do—walking past the foot of the old steps at Harrow 'bill'—'Here, sir! Here, sir!'—wrapping boots in the Westminster Gazette, greenish paper, shining boots—grandfather coming from somewhere dark—a smell of earth—the mushroom house! Robin Hill! Burying poor old Balthasar in the leaves! Dad! Home...

Consciousness came again with noticing that the river had no water in it...

Cricket! Holly! She wouldn't bowl properly. Oh! Pitch them up! Not sneaks!...Rowing! 'Back her, Two and Bow!' He was Two!...

Consciousness came once more with a sense of the violet dusk outside, and a rising blood-red crescent moon. His eyes rested on it

*fascinated; in the long minutes of brain nothingness it went moving up
and up...*

"He's going, doctor!" Not pack boots again? Never? 'Mind your
form, Two!' Don't cry! Go quietly—over the river—sleep!...Dark? If
somebody would—strike—watch!...

I watched my father dying. It was impossible to know what was
in his thoughts other than the knowledge as Diane, Sally and I held
his hands that there were moments he clung to us. Did the demise of
'Forsythia', the world of permanence in which he was born, pass by
him? "God help you all," he said, as if he knew that safe permanence
was gone. Then, there was that last real moment of lucidity after a long
night listening to his current favorite music, a modern piece for choirs:
Take me, Lord. He opened his eyes wide and it was then that he repeated
several times in a strong voice: "Tea." We fed him a few drops of his
favorite beverage.

CHAPTER FIVE

SOAMES ACTS

It was not long before Mr. Polteed's agent reported on the Richmond meetings of numbers 47 and 17. Soames read the report *at his City club, sacred to him for the meals he had eaten there with his father in the early seventies:*

'*Dear Sir,*
'*In accordance with your suggestion we have duly taken the matter up at the other end with gratifying results. Observation of 47 has enabled us to locate 17 at the Green Hotel, Richmond. The two have been observed to meet daily during the past week in Richmond Park. Nothing absolutely crucial has so far been notified. But in conjunction with what we had from Paris at the beginning of the year, I am confident we could now satisfy the Court. We shall of course, continue to watch the matter until we hear from you.*

'*Very faithfully yours,*
'*CLAUD POLTEED*'

That fellow Jolyon! He would disgrace him in the eyes of his own children. Soames knew *he could not treat this scandalous matter in his own office. He must commit the soul of his private dignity to a stranger, some other professional dealer in family dishonour. Who was there he could go to? Linkman and Laver in Budge Row, perhaps—reliable, not too conspicuous, only nodding acquaintances.*

Before doing so, Soames knew he would have to come clean with Mr. Polteed. He suspected the man knew the truth, anyway.

"I've had your letter," Soames said. *"I'm going to act. I suppose you know who the lady you've been watching really is?"*

Mr. Polteed's expression at that moment was a masterpiece. It so clearly said: 'Well, what do you think? But mere professional knowledge, I assure you—pray forgive it!' He made a little half airy movement with his hand, as who should say: 'Such things—such things will happen to us!'

"Very well, then," said Soames, "there's no need to say more. I'm instructing Linkman and Laver of Budge Row to act for me. I don't want to hear your evidence, but kindly make your report to them at five o'clock, and continue to observe the utmost secrecy."

That evening in Park Lane, watching his father dine, Soames was overwhelmed by his old longing for a son—a son of his own begetting who could understand him because he was the same flesh and blood— understand, and comfort him, and become more rich and cultured than himself because he would start even better off.

To get old like James, his father, and be quite alone with possessions heaping up around him—No! He would force divorce through now, and be free to marry and have a son to care for him before he grew to be like the old old man his father, wistfully watching now his sweetbread, now his son.

Sweetbreads were a popular supper meal in the 'Forsyte' home, especially for invalids, the elderly, or children, who might not be attending dinner in the dining room. They were calves' thyroid glands, soft and mushy when served with warm milk. They had the texture of fish roes and were easy to eat almost melting in the mouth.

Chapter Six

A Summer Day

His boy was seldom absent from Jolyon's mind in the days which followed the first walk with Irene in Richmond Park.

June and Holly were still at sea on passage to Cape Town. Jolly was alone fighting the enteric.

Only in Irene's presence had he relief.

With Jolly was bound up all that sense of continuity and social creed of which he had drunk deeply in his youth and again during his boy's public school and varsity life—all that sense of not going back on what father and son expected of each other. With Irene was bound up all his delight in beauty and in Nature. And he seemed to know less and less which was the stronger in him.

I saw this pattern in my own father's life, and perhaps even more so in the life of his youngest brother, my Uncle Dennis. They were brought up in a bastion of 'Forsythia' still dominated by my great-grandfather, Oliver Longley—the chairman of the family businesses. My father was innovative, but the older family members, who were his senior partners, rarely allowed his innovations growth. The business was prosperous, entrenched in 'Forsyte' principles, and there seemed little need for innovation or any fear that the social order of our world was ever going to change. It was upset by World War II, but not changed. Suzerainty of The Breach passed from Great-grandfather to Grandpop. Granny Longley continued to shop at the expensive Oxford Street stores, and

Mrs. James continued to cook huge family Sunday roasts. Yes, there was food rationing, but owning a small farm made one fairly self-sufficient. We had all the milk and eggs we needed; too many apples; strawberries and potatoes that we had started growing during the war, and access to meat, game and poultry through our business. Perhaps the most noticeable difference in our immediate post-war world was the reduction in the number of domestic servants—the lack of pre-war cap and apron.

Politically, the Empire was still intact. India was showing great unrest, but our wartime hero, Sir Winston Churchill, spoke nobly against any partition or independence for the sub-continent—India was the crown jewel of the British Empire. However, against 'Forsyte' principles, a socialist government swept into power under Clement Atlee, putting 'Winnie' into opposition, and the situation in India only got worse. Ultimately, Atlee appointed the king's cousin, Earl Mountbatten of Burma, to take the role of viceroy with plenipotentiary powers to create a smooth transition to some measure of Indian independence. Churchill was devastated. With great dignity, Mountbatten, steered the leaders of the religious and political factions in India to an agreement, assisted by the man who had become the spirit of India, and in retrospect one of the greatest motivators of humane change in the twentieth century—Mahatma Ghandi. Despite Mountbatten's skill, however, India was divided into moslem Pakistan and hindu India amid terrible bloodshed and the assassination of India's spiritual embodiment for peace, Ghandi himself.

How 'Forsyte's' reacted to the loss of India has to be coupled with many other political changes that started to surface in their imperial world in the last two decades of their era. I was too young to be affected by the loss of India, and can only say that in my childhood, collecting stamps only led us to believe that most of the world was still British. However, following India, independence movements grew up throughout the Empire, some of the results more successful than others, but all pointing to a change in our world. The purpose of 'Forsythia'—running the great British Empire for our commercial gain and our imperial subjects' social improvement—was drying up.

Some 'Forsytes' just faded away, sent their children to state schools, accepted their changing accents and begrudgingly embraced a different England. Others took their dislike of the changes out on the new super-power—the United States of America, whom the old guard considered naïve at best. Some, refused to accept there was real change, and tried to bestow on their families all the 'Forsyte' principles of their own upbringing. At first, my mother and father were probably in that latter category, and my mother probably remained in that ethos most of her life, but as time went by, that innovative spirit that had been crushed early in my father's life, began to embrace some of the social changes— the creation of a fairer, more just world where wealth was more evenly distributed. Of course, he could see that this was often abused without entrenched 'Forsyte' principles. He was shocked at the rising role of debt—no 'Forsyte' believed in debt. It was philosophically, however, that my father most changed, embracing liberal religious thoughts and allowing his appreciation of beauty in nature to govern his inner life. All three of us children were creative—potentially two artists and an actress! And all of us were also lovers of nature—a nature that also embraced a liberal spirituality.

Uncle Dennis was also a free thinker. His childhood was as entrenched in 'Forsythia' as my father's, but he found a spiritual freedom in his love of music and creative hobbies. He spoke the most beautiful English of any member of my family, complimented by his first wife's horsey county accent, but Dennis and Brigid embraced a very non-'Forsyte' approach to the bringing up of their family. Few 'Forsyte' principles were applied. There were no nannies, and much of their education was local. My cousins did not go to boarding school like the rest of us. They were also the first Longley generation to be brought up with television. Dennis and Brigid believed that their children had to adapt to the new world. Eventually, in his second wife, my Aunt Pat, Dennis truly found a soul mate in this new order. Pat is highly intelligent and a free thinker and was even able to wean Dennis from voting for the Conservative party, a step I don't believe my father was ever able to make. Together, Dennis and Pat had a very free and clear idea of justice in a post-'Forsyte' world, even though their home, strangely named the Manor House, but in reality a beautiful Kentish village house, is filled with little trappings of that great 'Forsythia' past. They both loved family history and local Kentish history; but it is history—no longer the 'Forsyte' way of life.

It is not surprising that with this liberal embrace fostered by a love of beauty, music, and nature, my father, Pat, and Dennis, became interesting kindred spirits in later life in a way that my mother never really could. They were able to adapt and transcend 'Forsythia'.

Jolyon Forsyte was on the brink of the same—entrenched in 'Forsythia', but a willing rebel—living on his father's wealth, but generous to share. His love of beauty and recording it in nature caused an emotional split with the old 'Forsyte' principles of his uncles and cousins whose love was property. And, now, this was embodied in Jolyon's feelings for Irene.

From such sentimental paralysis Jolyon was rudely awakened, however, one afternoon, just as he was starting off to Richmond, by a young man with a bicycle—Was it the telegram boy?

"Mr. Jolyon Forsyte? Thank you!" Placing an envelope in Jolyon's hand he wheeled off the path and rode away. Bewildered, Jolyon opened it.

"Admiralty Probate and Divorce, Forsyte v. Forsyte and Forsyte!"

A 'Forsyte'sensation of shame and disgust was followed by the instant reaction: 'Why, here's the very thing you want, and you don't like it!' But Irene *must have one too; and he must go to her at once.*

He turned things over as he went along.

For, whatever the Scriptures said about the heart, it took more than mere longings to satisfy the law. They could very well defend this suit, or at least in good faith try to. But the idea of doing so revolted Jolyon. If not her lover in deed he was in desire, and he knew that she was ready to come to him.

Surely she would not ask him to defend the suit, knowing that he adored her! Thank Heaven she had not that maddening British conscientiousness which refused happiness for the sake of refusing—a trait found in my mother and her mother, Granny Mabs. *Surely Irene must rejoice at this chance of being free—after seventeen years of death in life!*

The notion of standing in a witness box and swearing to the truth that no gesture, not even a word of love had passed between them seemed to Jolyon *more degrading than to take the tacit stigma of being an adulterer—more degrading considering the feeling in his heart, and just as bad and painful for his children.*

The brutality and hypercritical consciousness of the whole process; the probability that they would not be believed—the mere vision of her, whom he looked on as the embodiment of Nature and of Beauty, standing there before all those suspicious, gloating eyes was hideous

*to him. No, no! A thousand times better to accept what Soames and the
gods had sent!*

*The sky had become overcast, purplish, with little streaks of white.
'Phew!' he thought, 'thunder!'*

Behind our houses in Wickham Way there was in my childhood
an area of wasteland separating the Park Langley Estate from Langley
Court, at that time the home of the pharmaceutical company of
Burroughs Wellcome. It was a flat area of long grass behind our house,
and a more rugged pit behind Granny Mabs' house. Diane, Sally and
I, often joined by our cousin John Cuthbertson, loved to play in this
area although technically the pit behind Redcroft was considered out
of bounds by my grandparents. For some strange reason we all share a
common memory of the territory—the sight of the blue sky of a sunny
summer day turning menacing with that overcast, purplish light with
little streaks of creamy yellow. As before noted, we used to call this "the
brewing of a stormy petrol." There followed thunder and pouring rain.

*As this 'stormy petrol' brewed over Richmond Park, Jolyon saw
Irene coming towards the Gate. 'We must scuttle back to Robin Hill,'
he thought.*

* * *

*The same storm had passed over the Poultry at four o'clock, bringing
welcome distraction to the clerks in every office. Soames was drinking
a cup of tea when a note was brought to him:* for in 'Forsythia', as
in the famous song, 'at four o'clock everything stops for tea'—storm
or no storm.

The note from Linkman and Laver confirmed that Jolyon Forsyte
and Irene Forsyte had been served in the case of *Forsyte v. Forsyte and
Forsyte.*

*Ever since he had given those instructions Soames had been tempted
to annul them. It was so scandalous, such a general disgrace! Was it
too late? Now that they had been brought up sharp by service of this
petition, had he not a lever with which he could force them apart? 'But
if I don't act at once,' he thought, 'it will be too late, now they've had
this thing. I'll go and see him; I'll go down!'*

*And, sick with nervous anxiety, he sent out for one of the 'new-
fangled' motor-cabs.*

*A man's life was what he possessed, and sought to possess. Only
fools thought otherwise—fools, and socialists, and libertines!*

Although I have become a definite socialist, I hope I am not a fool or a libertine. Socialism was a dirty word in my upbringing, and even more so in the years that I spent with the Albertini family. I remember Mr. Albertini expressing this well with the sentence that "the only difference between socialism and communism is the difference between dog poop and cat poop." I rubbed shoulders with a few idealistic socialists in my Cambridge years including my own roommate, Sebastian Jones. In fact, it was primarily because of my relationship with Sebastian and his sister Tina, that neither Mr. or Mrs. Albertini ever came to visit me while I was up at Cambridge—quite interesting socially, inasmuch as Sebastian's grandfather lived in a crown property at Datchet on the River Thames opposite Windsor Great Park and next door to Sandlea Court, Mr. Albertini's father's home leased from the crown in the 1930s before they moved to White Lodge in Richmond Park. For me, at least in those days, embracing some principles of social justice, did not mean sacrificing my entrenched imperial conservatism. Social justice could be achieved paternally, and I used to wrap my liberal beliefs within an outer veneer of social quality that I called "Hovendenism" after my maternal grandmother. With Sebastian Jones, in our elaborate paneled rooms off 'B' staircase in St. Catherine's College, I hosted contribution lunches for 'Oxfam' and 'War on Want', but we served smoked salmon to our guests sent to me by the Albertinis in Ireland and kept for me refrigerated in the college kitchens! In actuality, of course, we raised more money for these charities than most others in the field, who served watered down tomato soup and saltines!

I still did not have the right to vote while I was up at Cambridge, being under twenty-one, but I do remember the British general election results that brought down Harold MacMillan's conservative government, and feeling the bitter shame of now having to live in Britain under Harold Wilson's labour government. The feeling of shame at the time was real, for almost all my remembered 'Forsyte' childhood Great Britain had been under a conservative government.

To this day, some find it hard to envisage me as a socialist because of the trappings of 'Forsythia' that still surround me, but in reality if I must describe my politics it is well within the socialist camp. Yes, I wanted to be a socialist, but I still wanted to live under the proscenium arch of a 'Forsyte' stage.

The cab carrying Soames made its way out of central London *passing villas now, going a great pace. 'Fifteen miles an hour, I should think!'*

he mused, 'this'll take people out of town to live!' The cab sped on, down the hill past Wimbledon Common. This interview with his cousin Jolyon. *Surely a man of fifty-two with grown-up children, and hung on the line, would not be reckless. 'He won't want to disgrace the family,' he thought; 'he was as fond of his father as I am of mine, and they were brothers. That woman brings destruction—what is it in her?'*

The cab turned in at the drive to Robin Hill, *which might have been his own, and the sound of music met him. He had forgotten the fellow's daughters.*

After asking the cab to wait, *he rang the bell.*

Following the maid through the curtains into the inner hall, he felt relieved that the impact of this meeting would be broken by June or Holly, whichever was playing in there.

The inner and outer hall was a common architectural feature of 'Forsythia' homes as at Hockeredge. In a pre-central heating world, the cold of winter creeping under the front door was isolated from the rest of the house by the doors from the outer to the inner hall—doors, often screened by those heavy velvet curtains that were drawn apart in order to answer the front door bell's ring. As mentioned, the movement of the drapes was a very distinctive and deliberate sound that has remained with me throughout my life—the sound of a visitor arriving.

It was *with complete surprise* Soames *saw Irene at the piano, and Jolyon sitting in an armchair listening. The look of his farmer forebears—dogged Forsytes down by the sea, from 'Superior Dosset' back—grinned out of his face.*

"Very pretty!" he said.

He heard Jolyon *murmur:*

"This is hardly the place—we'll go to the study, if you don't mind."

Soames pulled the door to behind him with a slam; the sound carried him back all those years to the day when he had shut out Jolyon—shut him out for meddling with his affairs.

"Well," he said, "what have you to say for yourselves?"

"What we have received today," Jolyon replied, "has taken away your right to ask. I should imagine you will be glad to have your neck out of chancery."

"Oh!" said Soames, "you think so! I came to tell you that I'll divorce her with every circumstance of disgrace to you both, unless you swear to keep clear of each other from now on."

Neither of them answered.

"*Well,*" Soames *said; "you—Irene?*"

Her lips moved, but Jolyon laid his hand on her arm.

"*Let her alone!*" *said Soames furiously.* "*Irene, will you swear it?*"

"*No.*"

"*Oh! And you?*"

Jolyon said, "*Still less.*"

"*So then, you're guilty, are you?*"

"*Yes, guilty.*" *It was Irene speaking in that serene voice, with that unreached air which had maddened him so often.*

"*You are a devil.*"

"*Go out! Leave this house, or I'll do you an injury,*" Jolyon responded.

"*A trustee,*" Soames *said,* "*embezzling trust property! A thief, stealing his cousin's wife.*"

"*Call me what you like. You have chosen your part, we have chosen ours. Go out!*"

Soames' *eyes fastened on Irene's face—the last time, no doubt!*

"*You,*" *he said suddenly,* "*I hope you'll treat him as you treated me—that's all.*"

He saw her wince, and with a sensation not quite triumph, not quite relief, he wrenched open the door, passed out through the hall, and got into his cab.

CHAPTER SEVEN

A SUMMER NIGHT

fter Soames left, *Jolyon said suddenly, "Thank you for that good lie."* They felt a relief and went outside.

After that painful scene the quiet of Nature was wonderfully poignant. From the bees came a low hum in which all other sounds were set.

Bees used to hum in the windows of the dining room at Hockeredge where the nectar of japonica, jasmine, and summer honeysuckle was freely available below their panes. My last memory of Hockeredge before leaving for a new life in the United States is that of the buzzing of the bees. It was an eternal summer sound, overpowering all other sounds and relaxing the senses.

In their suspended moment between fear of the future and in knowing themselves, Jolyon and Irene heard *the mooing of a cow deprived of her calf, the calling of a cuckoo from an elm tree at the bottom of the meadow. Who would have thought that behind them, within ten miles, London began—that London of the Forsytes, with its wealth, its misery; its dirt and noise; its jumbled stone isles of beauty, its grey sea of hideous brick and stucco? That London which had seen Irene's early tragedy, and Jolyon's own hard days; that web; that princely workhouse of the possessive instinct!*

Jolyon pondered those words: 'I hope you'll treat him as you treated me.' That would depend on himself? Did Nature permit a Forsyte not to make a slave of what he adored? 'We are a breed of spoilers,' thought Jolyon, 'close and greedy; the bloom of life is not safe with us. Let her come to me as she will, not at all if she will not. Let me be just her stand-by, her perching-place; never—never her cage! Let me, ah! let me only know how not to grasp and destroy!

To-morrow he would see Herring—they would go and see him together. And then—abroad, leaving no doubt, no difficulty about evidence, making the lie she had told him into the truth.

He looked around at her. 'And this is to be mine,' he thought as the sounds enveloped them, *'It frightens me.'*

Back in the house, he asked the maid to show Irene to Holly's room—Holly now gone—on her way to South Africa.

The maid handed him a telegram.

Opening the telegram, he read:

> *'JOLYON FORSYTE, Robin Hill.—Your son passed painlessly*
> *away on June 20th. Deep sympathy'*
> *Signed by—some name unknown to him.'*

He dropped it, spun round and stood motionless.

Gone out like a candle flame; far from home, from love, all by himself, in the dark! His boy! From a little chap always so good to him—so friendly! Twenty years old and cut down like grass—to have no life at all! 'I didn't really know him,' he thought, 'and he didn't know me; but we loved each other. It's only love that matters.'

Oh! How important is that 'Forsyte' son! Was it love or possession—the knowledge that name and chattels will pass on? This, too, is what gnawed at Soames' heart.

Jolly—To die out there—lonely—wanting them—wanting home! This seemed to Jolyon's *Forsyte heart more painful, more pitiful than death itself. No shelter, no protection, no love at the last! Better far if he had died in battle, without time to long for them to come to him, to call out for them, perhaps in his delirium!*

The study *door creaked. He saw Irene come in, pick up the telegram and read it. He heard the faint rustle of her dress. She sank on her knees close to him, and he forced himself to smile at her. She stretched up her arms and drew his head down on her shoulder. The perfume and warmth of her encircled him; her presence gained slowly his whole being.*

CHAPTER EIGHT

JAMES IN WAITING

J ames *had been unwell lately. This would have to be kept from him! Never till that moment had he realised how much the dread of bringing James's grey hairs down with sorrow to the grave had counted with* Soames; *how intimately it was bound up with his own shrinking from scandal. His affection for his father, always deep, had increased of late years. It seemed pitiful that one who had been so careful all his life and done so much for the family name—so that it was almost a byword for solid, wealthy respectability—should at his last gasp have to read it all in the newspapers.*

When my father, at ninety-three, fell ill with pneumonia and appeared to be dying, I was myself, like Soames, going through some great difficulties in my life, especially financial, that I never wanted him to know. For the first time in my life, I was in debt, and debt was total anathema to 'Forsytes'. Fortunately, for most 'Forsytes' their 'Forsythia' world pre-dated the easy credit world of the post-'Forsythia' decades. Unfortunately, my father was shrewd and probably knew a great deal more than I would have wanted him to know, but like his father before him, and most other members of my family's 'Forsythia' generations, especially Granny Mabs and my mother, neither debt nor divorce were acceptable. I was experiencing both phenomena and did the best I could to shield my father from knowing the worst.

'*I must tell mother,*' Soames *thought, 'and when it comes on, we must keep the papers from him somehow. He sees hardly anyone.*'

James was waiting for his son on the landing when he arrived at Park Lane after dining at the Remove Club.

"*Now come back to bed, James,*" Emily called.

"*Um! I might die before tomorrow morning.*"

Soames took his agitated father back to his bedroom where Emily started to brush his hair.

'*What is it?*' thought Soames. '*What has he got hold of now?*'

"*I want to say something, your mother hasn't heard,*" James said.

"*Your father's been in a great state all the evening. I'm sure I don't know what about.*" The faint '*whish-whish*' of the brushes continued the soothing of her voice.

"*No! you know nothing,*" said James. "*Soames can tell me. I'm getting on Soames. At my age, I can't tell. I might die at any time. There'll be a lot of money. There's Rachel and Cicely got no children; and Val's out there—that chap his father will get hold of all he can. And somebody'll pick up Imogen, I shouldn't wonder.*"

Soames listened vaguely—he had heard all this before.

"*If that's all—!*" said Emily.

"*Ah! cried James; "it's nothing. I'm coming to that.*"

"*It's you, my boy,*" he said suddenly; "*you ought to get a divorce.*"

That word, from those of all lips, was almost too much for Soames's composure. James hurried on.

"*I don't know what's become of her—they say she's abroad. Your Uncle Swithin used to admire her—he was a funny fellow.*" Soames knew it was Irene to whom the old man was alluding. "*She wouldn't be alone, I should say.*"

"*Come, James! Soames knows best. It's his business,*" Emily scolded.

"*Ah! but there's all my money, and there's his—who's it to go to? And when he dies the name goes out.*"

"*The name,*" said Emily, "*there are all the other Forsytes.*"

"*As if that helps me,*" muttered James. "*I shall be in my grave, and there'll be nobody unless he marries again.*"

"*You're quite right,*" said Soames quietly; "*I'm getting a divorce.*"

"*Well,*" said Emily, "*who would have imagined you wanted it? My dear boy, that is a surprise, after all these years.*"

"It'll be a scandal," muttered James, "but I can't help that. When'll it come on?"

"Before the Long Vacation, it's not defended."

James's lips moved in secret calculation. "I shan't live to see my grandson," he muttered.

Emily ceased brushing. "Of course you will, James. Soames will be as quick as he can."

Soames bent over and kissed his father's brow where the hair began. A relaxing quiver passed over James's face, as though the wheels of anxiety within were running down.

"I'll get to bed," he said; "I shan't want to see the papers when that comes. They're a morbid lot; but I can't pay attention to them, I'm too old."

CHAPTER NINE

OUT OF THE WEB

For 'Forsytes' the name was all-important, whether it be the necessity for family continuity, or the avoidance of scandal—the name must flourish.

On Forsyte 'Change the announcement of Jolly's death. Among a batch of troopers, caused mixed sensation. It revived the old grudge against his father for having estranged himself. For such was still the prestige of old Jolyon that the other Forsytes could never quite feel, as might have been expected, that it was they who had cut off his descendents for irregularity. The news increased, of course, the interest and anxiety about Val; but then Val's name was Dartie, and even if he were killed in battle or got the Victoria Cross, it would not be at all the same as if his name was Forsyte. Not even casualty or glory to the Haymans would be really satisfactory. Family pride felt defrauded. The name was Forsyte.

Possibly some eye had seen 'Forsyte v. Forsyte and Forsyte' in the cause list; and had added it to 'Irene in Paris with a fair beard'. It was known—whispered among the old, discussed among the young—that family pride must soon receive a blow.

Soames braved a Sunday visit to Timothy's and *felt knowledge in the air as he came in.* He did not stay long, and they all feared that Aunt Juley would say something inappropriate. *Aunt Hester excused herself*

and said she must go and bathe Timothy's eye—he had a sty coming.
Soames impassive, slightly supercilious, did not stay long.

Soames planned for his retirement. The scandal would hurt
his business and he had made plenty of money. *To go on seeing all*
those people who had known him as a 'long-headed chap', an astute
adviser—after that—no! He would retire, live privately, go on buying
pictures, make a great name as a collector—after all, his heart was
more in that than it had ever been in the Law. He amalgamated his firm
with *Cuthcott, Holliday and Kingson—Cuthcott, Holliday, Kingson,*
Forsyte, Bustard and Forsyte. The full name now was so long and two
of the partners now being deceased, he then abbreviated it to *Cuthcott,*
Kingson and Forsyte, of whom Kingson would be active and Soames
the sleeping partner. For leaving his name, prestige, and clients behind
him, Soames would receive considerable value.

I sometimes wonder if the family firms of Campbell, Key and
Longley, E. Weatherley and Company, and R.F. Potter, might have been
more manageable in an amalgamated form as there were no directors,
other than my aunts, Biddy and Bernice, who did not carry the Longley
name. Tradition often dictated Forsytes in such matters, a firm's name
being better preserved for historical continuity, and besides, in our case
it also allowed my father as principle director of Campbell, Key and
Longley, to have the personalized number plate on his last Armstrong
Siddeley Star Sapphire automobile to read CKL 1. James and Soames
had been perfectly happy to carry old Bustard's name for many years
and it was only looming scandal that really brought on this merger.

Oh! How important to a 'Forsyte' was his name!

If the divorce went through, Soames *had determined on his line*
with Madame Lamotte. She had, he knew, but one real ambition—to
live on her 'rentes' in Paris near her grandchildren. He would buy the
goodwill of the restaurant Grand Bretagne at a fancy price and employ
a manager. *Madame would live like a queen-mother in Paris on the*
interest, invested as she would know how. On Annette he would promise
to settle fifteen thousand pounds.

Jolyon's solicitor informed him that Jolyon and Irene were in Italy.
And an opportunity had been duly given for noting that they had first
stayed at an hotel in London. The matter was clear as daylight, and
would be disposed of in half an hour or so; but during that half-hour
he, Soames, would go down to hell; and after that half-hour all bearers
of the Forsyte name would feel the bloom was off the rose.

The name was a possession, a concrete, unstained piece of property,
the value of which would be reduced some twenty per cent, at least.

Unless it were Roger, who had once refused to stand for Parliament, and—oh, irony!—Jolyon hung on the line, there had never been a distinguished Forsyte for good or bad. *But that very lack of distinction was the name's greatest asset. It was a private name, intensely individual, and his own property; it had never been exploited for good or evil by intrusive report. He and each member of his family owned it wholly, sanely, secretly, without anymore interference from the public than had been necessitated by their births, their marriages, their deaths.* It was a 'Forsyte' cry in 'Forsythia'—Keep your name out of the papers!

Soames *had asked no better than to live in spotless domesticity, and now he must go in the witness-box, after all these futile, barren years, and proclaim his failure to keep his wife—incur the pity, the amusement, the contempt of his kind. It was all upside down. She and that fellow ought to be the sufferers, and they—were in Italy! In these weeks the Law he had served so faithfully, looked on so reverently as the guardian of all property, seemed to him quite pitiful. What could be more insane than to tell a man that he owned his wife, and punish him when someone unlawfully took her away from him?*

Soames decided to give the damages of his case to the blind. He wanted to avoid the further scandal whereby *people might say; "Oh yes, he got quite a good price for her!" The case would be reached before August. As the day grew nearer,* his sister *Winifred was his only comfort. The day before, he went to see her.*

Soames found her with a letter in her hand.

"That from Val?" he asked gloomily. "What does he say?"

"He says he's married," said Winifred.

"Whom to, for goodness sake?"

Marriages of young 'Forsytes' serving in far lands of the Empire were not uncommon, but often feared arousing suspicion. The families were not known, had not been vetted by the established relatives in England. Apart from the fact that my great-aunt, Ruby, my cousin John Cuthbertson's mother was much younger than my Great-uncle Bert—cause enough for scandal—she was not known. They had married in India and the news had filtered to Granny Mabs and other members of the Cuthbertson family in a similar way—by letter. There was almost a clandestine feeling about it—'Did they have to get married?'

Winifred looked up at Soames.

"To Holly Forsyte, Jolyon's daughter."

"What?"

"He got leave and did it. I didn't even know he knew her. Awkward, isn't it?"

Well, there was the hope that Jolyon and Irene wouldn't know about this until they returned from Italy. They didn't need this compounding the scandal of the divorce. Soames hoped, too, that Val and Holly would stay out there in South Africa.

"I don't know what I've done," said Soames. *"I never have. It's all upside down."* He asked how Dartie was behaving.

"It might be worse; but it's always money. Would you like me to come down to the Court tomorrow, Soames?"

The case was reached before noon next day, and was over in little more than half an hour. Four hours until he became public property!

That evening he bought a paper *in front of St. Paul's. Yes! There he was! 'Well-known solicitor's divorce. Cousin co-respondent. Damages given to the blind.'—so, they had got that in! At every other face, he thought, 'I wonder if they know!'*

He sought escape. *He would get down to the river* at Mapledurham *and row about, and fish,* but *it flashed across him that he had something of importance to do before he went out of town. Madame Lamotte! He must explain the Law. Another six months before he was really free!*

At the Restaurant Grand Bretagne he found Annette.

"You are quite a stranger," she said *languidly.*

Soames smiled.

"I haven't wished to be. I've been busy. Where's your mother, Annette? I've got some news for her."

"Mother is not in."

What did she know? How much had her mother told her?

"I'll write your mother, then. *I'm going down to my river house for a long holiday. I want you both to come there presently and stay. It's just at its best. You will, won't you?"*

"It will be veree nice." A pretty little roll of that 'r', but no enthusiasm.

He couldn't read her and said: *"Goodnight."*

Annette felt he was uncomfortable.

"Shall I give you some coffee?" she asked.

"No," said Soames *firmly. "Give me your hand?"*

She held out her hand, and Soames raised it to his lips.

'I can't tell', he thought as he went out; *'but I mustn't think—I mustn't worry.'*

But worry he did, walking towards Pall Mall. English, not of her religion, middle-aged, scarred, as it were, by domestic tragedy. What had he to give her? Only wealth, social position, leisure, admiration! It was much, but was it enough for a beautiful girl of twenty? He felt so ignorant about Annette. He had, too, a curious fear of the French nature of her mother and herself. They knew so well what they wanted. They were almost Forsytes. They would never grasp a shadow and miss a substance!

* * *

Soames wrote to Madame Lamotte from his Club

'*MY DEAR MADAME,*

'*You will see by the enclosed newspaper cutting that I obtained my decree of divorce to-day. By the English law I shall not, however, be free to marry again till the decree is confirmed six months hence. In the meanwhile I have the honour to ask to be considered a formal suitor for the hand of your daughter. I shall write again in a few days and beg you both to come and stay at my river house.*

'*I am, dear Madame,*

'*Sincerely yours,*

'*SOAMES FORSYTE.*'

He found it hard to eat dinner at the club. Leaving most of it, he afterwards hailed a cab for Paddington *and took the first train to Reading. He reached his house just as the sun went down, and wandered out on the lawn. The air was drenched with the scent of pinks and picotees in his flower borders. A stealing coolness came off the river.*

Long summer evenings in the garden were one of the great pleasures of 'Forsytes' throughout 'Forsythia'. This was a symbol of England, the hub of the Empire, an Empire that was mostly in warmer climes where long evenings were eclipsed by a sharp transition from afternoon to night. From colonial postings, 'Forsytes' looked forward to leave and a return to England to enjoy the privacy of those long summer evenings in their gardens.

Soames looked around him at the peace. *Rest—peace! Let him cease from himself, and rest.* And no doubt he sat down in one of those wicker garden chairs watching the river, *whitening fast in twilight, like the darkening cornflower-blue sky where stars were coming up.*

Chapter Ten

Passing of an Age

The marriage of Soames with Annette took place in Paris on the last day of January, 1901, just fourteen years to the day before my father was born, and just a few days before the passing of "The Great White Queen"—Victoria Regina, Queen and Empress. It took place *with such privacy that not even Emily was told until it was accomplished.* Annette's *beauty in the best Parisian frocks was giving him more satisfaction than if* Soames *had collected a perfect bit of china, or a jewel of a picture; he looked forward to the moment when he would exhibit her in Park Lane, in Green Street, and at Timothy's.*

"What is love?" He said to himself as if asked if he was in love. *"If you mean do I feel for her as I did towards Irene in those old days when I first met her and she would not have me; when I sighed and starved after her and couldn't rest a minute until she yielded—no! If you mean do I admire her youth and prettiness, do my senses ache a little when I see her moving about—yes! Do I think she will make me a creditable wife and a good mother for my children?—again yes! What more do I need?—and what more do three-quarters of the women who are married get from the men who marry them?"*

Was he looking *for spiritual union in this marriage?*

"That's as it may be. If I get satisfaction for my senses, perpetuation of myself, good taste and good humour in the house, it is all I can expect

at my age. I am not likely to be going out of my way towards any far-fetched sentimentalism."

The day after the wedding he brought her to one of those quiet hotels in London.

Then, the queen died.

Fur-coated and top-hatted, with Annette beside him in dark furs, Soames crossed Park Lane on the morning of the funeral procession, to the rails in Hyde Park. Little moved though he ever was by public matters, this event, supremely symbolical, this summing up of a long rich period, impressed his fancy. In '37, when she came to the throne, 'Superior Dosset' was still building houses to make London hideous; and James, a stripling of twenty-six, just laying the foundations of his practice in the Law. Well-nigh two generations had slipped by—of steamboats, railways, telegraphs, bicycles, electric light, telephones, and now these motor-cars—of such accumulated wealth that eight per cent. had become three, and Forsytes were numbered by the thousand! Sixty-four years that favoured property, and made the upper-middle class; buttressed, chiselled, polished it, till it was almost indistinguishable in manners, morals, speech, appearance, habit, and soul from the nobility.

And to witness the passing of this Age, London was pouring forth her citizens through every gate into Hyde Park. The 'good old' queen, full of years and virtue, had emerged from her seclusion for the last time to make a London holiday. From Houndsditch, Acton, Ealing, Hampstead, Islington, and Bethnal Green; from Hackney, Hornsey, Leytonstone, Battersea and Fulham; and from those green pastures where Forsytes flourish—Mayfair and Kensington, St. James's and Belgravia, Bayswater and Chelsea and the Regent's Park, and the newer leafy suburbs of Dulwich, Sydenham and Beckenham, *the people swarmed down onto the roads where death would presently pass with dusky pomp and pageantry. A pity the war dragged on, and that the Wreath of Victory could not be laid upon her coffin! All else would be there to follow and commemorate—soldiers, sailors, foreign princes, half-masted bunting, tolling bells, and above all the surging, great, dark-coated crowd, with perhaps a simple sadness here and there deep in hearts beneath black clothes put on by regulation.*

Under the grey heavens, whose drizzle just kept off, the dark concourse gathered to see the show.

Fifty two years later they would gather again, in my own childhood, to witness the crowning of the next great queen, Her Majesty Queen Elizabeth II, who would reign over an equally long period of equal change—the Victorian age being the period of the making of 'Forsythia', and the 'Second' Elizabethan period being witness to its demise, even the extinction of 'Forsythia'. In between, lay the fruits of 'Forsythia' in the British Empire at its geographical and influential height—that global landmass around the planet—one quarter of the inhabited world—on which at no time could it be said that the sun could ever fully set.

On June 2nd, 1953, at the same time as news reached the capital that the world's last stronghold of physical resistance to man, Mount Everest, had been scaled by the imperial mountaineer from New Zealand, Sir Edmund Hilary and his Nepalese sherpa, Tenzing Norgay, *under grey heavens, whose drizzle* threatened further rain, *the concourse gathered to see the show.*

My father had taken us along the coronation procession route a few days before, so we could see the decorations—the great hoops over The Mall, the banners and portraits, the flagpoles and bunting of royal cheer. We waited in awe to see the day Her Majesty, wearing the Imperial Crown to Westminster Abbey, and St. Edward's Crown—the coronation crown—on the long procession route in her gilded carriage from the Abbey through the streets of London and back to Buckingham Palace. We watched it in black and white on the television set that Aunt Eileen had bought for Granny Mabs and Grandpa Jack. Later, at Newlands, our whole school was escorted to the cinema in Seaford to see the ceremony and procession in color—the official film of the Coronation of Her Majesty Queen Elizabeth the Second. To me, what is most memorable about that great day and what has gone down in history as most memorable on a day that ultimately poured with rain, was the sight of Queen Salote of Tonga riding in an open carriage soaked to her skin. Queen Salote was a giant of a woman, typical of her Polynesian race. Beside her in the carriage rode her aide dressed in a morning suit with a soggy top hat. It has often been quoted that when their carriage passed Whitehall, Somerset Maughan asked Noel Coward:

"Who is that huge lady in the soaked carriage."

"Oh! That's Queen Salote of Tonga," Coward said, "and the little man beside her is her lunch."

Tonga is an ancient Polynesian kingdom of a few flat islands in the South Pacific best known for its flying foxes or bats, and only a century before was known for cannibalism. In 1953, however, it was still seen to be very important for rulers of all areas of the British Empire to pay homage to the new queen, Queen Elizabeth the Second. Queen Salote had literally come from the antipodes, the furthest imperial territory from England on the planet.

Tonga continues to be a very proud member of the British Commonwealth and equally proud of its near thousand year succession of kings and queens. I recall an interesting anecdote from 1985 when I was a cruise director with Royal Viking Line. The Crown Prince of Tonga was on board during a South East Asian cruise as part of a series of voyages hosted by royalty. We visited his father's kingdom on Easter Sunday. The Crown Prince arranged for the entire entertainment department on board to attend a luau on his private island, while most the passengers were sent on tours to Sunday services to hear the very impressive Polynesian Methodist choirs. We were all sitting in this little grass shack well plied with coco locos, looking out at the suckling pig roasting in its pit, when the subject of conversation turned to recent films. *Nicholas and Alexandria* was mentioned—that great film depicting the grandeur and tragedy of the reign of the last Russian Tsar, based on Robert Massie's marvelous book. The Crown Prince, leaned back in his chair in this primitive setting and announced:

"My father...my father always says that the Romanovs were a very nouveau riche monarchy."

It seemed strange to me under the circumstances, especially as a cruise director I had visited those magnificent Romanov palaces of St. Petersburg, then Leningrad, but the Romanovs were only Tsars of Russia for three hundred years. The King of Tonga sat on a throne that had an over nine hundred year pedigree!

Royalty, never as close to 'Forsythia' as the aristocracy, and less emotionally favored by the upper-middle class as by the lower-middle class and the masses, is nonetheless a binding force for the British nation. Royal funerals, births with resultant christenings, marriages, and most significantly of all, coronations, are celebrated with great pomp and pageantry as entries in the family Bible of the Nation, and throughout 'Forsythia', of the Empire.

Out in the crowd against the railings, with his arm hooked in Annette's, Soames waited. Yes! The age was passing! What with this Trade Unionism and Labour fellows in the House of Commons, things were very different. He recalled the crowd on Mafeking night, and

George Forsyte saying: "They're all Socialists, they want our goods."
Like James, Soames didn't know, he couldn't tell—with Edward on the
throne! Things would never be as safe again as under good old Viccy!
Convulsively he pressed his young wife's arm. There, at any rate, was
something substantially his own, domestically certain again at last;
something which made property worthwhile—a real thing once more.

Suddenly, a little behind them to the left, he saw a tallish man with a
soft hat and short grizzling beard, and a tallish woman in a little round
fur cap and veil. Jolyon and Irene talking, smiling at each other, close
together like Annette and himself! They looked happy! What had they
come here for—inherently illicit creatures, rebels from the Victorian
ideal? What business had they in this crowd? Each of them twice exiled
by morality—making a boast, as it were, of love and laxity!

Annette, who had also noted the couple, turned to Soames and
said: "Those two people Soames; they know you, I am sure. Who are
they?"

Soames nosed sideways.

"What people?"

"There, you see them; just turning away. They know you."

"No," Soames answered; "a mistake, my dear."

"A lovely face! And how she walk! Elle est tres distinguee!"

"You'd better attend," Soames said, "they're coming now!"

The 'Royal Show', like God, transcends all our national petty
divisions. As Princess Elizabeth, our future queen used to say of her
grandfather, King George V, "He is 'Papa England'," and unknown
to her at the time, through a quirk of history—the abdication crisis of
1936—she was to become "Mama England."

There it was—the bier of the Queen, coffin of the Age slow passing!
And as it went by there came a murmuring grown from all the long line
of those who watched, a sound such as Soames had never heard, so
unconscious, primitive, deep and wild, that neither he nor any knew
whether they had joined in uttering it. Strange sound, indeed! Tribute
of an age to it's own death...Ah! Ah!...The hold on life had slipped. That
which had seemed eternal was gone! The Queen—God bless her!

Soames lingered just long enough to gratify Annette, then took her
out of the Park to lunch at his father's in Park Lane...

James had spent the morning gazing out of his bedroom window.
Swithin and he had seen her crowned—slim slip of a girl, not so old
as Imogen! His brother *Jolyon* and he had seen her married to that

German chap, her husband—he had turned out all right before he died, and left her with that son of his. Now he had come to the throne. They said he had steadied down—he didn't know—couldn't tell! He'd make the money fly still, he shouldn't wonder. It didn't seem much longer ago than Jubilee Year, when he had joined with Roger in renting a balcony in Piccadilly. Jolyon, Swithin, Roger all gone, and he would be ninety in August! And there was Soames married again to a French girl. The French were a queer lot, but they made good mothers, he had heard. Things changed! They said this German Emperor was here for the funeral, his telegram to old Kruger had been in shocking taste. He shouldn't be surprised if that chap made trouble some day. Change! H'm! And now Emily had asked Dartie to lunch, with Winifred and Imogen, to meet Soames's wife—she was always doing something. And there was Irene living with that fellow Jolyon, they said. He'd marry her now, he supposed.

    'She was a pretty thing, too,' James thought; 'I was fond of her. Perhaps Soames didn't suit her—I don't know—I can't tell. We never had any trouble with our wives.' Women had changed—everything had changed! And now the Queen was dead—well, there it was!

    Through the bare branches of the plane trees he could just see the procession, could see the hats coming off the people's heads—a lot of them would catch colds, he shouldn't wonder!

    Plane trees had been planted in abundance along London's streets in the late Victorian era. It was said that they thrived on the soot in the air from the city's numerous chimneys. In my early childhood at Chelston, there were large plane trees on either side of Overbury Avenue in Beckenham. Other streets were lined with horse chestnuts, or conker trees as we called them, that also had resilience to the silent pollution. The conkers were the chestnut seeds that we prized from prickly green shells—the fruits that dropped from the trees in September and October. Diane and I used to hoard them like jewels as when fresh they had a beautiful sheen, other children attached them to string and used them for conker fights. Naturally, Cousin John Cuthbertson, the wonder boy, was an expert at gathering conkers. He was able to knock them down from the trees for us. At school, our conkers became valuable currency. Good conkers could be swapped or exchanged for stamps, glass marbles, transfers or other items that we often thought to be of greater value.

    On our visits to town when we rode those double-decker buses, the top side of the bus would brush against the London plane trees, and to us children seated in the front of the bus it was as if we were birds looking down like James through this tracery of branches to the street below. This idea was picked up by creative artists in 1951 for the celebration of The Festival of Britain. It was to celebrate the hundredth anniversary of the Great Exhibition in Hyde Park that had spawned the Crystal Palace in 1851. The Festival grounds in 1951 were along the south bank of the Thames, and today are best commemorated by the Festival Hall concert theatre built for the exhibition. Ironically, the great Ferris wheel, The London Eye, erected decades later, is also in this area. In 1951, however, the centerpiece of the Festival exhibition was the Skylon—some sort of rocket exhibit, but for us, adjacent to the Festival grounds were the Festival Gardens in Battersea Park, which is where we were taken as children. My greatest memory of the Festival Gardens was that of the Tree Walk—a planked and roped walkway through the branches of the plane trees with views looking down like a bird at the festival goers wandering through the booths of the Battersea gardens. I remember at one of those booths my father bought Diane a Charlie Chaplin puppet and I am not sure it wasn't at another booth that my sister Sally acquired her first teddy bear—Timmy.

The funeral procession passed. *There she went, the old Queen; she'd had a lot of anxiety—she'd be glad to be out of it,* James *should think!*

The meeting with his new daughter-in-law took place in the dining-room. James was seated by the fire when she was brought in. Stooping and immaculate in his frock-coat, thin as a line, he received Annette's hand in his:

"How are you?" he said. "You've been to see the Queen, I suppose? Did you have a good crossing?"

Yes, in a conversation with anyone who had just arrived from Europe, 'Forsytes' automatically asked if they had a good crossing. On the occasions when my grandparents Longley would go to Paris to visit my Uncle Gyles and Aunt Ginette, the first question on their return was not about Paris or how my father's brother and sister-in-law were, but "Did you have a good crossing?" The English Channel can be notoriously rough at times, but that tendency for rough seas was also much appreciated by the insular British attitude toward Europe. Those rough seas were what made us "an Island people"—separated us from the French and the Europeans and, since 1066, had kept us free from foreign invasion, even scattering the Spanish Armada in 1588.

Annette murmured something in French which James did not understand, but to which he replied, *"Yes, yes, you want your lunch, I expect. Soames, ring the bell; we won't wait for that chap Dartie."*

But just then they arrived. Dartie's *eyes rested on Annette. The second beauty that fellow Soames had picked up! What women could see in him! Well, she would play him the same trick as the other, no doubt; but in the meantime, he was a lucky devil!*

Afterwards, as they left to go to Timothy's, Annette said in the cab, *"That Monsieur Dartie, je n'aime pas ce type-la."*

"No, by George!" said Soames.

"Your sister is veree aimiable, and the girl is pretty. Your father is veree old. I think your mother has trouble with him; I should not like to be her."

Soames nodded at the shrewdness, the clear hard judgment in his young wife, but *the thought just flashed through him, too: 'When I'm eighty she'll be fifty-five, having trouble with me!'*

Things went pretty well with the old aunts at Timothy's until the subject of Soho came up.

"What do you think of London, Annette," Aunt Hester asked.

"Oh! I know London, I have visited before."

Soames *had never ventured to speak to her on the subject of the restaurant. The French had different notions about gentility, and to shrink from connection with it might seem to her ridiculous; he had waited to be married before mentioning it; and now he wished he hadn't.*

"And what part do you know best," asked Aunt Juley.

"Soho," said Annette simply.

"Soho?" repeated Aunt Juley; "Soho?"

'That'll go round the family,' thought Soames.

"It's very French and interesting," he said.

"Yes," murmured Aunt Juley, "your Uncle Roger had some houses there once; he was always having to turn the tenants out, I remember."

Soames changed the subject to Mapledurham.

"Of course," said Aunt Juley, "you will be going down there soon to settle in. We are all so looking forward to the time when Annette has a dear little..."

"Juley!" cried Aunt Hester desperately, "ring for tea!"

Soames dared not wait for tea, and took Annette away.

"I shouldn't mention Soho if I were you," he said in the cab. *"It's rather a shady part of London; and you're altogether above that restaurant business now; I mean,"* he added, *"I want you to know nice people, and the English are fearful snobs. Our professional and leisured classes still think themselves a cut above our business classes, except, of course, the very rich. It may be stupid, but there it is, you see. It isn't advisable in England to let people know that you ran a restaurant or kept a shop or were in any kind of trade. It may have been extremely creditable, but it puts a sort of label on you; you don't have such a good time or meet such nice people—that's all."*

"I see," said Annette; *"it is the same in France."*

"Oh!" murmured Soames, at once relieved and taken aback. *"Of course, class is everything, really."*

"Yes," said Annette; *"comme vous etes sage."*

The formal "vous" of the statement "you are wise" did not register with Soames. *His knowledge of French was not yet such as to make him grieve that she had not said 'tu'. He slipped his arm round her and murmured with an effort,* also using the more formal mode:

"Et vous etes ma belle femme."

Annette went off into a little fit of laughter, then asked him, *"What is that old lady, your aunt, looking forward to?"*

"God knows!" he said; *"she's always saying something;"* but he knew better than God.

CHAPTER ELEVEN

SUSPENDED ANIMATION

The war dragged on. Nicholas had been heard to say that it would cost three hundred millions if it cost a penny before they'd done with it! The income tax was seriously threatened as 'Forsytes' did not believe in debt. It had to be paid for.

The significance of many aspects of this Boer War became in the history books so overshadowed by the travesties of the Great War and the Second World War of the next two generations of 'Forsythia' that it is worth considering them in the perspective of their time. The Boer War was the first really major modern war. The Crimean War of the mid-nineteenth century was a lot closer to the Napoleonic wars in concept than this new warfare. Cavalry, sabres, formations and regulars were now a thing of the past. The regular army was heavily supported by volunteers—recruits like Jolly and Val. Despite Holly asking her brother if he would carry a sword, rifles were now the obligatory weapon. The red uniforms of British pride had given way to khaki. Warfare was no longer an army pitched against an army, but small units against small units spread across the vast Veldt. Horses carried dispatches and pulled gun carriages, but did not charge. With this new warfare, came prisoners, interrogation and concentration camps. And with this new warfare, came almost instant news by telegraph, emotionally effecting those at home. Casualties, high in the Crimean War, were even higher in this war with the Boers. The new warfare was a learning curve before the even worse scenarios of the Great War and World War II, but at the time they were appalling in their own right. And, what almost made it worst of all, for a long time it seemed we were losing—the great British Empire losing to these South African Dutch farmers! In time, for many, the only defense was to bury one's head in the sand.

Indeed, the attitude of the nation was typified by Timothy's map, whose animation was suspended—for Timothy no longer moved the flags.

Suspended animation went further; it invaded Forsyte 'Change and produced a general uncertainty as to what was going to happen next. The announcement in the marriage column of the Times, *'Jolyon Forsyte to Irene, only daughter of the late Professor Heron', had occasioned doubt whether Irene had been justly described. And yet, on the whole, relief was felt that she had not been entered as, 'Irene, late the wife', or 'the divorced wife', of 'Soames Forsyte'.*

What would happen now that both Soames and Jolyon were married again! That was very intriguing. George was known to have laid Eustace six to four on a little Jolyon before a little Soames. Dartie had bet as to whether James would attain the age of ninety, though which of them had backed James no one knew.

Early in May, Winifred came round to say that Val had been wounded in the leg by a spent bullet, and was to be discharged. His wife was nursing him. He would have a little limp—nothing to speak of. He wanted his grandfather to buy him a farm out there where he could breed horses. Her father was giving Holly eight hundred a year, so they could be quite comfortable, because his grandfather, James, *would give Val five, he had said; but as to the farm,* James *didn't know—couldn't tell: he didn't want Val to go throwing away his money.*

"Val loves horses," said Winifred. "It'd be such an occupation for him."

Aunt Juley thought horses were very uncertain, had not Montague Dartie found them so?

"Val's different," said Winifred; "he takes after me."

Aunt Juley wanted to know what Montague had said about the idea.

Winifred did not tell her, for Montague had merely remarked: "Wait till the old man dies."

At this moment, Francie was announced. Her eyes were brimming with a smile.

"Well," she said, "what do you think of it?"

"Of what, dear?"

"In the Times *this morning."*

"We haven't seen it, we always read it after dinner; Timothy has it till then."

Francie rolled her eyes.

"Do you think you ought to tell us?" said Aunt Juley. "What was it?"

"Irene's had a son at Robin Hill."

Aunt Juley drew in her breath. "But," she said, "they were only married in March!"

"Yes, Auntie; isn't it interesting?"

"Well," said Winifred, "I'm glad. I was sorry for Jolyon losing his boy. It might have been Val."

Aunt Juley seemed to go into a sort of dream.

"I wonder," she murmured, "what dear Soames will think? He had so wanted to have a son himself. A little bird has always told me that."

'Little birds' were always telling 'Forsytes' things, they sort of made gossip respectable.

"Well," said Winifred, "he's going to—bar accidents."

Gladness trickled out of Aunt Juley's eyes.

"How delightful!" she said. "When?"

"November."

Either George or Eustace had won their bet, but would James live to ninety and witness the birth of his future heir, and who would reap the rewards of that wager—George or Dartie?

This new event—the birth of an heir to Soames—was so important to him, and to his dear father, too, that James might not have to die without some certainty about things—especially the continuation of the family name. After all, one's own name did count! And as James's ninetieth birthday neared they wondered what precautions he was taking. He would be the first of the Forsytes to reach that age, and set, as it were, a new standard in holding on to life.

In my lifetime, both Grandpa Jack Collings and my father reached ninety. Grandpa died in his ninetieth year and at the time of his birthday was suffering from dementia much hastened by the loss of Granny Mabs the year before. My father, however, although he had lost my mother the year before, was still very much of a sound mind. His birthday was celebrated with a magnificent private family luncheon laid on in the splendor of Barber-Surgeons Hall. It was the last time that his sister Biddy came down to London from Scotland and the whole family was together. When my father died three years later, still with a very keen mind and sharp wit, Aunt Biddy was unable to make the journey south for the Memorial Service, although she was represented by my cousin John Thompson and his wife, Dodo. My father was the oldest living member of my family to date, but his generation of Longleys are a long lived lot—his brothers and sister are fast catching him up, Uncle Gyles having celebrated his ninety-third birthday.

James's birthday fell on *August the 5*th. There was no great family gathering of Forsytes, but they all inquired after him. Timothy and Aunts Juley and Hester even sent their old retainer, Smither, round to James' to send gifts and greetings and asked her to go on to Green Street *and ask dear Mrs. Dartie to be sure and look in before she went out of town.*

All this Smither did—an undeniable servant trained thirty years ago under Aunt Ann to a perfection not now procurable. In some ways, we felt that way about 'Lloydy', the last of her breed. Each progressing generation of 'Forsytes' always seemed to consider their servants of the previous generation to have been better and more faithful than their present help until it reached the point in post-'Forsythia' where servants were no longer servants at all, but secretaries, companions, and assistants.

According to Smither, *Mr. James, so Mrs. James said, had passed an excellent night, he sent his love; Mrs. James had said that he was very funny and had complained that he didn't know what all the fuss was about. Oh! and Mrs. Dartie sent her love, and she would come to tea.*

Winifred came at the obligatory hour of four, *bringing Imogen and Maud, just back from school, so that it was extremely difficult to ask for news about Annette.* To discuss a lady's confinement was not considered appropriate in front of children—an indelicate topic throughout the period of 'Forsythia'. *Aunt Juley, however, summoned courage to enquire whether Winifred had heard anything, and if Soames was anxious.*

"Uncle Soames is always anxious, Auntie," interrupted Imogen, in a way that the previous generation would have never dared. *"He can't be happy now he's got it."*

Imogen's voice rose clear and clipped:

"Imagine! Annette's only two years older than me; it must be awful for her, married to Uncle Soames."

Aunt Juley lifted her hands in horror, as my own mother would have done.

"My dear," she said, "you don't know what you're talking about. Your Uncle Soames is a match for anybody. He's a very clever man, and good-looking and wealthy, and most considerate and careful, and not at all old, considering everything. I hope that you will marry as good a man."

Granny Longley might have said something similar if my sisters or I had raised such critical judgment on a family member, but her words, unlike Aunt Juley's, would be second to that Hovenden glare.

"I shan't marry a good man, Auntie," murmured Imogen; "they're dull."

"If you go on like this," replied Aunt Juley, still very much upset, "you won't marry anybody. We'd better not pursue the subject."

She then suggested they *drink dear James's health—and the health of Soames's wife. "It is an occasion! Only fancy if Soames has a dear little boy, to carry the family on! I do feel it so important, now that Irene has had a son."*

That night before she slept, Aunt Juley thought *she would be so happy if she could see dear Soames happy. He would have all that he wanted: property, and wife, and children! And he would live to a green old age, like his dear father, and forget all about Irene and that dreadful case.*

CHAPTER TWELVE

BIRTH OF A FORSYTE

Soames paced the lawn as he mulled over what the doctor attending Annette had just said.

"I can make pretty certain of her life if I operate, but the baby will be born dead. If I don't operate, the baby will most probably be born alive, but it's a great risk for the mother—a great risk. In either case, I don't think she can ever have another child. In her state she obviously can't decide for herself, and we can't wait for her mother. It's for you to make the decision, while I'm getting what's necessary. I shall be back within the hour."

It is hard to believe that this predicament now facing Soames was not uncommon throughout the years of 'Forsythia'. Bearing children, such an important role in those 'Forsyte' principles of property and inheritance, still remained one of life's greatest risks—far greater than war, crime, disease or accident. As mentioned earlier, my own grandmother, Granny Mabs, lost her son William Collings within a few days of his birth, and Great-grandfather Oliver Longley had eleven siblings—the children of Gyles Longley and Martha Ann Southon—eight of whom died within the first year of life. The three survivors were my great-grandfather, my Great-great-uncle Julius and my Great-great-aunt Emily. Julius never married and when he went out to Australia during the Ballarat gold rush it was only to die out there a young man of twenty-five. He was possibly never strong as one of a pair of twins, his twin Nathaniel having died not long after their birth. In fact, twins ran in the family during that generation. Gyles and Martha Ann Longley had another set of twin girls, Helen and Kate, who lived only two months. My great-grandfather's sister, Emily, the infamous "Aunt Golly," lived to old age, but had her drinking problem. She married Augustus Laurel Oliphant in 1884, who always looked somewhat of a dashing 'man about town' with a waxed moustache, but to her nieces and nephews she was to forever be known as "Aunt Golly," a derivative formed from her married name and her often glazed alcoholic look. She was unpredictable.

Loss of children at childbirth or early in their first year was common to almost all 'Forsyte' families and if it was not for their recorded births and deaths in those obligatory 'Forsyte' family Bibles, one would know little of them, for the tragedy was simply boxed away, neatly recorded on the vellum and then forgotten. In fact, in the Longley family Bible, there is sad evidence of this reality. In the register of births the twins are recorded as Ellen and Kate Longley, born the sixth of May, 1870. In the register of deaths, they are recorded as Helen and Kate Longley, who died within two days of each other in July 1870. At this time, whoever entered their names in the Bible returned to the register of births and added an 'H' in front of the 'E' of Ellen, but did not strike out one of the 'L's'. Did even their names become forgotten? Private grief, I am sure was felt, but 'Forsytes' never showed this grief in public, thus dismissing these infantile tragedies in their perceived lives.

For Soames Forsyte, however, a decision had to be made that weighed in the proportion of King Solomon's choice. *On the one hand life, nearly certain, of his young wife, death quite certain of his child; and—no more children afterwards! On the other, death perhaps of his wife, nearly certain life for the child; and—no more children afterwards! Which to choose?*

Leaves fell, lives drifted down! Death! To decide about death!

He thought of Irene. *Would he have hesitated then? Not a moment! Operate, operate! Make certain of her life! No decision—a mere instinctive cry for help, in spite of his knowledge, even then, that she did not love him! But this! Ah! there was nothing overmastering in his feeling for Annette! And yet—so pretty! What would she wish—to take the risk?*

'I know she wants the child,' Soames *thought. 'If it's born dead, and no more chance afterwards—it'll upset her terribly. No more chance! All for nothing! Married life with her for years and years without a child.*

Nothing to steady her! She's too young. Nothing to look forward to, for her—for me! For me!

He looked at his watch. In half an hour the doctor would be back. He must decide!

Soames came back in and unlocked the Tantalus.

Late Victorian and Edwardian households often had a Tantalus. They were almost a secret source for alcoholic beverage in need. I have Grandpa Jack's Tantalus and remember the day he introduced me to it. Grandpa, like his father, liked a drink when he could get it, but Granny Mabs very much controlled their household, and sherry, cocktails and cigarettes were rationed out at appropriate times. On this particular day, when I was about sixteen, perhaps as a rite of passage, Grandpa Jack took me into the dining room, unbeknown to Granny, and unlocked the Tantalus. He poured me a gin and tonic, for a Tantalus always held three decanters locked in a wooden box by a bar, so only he who had the key could gain access. Butlers or senior servants usually controlled the wine cellar, cocktail cabinets and beverage trays of 'Forsyte' households, but only the master controlled the Tantalus. The three decanters held three spirits, usually whisky, vodka, and gin. I do not know whether Granny Mabs ever knew of this rite of passage, although she was probably shrewd enough to know that the gin decanter held a little less gin after our secret drink.

Soames *hardly ever touched spirits, but now he poured himself out some whisky and drank it neat.*

'That fellow Jolyon,' he thought: 'he had children already. He has the woman I really loved; and now a son by her! And I—I'm asked to destroy my only child! Annette can't die; it's not possible. She's strong!'

The doctor returned. Soames waited *for him to come downstairs.*

"Well, doctor?"

"The situation's the same. Have you decided?"

"Yes," said Soames; "don't operate!"

"Not? You understand—the risk's great?"

In Soames's set face nothing moved but his lips.

"You said there was a chance?"

"A chance, yes; not much of one."

"You say the baby must be born dead if you do?"

"Yes."

"Do you still think that in any case she can't have another?"

"One can't be absolutely sure, but it's most unlikely."

"She's strong," said Soames; *"we'll take the risk."*

The doctor nodded and went upstairs.

Soames went up to his picture gallery and looked out at the autumn landscape. *'By this time tomorrow,'* he thought, *'I may have her death on my hands. But she'd take the risk of losing me sooner than lose her child! She doesn't really love me!'*

The one thing really vital to them both, vital to their marriage and their futures, was a child! *'I've been through a lot for this,'* he thought, *'I'll hold on—hold on. There's a chance of keeping both—a chance.'*

He began walking round the gallery. Collecting pictures; growing richer, richer! What use if—!

It was already growing dark when at last he opened the door. A milky twilight crept about the stairway and the landings below. A sound caught his ear. Peering down, he saw a black shape moving, and his heart stood still. What was it? Death? The shape of death coming from her door? No! Only a maid without cap or apron. She came to the foot of his flight of stairs and said breathlessly:

"The doctor wants to see you, sir."

He ran down. She stood flat against the wall to let him pass, and said:

"Oh, sir! it's over."

"Over?" said Soames, *with a sort of menace; "what d'you mean?"*

"It's born, sir."

He dashed up the four steps in front of him and came suddenly on the doctor in the dim passage. The man was wiping his brow.

"Well?" Soames *said; "quick!"*

"Both living, it's all right, I think."

Soames stood quite still.

"I congratulate you," he heard the doctor say; *"it was touch and go."*

"Thanks," he said; *"thanks very much. What is it?"*

"Daughter, luckily; a son would have killed her—the head."

A daughter!

"The utmost care of both," he heard the doctor say, *"and we shall do. When does the mother come?"*

"Tonight, between nine and ten, I hope."

"I'll stay till then. Do you want to see them?"

"Not now," said Soames. And he went downstairs.

*Relief unspeakable, and yet—a daughter! To have taken that risk—
to have been through this agony—and what agony!—for a daughter!*

A daughter—like my own father would have said: "'It' will have
to prove itself."

All females were 'its' until they had proven themselves. Soames
needed a son. Soames' father, James, needed a grandson—property,
inheritance, the preservation of the family name.

As Soames stood in the hall musing these thoughts *a telegram was
brought him.*

'Come up at once, your father sinking fast.—MOTHER'

He read it with a choking sensation.

*Half past seven, a train from Reading at nine, and madame's train,
if she had caught it, came in at eight-forty—he would meet that and go
on.*

The doctor came out to him.

"They're sleeping."

*"I won't go in," said Soames with relief. "My father's dying: I have
to go up. Is it all right?"* he said expressing that 'Forsyte' stiff upper
lip.

*"Yes, I think you may go with an easy mind. You'll be down
soon?"*

"Tomorrow," said Soames. Here's the address."

He ordered the carriage.

*The London train came in just as he reached the station, and Madame
Lamotte, substantial, dark-clothed, very yellow in the lamplight, came
towards the exit with a dressing-bag.*

"This all you have?" asked Soames.

"But yes. I had not the time. How is my little one?"

"Doing well—both. A girl!"

"A girl! What joy! I had a frightful crossing!"

"And you, mon cher?" she said as she climbed into the brougham.

"My father's dying. I'm going up. Give my love to Annette."

"Tiens!" murmured Madame Lamotte; "quel malheur!"

Soames took his hat off and moved towards his train. 'Bad-timing—
eh! *The French!' he thought.*

Chapter Thirteen

James is Told

J ames caught a little cold, but it went to his chest, to his lungs and there he was with pneumonia. So it was with my father. It took so little at their great age to cause so much. The doctor had said, *"He mustn't catch cold, and he had gone and caught it—frail James.* James claimed it had come from airing the room too much. Who knows?

For a whole day he was highly nervous about himself and went in advance of all precautions and remedies; drawing every breath with extreme care and having his temperature taken every hour. Emily was not alarmed. She knew he was determined to fight it off. My father was determined, too.

My father was taken to hospital, unlike James, and at first the private wing was not available to him. He became much amused by those around him in the public ward, considering himself so much more rational, fit, and determined to fight it off than his less fortunate fellow occupants of hospital beds. He called it all, "Such a carry on," perhaps in part because he had loved the 1950s comedy series of 'Carry on' films starring Leslie Philips that he often watched in re-runs on television. His favorite was *Carry on Nurse.* However, for comfort, and more concentrated treatment, especially after he was put on oxygen, once the private wing was available, he elected to be moved there.

The next morning when Emily *went* into James' room *the nurse whispered: "He won't have his temperature taken."*

Then Emily *was alarmed.* Was this the beginning of the end? Was James ceasing to fight? *For nearly fifty years; she couldn't remember or imagine life without James—James, behind all his fussiness, his pessimism, his crusty shell, deeply affectionate, really kind and generous to them all!* Just like my father!

But even though *all that day and the next* James *hardly uttered a word, there was in his eyes a noticing of everything done for him, a look on his face which told* Emily *he was fighting; and she did not lose hope.* In the same way, nor did Diane, Sally, and I, as we kept vigil at our father's bedside accompanied at times by my Uncle Gyles.

About tea-time on the third day, for most 'Forsytes' the most important moment of any day, Emily who *had just changed her dress, keeping her appearance so as not to alarm him,* and honoring the 'Forsyte' sacred hour of four o'clock when everything stops for tea, on entering James' room *saw a difference. 'It's no use; I'm tired,' was written plainly across that white face, and when she went up to him, he muttered: "Send for Soames."*

"Yes, James," she said comfortably; "all right—at once." She saw that his eyes looked grateful. She sent Soames the telegram.

I arrived in England from America before my father officially asked for me, but in the knowledge that he was deteriorating. His first fighting words to me were: "Why have you come? You shouldn't have spent all that money. I'm not dead yet." Within a day of my arrival, however, he became less communicative, speaking only, like James, with his fighting eyes.

When Soames *entered out of the black windy night, the big house was still as a grave.* Warmson took his fur coat. The old retainer's *lips twitched. "He's asking for you, sir?" and suddenly he blew his nose,* that 'Forsyte' way of disguising choking tears. *"It's a long time, sir,"* he said, *"that I've been with Mr. Forsyte—a long time."*

Soames went upstairs. *His mother and Winifred were sitting on the far side of* James' *bed; the nurse was moving away from the near side where was an empty chair. 'For me!' thought Soames.*

James's breathing was as if strangled; his eyes were closed. And in Soames, looking on his father so worn and white and wasted, listening to his strangled breathing, there rose a passionate vehemence of anger against Nature, cruel, inexorable Nature, kneeling on the chest of that wisp of a body, slowly pressing out the breath, pressing out the life of the being who was dearest to him in the world. His father, of all men, had lived a careful life, moderate, abstemious, and this was his reward—to have life slowly, painfully squeezed out of him!

He took a step nearer to his father. For three days James had not been shaved, and his lips and chin were covered with hair, hardly more snowy than his forehead. It softened his face, gave it a queer look already not of this world. His eyes opened.

"Here I am, Father."

"Um—what—what news? They never tell..." the voice died and a flood of emotion made Soames's face work so that he could not speak. Tell him?—yes. But what? He made a great effort, got his lips together and said:

"Good news, dear, good—Annette, a son."

"Ah!"

The eyes closed, and that strangled sound of breathing began again. The lie Soames had told, based, as it were, on some deep, temperamental instinct that after death James would not know the truth, had taken away all power of feeling for the moment. Soames' arm brushed against something. It was his father's naked foot. In the struggle to breathe he had pushed it out from under the clothes.

When rational on that first day after I arrived in England, my father asked me how my work was going in sales for Wyndham Vacation Resorts, a timeshare company with whom I was employed in front line sales. I told him how well it was going, knowing that in reality this very visit to England was sealing my fate in lost sales and a potential loss of my position. I never told him I was no longer a manager and that I had been warned that without a higher percentage of sales returns my position was on the line. Wyndham was my lie—my father, my inspiration and hope. All that he had done for me welled before me as I recalled the times he had been proud of me. I never wanted to let him down.

Then, as I let go of his hand, I, too, felt my father's leg protruding from the hospital bedding. I noticed he had a large mole on his right thigh exactly where I had one. I had his genes, I was his son, and no matter what my circumstances I carried on his name—the mantle of 'Forsyte' possession. How could Soames have said to his father, whose expectations were so high: "Annette, a daughter and she can never bear me a son. This was her only chance."

The nurse pulled James up to ease the pressure on his chest. As he was being raised up, *James's eyes bent on* Soames *a look that seemed to* come from the very depths of what was left within. 'I'm done, my boy,' it seemed to say, 'take care of them, take care of yourself; take care—I leave it all to you.'

I recall what Grandpa Jack had said about his father, my Great-grandfather Collings on his deathbed, and how the old rascal with a final twinkle of his eye said: "Jack, my boy, I've had a darned good life. You see that you do the same."

'Forsyte' security—by 2008 it was long gone. Remember, my father's last really rational words to my sisters and me from that hospital bed were: "God help you all."

The strained expression on James' *face passed, a curious white tranquility took its place. His eyelids quivered, rested; the whole face rested, at ease. Only by the faint puffing of his lips could they tell that he was breathing. He heard the nurse quietly crying over there by the fire; curious that she, a stranger, should be the only one of them who cried.*

My father's nurse cried, too.

Suddenly James *started up; a sound, a dreadful sound such as* Soames *had never heard, was coming from his father's lips, as if an outraged heart had broken with a long moan. What a strong heart to have uttered that farewell! It ceased. Soames looked into the face. No motion; no breath! Dead!*

He ran upstairs to the bedroom, still kept for him, flung himself face down on the bed, and broke into sobs which he stifled with the pillow...

A little later he went downstairs and passed into the room. James lay alone, wonderfully calm, free from shadow and anxiety.

"Good-bye!" he whispered, and went out.

CHAPTER FOURTEEN

HIS

Soames *had much to see to, that night and all next day. A telegram at breakfast reassured him about Annette, and he only caught the last train back to Reading.*

He reached his house at midnight. The weather had changed, was mild again, as though, having finished its work and sent a Forsyte to his last account, it could relax. A second telegram, received at dinner-time, had confirmed the humane *good news of Annette, and instead of going in,* the disappointment over the birth of a daughter with no future prospects of a son, now uppermost again; he put off seeing them. *Soames passed down through the garden in the moonlight to his houseboat.* He slept.

He woke soon after dawn and went on deck. Dawn has power to fertilise the most matter-of-fact vision, and civilised, by his researches among landscape painting, Soames was stirred. It was another world from the river he knew, under that remote cool light; a world into which man had not entered, an unreal world, like some strange shore sighted by discovery. Its colour was not the colour of convention, was hardly colour at all; its shapes were brooding yet distinct; its silence stunning; it had no scent.

This was what Turner and Whistler captured in their landscapes—it was what my sister, Diane, could capture so well in her mystical scenes of London, notably in an award winning painting of hers of the Thames at Tower Bridge.

Why it should move Soames *he could not tell, unless it were that he felt so alone in it, bare of all relationship and all possessions. Into such a world his father might be voyaging, for all resemblance it had to the world he had left.*

Once on a time none of this was owned, *all this was jungle and marsh and water, and weird creatures roamed and sported without human cognisance to give them names; rotting luxuriance had rioted where those tall, carefully planted woods* now *came down to the water, and marsh-misted reeds on that far side had covered all the pasture. Once in a way, as now* for Soames, *the ghost of the past came out to haunt and brood and whisper to any human who chanced to be awake: 'Out of my unowned loneliness you all came, into it some day you will all return.'*

Soames went back into the cabin of the houseboat *and made himself tea on a spirit-lamp.*

In the early 1960's, my father rented a cabin cruiser on the Thames on two or three different occasions. I can smell the spirit-lamp for making tea and hear the sound of the river lapping around the bow. The spirit-lamp was an essential part of most our childhood outings. An entire picnic, if in an enclosed area, became permeated with the smell of paraffin as my mother or father brewed the tea. The smell invaded the bread and jam, the banana sandwiches, the sticky buns—only the sardine sandwiches bearing their own overpowering sense of presence, were immune.

Soames, sipping tea to the gentle rhythms of his houseboat, then wrote two paragraphs:

'On the 20ᵗʰ instant at his residence in Park Lane, James Forsyte, in his ninety-first year. Funeral at noon on the 24ᵗʰ at Highgate. No flowers by request.'

And,

'On the 20ᵗʰ instant at The Shelter, Mapledurham, Annette, wife of Soames Forsyte, of a daughter.'

They would appear shortly on that famous front page of the *Times* glanced over daily by thousands of fellow 'Forsytes'.

Then, *underneath on the blotting-paper he traced the word 'son'.*

Blotting paper was an essential part of 'Forsythia' and became extinct at about the same time. Every morning during my schooldays at Newlands, we were furnished with that fresh clean sheet of Ford's blotting paper. It was essential as our dip pens often took up more ink from our inkwells than was necessary and it often fell to the pages of our schoolwork in a blob. This had to be soaked up. As for Soames, too, blotting-paper became a useful place to write notes, or even as in my case, to play an interesting game during the boredom of learning Latin verbs or elementary French. I used to draw a mouthful of teeth on my blotting paper and then proceed to make little holes in them with my pen's nib. Wetting little balls of blotting paper with ink I would fill the holes as if I was a dentist, even though I never had any aspirations to ever be a dentist. The balls of blotting paper hardened as the ink dried and temporarily affixed themselves to the drawn teeth. To the hum of Latin and French declensions and conjugations I could almost hear our dentist, Dr. Whelpton, call out: "Nurse, Amalgam please." Amalgam, that in years hence was proved to be a dangerous intake of Mercury, filled our 'Forsyte' teeth, especially those of us born in that last generation of 'Forsythia'. Our teeth were not strong, weakened they always said by the heavy rationing of healthy foods during and after World War II.

For the next generation after the demise of 'Forsythia', Amalgam gave way to porcelain—blotting paper and dip pens gave way to fountain pens and ballpoints.

It was eight o'clock in a now *ordinary autumn world when* Soames *went across to the house. Madame Lamotte was beginning her breakfast.*

She looked at his mourning clothes and *said, "Don't tell me!" and pressed his hand. "Annette is prettee well. But the doctor say she can never have no more children. You knew that?" Soames nodded. "It is a pity. Mais la petite est adorable. Du Café?"*

Soames got away from her as soon as he could. She offended him— solid, matter-of-fact, quick, clear—French. He resented the way she had looked at him, as if it were his fault that Annette could never bear him a son! His fault! He even resented her cheap adoration of the daughter he had not yet seen.

He was afraid of what Annette was thinking of him, author of her agonies, afraid of the look of the baby, afraid of showing his disappointment with the present and—the future.

He spent an hour walking up and down the drawing-room before he could screw his courage up to mount the stairs and knock on the door of their room.

Madame Lamotte opened it.

"Ah! At last you come! Elle vous attend!"

Annette was very pale and very pretty lying there.

"Here you are then, Soames," she said. "I am not so bad now. But I suffered terribly, terribly. I am glad I cannot have any more. Oh! how I suffered!"

Soames stood silent, stroking her hand; words of endearment, of sympathy, absolutely would not come; the thought passed through him: 'An English girl wouldn't have said that!' Where, at least was her emotional duty to her 'Forsyte' husband? Would my great-great-grandmother, Martha Southon, have said that as she lost most of her infant children?

At this moment Soames knew with certainty that he would never be near to her in spirit and in truth, nor she to him. He had collected her—that was all!

"Don't you want to see the baby Soames?" Annette said, "She is asleep."

"Of course," said Soames bravely, "very much."

For the first moment what he saw was much what he had expected to see—a baby. But as he stared and the baby breathed and made little sleeping movements with its tiny features, it seemed to assume an individual shape, grew to be like a picture, a thing he would know again; not repulsive, strangely bud-like and touching. The eyes winked, stared, had a sort of sleepy depth in them. And suddenly Soames' heart felt queer, warm, as if elated.

"Ma petite fleur!" Annette said softly.

"Fleur," repeated Soames: "Fleur! We'll call her that."

The sense of triumph and renewed possession welled within him.

By God! This—this thing was his!

INTERLUDE

AWAKENING

Little Jon, Jolyon and Irene's son, was now nine years old. His parents had gone to Ireland on vacation—four weeks! The boy awaiting their arrival home, promised Bella, his favorite maid, to be in time for tea underneath the old oak tree.

How had those first nine years of his life been? They were largely molded by 'Da', his nanny, and Bob, the groom, who played the concertina.

Jon—the spelling of his name dictated by his father, Jo, Jolly and Holly having used up most the syllabics of 'Jolyon'—was born in 1901. *He had come to consciousness when his country, just over the Boer War, was preparing for the Liberal revival.* The old queen was gone, and King Edward VII brought with him his own version of the meaning of liberal. *Coercion was unpopular, parents had exalted notions of giving their offspring a good time. They spoiled their rods, spared their children, and anticipated the results with enthusiasm. In choosing,* if he had a choice, *for his father an amiable man of fifty-two, who had already lost an only son, and for his mother a woman of thirty-eight, whose first and only child he was, little Jon had done well and wisely.* He was also born with that proverbial silver spoon of 'Forsythia' in his mouth, *though 'Da' sometimes said that other children would do him a 'world of good.'*

'Da', who wore the violet dress on Sundays, and enjoyed the name of Spraggins in that private life lived at odd moments even by domestic servants, had recently gone. She had left *the very day after his birthday in floods of tears 'to be married' of all things—'to a man.'* When the private life of domestics spilled into their employment it was almost frowned upon—a betrayal. 'Da' was no longer there to put up with his imaginative games, and imaginative they were. A transition of affection from 'Da' to his mother, however, had begun when he was seven. 'Da' had *held him down on his back, because he wanted to do something of which she did not approve. This first interference with the new free individualism of a Forsyte drove him almost frantic.* He appealed to his mother:

"Mum, don't let 'Da' hold me down on my back again."

His mother and father came to his aid, and 'Da' was told.

This new freedom found in the Edwardian childhood, at least prior to boarding school, was reflected to some extent in my own family. Great-aunt Agnes, Grandpop, and Great-uncle 'Tig'—young Oliver— were all born into a strictly Victorian household, but their siblings, George, Arthur Douglas, and Bernice, were raised for the most part in an Edwardian nursery. It was obvious in my own childhood, that the families of George and Bernice—Douglas' stepson Roy Follitt having been killed in the Second World War—were far more liberal than us and our cousins, who were descendents of my grandfather.

Actually, my Great-uncle George's family was the first among my relatives outside my grandparents to be known to me. Great-uncle George lived in a house in Oakwood Avenue, Beckenham, just up the hill from Chelston in Overbury Avenue. Great-uncle George shared something in common with Great-uncle Bert Cuthbertson—they had both married much younger wives. Marjorie Searle, whose parents were good friends of Oliver and Minnie Longley, lived near them in the Avenue. When Great-uncle George married Marjorie she was considerably younger than him. In fact, her younger brother, Douglas Searle, was more of a friend and companion to his nephews—my father and Uncle Gyles—than to the older generation, rather like John Cuthbertson, my mother's cousin, was to our generation when he lived with Granny Mabs in Wickham Way. George and Marjorie's children were really my father's cousins, but they seemed only a little older than us, especially their youngest daughter, Jill Longley, who was a teenager when we were small children. Jill had an older brother and sister. Jane married Hugh Compton, one of those strange people like the Tonbridge School chaplain of my day, the Reverend Harry Gripper, who could memorize the entire British Rail timetable—they were both pretty good with the buses, too—public transport gurus. Jill and Jane's brother, John Longley, remains somewhat of a mystery, and I believe ended up in Belfast, Ireland. I do remember Jane Longley visiting the United States in the late 1940s as a nanny. I remember after she returned from America she was full of their new invention—plastic—so much so that Diane and I became forever influenced by her in describing things we thought shoddy that came out of the United States as "plastic." Diane still speaks of the United States as a "land of plastic." Of course, all of this in our formative years was in part because of 'Forsythia's' downplaying of the new superpower—a sort of fear that one day the United States might actually take over from us, the inheritors of the British Empire. We were schooled in the thought that Winston Churchill and Field Marshal Montgomery were the real heroes of the Second World War, far more than General Eisenhower or Patton. Hugh and Jane, however, remained the closest to us over the years and are to this day very loyal members of the family. I became a godfather to Alison, one of their daughters, and Sally a godmother to Claire. During the late 1940s and early '50s, we often went to visit Great-uncle George and Great-aunt Marjorie in Oakwood Avenue and watched television with Jill. Hardly anybody had television in the late 1940s, but they possessed a television set when it was quite a novelty. In those days, the BBC only broadcast television for two or three hours in the evening, and one of our favorite programs was a puppet show called *Muffin the Mule*. There was also great excitement when our Kindergarten teacher, Miss Pope at St. Christopher's, The Hall, wrote a children's program for the BBC about a beetroot character named 'Bertie' and other animated vegetables. However, Miss Pope was not the only nationally recognized writer from Beckenham in that era. Enid Blyton was probably the most famous young children's writer in England in the late 1940s with her series of stories about 'Noddy' and 'Big Ears', and later *The Famous Five,* England's equivalent in age and appeal to the *Nancy Drew* stories. The Noddy books at one time became banned by some public libraries as Noddy and Big ears, two elf-like characters, were considered 'gay', all because Big Ears liked to ring the bell on the top of Noddy's pointed hat! Times have changed.

Little Jon Forsyte's world was one of extreme make-believe, too. He seemed of the *opinion that the world was a place of perfect and perpetual gentility and freedom.* As far as his education was concerned, he had the usual governess of his class—French, of course, *who came for two hours every morning to teach him her language, together with history, geography and sums;* and his mother gave him piano lessons.

Then, the inevitable plague of the nursery struck, shortly after he had endured the experience of sitting *on a humble-bee, a poignant experience, which his mother had understood much better than 'Da'. Following a day of utter wretchedness, he had enjoyed a disease composed of little spots, bed, honey in a spoon, and many tangerine oranges. It was then that the world had flowered.*

Those spots, whether the rash of measles, or the pimples of chicken pox, meant four weeks quarantine, when the nursery bedroom was all one's world. This still applied in my own youth, even as the severity of these childhood diseases was waning to the advance of medical science—quarantine—days entirely on one's own, or in our case, when at boarding school, in that dormitory shared only by others inflicted with the disease.

After the initial period of high fever and darkened rooms, came a long period of convalescence when we felt quite well, but remained quarantined.

For Jon, this expanded his imagination. His 'Auntie' June—really his half-sister, but oh, so much older than him that she felt more like an aunt—on hearing he was *a little lame duck came rushing down from London, bringing with her the books which had nurtured her own Berserker spirit. Aged, and of many colours, they were stored with the most formidable happenings. Of these she read to little Jon, till he was allowed to read to himself; whereupon she whisked back to London and left them with him in a heap. Those books cooked his fancy, till he thought and dreamed of nothing but midshipmen and dhows, pirates, rafts, sandal-wood traders, iron horses, sharks, battles, Tartars, Red Indians, balloons, North Poles and other extravagant delights.*

He turned the nursery and its furnishings into re-enactment of these adventures.

Then, his father added *Ivanhoe, Bevis, a book about King Arthur, and Tom Brown's Schooldays.* The boy's extraordinary imagination increased.

Diane and I also shared great imagination in our childhood. We created a whole fantasy world we named "Bonkon Land." We both created our own 'Bonkon' families, who lived in the woods. We were also inspired by the Jabberwock in *Alice through the Looking Glass,* and extended these dragons into our play after appreciation of our favorite theatre experience when we saw a West End production of *Where the Rainbow Ends.* Later, as with Jon, our toy soldiers took over, and my younger sister, Sally, joined us in making our nursery the adventure playground of the British Empire. However, unlike little Jon, we also had an incredible interest in nature, and most our imperial games centered on natural exploration of tropical flora and fauna, rather than imperial power.

After reading Ivanhoe, for three days Jon *built, defended and stormed Front de Boeuf's castle, taking every part in the piece except those of Rebecca and Rowena; with piercing cries of: "En avant, de Bracy!" and similar utterances. After reading the book about King Arthur he rode his old rocking-horse to death, armed with a long bamboo. Bevis he found tame; besides it required woods and animals, of which he had none in the nursery. For Tom Brown, he was yet too young. There was relief in the house when, after the fourth week, he was permitted to go down and out.*

In the garden, he extended his adventures, but with less disturbance to the household. *He lived a life of the most violent action.*

"Jon," said his father to his mother, under the oak tree, "is terrible. I'm afraid he is going to turn out a sailor, or something hopeless. Do you see any sign of his appreciating beauty?"

"Not the faintest."

"Well, thank heaven he's no turn for wheels or engines! I can bear nothing but that. But I wish he'd take more interest in Nature."

"He's imaginative, Jolyon."

"Yes, in a sanguinary way. Does he love anyone just now?"

"No; only everyone. There never was anyone born more loving or more lovable than Jon."

"Being your boy, Irene."

Jon heard it all in the tree above them, *but that fragment of talk lodged, thick, in his small gizzard. Loving, lovable, imaginative, sanguinary!*

With 'Da's' departure, Jon took his imagination indoors again, using *two boxes of soldiers, and some artillery, together with The Young Buglers, which had been among his birthday presents.*

This phase, caused his parents anxiety, as it had my mother and father, *because it kept him indoors when he ought to have been out.*

Eventually, however, we simply took our soldiers outside into the garden where they went for long treks across the lawn to jungles of flowerbeds and lakes and mystical waterfalls of the tropics around our pond. They remained explorers of the Empire.

Jon with his more aggressive soldier games stayed indoors, a period that *lasted through May and half of June, till his father killed it by bringing home to him 'Tom Sawyer' and 'Huckleberry Finn'. When* Jon *read those books something happened to him, and he went out of doors again in passionate quest of a river. He had to make one out of their pond. On this pond, he was allowed a little collapsible canoe, in which he spent hours and hours paddling, and lying down out of sight of Indian Joe and other enemies. On the shore of the pond, too, he built himself a wigwam about four feet square, of old biscuit tins, roofed in by boughs. He led a lonely life of 'make believe' during those five weeks of summer weather, with gun, wigwam, water and canoe; and however hard his active little brain tried to keep the sense of beauty away, she did creep in on him for a second now and then, perching on the wing of a dragon-fly, glistening on the water-lilies or brushing his eyes with her blue as he lay on his back in ambush.*

While his parents were away, 'Auntie' June had been left in charge. At one time, she brought two 'grown ups' down to the pond. *The names of the two grown-ups were 'Auntie' Holly and 'Uncle' Val. He took a fancy to 'Auntie' Holly, who seemed to be a sister, too.* Perhaps in this other sister, he experienced that first awakening of feminine beauty. He now wanted something soft.

I remember that moment well, standing in line with my father to visit the new broadcasting tower on the site of the old Crystal Palace. A girl, perhaps two years older than me, with long dark hair held in place by an 'Alice' band, stood in front of us. For the first time, my stomach ached for something soft.

As Jon waited, just before his mother returned from Ireland, he *had stolen into her room, looked at everything, without touching, and on into the dressing-room. Then, he had opened his mother's wardrobe, and taken a long sniff which seemed to bring him nearer to—he didn't know what.*

He was outside in the garden, when they arrived. The motor car pulled up and stopped. His father greeted him with 'Forsyte' reserve:

"Bless us! Well, old man, you are brown."

Then, with a long, shy look he saw his mother, in a blue dress, with a blue motor scarf over her cap and hair, smiling. He jumped as high as ever he could, twined his legs behind her back and hugged. He heard her gasp, and felt her hugging back. His eyes looked into hers, and squeezing with all his might he heard her creak and laugh, and say:

"You are strong, Jon!"

He slid down at that and rushed into the hall, dragging her by the hand.

While he was eating his jam beneath the oak tree, he noticed things about his mother.

She was ever so beautiful, more beautiful than 'Da' or 'Mademoiselle', or 'Auntie' June or even 'Auntie' Holly, to whom he had taken such a fancy. This new beautifulness of his mother had a kind of particular importance, and he ate less than he had expected to.

The discovery that his mother was beautiful was one which he felt must absolutely be kept to himself, just like my feelings for that longhaired girl at the Crystal Palace.

He sneaked into her room while she was unpacking. *He entered her bedroom from his own, the door being open. She was still kneeling before a trunk, and he stood close to her, quite still.*

She knelt up straight and said:

"Well, Jon?"

"I thought I'd just come and see."

He watched her, feeling those strange feelings.

Then, they talked a little of what he had done with Auntie June while she had been away. Jon told her Auntie June had taken him to church. His response to this induction into religion was not all it could have been.

"You and Daddy never go to church, do you?" he asked.

"No, we don't."

"Why don't you?"

His mother smiled.

"Well, dear, we both of us went when we were little. Perhaps we went when we were too little."

"I see," said little Jon, "it's dangerous."

"You shall judge for yourself about all those things as you grow up."

Little Jon replied in a calculating manner:

"I don't want to grow up much. I don't want to go to school." A
sudden overwhelming desire to say something more, to say what he
really felt, turned him red. "I—I want to stay with you, and be your
lover, Mum. I don't want to go to bed to-night, either. I'm simply tired
of going to bed every night."

"Have you had any more nightmares?"

"Only about one. May I leave the door open into your room tonight,
Mum?"

"Yes, just a little."

Little Jon heaved a sigh of satisfaction.

"What did you see in Ireland*?"*

"Nothing but beauty, darling."

"What exactly is beauty? Can I see it, for instance?" Jon asked. He
knew he could feel it.

"You do, every day. The sky is beautiful, the stars, and moonlit
nights, and then the birds, the flowers, the trees—they're all beautiful.
Look out of the window—there's beauty for you, Jon."

"Oh! yes, that's the view. Is that all?"

"All? No. The sea is wonderfully beautiful, and the waves, with their
foam flying back."

Little Jon suddenly reached out and caught her neck in his hands.

"I know," he said mysteriously, "you're it really, and all the rest is
make believe."

She sighed, laughed, said:

"Oh! Jon!"

Little Jon put his finger to the outer corner of her eye.

"I love your little rays, Mum."

"Oh! Those? But they're a sign of age."

"They come when you smile."

"But they usen't to."

"Oh! well, I like them. Do you love me, Mum?"

"I do—I do love you, darling."

"Ever so?"

"Ever so!"

"More than I thought you did?"

"Much—much more."

"Well, so do I; so that makes it even."

He sat with them over dinner. He stayed up later than usual. Finally,
he went to bed, his mother listening to him as he said his prayers.

"You won't shut the door more than that, will you?" he said as she left to go back down and play the piano for Jolyon.

Jon found it hard to sleep. He was experiencing new sensations. He went to the window, drew the drapes. He looked out at the moonlit landscape—like his mother had said: "Beautiful." *The trees threw thick shadows, the lawn looked like spilt milk, and a long, long way he could see; oh! very far; right over the world, and it looked different and swimmy. There was a lovely smell, too, in his open window.* He ate a macaroon he had been hoarding as he heard the music his mother was playing, drifting out into that magical landscape. When she stopped playing, he retreated back to his bed so he could pretend he was asleep when she came back to kiss him as she had promised. The moonbeam through the window seemed to follow him. Then, *the music began again, but he could only just hear it now; sleepy music, pretty—sleepy—music—sleepy—slee...*

The moonbeam reached his face as he dreamed. There was a milk pan, a cat, and then his bed turning round and round, up and down, *and getting fiery, and Mother Lee out of 'Cast up by the Sea' was stirring. Oh! so horrible she looked! Faster and faster!—till he and the bed and Mother Lee and the moon and the cat were all one wheel going round and round and up and up—awful—awful—awful!*

He shrieked.

A voice saying: "Darling, darling!" got through the wheel, and he awoke, standing on his bed, with his eyes open.

There was his mother, with her hair like Guinevere's from Camelot, loose and long. *Clutching her, he buried his face in it.*

"It's all right, treasure. You're awake now. There! There! It's nothing!"

Her voice went on, velvety in his ear.

"It was the moonlight, sweetheart, coming on your face."

Little Jon burbled into her nightgown:

"You said it was beautiful. Oh!"

"Not to sleep in, Jon. Who let it in? Did you draw the curtains?"

"I wanted to see the time; I—I looked out, I—I heard you playing, Mum; I—I ate my macaroon."

Granny Mabs always gave us macaroons, but not to sleep on.

"Well, Jon, what can you expect if you eat macaroons after you've gone to bed," his mother said.

Only one, Mum; it made the music ever so more beautiful. I was waiting for you—I nearly thought it was tomorrow."

"My ducky, it's only just eleven now."

Little Jon was silent, rubbing his nose on her neck.

"Mum, is Daddy in your room?"

"Not tonight."

"Can I come?"

"If you wish, my precious."

Half himself again, little Jon drew back.

"You look different, Mum; ever so younger."

"It's my hair, darling."

"I like it," he said. "I like you best of all like this."

Taking her hand he had begun dragging her towards the door. He shut it as they passed, with a sigh of relief.

"Which side of the bed do you like, Mum?"

"The left side."

"All right."

Wasting no time, giving her no chance to change her mind, little Jon got into the bed, which seemed much softer than his own."

"It wasn't anything, really, was it?" he said.

From before her glass his mother answered:

"Nothing but the moon and your imagination heated up. You mustn't get so excited, Jon."

Irene started to plait her hair.

"Oh! Mum, do hurry up!" Jon pleaded.

"Darling, I have to plait my hair."

"Oh! not to-night. You'll only have to unplait it again tomorrow."

That long hair—the long hair of awakening—softness—beauty.

His mother stood up white and flowery before the winged mirror; he could see three of her, with her neck turned and her hair bright under the light, and her dark eyes smiling.

"Do come, Mum; I'm waiting."

"Very well, my love, I'll come."

Little Jon closed his eyes. Everything was turning out most satisfactory, only she must hurry up! He felt the bed shake, she was getting in. And, still with his eyes closed, he said sleepily:

"It's nice, isn't it?"

He heard her voice say something, felt her lips touching his nose, and, snuggling up beside her who lay awake and loved him with her thoughts, he fell into the dreamless sleep which rounded off his past.

BOOK THREE
TO LET

PART ONE

CHAPTER ONE

ENCOUNTER

The childhood freedoms of the Edwardian decade that had finally expressed themselves for little Jon in a close bond with his mother, something almost unknown in the generation before, were more obviously flaunted by Soames' daughter, Fleur.

Her bond was with her father, but not for love, but for what she knew he could provide. Soames had a fortune of a quarter of a million pounds and it was very diversely invested. Although his greatest fear, as that of most 'Forsytes' in the early twentieth century, was socialism and its encroachment on his privileged property, he knew that his diversity *afforded substantial guarantee even against that 'wildcat notion'—a levy on capital.* What purpose had he in life now, but to indulge in his daughter? His marriage was no more than a convenience. *He had known but one real passion in his life—for that first wife of his—Irene.*

It was two years now since the Great War, and Fleur, whom he had kept at a boarding school in the West Country through those troublesome years, was now a young lady. In May, 1920, while they were in town on a shopping spree, he arranged to meet her at a *Gallery off Cork Street.*

Despite the war and this creeping socialism, expressed by surly cab drivers that made Soames rather walk than face their jibes, *the price of pictures, had, if anything, gone up, and he had done better with his collection since the war began than ever before.* So, too, had it been for my great-grandfather, Oliver Longley, who continued to adorn the walls of Hillside and The Breach with new acquisitions—part curiosity and part investment, and probably seen as with Soames, as a tangible buffer against the possible collapse of their world if "these labor chaps" took power.

Soames paused at Rotten Row. *No greater change in all England than in the Row! Born almost within hail of it, he could remember it from 1860 on. Brought there as a child between the crinolines to stare at tight-trousered dandies in whiskers, riding with a cavalry seat; to watch the doffing of curly-brimmed and white top hats; the leisurely air of it all, and the little bow legged man in a long red waistcoat who used to come among the fashion with dogs on several strings and try to sell them: King Charles spaniels, Italian greyhounds—you never saw them now. You saw no quality of any sort, indeed, just working people sitting in dull rows with nothing to stare at but a few young bouncing females in pot hats, riding astride, or desultory Colonials charging up and down on dismal-looking hacks; with here and there little girls on ponies, or old gentlemen jogging their livers; no thoroughbreds, no grooms, no bowing, no scraping, no gossip—nothing; only the trees the same—the trees indifferent to the generations and declensions of mankind. A democratic England—dishevelled, hurried, noisy, and seemingly without an apex. Wealth there was—oh, yes! Wealth—he himself was a richer man than his father had ever been; but manners, flavour, quality, all gone, engulfed in one vast, ugly, shoulder-rubbing, petrol-smelling Cheerio. Little half-beaten pockets of gentility and caste lurking here and there; but nothing ever again firm and coherent to look up to. And into this new hurly-burly of bad manners and loose morals his daughter—flower of his life—was flung! And when those Labour chaps got power—if they ever did—the worst was yet to come.*

He thought of his sister Winifred's new friend—Prosper Profond. A foreigner, of course, and made a lot of money out of the war. 'Munitions', he thought, 'but no manners.'

It was only three years since the Bolshevik revolution in Russia—they had murdered the Tsar, Tsarina, and their children. Before the war, Tsar Nicholas II, had reviewed the fleet at Spithead with his look-alike cousin, King George V. Now, Russia was in chaos—Socialism!

It was strangely refreshing to see his cousin George Forsyte, still sitting in the window of the Iseum Club. *Yes, there he was, tall, ponderous, neat, clean-shaven, with his smooth hair, hardly thinned, smelling no doubt, of the best hair-wash, and a pink paper in his hand,* trademark of the *Financial Times. Well, he didn't change!* Half-beaten pockets of gentility. *And perhaps for the first time in his life Soames felt a kind of sympathy tapping in his waistcoat for that sardonic kinsman. He was a guarantee that the old order would take some shifting yet*—in reality, another forty years.

George, who had arranged to meet him, beckoned Soames in.

"Haven't seen you since the War," he said. *"How's your wife?"*

"Thanks," said Soames coldly, *"well enough."*

Some hidden jest curved, for a moment, George's fleshy face.

"That Belgian chap, Profond," he said, *"is a member here now. He's a rum customer."*

"Quite!" muttered Soames. *"What did you want to see me about?"*

"Old Timothy; he might go off the hooks at any moment. I suppose he's made his Will."

"Yes."

"Well, you or somebody ought to give him a look up—last of the old lot; he's a hundred you know. They say he's like a mummy. Where are you goin' to put him? He ought to have a pyramid by rights."

Soames shook his head. "Highgate, the family vault."

Property—George fishing to know to whom his bachelor uncle, Timothy, had left his money—no doubt. Was it to all of them?

"Is that all," said Soames. *"I must be getting on."*

As a parting gesture, George expressed his concern, too:

"Haven't you attorneys invented a way yet of dodging this damned income tax? It hits the fixed inherited income like the very deuce. I used to have two thousand five hundred a year; now I've got a beggarly fifteen hundred, and the price of living doubled. These Labour chaps mean to have the lot before they've done."

Soames left and *moved along Piccadilly.*

He himself, he reflected, *had always been a worker and a saver, George always a drone and a spender; and yet if confiscation once began, it was he—the worker and the saver—who would be looted! That was the negation of all virtue, the overturning of all Forsyte principles. Well, they wouldn't confiscate his pictures, for they wouldn't know their worth.*

He arrived at the Cork Street gallery. An exhibit for the Future, what was it about?

He tried to make sense of a sculpture *described in his catalogue as 'Jupiter'. It looked to him like a lamp-post bent by collision with a motor omnibus. 'If that's Jupiter,' he thought, 'I wonder what Juno's like?' And suddenly he saw her opposite. She appeared to him like nothing so much as a pump with two handles, lightly clad in snow. He was still gazing at* Juno when he heard a young onlooker, disheveled-looking, but accompanied by a good-looking chap, admiring 'Jupiter'.

"You've *missed it, old bean; he's pulling your leg,"* the good-looking boy said. *"When Jove and Juno created he them, he was saying: 'I'll see how much these fools will swallow.' And they've lapped up the lot."*

"You young duffer!" his friend retorted. *"Vospovitch is an innovator. Don't you see that he's brought satire into sculpture? The future of plastic art, of music, painting, and even architecture, has set in satiric. It was bound to. People are tired—the bottom's tumbled out of sentiment."*

"Well, I'm quite equal to taking a little interest in beauty." Then the good-looking chap looked up at Soames. *"You've dropped your handkerchief, sir."*

Still staring across the room, *Soames saw a handkerchief held out in front of him. He took it with some natural suspicion, and approached it to his nose. It had the right scent—of distant eau-de-Cologne—and his initials in a corner.*

"Thank you," he said; and moved by a sort of irritation, added: "Glad to hear you like beauty; that's rare, nowadays."

"I dote on it," said the young man; "but you and I are the last of the old guard, sir."

Soames smiled.

"If you really care for pictures," he said, "here's my card. I can show you some quite good ones any Sunday, if you're down the river and care to look in."

"Awfully nice of you, sir. I'll drop in like a bird. My name's Mont—Michael." And he took off his hat.

Soames, already regretting his impulse, raised his own slightly in response.

He watched them leave the gallery.

What had possessed him to give his card to a rackety young fellow, who went about with a companion *like that?*

Soames moved on in the gallery to look at *a large canvas with a great many square tomato-coloured blobs on it, and nothing else. He looked at his catalogue:*

'No 32—"The Future Town"—Paul Post.'

'I suppose that's satiric, too,' he thought. 'What a thing!'

Soames, however, was aware that change in artistic fashion had monetary value. *There was money to be made out of every change of fashion.*

Above the tomato blobs was what he took to be a sunset, but he overheard was an airplane. *Below the tomato blobs was a band of white with vertical black stripes, to which* Soames *could assign no meaning whatever, till someone else came by, murmuring: "What expression he gets with his foreground!" Expression? Of what?*

Expression! Ah! they were all Expressionists now, he had heard, on the Continent. So it was coming here too, was it?

Then *he became conscious of a woman and a youth standing between him and the 'Future Town'. No mistaking that back, elegant as ever though the hair above had gone grey. Irene! His divorced wife—Irene! And this, no doubt was her son—by that fellow Jolyon Forsyte—their boy, six months older than his girl.* She turned to her boy. *Her lips were smiling as Soames, first possessor of them, had never seen them smile. And how that boy smiled back at her! It went beyond what Fleur gave him, and it was undeserved. Their son might have been his son; Fleur might have been her daughter, if she had kept straight!*

As he waited for Fleur, who had been at her cousin Imogen's for lunch, *he heard the boy laugh, and say eagerly: "I say Mum, is this by one of 'Auntie' June's lame ducks?"*

"Paul Post—I believe it is, darling."

And then, she saw him. Her gloved hand crisped the folds of her frock, her eyebrows rose, her face went stony. She moved on.

Officially, throughout 'Forsythia' the gloved hand remained a badge of class until the demise. Gloves were part of my sisters' boarding school uniform, and they were the bane of our outings to London with my mother and Granny Mabs. They were always getting left in the train compartment or on bus seats. It was a constant cry: "Where are your gloves?" There were thin leather winter gloves and white cotton summer gloves. For formal events there were still those long elbow gloves, worn sometimes by my mother to 'City' banquets or masonic ladies' nights. Gloves had little to do with warming digital extremities, they were a badge of the three percent.

My mother hated masonic ladies' nights, indeed, she hated anything to do with the freemasons, but my father had become involved in freemasonry through his interests in the 'City' and was a member of the Poulterers Lodge and also as part of the 'old boy' network where he supported the Old Tonbridgian Lodge along with his brother, my Uncle Gyles. In time, he became a Grand Lodge freemason in the 'City'. I remember his suitcase with the regalia that used to cause much mockery from my mother. As a duty, however, especially in the early days of his freemason connection, she attended elaborate white tie dinners with him at the Connaught Rooms in London. I remember her wearing her wedding dress, remodelled into a stunning evening gown, to one of those dinners, and of course, the obligatory long elbow length white gloves. In later life, she often made excuses to avoid having to attend masonic ladies' nights.

Irene and her son *passed from* Soames' *view into the next room, and Soames continued to regard the Future Town, but saw it not. He was despising the vehemence of his own feelings after all these years. Ghosts! And yet as one grew old—was there anything but what was ghost-like left? Yes, there was Fleur! He fixed his eyes on the entrance.*

Then he saw a gaudy woman, a sort of artistic tramp, *surely June Forsyte! His cousin June—and coming straight to his recess.*

"Soames!"

Soames turned his head a very little.

"How are you?" he said. "Haven't seen you for twenty years."

"No. Whatever made you come here?"

"My sins," said Soames. "What stuff?"

"Stuff? Oh, yes—of course; it hasn't arrived yet."

"It never will," said Soames; "it must be making a dead loss."

"Of course it is."

"How do you know?"

"It's my Gallery."

"Well," he said, "if you take my advice, you'll close this exhibition."

June looked back at him. "Oh! You Forsyte!" she said and moved on.

Forsyte! Of course he was a Forsyte—so was she!

He contemplated his family, realizing how little he knew now of them. *The old aunts at Timothy's had been dead so many years; there was no* 'Forsyte Change, *no clearing-house for news.* And so, in some ways it was for us without Hillside, and later, without The Breach.

What had they all done in the War? Young Roger's boy had been wounded. St. John or Singent Hayman's second son killed. Young Nicholas's eldest had got an O.B.E., or whatever they gave them. They had all joined up somehow, he believed. That boy of Jolyon's and Irene's, he supposed had been too young: his own generation, of course, too old, though Giles Hayman had driven a car for the Red Cross—and Jesse Hayman had been a special constable—those 'Dromios' had always been of a sporting type.

Grandpa Jack was a special constable during the Great War. His truncheon, then a beautiful polished wooden affair with a leather hand strap, had hung in the hall at Redcroft during my childhood, and later graced the dining room at Hockerdege. Grandpop and 'Tig' had both served in the Honourable Artillery Company and survived the conflict without a scratch. Grandpop's efforts had included that act of sacrificial bravery that had won him the Military Cross, something more prestigious than the O.B.E. that in 'Forsythia' we usually called the award for "other bugger's efforts." Uncle Gyles, as noted, followed in his father's footsteps in the Second World War winning the Military Cross for bravery in the Italian campaign.

My great-uncle, Frank Cuthbertson, almost survived the Great War, having served in the trenches on the front line. Unfortunately, he was awaiting leave in a rest trench in 1918 when an unlikely shell hit the trench. His brother, my great-uncle, Bert Cuthbertson, was on a troop ship at the time, sailing from Durban in South Africa on his way to East Africa to take up some engineering work. The war was near an end, but the struggle with Germany in the African colonies, more a diplomatic war than a war of action, was still in progress. The ship was surprisingly torpedoed by one of the new German submarines. Great-uncle Bert survived the disaster along with this letter that despite waterlogging is still quite legible. It is of interest to me, as it shows something of the rakish colonial character of my mother's favorite uncle. It was written to my grandmother from Durban the day they sailed.

'Fern Villa Hotel,
Marine Parade.
Ocean Beach,
Durban.

April 20ᵗʰ 1918

'*My Dear Mabel,*

'*This is our last day in Durban, we leave this afternoon by* H.M.T. Ingoma *with several hundred troops for East Africa. The boat will be crowded, four in a cabin I hear, but no matter!*

'*We arrived here on the fourth last and have had a very nice time. It is a lovely seaside place, as nice as any at home. Beautifully laid out. There are some very pretty girls here, but they are the most moral lot I have struck, only found about two glad eyes all the time apart from the theatre crowd, which we did very well with. Swimming, supping, and tea-ing. Last night we had a very merry night, singing round the piano in the drawing room till after twelve, finishing up by prowling around the roof and waking everyone up. I have taken some very good pictures with my camera and have sent mother some. I have mislaid the best or sent them down to the steamer with the hold baggage or something. I have three pals here going to British East Africa. Two are from Cambridge and one from Oxford, we manage to have quite a good time. However, the speaker's son is also in the crowd, but staying at the Royal. He is a queer bird – never gets flustered, and is to be found sitting on the verandah of the Royal at all hours of the day – I don't think he has been to the front more than once. This hotel is right on the front, a lovely position. The climate is topping, it is the best place that I have ever been stranded in. There is golf, tennis, swimming, racing, cricket, bowls, football and whiskey and soda to be had and I could settle down comfortably. The only drawback is that the methodists run the show, and make silly regulations, for instance a lady may not have a drink at all. We have to order two drinks each and sumptuously dispose of hers. Tons of food here and we live jolly well – seven course dinners and five course breakfasts, some place. How are the Squirts? I hope both you and Jack are fit, I have a good chess opening to show Jack – it will get him cold.*

'*Bye bye. Love to all,*
Your affectionate brother,
Bert'

I note the reference to chess. Grandpa Jack had a rather fine chess set that is still in my possession today.

In this war, unlike the earlier Boer War, everybody had done 'their bit', so far as Soames Forsyte *could make out, as a matter of course.* The best part of a whole generation of England's youth had been sacrificed in the winter mud and summer poppy fields of Flanders, just to assuage German impudence. *It seemed to show the growth of something or other—or perhaps the decline of something else. Had* 'Forsytes' *become less individual, or more Imperial, or less provincial? Or was it simply that one hated Germans?* The impudence. Their country had only existed for two generations! At least our traditional foe—France—had been around as long as we had. What was Germany but a bunch of little 'Cinderella' states—baronies, dukedoms, and principalities that had been absorbed by the ambitious Prussians with their militaristic rulers from the House of Hoenzollen—even if by marriage related to Queen Victoria? It was a good thing *that* kaiser had been deposed. At least Count Hindenburg did not come from *that* family.

Little did the world know that before the demise of 'Forsythia', Germany would rise yet again under the militaristic fascist dictatorship of Adolf Hitler, who started out as President Hindenburg's chancellor. It was no wonder that in my childhood we all openly called the Germans "Stinkies."

However, trophies came from final victory. Further imperial expansion was one of those spoils. In the hall at Redcroft there were two mounted impala horns and two small mounted dik-dik horns—wild animals of Africa that Great-uncle Bert Cuthbertson had shot and sent back to his sister. They are now in my possession and the mounts are inscribed GEA 1918, showing they were shot right at the end of the Great War in German East Africa. German East Africa was ceded to Great Britain a few months later at the Treaty of Versailles. The area became the British colonies of Uganda and Tanganyka. This was the last land in Africa to hold up what had been Cecil Rhodes' dream—one could now travel by train from Capetown, at the south westernmost tip of Africa, to Cairo at the most north eastern corner, entirely on British soil.

While Soames had been musing over his families' war efforts, Fleur must have come in. At first he didn't notice her, but rather noticed June, Irene, and her boy come back in. Then, when they stood by the sculpture 'Juno' again, he noticed Fleur. She was in front of them. Soames *could see her eyes glint sideways at the boy, and the boy look back at her. Then Irene slipped her hand through his arm, and drew him on. Soames saw him glancing round, and Fleur looking after them as the three went out.*

A voice said cheerfully: "Bit thick isn't it, sir?"

The young man who had handed him his handkerchief was again passing. Soames nodded.

"I don't know what we're coming to."

"Oh! That's all right, sir," answered the young man cheerfully; "they don't either."

Fleur's voice said : "Hullo, Father! Here you are!" precisely as if he had been keeping her waiting.

Then, she started to quiz him about the young man.

"He picked up my handkerchief. We talked about the pictures"

Fleur dragged at his arm. "Oh! Let's go! It's a ghastly show."

"Well," he said in the street, "whom did you meet at Imogen's?"

"Aunt Winifred, and that Monsieur Profond."

"Oh!" muttered Soames; "that chap! What does your aunt see in him?"

"Cousin Val and his wife were there, too."

"What!" said Soames. "I thought they were back in South Africa."

"Oh, no! They've sold their farm. Cousin Val is going to train race-horses on the Sussex Downs. They've got a jolly old manor house; they asked me down there. I promised to go Saturday to Wednesday next."

Why the deuce couldn't his nephew have stayed out in South Africa? His own divorce had been bad enough, without his nephew's marriage to the daughter of the co-respondent; a half sister too of June, and of that boy whom Fleur had just been looking at. If he didn't look out, she would come to know all about that old disgrace! Unpleasant things! They were round him this afternoon like a swarm of bees!

"I don't like it!" he said.

"I want to see the race-horses," murmured Fleur; "and they've promised I shall ride. Cousin Val can't walk much, you know; but he can ride perfectly."

"Racing!" said Soames, grimly. "It's a pity the War didn't knock that on the head. He's taking after his father, I'm afraid."

"I don't know anything about his father."

"No," said Soames, grimly. "He took an interest in horses and broke his neck in Paris, walking downstairs. Good riddance for your aunt."

He frowned, recollecting the inquiry into those stairs which he had attended in Paris six years ago. Montague Dartie—*either his winnings, or the way he had celebrated them had gone to his brother-in-law's head.* So had ended the 'man about town.'

A sound from Fleur distracted his attention. "Look! *The people who were in the Gallery with us.*"

Soames saw, flinched and hastened Fleur into a pastry-cook's.

"*Two teas,*" he said, "*and two of those nougat things.*"

But, those three, June, Irene and that boy, they were following them. They came into the pastry cook's, too.

Soames *heard Irene say something to her boy, and his answer:*

"*Oh! no, Mum; this place is all right. My stunt.*" *And the three sat down.*

When Soames went to the counter to pay, Fleur passed their table.

Soames turned round to see *Fleur standing by the door, holding a handkerchief which the boy had evidently just handed to her.*

"*F.F.,*" *he heard her say.* "*Fleur Forsyte—it's mine all right. Thank you ever so.*"

Good God! She had caught the trick from what he had told her in the Gallery—monkey!

"*Forsyte? Why—that's my name too. Perhaps we're cousins*"

"*Really! We must be. There aren't any others. I live at Mapledurham; where do you?*"

"*Robin Hill.*"

"*Come along!*" *said Soames.*

Fleur did not move.

"*Didn't you hear, Father? Isn't it queer—our name's the same. Are we cousins?*"

"*What's that?*" Soames *said.* "*Forsyte! Distant, perhaps.*"

"*My name's Jolyon, sir. Jon for short.*"

"*Oh! Ah!*" *said Soames.* "*Yes. Distant. How are you? Very good of you. Good-bye!*"

He moved on.

"*Thanks awfully,*" *Fleur was saying.* "*Au revoir!*"

"*Au revoir!*" *he heard the boy reply.*

Chapter Two

Fine Fleur Forsyte

Fleur quizzed her father about the cousins she had just met.

"Why don't you like those cousins, Father? You must know them; I saw them looking at you."

"I've never seen the boy in my life," replied Soames with perfect truth.

"No; but you've seen the others, dear."

What had she picked up? Had her Aunt Winifred, or Imogen, or Val Dartie and his wife, been talking? Every breath of the old scandal had been carefully kept from her at home.

"Well," he said, "your grandfather and his brother had a quarrel. The two families don't know each other. And they'll continue not to know each other," but *he instantly regretted the challenge in those words. Fleur was smiling. In this age, when young people prided themselves on going their own ways and paying no attention to any sort of decent prejudice, he had said the very thing to excite her wilfulness.*

"What sort of a quarrel?"

"About a house. It's ancient history for you."

After a brief diversion she returned to the topic:

"Where is Robin Hill, Father?"

Robin Hill! Robin Hill, round which all, that tragedy had centred! What did she want to know for?

"In Surrey," he muttered; "not far from Richmond. Why?"

"Is the house there?"

"What house?"

"That they quarreled about."

"Yes. But what's all that got to do with you? We're going home tomorrow—you'd better be thinking about your frocks."

"Bless you. They're all thought about. A family feud? It's like The Bible or Mark Twain—awfully exciting. What did you do in the feud, Father?"

"Never you mind."

He tried to distract her again by purchasing some rosaline in a shop they were passing, but outside, Fleur continued her quest.

"Don't you think that boy's mother is the most beautiful woman of her age you've ever seen?"

Soames shivered.

"What's her husband like? He must be your first cousin, if your fathers were brothers."

"Dead for all I know," said Soames, with sudden vehemence. *"I haven't seen him for twenty years."*

"What was he?"

"A painter."

"That's quite jolly."

The words: *'If you want to please me you'll put those people right out of your head,'* sprang to Soames's lips, but he choked them back—he must not let her see his feelings.

"He once insulted me."

"I see! You didn't avenge it, and it rankles. Poor Father!"

As they reached the hotel, he said grimly:

"I did my best. And that's enough about these people. I'm going up to your mother till dinner.*"*

Fleur stayed in the hall of the hotel seated in a chair, as Soames went up in the lift. Some time later she did not see him come down, she had been in a sort of dream, but she suddenly got up and impulsively went to a writing table. *Seizing ink and writing-paper, she began to write as if she had not time to breathe before she got her letter written. And suddenly she saw* her father. *The air of desperate absorption vanished, she smiled, waved a kiss, made a pretty face as if she were a little puzzled and a little bored.*

My sister, Sally, was probably the most willful of us three growing up in that last decade of 'Forsythia'. Actually, for the most part she grew up in the next decade, and the world was fast changing—no longer really 'Forsythia'. Willfulness flowers in change, just as it did for 'Forsytes' themselves flowering in that era right after the Great War. The changes in 'Forsythia' then, were even more dramatic than those that came in with the Edwardian era, and greater again in its 1960s demise. One always knew if Sally was trying to conceal her thoughts from the rest of us. Like Fleur her *air of desperate absorption vanished, she smiled, waved a kiss, made a pretty face as if she were a little puzzled and a little bored*—we used to call it her "siddle face."

Ah! as Fleur's mother or my mother might have said, *she was 'fine'— 'fine.'*

CHAPTER THREE

AT ROBIN HILL

While Irene had taken Jon to London, *Jolyon Forsyte had spent his boy's nineteenth birthday at Robin Hill, quietly going into his affairs. He did everything quietly now, because his heart was in a poor way, and, like all his family, he disliked the idea of dying. He had never realised how much till one day, two years ago, he had gone to his doctor about certain symptoms, and been told:*

"At any moment, on any overstrain."

He had taken it with a smile—the natural Forsyte reaction against an unpleasant truth. "Very Daphne," as my family would have said, or as my mother might have said in the presence of her formidable cousin—the unmovable Doggett—"Well, Daf, we must just soldier on, right?"

Jolyon kept his condition to himself.

Prior to Jon's nineteenth birthday, Jolyon had tried to ascertain in what direction his son wished to go. He had left school, now. Would he go to university? Should he travel now? The boy himself, really didn't seem to know what he wanted to do, possibly stifled in thought by his deep affection for his mother.

Then, just two weeks before his birthday, Jon had made a suggestion:

"I should like to try farming, Dad; if it won't cost you too much. It seems to be about the only sort of life that doesn't hurt anybody; except

477

art, and of course that's out of the question for me. He did not show the prowess of his father.

Jolyon subdued his smile and answered:

"All right; you shall skip back to where we were under the first Jolyon in 1760. It'll prove the cycle theory, and incidentally, no doubt, you may grow a better turnip than he did."

A little dashed, Jon had answered:

"But don't you think it's a good scheme, Dad?"

"'Twill serve, my dear; and if you should really take to it, you'll do more good than most men, which is little enough."

To himself, however, he had said: "But he won't take to it. I give him four years. Still, it's healthy and harmless."

Most 'Forsytes' who did not opt for some form of colonial service, running the Empire militarily, legally, or mercantilely, followed into family businesses, medicine, or law firms, a few the Church, but almost none into farming. Farming, throughout 'Forsythia' was divided between the landed gentry and aristocracy, and the residue of that old yeoman class of independent farmers from whose ancestors most 'Forsytes' had evolved. The eldest sons of the gentry and aristocracy usually overseered large inherited acres, and often, younger sons not otherwise employed, ran other people's landed properties as estate managers. In either case, they received their qualifications to do so from a combination of 'blue blood' and the Royal Agricultural College at Cirencester. 'Forsytes' were rarely big landowners, although many did have small non-profit farms giving a taste of country living, such as Jolyon at Robin Hill or my family at The Breach. They employed foremen, younger sons of yeoman farmers, to manage their properties, like Williams, who for many years managed the farm at The Breach, or in my childhood, Collard, before my Uncle Dennis bought the farm from my grandfather.

That Jon should be a serious farmer was not a consideration of his class—just a passing fancy. But, I am reminded that when looking into my own future rather younger than Jon Forsyte, farming was an attraction, especially after seeing a film at Newlands about a large Sussex farm. For various personal reasons, however, I chose the Church. This, then governed my teen years, and there was no reason for my father and I to discuss my future. Apart from those early life occasions when he had taken me to Smithfield in the belief that like his grandfather, father and uncles, and himself and his cousins, I would follow into that family business, there was no discussion. I was going to be ordained

a priest in the Church of England. It was for this reason that I read
theology at Cambridge. Ironically, however, after the Church of England
deferred my plans for ordination on the truly non-'Forsyte' principle that
I 'came from too privileged and sheltered a background' at a time when
the Church in immediate post-'Forsythia' was embracing socialism,
I made my post-university career in agriculture, when becoming the
estate manager of Tullamaine Castle in Ireland! I fell into farming, but
without that degree in agriculture from the Royal Agricultural College
at Cirencester. I learned like Jon Forsyte to become a gentleman farmer
on the job.

Jolyon played safe. He thought it best to keep this venture of young
Jon in the family. *He wrote to his daughter Mrs. Val Dartie, asking if
they knew of a farmer near them on the Downs who would take Jon as
an apprentice,* but on whom Val and Holly could keep an eye.

*Holly's answer had been enthusiastic. There was an excellent man
quite close; she and Val would love Jon to live with them.*

The boy was due to go to-morrow.

Jolyon waited for their return from London. He sat beneath the old
oak tree on the terrace, sipping lemon tea.

*From where he sat he could see a cluster of apple trees in blossom.
Nothing in nature moved him so much as fruit trees in blossom,*
something he shared with both my grandfather and great-grandfather,
who loved their orchards. *Decidedly no man ought to have to die while
his heart was still young enough to love beauty! Blackbirds sang
recklessly in the shrubbery, swallows were flying high, the leaves above
him glistened; and over the fields was every imaginable tint of early
foliage, burnished by the level sunlight, away to where the distant
'smoke-bush' blue was trailed along the horizon. Irene's flowers in their
beds had startling individuality. Only Chinese and Japanese painters,
and perhaps Leonardo, had known how to get that startling little ego
into each painted flower, and bird, and beast—the ego, yet the sense
of species, the universality of life as well. They were the fellows! 'I've
made nothing that will live!' thought Jolyon; 'I've been an amateur—a
mere lover, not a creator. Still, I shall leave Jon behind me when I go.'
What luck that the boy had not been caught by that ghastly war! He
might so easily have been killed, like poor Jolly twenty years ago out
in the Transvaal. Jon would do something some day—if the Age didn't
spoil him—an imaginative chap. And just then he saw them coming up*

the field: Irene and the boy, walking from the station, with their arms linked.

That night, Irene told Jolyon what had happened at June's gallery and after at the confectioner's.

Jolyon's heart side-slipped again. His wife's face had a strained and puzzled look.

"You didn't—?" he began.

"No; but Jon knows their name. The girl dropped her handkerchief and he picked it up."

"June was with you. Did she put her foot into it?"

"No; but it was all very queer and strained, and Jon could see it was."

Jolyon drew a long breath, and said:

"I've often wondered whether we've been right to keep it from him. He'll find out some day."

"The later the better, Jolyon: the young have such cheap, hard judgment. When you were nineteen what would you have thought of your mother if she had done what I have?"

"What have you told him?"

"That they were relations, but we didn't know them; that you had never cared much for your family, or they for you. I expect he will be asking you."

Irene looked up at him.

"We've known it would come some day."

Jolyon realized they must take precautions—*every precaution possible.*

He must write to Holly, telling her that Jon knew nothing as yet of family history. Holly was discreet, she would make sure of her husband, she would see to it! Jon would take the letter with him tomorrow.

Jon's education like most 'Forsytes' was single sex—boarding school for boys only, *and his holidays had been spent at Robin Hill with boy friends, or his parents alone.* His mother was the only outlet of his feelings for the opposite sex, his much older sisters having not been at home with him. This encounter with Fleur, was, therefore, his first pang of innocent love—an instant attraction. It was for him what the young girl in line at the Crystal Palace had been for me—the first encounter to make those butterflies flutter in the secret bowels of one's stomach. He *lay awake, the prey of a sensation disputed by those who have never known it, 'love at first sight.'*

Fleur! Her name alone was almost enough for one who was terribly susceptible to the charm of words. Fleur! And she lived at Mapledurham—a jolly name, too, on the river somewhere. He could find it in the atlas presently. He would write to her. But would she answer? Oh! She must. She had said "Au revoir!" Not good-bye! What luck that she had dropped her handkerchief!

At dawn, he stole out of the house and he sniffed the landscape in a different way. It was all in conversation with him—the bluebells spoke, *among the larch trees there was mystery—the air, as it were, composed of that romantic quality. Fleur! It certainly rhymed with her! Rhythm thronged his head; words jostled to be joined together; he was on the verge of a poem. The thing was too deep to be revealed to a mortal soul—even to his mother.*

Chapter Four

The Mausoleum

There are houses whose souls have passed into the limbo of Time, leaving their bodies in the limbo of London. Oh! There were so many in my childhood—streets of 'Forsyte' homes in leafy Beckenham, whose bomb damage was still gaping, whose gardens were overgrown, and whose fate lay in the future—the wrecking ball of a post-'Forsythia' world. Many, like our dear old Chelston, were turned into three or four flats, others, like that of Dr. Clement, or our dentist, Mr. Potts, continued in a time warp of dado and gas light fittings; mantels supporting clock and urn sets holding down the obligatory fringe; lace curtains, deep red and blue Turkish rugs, and large black and white tiles. Whether war damaged or surviving in this time warp, they all had impressive entryways. Some had gates with lodges and almost all had substantial brick pillars mounted by stone slabs. Those were the "larders" of our childhood and in the years following 'Forsythia', when so many of those great Victorian and Edwardian homes were demolished, making way for little estates of bungalows in their gardens, or plain uninteresting blocks of flats, those 'larders' survived—a reminder of the Beckenham into which we were born.

The old Forsyte home on the Bayswater Road where the aunts had held court and Timothy had lived out his bachelor life, and still was at a hundred years of age, was in such a time warp. It was solidly Victorian in a now post-Edwardian world—they called it a brave new world, licking its wounds in new hopes after "the war to end all wars." The few Forsytes who still visited; Francie, Euphemia and Winifred, never got to see Uncle Timothy. They were received by Smither, the maid, now an aging lady herself; they paid their respects to Cook, but they never got upstairs to the bedroom where *old Timothy's soul still had one foot.* A Mausoleum, George had called the old house when he suggested to Soames at the Iseeum that he should look up the last of the old Forsytes—find out about Timothy's will before *'he went off the hooks.'*

So, leaving Annette and Fleur at the hotel the day after the encounter with Irene and her boy, Soames made a pilgrimage to that *house of the 'old people' of another century, another age.*

The sight of Smither—still corseted up to the armpits because the new fashion which came in as they were going out about 1903 had never been considered 'nice' by Aunts Juley and Hester—brought a pale friendliness to Soames's lips; Smither, still faithfully arranged to old pattern in every detail, an invaluable servant—none such left—smiling back at him, with the words: "Why, it's Mr. Soames, after all this time! And how are you, sir? Mr. Timothy will be so pleased to know you've been."

"How is he?"

"Oh! he keeps fairly bobbish for his age, sir: but of course he's a wonderful man. As I said to Mrs. Dartie when she was here last: it would please Miss Forsyte and Mrs. Juley and Miss Hester to see how he relishes a baked apple still.

My great-grandfather, Oliver Longley, loved apples. He had an apple after almost every meal, peeling off the skin with an old penknife that he kept in his pocket. My Great-uncle George, his youngest son, loved stewed apples so much that we actually nicknamed him "Uncle Stapps" in our childhood. In the nursery, too, like so many of 'Forsythia', baked apples were a fairly regular dish that seemed to die in popularity with the breed. The skin of a baked apple became thin and brittle, and the apple inside mushy and easy to eat with a spoon. The core had been removed by a special gadget found in 'Forsythia' kitchen drawers, and the resulting hole stuffed with raisins and sultanas—easy to eat and so good for you, they said. Personally, in the nursery, I preferred mushy cornflakes with warm milk and Barbados pieces—brown sugar always served in blue bags. Diane liked groats—a sort of cross between porridge and semolina. Like the baked apples and those sweetbreads, they were all easy to eat, and in a post-war world of rationing, both economic and easy to get. Besides, at Chelston we had our own orchard of apple trees, now, sixty years on, commemorated by a short suburban cul-de-sac between boring little houses where our croquet lawn, chicken runs and kitchen garden once stood, and named 'Little Orchard'.

Countless people live in today's Beckenham that never knew our world or understand the subtleties in the names of new streets and cul-de-sacs like 'Little Orchard', but if you can think back in time just sixty years you can reconstruct the architecture and landscape of 'Forsythia'.

Smither started to recall for Soames how they had coped in the air raids towards the end of the Great War. She was *getting garrulous.* "Quite," he *murmured. "I just want to look round and see if there's anything to be done."*

Unlike his sister Winifred, or those nieces of theirs, he expressed his desire to see Timothy.

Smither coloured up above her corsets.

"It will be an occasion!" she said. "Shall I take you round the house, sir, while I send Cook to break it to him?"

"No, you go to him," said Soames. "I can go round the house by myself."

One could not confess to sentiment before another, and Soames felt that he was going to be sentimental nosing round those rooms so saturated with the past.

In the dining room, he looked at *two faintly coloured drawings of a boy and a girl, rather charming, which bore the initials 'J.R.'—Timothy had always believed they might turn out to be Joshua Reynolds, but Soames, who admired them,* long ago *had discovered that they were only John Robinson,* but possibly worthy of his collection at an estate sale.

In the study, a room he had hardly ever entered, he briefly looked at the books—nothing of great interest—and noted *a large chair with a mahogany reading-stand attached, on which a yellowish and folded copy of the* Times, *dated July 6. 1914, the day Timothy first failed to come down, as if in preparation for the war, seemed waiting for him still. He went up to a globe and gave it a spin; it emitted a faint creek and moved about an inch, bringing into his purview a daddy-long-legs which had died on it in latitude 44.*

'Mausoleum!' he thought. 'George was right!'

Upstairs on each side of the drawing room door *were the groups of miniatures. Those he would certainly buy in! The miniatures of his four aunts, one of his Uncle Swithin adolescent, and one of his Uncle Nicholas as a boy.* They had all been painted by a young lady friend of the family at a time, 1830, just before the daguerreotype became fashionable that captured some three generations of my Hovenden forebears in silver, mercury, and iodine. *Miniatures were considered very genteel,* more *lasting too, painted as they were on ivory. Many a time had he heard the tale of that young lady: "very talented, my dear; she had quite a weakness for Swithin, and very soon after she went into a consumption and died: so like Keats—we often spoke of it."*

Well, there they were! Anne, Juley, Hester, Susan—quite a small child; Swithin with sky blue eyes, pink cheeks, yellow curls, white waistcoat—large as life; and Nicholas, like Cupid with an eye on heaven. Yes, she must have had talent, and miniatures always had a certain back-watered cachet of their own, little subject to the currents of competition on aesthetic change.

However, for Soames it was more than noting the miniatures as items of worth. They stood guard at the entrance to the drawing room—their room—the room of those aunts and uncles who had reigned there over 'Forsyte 'Change'. *The room was dusted, the furniture uncovered, the curtains drawn back, precisely as if his aunts still dwelt there patiently waiting. And a thought came to Soames: When Timothy died—why not? Would it not be almost a duty to preserve this house—like Carlyle's— and put up a tablet and show it?* "Specimen of mid-Victorian abode— entrance, one shilling with catalogue. Perfect in its special taste and culture, if, that is, he took down and carried over to his own collection the four Barbizon pictures he had given them.*

He noted with amusement, too, along with all sorts of preserved family relics in the marqueterie cabinets of the room, *one very yellow elephant's tusk, sent home from India by Great-uncle Edgar Forsyte, who had been in jute.* It was interesting how aspects of the Empire like those family members who went out to its farthest reaches, always came back to the hub—London—England, that blessed plot. And now, after two decades of colonial farming out in the new Dominion of South Africa—served those Boers right—his nephew Val Dartie and wife had returned to breed racehorses on the Sussex Downs.

'No,' he thought again as he soaked in the atmosphere, *'there's nothing like it left; it ought to be preserved.' And, by George, they*

*might laugh at it, but for a standard of gentle life never departed from,
for fastidiousness of skin and eye and nose and feeling, it beat to-day
hollow—to-day with its Tubes and cars, its perpetual smoking, its cross-
legged, bare-necked girls visible up to the knees and down to the waist if
you took the trouble, with their feet, too, screwed round the legs of their
chairs while they ate, and their 'So longs', and their 'Old Beans', and
their laughter—girls who gave him the shudders whenever he thought of
Fleur in contact with them; and the hard-eyed, capable, older women,*
that first generation of 'Daphnes', *who managed life and gave him the
shudders too. No! his old aunts, if they never opened their minds, their
eyes, or very much their windows, at least had manners, and a standard,
and reverence for past and future.*

*With rather a choky feeling he closed the door and went tip-toeing
upstairs. He tapped.* The *door was opened by Smither, very red in the
face.*

*Mr. Timothy was taking his walk and she had not been able to get
him to attend. If Mr. Soames would come into the back-room, he could
see him through the door.*

*The last of the old Forsytes was on his feet, moving with the most
impressive slowness, and an air of perfect concentration on his own
affairs, backward and forward between the foot of his bed and the
window, a distance of some twelve feet. One hand held a stout stick,
and the other grasped the skirt of his Jaeger dressing-gown, from under
which could be seen his bedsocks thrust into Jaeger slippers.*

'Forsytes' sending their children away to boarding school all made
the same pilgrimage to the relevant London department store every
school holiday to purchase necessary school uniform and clothing items
as laid down by 'The List'. As noted, Newlands and Micklefield both
had Goringes as their school outfitters. All these school outfitters used
the same suppliers, however. Underwear was 'Chilproof' and dressing
gowns and slippers were 'Jaeger'. Everyone in the school had a uniform
Jaeger dressing gown. Colors might vary, but the trim boasted that
plaited silk from head to toe like the tassles of the tie, and deep pockets
on either side were also trimmed in the silk plait in a simplified fleur-
de-lys pattern. The slippers looked like they were made in one piece of
soft leather, very pliable, usually brown, and always with a warm, wool,
tartan felt lining.

"He looks strong. Does he take any interest in things generally?"
Soames asked.

"Oh! yes, sir; his food and his Will. It's quite a sight to see him turn it over and over, not to read it, of course; and every now and then he asks the price of Consols, and I write it on a slate for him—very large. Of course, I always write the same, what they were when he last took notice, in 1914.

"What would happen if I were to go in?" asked Soames. "Would he remember me? I made his Will, you know, after Miss Hester died in 1907."

"Oh! that, sir," replied Smither doubtfully, "I couldn't take on me to say. I think he might; he really is a wonderful man for his age."

Soames called out, *"Uncle Timothy!"*

Timothy trailed back half-way, and halted.

"Eh?" he said.

"Soames," cried Soames at the top of his voice, holding out his hand, "Soames Forsyte!"

"No!" said Timothy, and stumping his stick loudly on the floor, continued his walk.

"It doesn't seem to work," said Soames.

"No, sir," replied Smither, rather crestfallen; "you see, he hasn't finished his walk. It always was one thing at a time with him. I expect he'll ask me this afternoon if you came about the gas, and a pretty job I shall have to make him understand."

"Well," said Soames, turning away, "it's rather sad and painful to me. I'll go down. By the way, let me see his Will."

"I should have to take my time about that, sir; he keeps it under his pillow, and he'd see me while he's active."

"I only want to know if it's the one I made," said Soames, "you take a look at its date sometime and let me know."

"Yes, sir; but I'm sure it's the same, because me and Cook witnessed, remember, and there's our names on it still, and we've only done it once."

"Quite," said Soames. He did remember. Smither and Jane had been proper witnesses, having been left nothing in the Will that they might have no interest in Timothy's death. It had been—he admitted—an almost improper precaution, but Timothy had wished it, and, after all, Aunt Hester had provided for Smither and Cook *amply.*

It was quite customary for 'Forsytes' to give small bequests to long term retainers, either in cash or a cottage. Those lodge cottages by the 'larders' of the big houses in Beckenham were often given as retirement homes for old retainers for the duration of their remaining lives. As earlier noted, my great-grandfather, Oliver Longley, also built cottages at Wilsley Pound, Cranbrook, for some of his farm help, including Collard, his last farm foreman.

"Very well," Soames *said; "good-bye, Smither. Look after him, and if he should say anything at any time, put it down and let me know."*

"Oh! yes, Mr. Soames; I'll be sure to do that. It's been such a pleasant change to see you. Cook will be quite excited when I tell her."

Soames shook her hand and went downstairs. 'So it all passes,' he was thinking; 'passes and begins again. Poor old chap!'

Nothing—nothing! Just the scent of camphor, and dust-motes in a sunbeam through the fanlight over the door. The little old house! A mausoleum! And turning on his heel, he went out.

That afternoon, he and his family caught the train from Paddington to return to Mapledurham.

Chapter Five

The Native Heath

Val Dartie had set his heart on a certain bloodline. The Newmarket bloodstock sales were where he hoped to purchase. *He had not been* to Newmarket *since the autumn of 1899, when he stole over from Oxford for the Cambridgeshire.*

"*Don't overtire your leg, Val, and don't bet too much,*" said his wife.

With the pressure of Holly's *chest against his own, and her eyes looking into his, Val felt both leg and pocket safe. He should be moderate; Holly was always right—she had a natural aptitude. It did not seem so remarkable to him perhaps, as it might to others, that—half Dartie as he was—he should have been perfectly faithful to his young first cousin during the twenty years since he married her romantically out in the Boer War; and faithful without any feeling of sacrifice or boredom—she was so quick, so slyly always a little in front of his mood. Being cousins they had decided, or rather Holly had, to have no children; and though a little sallower, she had kept her looks, her slimness, and the colour of her dark hair.* She was independent, kept an interest in reading and her music, and rode better every year. *Out on their farm in Cape colony she had looked after all the 'nigger' babies and women in a miraculous manner. Val had come to have the feeling that she was his superior, and he did not grudge it—a great tribute.*

Tanned and wrinkled by colonial weather and the wiles inseparable from horses, and handicapped by the leg which, weakened in the Boer War, had probably saved his life in the War just past, Val was still very much as he had been in the days of his courtship. He gave the impression of one who has lived actively with horses in a sunny climate.

There seems something very solid about such a marriage, and in many ways I can see a great parallel here with the marriage of my Scottish cousin, John Thompson, who married the girl next door, Dorothy Lawrie, only next door was something of a Scottish baronial castle—Spott House. Just outside the village of Spott, the chateau-like house was close to Dunbar in East Loathian. My cousin Johnny lived a mile or two up the hill from Spott at Pathhead, a house very similar to The Breach surrounded by the large sheep farm in the Lamamuir hills where my uncle, Mark Thompson, one of Great-grandfather Oliver Longley's senders at Smithfield, had whisked my father's sister, my Aunt 'Biddy', from her sheltered suburban life in Beckenham to the moors east of Edinburgh. Because Beckenham was under the threat of the VI and V2 rockets in 1944, my mother, pregnant with me at the time, was dispatched up to Scotland to stay at Pathhead with her sister-in-law, who was also expecting her second child, my cousin 'Jaykie'. After we were both born at Drumsleagh Gardens in Edinburgh, Granny Longley sent Miss Coath up to Scotland to help my mother and Aunt 'Biddy' out. In the safety of this beautiful country I breathed my first air, but I was only there a few months. We moved south to Birmingham and then back to Beckenham. I did not return to Scotland until that day when Johnny married Dorothy Lawrie, his beloved 'Dodo'. Diane was one of her bridesmaids. I was at Cambridge at the time, but I escorted Sally on the night train to Scotland as she was able to get off from school for the great day, all the rest of the family of course, Diane being a bridesmaid, already entrenched in the little seaside town of Dunbar or at Pathhead. Diane, however, was a guest at Spott House, and she truly looked lovely as one of Dodo's bridesmaids.

After Johnny and Dodo were married in 1965 they took over the management of one of the properties of John Lawrie Farms Ltd. near Kinross—Tillyrie. Although Diane visited both Dodo and Aunt Biddy a few times, I did not go back until Aunt Biddy's ninetieth birthday in 2009. I then stayed at Tillyrie. Johnny and Dodo had bred and trained racehorses there for years much as Val Dartie and Holly were proposing to do at their farm on the Sussex Downs. Dodo also had many of the humanitarian and down to earth traits of Holly. Johnny, like Val, *always gave the impression of one who had lived actively with horses* and sheep *in a* harsh *climate.*

As they drove to the station, Val asked Holly:

"When is young Jon coming?"

"To-day."

"Is there anything you want for him? I could bring it down on Saturday."

"No; but you might come by the same train as Fleur—one-forty."

"That's a young woman who knows her way about," Val *said. "I say, has it struck you?"*

"Yes," said Holly.

"Uncle Soames and your Dad—bit awkward isn't it?"

"She won't know, and he won't know, and nothing must be said, of course. It's only for five days, Val."

"Stable secret. Righto!" If Holly thought it safe, it was. But *glancing slyly round at him, she said: "Did you notice how beautifully she asked herself?"*

"No!"

"Well she did. What do you think of her, Val?"

"Pretty, and clever; but she might run out at any corner if she got her monkey up, I should say."

"I'm wondering," Holly *murmured, "whether she is the modern young woman. One feels at sea coming home to all this."*

"You! You get the hang of things so quick."

They arrived at the station.

"What do you think of that Belgian fellow, Profond?"

"I think he's rather 'a good devil'."

Val grinned.

"He seems to me a queer fish for a friend of our family. In fact, our family is in pretty queer waters, with Uncle Soames marrying a Frenchwoman, and your Dad marrying Soames's first. Our grandfathers would have had fits!"

"So would anybody's, my dear."

He caught his train

On getting back to England, after the profitable sale of his South African farm and stud, and observing that the sun seldom shone, Val had said to himself: 'I've absolutely got to have an interest in life, or this country will give me the blues. Hunting's not enough, I'll breed and I'll train.' Now, he was on his way to make that start.

'I must have a strain of Mayfly blood.'

His twenty years of Colonial life divesting him of the dandyism in which he had been bred made him go straight to the heart of things. *Observant, quick, resourceful, he went straight into a transaction.* Thus, *a horse, a drink; and he was on his way to the heart of a Mayfly filly, when a slow voice said at his elbow:*

"Mr. Val Dartie? How's Mrs. Val Dartie? She's well, I hope." And he saw beside him at that Newmarket paddock *the Belgian he had met at his sister Imogen's.*

"Prosper Profond—I met you at lunch," said the voice.

"How are you?" murmured Val.

"I'm very well," replied Monsieur Profond. *"Here's a gentleman wants to know you—cousin of yours—Mr. George Forsyte."*

Val saw a large form, and a face clean, bull-like, he remembered it dimly from old days when he would dine with his father at the Iseeum Club.

"I used to go racing with your father," George was saying. *"How's the stud? Like to buy one of my screws?"*

Monsieur Profond invited Val to join George and he for *"a small lunch—just a small one in my car."*

"Thanks, very good of you. I'll come along in about quarter of an hour."

Val remained gazing at the Mayfly filly. He felt Profond and George were laughing at him. *The Mayfly strain—was it any better than any other. He might just as well have a flutter with his money instead.*

"No, by gum!" he muttered suddenly, using an expression normally only found in northern England, and not of his class, but one which had crept in more freely through the racial divide of class in the colonial Empire where division was not so much between that 'Forsyte' upper-middle class and a lower-middle and working class, but between black or native, and white. *"If it's no good breeding horses it's no good doing anything. What did I come for? I'll buy her."*

He went to the paddock gate to watch the Mayfly filly canter down. He could not help observing along the way, young men, two or three of them with only one arm.

One arm, or leg, lost in the trenches or 'going over the top,' blighted much of the generation just a little younger than Val. I remember at

Tonbridge even in the 1950s, this generation still working its way through our academic staff. The Head of the Science Department was a man we called "Tinfin Morris," derived from his artificial limb incurred during World War I. He taught both my father and myself.

After a 'small' lunch, Monsieur Profond accompanied Val back to the paddock for the sales.

A small lunch at Newmarket has remained with me my whole life. For some unknown reason it has become one of my most vivid memories of both my parents and my childhood and it has something to do with the pungent smell of a tiny wooden café.

We were driving up to Norfolk on one of those tours that my father used to make, chatting up the gamekeepers of his senders. It was spring—April, the Easter holidays, and we were to stay a few days at the Cliftonville Hotel in Cromer. It was part vacation, part business. We approached Newmarket about lunchtime on our journey north. It was raining, but Newmarket was bustling—the time of the sales. We stopped at this little café overlooking the paddocks for a small lunch. The café was very full of 'Monsieur Profonds' and 'Val Darties'. Their coats were wet from the rain and the café was steaming, creating a pungent odor. Then, we ordered soup—a soup that itself had a strange pungency—a green liquid of some vegetable base. Smell lingers in the memory, and perhaps the smell I record here would best be described as 'fug'. Whatever, it has remained with me, kindling one of the few real childhood memories I have of the five of us together, my mother, my father, my sisters Diane and Sally, and me. We were only all together on our school holidays, being separated at boarding schools most of the year. We were also traveling to an exciting spring break at one of our favorite places, Cromer on the Norfolk coast. We were traveling together in our spacious car, the black Armstrong Siddely Sapphire, but we were in close quarters—on a family road trip. Somehow, that closeness came together in my memory of the pungent 'fug' and the smell of the green soup in that little café at Newmarket. In my senior years, somehow it is to that café that my mind leads me when I think of my immediate family without the grandparents, the aunts and uncles, and all the other trappings of 'Forsythia'.

Val Dartie *was not flush of capital that he could touch, having spent most of what he had realised from his South African farm on his establishment in Sussex. And* on arriving back at the paddocks with Monsieur Profond, *very soon he was thinking: 'Dash it! she's going beyond me!' His limit—six hundred—was exceeded; he dropped out of the bidding. The Mayfly filly passed under the hammer at seven hundred and fifty guineas. He was turning away vexed when the slow voice of Monsieur Profond said in his ear:*

"Well, I've bought that small filly, but I don't want her; you take her and give her to your wife."

Val looked at the fellow with suspicion.

"I made a small lot of money in the War," began Monsieur Profond, reading Val's look. *"I 'ad armament shares. I like to give it away. I'm always makin' money. I want very small lot myself. I like my friends to 'ave it."*

"I'll buy her off you at the price you gave," said Val with sudden resolution.

"No," said Monsieur Profond. "You take her. I don't want her."

"Hang it! one doesn't..."

"Why not?" smiled Monsieur Profond. "I'm a friend of your family."

"Seven hundred and fifty guineas is not a box of cigars," said Val impatiently.

"All right; you keep her for me until I want her, and do what you like with her."

"So long as she's yours," said Val. "I don't mind that."

"That's all right," murmured Monsieur Profond, and moved away.

Val watched; he might be 'a good devil', but then again he might not. He saw him rejoin George Forsyte, and thereafter saw him no more.

Val stayed with his mother in London, traveling daily up to Newmarket.

It was to Winifred a vehement satisfaction to have her favourite son back from South Africa after all this time, to feel him so little changed, and to have taken a fancy to his wife. But, her brother's 'little girl' Fleur frankly puzzled her. The child was as restless as any of these modern young women—"She's a small flame in a draught," Prosper Profond had said one day after dinner—but she did not flop, or talk at the top of her voice.

In discussing her with Val, at breakfast on Saturday morning, Winifred dwelt on the family skeleton.

"That little affair of your father-in-law and your Aunt Irene, Val— it's old as the hills, of course, Fleur need know nothing about it—making

a fuss. Your Uncle Soames is very particular about that. So, you'll be careful."

"Yes! But it's dashed awkward—Holly's young half-brother is coming to live with us while he learns farming. He's there already."

"Oh!" said Winifred. "That is a gaff! What is he like?"

"Only saw him once—at Robin Hill, when we were home in 1909; he was naked and painted blue and yellow in stripes—a jolly little chap."

Winifred thought that 'rather nice', and added comfortably:

"Well, Holly's sensible; she'll know how to deal with it. I shan't tell your uncle. It'll only bother him. It's a great pleasure to have you back, my dear boy, now that I'm getting on."

"Getting on! Why! You're as young as ever. That chap Profond, Mother, is he all right?"

"Prosper Profond! Oh! the most amusing man I know."

Val told her about his purchase of the filly and how he wanted him to have the horse.

"That's so like him," murmured Winifred. "He does all sorts of things."

"Well," said Val shrewdly, "our family haven't been too lucky with that kind of cattle; they're too light-hearted for us."

It was true, and Winifred's blue study lasted a full minute before she answered:

"Oh! well! He's a foreigner, Val: one must make allowances."

'Forsytes' had such confidence in themselves and their Empire. If God is of a nationality, then assuredly "God is an Englishman"—indeed, a title of another chronicler of 'Forsythia'—R.F.Delderfield.

"All right," said Val, "I'll use Profond's filly and make it up to him, somehow."

Soon after, he left her and made his way to *Victoria Station.*

CHAPTER SIX

JON

*M**rs. Val Dartie, after twenty years of South Africa, had fallen
deeply in love, fortunately with something of her own, for the
object of her passion was the prospect in front of her windows,
the cool clear light on the green Downs. It was England again, at last!
England more beautiful than she had dreamed.*

My formative years were spent in this same area—the South
Downs—but, because it was school that took my sisters and me to
Sussex, we really didn't appreciate the beauty that was all around us.
On visiting weekends, my mother and father would take us on drives
through the rolling hills that come down to the sea, faced in chalk and
protecting small flint villages and ancient Saxon churches. Sussex—
South Saxons—this was 'Olde Englande'—pre-conquest England, itself
the area of that famed Battle of Hastings way back in 1066 that made our
Saxon dynasty French. Many years later, returning to this area, really
to see if Newlands geographically or architecturally had changed, my
breath was taken away when driving up out of the village of Alfriston.
In my childhood, my parents had stayed at the Old Star Inn in Alfriston
because their hotel, the Esplanade, on Seaford's front, was being pelted
with pebbles from the beach in a fierce English Channel storm. Windows
were breaking and basements flooding. On this particular day, however,
the sun was shining and all of a sudden as I reached the top of High and
Over, there lay the whole Cuckmere valley before me with the bumps

of the Seven Sisters beyond—Downland at its best. I had seen this hundreds of times as a boy, but revisited outside the trappings of school uniform and a school cap, it looked so different, so very beautiful. My cousin John Cuthbertson now lives in this same majestic area just outside the ancient town of Lewes. After twenty years in South Africa this magical part of old England looked so wonderful for Holly Dartie, too. We can forgive the weather for those rare moments of unbelievable English summer light. It was this that she wanted to share with her young half-brother, whom she barely knew.

Waiting for Jon at the station, *she promised herself that the first use she would make of Jon would be to take him up* to see the Downland view above her own place—*the view under this May-day sky.*

During the three days she had spent at Robin Hill on their return from South Africa, she had not seen Jon. He was away at his public school, finishing up his last term. The only time she had seen him was with Val when they had visited in 1909—that naked boy painted in stripes playing with a canoe at the pond. She felt a little strange around her step-mother, too—Irene, still for her 'the lady in grey' that used to give her piano lessons when she visited her grandpa. And then, she was astute enough, especially as an ex-volunteer nurse, to notice *something funereal in* her father's movements and *ironic gentleness* along with philosophic spiritualist murmuring, but she kept these thoughts to herself.

The most poignant memory of that little visit had been watching, unobserved, her stepmother reading to herself a letter from Jon. It was—she decided—the prettiest sight she had ever seen. Irene, lost as it were in the letter of her boy, stood at a window where the light fell on her face and her fine grey hair; her lips were moving, smiling, her dark eyes, laughing, dancing, and the hand which did not hold the letter was pressed against her breast. Holly withdrew as of a vision of perfect love, convinced that Jon must be nice.

When she saw Jon *coming out of the station with a kitbag in either hand, she was confirmed in her predisposition. He was a little like* her brother *Jolly, that long lost idle of her childhood, but eager-looking and less formal, with deeper eyes and brighter coloured hair, for he wore no hat*—and throughout 'Forsythia' even in my childhood, we 'Forsytes' rarely went without a hat—*altogether a very interesting 'little' brother!*

As soon as they reached the house, Jon gave Holly a crumpled letter that he pulled from his pocket. She read it *while he was washing—a quite short letter.*

'*MY DEAR* ,
'*You and Val will not forget, I trust, that Jon knows nothing of family history. His mother and I think he is too young at present. The boy is very dear and the apple of her eye. Verbum sapientibus.*
'*Your loving father, J.F.*'

That was all; but it renewed in Holly an uneasy regret that Fleur was coming.
After tea, Holly took Jon out onto the Downs. *They had a long talk, sitting above an old chalk-pit grown over with brambles and goosepenny. Milkwort and liverwort starred the green slope, the larks sang, and thrushes in the brake, and now and then a gull flighting inland would wheel very white against the paling sky, where the vague moon was coming up.*
Jon, who had fallen silent, said rather suddenly:
"I say, this is wonderful! There's no fat on it at all. Gull's flight and sheep-bells..."
"'Gull's flight and sheep-bells'! You're a poet, my dear!"
Jon sighed.
"Oh, Golly! No go!"
"Try, I used to at your age."
In the aftermath of the war, poetry of the expressionist kind had become quite the rage. The emotions of that slaughtered generation were poured out by the survivors—philosophical and spiritual, on human relationships and a new utopia—it was all being fashionably penned by poets of the new school—poetic prose often without rhyme or meter, but the language of soul and heart.
"Did you?" Jon replied. *"Mother says 'try' too; but I'm so rotten. Have you any of yours for me to see?"*
"My dear," Holly murmured, *"I've been married nineteen years. I only wrote verses when I wanted to be."*
"Oh!" said Jon, but his heart was racing.
Holly saw his reaction, but Holly did not equate it with Fleur. *Was Jon 'touched in the wind', then, as Val would have called it?* She felt

relieved; if Jon was touched by some young heart it would make it easier with Fleur.

Another long talk after dinner over a wood fire in the low hall, and there seemed little left to know about Jon except anything of real importance, Holly parted from him at his bedroom door, having seen twice over that he had everything, with the conviction that she would love him, and Val would like him. He was eager, but did not gush; he was a splendid listener, sympathetic, reticent about himself. He liked riding, rowing and fencing, among my own sports during school and university, and like me, he did not like ball games. *He saved moths from candles, and couldn't bear spiders, but put them out of doors in screws of paper sooner than kill them. In a word, he was amiable. She went to sleep, thinking he would suffer horribly if anybody hurt him; but who would hurt him?*

Jon, on the other hand, sat awake at his window with a bit of paper and a pencil, writing his first 'real' poem by the light of a candle because there was not enough moon to see by, only enough to make the night seem fluttery and as if engraved on silver. He had a feeling such as the winds of Spring must have, trying their first songs among the blossom. And he thought with a sort of discomfiture: 'I shan't be able to show it to Mother.' He slept terribly well, when he did sleep, overwhelmed by novelty.

CHAPTER SEVEN

FLEUR

To avoid the awkwardness of questions which could not be answered, all that had been told Jon was:

"There's a girl coming down with Val for the weekend."

For the same reason, all that had been told Fleur was: "We've got a youngster staying with us."

The two yearlings, as Val Dartie called them in his thoughts, met therefore in a manner which for unpreparedness left nothing to be desired. They were thus introduced by Holly:

"This is Jon, my little brother; Fleur's a cousin of ours, Jon."

Jon, who was coming in through a French window out of strong sunlight, was so confounded by the providential nature of this miracle, that he had time to hear Fleur say calmly: "Oh, how do you do?" as if he had never seen her, and to understand dimly from the quickest imaginable movement of her head that he never had seen her. He bowed therefore over her hand in an intoxicated manner, and became more silent than the grave. He knew better than to speak.

He listened therefore to Fleur's swift and rapt allusions to the jolliness of everything, plied her with scones and jam, and got away as soon as might be.

In his room, he *began to copy out his poem—which of course he would never dare to show her—till the sound of horses hooves roused him, and, leaning from his window, he saw her riding forth with Val.*

500

Why? If he hadn't bolted, he could be riding with them, too. *'Silly brute!'* he thought; *'I always miss my chances.'*

Why couldn't he be self confident and ready?

He did not get to see her again until dinner. Awkwardly, they avoided eye contact or conversation at the table. Jon didn't speak to anyone, but Fleur *was talking so well* to the others, *swooping with swift wing this way and that. Wonderful that she had learned an art which he found so disgustingly difficult. She must think him hopeless, indeed.*

"Jon is going to be a farmer," he heard Holly say; "a farmer and a poet."

Jon *glanced up reproachfully, caught the comic lift of her eyebrow just like their father's, laughed, and felt better.*

The conversation turned to Val's Newmarket encounter with Monsieur Profond.

Alone with Val after dinner, he sipped port deferentially.

"I used to know your brother up at Oxford," Val said, *"the one who died in the Boer War. We had a fight in New College Gardens. That was a queer business,"* he added, musing; *"a good deal came out of it."*

Jon's eyes opened wide; all was pushing him towards historical research, when his sister's voice said gently from the doorway:

"Come along, you two."

Fleur having declared that it was "simply too wonderful to stay indoors," *they all went out. Moonlight was frosting the dew, and an old sundial threw a long shadow. Two box hedges at right angles, dark and square, barred off the orchard. Fleur turned through that angled opening.*

"Come on!" she called. Jon glanced at the others and followed.

"Isn't it jolly?" she cried when they were alone.

"Rather!"

She reached up, twisted off a blossom and, twirling it in her fingers, said:

"I suppose I can call you Jon?"

"I should think so just."

"All right. But you know there is a feud between our families?"

Jon stammered: *"Feud? Why?"*

"It's ever so romantic and silly. That's why I pretended we hadn't met. Shall we get up early to-morrow morning and go for a walk before breakfast and have it out? I hate being slow about things, don't you?"

Jon murmured a rapturous assent.

"Six o'clock, then. I think your mother's beautiful."
Jon said fervently, *"Yes, she is."*
"I love all kinds of beauty," went on Fleur, *"when it's exciting."*
She caught Jon's hand.
"Of all things in the world, don't you think caution's the most awful? Smell the moonlight!"
She thrust the blossom against his face; Jon agreed giddily that of all things in the world caution was the worst, and bending over, kissed the hand which held his.
"That's nice and old fashioned," said Fleur calmly. *"You're frightfully silent, Jon. Still, I like silence when it's swift."* She let go his hand. *"Did you think I dropped my handkerchief on purpose?"*
"No!" cried Jon, intensely shocked.
"Well, I did, of course. Let's go back, or they'll think we're doing this on purpose, too." In her white dress, *she ran like a ghost among the trees.*
Back on the lawn she greeted Holly:
"It's quite wonderful in there."
Back inside, *she bade* Jon *a casual and demure good-night, which made him think he had been dreaming...*
In her bedroom, Fleur wrote to her girlfriend Cherry, an old school friend from that seminary in the West Country.

'I believe I'm in love. I've got it in the neck, only the feel-
ing is really lower down. He's a second cousin—such a child,
about six months older and ten years younger than I am. Boys
always fall in love with their seniors, and girls with their
juniors or with old men of forty. Don't laugh, but his eyes are
the truest things I ever saw; and he's quite divinely silent!
There's a feud between our families, which makes it really
exciting. Yes! And I may have to use subterfuge and come on
you for invitations—if so, you'll know why! My father doesn't
want us to know each other, but I can't help that. Life's too
short. I'm staying with his sister—who married my cousin; it's
all mixed up, but I mean to pump her to-morrow.
'Jon is the sort that lights up and goes out; about five feet
ten, still growing, and I believe he's going to be a poet. If you
laugh at me I've done with you forever. I perceive all sorts
of difficulties, but you know when I really want a thing I get

it. This is my first, and I feel as if it were going to be my last, which is absurd, of course, by all the laws of Nature and morality. If you mock me I will smite you, and if you tell anybody I will never forgive you. So much so, that I almost don't think I'll send this letter. Anyway, I'll sleep over it. So good-night, my Cherry-oh!'

CHAPTER EIGHT

IDYLL ON GRASS

There was not a cloud in the sky as Fleur and Jon set out on their pre-breakfast walk. *The Down dipped and rose again toward Chanctonbury Ring; a sparkle of far sea came into view.* So it was at Newlands where from the 'Big Schoolroom' window we looked out at the Down of Seaford Head with that little sparkle of sea off to the right—the very view that had fired my imagination at the age of eight into believing it to be the sight of a mystical experience for me, a vision whereby God called me to serve Him in some special way—This vision of a bare wooden cross rising up on Seaford Head with the voice of God booming from it like Kitchener looking for recruits in World War I—"God needs you!"

This was the simple vision that took me away from following into the 'Forsyte' family business, into a life of non-'Forsyte' philosophical doubt and exploration. It all happened on a bright sunny afternoon looking out at those Downs. We had just had our government supplied third of a pint of milk, something that every child of my generation received in school—a socialist promise of better health in a society recovering from the rigors of wartime food rationing. The little milk bottles with their oily cardboard tops and wax reinforced paper straws collected souring odors around their rims, but it was a compulsory drink, and at school we did what we were told to do—we drank. As a prefect came round with a crate and I placed my empty bottle back,

I looked up out of the great schoolroom window to see that familiar vista of Seaford Head beside the English Channel that sparkled in the afternoon sun. The great cross rose up before my eyes. It was worn, made from big, old, rough-hewn timbers. The form of Jesus was not on the cross, but when it reached the upright state, the voice of God boomed from it: "God needs you!" That was my vocation. The cross faded, but my loyalty to the call, although it has taken many interesting turns throughout my varied spiritual life, has never wavered.

At first, I followed every traditional belief of the Anglican Church, then I deviated in my flirt with adolescent reason. After the Church of England turned me down as an unsuitable candidate for ordination in 1962, thinking I came "from too privileged and sheltered a background," at Cambridge I thrived on 'avant-garde' interpretations of theology and gained my masters degree. For eleven years I was a licensed lay-reader and preacher in the Church of Ireland. During that time, I had the rare experience of being acting dean of a cathedral and I was trained for religious broadcasting. I was a conference leader at the 1970 Centenary Conference of the disestablishment of the Church of Ireland, during which I read the lessons in pre-microphone days at the ceremonial Eucharist in St. Anne's Cathedral, Belfast. As a member of the General Synod in the Church of Ireland, I was asked to step down from the rostrum by the Archbishop of Dublin for an attack I made on the 'Thirty Nine Articles of the Anglican Church'. Most gratifying of all for me, however, was the statement made many years later when I returned to Ireland. A member of my old congregation at Cashel Cathedral said to me: "We have always remembered you for your extraordinary sermons."

Later, in the United States, I flirted with ordination again in the Diocese of Georgia. I became a licensed lay reader and preacher at Christ Church, Frederica, on St. Simons Island. I interviewed for theological college at St. Lukes within the University of the South at Sewanee, Tennessee, and Union Theological College in New York. Almost within my grasp, ordination was then removed from me again on problems with immigration status. I drifted into other areas of spirituality while traveling the world as a cruise director. Then, in 1988, inspired by the rock musicals *Jesus Christ, Superstar* and *Godspell,* I started on my life's work, a massive interpretation of a plausible life of Mary Magdalene and her times. It was hard to get this huge volume published as an unknown author, and eventually I had to abandon it just in time to let others like

Dan Brown take the glory with *The Da Vinci Code*. Finally, however, after much revision, my work was published as *The Magdala Trilogy*, comprised of three books, *A Star's Legacy, Beyond the Olive Grove,* and *The Mist of God*. I became a keen follower of *The Jesus Seminar*, becoming a member of its lay branch, *The Westar Institute*.

My interpretation of the Divine and especially of the Divinity of Jesus of Nazareth, does differ somewhat from conventional thought, and is one of the reasons that I have always believed was why his image was not there on that rough-hewn cross when it rose up before me on the Down of Seaford Head. Divinity is too vast for the capsule of Christianity, but the role of Jesus as a catalyst for opening that capsule up is powerful to say the least. I go on paying heed to the booming voice of the Almighty, whoever and whatever that may be: "God needs you!"

On that early summer morning looking out toward Chanctonbury Ring, Fleur and John *discussed the nature of their homes and previous existences which had a kind of fascinating unreality up on that lonely height. There remained but one thing solid in Jon's past—his mother; but one thing solid in Fleur's—her father.*

Then, distracted by a sparrow hawk, Jon showed his interest in birds. Fleur *spoke of dogs, and the way people treated them. It was wicked to keep them on chains! She would like to flog people who did that. Jon was astonished to find her so humanitarian.*

"It's their sense of property," Jon *said, "which makes people chain things. The last generation thought of nothing but property, and that's why there was the War."*

"Oh!" said Fleur, "I never thought of that. Your people and mine quarelled about property. And anyway we've all got it—at least, I suppose your people have."

"Oh! yes, luckily; I don't suppose I should be any good at making money."

"If you were, I don't believe I should like you."

Jon slipped his hand tremulously under her arm.

Fleur looked straight before her and chanted:

"Jon, Jon, the farmer's son,
Stole a pig, and away he run."

Jon's arm crept around her waist.

"This is rather sudden," said Fleur calmly; "do you often do it!"

Jon dropped his arm. But when she laughed, his arm stole back again; and Fleur continued singing.

Then Jon sang. The larks joined in, sheep-bells, and an early morning church far away over in Steyning. They went on from tune to tune, till Fleur said:

"My God! I am hungry now!"

"Oh! I am sorry!"

She looked round into his face.

"Jon, you're rather a darling."

And she pressed his hand against her waist. Jon almost reeled from happiness.

They walked on.

"If the grass is dry," said Fleur, "let's sit down for half a minute."

Jon took off his coat and they shared it.

"Smell! Actually wild thyme!"

With his arm round her waist again, they sat some minutes in silence.

Then realizing the time, Fleur jumped up. "We shall be most fearfully late, and look so silly, and put them on their guard. Look here, Jon! We only came out to get an appetite for breakfast, and lost our way. See?"

"Yes," said Jon.

"It's serious. There'll be a stopper put on us. Are you a good liar?"

"I believe not very, but I can try."

Fleur frowned.

"You know," she said. "I realise that they don't mean us to be friends."

"Why not?"

"I told you why."

"But that's silly."

"Yes, but you don't know my father!"

"I suppose he's fearfully fond of you."

"You see, I'm an only child. And so are you—of your mother. Isn't it a bore? There's so much expected of one. By the time they've done expecting, one's as good as dead."

"Yes," muttered Jon, "life's beastly short. One wants to live forever, and know everything."

"And love everybody?"

"No," cried Jon; "I only want to love once—you."

"Indeed! You're coming on! Oh! Look! There's the chalk pit; we can't be very far now, let's run."

Fleur flung back her hair.

"Well," she said, "in case of accidents, you may give me one kiss, Jon," and she pushed her cheek forward. With ecstasy he kissed that soft hot cheek.

"Now, remember! We lost our way; and leave it to me as much as you can. I'm going to be rather beastly to you; it's safer; try and be beastly to me! Look! There they are! Wave your hat! Oh! you haven't got one. Well, I'll cooee! Get a little away from me and look sulky."

Five minutes later, entering the house and doing his utmost to look sulky, Jon heard her clear voice in the dining-room:

"Oh! I'm simply ravenous! He's going to be a farmer—and he loses his way! The boy's an idiot!"

Chapter Nine

Goya

After lunch Soames escaped to his picture gallery. *Fleur was not yet home. She had been expected on Wednesday; had wired that it would be Friday; and again on Friday that it would be Sunday afternoon; and here was her aunt, and her cousins, the Cardigans, and this fellow Profond, and everything flat as a pancake for the want of her. He stood before his Gauguin—sorest point of his collection. He was wondering whether Profond would take it* off his hands—the *fellow seemed not to know what to do with his money—when he heard his sister's voice say: "I think that's a horrid thing, Soames," and saw that Winifred had followed him up.*

Soames uttered a glum laugh. "You didn't come up to tell me that?"

"No. Do you know that Jolyon's boy is staying with Val and his wife?"

Soames spun round.

"What?"

"Yes," drawled Winifred; "he's gone to live with them there while he learns farming." She then tried to reassure him: *"I had warned Val that neither of them was to be spoken to about old matters."*

"Why didn't you tell me before?"

"Fleur does what she likes. You've always spoiled her, besides, my dear boy, what's the harm?"

*"The harm!" muttered Soames. "Why she..." he checked himself.
The Juno, the handkerchief, Fleur's eyes, her questions, and now this
delay in her return...*

"If I were you, I should tell her of that old matter," said Winifred.
*"It's no good thinking that girls in these days are as they used to be.
Where they pick up their knowledge I can't tell, but they seem to know
everything. If you don't like to speak of it, I could for you."*

Soames shook his head.

"No," he said, "not yet. Never if I can help it."

Winifred left.

*Soames passed into the corner where, side by side, hung his real
Goya and the copy of the fresco 'La Vendemia'. His acquisition of the
real Goya rather beautifully illustrated the cobweb of vested interests.*

The painting had been acquired by a member of the aristocracy
whose ancestor had found it during some Spanish war—*it was in a word
loot. It was only a fair Goya, but almost unique in England.* As members
of the House of Lords, the lineage of the family had decided to leave
this Goya and other paintings to the Nation, but after the bitter attack on
the Lords and their privileges in 1909 by the Liberals, heralding income
tax and death duties, *the noble owner became alarmed and angry. "If,"
he said to himself, "they think they can have it both ways they are very
much mistaken. So long as they leave me in quiet enjoyment the nation
can have some of my pictures at my death. But if the nation is going to
bait me, and rob me like this, I'm damned if I won't sell the bloody lot.
They can't have my private property and my public spirit—both."*

Thus Soames acquired the Goya. *And next to it was hanging the
copy of 'La Vendimia'. There she was—the little wretch—uncannily like*
Fleur, *looking back at him in her dreamy mood, the mood in Fleur he
loved best because he felt so much safer when she looked like that.*

*He was still gazing when the scent of a cigar impinged on his
nostrils, and a voice said:*

"Well, Mr. Forsyde, what you goin' to do with this small lot?"

*That Belgian chap, whose mother—as if Flemish blood were not
enough—had been Armenian! Subduing a natural irritation, he said:*

"Are you a judge of pictures?"

"Well, I've got a few myself."

"Any Post-Impressionists?"

"Ye-es, I rather like them."

"What do you think of this," said Soames, pointing to the Gauguin.

Monsieur Profond protruded his lower lip and short pointed beard.

"Rather fine, I think; do you want to sell it?"

"Yes," Soames said.

"What do you want for it?"

"What I gave."

"All right," said Monsieur Profond. "I'll be glad to take that small picture. Post-Impressionists—they're awful dead, but they're amusin'. I don't care for pictures much, but I've got some, just a small lot."

"What do you care for?" asked Soames somewhat irritated by the foreigner despite the deal.

"I don't worry," replied Monsieur Profond smiling; "we're born, and we die. Half the world's starvin'. I feed a small lot of babies out in my mother's country; but what's the use? Might as well throw my money in the river."

The last real generation of 'Forsytes' even into my own childhood, but particularly my parents contemporaries, were all brought up under the threat of the 'starving Armenians'. Turkey had routed Armenia and resultant hardship there found its way into the language of almost every 'Forsyte' nursery. If 'Forsyte' children between the wars did not eat all the food on their nursery plate, Nanny would say in a knowing voice about something of which she really knew nothing at all—"Eat up; remember the starving Armenians."

"What shall I make my cheque for?" pursued Monsieur Profond.

"Five hundred," said Soames shortly.

Five hundred pounds had been exactly the sum of money that Charles Spencelaugh had owed my Great-grandfather Oliver in 1894 when he commissioned those two portraits from him of Minnie and himself to cover the debt. It is interesting that the perceived value, at least to my great-grandfather, of those portraits should equal that of a post-impressionist Gauguin some thirty-five years later.

Monsieur Profond held out the cheque and smiling he drifted out of the Gallery again blue and solid like the smoke of his excellent cigar.

'He's a cosmopolitan,' he thought a few minutes later *watching Profond emerge from under the verandah with Annette, and saunter down the lawn toward the river. What his wife saw in the fellow he didn't know, unless it was that he could speak her language; and there passed*

*in Soames what Monsieur Profond would have called a 'small doubt'
whether Annette was not too handsome to be walking with any one so
'cosmopolitan.' He watched them walk along the path at the bottom of
the garden. A young man in flannels joined them down there—a Sunday
caller no doubt, from up the river. He went back to his Goya. He was
still staring at that replica of Fleur, and worrying over Winifred's news,
when his wife's voice said:*

"Mr. Michael Mont, Soames. You invited him to see your
pictures."

There was the cheerful young man of the Gallery off Cork Street!

"Turned up, you see, sir; I live only four miles from Pangbourne.
Jolly day, isn't it?"

*Soames scrutinised his visitor. He seemed always grinning almost to
annoyance. Why didn't he grow the rest of those idiotic little moustaches,
which made him look like a music-hall buffoon? What on earth were
young men about, deliberately lowering their class with these tooth-
brushes, or little slug whiskers? Ugh! Affected young idiots! In other
respects he was presentable, and his flannels very clean.*

"Happy to see you!" *he said.*

The young man looked at 'La Vendimia'. *"I say," he said, "'some'
picture!"*

"Yes," *Soames said dryly,* "that's not a Goya. It's a copy. I had it
painted because it reminded me of my daughter."

"By Jove! I thought I knew the face, sir. Is she here?"

The frankness of his interest almost disarmed Soames.

"She'll be in after tea," *he said.* "Shall we go round the
pictures?"

And Soames began that round that never tired him, somewhat
surprised by his guest's enthusiasm. *It was after the young man had
whistled before a Whistler, with the words, "D'you think he ever really
saw a naked woman, sir?" that Soames remarked:*

"What are you, Mr. Mont, if I may ask?"

"I, sir? I was going to be a painter, but the war knocked that. Then
in the trenches, you know, I used to dream of the Stock Exchange, snug
and warm and just noisy enough. But the Peace knocked that; shares
seem off, don't they? I've only been demobbed about a year. What do
you recommend, sir?"

"Have you got money?"

"Well," answered the young man, "I've got a father; I kept him alive during the War, so he's bound to keep me alive now. Though, of course, there's the question whether he ought to be allowed to hang on to his property. What do you think about that, sir?"

Soames didn't answer.

"The old man has fits when I tell him he may have to work yet. He's got land, you know; it's a fatal disease."

"This is my real Goya," said Soames dryly.

"By George! He was a swell. I saw a Goya in Munich once that bowled me middle stump. Couldn't he just paint! He makes Velasquez stiff, don't you think?"

"I have no Velasquez," said Soames.

The young man stared. "No," he said; *"only nations or profiteers can afford him, I suppose. I say, why shouldn't all the bankrupt nations sell their Velasquez and Titians and other swells to profiteers by force, and then pass a law that anyone who holds a picture by an Old Master must hang it in a public gallery! There seems something in that."*

"Shall we go down to tea?" said Soames, mulling on the man's political philosophy. *'He's not dense.'*

The tea party looked like a Goya painting down to the daring of light and shade and all the accoutrements. They were all there, except Fleur.

After tea, Jack Cardigan invited Prosper Profond and Michael Mont to join him at the tennis court, and suggested Fleur might join them if she comes.

Ah! and why didn't she come? Soames *did not like the look of things! He saw her dog, a retriever, lying on the drive in a patch of sunlight, and called to him. "Hallo, old fellow—waiting for her too?"*

Ah! There was the car at last! It drew up, it had luggage, but no Fleur.

"Miss Fleur is walking up, sir, by the towing path," the chauffeur said.

Walking all those miles? Soames stared. The man's face had the beginning of a smile on it. What was he grinning at? And very quickly Soames turned saying, "All right, Sims!" and went into the house.

He mulled over his thoughts looking at the towing path from his gallery. *The staccato shouts of Jack Cardigan pursuing the ball, the laugh of young Mont rose in the stillness and came in. He hoped they were making that chap Profond run.*

In front of him, *the girl in 'La Vendimia' stood with her arm akimbo and her dreamy eyes looking past him. 'I've done all I could for you,' he thought, 'since you were no higher than my knee. You aren't going to—to—hurt me, are you?'*

But the Goya copy answered not.

'Why doesn't she come?'

CHAPTER TEN

TRIO

On Thursday evening, as *they were standing in the bay window of the drawing-room* at Wansdon under the Downs, *dressed for dinner,* Fleur hatched a plan to Jon.

"Jon, I'm going home on Sunday by the 3.40 from Paddington; if you were to go home on Saturday you could come up on Sunday and take me down, and just get back here by the last train, after. You were going home anyway, weren't you?"

Jon nodded.

"Anything to be with you," he said; *"only why need I pretend..."*

Fleur slipped her little finger into his palm:

"You have no instinct, Jon; you must leave things to me. It's serious about our people. We've simply got to be secret at present, if we want to be together."

And as it had been all week, when the door opened they acted as if they didn't really care for each other that much. For nine days *never had Fleur been so 'fine', Holly so watchful, Val so stable secretive, Jon so silent and disturbed.*

Diane and I never really had secret courtships under the noses of our family; in fact we hardly ever had courtships. Sally, however, a part of the next generation of liberation—really the first generation after 'Forsythia', but still living with its trappings—had several. Diane and I called them her "secret boyfriends," and although there was little

515

about them that was scandalous, there was enough. One was a school relationship with a boy in Seaford that certainly would not have been espoused by my parents, who believed in the rules and regulations of boarding schools and their bounds; the other was with a man in Beckenham, considerably older than Sally and divorced. I remember the absolute fear and panic of my parents one night when Sally did not come home. Hospitals were alerted and the police informed, although Diane and I, somewhat disturbed that our sister had so upset my parents, were pretty sure she had spent the night with this man—a man who incidentally was very respectable and was ultimately quite well accepted by my family, although by then the relationship had been curtailed to 'friendship'.

The next evening, after dinner at *about eleven* Jon *had packed his bag, and was leaning out of his window, half miserable, and half lost in a dream of Paddington Station, when he heard a tiny sound, as of a finger-nail tapping on his door. He rushed to it and listened. Again the sound. It was a nail. He opened. Oh! What a lovely thing came in!*

"I wanted to show you my fancy dress," it said, and struck an attitude at the foot of his bed.

Jon drew a long breath and leaned against the door. The apparition wore white muslim on its head, a fichu round its bare neck over a wine-coloured dress, fulled out below its slender waist. It held one arm akimbo, and the other raised, right-angled, holding a fan which touched its head.

"This ought to be a basket of grapes," it whispered, "but I haven't got it here. It's my Goya dress. And this is the attitude in the picture. Do you like it?"

"It's a dream."

The apparition pirouetted. "Touch it and see."

Jon knelt down and took the skirt reverently.

"Grape colour," came the whisper, "all grapes—La Vendicia—the vintage."

Jon's fingers scarcely touched each side of the waist; he looked up with adoring eyes.

"Oh! Jon," it whispered; bent, kissed his forehead, pirouetted again, and, gliding out, was gone.

Jon stayed on his knees a long time. And his forehead where it had been kissed had a little cool place between the brows, like the imprint of a flower—a 'fleur'. Love filled his soul, that love of boy for girl which knows so little, hopes so much, would not brush the down off for the world.

Yes, Jon was a sensitive soul, but also reticent, afraid to really show his feelings with *a determination not to know when he was beaten.* To this end, possessed of that stiff upper lip, he was truly a 'Forsyte'. *Sensitive, imaginative, affectionate boys get a bad time at* boarding *school, but Jon had* weathered the system, *instinctively kept his nature dark, and been but normally unhappy there.* Those who were happiest in those rigid schools of 'Forsythia', and they were the majority, were the ones who played rugger and cricket with a passion—the likes of Jack Cardigan or my cousin, John Cuthbertson—the rest of us, including myself, experienced the pride of discovering that we were part of the three percent, and made the best of the system knowing that it would give us entry into the club. So, if sensitive, we kept our nature dark.

Back at home that Saturday, Jon had a sensitive moment with his mother. He had dreaded not being frank and natural with her, but it was she who broached the subject:

"So you've had our little friend of the confectioner's there, Jon. What is she like on second thoughts?"

With relief, and a high colour, Jon answered:

"Oh! awfully jolly, Mum."

Her arm pressed his.

The fact that Jon had always addressed his mother as "Mum" was an indication of the unusually non-'Forsyte' nature of their bond. As seen, 'Forsyte' mothers were somewhat remote to their children, who had been brought up in the nursery and at private boarding schools. "Mummy" was the preferred designation of Jon's generation, 'Mum' being too familiar. After all, the generation before, even in my family with Grandpop, had addressed their parents as "Mater and Pater." Granny Mabs was always "Mother" to my mother and Aunt Eileen, one step down from 'Mater' and 'Pater'; and "Mummy," rarely 'Mum', was certainly the preference of my own generation.

But *Jon had never loved* or bonded with his mother *so much as in that minute which seemed to falsify Fleur's fears and to release his soul. He turned to look at her, but something in her smiling face—something which perhaps only he would have caught—stopped the words bubbling up in him* to tell all. *Could fear go with a smile? If so, there was fear on her face. And out of Jon tumbled quite other words, about farming, Holly and the Downs. Talking fast, he waited for her to come back to*

Fleur. But she did not. Nor did his father mention her, though of course, he too, must know. What deprivation, and killing of reality was in this silence about Fleur—when he was so full of her; when his mother was so full of Jon, and his father so full of his mother! And so the trio spent the evening of that Saturday.

After dinner his mother played the piano. Jon *gazed at his mother but he saw Fleur—Fleur in the moonlit orchard, Fleur in the sunlit gravel-pit, Fleur in that fancy dress, swaying, whispering, stooping, kissing his forehead.*

When he went up to bed his mother came into his room. She stood at the window, and said:

"Those cypresses your grandfather planted down there have done wonderfully. I always think they look wonderful under a drooping moon. I wish you had known your grandfather, Jon."

"Were you married to father when he was alive?" asked Jon suddenly.

"No, dear; he died in '92—very old—eighty-five, I think."

Jon slipped his hand through his mother's arm. "Tell me about the family quarrel, Mum."

He felt her arm quivering. "No, dear; that's for your father some day, if he thinks fit."

"Then it was serious," said Jon, with a catch in his breath.

"Yes." And there was a silence, during which neither knew whether the arm or the hand within it were quivering most.

Irene was still looking at the cypress trees—Italian trees.

"Jon, Father says we may go to Italy, you and I, for two months. Would you like?"

A fortnight ago it would have been perfection; now it filled him with dismay; he felt that the sudden suggestion had to do with Fleur. He stammered out:

"Oh! yes; only—I don't know. Ought I—now I've just begun my farming apprenticeship. *I'd like to think it over."*

"Yes, dear; think it over. But better now than when you've begun farming seriously. Italy with you—! It would be nice!"

Jon put his arm round her waist, still slim and firm as a girl's—as Fleur's.

"Do you think you ought to leave Father?" he said feebly, feeling very mean.

"Father suggested it; he thinks you ought to see Italy at least before you settle down to anything."

He knew, yes—he knew—They wanted to keep him from Fleur.

And as if she felt that process going on, his mother said:

"Good-night darling. Have a good sleep and think it over. But it would be lovely."

* * *

Irene, after she had stood a moment in her own room, passed through the dressing-room between it and her husband's.

"Well?"

"He will think it over, Jolyon."

Watching her lips that wore a little drawn smile, Jolyon said quietly:

"You had better let me tell him, and have done with it. After all, Jon has the instincts of a gentleman. He has only to understand..."

"Only! He can't understand; that's impossible."

"I believe I could have at his age."

Irene caught his hand. "You were always more of a realist than Jon; and never so innocent."

"That's true," said Jolyon. "It's queer, isn't it? You and I would tell our story to the world without a particle of shame; but our own boy stumps us."

"We've never cared whether the world approves or not."

"Jon would not disapprove of us!"

"Oh! Jolyon, yes. He's in love. I feel he's in love. And he'd say: 'My mother once married without love! How could she have!' It'll seem to him a crime! And so it was!"

"If the boy is really in love, he won't forget, even if he goes to Italy," said Jolyon *with a wry smile. "We're a tenacious breed; and he'll know by instinct why he's being sent. Nothing will really cure him but the shock of being told."*

"Let me try, anyway," Irene pleaded.

Jolyon stood a moment without speaking. Between this devil and this deep sea—the pain of a dreaded disclosure and the grief of losing his wife for two months—he secretly hoped for the devil, yet if she wished for the deep sea he must put up with it. After all, it would be training for that departure from which there would be no return, which was now uttermost in his thoughts. *And, taking her in his arms, he kissed her eyes, and said:*

"As you will, my love."

CHAPTER ELEVEN

DUET

J *on reached Paddington station half an hour before his time and a full week after as it seemed to him. Every minute was an hour long. After nineteen had passed, he saw her with a bag and a porter wheeling her luggage. She came swiftly; she came cool. She greeted him as if he were a brother.*

"First class," she said to the porter, "corner seats, opposite."

Jon admired her frightful self-possession.

"Can't we get a carriage to ourselves?" he whispered.

"No good; it's a stopping train. After Maidenhead perhaps. Look natural, Jon."

They got in—with two other beasts!—oh! heaven! He tipped the porter unnaturally in his confusion.

Fleur hid herself behind a magazine—*the* Lady's Mirror. *Jon imitated her behind the* Landsman. *The train started.*

'Forsytes' were brought up in the nursery to speak only when spoken to, and never to speak to strangers. This practice was certainly found when they used public transportation. City businessmen traveling daily to London from her suburbs regularly hid behind their newspapers. Was this nursery training the foundation of British reserve? It was not 'done' when traveling on a train or bus to communicate with strangers, or even one's own family within earshot of strangers.

I am reminded again of that incident when crossing the channel to Dover after a visit to Italy. Even though traveling First class, that middle aged English couple were seated across the aisle from me in the ferry's lounge, he in a suit and bowler hat, and she in a tweed skirt and twin set—the fashion in that last decade of 'Forsythia'. He was peering into his copy of the *Times*. She kept asking him that barrage of questions. To each question without blinking from behind his paper, he replied: "Yes, darling." Finally, frustrated and again without so much as raising an eyebrow behind his newspaper he said in exactly the same monotone: "Shut up, darling." The communication ceased.

Eventually, however, *Fleur let the* Lady's Mirror *fall and leaned forward.*

"Well?" she said.

"It's seemed about fifteen days."

She nodded, and Jon's face lighted up at once.

"Look natural," murmured Fleur, still fully aware of public transportation etiquette, *and went off into a bubble of laughter. It hurt Jon. How could he look natural with Italy hanging over him? He had meant to break it to her gently, but now he blurted it out.*

"They want me to go to Italy with Mother for two months."

Fleur drooped her eyelids, turned a little pale and bit her lips.

"Oh!" she said.

That "Oh!" was like the quick drawback of the wrist in fencing ready for riposte. It came.

"You must go!"

"Go?" said Jon in a strangled voice.

"Of course."

"But—two months—it's ghastly."

"No," said Fleur, "six weeks. You'll have forgotten me by then. We'll meet in the National Gallery the day after you get back."

Jon laughed nervously, hoping the strangers were not listening.

"But suppose you've forgotten me," he muttered into the noise of the train.

Fleur shook her head.

"Some other beast..." murmured Jon.

Her foot touched his.

"No other beast," she said, lifting the Lady's Mirror.

The train stopped; two passengers got out, and one got in.

'I shall die,' thought Jon, 'if we're not alone at all.'

The train went on; and again Fleur leaned forward.

"I never let go," she said; "do you?"

Jon shook his head vehemently.

"Never!" he said. "Will you write to me?"

"No; but you can—to my club."

She had a club, she was wonderful.

The idea that ladies should have membership of clubs was almost unknown among the previous generation of 'Forsytes'. Again, this was illustrated by Jules Verne in *Around the World in Eighty Days*, when he shocked his readers by having Phileas Fogg introduce his Indian princess to the Reform Club the night he won his wager. In the brave new world following universal suffrage and the Great War, ladies' clubs had been formed, and some men's clubs opened a ladies' section, although for the most part the famous clubs remained single sex until the demise of 'Forsythia'. The Cork and County Club in Ireland had a small ladies' lounge where Mrs. Albertini and I would hole up after shopping sprees, or my frequent dentist visits, in the city of Cork in the early 1960s. There, we would wait for Mr. Albertini, who usually spent a good part of the day in the men's bar with his fishing friend Group Captain George Russell. Ironically, after I visited India in 1970 with my sister, I was invited to speak to the 'Cork and County Literary and Scientific Society' on *My Impressions of India: Past and Present*. The meeting took place at the venerable old Cork and County Club that provided reciprocal membership with such prestigious establishments as Crockfords in London and the Knickerbocker in New York. The 'Literary and Scientific' reminded me of those popular Victorian societies that observed many things in discussion behind closed doors such as Mr. Samuel Pickwick's dissertation on the tittle bats of Hampstead Heath in Charles Dicken's *Pickwick Papers*! I might add, however, almost as a throw back to Dickensian times, on the occasion that I addressed the 'Literary and Scientific' at the Cork and County Club, as the speaker, I wore white tie and tails!

"Did you pump Holly?" Jon Forsyte muttered.

"Yes, but I got nothing. I didn't dare pump hard."

"What can it be?" cried Jon.

"I shall find out all right."

A long silence followed until Fleur said: "This is Maidenhead; stand by, Jon!"

The train stopped. The remaining passenger got out. Fleur drew down her blind.

"Quick!" she cried. "Hang out! Look as much as a beast as you can."

Jon blew his nose and scowled; never in all his life had he scowled like that! An old lady recoiled, a young one tried the handle. It turned, but the door would not open. The train moved, the young lady darted to another carriage.

"What luck!" cried Jon. "It jammed."

"Yes," said Fleur. "I was holding it."

The train moved out and Jon fell on his knees.

"Look out for the corridor," she whispered; "and—quick!"

Her lips met his. And though their kiss only lasted perhaps ten seconds Jon's soul left his body and went so far beyond, that, when he was again sitting opposite that demure figure, he was pale as death. He heard her sigh, and the sound seemed to him the most precious thing he had ever heard—an exquisite declaration that he meant something to her.

"Six weeks isn't really long," she said; "and you can easily make it six if you keep your head out there, and never seem to think of me."

Jon gasped.

"This is just what's really wanted, Jon, to convince them, don't you see? If we're just as bad when you come back they'll stop being ridiculous about it. Only, I'm sorry it's not Spain; there's a girl in a Goya picture at Madrid who's like me, Father says. Only she isn't— we've got a copy of her."

It was to Jon like a ray of sunshine piercing through a fog. "I'll make it Spain," he said, "Mother won't mind; she's never been there. And my father thinks a lot of Goya."

"Oh! yes, he's a painter, isn't he?"

"Only water-colour," said Jon with honesty.

Throughout the generations of 'Forsythia', watercolor was the medium used by refined young ladies schooled by amateur governesses. Such ladies rarely painted in oils. Oil was the masculine medium of real artists. My sister Diane was an extremely talented watercolor painter, but once she studied professionally at the Byam Shaw School of Art and at the Royal Academy, it was her oil paintings that won her awards. As a painter myself, I always found this attitude toward watercolors a little frustrating. I paint mostly in oils, but I have to admit that it is easier to create a poor oil painting than it is to create a really good watercolor. Watercolor, at its best, is one of the hardest of media to master, but for four generations of 'Forsytes' it was renegaded to the position of a social accomplishment.

"When we come to Reading, Jon," said Fleur eagerly, *"get out first and go down to Caversham lock and wait for me. I'll send the car home and we'll walk by the towing-path."*

Jon seized her hand in gratitude, and they sat silent, with the world well lost, and one eye on the corridor.

"We're getting near," said Fleur; *"the towing-path's awfully exposed. One more! Oh! Jon, don't forget me."*

Jon answered with his kiss.

Caversham Lock is well remembered by my family. One of the boating trips we took on the Thames in the early 1960s was too early in the season—April. Of course, fresh new leaves were formed on the trees, especially the glorious Thames weeping willows, and the blossoms of may, pear, and apple were found in orchards and meadows along the way. New calves and lambs skipped around in pastures rich in the first green of spring. Primroses, daffodils, and dandelions peppered the river banks with yellow. The locks along the river also pride themselves on their gardens and most were full of spring bulbs in white, pink, yellow, and blue—hyacinths, daffodils, narcissi, and tulips. The weather was glorious as we set out on an Easter week journey up river with a stop at Benson, near Oxford, as our goal. Uncle Jim and Aunt Eileen were stationed at RAF Benson at that time, and we planned to visit them and then all have dinner together at one of those wonderful riverside inns, and of course, my father wanted to show off our spacious cabin cruiser, *Maid Margot* that we had all so enjoyed the summer before. Shortly after dinner at *The Wedge and Beetle* near Benson, however, the weather changed and in no time we were in the midst of a late spring blizzard of heavy wet snow! It would take us at least two days to get back down river all the way to Teddington from whence our boat was hired. In fearful conditions, we slowly made our way until at Caversham we were informed by the lock-keeper that all river traffic was now closed, the Thames having risen, causing a torrential flow making further passage through locks and past weirs dangerous.

Granny Mabs, who had spent Edwardian summers on the river at Tag's Island near Teddington and considered herself knowledgeable on the Thames, chastised my father after we had to be bailed out at Caversham.

"Nobody goes boating on the river in April," she said. "What were you all thinking of?"

The Longleys used to hire houseboats on the Norfolk Broads in the early 1930s. I remember an anecdote that Miss Coath shared with us on one of those occasions when she could share her ability to mimic a north country accent to advantage in our queen's English 'Forsyte' world. "A man fell off the boat behind us," she said. "His wife held out a swabbing mop for him to catch onto to help him back into the boat. Then, as he clambored back onto the decking, she yelled at him in a loud Lancashire accent that we could all hear: 'What y'a want to fall in water f'a you great big gump?'"

Fleur *rejoined* Jon *on the towing-path* after telling the chauffeur that she *was train-giddy.*

"Did you look pretty natural as you went out?" she asked.

"I don't know. What is natural?"

"It's natural to you to look seriously happy. When I first saw you I thought you weren't a bit like other people."

"Exactly what I thought when I saw you. I knew at once I should never love anybody else."

Fleur laughed.

"We're absurdly young. And love's young dream is out of date, Jon. Besides, it's awfully wasteful. Think of all the fun you might have. You haven't begun, even; it's a shame really. And there's me. I wonder!"

Confusion came on Jon's spirit. How could she say such things just as they were going to part?

"If you feel like that," he said, *"I can't go. I shall tell Mother that I ought to try and work. There's always the condition of the world!"*

"The condition of the world!"

Jon thrust his hands deep into his pockets.

"But there is," he said seriously. *"Think of all the people starving!"*

Fleur shook her head. "No, no, I never, never will make myself miserable for nothing."

"Nothing! But there's an awful state of things, and of course one ought to help."

"Oh! yes, I know all that. But you can't help people, Jon; they're hopeless. When you pull them out they only get into another hole. Look at them, still fighting and plotting and struggling, though they're dying in heaps all the time. Idiots!"

"Aren't you sorry for them?"

"Oh! sorry—yes, but I'm not going to make myself unhappy about it; that's no good."

And they were silent, disturbed by this first glimpse of each other's natures and how it was wasting their valuable time. *It was as if they had quarrelled—and at this supreme and awful moment, with parting visible out there in that last gap in the willows!*

"I must believe in things," said Jon with a sort of agony; "we're all meant to enjoy life."

Fleur laughed. "Yes; and that's what you won't do, if you don't take care. But perhaps your idea of enjoyment is to make yourself wretched. There are lots of people like that, of course."

Fleur was staring at the river, but then she looked round at Jon. *Never was anything so intoxicating as that vivacious look.*

"Don't let's be silly," she said, "time's too short. I mustn't dawdle anymore. It's no good going beyond the next hedge, it gets all open. Let's get on to it and say good-bye. My club's the 'Talisman', Stratton Street, Piccadilly. Letters there will be quite safe, and I'm always up once a week."

Jon nodded.

"To-day's the twenty-third of May," said Fleur; "on the ninth of July I shall be in front of the 'Bacchus and Ariadne' in the National Gallery at three o'clock; will you?"*

"I will."

They kissed, a spray of hawthorn blossom above their heads.

"Good-bye, Jon." For a second they stood with hands hard clasped. Then their lips met again, *and when they parted Fleur broke away and fled through the wicket gate.*

Jon saw a gable, a chimney or two, a patch of wall—Mapledurham, an enclave of 'Forsythia' along the banks of the Thames. *He saw her hand make a little flitting gesture; then she sped on.*

Jon must have felt like Harry in *Three Men in a Boat* after leaving the girls at a 'Forsyte' Thameside party that they had attended. He returned to Reading, to London, and from London back to Wansdon.

Railways linked all England, during 'Forsythia'. There was barely a village that could not be reached by main or branch line as little trains puffed their way over viaducts, through tunnels, and beside green pastures. Travel was cheap and classes were segregated.

CHAPTER TWELVE

CAPRICE

Fleur sped on and was about to take the ferry, when she saw a skiff with a young man standing up in it, and holding to the bushes.

"Miss Forsyte," he said, "let me put you across. I've come on purpose."

She looked at him in blank amazement.

"It's all right, I've been having tea with your people. I thought I'd save you the last bit. It's on my way, I'm just off back to Pangbourne. My name's Mont. I saw you at the picture-gallery—you remember—when your father invited me to see his pictures."

"Oh!" said Fleur; "yes—the handkerchief."

To this young man she owed Jon; and taking his hand, she stepped down into the skiff.

The young man prattled on about everything concerning himself, the world, her family, her father's paintings, and Russian ballet. Fleur had never heard anyone say so much in so short a time.

"Do you know that we're getting farther off, not nearer? This river flows."

"Splendid!" cried Mont, dipping his sculls vaguely; "it's good to meet a girl who's got wit."

"But better to meet a young man whose got it in the plural."

Young Mont raised a hand to tear his hair.

"Look out!" cried Fleur. "Your scull!"

"All right! It's thick enough to bear a scratch."

"Do you mind sculling?" said Fleur severely. "I want to get in."

"Don't you bless the day that gave you a French mother, and a name like yours?"

"I like my name, but Father gave it me. Mother wanted me called Marguerite."

"Which is absurd. Do you mind calling me M.M. and letting me call you F.F.? It's the spirit of the age."

"Please row."

"I am." And he did for several strokes, looking at her with rueful eagerness. "Of course, you know," he ejaculated, pausing, "that I came to see you, not your father's pictures."

Fleur rose.

"If you don't row, I shall get out and swim."

"Really and truly. Then I could come in after you."

"Mr. Mont, I'm late and tired; please put me on shore at once."

When she stepped out on the garden landing-stage he rose, and grasping his hair with both hands, looked at her.

Fleur smiled.

"Don't!" cried the irrepressible Mont. "I know you're going to say: 'Out, damned hair!'"

Fleur whisked round, threw him a wave of her hand. "Good-bye, Mr. M.M.!" she called, and was gone among the rose trees.

The sound of voices came from the drawing-room. Mother! Monsieur Profond! From behind the verandah screen which fenced the ingle-nook she heard these words:

"I don't, Annette."

Did father know that he called her mother 'Annette'? Always on the side of her father—as children are ever on one side or the other in houses where relations are a little strained—she stood, uncertain. One word she caught: *"Demain"*—tomorrow. And then Profond's voice: *"I'm taking a small stroll."*

When Fleur entered the drawing room, her mother was sitting on the sofa.

"Ah! Here you are, Fleur! Your father is beginning to fuss."

"Where is he?"

"In the picture-gallery. Go up!"

"What are you going to do to-morrow, Mother?"

"To-morrow? I go up to London with your aunt."

"They're all going back, I suppose."

"Yes, all; you will console your father. Kiss me, then."

Fleur crossed the room, stooped, received a kiss on the forehead, and went out past the impress of a form on the sofa-cushions in the corner. She ran upstairs.

If that man had really been kissing her mother it was—serious, and her father ought to know. "Demain!" "All right!" And her mother going up to Town! She turned into her bedroom and hung out of the window to cool her face, which had suddenly grown very hot. Jon must be at the station by now! What did her father know about Jon? Probably everything—pretty nearly!

She changed her dress, so as to look as if she had been in some time, and ran up to the gallery.

"Well," Soames *said stonily, "so you've come* home*! Why do you keep me on tenderhooks like this, putting me off and off?"*

"Darling, it was very harmless."

"Harmless! Much you know what's harmless and what isn't."

"Well, then, dear, suppose you tell me; and be quite frank about it."

And she sat in *the window seat.*

"You're my only comfort," said her father, *"and you go on like that."*

Fleur's heart began to beat.

"Like what, dear?"

"You know what I told you," he said; *"I don't choose to have anything to do with that branch of the family."*

"Yes, ducky, but I don't know why I shouldn't."

Soames turned on his heel.

"I'm not going into the reasons," he said; *"you ought to trust me, Fleur! You knew my wishes, and yet you stayed on there four days. And I suppose that boy came with you to-day."*

Fleur kept her eyes on him.

"I don't ask you anything," said Soames; *"I make no inquisition where you're concerned."*

The click of billiard balls rose up from open windows below, *where Jack Cardigan had turned the light up.*

"Will it make you any happier," Fleur *said suddenly, "if I promise you not to see him for say—the next six weeks?"*

"Six weeks? Six years—sixty years more like. Don't delude yourself, Fleur; don't delude yourself!"

Fleur turned in alarm.

"Father, what is it?"

Soames came close enough to see her face.

"Don't tell me," he said, "that you're foolish enough to have any feeling beyond caprice. That would be too much!" And he laughed.

Fleur, who had never heard him laugh like that, thought: 'Then it is deep! Oh! what is it?' And putting her hand through his arm she said lightly:

"No, of course, caprice. Only, I like my caprices and I don't like yours, dear."

"Mine!" said Soames bitterly, and turned away.

Fleur *felt a sudden hunger for Jon's face, for his hands, and the feel of his lips again on hers.* Maybe, this was the moment for her to win back her father by revealing what she thought she knew.

"O la! La! What a small fuss! As Profond would say, Father, I don't like that man."

She saw him stop, and take something out of his breast pocket.

"You don't," he said. "Why?"

"Nothing," murmured Fleur; "just caprice!"

"No," said Soames; "not caprice!" And he tore what was in his hands across. "You're right. I don't like him either!"

Together, they watched Monsieur Profond walking in the garden.

"Prowling!" Fleur *muttered.*

Father and daughter were now on the same page. *Her father* started again to tear *the paper in his hands. Fleur saw it was a cheque.*

"I shan't sell him my Gauguin," Soames *said. "I don't know what your aunt and Imogen see in him."*

"Or Mother."

"Your Mother!" said Soames.

'Poor Father!' she thought. 'He never looks happy—not really happy. I don't want to make him worse, but of course I shall have to, when Jon comes back. Oh! well, sufficient unto the night!'

"I'm going to dress," she said.

Fleur dressed in a fancy dress costume she called *her 'freak' dress. It was of gold tissue with little trousers of the same, tightly drawn in at the ankles, a page's cap slung from the shoulders, little gold shoes, and a gold-winged Mercury helmet; and all over her were tiny gold bells, especially on the helmet; so that if she shook her head, she pealed.*

Dressing up in costumes for fancy dress evenings, stretching the imagination and humor of the participants, was a popular pastime in 'Forsythia', especially after 1900. It had grown, too, from 'Forsytes' bringing back to England the national dress and costumes of some of the subject peoples to whom they administered. My grandparents Longley loved fancy dress. They took many cruises before the war and prized themselves on their ingenuity for fancy dress nights on board ship. There are also old cine films taken in the 1930s showing sundry members of the family in costumed poses at The Breach, including my mother when she was courting my father. They dressed up as Grecian goddesses, characters from *A Mid-Summer's Night Dream*, clowns, and in humorous spoofs like Grandpop and a Goodchild cousin in bowler hats, wing collars, ties and suit tops with beach shorts that they captioned 'City Gents on holiday'—caprice!

When she was dressed Fleur felt quite sick because Jon could not see her; it even seemed a pity that the sprightly young man Michael Mont would not have a view. But the gong had sounded, and she went down.

She made a sensation in the drawing-room. Winifred thought it "Most amusing." Imogen was enraptured. Jack Cardigan called it 'stunning', 'ripping', 'topping', and 'corking.' Monsieur Profond, smiling with his eyes, said: "That's a nice small dress!" However, her mother was not amused:

"What did you put on that thing for? You're not going to dance."

Fleur spun round, and the bells pealed.

"Caprice!"

Soames stared at her, and, turning away, gave his arm to Winifred. Jack Cardigan took her mother, Prosper Profond took Imogen. Fleur went in by herself, with her bells jingling...

Late that night, still dressed in her 'freak' dress, Fleur leaned out of her window. Night sounds and scents abounded, but *Fleur heeded not these sounds; her spirit, far from disembodied, fled with swift wing from railway-carriage to flowery hedge, straining after Jon, tenacious of his forbidden image, and the sound of his voice which was taboo. And she crinkled her nose, retrieving from the perfume of the river-side night that moment when his hand slipped between the may-flowers and her cheek.*

But at last even she felt sleepy, and, forgetting her bells, drew quickly in.

Through the open window of his room, alongside Annette's, Soames, wakeful too, heard their thin faint tinkle, as it might be shaken from the stars, or the dewdrops falling from a flower, if one could hear such sounds.

'Caprice!' he thought. 'I can't tell. She's wilful. What shall I do? Fleur!'

And long into the 'small' night he brooded.

PART TWO

Chapter One

Mother and Son

Spain had become Italy by Jon *simply saying: "I'd rather go to Spain, Mum; you've been to Italy so many times; I'd like it new to both of us."*

Jon also *never forgot that he was going to shorten the proposed two months into six weeks, and therefore must show no sign of wishing to do so.*

Fleur's wisdom in refusing to write to him was profound, for he reached each place entirely without hope or fever, and could concentrate immediate attention on the donkeys and tumbling bells, the priests, patios, beggars, children, crowing cocks, sombreros, cactus hedges, old high white villages, goats, olive-trees, greening plains, singing birds in tiny cages, water-sellers, sunsets, melons, mules, great churches, pictures, and swimming grey brown mountains of a fascinating land.

It was already hot and most the English tourists of the spring had left.

When they came to see the Prado in Madrid, Jon *could not tell whether* his mother *noticed his absorption in that Goya picture, 'La Vendimia', or whether she knew he had slipped back there after lunch and again next morning, to stand before it full half an hour, a second and third time. It was not Fleur, of course, but like enough to give him heartache—so dear to lovers—remembering her standing at the foot of his bed with her hand held above her head.*

He kept a postcard of the painting with him at all times.

In Granada he was fairly caught, sitting on a sun-warmed stone bench in a little battlemented garden on the Alhambra hill, whence he ought to have been looking at the view. His mother, he had thought, was examining the potted stocks between the polled acacias, when her voice said:

"Is that your favourite Goya, Jon?"

He checked, too late, a movement such as he might have made at school to conceal some surreptitious document, and answered: "Yes."

"It certainly is most charming; but I think I prefer the 'Quitasol'. Your father would go crazy about Goya; I don't believe he saw them when he was in Spain in '92."

What had been the previous existences of his father and his mother? If they had a right to share in his future, surely he had a right to share in their pasts.

He looked from his balcony over the Moorish city at night, he thought of Fleur, and he was inspired to write:

'Voice in the night crying, down in the old sleeping
Spanish city darkened under her white stars!
What says the voice—its clear—lingering anguish?
Just the watchman, telling his dateless tale of safety?
Just a road-man, flinging to the moon his song?
No! 'Tis one deprived, whose lover's heart is weeping
Just his cry: 'How long?'"

Next day he wrote it out again and enclosed it in one of those letters to Fleur which he always finished before he went down, so as to have his mind free and companionable with his mother.

About noon that same day, on the tiled terrace of their hotel, he felt a sudden dull pain in the back of his head, a queer sensation in the eyes, and sickness. The sun had touched him too affectionately. For three days he remained sick, diligently nursed by his mother. He wished terribly that Fleur could see him, thinking he was dying, but as he began to recover, *he was not slow* to perceive *that he had now his excuse for going home.*

"I'd like to be back in England, Mum, the sun's too hot."

"Very well, darling," she said, *"as soon as you're fit to travel."* And at once he felt better, and—meaner.

Condemned by Spanish Providence to spend a day in Madrid between their trains, it was but natural to go again to the Prado. Jon was elaborately casual this time before his Goya girl. Now that he was going back to her, he could afford a lesser scrutiny. It was his mother who lingered before the picture, saying:

"The face and the figure of the girl are exquisite."

Jon heard her uneasily. Did she understand?

The happiest moment of his travel was that when he stepped on to the Folkestone boat.

'Forsytes' appreciated Europe for its culture and scenic beauty, but never considered themselves Europeans. It was always a relief to finally be coming home and to again enjoy "a nice cup of tea."

In my second year at Cambridge, I took a long summer trip with five other students, driving through Europe to the Middle East and working for the summer on community farms in Israel as a *kibbutznik*. It was a fascinating trip, but when we reached Calais to board the cross-channel boat for the last leg of our long round trip journey, it felt so good—relief—a weight off the shoulders—home. In a similar way, after I had moved to the United States and become a cruise director traveling all over the world and being away months at a time, those first moments driving out from the port area at Fort Lauderdale were always sublimely happy. I felt like a train as I pulled out of the urban sprawl of south Florida and left a world cruise behind heading north to the swamps and pine forests of my adopted Georgia and my happy isles off the coast—Sea Island and St. Simons.

Sensing her son's relief, standing by the bulwark rail, with her arm in his, Irene said to Jon*:*

"I'm afraid you haven't enjoyed it much. But you've been very sweet to me."

Jon squeezed her arm.

"Oh! yes, I've enjoyed it awfully—except for my head lately."

And now that the end had come, he really had, feeling a sort of glamour over the past weeks—a kind of painful pleasure, such as he had tried to screw into those lines about the voice in the night crying. And he wondered why it was he couldn't say to her quite simply what she had said to him:

"You were very sweet to me." Odd—one never could be nice and natural like that! He substituted the words: "I expect we shall be sick,"—
the price and the mystique of that channel crossing.

They were, and reached London somewhat attenuated, having been away six weeks and two days, without a single allusion to the subject which had hardly ever ceased to occupy their minds.

CHAPTER TWO

FATHERS AND DAUGHTERS

eprived of his wife and son by the Spanish adventure, Jolyon found the solitude at Robin Hill intolerable. June took it upon herself to take care of her father. *He was a 'lame duck' now, and on her conscience. She appeared at Robin Hill a fortnight after Irene and Jon had gone. After three days at Robin Hill she carried her father back with her to Town,* where she was now living *in a tiny house with a big studio at Chiswick. In those three days* June *had stumbled on the secret he had kept for two years, and had instantly decided to cure him. She knew, in fact, the very man.*

The great thing about this healer was that he relied on Nature. He had made a special study of the symptoms of Nature—when his patient failed in any natural symptom he supplied the poison which caused it—and there you were! She was extremely hopeful. Her father clearly had not been living a natural life at Robin Hill, and June *intended to provide the symptoms. He was—she felt—out of touch with the times, which was not natural; his heart wanted stimulating.*

There was considerable interest among 'Forsytes' in late nineteenth and early twentieth-century alternatives to normal medicinal practices, especially in the realms bordering on functions of the brain and psychology. Granny Mabs' Uncle Singleton was a phrenologist, who read cranial bumps on the scalp that his profession felt determined many aspects of an individual's behavior. In their early childhood, he drew cranial maps of both my mother and Aunt Eileen. Both sides of my family in the 1920s and '30s believed firmly in the healing capability of osteopaths. In my childhood, my sisters and I were regularly taken to visit an osteopath. My mother, being a keen golfer, often had shoulder aches that she firmly believed our osteopath, Ronald Leisk, could help. Some of the techniques of osteopathy bore a great resemblance to the Palmer method of chiropractors. Both believed in manipulation of bones to create a balanced muscle pattern and better health. Mainstream medicine of the era did not support chiropractors, but paid some attention to osteopaths. The work of phrenologists like my great-great-uncle passed to the increasing acceptance of psychology and psychiatry, with a greater understanding of the composition of the human brain rather than the brain casing. Enormous advances in these fields followed with the work of Dr. Sigmund Freud.

There were two interesting by-products to those regular visits to Mr. Leisk in our childhood. The first was the use of a sun lamp that Mr. Leisk liked to use on us before manipulation, perhaps to soften up the muscles, but also in the bounds of alternative medicine to provide us with the natural vitamins of solar heat without the harmful rays. The second by-product was not medicinal. Ronald Leisk was an artist, and a visit to his large Victorian home on the Croydon Road also meant a review of his most recent works. He knew that Diane and I liked to paint and there were times when we, too, took our most recent works with us for him to review. Visits to Leisk became more social than medicinal. However, all her life, my mother believed in osteopathy and after Ronald Leisk passed on, received the care of a Mr. Mace, who moved osteopathy on into that meeting point of mind, body and spirit—a place where modern osteopaths and chiropractors mesh.

June, along with her 'lame duck' Austrian maid, in her efforts to place the right symptoms before her father *stimulated Jolyon in all sorts of ways, preparing him for his cure. In the evenings, for his benefit, as* June *declared, though he suspected she also got something out of it, she assembled the Age so far as it was satellite to genius; and with some solemnity it would move up and down the studio before him in the foxtrot, and that more mental form of dancing—the one-step—which so pulled against the music, that Jolyon's eyebrows would be almost in his hair for wonder at the strain it must impose on the dancers' will-power. And when June brought some girl or young man up to him, he would rise to their level so far as was possible, and think: 'Dear me! This is very dull for them!' Having his father's perennial sympathy with Youth, he used to get very tired from entering into their points of view. But it was all stimulating. Even genius itself attended these gatherings now and then, and June always introduced it to her father. This she felt, was exceptionally good for him, for genius was a natural symptom he had never had—fond as she was of him.*

It was not too much to say that Jolyon *preferred* June *to the Age with which she was surrounded, youthful though, for the greater part, it was.* Then, *her dentist* wanted to remove his teeth finding *'Staphylococcus aureus present in pure culture' (which might cause boils, of course). Jolyon's native tenacity was roused, and in the studio that evening he developed his objections. He had never had any boils, and his own teeth would last his time. Of course—June admitted—they would last his time if he didn't have them out! But if he had more teeth he would have a better heart and his time would be longer. His recalcitrance—she said—was a symptom of his whole attitude. When was he going to see the man who had cured Paul Post,* the expressionist artist who had created *The Future Town? Jolyon was very sorry, but the fact was he was not going to see him. June chafed. Pondridge—she said—the healer, was such a fine man, and he had difficulty in making two ends meet, and getting his theories recognised.*

"I perceive," said Jolyon, "that you're trying to kill two birds with one stone."

"Dad!" cried June, "you're hopeless."

"That," said Jolyon, "is a fact, but I wish to remain hopeless as long as possible. I shall let sleeping dogs lie, my child. They are quiet at present."

"That's not giving science a chance," cried June. "You've no idea how devoted Pondridge is. He puts his science before everything."

"Just as Mr. Paul Post puts his art, eh? Art for Art's sake—Science for the sake of Science. I know those enthusiastic egomaniac gentry. They vivisect you without blinking. I'm enough of a Forsyte to give them the go-by, June."

"Dad," said June, "if you only knew how old-fashioned that sounds! Nobody can afford to be half-hearted nowadays."

"I'm afraid," murmured Jolyon, with his smile, "that's the only natural symptom with which Mr. Pondridge need not supply me. We are born to be extreme or to be moderate, my dear; though, if you'll forgive my saying so, half the people nowadays who believe they're extreme are

really very moderate. I'm getting on as well as I can expect, and I must leave it at that."

The subject was now closed, in very much the same way as Granny Longley would have stemmed a topic once it no longer interested her. Indeed, one of her funnier comments in stemming a conversation was when Diane asked her shortly after the landing of man on the moon: "Granny, what do you think of man landing on the moon?" She turned to my sister, her cigarette dangling from her mouth, dropping ash over her jig-saw puzzle, and replied: "As far as I am concerned, the moon was made for spooning under and nothing else"—end of conversation.

How he came to let her know why Irene had taken Jon to Spain puzzled Jolyon, for he had little confidence in her discretion, but he did. She was immediate family, after all. After she had brooded on the news, it brought a rather sharp discussion.

According to June, it was foolish and even cowardly to hide the past from Jon. She blamed Irene, showing just a little of her own bitterness *over the body of Philip Bosinney. "If it were left to you, you would* tell him," she said.

"I might, but simply because I know he must find out, which would be worse than if we told him."

"Then why don't you tell him? It's just sleeping dogs again."

"My dear," said Jolyon, "I wouldn't for the world go against Irene's instinct. He's her boy."

"Yours too," cried June.

"What is a man's instinct compared with a mother's?"

"Well, I think it's very weak of you."

"I dare say," said Jolyon, "I dare say."

And that was all she got from him.

And there stirred in her a tortuous impulse to push the matter toward decision. Jon ought to be told. She determined to see Fleur, and judge for herself. After all, she was Soames's cousin, and they were both interested in pictures. She would go and tell him he ought to buy a Paul Post, and of course she would say nothing to her father. She went on the following Sunday.

* * *

At Soames' Mapledurham home, June *was conducted to a drawing-room, which, though not her style, showed every mark of fastidious elegance. Thinking, 'Too much taste—too many knick-knacks,' she saw in an old lacquer-framed mirror the figure of a girl coming in from the verandah.*

"How do you do?" said June, turning round. "I'm a cousin of your father's."

"Oh, yes; I saw you in that confectioner's."

"With my young step-brother. Is your father in?"

"He will be directly. He's only gone for a little walk."

June slightly narrowed her blue eyes.

"Your name's Fleur, isn't it? I've heard of you from Holly. What do you think of Jon?"

Fleur sniffed roses she was carrying before replying:

"He's quite a nice boy."

"Not a bit like Holly or me, is he?"

"Not a bit."

'She's cool,' thought June.

And suddenly the girl said: "I wish you'd tell me why our families don't get on? You know, the surest way to make people find out the worst is to keep them ignorant. My father's told me it was a quarrel about property. But I don't believe it; we've both got heaps. They wouldn't have been so bourgeois as all that."

June flushed. That *word, applied to her grandfather and father, offended her.*

'Bourgeois' was a boring term for the middle class—Napoleon's 'Nation of shopkeepers.' Although middle class—not members of the aristocracy or old families of the landed gentry—'Forsytes' never regarded themselves in that light. They were upper-middle class with a decided emphasis on the word 'upper.' It would be hard, after all, to count the three percent as middle class. It was the lower-middle class that were the 'Bourgeoisie'—the forty percent, who could be described as Napoleon's 'Nation of shopkeepers', clerks and foremen.

"My grandfather," June *said, "was very generous, and my father is, too; neither of them was in the least 'bourgeois'."*

"Well, what was it then?" repeated the girl.

June, now insulted, was less disposed to reveal all.

"Why do you want to know?"

Fleur *smelled at her roses* again, avoiding eye contact with June. *"I only want to know because they won't tell me."*

"Well, it was about property, but there's more than one kind."

"That makes it worse. Now I really must know."

June looked squarely at Fleur, giving her something of a Hovenden glare.

"You know," she said. "I saw you drop your handkerchief. Is there anything between you and Jon? Because, if so, you'd better drop that too."

Fleur grew paler, but she smiled.

"If there were, that isn't the way to make me."

At the gallantry of her reply, June held out her hand.

"I like you; but I don't like your father; I never have. We may as well be frank."

"Did you come down to tell him that?"

June laughed. "No; I came down to see you."

"How delightful of you!"

This girl could fence.

"I'm two and a half times your age," said June, "but I quite sympathise. It's horrid not to have one's own way."

The girl smiled again. "I really think you might tell me."

How the child stuck to her point!

"It's not my secret. But I'll see what I can do, because I think both you and Jon ought to be told. And now I'll say good-bye."

"Won't you wait and see Father?"

June shook her head. "How can I get over to the other side?"

"I'll row you across."

"Look!" said June impulsively, "next time you're in London, come and see me. This is where I live. I generally have young people in the evening. But I shouldn't tell your father that you're coming."

The girl nodded.

Watching Fleur scull the skiff back across, June thought: 'She's awfully pretty and well made. I never thought Soames would have a daughter as pretty as this. She and Jon would make a lovely couple. Her youth!' Then she reflected on herself: 'So long ago—when Phil and she—And since? Nothing—no one had been quite what she had wanted. And so she had missed it all.

'Jon and Fleur! Two little lame ducks—charming callow yellow little ducks! A great pity! Surely something could be done!'

* * *

That evening back at Robin Hill over dinner, June said to her father, Jolyon:

"Dad, I've been down to see young Fleur. I think she's very attractive. It's no good hiding our heads under our wings, is it?"

The startled Jolyon set down his barley-water, and began crumbling his bread.

In an era prior to vitamin supplements, 'Forsytes' had great faith in barley water as a pick-me-up incentive for better health. It was administered as the drink of choice in the nursery and in old age, but it was also used extensively in the sick room. Epidemics of childhood diseases and influenza were common, especially during the spring term at our private boarding schools. When sick at Newlands, we were always given barley water two or three times a day poured from big jugs by the matrons into large glasses beside our sick beds. Fortunately, most of us liked barley water and it was one of the better benefits of being sick.

Jolyon, after he set down his barley water, *rose.*

"Do you realise whose daughter she is?" he said.

"Can't the dead past bury its dead?"

"Certain things can never be buried," Jolyon quipped.

"I disagree," said June. *"It's that which stands in the way of all happiness and progress. You don't understand the Age, Dad. It's got no use for outgrown things. Why do you think it matters so terribly that Jon should know about his mother? Who pays any attention to that sort of thing now? The marriage laws are just as they were when Soames and Irene couldn't get a divorce, and you had to come in. We've moved, and they haven't. So nobody cares. Marriage without a decent chance of relief is only a sort of slave-owning; people oughtn't to own each other. Everybody sees that now. If Irene broke such laws, what does it matter?"*

"It's not for me to disagree there," said Jolyon; *"but that's all quite beside the mark. This is a matter of human feeling."*

"Of course it is," cried June, *"the human feeling of those two young things."*

"My dear," said Jolyon with gentle exasperation, *"you're talking nonsense."*

"I'm not. If they prove to be really fond of each other, why should they be made unhappy because of the past?"

"You haven't lived that past. I have—through the feelings of my wife, as only one who is devoted can."

"If," June interjected, *"she had been the daughter of Phil Bosinney, I could understand you better. Irene loved him, she never loved Soames."*

"That shows how little you understand. It's the brutality of a union without love. This girl is the daughter of a man who once owned Jon's mother as a negro slave was owned. You can't lay that ghost; don't try to, June! It's asking us to see Jon joined to the flesh and blood of the man who possessed Jon's mother against her will. It's no good mincing words; I want it clear once for all. And now I mustn't talk any more, or I shall have to sit up with this all night."

Jolyon put his hand over his heart and looked away.

At this, *June was seriously alarmed. She came and slipped her arm through his*—her lame duck father.

* * *

After taking her elderly cousin across the river, *Fleur did not land at once, but pulled in among the reeds. She took out Jon's letters—not flowery effusions, but haunted in their recital of things seen and done by a longing very agreeable to her, and all ending 'Your devoted J'.*

Fleur then sculled back *and pulled up at the landing-stage. Crossing the lawn she wondered if she should tell her father of June's visit. If he learned of it from the butler, he might think it odd if she did not. It gave her, too, another chance to startle out of him the reason of the feud. She went, therefore, up the road to meet him.*

Soames had gone to look at a patch of ground on which the Local Authorities were proposing to erect a Sanatorium for people with weak lungs. He could not, however, remain indifferent to this new and dangerous scheme. He was quite of the opinion that the country should stamp out tuberculosis; but this was not the place. It should be done further away. He took, indeed, an attitude common to all true Forsytes, that disability of any sort in other people was not his affair, and the state should do it's business without prejudicing in any way the natural advantages which he had acquired or inherited. A Sanatorium would depreciate the neighborhood, and he should certainly sign the petition which was being got up against it.

I vaguely remember something similar in my own childhood. The Park Langley estate with its principle road, Wickham Way, backed onto Langley Court, one of those elegant Victorian mansions surrounded by several acres that had been commonplace around the late nineteenth-century village of Beckenham. When the land at Langley Court had become the headquarters of the well-known pharmaceutical company—Burroughs Wellcome—the old mansion served as its executive offices and in our childhood was surrounded by company laboratories. There was a proposal to open a roadway along a right of way out from Burroughs Wellcome into Wickham Way. As Wickham Way was the last 'Forsyte' stronghold of Beckenham, it was not surprising that petitions were raised against this proposal. The flow of traffic and factory workers into our secluded 'Forsyte' street, however practical for Burroughs Wellcome, was not to be tolerated, and it was duly defeated.

Soames, having inspected the proposed Sanatorium site near Mapledurham, was walking back when *he saw Fleur coming.*

She was showing him more affection of late, and the quiet time down here with her in this summer weather had been making him feel quite young. Annette was always running up to Town for one thing or another, so that he had Fleur to himself almost as much as he could wish. To be sure, young Mont had formed a habit of appearing on his motor-cycle almost every other day. With a girl friend of Fleur's who was staying in the house, and a neighboring youth or so, they made two couples after dinner, in the hall, to the music of the electric pianola, which performed foxtrots unassisted. Annette, even, now and then passed gracefully up and down in the arms of one or other of the young men. To Soames' ever-anxious eyes Fleur showed no signs of remembering that caprice of hers.

When she reached him on the dusty road, he slipped his hand within her arm.

"Who do you think has been to see you, Dad! She couldn't wait! Guess!"

"I never guess," said Soames uneasily. "Who?"

"Your cousin, June Forsyte."

He gripped her arm. *What did she want?*

"I don't know. But it was rather breaking through the feud, wasn't it?"

"Feud? What feud?"

"The one that exists in your imagination, dear."

Soames dropped her arm. *Was she mocking, or trying to draw him on?*

"I suppose she wanted me to buy a picture," he said at last.

"I don't think so. Perhaps it was just family affection."

"She's only a first cousin once removed," muttered Soames.

"And the daughter of your enemy."

"What d'you mean by that?"

"I beg your pardon, dear. I thought he was."

"Enemy!" repeated Soames. "It's ancient history. I don't know where you get your notions."

"From June Forsyte."

Soames was startled, but she had underrated his caution and tenacity.

"If you know," he said coldly, "why do you plague me?"

"I don't want to plague you, darling. As you say, why want to know more? Why want to know anything of that 'small' mystery—Je m'en fiche, as Profond says?"

"That chap!" said Soames profoundly. She had struck a nerve again.

That evening Chance, which visits the lives of even the best invested Forsytes, put a clue into Fleur's hands. Her father came down to dinner without a handkerchief, and had occasion to blow his nose.

"I'll get you one, dear," she had said, and ran upstairs. In the sachet where she sought for it—an old sachet of very faded silk—there were two compartments; one held handkerchiefs; the other was buttoned, and contained something flat and hard. By some childish impulse Fleur unbuttoned it. There was a frame and in it a photograph of herself as a little girl. She gazed at it, fascinated. Then, *she saw that another photograph was behind. It was of a young woman, very good-looking, in a very old style of evening dress. Only on the stairs did she identify that face. Surely—surely Jon's mother! Why, of course! Jon's father had married the woman her father had wanted to marry, and cheated him out of her.*

I remember the trappings of his 'Forsyte' upbringing in my father's lowboy bedroom wardrobe. There was a fascinating wooden box that held squares of folded handkerchiefs somewhat like Soames' sachet. There were little compartments and places for boxes of shirt studs, tie pins, and cuff links—places for eau de cologne, that my father used to like to buy for everyone at Christmas that he wrapped as table gifts. There was a clothes brush that hung on a hook of the door, rarely used by 'the Clown'. A chrome rack displayed ties hung in rows. On top of this low wardrobe he kept his electric razor, a last decade of 'Forsythia' must in a gentleman's toilet—a gift that we all hoped might be under the Christmas tree when we reached the age of about sixteen, but also a square collar box in which were those stiff wing collars that we still used with our boiled starched shirts and white waistcoats on those occasions when we dressed in white tie and tails. From his morning coat and evening dress tails there emanated a smell of mothballs.

Fleur presented her father with the silk handkerchief and *that evening passed for Fleur in putting two and two together; recalling the look on her father's face in the confectioner's shop—a look strange and coldly intimate, a queer look. He must have loved that woman very much to have kept her photograph all this time, in spite of having lost her. Unsparing and matter-of-fact, her mind darted to his relations with her own mother. Had he ever really loved her? She thought not. Jon was the son of the woman he had really loved. Surely, then, he ought not to mind his daughter loving him; it only wanted getting used to. And a sigh of sheer relief was caught in the folds of her nightgown slipping over her head.*

CHAPTER THREE

MEETINGS

Jon had never really seen his father's age till he came back from
Spain. Worn by waiting, his father's face looked so wan and old.
His father had always been 'so jolly' to him.

His father asked him what he thought of the great Goya. Jon's
conscience pricked him badly. The great Goya only excited because he
had created a face which resembled Fleur's.

It was only the fifth of July, and no meeting was fixed with Fleur
until the ninth. He was to have three days at home before going back to
farm. Somehow he must contrive to see her!

On the excuse of ordering trousers at his tailor, Jon went to Town
one of those days. After his visit to the tailor he turned his face towards
Piccadilly. Stratton Street, where her club was, adjoined Devonshire
House. On the way, he ran into Val Dartie moving towards the Iseeum
Club, to which Val had just been elected.

"Hallo! Young man! Where are you off to?"

Jon flushed. "I've just been to my tailor's."

There were two trade professionals that male 'Forsytes' considered
personal—their tailor and their barber. They rarely changed their
allegiance to either, often inheriting them from father to son. There was
an ownership and a pride in acknowledging the personal connection—
"my tailor."

I remember my father with pride quoting the pre-World War II cost at his tailor for making his set of evening tails and his morning suit, both of which he was able to wear with minor repairs to linings and lapels for his entire life. After the war, however, most our clothing was 'off the peg' although a special trip was made back to the tailor at Austin Reed's by my father to make a 'City Gent's' black coat and striped trousers—not so much for 'City' wear as after the war that obligatory dress was rare, but because of his need for that formality in his freemasonry meetings—the appropriate dress when going through 'the chair.'

In that post war world I did not inherit a tailor, although my father took me once or twice to his barber in the shop, also at Austin Reed's, where he proudly explained to me that "in here they don't use electric clippers, only hand clippers." However, I was introduced to 'my tailor' in Ireland during my years with the Albertini family. Mr. Cahill had a tailor's shop in Cappoquin, a small village on the river Blackwater just down from Lismore in County Waterford. In my first two years in Ireland, thanks to the generosity of Mr. Albertini, Mr. Cahill made me two tweed suits, several three-piece suits, two splendid old-fashioned Norfolk jackets with knickerbockers, two unusual dinner jackets, jodhpurs and riding breeches, a hacking jacket and ultimately a hunting coat. 'Our' tailor was the real deal, the old-fashioned type, who really did sit cross-legged on a shelf surrounded by bolts of incredible cloths. He did not believe in zips—only buttons, and everything was hand-stitched, and Ireland then being somewhat behind the times, he charged only those pre-war prices to which my father had alluded! Like my father's evening clothes, Mr. Cahill's clothes have lasted my lifetime; but unlike my father, I put on a little weight and outgrew most of them! In some ways, that wardrobe that Mr. Cahill stitched for me, was the last of 'Forsythia' in my own life—now a vanished wardrobe for a vanished world that lingered on for me in the rural Ireland of the 1960s.

Val looked Jon *up and down. "That's good! I'm going in here to order some cigarettes; then come and have some lunch."*

Jon thanked him. He might get news of Fleur *from Val!*

Jon entered the Iseeum with curiosity. Except to lunch now and then at the Hotch-Potch with his father he had never been in a London club. The Iseeum, comfortable and unpretentious, did not move, could not, so long as George Forsyte sat on its committee, where his culinary acumen was almost the controlling force. The club had made a stand against the newly rich, and it had taken all George Forsyte's prestige, and praise of him as a 'good sportsman,' to bring in Prosper Profond.

The two were lunching together when Val and Jon *entered the dining-room, and attracted by George's forefinger, sat down at their table. There was an air of privilege around that corner table. Jon was fascinated by the hypnotic atmosphere. The waiter pervaded with such freemasonical deference. His liveried arm and confidential voice alarmed Jon, they came so secretly over his shoulder.*

Essentially, George and Prosper Profond paid little attention to Jon. *The talk was all about breeding, points, and prices of horses.*

"I want to see Mr. Soames Forsyde take an interest in 'orses," said Mr. Profond.

"Old Soames!" said George. "He's to dry a file!"

With all his might Jon tried not to grow red, as Mr. Profond continued:

"His daughter's an attractive small girl. Mr. Soames Forsyde is a bit old-fashioned. I want to see him have a pleasure some day."

George Forsyde grinned.

"Don't you worry; he's not so miserable as he looks. He'll never show he's enjoying anything—they might try and take it from him. Old Soames! Once bit, twice shy!"

"Well, Jon," said Val hastily, "if you've finished we'll go and have coffee."

"Who were those?" Jon asked, on the stairs. "I didn't quite..."

"Old George Forsyte is a first cousin of your father's and of my Uncle Soames. He's always been here. The other chap, Profond, is a queer fish. I think he's hanging around Soames's wife, if you ask me!"

Jon looked at him, startled. "But that's awful," he said: "I mean— for Fleur."

"Don't suppose Fleur cares very much; she's very up to date."

"Her mother!"

"You're very green, Jon."

Jon grew red. "Mothers," he stammered angrily, "are different."

"You're right," said Val suddenly; "but things aren't what they were when I was your age. There's a 'To-morrow we die' feeling. That's what old George means about my Uncle Soames. He doesn't mean to die to-morrow."

Jon said, quickly: "What's the matter between him and my father?"

"Stable secret, Jon. Take my advice, and bottle up. You'll do no good by knowing. Have a liqueur?"

Jon shook his head.

"I hate the way people keep things from one," he muttered, "and then sneer at one for being green."

"Well, you can ask Holly. If she won't tell you, you'll believe it's for your own good, I suppose."

Jon looked upset. "I must go now; thanks awfully for the lunch."

"All right! See you on Friday."

"I don't know," murmured Jon.

And he did not. This conspiracy of silence made him desperate. It was humiliating to be treated like a child! He retraced his moody steps to Stratton Street.

The porter told him Miss Forsyte was not in, but she often did come in on a Monday afternoon.

Jon said he would call again, and, crossing into the Green Park, flung himself down under a tree. He heard Big Ben chime 'three' above the traffic. The sound moved something in him, and, taking out a piece of paper, he began a stanza. He was searching the grass for another verse, when something hard touched his shoulder—a green parasol. There above him stood Fleur!

"They told me you'd been, and were coming back. So I thought you might be out here, and you are—it's rather wonderful!"

"Oh, Fleur! I thought you'd have forgotten me."

"When I told you I shouldn't!"

Jon seized her arm.

"It's too much luck! Let's get away from this side."

They moved to a less exposed area.

"Hasn't anybody cut in?" he said, gazing at her lashes, in suspense above her cheeks.

"There is a young idiot, but he doesn't count."

Jon felt a twitch of confident *compassion for the—young idiot.*

"You know I've had sunstroke; I didn't tell you."

"Really! Was it interesting?"

"No. Mother was an angel. Has anything happened to you?"

"Nothing. Except that I think I've found out what's wrong between our families, Jon. I believe my father wanted to marry your mother, and your father got her instead."

"Oh!"

Fleur then explained to him about the photograph in her father's silk sachet.

"Suppose they were engaged?" Fleur suggested.

"If we were engaged, and you found you loved somebody better, I might go cracked, but I shouldn't grudge it you."

"I should. You mustn't ever do that with me, Jon."

"My God! Not much!"

"I don't believe my father *has ever really cared for my mother."*

Jon was silent. Val's words at lunch—that Mr. Profond?

"You see, we don't know," went on Fleur; *"it may have been a great shock. She may have behaved badly to him. People do."*

"My mother wouldn't."

Fleur shrugged her shoulders. *"I don't think we know much about our fathers and mothers. We just see them in the light of the way they treat us, but they've treated other people, you know, before we were born—plenty, I expect. You see, they're both old. Look at your father, with three separate families!"*

It was true that in 'Forsythia' we really did not know much about our fathers and mothers. In infancy, we were surrounded by nannies or 'au pairs'. From four, we were in school—not playschool as today, but real school. From eight until eighteen, we were at boarding school. We got to know our parents somewhat during school holidays, but it was all rather formal. As mentioned before, the nearest we really got to knowing our parents was on our annual two-week summer holiday—that vacation at the seaside—and it is questionable, seeing this was as much their holiday as ours, that we didn't know them even then under normal circumstances. We got to know them best when they were old and when we started to care for them. Then, little by little they would reveal things about their past—things that often surprised us.

Jon and Fleur got in a taxi just for privacy. As they thought about where they would like to go, Fleur said:

"Are you going back to Robin Hill? I should like to see where you live, Jon. I'm staying with my aunt for the night, but I could get back in time for dinner. I wouldn't come to the house, of course."

Jon gazed at her enraptured.

"Splendid! I can show it you from the copse, we shan't meet anybody. There's a train at four."

The plot hatched, they took the taxi to the station and traveled alone, beating the 'rush hour' in a first-class compartment to Robin Hill.

They walked out up the lane from the station. At the copse *they turned in among the larches, and suddenly, at the winding of the path, came on Irene, sitting on an old log seat.*

Jon's dignity collapsed in shock. *To have brought Fleur down openly—yes! But to sneak her in like this! Consumed with shame, he put on a front as brazen as his nature would permit.*

Fleur was smiling, a little defiantly; his mother's startled face was changing quickly to the impersonal and gracious. It was she who uttered the first words:

"I'm very glad to see you. It was nice of Jon to think of bringing you down to us."

"We weren't coming to the house," Jon blurted out. *"I just wanted Fleur to see where I lived."*

His mother said quietly:

"Won't you come up and have tea?"—always the English solution to embarrassments and problems.

"Thanks very much; I have to get back to dinner," Fleur answered. *"I met Jon by accident, and we thought it would be rather jolly just to see his home."*

How self-possessed she was!

"Of course; but you must have tea. We'll send you down to the station. My husband will enjoy seeing you."

Irene gave Jon a 'Hovenden' glare. *Then she led on, Fleur followed her. Jon felt like a child, trailing after those two, who were talking so easily about Spain and Wansdon, and the house up there beyond the trees and the grassy slope. He watched the fencing of their eyes, taking each other in—the two beings he loved most in the world.*

They met his father under the old oak tree.

"This is Fleur Forsyte, Jolyon; Jon brought her down to see the house. Let's have tea at once—she has to catch a train. Jon, tell them, dear, and telephone to the Dragon for a car.

When Jon *returned under cover of the maids and teapots, there was not a trace of awkwardness beneath the tree; it was all within himself, but not the less for that. They were talking of the Gallery off Cork Street.*

"We back numbers," his father was saying, *"are awfully anxious to find out why we can't appreciate the new stuff; you and Jon must tell us."*

"It's supposed to be satiric, isn't it?" said Fleur.

He saw his father's smile.

"Satiric? Oh! I think it's more than that. What do you say, Jon?"

"I don't know at all," stammered Jon. His father's face had a sudden grimness.

"The young are tired of us, our gods and our ideals. Property, beauty, sentiment—all smoke. We mustn't own anything nowadays, not even our feelings. They stand in the way of—Nothing. Nothing's the god of today. We're back where the Russians were sixty years ago, when they started Nihilism."

Russia was in chaos struggling with it's socialist revolution. The old 'Forsyte' world felt threatened. Why...quietly, almost unnoticed while 'Forsyte' youths fought in the trenches of the Great War, Ireland had provisionally declared itself independent of the Empire and all that world stood for—and before the war they were so close to achieving their 'Home rule'. And now, like Russia, Ireland was embroiled in the civil war of revolution. Were these cracks the beginning of the end, or had it started with those upstart Boers?

"No, Dad," cried Jon suddenly, "we only want to live, and we don't know how, because of the Past—that's all!'

"By George!" said Jolyon, "that's profound, Jon. Is it your own? The Past! Old ownerships, old passions, and their aftermath. Let's have cigarettes."

Jon felt less young.

Fleur looked at her watch, and rose. His mother went with her into the house. Jon stayed with his father puffing at his cigarette.

"See her into the car, old man," said Jolyon; "and when she's gone, ask your mother to come back to me."

Jon went. He waited in the hall. He saw Fleur *into the car. There was no chance for any word; hardly for a pressure of the hand. He waited all that evening for something to be said to him. Nothing was said. Nothing might have happened.* The punishment was awkward silence.

CHAPTER FOUR

IN GREEN STREET

U ncertain, whether the impression that Prosper Profond was *dangerous should be traced to his attempt to give Val the Mayfly filly; to a remark of Fleur's: 'He's like the hosts of Midian—he prowls and prowls around'; to a preposterous enquiry of Jack Cardigan: "What's the use of keepin' fit?" or, more simply to the fact that he was a foreigner.*

Oh! How 'Forsyte's' throughout 'Forsythia' mistrusted foreigners. Foreigners were accepted as French or sometimes Swiss governesses, and in the post-World War II era as 'au pairs', but were not truly accepted as anything else. This fell hardest on Europeans, and after World War II on Americans, because subjects of the British Empire still had the right to call themselves British, and throughout 'Forsythia' they were a sizeable segment of the world's population. An Indian was not necessarily, therefore, a foreigner, and if of the princely caste, was generally accepted. Subjects in the Dominions were readily accepted— Canadians, Australians, New Zealanders and white South Africans, excepting the Boers, of course. In fact, if of the 'Forsyte' class, even in these far off lands they educated themselves to speak the 'King's' English, and so visited the mother country with the same clipped accents as prevailed among Britain's three percent. It was an old New Zealander who put Diane and me up for membership in the Royal Commonwealth Club in that last decade of 'Forsythia'—Leslie Fielding. The club had premises on Northumberland Avenue, and rooms paneled in timber from all parts of the Empire. It was there that I first met a member of the Royal family, that is, discounting the favored seats that Grandpop purchased for us when we attended the Royal Tournament and found ourselves separated by a low partition from the Royal Box and our future queen, the Princess Elizabeth. Her Royal Highness Princess Alexandria hosted a reception at the Royal Commonwealth Club in 1962, and members, with affiliation to all parts of the Commonwealth, as the Empire had then become, were encouraged to attend in National dress—albeit 'formal' national dress.

Foreigners outside the Empire, however, were still regarded with deep suspicion or even jest. Americans, for instance, were not taken seriously by 'Forsytes', who considered them primitive—cowboys and Indians in a land of ten gallon hats, large steam locomotives with over-exaggerated smokestacks and weird cow catchers, Mississippi gamblers and incredible naivete. They looked down on the nouveau riche element of its success, the get-rich-quick possibilities of a society where money was god and class irrelevant. As 'Forsytes' they even somewhat resented the reality that some of those get-rich-quick fortunes had helped to boost flagging British aristocratic families like those of Astor and Churchill. It did not occur to them that their own rise from yeomanry to 'Forsythia' on the wheels of property, imperial commerce and investments was similar—but then 'yeomanry' was an independent landed class and certainly a cut above an Irish emigrant who made good in America. The achievement of the Panama Canal and with it the medical advances against malaria and yellow fever, early advances in flight, the Model 'T' Ford, the Hoover dam, the Empire State building, Hale's telescope on Palomar Mountain, were overshadowed by perceptions of Hollywood tinsel, and back in 1920 an almost bemused reflection on those American soldiers who came 'over there' only in the last year of the Great War and yet whose nation had the audacity to play such a major part in the Treaty of Versailles.

Prosper Profond, even if of Armenian background, for which race there was some sympathy in 1920, looked, spoke, and behaved like a foreigner—even like a get-rich-quick American, having made his fortune, without class, out of munitions, which he probably sold to both sides in the conflict.

And now—Profond and Annette? It was *certain that Annette was looking particularly handsome, and that Soames had sold him a Gaugin*

and then torn up the cheque, so that Monsieur Profond himself had said:
"I didn't get that small picture I brought from Mr. Forsyde."

Annette was a foreigner, too—one of those 'French' foreigners. It was really up to them how well they would fit in. Annette's mother would never have fitted in, but Annette was smart enough to play her role, managing Soames' home graciously and at least being accepted by his inner circle. His sister Winifred, in particular, as much for Soames' sake as Annette's, had included her in her circle. It was in this way that Annette had met Prosper Profond.

As aforementioned, my Aunt Ginette was a 'French' foreigner, but at least she had an English father. Besides, Ginette knew how to play the game, too, and because she did not take 'Forsyte' comments about foreigners seriously, but joked along with them rather than rise to the bait, was taken fully into the bosom of my very 'Forsyte' family. In fact, her parents retired to England, living in Hove on the Sussex coast, a place noted as a retirement retreat for 'Forsytes'. In my last year at Newlands, the school doctor recommended my tonsils should be removed. I was sent to Hove for the operation at a nursing home on The Drive—a 'Forsyte' street of fine old late Victorian and Edwardian homes. I loved staying at '70, The Drive' that week where I was able to soak in the nostalgia of 'Forsythia'—the high ceilings, molded plaster, fireplaces with elaborate mantels, tiled passage floors, and a peaceful garden lined by trees and featuring gravel paths, urns, and rose bowers—my place of convalescence.

Winifred still found Profond 'amusing', and would write him little notes saying: 'Come and have a "jolly" with us'—it was breath of life with her to keep up with the phrases of the day. However, even if Prosper expressed his dissolution with things in an amusing sort of a way, and the English understatement of upper-class dialogue often seemed desultory, *to see nothing in anything, not as a pose, but because there was nothing in anything, was not English; and that which was not English one could not help feeling secretly was dangerous. Monsieur Profond, in fact, made the mood too plain in a country which decently veiled such realities.*

When Fleur, after her hurried return from Robin Hill came down to dinner that evening, she found Monsieur Profond standing in the window.

"Well, Miss Forsyde," he said, *"I'm awful pleased to see you. Mr. Forsyde well? I was sayin' today I want to see him have some pleasure. He worries."*

"You think so?" said Fleur shortly.

"Worries," repeated Monsieur Profond.

Fleur spun round. *"Shall I tell you,"* she said, *"what would give him pleasure?"* But the words, *"To hear that you had cleared out,"* did not come out—Fleur controlled herself.

"I was hearin' at the club to-day about his old trouble," Profond continued.

"What do you mean?"

"Before you were born," he said; *"that small business."*

Fleur was unable to resist a rush of nervous curiosity. *"Tell me what you heard?"*

"Why!" murmured Monsieur Profond, *"you know all that."*

"I expect I do. But I should like to know that you haven't heard it all wrong."

"His first wife," murmured Profond.

Choking back the words, *"He was never married before,"* Fleur said: *"Well, what about her?"*

"Mr. George Forsyde was tellin' me about your father's first wife marryin' his cousin Jolyon afterward. It was a small bit unpleasant, I should think. I saw their boy—nice boy!"

At this point, Fleur was rescued from fury as *Winifred came in.*

"Oh! here you both are already! Imogen and I have had the most amusing afternoon at the Babies' bazaar."

"What babies?" said Fleur mechanically.

"The 'Save the Babies'. I got such a bargain, my dear. A piece of old Armenian work from before the Flood. I want your opinion on it, Prosper."

"Auntie," whispered Fleur suddenly, as if roused from some other place. *"Auntie, he—told me that father has been married before. Is it true that he divorced her, and she married Jon Forsyte's father?"*

Winifred felt seriously embarrassed.

"Your father didn't wish you to hear," she said, with all the aplomb she could muster. *"These things will happen. I've often told him he ought to let you know."*

Oh!" said Fleur.

"We've forgotten about it years and years ago," Winifred *said comfortably. "Come and have dinner."*

"No, Auntie. I don't feel very well. May I go upstairs?"

"My dear!" murmured Winifred, concerned, "you're not taking this to heart? Why, you haven't properly come out yet! That boy's a child!"

"What boy? I've got a headache. I can't stand that man to-night."

"Well, well," said Winifred, "go and lie down. I'll send you some bromide, and I shall talk to Prosper Profond. What business had he to gossip? Though I must say I think it's much better that you should know."

Bromide was widely used in 'Forsythia' as a sedative. It was also considered a suppressant of hormones and used to lower libidos. By late 'Forsythia', especially after World War II, it had become the butt of music hall jokes, for it was forever rumored that the army put bromide in the troops' tea urns to reduce the sexual libido of soldiers on duty. This rumor persisted in my schooldays when we were led to believe bromide was put in the tea distributed at Combined Cadet Corps training camp. In a sexually segregated system such as we experienced in our schooldays, there was no small amount of homosexual experimentation. Bromide was expected to reduce these desires when younger boys were billeted with older boys in their army training units.

The subject of homosexuality in British private boarding schools during 'Forsythia' is worthy of mention, as it tainted three generations of imperial rulers. Almost no boy came through the system innocent of some homosexual activity in their formative years. It was our only outlet, and to some extent a blind eye was turned toward it. It became, however, the subject of great writers—especially of Evelyn Waugh in *Brideshead Revisited.* Did such homosexuality last? No. For the most part experimental homosexuality died a death when its practitioners came into the real world, but there was always that knowledge that we had all been members of the same club. That reality continued in the male bastions of imperial society. If a new member was put up at some colonial club, there was often someone who would offer a response: "I knew that boy when we were in school." One never knew exactly what was meant, and if there was no reason to see lingering homosexual trends, others would quickly interject: "There's nothing queer about Carruthers."

Whether Winifred had Fleur's sexual desires on Jon in mind, or just concern for Fleur's depressed state on hearing at least a part of the truth, bromide was an obvious solution. Had she ever secretly administered bromide in her late husband's tea? Montague Dartie might well have been deserving of such treatment.

Left alone, Fleur thought again of that photograph beneath her own in her father's silk sachet. *Could he hate Jon's mother and yet keep her photograph! Had they told Jon—had her visit to Robin Hill forced them to tell him? Everything now turned on that! She knew, they all knew, except—perhaps—Jon!*

If they had told him, what would he do? She could not tell. But if they had not told him, should she not—could she not get him for herself—get married to him, before he knew? Instinctively she felt they would shrink from telling Jon, even now shrink from hurting him—for of course it would hurt him awfully to know!

Her aunt must be made to not tell her father that she knew. So long as neither she herself nor Jon were supposed to know, there was still a chance—freedom to get what her heart was set on. Everyone's hand was against her—everyone's! It was as Jon had said—he and she just wanted to live and the past was in their way, a past they hadn't shared in, and didn't understand. And suddenly she thought of June. Would she help them? For somehow June had left on her the impression that she would be sympathetic with their love. Then, instinctively, she thought: 'I won't give anything away, though, even to her. I daren't. I mean to have Jon; against them all.'

When Winifred came to check on her, *Fleur opened her campaign with these words:*

"You know, Auntie, I do wish people wouldn't think I'm in love with that boy. Why, I've hardly seen him!"

Winifred, though experienced, was not 'fine'. She accepted the remark with considerable relief. She then, told Fleur what she felt she should know.

Her description was a masterpiece of understatement. Fleur's father's first wife had been very foolish. There had been a young man who had got run over, and she had left Fleur's father. Then, years after, when it might have all come right again, she had taken up with their cousin Jolyon; and, of course, her father had been obliged to have a divorce. Nobody remembered anything of it now, except just the family. And, perhaps it had all turned out for the best; her father had Fleur; and

Jolyon and Irene had been quite happy, they said, and their boy was a nice boy. "Val having Holly, too, is a sort of plaster, don't you know?"

Her aunt had left out all that mattered—all the feeling, the hate, the love, the unforgivingness of passionate hearts. 'Poor Father!' she thought. 'Poor me! Poor Jon! But I don't care, I mean to have him!' From the window of her darkened room she saw 'that man' issue from the door below and 'prowl' away. If he and her mother—how would that affect her chance? Surely it must make her father cling to her more closely, so that he would consent in the end to anything she wanted.

She took some earth from the flower-box in the window, and with all her might flung it after that disappearing figure. It fell short, but the action did her good.

CHAPTER FIVE

PURELY FORSYTE AFFAIRS

Soames *seldom visited the City now, but he still had a room of his own at Cuthcott Kingson and Forsyte's, and one special clerk and a half assigned to the management of purely Forsyte affairs.* He was on his way there, ruminating, before he would pick up Fleur at Green Street to take her back to Mapledurham.

If Soames thought this or thought that, one had better save oneself the bother of thinking, too. He guaranteed, as it were, irresponsibility to numerous Forsytes of the third and fourth generations. His fellow trustees, such as his cousin Roger or Nicholas, his cousins-in-law Tweetyman and Spender, or his sister Ciceley's husband, all trusted him; he signed first, and where he signed first they signed after, and nobody was a penny the worse. Just now they were all a good many pennies the better.

In our family, this role seemed to fall to Aunt Daphne's husband, Gordon Noble. He handled insurance needs for almost all the branches of the Collings family, including us. And in other legal matters, if a signatory was required, it was usually Gordon Noble who was called upon. He was a member of Lloyds, that prestigious club of global insurance that first started in an eighteenth-century coffeehouse named Lloyds. It was considered throughout 'Forsythia' that if you were backed by Lloyds you were secure. Lloyds' reputation gained worldwide during the imperial period, when almost all the world's shipping was insured at the brokerage. Shipping was the lifeline of the British Empire. Where Gordon Noble signed, the rest of us signed.

Soames *ruminated. Money was extraordinary tight; and morality extraordinary loose! The War had done it. Banks were not lending; people breaking contracts all over the place. There was a feeling in the air and a look on faces that he did not like. He was only an Englishman like any other, so quietly tenacious of what he had that he knew he would never part with it without something more or less equivalent in exchange. Take his own case, for example! He was well off. Did that do anybody harm? He did not eat ten meals a day; he ate no more than, perhaps not so much as, a poor man. He spent no money on vice; breathed no more air, used no more water to speak of than the mechanic or a porter. He certainly had pretty things about him, but they had given employment in the making, and somebody must use them. He bought pictures, but Art must be encouraged. He was, in fact, an accidental channel through which money flowed, employing labor. What was there objectionable in that?* If his name was not Soames Forsyte it could well have been Oliver Longley. *In his charge money was in quicker and more useful flux than it would be in charge of the State and a lot of slow-fly money-sucking officials. The State paid him no salary for being trustee of his own or other people's money—he did all that for nothing. Therein lay the whole case against nationalisation—owners of private property were unpaid, and yet had every incentive to quicken up the flux. Under nationalisation—just the opposite! In a country smarting from officialism he felt that he had a strong case.*

He reached *the offices of Cuthcott Kingson and Forsyte.*

His old clerk Gradman was seated, where he always was, at a huge bureau with countless pigeonholes. Half-the-clerk stood beside him.

Soames hung up his hat, just as my grandfather always did when first he entered the offices of E. Weatherley and Company at Smithfield. After he died, for he never completely retired, Grandpop's old raincoat and an umbrella, his famous 'ski' stick, hung ceremonially from the hat stand at E. Weatherley and Company until the day the business was sold.

"I want to look at my Will and Marriage Settlement, Gradman," Soames said.

Old Gradman moving to the limits of his swivel chair, drew out two drafts from the bottom left-hand drawer. Recovering his body, he raised his grizzle-haired face, very red from stooping.

"Copies, sir."

Soames took them.

Soames unfolded his Marriage Settlement. He had not looked at it for over eighteen years, not since he remade his Will when his father died and Fleur was born. He wanted to see whether the words 'during coverture' were in. Yes, they were—odd expression, when you thought of it, and derived perhaps from horse-breeding! Interest on fifteen thousand pounds so long as she remained his wife, and afterwards during widowhood 'dum casta'. His will made it up to an annuity of a thousand under the same conditions. All right!

"Gradman! I don't like the condition of the country; there are a lot of people about without any common sense. I want to find a way by which I can safeguard Miss Fleur against anything which might arise."

"Ye-es," Gradman *said; "there's a nahsty spirit."*

"Suppose those Labour fellows come in, or worse! It's these people with fixed ideas who are the danger. Look at Ireland!"

The reality that Ireland's proclamation of independence in 1916 was now virtual reality, despite civil war—the era of Michael Collins and the Republican idealist Eamonn de Valera—weighed heavily on 'Forsytes' of Soames' era. It was a blow against the subject peoples of any part of the British Empire, let alone one so close to home.

When I moved to Ireland in 1962, Eamonn de Valera was President of the Republic—the grand old man of the revolution, highly respected. The 1924 compromise that he had brokered with Great Britain, however, although it brought the civil war to a close, was not yet resolved. Pockets of the rebel Irish Republican Army, still wanted to lay claim on those six counties of Northern Ireland that Britain had retained. Also, there were many families among the Anglo-Irish who remembered vividly their homes being looted and burned by the rebels. The skeletons of many of those eighteenth and nineteenth-century mansions dotted the countryside, roofless, windows agape and ivy tearing at their stones. Tullamaine Castle itself had been burned and looted in 1920. The castle, however, was rebuilt in 1930, and extensively restored in 1967 by Mr. Albertini. The Irish, however, did not refer to the uncertainties of 1920-22 as civil war, but with the endearing understatement that they were "the troubles."

"Suppose I were to make a settlement on Fleur at once with myself as beneficiary for life," Soames continued. *"They couldn't take anything but the interest from me, unless of course they alter the law."*

"Aoh!" Gradman *said, "they wouldn't do tha-at!"*

"I don't know," muttered Soames; *"I don't trust them, but that's not the point. Draw a form of settlement that passes all my property to Miss Fleur's children in equal shares, with antecedent life-interests first to myself and then to her without power of anticipation, and add a clause that in the event of anything happening to divert her life-interest, that interest passes to the trustees, to apply for her benefit, in their absolute discretion."*

Gradman grated: *"Rather extreme at your age, sir: you lose control."*

"That's my business," said Soames, sharply.

"What trustees then? There's young Mr. Kingson; he's a nice steady young fellow."

"Yes, he might do for one. I must have three. There isn't a Forsyte now who appeals to me."

"Not young Mr. Nicholas? He's at the Bar. We've given 'im briefs."

"He'll never set the Thames on fire," said Soames.

"You can't expect it at his age, Mr. Soames."

"Well, put him in; but I want somebody who'll take a personal interest. There's no one that I can see."

"What about Mr. Valerius, now he's come home?'

"Val Dartie? With that father? No," said Soames. *"I don't like the connection."* He rose. Gradman said suddenly:

"If I were making a levy on capital, they could come on the trustees, sir. So there you'd be just the same. I'd think it over if I were you."

"That's true," said Soames, *"I will. Mr. Timothy? Is everything in order in case of..."*

"I've got the inventory of his estate all ready; had the furniture and pictures valued so that we know what reserves to put on. I shall be sorry when he goes, though. Dear me! It is a time since I first saw Mr. Timothy!"

"We can't live forever," said Soames, taking down his hat. *"I must call for Miss Fleur and catch the four o'clock. Good-day Gradman."*

"Good-day, Mr. Soames. I hope Miss Fleur..."

"Well enough, but gads about too much."

"Ye-es," grated Gradman; "she's young."

Soames went out musing: 'Old Gradman! If he were younger I'd put him in the trust. There's nobody I can depend on to take a real interest.'

* * *

Two hours later by his watch, Thomas Gradman closed the last drawer of his bureau, and putting into his waistcoat pocket a bunch of keys so fat that they gave him a protuberance on the liver side, brushed his old top hat with his sleeve, took his umbrella, and descended to the street.

He never missed that daily promenade to the Tube for Highgate, and seldom some critical transaction on the way in connection with vegetables and fruit. Generations might be born, and hats might change, wars be fought, and Forsytes fade away, but Thomas Gradman, faithful and grey, would take his daily walk and buy his daily vegetable. Times were not what they were, and his son had lost a leg in the war, but these tubes were convenient things. It was fifty years since he went into Mr. James's office, and Mr. James had said to him: "Now, Mr. Gradman, you're only a shaver—you pay attention, and you'll make your five hundred a year before you're done." And he had, he was getting around eight hundred a year, and feared God, and served the Forsytes, and kept a vegetable diet at night. And, buying a copy of John Bull—*not that he approved of it, an extravagant affair—he entered the Tube elevator and was borne down into the bowels of the earth.*

London's underground transport became the envy of the world with trains that criss-crossed the entire city in tubes that created a warren of mole tracks through the subsoil. Some were deep. Hampstead Station was the deepest. There, and at a few others, elevators had to be taken to speed commuters to the depths of the tubes. At most, however, a series of escalators took one to different levels where tubes crossed over and under each other. One of the largest complexes was Piccadilly Circus. I remember a wonderful cut out diagram in a book on the 'Underground' that showed all the tubes and escalators at Piccadilly. It almost looked like the board of the common childhood game—snakes and ladders. The tubes were the snakes and the ladders the escalators.

Escalators fascinated us as children. It was a treat to travel on the tube, and my father sometimes took us, although my mother and Granny Mabs preferred the double-decker buses. It was more a treat to actually take those escalators ever further down into the ground below London's streets than travel in the trains. The trains, after all, just traveled through dark tunnels. We always hoped that the line we needed to take was the deepest.

As a measure of how much the London Underground was prized by all who visited the city, unlike perhaps the subways of New York or the Metro of Paris, I remember with perhaps a tinge of jealousy, the gift that the Soviet leader Nikita Kruschev presented to my closest contemporary within the Royal family, Prince Charles—a model train set of the London Underground. Did it burrow beneath Buckingham Palace! However, the Tube was also much endeared by Londoners as the safe refuge that it had afforded against Hitler's bombs. There was that tragic accident at The Bank—a station not deep enough, but for the most part, the London Underground had proved to be the city's best bomb shelter during those tumultuous years of the Second World War.

Ironically, the Russian premier on that State Visit in 1955 was in Oxford at the same time as my father and all of us were returning from the Spring Game Fair at Ditchley Park, where we had enjoyed one of my mother's wonderful picnics complete with beetroot rolls—a speciality of hers that I particularly liked. We actually witnessed the Krucschev motorcade come down the High—a moment in history and perhaps one that defined the coming demise of 'Forsythia', just one year before the Suez crisis, when Her Majesty The Queen was placed in the position of being host to the communist leader, whose ideology was exactly that which most 'Forsytes' had dreaded.

CHAPTER SIX

SOAMES'S PRIVATE LIFE

At Green Street Soames *found that Fleur was out and would be all the evening; she was staying one more night in London.* He took the train home alone.

He reached his house about six o'clock. Taking his letters he went up to his dressing-room.

An uninteresting post. A receipt, a bill for purchases on behalf of Fleur. A circular about an exhibition of etchings. A letter beginning:

'SIR,
'I feel it my duty...'

That would be an appeal or something unpleasant. He looked at once for the signature. There was none! Not being a public man, Soames had never yet had an anonymous letter, and his first impulse was to tear it up, as a dangerous thing; his second to read it, as a thing still more dangerous.

'SIR
'I feel it my duty to inform you that having no interest in the matter your lady is carrying on with a foreigner...'

Reaching that word Soames stopped mechanically and examined the postmark. Battersea? Perhaps! He read on.

'These foreigners are all the same. Sack the lot. This one
meets your lady twice a week. I know it of my own knowledge—and to see an Englishman put on goes against the
grain. You watch it and see if what I say isn't true. I shouldn't
meddle if it wasn't a dirty foreigner that's in it. Yours obedi-
ent.'

Soames dropped the letter. He did not know whether he was more annoyed by the content or the anonymity. *"Prowling cat!"* he muttered. *Had he not in connection therewith, this very day, perused his Will and Marriage Settlement? And now this anonymous ruffian, with nothing to gain, apparently, save the venting of his spite against foreigners, had wrenched it out of the obscurity in which he had hoped and wished it would remain. He would not be forced into another scandal. No! However he decided to deal with this matter—and it required the most far-sighted and careful consideration—he would do nothing that might injure Fleur.*

He had nothing but this now *torn-up letter from some anonymous ruffian, whose impudent intrusion into his private life he so violently resented.* As he reflected on this in his picture gallery, now pleased that *Fleur was not at home tonight,* a servant announced that Mr. Michael Mont had arrived. *"Will you see him?" the servant asked.*

"No," said Soames; "yes... I'll come down."

Anything that would take his mind off for a few minutes.

Soames's feeling toward this young man was singular. He was no doubt a rackety, irresponsible young fellow according to old standards, yet somehow likeable, with his extraordinary cheerful way of blurting out his opinions.

"Come in" he said; "have you had tea?"

Mont came in.

"I thought Fleur would have been back, sir; but I'm glad she isn't. The fact is, I—I'm fearfully gone on her; so fearfully gone that I thought you'd better know. It's old-fashioned, of course, coming to father's first, but I thought you'd forgive that. I went to my own Dad, and he says if I settle down he'll see me through. He rather cottons to the idea, in fact. I told him about your Goya."

"Oh!" said Soames, inexpressibly dry. "He rather cottons?"

"Yes, sir; do you?"

Soames smiled faintly.

"You see," resumed Mont, twiddling his straw boater, while his hair, ears, eyebrows, all seemed to stand up from excitement, "when you've been through the War you can't help being in a hurry."

"To get married, and unmarried afterwards," said Soames slowly.

"Not from Fleur, sir. Imagine, if you were me!"

"Fleur's too young," Soames said.

"Oh! no, sir. We're awfully old nowadays. My Dad seems to me a perfect babe; his thinking apparatus hasn't turned a hair. But he's a Baronight, of course; that keeps him back."

"Baronight," repeated Soames; "what may that be?" as if he didn't know.

"Bart, sir. I shall be a Bart some day. But I shall live it down, you know."

'Forsytes' were not that conscious of landed titles. A Baronet is the lowest of the landed hereditary titles and in society, in an almost mocking way, is usually referred to as 'Bart', the abbreviation that is allowed to follow the Baronet's written name. However, a Baronet is a hereditary knight, and his spouse is a 'Lady'. Even if a 'Forsyte' might not be particularly impressed by the title 'Bart' it was always a nice feather in the cap for a daughter to be a 'Lady'.

In post-'Forsythia' years, my Uncle Gyles was rewarded in the Queen's honors with the title CBE—Commander of the British Empire—for his work as President of the British Chamber of Commerce in Paris. This is the highest award that can be made without bestowing a knighthood. There are three ranks of awards that are given in the name of the now obsolete British Empire. The most common is the OBE—Order of the British Empire, the one that as aforementioned, many mockingly used to call an award for 'other buggers' efforts'—often an almost automatic award for certain civic, administrative, and military positions. The second, requiring some major personal effort on behalf of the nation in the sciences, arts, or British commerce is the MBE—Member of the British Empire that truly is quite an honor to receive. The highest is the CBE—Commander of the British Empire. Immediately above that comes the KBE—Knight of the British Empire—which carries for life the same weight as that lowest level of the peerage—'Baronet'.

We always liked to believe that Uncle Gyles was almost within reach of being knighted, one pip above the CBE that he received. If he had been, my Aunt Ginette would have been Lady Longley for the duration of her life. All these titles are bestowed by the monarch at an investiture in Buckingham Palace. We were all very proud of Uncle Gyles on the day that it was his turn to attend, following in the footsteps of his father, Grandpop Longley, who was awarded the Military Cross at an investiture from King George V for his specific bravery during the Great War. In reality, however, it was the second time Uncle Gyles had been summoned to the Palace for an award, for like Grandpop, he too had been awarded the Military Cross for bravery during the Italian campaign of World War II, bestowed on him by King George VI. Unfortunately, he could not be present at the investiture while serving abroad, but he did receive a nice personal letter from the king.

The idea that one-day Fleur might be Lady Mont did not fully register with Soames, who probably in 'Forsyte' amusement only saw this irrepressible youth as a future 'Bart'.

"Go away and live this down," he replied.

Young Mont said imploringly: "Oh! no, sir. I simply must hang around, or I shouldn't have a dog's chance. You'll let Fleur do what she likes, I suppose, anyway, Madame passes me."

"Indeed!" said Soames frigidly.

"You don't really bar me, do you?" and the young man looked so doleful that Soames smiled.

"You may think you're old," he said; "but you strike me as extremely young. To rattle ahead of anything is not proof of maturity."

"All right, sir; I give in to you on age. But to show you I mean business—I've got a job."

"Glad to hear it."

"Joined a publisher; my governor is putting up the stakes."

Soames put his hand over his mouth—he had so very nearly said: "God help the publisher!" His grey eyes scrutinised the agitated young man.

"I don't dislike you, Mr. Mont, but Fleur is everything to me. Everything—you understand?"

"Yes, sir, I know; but so she is to me."

"That's as may be. I'm glad you've told me, however. And now I think there's nothing more to be said."

"I know it rests with her, sir."

"It will rest with her a long time, I hope."

"You aren't cheering," said Mont suddenly.

"No," said Soames, "my experience of life has not made me anxious to couple people in a hurry. Good-night, Mr. Mont. I shan't tell Fleur what you've said."

Although it was post-'Forsythia', I was brought up in this tradition that at least, in practice, it was polite to ask a father for his daughter's hand in marriage before making an engagement official. I did so in 1978 with an even less favorable reception than that which met Mr. Michael Mont.

"Get out of my house!" my expected father-in-law-to-be shouted, after a day when he had freely entertained me and my girlfriend, Leslie, at his vacation home on Key Largo in Florida, even taking us out in his power boat for a spin in the bay. Turning to his daughter he continued: "Marry the guy if you must, but I don't want to ever see either of you again!"

Needless to say, after such an inauspicious start, Leslie and I never got married, although we were engaged. I met Leslie on a Scandinavian cruise in 1978 on the fabulous old Swedish-America Liner *Kungsholm* where I was on the cruise staff as ship's artist. My principal task, other than to socialize with the passengers, was to design, construct and paint all the port signs, stage sets, and photographers' sets needed throughout the cruise. The cruise was a graduation present or kind of coming-out gift from Leslie's mother for her youngest daughter when she completed high school. We became engaged at Sea Island over Thanksgiving the following fall. Despite her father's disapproval, I spent the summer of 1979 at her mother and stepfather's home in Ladue, a very salubrious suburb of St. Louis, where I redesigned their garden. Mrs. Meletio was dying of cancer at the time, and the redesigned gardens became the last beautiful experience in her life. Meanwhile, Leslie and I had broken off our engagement, with no small pressure from her father and stepmother. I made the story of that incredible and strange year in my life into a novel that I titled *Love is Where Your Rosemary Grows*—a novel that won the publisher's Editor's Choice award.

However, the idea of a luxury cruise as a sort of rite of passage was quite common in 'Forsythia', especially in the 1930s. Both my mother and my father went on such cruises. My mother actually met a promising prospect on such a cruise. Later, she was invited to join him at a country house party, but the timing was wrong, she was scheduled that weekend to be on vacation with her cousin John Hoby—my godfather—the one we called Uncle 'Jong' after the beautiful antique Mahjong sets he had.

My father took a Scandinavian cruise, but it led to no shipboard romance. However, all his life he told us how beautiful the approach to Stockholm was as his Orient Line cruise ship made its way through the Stockholm archipelago. It was very special for me, therefore, that through my cruising career, I was able to encourage him to cruise the archipelago again in the 1990s. On that Baltic cruise, in which we all sailed as a family with Uncle Gyles and Aunt Ginette joining us, too, we were able to visit St. Petersburg. In the 1930s, Leningrad was not on the itinerary of cruise ships it still being too close to the communist revolution. I knew my father would love St. Petersburg, however, and I was right. I think the 'City of the Tsars' impressed him even more than the Stockholm archipelago. In fact, with a nostalgic longing perhaps for the 'Forsythia' world of his childhood, I remember him saying to me not long before he died and Russia was re-establishing itself as a capitalist society after the collapse of the Soviet Union: "Peter, do you think they might bring back the Tsars?"

'The younger generation!' thought Soames heavily after Mont left on his motor cycle. He went out on the lawn. Where was Annette? With that chap, for all he knew—she was a young woman! Impressed with the queer charity of that thought, he entered the summer-house and sat down. The fact was—and he admitted it—Fleur was so much to him that his wife was very little—very little; French—had never been much more than a mistress, and he was getting indifferent to that side of things! He cared so much for Fleur that he would have no further scandal. If only he could get at that anonymous letter-writer, he would teach him not to meddle and stir up mud at the bottom of water which he wished should remain stagnant. A distant flash, a low rumble, and large drops of rain spattered on the thatch above him. He remained indifferent, tracing a pattern with his finger on the dusty surface of a little rustic table. Fleur's future! 'I want fair sailing for her,' he thought. 'Nothing else matters at my time of life.'

The rain dripped from the thatch.

Summerhouses were very fashionable in latter 'Forsythia', taking the place of earlier 'Forsythia's' obligatory conservatories. Instead of bringing the garden into the house, 'Forsytes' in the 1920s and '30s started to take the house out into the garden.

Many summerhouses had a rustic cottage feeling featuring thatched roofing. They had the form of a single room the south side being open to the rays of the sun—a great place for enjoying afternoon tea, or a place of sheltered solitude for reading, or at times even the secret place of a tryst.

One of those substantial Victorian estates around the original village of Beckenham was Kelsey Manor. It was a large Baronial-style mansion set at the head of sloping lawns with obligatory Lebanon cedar trees that went down to a lake formed by damming a section of the little River Beck. The mansion had belonged to the Hoare banking family, but in its latter days it was a convent and was used as a convalescent home for injured soldiers during the Great War like *Downton Abbey* in the popular 2011 Masterpiece Theatre public television mini-series. After the First World War, Kelsey Manor was pulled down to make way for a 1920s development of prosperous 'Forsyte' homes along Manor Way. The Kelsey Manor gardens, however, were preserved as a public park around the lake, and at appropriate places rather delightful summerhouses were built with beautifully thatched roofs. Grandpa Jack loved to take me and my sisters into the park to feed the ducks, and those thatched summerhouses with their rustic furnishings always fascinated us as children. Sadly, in a post-'Forsythia' world, those same thatched roofs were set on fire by hooligans and replaced by boring municipal roofs, but Kelsey Park remains a beautiful place and a haven to many interesting birds.

Granny Mabs and Grandpa Jack also had their own summerhouse at Redcroft. It was not thatched, but faced the sun and a magnificent garden view of my grandparents' immaculate herbaceous borders. Every day during the summer, weather permitting, my grandparents sat in the summerhouse all afternoon. Granny would give out their after-lunch cigarettes—she controlled their smoking—always the same brand, 'Craven A', and always just one cigarette two or three times a day. Then, they would settle down to their library books leaning back in their deck chairs until teatime. Sometimes, we joined them for tea.

Aunt Daphne, at the house next door to ours in Wickham Way, also had a large summerhouse in her back garden that could rotate according to the position of the sun throughout the day. We never had a summerhouse at Hockeredge, but we certainly brought the house out into the garden with our daily use of our patio terrace for lunches, afternoon teas, and family gatherings with a view over the geraniums down our striped lawn to boundary trees past a flowering border and poles of roses. 'Forsytes' loved their gardens.

When the storm was over, Soames Forsyte *left* the summerhouse *and went down the wet path to the river bank.*

Annette must be back now from wherever she had gone, for it was nearly dinner-time. A new and scaring thought occurred to him. Suppose she wanted her liberty to marry this fellow! Well, if she did, she couldn't have it. He had not married her for that. The image of Prosper Profond dawdled before him reassuringly. Not a marrying man! No, no! Anger replaced that momentary scare. 'He had better not come my way,' he thought.

When he returned, *Annette was in the drawing-room, dressed for dinner. A fine piece in any room! Soames, held that torn letter in a hand thrust deep into the side-pocket of his dinner-jacket.*

Whereas the practice of dressing for dinner automatically meant, white tie and tails in the pre-Great War era of 'Forsythia', a new trend developed in the 1920s—black tie, with a black silk-lapelled suit, that in the tropics became a white silk-lapelled suit—the dinner jacket. In the '20s and '30s the dinner jacket was generally worn for family dining, but for entertaining, most 'Forsytes' returned to white tie and tails. After World War II the lounge suit took over from the dinner jacket in most households, although among some, including most of those I encountered in that last decade when I lived among the Anglo-Irish 'Forsytes', black tie was still in vogue for entertaining, and white tie and tails was still preferred for balls and 'occasion' dinners. Sadly, with the demise of 'Forsythia' in the 1960s almost any dressing for dinner disappeared. In Ireland at Tullamaine Castle, for a while in those twilight years of 'Forsythia' we actually revived the custom of dressing for dinner nightly—'Black Tie' with dinner jacket or velvet smoking jacket.

What was Annette *thinking of?* Soames *had never understood a woman in his life—except Fleur—and Fleur not always. He took out the torn letter.*

"I've had this."

Annette's eyes widened, stared at him, and hardened.

Soames handed her the letter.

"It's torn, but you can read it." Out of the corner of his eye he saw Annette holding the letter rigidly; her eyes moved from side to side

*under her darkened lashes and frowning, darkened eyebrows. She
dropped the letter, gave a little shiver, smiled, and said:*

"Dirrty!"

"I quite agree," said Soames; "degrading. Is it true?"

"And what if it were?" she brazenly replied.

"Is that all you have to say?"

"No."

"Well, speak out!"

"What is the good of talking?"

Soames said icily: "So you admit it?"

*"I admit nothing. You are a fool to ask. A man like you should not
ask. It is dangerous."*

*"Do you remember what you were when I married you? Working
at accounts in a restaurant."*

"Do you remember that I was not half your age?"

Soames broke off the hard encounter of their eyes. This benefited
neither of them.

*"I require you to give up this—friendship. I think of the matter
entirely as it effects Fleur."*

"Ah!—Fleur!"

*"Yes," said Soames stubbornly; "Fleur. She is your child as well
as mine."*

"It is kind to admit that!"

"Are you going to do what I say?"

"I refuse to tell you."

"Then I must make you."

Annette smiled.

*"No. Soames," she said. "You are helpless. Do not say things that
you will regret. There shall be no more such letters, I promise you. That
is enough."*

Soames writhed.

"When two people have married and lived like us," Annette
continued, *"they had better be quiet about each other. There are things
one does not drag up into the light for people to laugh at. You will be
quiet, then; not for my sake—for your own. You are getting old; I am
not, yet. You have made me very practical."*

Soames repeated dully:

"I require you to give up this friendship."

"And if I do not?"

"Then—then I will cut you out of my Will."

In family disputes among 'Forsytes' this was the most common attack roused from defense, although rarely put into practice for 'blood is thicker than water'. Property was what made 'Forsythia' spin. To be cut out of that inherited right to that property was ostracism from the club—the three percent. Ultimately, not even 'Old' Jolyon had been able to sustain that action against his son.

Annette laughed.

"You will live a long time, Soames."

"You—you are a bad woman," said Soames suddenly.

Annette shrugged her shoulders.

"I do not think so. Living with you has killed things in me, it is true; but I am not a bad woman. I am sensible—that is all. And so will you be when you've thought it over."

"I shall see this man," said Soames sullenly, "and warn him off."

"Mon cher, you are funny. You do not want me, you have as much of me as you want; and you wish the rest of me to be dead. I admit nothing, but I am not going to be dead, Soames, at my age; so you had better be quiet, I tell you. I myself will make no scandal; none. Now, I am not saying any more, whatever you do."

Without saying another word Soames *went out and up to the picture gallery. This came of marrying a Frenchwoman! And yet, without her there would have been no Fleur! She had served her purpose.*

'She's right,' he thought; 'I can do nothing. I don't even know if there's anything in it.'

And so it was that my father kept bottled within himself his own belief that my mother had enjoyed more than friendship with their old bridge opponent and her golfing partner, Eric Pilbrow. He waited until his deathbed before revealing his thoughts to us, his unsuspecting children—another 'Forsyte' potential scandal averted.

They had dinner and that night Soames went into Annette's room. *She received him in the most matter-of-fact way, as if there had been no scene between them. And he returned to his room with a curious sense of peace. If one didn't choose to see, one needn't. And he did not choose—in future he did not choose. There was nothing to be gained by it—nothing! Opening the drawer he took from the sachet a handkerchief, and the framed photograph of Fleur. When he had looked at it a little he slipped it down, and there was that other one—that old one of Irene. An owl hooted while he stood in his window gazing at it.*

The owl hooted, the red climbing roses seemed to deepen in colour, there came a scent of lime-blossom. God! That had been a different thing! Passion—Memory! Dust!

CHAPTER SEVEN

JUNE TAKES A HAND

Boris Strumolowski, a Slav sculptor recently coming to England from New York, was June's most recent 'lame duck'. *June had known him three weeks, and he still seemed to her the principal embodiment of genius, and hope of the future.* He shared a rather 'Forsyte' view with her of the United States—*a country, in his opinion, so barbarous in every way that he had sold practically nothing there, and become an object of suspicion to the police; a country, as he said, without a race of its own, without liberty, equality, or fraternity, without principles, traditions, taste, without—in a word—a soul.* And harsh though this description may seem, to an observer of the time, the principles touted by American patriots, who had so lately served with British and French soldiers in the Great War—those principles of liberty, equality and fraternity were lacking in the abject poverty of the American negro and many of her native Americans found by any who visited American cities and towns of the era. 'Forsytes', also, really had a double standard on race. In the lands of the Empire, they were masters of the native races ruling as a caste above them and, as yet, at home, few native imperial subjects outside the princely caste had as yet ventured to the mother country to create a sense of racial inequality. The problem was not, therefore, as glaring as in the United States.

June Forsyte *had begun to take steps to clear her Gallery, in order to fill it with Strumolowski masterpieces. She had at once encountered trouble* with Paul Post, Vospovitch and others. *With all the emphasis of a genius which she did not as yet deny them, they had demanded another six weeks at least of her Gallery. The American stream of* visitors, *still flowing in, would soon be flowing out.* Americans bought art abroad even if they ignored it at home. This *American stream was their right, their only hope, their salvation—since nobody in this beastly country cared for Art. June had yielded to the demonstration. After all Boris* Strumolowski *would not mind them having the full benefit of an American stream, which he himself so violently despised.*

Boris surprised her with his reaction, so desperate was he to exhibit his work. Suddenly, the American stream would work for him and he turned his venom on the selfishness of the British. *This—he said—was characteristic of England, the most selfish country in the world; the country which sucked the blood of other countries; destroyed the brains and hearts of Irishmen, Hindus, Egyptians, Boers and Burmese, all the finest races in the world; bullying, hypocritical England! This was what he had expected, coming to such a country, where the climate was all fog, and the people all tradesmen perfectly blind to Art, and sunk in profiteering and the grossest materialism.*

June was too much of a Forsyte to let this pass. She *grew crimson and suddenly rapped out:*

"Then why did you ever come? We didn't ask you."

The remark was so singularly at variance with all that she had led him to expect of her.

"England never wants an idealist," he moped.

But in June something primitively English was thoroughly upset; old Jolyon's sense of justice had risen, as it were, from bed. "You come and sponge on us," she said, *"and then abuse us. If you think that's playing the game, I don't."*

She now discovered that which others had discovered before her—the thickness of hide beneath which the sensibility of genius is sometimes veiled.

"Sponge," Boris repeated, *"one does not sponge, one takes what is owing—a tenth part of what is owing. You will repent to say that, Miss Forsyte."*

"Oh, no," said June, *"I shan't."*

"Ah! We know very well, we artists—you take us to get what you can out of us. I want nothing from you."

"Very well, then, you can take your things away."

And, almost in the same moment June *thought: 'Poor boy! He's only got a garret, and probably not a taxi fare.'*

Young Strumolowski shook his head violently:

"I can live on nothing," *he said shrilly.* "I have often had to for the sake of my Art. It is you bourgeois who force us to spend money."

The words hit June like a pebble in the ribs. After all she had done for Art, all her identification with its troubles and lame ducks. She was struggling for adequate words when the door was opened and her Austrian servant murmured:

"A young lady, gnädiges Fräulein."

"Where?"

"In the little meal-room."

Leaving Boris, June said nothing and went out. Entering the 'little meal-room', she perceived the young lady to be Fleur—looking very pretty, if pale. At this disenchanted moment a little lame duck of her own breed was welcome to June.

The girl must have come, of course, because of Jon; or, if not, at least to get something out of her. And June felt just then that to assist somebody was the only bearable thing.

"So you've remembered to come," *she said.*

"Yes. What a jolly little duck of a house! But please don't let me bother you, if you've got people."

"Not at all," *said June.* "I want to let them stew in their own juice for a bit. Have you come about Jon?"

"You said you thought we might be told. Well, I've found out."

"Oh!" *said June blankly.* "Not nice, is it?"

Observing Fleur, June *remembered with sudden vividness how nice she herself had looked in those old days when her heart was set on Philip Bosinney, that dead lover, who had broken from her to destroy forever Irene's allegiance to this girl's father. Did Fleur know of that, too?*

"Well," *she said,* "what are you going to do?"

It was seconds before Fleur answered.

"I don't want Jon to suffer. I must see him once more to put an end to it."

"You're going to put an end to it?"

"What else is there to do?"

The girl seemed to June, suddenly, intolerably spiritless.

"I suppose you're right," she muttered. *"I know my father thinks so; but—I should never have done it myself. I can't take things lying down."*

June was puzzled by the girl's calculated look and *how unemotional her voice sounded.*

"People will assume that I'm in love," Fleur said.

"Well, aren't you?"

Fleur shrugged her shoulders. 'I might have known it,' thought June; 'She's Soames's daughter—fish! And yet—he!'

"What do you want me to do then?" June *said with a sort of disgust.*

"Could I see Jon here tomorrow on his way down to Holly's? He'd come if you sent him a line to-night. And perhaps afterward you'd let them know quietly at Robin Hill that it's all over, and that they needn't tell Jon about his mother."

June was angry and still a little suspicious, but agreed.

She *licked a stamp. "Well, here it is. If you're not in love, of course, there's no more to be said. Jon's lucky."*

Fleur took the note. "Thanks awfully!"

'Cold-blooded little baggage!' thought June. Jon, son of her father, to love, and not to be loved by the daughter of—Soames! It was humiliating.

"Is that all?"

Fleur nodded; and the waistline frills of one of those new-fangled dresses tight below the knees *trembled as she swayed toward the door.*

"Good-bye!"

"Good-bye!...Little piece of fashion!" muttered June closing the door. *"That family!"*

She experienced a sense of futility and disgust, and went to the window to let the river-wind from the Thames *blow those squeaky words away.* Then, recomposed, she *mothered young Strumolowski for half an hour, promising him a month at least, of the American stream.*

Chapter Eight

The Bit between the Teeth

Fleur felt no remorse when she left June's house. Reading condemnatory resentment in her little kinswoman's blue eyes— she was glad that she had fooled her, despising June because that elderly idealist had not seen what she was after.

End it, forsooth! She would soon show them all that she was only just beginning, but would she be able to manage Jon? She had taken the bit between the teeth, but could she make him take it too? She knew the truth and the real danger of delay—he knew neither; therein lay all the difference in the world.

People always accepted an accomplished fact in time! From that piece of philosophy Fleur *passed to another consideration less philosophic. If she persuaded Jon to a quick and secret marriage, and he found out afterward that she had known the truth . What then? Jon hated subterfuge. Again, then, would it not be better to tell him? Fleur was afraid. His mother had power over him; more power than perhaps she herself.*

As she walked past the Iseeum on her way to Green Street, *she saw Monsieur Profond with a tall stout man in the bay window. Turning into Green Street she heard her name called, and saw that 'prowler' coming up.*

"Good evenin'! Miss Forsyde. Isn't there a small thing I can do for you?"

"Yes, pass by on the other side."

"I say! Why do you dislike me?"

"Do I?"

"It looks like it."

"Well, then, because you make me feel like life isn't worth living."

Monsieur Profond smiled.

"Look here, Miss Forsyde, don't worry. It'll be all right. Nothing lasts."

"Things do last," cried Fleur; *"with me anyhow—especially likes and dislikes."*

"Well, that makes me a bit un'appy."

"I should have thought nothing could make you happy or unhappy."

"I don't like to annoy other people. I'm goin' on my yacht."

Fleur looked at him, startled.

"Where?"

"Small voyage to the South Seas or somewhere," said Monsieur Profond.

Fleur suffered relief and a sense of insult. Clearly he meant to convey that he was breaking with her mother. How dared he have anything to break, and yet how dared he break it?

"Good-night, Miss Forsyde! Remember me to Mrs. Dartie. I'm not so bad really. Good-night!"

'He can't even love with conviction,' she thought. 'What will Mother do?'

Back at her aunt's, Fleur consulted *Whitaker's Almanac*. *A Forsyte is instinctively aware that facts are the real crux of any situation. From the invaluable tome she learned that they must each be twenty-one; or someone's consent would be necessary, which of course was unobtainable; then she became lost in directions concerning licenses, certificates, notices, districts, coming finally to the word 'perjury'. The more she studied the less sure she became; till, idly turning the pages, she came to Scotland. People could be married there without any of this nonsense. She had only to go and stay there twenty-one days, then Jon could come, and in front of two people they could declare themselves married. She ran over her schoolfellows. There was Mary Lambe who lived in Edinburgh and was 'quite a sport'! She had a brother too. She could stay with Mary Lambe, who with her brother would serve for witnesses.*

More at ease now, she packed, avoided her aunt, and took a bus to Chiswick. She was too early, and went on to Kew gardens where she *lunched off anchovy paste sandwiches and coffee.*

Anchovy paste used to come in beautiful stone jars marketed as 'Patum Pepperum' and was a favorite spread of my father's, so much so that almost all his life my sisters and I used to make sure a jar of the spread was in his Christmas stocking. With the demise of 'Forsythia', however, the stone jars became plastic, even though still wrapped in the same checker board paper featuring the little fishes, and still advertising itself with that very 'Forsyte' pretension of 'The Gentleman's Relish'.

After lunch, Fleur *returned to Chiswick and rang June's bell. The Austrian admitted her to the 'little meal-room'. If she could not have her way, and get Jon for good and all, she felt like dying of privation. By hook or by crook she must and would get him! She heard the bell ring, and, stealing to the window, saw him standing on the door-step smoothing his hair and lips.*

When he came in, she said:

"Sit down, Jon, I want to talk seriously."

Jon sat by her side.

"If you don't want to lose me we must get married."

Jon gasped.

Why? Is there anything new?"

"No, but I felt it at Robin Hill, and among my people."

"But..." stammered Jon, *"at Robin Hill—it was all smooth—and they've said nothing to me."*

"But they mean to stop us. Your mother's face was enough. And my father's."

"Have you seen him since?"

Fleur nodded a lie.

"But," said Jon eagerly, *"I can't see how they can feel like that after all these years."*

Fleur finally looked him in the eye:

"Perhaps you don't love me enough?"

"Not love you enough! Why—I..."

"Then make sure of me."

"Without telling them?"

"Not till after."

Jon was silent.

"It would hurt Mother awfully," he said.

Fleur drew back.

"You've got to choose."

Jon slid off the table on to his knees.

"But why not tell them? They can't really stop us, Fleur!"

"They can! I tell you they can."

"How?"

"We're utterly dependent—by putting money pressure, and all sorts of other pressure. I'm not patient, Jon."

"But it's deceiving them."

Fleur got up.

"You can't really love me or you wouldn't hesitate."

Lifting his hands to her waist, Jon forced her to sit down again. She hurried on:

"I've planned it all out. We've only to go to Scotland. When we're married they'll soon come round. People always come round to facts. Don't you see, Jon?"

"But to hurt them so awfully!"

So he would rather hurt her than those people of his! "All right, then; let me go!"

Jon got up and put his back against the door.

"I expect you're right," he said slowly; "but I want to think it over."

She saw his eyes, adoring and distressed.

"Don't look like that. I only don't want to lose you, Jon."

"You can't lose me as long as you want me."

"Oh, yes, I can."

Jon put his hands on her shoulders.

"Fleur, do you know anything you haven't told me?"

She looked straight at him and lied: *"No." he would forgive her. And throwing her arms around his neck, she kissed him on the lips. She was winning! She felt it in the beating of his heart against her, in the closing of his eyes. "I want to make sure! I want to make sure!" she whispered, "Promise!"*

Jon did not answer.

At last he said:

"It's like hitting them. I must think a little, Fleur. I really must."

Fleur slipped out of his arms.

"Oh! Very well!" And suddenly she burst into tears of disappointment, shame, and overstrain. Despite her will to cry, "Very well, then, if you don't love me enough—good-bye!" she dared not.

That stormy little meeting ended inconclusively.

Pushing Jon from her, she was gone.

No one was at Green Street. Fleur went on to Paddington.

Chapter Nine

The Fat in the Fire

Fleur found both her mother and father to be in a strained relationship on her return. She joined her father in the vinery. *He was pale as a sheet* standing *in the steamy heat, redolent of the mushy scent of earth, of potted geraniums, and of vines coming along fast.*

Many 'Forsytes' tried to grow grapes and espaliered peaches in glasshouses or greenhouses as we called them. Some even grew orchids. Hot water heating pipes kept out the frost, and the vines flourished, but not for production of wines, only for table grapes and sophisticated prestige. Great Grandpa John Collings had a fine vine house at Reculver Lodge. The aristocracy both in England and northern Europe had long had huge green houses to grow oranges, and the 'Forsyte' vinery was something similar on a lesser scale. As estate manager at Tullamaine Castle in Ireland, I helped restore glasshouses for vines and peaches. Mr. Albertini was fortunate in having a Spanish butler at the time, who was able to tend the vines and we grew bumper crops of table grapes. Below the vines, we too, like Soames, kept potted geraniums through the winter. At Chelston, Grandpop did not grow grapes, but the greenhouse did keep geraniums and carnations through the winter with numerous cuttings every year, and in the spring was filled with young seedlings for the extensive vegetable garden. In the summer, it was full of tomato plants climbing up stakes. One of my first memories as a child was going with my father to Turners, the wonderful old seed merchant in Beckenham High Street. The store had an earthy odor of sack and seed that has disappeared in today's packaged world. The same smell mingled with the geraniums and summer tomatoes in the Chelston greenhouse and potting shed and is a vivid memory of a 'Forsyte' childhood along with that odor of the drying onion sets in the fall.

Fleur, seeing her father in the vinery so obviously distressed, thought: *'Is it because of me, or because of Profond?'* Her mother had merely shrugged her shoulders when Fleur had asked: "What's the matter?" So, Fleur asked her father what was up with her mother.

"Matter, what should be the matter?" and he gave her a sharp look.

"By the way," murmured Fleur, *"Monsieur Profond is going a 'small' voyage on his yacht, to the South Seas."*

Soames examined a branch on which no grapes were growing.

"This vine's a failure," he said showing little reaction. *"I've had young Mont here. He asked me something about you."*

"Oh! How do you like him, Father?"

"He's—a product—like all these young people."

"What were you at his age, dear?"

Soames smiled grimly.

"We went to work and didn't play about—flying and motoring, and making love."

"Didn't you ever make love?"

"I had no time or inclination to philander."

"Perhaps you had a grand passion."

Soames looked at her intently.

"Yes—if you want to know—and much good it did me." He moved away, along by the hot-water pipes. Fleur tiptoed silently after him.

"Tell me about it, Father!"

Soames became very still.

"What should you want to know about such things, at your age?"

"Is she alive?"

He nodded.

"And married?"

"Yes."

"It's Jon Forsyte's mother, isn't it? And she was your wife first."

"Who told you that? If your aunt...! I can't bear the affair talked of."

"But, darling," said Fleur, softly, *"it's so long ago."*

"Long ago or not, I..."

Fleur stood stroking his arm.

"I've tried to forget," he said suddenly; "I don't wish to be reminded."
And then, as if venting some long and secret irritation, he added: "In
these days people don't understand. Grand passion, indeed! No one
knows what it is."

"I do," said Fleur, almost in a whisper.

Soames, who had turned his back on her, spun round.

"What are you talking of—a child like you!"

"Perhaps I've inherited it, Father."

"What?"

"For her son, you see."

They stood staring at each other in the steamy heat.

"This is crazy," said Soames at last.

"Don't be angry, Father, I can't help it."

But she could see he wasn't angry; only scared, deeply scared.

"I thought that foolishness," he stammered, "was all forgotten."

"Oh no! It's ten times what it was."

Soames kicked at the hot-water pipe. The hapless movement touched
Fleur who had no fear of her father—none.

"Dearest!" she said. "What must be, must, you know."

"Must!" repeated Soames. "You don't know what you're talking of.
Has that boy been told?"

The blood rushed into her cheeks.

"Not yet."

"It's most distasteful to me," he said suddenly; "nothing could be
more so. Son of that fellow! It's—it's—it's perverse!"

Fleur slipped her hand under his arm.

"Jon's father is quite ill and old; I saw him."

"You...?"

"Yes, I went there with Jon. I saw them both."

"Well, and what did they say to you?"

"Nothing. They were very polite."

"They would be." Soames resumed examining a joint pipe and then
said suddenly:

"I must think this over—I'll speak to you again tonight."

It was a 'Forsyte' trait to be extra polite when really being deeply
concerned. My mother was often that way although her looks would
betray her beyond the politeness of her words. Sometimes, it was hard to

read what 'Forsytes' really thought, which was a sort of mental version of the stiff upper lip.

Fleur left her father in the steamy greenhouse and wandered into the fruit garden, among the raspberry and current bushes, without impetus to pick and eat.

Those gravel paths through the great fruit and vegetable garden at Chelston were a favorite area of play for Diane and me. The vegetable garden was not kept up quite as it had been before the Second World War, when a superb gardener named Taylor kept up the demesne at Chelston, but in our childhood it was fairly well cared for by our post-war gardener—Spencer. We often pulled each other along these paths in homemade carts, assisted by my mother or more likely, 'Auntie' Morissette, our au pair, and at the end of the vegetable garden and orchard was that wood—our secret area that was the inspiration for our fictitious 'Bonkonland'.

Then, *suddenly, round the corner of the high box hedge* of the Shelter's vegetable garden, Fleur *came plump on her mother, walking swiftly, with an open letter in her hand. Her bosom was heaving, her eyes dilated, her cheeks flushed.*

Mail in 'Forsythia' was delivered to houses twice a day, another luxury that disappeared at the era's demise in the 1960s. Mail or as we English say, the post, was renegaded to a single daily delivery.

Noticing the letter, *Fleur thought: 'The yacht! Poor Mother!'*

Annette gave Fleur *a wide startled look, and said:*

"J'ai la migraine."

"I'm awfully sorry you have a headache, *Mother."*

"Oh, yes! You and your father—sorry!"

"But, Mother—I am. I know what it feels like."

Annette crumpled the letter in her hand. Fleur knew that she must ignore the sight.

"Can't I do anything for your head, Mother?"

Annette shook her head and walked on, swaying her hips.

'It's cruel,' thought Fleur, 'and I was glad! That man! What do men come prowling for, disturbing everything! I suppose he's tired of her. What business has he to be tired of my mother? What business!'

She ought of course, to be delighted, but what was there to be delighted at? Her father didn't really care! Her mother did, perhaps?

She contemplated her own situation.

Jon was right. They wouldn't let you live, these old people! They made mistakes, committed crimes, and wanted their children to go on paying!

After a rather silent and tense dinner where everything at the table seemed pale, Annette rose to leave, Fleur stood to follow her into the drawing-room—a 'Forsyte' title in itself for the room to which the ladies withdrew after meals, leaving the men to enjoy port and cigars at the dinner table. In fact, in the larger homes of 'Forsythia' there might well have been four reception rooms—a morning room, used casually en famille; a sitting room, used to receive guests; a drawing room, only used formally, especially after dinner parties or holidays like Christmas and Easter; and a study or library that was the bastion of the male head of the family. Granny Mabs and Grandpa Jack lived in their morning room at Redcroft. They hardly ever used their drawing room with its grand piano, gilt mirror, chinese vases and other 'Forsythia' accompliments.

Soames *called* Fleur *back.*

She sat down beside him at the table and plucked a honeysuckle from the centerpiece.

"I've been thinking," he said.

"Yes, dear?"

"It's extremely painful for me to talk, but there's no help for it. I don't know if you understand how much you are to me—I've never spoken of it, I didn't think it necessary; but—but you're everything. Your mother..." he paused, staring at his finger-bowl of Venetian glass.

Tullamaine Castle was also the last time in my life that I was exposed to the practice of serving finger bowls after dessert. They were used for the purpose of rinsing off ones fingers and lips at the end of a meal—sometimes silver and more often of elaborate cut glass like those of Soames. They were the last item left on the table after the meal apart from the port and liqueur glasses. At State banquets and some 'City' livery dinners the tradition continues, but for most homes it died with 'Forsythia'.

"Yes?" said Fleur waiting for her father to continue.

"I've only you to look to. I've never had—never wanted anything else, since you were born."

"I know," murmured Fleur.

Soames dipped his napkin in the finger bowl and *moistened his lips.*

"*You may think this a matter I can smooth over and arrange for you. You're mistaken. I—I'm helpless.*"

Fleur did not speak.

"*Quite apart from my own feelings,*" went on Soames with more resolution, "*those two are not amenable to anything I can say. They—they hate me, as people always hate those whom they have injured.*"

"*But he—Jon...*"

"*He's their flesh and blood, her only child. Probably he means to her what you mean to me. It's a deadlock.*"

"*No,*" cried Fleur, "*no, father!*"

"*Listen!*" he said. "*You're putting the feelings of two months—two months—against the feelings of thirty-five years! What chance do you think you have? Two months—your very first love affair, a matter of half a dozen meetings, a few walks and talks, a few kisses—against, against what you can't imagine, what no one could who hasn't been through it. Come, be reasonable, Fleur! It's mid-summer madness!*"

Fleur tore the honeysuckle into little, slow bits.

"*The madness is in letting the past spoil it all. What do we care about the past? It's our lives, not yours.*"

Soames raised his hand to his forehead.

"*Whose child are you?*" he said. "*Whose child is he? The present is linked with the past, the future with both. There's no getting away from that.*"

Fleur was impressed, *she had never heard philosophy pass those lips before.*

"*But, Father, consider it practically. We want each other. There's ever so much money, and nothing whatever in the way but sentiment. Let's bury the past, Father.*"

His answer was a sigh.

"*Besides,*" said Fleur gently, "*you can't prevent us.*"

"*I don't suppose,*" said Soames, "*that if left to myself I should try to prevent you; I must put up with things, I know, to keep your affection. But it's not I who control this matter. That's what I want you to realise before it's too late. If you go on thinking you can get your way, and encourage this feeling, the blow will be much heavier when you find you can't.*"

"*Oh!*" cried Fleur, "*help me, Father; you can help me, you know.*"

"I?" he said bitterly. "Help? I am the impediment—the just cause and impediment—isn't that the jargon? You have my blood in your veins."

He rose.

"Well, the fat's in the fire. If you persist in your wilfulness you'll have yourself to blame. Come! Don't be foolish, my child—my only child!"

Fleur left her father and *went down to the river bank, and stood gazing at a moonstreak on the darkening water. Suddenly she smelled tobacco smoke, and a white figure emerged as if created by the moon. It was young Mont in flannels, standing in his boat.*

"Fleur," came his voice, "don't he hard on a poor devil! I've been waiting hours."

"For what?"

"Come in my boat!"

"Not I."

"Why not?"

"I'm not a water-nymph."

"Haven't you any romance in you? Don't be modern, Fleur!"

He appeared on the path within a yard of her.

"Go away!"

"Fleur, I love you, Fleur!"

Fleur uttered a short laugh.

"Come again," she said, "when I haven't got my wish."

"What is your wish?"

"Ask another."

"Fleur," said Mont, and his voice sounded strange, "don't mock me!"

Fleur shook her head but her lips were trembling.

"Well, you shouldn't make me jump. Give me a cigarette."

Mont gave her one, lighted it, and another for himself.

"I don't want to talk rot," he said, "but please imagine all the rot that all the lovers that ever were have talked, and all my special rot thrown in."

"Thank you, I have imagined it. Good-night!"

They stood for a moment facing each other in the shadow of an acacia tree with very moonlit blossoms.

"Also ran: 'Michael Mont'?" he said. Fleur turned abruptly toward the house. On the lawn she stopped to look back. Michael Mont was *whirling his arms above him; she could see them dashing at his head; then waving at the moonlit blossoms of the acacia. His voice just reached her. "Jolly-jolly!" Fleur shook herself. She couldn't help him, she had too much trouble of her own!*

At the house, *her mother was sitting in the drawing-room at her writing bureau, quite alone. There was nothing remarkable in the expression of her face except its utter immobility. But she looked desolate! Fleur went upstairs. She could hear her father walking up and down, up and down the picture gallery.*

'Yes,' she thought, 'jolly! Oh Jon!'

CHAPTER TEN

DECISION

After Fleur left, June's Austrian maid offered Jon a cup of tea. *Hours of remorse and indecision lay before him! And with a heavy sense of disproportion he smiled,* and accepted.

She brought in a little pot of tea with two cups and without hesitation sat with him. She then began to speak to him in rapturous praise about his half-sister, Miss Forsyte, and his father.

"Your father is a very nice old man—the most nice old man I ever see. Miss Forsyte tell me all about him. Is he better?"

Her words fell on Jon like a reproach. "Oh! Yes, I think he's all right."

"I like to see him again," said the Austrian, putting a hand on her heart; "he have veree kind heart."

Even in as liberal a house as that of Jolyon Forsyte, Jon was not used to this informality between master and servant. The time had not yet come for this mingling of class. That was not to come until after the Second World War. He felt awkward.

Then, the maid revealed how she had seen a photograph of his mother when his father was staying with Miss Forsyte. *"Your mother— veree beautiful—she nice and well?"*

Jon gulped down his tea. This woman, with her concerned face and her reminding words, was like the first and second murderers.

"Thank you," he said: "I must go now. May—may I leave this with you?'

He put a ten-shilling note on the tray with a doubting hand and gained the door. He heard the Austrian gasp and hurried out.

Until the Second World War the separation of 'upstairs downstairs' was pretty strictly observed, familiarity between servants and their masters remaining strictly behind closed doors. With the war and the resulting solidarity that came to the nation irrespective of class—city gentleman and cockney sharing common turf in those underground stations during the Blitz; Squadron Leader and airmen, ace pilots alike, sharing their common goal in the defense of Britain's southern skies—post-war 'Forsythia'—that last decade—allowed for far more interaction between servants and their employers. The daily maids who worked for my mother in my childhood—for apart from the 'au pair' we no longer kept live-in maids—were always given a cup of tea when they arrived in the morning. My mother would then sit with them for the best part of an hour, exchanging gossip. In fact, by the demise of 'Forsythia' in the early 1960s, our daily maid was almost more of a companion to my mother than a servant. The maid became the charwoman, who in turn became the daily help, and the very word 'help' struck a chord of equality.

Jon, relieved to escape the overbearing familiarity of the Austrian maid only just had time to catch his train. *On reaching Worthing he put his luggage into the local train, and set out across the Downs for Wansdon, trying to walk off his aching irresolution. He tramped in, just as the first dinner-bell rang. His things had already been brought up. He had a hurried bath and came down to find Holly alone—Val had gone to Town and would not be back till the last train.*

Holly startled him at dinner by saying that she thought their father not at all well. She had been twice to Robin Hill for the week-end. He had seemed fearfully languid, sometimes even in pain, but had always refused to talk about himself.

"He's awfully dear and unselfish—don't you think, Jon?"

Feeling far from dear and unselfish himself, Jon answered:

"Rather!"

"I think he's been a simply perfect father, so long as I can remember."

"Yes," answered Jon, very subdued.

"He's never interfered, and he's always seemed to understand. I shall never forget his letting me go to South Africa in the Boer War when I was in love with Val."

"That was before he married Mother, wasn't it?" said Jon suddenly.

"Yes. Why?"

"Oh! nothing. Only, wasn't she engaged to Fleur's father first?"

Holly put down the spoon she was using and raised her eyes. What did the boy know? Enough to make it better to tell him? She could not decide.

"There was something," she said. "Of course we were out there, and got no news of anything."

She saw that he knew she was putting him off, and added:

"Have you heard anything of Fleur?"

"Yes."

His face told her, then, more than the most elaborate explanations. So he had not forgotten!

She said very quietly: "Fleur is awfully attractive, Jon, but you know—Val and I don't really like her very much."

"Why?"

"We think she's got rather a 'having' nature."

"'Having'? I don't know what you mean. She—she..." he pushed his dessert plate away, got up, and went to the window.

Holly, too, got up, and put her arm round his waist.

"Don't be angry, Jon, dear. We can't all see people in the same light, can we? You know, I believe each of us only has about one or two people who can see the best that's in us, and bring it out. For you, I think it's your mother. I once saw her looking at a letter of yours; it was wonderful to see her face. I think she's the most beautiful woman I ever saw—Age doesn't seem to touch her."

Jon's face softened; then again became tense. Everybody—everybody was against him and Fleur! It all strengthened the appeal of her words: "Make sure of me—marry me, Jon!"

He closed up utterly, going early to bed. He heard Val's arrival, the Ford discharging cargo, then the stillness of the summer night. Going to his window he leaned far out. Cold moon—warm air—the Downs like silver! Small wings, a stream bubbling, the rambler roses! God—how empty all of it without her.

Let him have pluck, and go and tell them! They couldn't stop him marrying her—they wouldn't want to stop him when they knew how he felt. Yes! He would go! Bold and open—Fleur was wrong!

Returning to his bed, *Jon slept, freed from the worst of life's evils— indecision.*

CHAPTER ELEVEN

TIMOTHY PROPHESIES

To 'Forsytes' in 1920, was it a brave new world? Or was it a chance to return to the sanity of the old world, before the Great War and all its madness, even a world before the Boer War, back in the time of the old queen? I guess it depended on the generation.

It was *the second anniversary of the resurrection of England's pride and glory—or, more shortly, the top hat. 'Lord's'—that festival which the War had driven from the field—raised its light and dark blue flags for the second time, displaying almost every feature of a glorious past*—the occasion, the annual Eton versus Harrow cricket match. Officially the Marylebone Cricket Club, 'Lord's', was the sacred center of the game that 'Forsytes' had taken around the world—to India, Ceylon, South Africa, Australia and New Zealand; Hong Kong, Singapore and Malaya; and far flung outposts like St. Helena, the West Indies, Fiji, and Western Samoa. The cities of the Empire all had their cricket grounds where the game was played meticulously following the rules governed by the Marylebone Cricket Club from its pavilion at 'Lord's'. To quote from the great 1950s musical *My Fair Lady*, at the Eton and Harrow Cricket match just as much as at the royal enclosure at Ascot: "Every Duke and Peer and Earl" was there and a good many 'Forsytes', too.

Here, in the luncheon interval, were all species of female and one species of male hat, protecting the multiple types of face associated with the 'classes'. The observing Forsyte might discern in the free or unconsidered seats a certain number of the squash-hatted, but they hardly ventured on the grass; the old school—or schools—could still rejoice that the proletariat was not yet paying the necessary half-crown. Here was still a close borough, the only one left on a large scale—for the papers were about to estimate the attendance at ten thousand. And the ten thousand, all animated by one hope, were asking each other one question: "Where are you lunching?" Something wonderfully uplifting and reassuring in the query and the sight of so many like themselves voicing it! What reserve power in the British realm—enough pigeons, lobsters, lamb, salmon mayonnaise, strawberries, and bottles of champagne to feed the lot! No miracle in prospect—no case of seven loaves and a few fishes—faith rested on surer foundations. Six thousand top hats; four thousand parasols would be doffed and furled, ten thousand mouths all speaking the same upper-class *English would be filled. There was life in the old dog yet! Tradition! And again Tradition! How strong and how elastic! Wars might rage, taxation prey, Trades Unions take toll and Europe perish of starvation; but the ten thousand would be fed; and, within their ring fence, stroll upon green turf, wear their top hats, and meet—themselves. The heart was sound, the pulse still regular. Eton! Eton! Har-r-o-o-o-w!*

Soames *had not been at either school,* having attended Marlborough College, in today's co-educational world, the public school of choice for Catherine Middleton, before she married Prince William and became the Duchess of Cambridge. Soames *took no interest in cricket, but he wanted Fleur to show her frock, and he wanted to wear his top hat—parade it again in peace and plenty among his peers. He walked sedately with Fleur between him and Annette. He remembered suddenly with what intoxication of pride he had walked round with Irene in the first years of his first marriage. And* at Lord's *how they used to lunch on the drag which his mother would make his father have, because it was so 'chic'—all drags and carriages in those days, not these lumbering great Stands! And how consistently Montague Dartie had drunk too much. He remembered George Forsyte—whose brothers Roger and Eustace had been at Harrow and Eton—towering on top of the drag waving a light blue flag with one hand and a dark blue flag with the other, and shouting, "Etroow—Harrton!" just when everybody was silent, like the buffoon he had always been. H'm! Old days, and Irene in grey silk shot with palest green. He looked, sideways, at Fleur's face. Rather colourless—no light, no eagerness! That love affair was preying on her—a bad business! He looked beyond, at his wife's face. She was taking Profond's defection with curious quietude; or was his 'small' voyage just a blind. Having promenaded around the pitch and in front of the pavillion they sought Winifred's table in the Bedouin Club. Outside it they found Jack Cardigan in a dark blue tie (he had once played for Harrow), batting with a Malacca cane to show how that fellow ought to have hit that ball.*

Great-grandfather Oliver Longley's fine gold-topped Malacca cane that Grandpop sometimes used as his 'Ski' stick during my childhood used to be leaning in a 'brolly' stand beside the front door at The Breach. I always admired it, and as aforementioned, eventually inherited it, but not before my Uncle Dennis reminded us that in his childhood he had used the cane as a makeshift golf club and gave that as an explanation for two little nicks in the gold top.

Assembled in Winifred's corner were Imogen, Benedict with his young wife, Val Dartie without Holly, Maud and her husband, and, after Soames and his two were seated, one empty place.

"I'm expecting Prosper," said Winifred, "but he's so busy with his yacht."

Soames stole a glance. No movement in his wife's face! Whether that fellow were coming or not, she evidently knew all about it. It did not escape him that Fleur, too, looked at her mother. If Annette didn't respect his feelings, she might think of Fleur's!

As he mulled over this he could vaguely hear Jack Cardigan recalling all the 'great mid-offs' of British cricket, as if they had been a definite racial entity in the composition of the British people. Soames had finished his lobster, and was beginning on his pigeon-pie, when he heard the words, "I'm a small bit late Mrs. Dartie," and saw that there was no longer an empty place. That fellow was sitting between Annette and Imogen. Soames ate steadily on, with an occasional word to Maud and Winifred. Conversation buzzed around him. He heard the voice of Profond say:

"I think you're mistaken, Mrs. Forsyde; I'll—I'll bet Miss Forsyde agrees with me."

"In what?" came Fleur's clear voice across the table.

"I was sayin', young girls are much the same as they always were—there's very small difference."

"Do you know so much about them?"

That sharp reply caught the ears of all, and Soames moved uneasily on his thin green chair—the same thin, green, folding chairs still found today in lawn marquees.

"Well, I don't know. I think they want their own small way, and I think they always did."

"Indeed!"

"Oh! but—Prosper," Winifred interjected comfortably, *"the girls in the streets—the girls who've been in munitions, the little flappers in the shops; their manners now really quite hit you in the eye."*

"It was inside before, now it's outside; that's all," said Profond, having now got the attention of them all, even Jack Cardigan.

"But their morals!" cried Imogen.

"Just as moral as they were, Mrs. Cardigan, but they've got more opportunity."

The saying, so cryptically cynical, received a little laugh from Imogen, and a creek from Soames's chair.

Winifred said: "That's too bad, Prosper."

"What do you say Mrs. Forsyde; don't you think human nature's always the same?"

Soames subdued a sudden longing to get up and kick the fellow. He heard his wife reply:

"Human nature is not the same in England as anywhere else." That was her confounded mockery!

"Well, I don't know much about this small country"—'No, thank God,' thought Soames—*"but I should say the pot was boilin' under the lid everywhere. We all want pleasure, and we always did."*

Damn the fellow! His cynicism was outrageous!

When lunch was over they broke up into couples for the digestive promenade. Soames knew perfectly that Annette and that fellow had gone prowling round together. Fleur was with Val; she had chosen him, no doubt, because he knew that boy. He himself had Winifred for partner.

"I wish we were back forty years, old boy!" she said. *"Sometimes I even wish Monty was back. What do you think of people nowadays, Soames?"*

"Precious little style. The thing began to go to pieces with bicycles and motor-cars; the War has finished it."

"I wonder what's coming?" said Winifred.

"There's money, but no faith in things. We don't lay by for the future. These youngsters—it's all a short life and a merry one with them."

"There's a hat!" said Winifred, as one of society's best paraded past them. *"I don't know—when you come to think of the people killed and all that in the War, it's rather wonderful, I think. There's no other country—Prosper says the rest are all bankrupt, except America; and of course her men always took their style in dress from us."*

"Is that chap," said Soames, *"really going to the South Seas?"*

"Oh! one never knows where Prosper's going!"

"He's a sign of the times," muttered Soames, *"if you like."*

Winifred's hand gripped his arm.

"Don't turn your head," she said in a low voice, *"but look to your right in the front row of the Stand."*

A man in a grey top hat, grey-bearded, with thin brown, folded cheeks, and a certain elegance of posture, sat there with a woman in a lawn-coloured frock, whose dark eyes were fixed on himself. Winifred's voice said in his ear:

"Jolyon looks very ill, but he always had style. She doesn't change— except her hair."

"Why did you tell Fleur about that business?"

"I didn't; she picked it up. I always knew she would."

"Well, it's a mess. She's set her heart upon their boy."

"The little wretch," murmured Winifred. *"She tried to take me in about that. What shall you do, Soames?"*

"Be guided by events."

They moved on, silent, in the almost solid crowd.

"Really," said Winifred suddenly; *"it almost seems like Fate. Only that's so old-fashioned. Look! There are George and Eustace!"*

George Forsyte's lofty bulk had halted before them.

"Hallo, Soames!" he said. *"Just met Profond and your wife. You'll catch them if you put on a pace. Did you ever go to see old Timothy?"*

Soames nodded, and the streams forced them apart.

"I always liked old George," said Winifred. *"He's so droll."*

"I never did," said Soames. *"Where's your seat? I shall go to mine. Fleur may be back there."*

Having seen Winifred to her seat, he regained his own. No Fleur, and no Annette! You could expect nothing of women nowadays! They had the vote. They were 'emancipated', and much good it was doing them! So Winifred would go back, and put up with Dartie all over again?

*To have the past once more—to be sitting here as he had sat in '83 and
'84, before he was certain that his marriage with Irene had gone all
wrong, before her antagonism had become so glaring that with the best
will in the world he could not overlook it. The sight of her with* Jolyon
*had brought all memory back. Even now he could not understand why
she had been so impracticable. She could love other men; she had it in
her! To himself, the one person she ought to have loved, she had chosen
to refuse her heart. Now, all decent ownership of anything had gone,
or was on the point of going. He had done his best. And his rewards
were—those two sitting in the Stand, and this affair of Fleur's!*

*And overcome by loneliness he thought: 'Shan't wait any longer!
They must find their own way back to the hotel—if they mean to come!'*
Leaving, he hailed *a cab outside the ground.*

"*Drive me to the Bayswater Road,*" *he said.*

He arrived at Timothy's to find Smither *standing in the open
doorway.*

"*Mr. Soames! I was just taking the air. Cook will be so pleased.*"

"*How is Mr. Timothy?*"

"*Not himself at all these last few days, sir; he's been talking a great
deal. Come in, Mr. Soames, come in! It's such a pleasant change!*"

"*No,*" *murmured Smither in the hall,* "*we haven't been very satisfied
with him, not all this week.*"

"*Has he said anything important?*"

"*I shouldn't like to say that, Mr. Soames; but he's turned against
his Will. He said the other day: 'They want my money.' It gave me such
a turn, because, as I said to him, nobody wants his money, I'm sure.
I took my courage in my 'ands. 'You know, Mr. Timothy,' I said, 'my
dear mistress'—that's Miss Forsyte, Mr. Soames, Miss Ann that trained
me—'she never thought about money,' I said, 'it was all character with
her.' He looked at me, I can't tell you how funny, and he said quite dry;
'Nobody wants my character.' Think of his saying a thing like that! But
sometimes he'll say something as sharp and sensible as anything.*"

*Soames, who had been staring at an old print by the hat-rack,
thinking, 'That's got value!' murmured:* "*I'll go up and see him,
Smither.*"

"*Cook's with him,*" *answered Smither;* "*she will be pleased to see
you.*"

*On the second floor he paused and tapped. The door was opened,
and he saw the round homely face of a woman about sixty.*

"Mr. Soames!" she said: "Why! Mr. Soames!"

Soames nodded. "All right, Cook!" and entered.

Timothy was propped up in bed, with his hands joined before his chest, and his eyes fixed on the ceiling, where a fly was standing upside-down.

"Uncle Timothy," Soames said, raising his voice, "Uncle Timothy!"

Timothy's eyes left the fly, and levelled themselves on his visitor.

"Uncle Timothy," Soames said again, "is there anything that I can do for you? Is there anything you'd like to say?"

"Ha!" said Timothy.

"I've come to look you up and see that everything's all right."

Timothy nodded.

"Have you got everything you want?"

"No," said Timothy.

"Can I get you anything?"

"No," said Timothy.

"I'm Soames, you know; your nephew, Soames Forsyte. Your brother James's son."

Timothy nodded.

"I shall be delighted to do anything I can for you."

Timothy beckoned. Soames went close to him.

"You—you tell them all from me—you tell them all..." and his finger tapped on Soames's arm, "to hold on—hold on—Consols are goin' up," and he nodded thrice.

"All right!" said Soames; "I will."

"Yes," said Timothy, fixing his eyes again on the ceiling, he added: "That fly!"

Soames took his leave of the old man *and went out with the cook.*

"Good-bye, sir: it has been a pleasure," Cook said.

"Take care of him, Cook. He is old."

Shaking her crumpled hand he went downstairs. Smither was still taking the air in the doorway.

"What do you think of him, Mr. Soames?"

"H'm!" Soames murmured: "He's lost touch."

"Yes," said Smither, "I was afraid you'd think that coming fresh out of the world to see him like."

"Smither," said Soames, "we are all indebted to you."

"Oh, no, Mr. Soames, don't say that! It's a pleasure—he's such a wonderful man."

"Well, good-bye!" said Soames, and got into his taxi.

'Going up!' he thought; 'going up!'

Reaching the hotel at Knightsbridge he went to their sitting-room, and rang for tea. Neither of them was in. And again that sense of loneliness came over him. These hotels! What monstrous great places they were now! He could remember when there was nothing bigger than Long's or Brown's, Morley's or the Tavistock—clubs and hotels; no end to them now.

Throughout 'Forsythia' it was always said that Brown's Hotel in Russell Square served the best afternoon tea in London. This tradition still held in my childhood. Newlands' old boy reunions were always held at Brown's, and not as evening events but over afternoon tea! It was served in the late 1950s in all its Edwardian splendor, and here as teenagers, all sophisticated at our public schools, we swapped our tales of adventure since leaving Newlands. We arrived at Brown's in suits and stiff collars such as our schools prescribed, with shirtsleeves that boasted almost equally starched cuffs fastened by gold links carrying the crests of Tonbridge, Marlborough, Rugby, Stowe, Haileybury, Charterhouse, Eton and Harrow—those 'private' public schools that would give us admission into the club, the three percent. There was even the odd Newlands old boy, then at Christ's Hospital, whose school uniform went back to the ecclesiastical style of the eighteenth century, complete with tabs, knee stockings and silver buckled shoes.

As a statement of the dream of 'Forsytes' that their world was not shattered by the Second World War, most of my generation had been 'put down' for our public schools at birth or shortly thereafter. Our names had been submitted, even our school houses selected, as soon as it was known that we were to be the next generation. Of course, it was still necessary for us to reach the accepted academic standard by the age of thirteen, but that is what our prep schools were for—preparatory schools to ensure that we would pass the necessary Common Entrance Examination for entry into our public schools. During my five years at Newlands I do not remember one boy ever failing to make the grade for entry to his previously selected public school.

Soames, who had just been watching at Lord's a miracle of tradition and continuity at the Eton versus Harrow cricket match, fell into reverie over the changes in that London where he had been born five-and-

sixty years before. Whether Consols were going up or not, London had become a terrific property. No such property in the world, unless it were New York! There was a lot of hysteria in the papers nowadays; but anyone who, like himself, could remember London sixty years ago, and see it now, realised the fecundity and elasticity of wealth. They had only to keep their heads, and go at it steadily. Why! he remembered cobblestones, and stinking straw on the floor of your cab. And old Timothy—what could he not tell them, if he had kept his memory! Things were unsettled, people in a funk or in a hurry, but here were London and the Thames, and out there the British Empire, and the ends of the earth. "Consols are goin' up!"

He heard a sound behind him, and saw that his wife and daughter had come in.

"So you're back!" *he said.*

Fleur did not answer; she stood for a moment looking at him and her mother, then passed into her bedroom. Annette poured out herself a cup of tea.

"I am going to Paris, to my mother, Soames."

"Oh! To your mother?"

"Yes."

"For how long?"

"I do not know."

"And when are you going?"

"On Monday."

Was she really going to her mother? Odd, how indifferent Soames felt! Odd, how clearly she had perceived the indifference he would feel so long as there was no scandal.

"Will you want money?"

"Thank you; I have enough."

"Very well. Let us know when you're coming back."

Annette put down the cake she was fingering, and, looking up through darkened lashes, said:

"Shall I give Maman any message?"

"My regards."

Annette stretched herself, her hands on her waist, and said in French:

"What luck that you have never loved me, Soames!" *Then rising, she too left the room. Soames was glad she had spoken it in French—it seemed to require no dealing with. Again that other face—pale, dark-*

eyed, beautiful still! And there stirred far down within him the ghost of warmth, as from sparks lingering beneath a mound of flaky ash. And Fleur infatuated with her boy! "Inherited," his girl had said. She—she was 'holding on'!

To the generation of 'Forsytes' who had survived the Second World War, was there a chance to return to the perceived sanity of the pre-war world? The British Empire was still intact, although there was dreadful strife in India—strife that led to partition in 1948, and the creation of the separate independent Indian states of India and Pakistan. In the 1950s, there was bloodshed for independence in Kenya—was the Empire breaking up? Yet, in 1958, just two years after Suez, my mother and father came with me to the Tonbridge versus Clifton cricket match at Lord's and brought along Grandpa Jack who loved cricket. There were only six of the prestigious public schools that played at Lord's, and as aforementioned, Tonbridge had always been one of them. Although not quite the fashion parade of the Eton and Harrow match, my mother prepared an elaborate picnic for us that included those beetroot rolls that I always loved. We had seats in the prestigious Warner Stand, just to the right of the Pavilion, and watched a game in which only Grandpa, like Jack Cardigan, had any great interest. The following year, I was to go on to our Combined Cadet Force training camp at Thetford in Norfolk. The cadet party were to leave by train right after the traditional two-day cricket match at Lord's. I remember sitting in my army uniform, with polished boots, clean blancoed webbing, and shining brasses, during the lunch interval at Lord's at one of those taverns around the ground that still served lobster, salmon mayonnaise, strawberries and cream, and, if you were of age and could afford it, champagne!

PART THREE

CHAPTER ONE

OLD JOLYON WALKS

Twofold impulse had made Jolyon say to his wife at breakfast:
"Let's go up to Lord's!"

'Wanted—something to abate the anxiety in which those two
had lived during the sixty hours since Jon had brought Fleur down.
'Wanted'—too, that which might assuage the pangs of memory in one
who knew he might lose them any day!

Fifty-eight years ago Jolyon had become an Eton boy. Year after
year he had gone to Lord's from Stanhope Gate with a father not well
versed in the game of cricket, but enthusiastic to give his son the best
education that society could provide. His father—in Crimean whiskers
then—had ever impressed him as the beau ideal. How delicious after
howling in a top hat and a sweltering heat, caused more by the strictures
of Eton clothing than the English weather, to go home with his father in
a hansom cab, bathe, dress, and forth to the 'Disunion' Club, to dine off
whitebait, cutlets, and a tart, and go—two 'swells', old and young, in
lavender kid gloves—to the opera or play. The golden sixties when the
world was simple, dandies glamorous, Democracy not born.

A generation later, with his own boy, Jolly, Harrow-buttonholed
with cornflowers—by old Jolyon's whim his grandson had been
canonised at a trifle less expense—again Jolyon had experienced the
heat and passions of the day, and come back to the cool and strawberry
beds of Robin Hill, and billiards after dinner, his boy making the most

heartbreaking flukes and trying to seem languid and grown-up. Those two days he and his son had been alone together in the world, one on each side—Eton and Harrow—and Democracy just born!

And so he had unearthed a grey top hat, borrowed a tiny bit of light blue-ribbon from Irene, and gingerly, keeping cool, by car and train and taxi had reached Lord's Ground. There, beside her in a lawn-coloured frock with narrow black edges, he had watched the game, and felt the old thrill stir within him.

When Soames passed, the day was spoiled. Irene's face was distorted by compression of the lips. No good to go on sitting here with Soames or perhaps his daughter recurring in front of them, like decimals. And he said:

"Well, dear, if you've had enough—let's go!"

Back at Robin Hill, Jolyon *felt exhausted. Not wanting her to see him thus, he waited till she had begun to play, and stole off to the little study* that had been his father's room. *He settled in his father's old armchair. Like that passage of the Cesar Franck sonata—so had been his life with her, a divine third movement. And now this business of Jon's—this bad business.*

In that room, unchanged since 'Old Jolyon's' day, it was almost as if he could hear his father speak. *"Are you facing it, Jo? It's for you to decide. She's only a woman! It's your wife, your son; your past. Tackle it my boy!"* It was his possession. *Was it a message from walking spirit; or but the instinct of his sire living on within him? Well! He would tackle it, write to Jon, and put the whole thing down in black and white! And suddenly he breathed with difficulty, with a sense of suffocation, as if his heart were swollen. He got up and went out into the air. The stars were very bright. He passed along the terrace round the corner of the house, till, through the window of the music-room, he could see Irene at the piano. But her hands were now idle. Jolyon saw her raise those hands and clasp them over her breast. 'It's Jon, with her,' he thought; 'all Jon! I'm dying out of her—it's natural!'*

Next day, after a bad night, he sat down to his task. He wrote with difficulty and many erasures.

'MY DEAREST BOY,

'You are old enough to understand how very difficult it is for elders to give themselves away to their young. I cannot say that we are conscious of having sinned exactly—people in real life very seldom are,

I believe—but most persons would say we had, and at all events our conduct, righteous or not, has found us out. The truth is, my dear, we both have pasts, which it is now my task to make known to you, because they so grievously and deeply effect your future. Many, very many years ago, as far back indeed as 1883...

At this point Jolyon recorded for Jon in explicit detail the unfortunate circumstances of his mother's marital mistake in marrying Soames Forsyte, Fleur's father. He went on, with difficulty, into explaining his mother's aversion to Soames in their sexual relations.

'In a vast number of marriages—and your mother's was one—girls are not and cannot be certain whether they love the man they marry or not; they do not know until after that act of union which makes the reality of marriage. Now, in many, perhaps in most doubtful cases, this act cements and strengthens the attachment, but in other cases, and your mother's was one, it is a revelation of mistake, a destruction of such attraction as there was. There is nothing more tragic in a woman's life than such a revelation, growing daily, nightly, clearer. I have had to say all this, because I am going to put you into a position to judge your mother, and you are very young, without experience of what life is...

Jolyon went on to describe Soames' commission to build Robin Hill and Irene's affair with Bosinney; Soames' attempt to assert his sexual rights; Bosinney's accident and tragic death; and how his father asked him to go and see how Irene was; his rebuff from Soames; Irene's walking out and her independent life and how he, Jolyon, had been made her trustee over funds that 'Old Jolyon' left to her. How eventually, after twelve years, he and Irene became attached. Soames divorced her and took up with another woman. He married Irene and Jon was born. Fleur was born to Soames and his second wife.

'My dear boy—it is not easy to write like this. But you see, I must. Your mother is wrapped up in you utterly, devotedly. I don't wish to write harshly of Soames Forsyte. I don't think harshly of him; perhaps I was sorry even then. As the world judges she was in error, he within his rights. He loved her—in his way. She was his property. That is the view he holds of life—of human feelings and hearts—property. It's not his fault—so was he born. To me it is a view that has always been abhorrent—so was I born.

'That is the story, Jon. I have told it you, because by the affection which we see you have formed for this man's daughter you are blindly moving toward what must utterly destroy your mother's happiness,

*if not your own. What I want you to realise is that feelings of horror
and aversion such as those* between your mother and Soames Forsyte
*can never be buried or forgotten. They are alive in her to-day. Only
yesterday at Lord's we happened to see Soames Forsyte. Her face, if
you had seen it, would have convinced you. The idea that you should
marry his daughter is a nightmare to her, Jon. I have nothing to say
against Fleur save that she is his daughter. But your children, if you
married her, would be the grandchildren of Soames, as much as your
mother, of a man who once owned your mother as a man might own a
slave. You are just on the threshold of life, you have only known this
girl two months, and however deeply you think you love her, I appeal
to you to break it off at once. Don't give your mother this rankling pain
and humiliation during the rest of her life. Pluck up your spirit, Jon,
and break away. Bless you, my dear boy, and again forgive me all the
pain this letter must bring you—we tried to spare you, but Spain—it
seems—was no good.*

> *'Ever your devoted father*
> *'JOLYON FORSYTE.'*

*He folded the confession, and put it in his pocket. It was—thank
Heaven!—Saturday; he had till Sunday evening to think it over; for
even if posted now it could not reach Jon* at Holly's *till Monday. He felt
a curious relief at this delay, and at the fact that, whether sent or not,
it was written.*

He found Irene in the rose garden.

*Jolyon took the confession from his pocket. "I've been writing this.
I think you ought to see it."*

*He gave it to her, and walked away among the roses. Presently,
seeing that she had finished reading and was standing quite still with
the sheets of the letter against her skirt, he came back to her.*

"Well?"

*"It's wonderfully put. I don't see how it could be put better. Thank
you, dear."*

"Is there anything you would like left out?"

She shook her head.

"No! he must know all, if he's to understand."

"That's what I thought, but—I hate it!"

He had the feeling that he hated it more than she. Sexual relations
were just something that 'Forsytes' found difficult to discuss.

"Would it be better to rewrite the whole thing, and just say you hated Soames?" he suggested.

Irene shook her head.

"Hate's only a word. It conveys nothing. No, better as it is."

"Very well. It shall go to-morrow."

She raised her face to his, and in sight of the big house's many creepered windows, he kissed her.

Throughout my childhood and most of my father's childhood before me, The Breach had been covered in Virginia creeper that entwined summer tentacles around the big sash windows. In the winter, the leaves fell off leaving the knotted grey stems and imprints of those summer tentacles to soften the mellowed brick and plaster of the big house in its period of dormant rest. Was The Breach a big house? Not really, but it always seemed so to us. It was the house of our 'Forsyte' saga.

Chapter Two

Confession

Late that same afternoon, Jolyon had a nap in his father's old armchair. Face down on his knee was a French book and just before he fell asleep he had been thinking: 'As a people shall we ever like the French.' He liked France, liked French food, French culture and he had shared some of his best times with Irene in France, but 'Forsytes' just didn't accept the French. He thought no Englishman could like them who could not see them in some sort with the detached aesthetic eye! And with that melancholy conclusion he had nodded off.

When he awoke he saw Jon, standing between him and the window. The boy had evidently come in from the garden and was waiting for him to wake. Jolyon smiled, still half asleep. How nice the chap looked— sensitive, affectionate, straight! Then his heart gave a nasty jump, and a quaking sensation overcame him. Jon! That confession! He controlled himself with an effort. "Why, Jon, where did you spring from?"

"I came home to tell you something, Dad."

With all his might Jolyon tried to get the better of the jumping, gurgling sensations within his chest.

"Well, sit down, old man."

Jon sat on a wing of the chair just as he had when a boy and as his father had at Stanhope Gate when he was a boy at 'Old Jolyon's' chair.

"Have you seen your mother?"

"No."

All his life Jolyon *had hated scenes like poison, avoided rows, gone on his own way quietly and let others go on theirs. But now—it seemed—at the very end of things, he had a scene before him more painful than any he had avoided.*

"Father," said Jon slowly, "Fleur and I are engaged."

'Exactly!' thought Jolyon, breathing with difficulty.

"I know that you and mother don't like the idea. Fleur says that Mother was engaged to her father before you married her. Of course I don't know what happened, but it must be ages ago. I'm devoted to her, Dad, and she says she is to me."

Jolyon uttered a queer sound, half laugh, half groan.

"You are nineteen, Jon, and I am seventy-two. How are we to understand each other in a matter like this, eh?"

"You love Mother, Dad; you must know what we feel. It isn't fair to us to let old things spoil our happiness, is it?"

He laid his hand on the boy's arm.

"Look, Jon! I might put you off with talk about you both being too young and not knowing your own minds, and all that, but you wouldn't listen, besides, it doesn't meet the case—Youth, unfortunately, cures itself. You talk lightly about 'old things like that', knowing nothing—as you say truly—of what happened. Now, have I ever given you reason to doubt my love for you, or my word?

"You can believe what I tell you. If you don't give up this love affair, you will make Mother wretched to the end of her days. Believe me, my dear, the past, whatever it was, can't be buried—it can't indeed."

Jon got up from the chair, Fleur's image dancing before him.

"I can't, Father, how can I—just because you say that? Of course I can't!"

"Jon, if you knew the story you would give this up without hesitation; you would have to! Can't you believe me?"

"How can you tell what I should think? Father, I love her better than anything in the world."

Jolyon's face twitched, and he said with painful slowness:

"Better than your mother, Jon?"

Jon clenched his fists.

"I don't know," he burst out, "I don't know! But to give Fleur up for nothing—for something I don't understand, for something that I don't believe can really matter half so much, will make me—make me..."

"Make you feel us unjust, put a barrier—yes. But that's better than going on with this."

"I can't. Fleur loves me, and I love her. You want me to trust you, why don't you trust me, Father? We wouldn't want to know anything— we wouldn't let it make any difference. It'll only make us love you and mother all the more."

Jolyon reached for the letter in his pocket, but he did not pull it out.

"Think what your mother's been to you, Jon! She has nothing but you; I shan't last much longer."

"Why not? It isn't fair to—Why not?"

"Well," said Jolyon, rather coldly, *"because the doctors tell me I shan't; that's all."*

"Oh! Dad!" cried Jon, and burst into tears.

Jolyon *reached out his hand helplessly—not wishing, indeed not daring to get up.*

"Dear man," he said, *"don't—or you'll make me!"*

Throughout 'Forsythia' it was an unwritten rule among male 'Forsytes' that you could not cry in public, and even in front of your parents. It was instilled into us from the cradle on. "Don't blubber!" our nannies would say during the 'terrible two's'; "Be a man!" our teachers might say at six: "Stop that blubbering," our headmaster might rebuke after administering us six strokes of the cane at prep school; "Don't be a Mother's boy!" We were expected to take 'the slings and arrows of outrageous fortune' with that stiff upper lip that would prepare us for whatever our destiny in the British Empire would bring.

"By the way, don't speak of that to Mother," Jolyon *said; "she has enough to frighten her with this affair of yours. I know how you feel. But, Jon, you know her and me well enough to be sure we wouldn't wish to spoil your happiness lightly. Why, my dear boy, we don't care for anything but your happiness—at least, with me it's just yours and Mother's and with her just yours. It's all the future for you both that's at stake."*

"What is it? What is it? Don't keep me like this!"

Jolyon, *who knew that he was beaten, thrust his hand again into his breast pocket, and sat for a full minute, breathing with difficulty, his eyes closed. Then he brought his hand out with the letter, and said with a sort of fatigue: "Well, Jon, if you hadn't come to-day, I was going to send you this. I wanted to spare you—I wanted to spare your mother and myself, but I see it's no good. Read it, and I think I'll go into the garden." He reached forward to get up.*

Jon, who had taken the letter, said quickly: "No, I'll go;" and was gone.

Jolyon sank back in his chair. His heart thumped and pained him. Life—its loves—its work—its beauty—its aching, and—its end! Life—it wore you down, yet did not want to make you die—that was the cunning evil! Out there somewhere in the fragrance of the summer Jon would be reading that letter, turning and twisting its pages in his trouble, his bewilderment and trouble—breaking his heart about it! The thought made Jolyon acutely miserable. Jon was such a tender-hearted chap. He remembered Irene saying to him once: "Never was anyone born more loving and more lovable than Jon." Poor little Jon. His world gone up the spout, all of a summer afternoon! Jolyon got out of his chair, and went to the window. The boy was nowhere visible. And he passed out into the garden. If one could take any help to him now—one must!

He traversed the shrubbery, glanced into the walled garden—no Jon! He passed the Cypressus trees, dark and spiral, into the meadow. Where had the boy got to? Had he rushed down to the coppice—his old hunting-ground? He crossed the rows of hay. They would cock it on Monday and be carrying the day after, if rain held off.

Edwardian farming with its traction engines, threshing machines and side-bar mowers had come a long way from manual Victorian methods, but apart from the primitive tractor taking over from the horses, by 1920, farming was somewhat standing still. It remained pretty much so throughout that period between the two world wars and was the sort of farming that took place at The Breach in my great-grandfather's time. In more remote parts of the British Isles, in Wales, Scotland and Ireland, it lingered on another generation. When I farmed in Ireland as late as 1967, we often still made hay drying it in little cocks, before putting it into big cocks to be pitched onto wagons—not always baling it.

At the far side of the meadow, Jolyon came to the pond, where flies and gnats were dancing over a bright reedy surface; and on into the coppice. Still no Jon! He called. No answer! On the log seat he sat down, nervous, anxious, forgetting his own physical sensations. He had been wrong to let the boy get away with that letter; he ought to have kept him under his eye from the start. Greatly troubled, he got up to retrace his steps. At the farm buildings he called again, and looked into the dark cow-house. The three Alderneys, reminiscent of Great-grandfather's Jerseys, the last of whom, Betty, was still on the farm at The Breach in my childhood, *were chewing the quiet cud. One turned a lazy head, a lustrous eye; Jolyon could see the slobber on its grey lower lip. He* now *saw everything with passionate clearness, in the agitation of his nerves—all that in his time he had adored and tried to paint—wonder of light and shade and colour.* It was almost a religious experience. *No wonder the legend put Christ into a manger—what more devotional than the eyes and moonwhite horns of a chewing cow in the warm dusk! He called again. No answer. Where had he got to? One must find the poor chap!*

He came up *to the rosery, and the beauty of the roses in sudden sunlight seemed to him unearthly.* Just that afternoon, *Irene had stood by a bush of dark red roses; had stood to read and decide that Jon must know it all! He knew all now! Had she chosen wrong? He bent and sniffed a rose, its petals brushed his nose and trembling lips; nothing so soft as a rose-leaf's velvet, except her neck—Irene! On across the lawn he went, up the slope, to the oak tree. He paused a minute with his hand on the rope of the swing—Jolly, Holly—Jon! The old swing! And suddenly, he felt horribly—deadly ill! 'I've overdone it,' he thought: 'By Jove! I've overdone it after all!' He staggered up towards the terrace, dragged himself up the steps, and fell against the wall of the house. He leaned there gasping, his face buried in the honeysuckle that he and she had taken such trouble with that it might sweeten the air which drifted in.*

It was the same sweet smell of honeysuckle that drifted in from the terrace at Hockeredge—through the summer's open windows of the dining room at 52, Wickham Way.

Now, for Jolyon, this *fragrance mingled with awful pain. 'My love!'* he thought; *'the boy!' And with a great effort he tottered in through the long window, and sank into old Jolyon's chair. The* French *book was there, a pencil in it; he caught it up, scribbled a word on the open page... His hand dropped...So it was like this—was it?...*

There was a great wrench; and darkness...

CHAPTER THREE

IRENE!

When Jon rushed away with the letter, he ran along the terrace and round the corner of the house. Leaning against the creepered wall he tore open the letter. It was long—very long! This added to his fear, and he began reading. When he came to the words: 'It was Fleur's father that she married,' everything seemed to spin before him. He was close to a window, and entering by it, he passed, through music-room and hall, up to his bedroom. He read with a dull feeling. He best grasped on that first reading, the pain his father must have had in writing such a letter. He let the last sheet fall, and in a sort of mental, moral helplessness began to read the first again. It all seemed to him disgusting—dead and disgusting. Then, suddenly, a hot wave of horrified emotion tingled through him. He buried his face in his hands. His mother! Fleur's father!

Property! Could there be men who looked on women as their property? His mother! He caught up the letter and read on again: 'horror and aversion—alive in her to-day...your children...grandchildren...of a man who once owned your mother as a man might own a slave...' It must be *true*, or his father would never have written it. He got up from the bed and *sat down on the floor*. He sat there like some unhappy little animal. He was wrenched from his blank wretchedness by the sound of the door opening from his mother's room. He could hear a rustle, her footsteps crossing, till beyond the bed he saw her standing before *his dressing-table. She had something in her hand. The least turn of her head, and she must see him! Her lips moved: "Oh, Jon!" She was speaking to herself; the tone of her voice troubled Jon's heart. He saw in her hand a little photograph. He knew it—one of himself as a tiny boy, which she always kept in her bag. His heart beat fast. And, suddenly as if she had heard it, she turned her eyes and saw him. At the gasp she gave, he said:*

"Yes, it's me."

She moved over to the bed, and sat down on it, quite close to him, her hands still clasping her breast, her feet among the sheets of the letter which had slipped to the floor. She saw them, and her hands grasped the edge of the bed. She sat very upright, her dark eyes fixed on him. At last she spoke.

"Well, Jon, you know, I see."

"Yes."

"You've seen Father?"

"Yes."

There was a long silence, till she said:

"Oh! my darling!"

"It's all right."

"What are you going to do?"

"I don't know."

There was another long silence, then she got up and said: "My darling boy, my most darling boy, don't think of me—think of yourself," and, passing round the foot of the bed, went back into her room.

Jon turned—curled into a sort of ball, as might a hedgehog—into the corner made by the two walls.

He must have been twenty minutes there before a cry roused him. It came from the terrace below. "Jon!" His mother was calling! He ran out and down the stairs, through the empty dining-room into the study. His mother was kneeling before the old armchair, and his father was lying back quite white, his head on his breast, one of his hands resting on an open book, with a pencil clutched in it—more strangely still than anything he had ever seen. She looked round wildly, and said:

"Oh! Jon—he's dead—he's dead!"

His mother's arms were round the knees; pressing her breast against them. "Why—why wasn't I with him?" he heard her whisper. Then he saw the tottering word 'Irene' pencilled on the open page and broke down himself. It was his first sight of human death, and its unutterable stillness blotted from him all other emotion. It made a dreadful mark on him; all seemed suddenly little, futile, short. He mastered himself at last, got up, and raised her.

"Mother! Don't cry—Mother!"

For those of us, like Jon, who never went through the trenches of World War I or saw the slaughter of subsequent wars and strife, who were not colonial administrators caring for sick natives, or members of the medical profession, the sight of death comes rarely. I did not see my first dead person until I was twenty-six, and that was after the body had been embalmed and was in a coffin. It was the body of the governess June Kennedy's grandmother in Ireland. I attended her Roman Catholic funeral where it was then the common practice to view the open coffin. Other than that, I have at the age of sixty-seven still only witnessed the dead bodies of my mother and my father.

My sister, Diane, was less fortunate. She found Granny Mabs dead on her bed, but for me it has really only been my mother's and father's bodies that I have seen shortly after death. My mother suffered for three days before she died, semi-comatose, but in trauma. It was extremely difficult to watch with my father and my sisters as we kept vigil at her hospital bed. As is so often the case, exhausted we left to sleep so that at the moment of death none of us were there. This hit Sally hard and was a solid reason for her dogged determination not to leave my father on his deathbed. When we returned to the hospital hearing the news, we saw my mother less stressed in death. The nurses had laid her out clutching a red carnation and with her teddy bear snuggled up beside her. Later, when we saw her dead face again as she lay in her coffin at the funeral home, she looked quite different. Embalmed, she bore an uncanny resemblance to her mother—Granny Mabs.

Sally was beside my father when he died. Again, we had kept vigil for several days, including that moment after we thought he was about to leave us and he suddenly awoke and demanded "Tea!" I would say that my father died a 'Forsyte'. He often challenged the opinions of the post-'Forsythia' world with a very 'Forsyte' response: "If my mother were alive today..." and you could almost feel that Hovenden glare rising from my father's own cynicism. However, his mind adapted exceptionally well to our changed world during the second half of his long life, perhaps in part because he let go of that sense of 'property'. We miss him deeply, with his love, cynical humor and real sense of family, along with all those accounts of his childhood—its aspirations and circumstances in that very different world going back to 1915.

Jon Forsyte, *when all was done that had to be, and his mother was lying down, saw his father alone, on the bed, covered with a white sheet. He stood for a long time gazing at that face which had never looked angry—always whimsical, and kind. "To be kind and keep your end up—there's nothing else in it," he had once heard his father say. How wonderfully Dad had acted up to that philosophy! He gazed with an awe and passionate reverence. His own trouble seemed small while he was looking at that face. The word scribbled on the page! The farewell word! Now his mother had no one but himself! He went up close to the dead face—not changed at all, and yet completely changed. Perhaps his father's consciousness was in the room with him. Above the bed hung a picture of his father's father. Perhaps his consciousness, too, was still alive; and his brother's—his half-brother, who had died in the Transvaal. Were they all gathered round this bed? Jon kissed the forehead, and stole back to his own room. The door between it and his mother's was ajar; she had evidently been in—everything was ready for him, even some biscuits and hot milk, and the letter no longer on the floor. Once in the night, turning in his heavy sleep, he was conscious of something white and still beside his bed, and started up.*

His mother's voice said: "It's only I, Jon dear!" Her hand pressed his forehead gently back; her white figure disappeared.

Alone! He fell heavily asleep again, and dreamed he saw his mother's name crawling on his bed.

CHAPTER FOUR

SOAMES COGITATES

The announcement in the Times of his cousin Jolyon's death affected Soames quite simply. So that chap was gone! At first, he considered this early decease a piece of poetic justice. For twenty years the fellow had enjoyed the reversion of his wife and house, and—he was dead! The obituary notice spoke of 'that diligent and agreeable painter whose work we have come to look on as typical of the best late-Victorian water-colour art.' Soames, who mechanically preferred others, had always sniffed when he came to one of his cousins', and as a connoisseur, he turned the Times with a crackle.

Soames had to go up to Town that morning on Forsyte affairs. In the office, he could almost hear Gradman thinking: 'Mr. Jolyon, ye-es—just my age, and gone—dear, dear! I dare say she feels it. She was a naice-looking woman. Flesh is flesh! They've given 'im a notice in the papers, Fancy!'

"About that settlement on Miss Fleur, Mr. Soames!" Gradman said.

"I've thought better of that," answered Soames shortly.

"Aoh! I'm glad of that. I thought you were a little hasty. The times do change."

How this death would effect Fleur had begun to trouble Soames. He was not certain that she knew of it—she seldom looked at the paper, never at the births, marriages, and deaths.

From the office, Soames *made his way to Green Street for lunch.*
"Did Profond ever get off?" he asked his sister Winifred.
"He got off, but where—I don't know."
Yes, there it was—impossible to tell anything? Not that he wanted to know. Letters from Annette were coming from Dieppe, where she and her mother were supposedly *staying.*
"You saw that fellow's death, I suppose," he asked, changing the subject.
"Yes," said Winifred. *"I'm sorry for—for his children. One must do him justice now he's dead."*
"I should like to have done him justice before," said Soames; *"but I never had the chance. Have you got a 'Baronetage' here?"*
"Yes; in that bottom row."
Soames took out a fat red book, and ran over the leaves.

'Debrett's Peerage and Baronetage' volumes were often found on the shelves of 'Forsyte' homes. They were rarely looked at—more subtle status symbols than anything. Occasionally, it was worth a search to see if there was some connection between a family member and the aristocracy, but 'Forsytes' viewed the aristocracy with amusement more than longing. Sometimes, a little 'blue' blood might cement a marriage proposal—they had their uses.

I remember a period in my life when my family started to take an interest in its ancestors. We always knew we were of yeoman stock from a book that Great-grandfather Charles Hovenden had put together—a beautiful leather-bound volume on the Hovenden family. They were of Flemish ancestry—Huguenots, who had fled Flanders in the religious wars following the Reformation, settled in Kent, and were in the cloth-weaving trade. They did well, had their own land at Hocker Edge and Borden, and like the Forsytes came to London in the very early Nineteenth Century as medical doctors. Through the herbs of medicine, they developed a perfume business, and like Galsworthy's Forsytes, by the late nineteenth century were paramount in their profession—the leading perfumers and barber's sundriesmen of London. However, apart from a possible marital link with Lord Holland in the early nineteenth century, they were not in the peerage, despite a coat of arms that appears in the Hovenden book. The Longleys continue to express pride in the belief that His Grace, The Most Reverend Charles Thomas Longley, Archbishop of Canterbury was a distant relative. As the Archbishop who founded the Lambeth Conferences that still basically dictate the general agreements of the worldwide Anglican Communion, he was significant, but no one in the family has ever provided the evidence behind this legend. The very name Longley, however, quite rare, and demonstrated so in the London telephone directories of my childhood that only listed eight of us, all mostly relatives, means 'The long field'—'Long Leigh,' presumably taken from yeoman land that the family acquired in those early enclosures of monastic lands under King Henry VIII, or in south east England's enclosures of village strip farming by squires, who parceled land out to tenant farmers for the production of sheep. Either way, the family became independent farmers, who rose from yeomanry to 'Forsythia' by the nineteenth century. Was there anything to link us to the peerage. Yes—there are Longley's in Worcestershire, even a village there named Longley Green—a Baronetcy—a coat of arms. As the name is rare, most yeoman who acquired long fields as independent farmers taking the name 'Langley'—'Langue Leigh' after a 'tongue shaped field'—some in my family still cling to a plausible link with the baronetcy. Like the Archbishop, there is no known link, and such a link can only be speculation that very distant cousins many times removed might form such links.

My mother's connection to the Massey family in Ireland is easier to trace. The baronetcy of Massey in Tipperary is well recorded in Debretts, along with numerous monuments to the family in Tipperary Church—the Protestant Church of Ireland, of course. What is not easy to prove, however, is that Harriet 'Penny' Massey was a legitimate daughter of Sir Hugh Massey, Bt,. Some members of the family believe she was the daughter of Lord Massey's brother, George Eyre Massey, somewhat of a rake, who lived at Kilakee in the Dublin hills and was a member of the Hell Fire Club and other black magic institutions. As the daughter of a baronet, Harriet would not have been a lady in her own right, even if legitimate, although her mother would have been Lady Massey. It is almost certain, however, legitimate or otherwise, that my Great-grandmother Collings was a Massey by blood. There was that book that had been given to her in her childhood with the inscription from Lord Massey, a story that Great-aunt Dorrie always clung to. Grandpa Jack was less sure and the book has long since disappeared.

Soames looked up 'Mont.'

"*Mont— Sir Lawrence, 9th Bt.,cr.1620, e.s. of Geoffrey, 8th Bt., and Lavinia, daur, of Sir Charles Muskham, Bt., of Muskham Hall, Shrops: marr. 1890 Emily. Daur. Of Conway Charwell, esq., of Condaford*

Grange, co. Oxon; 1 son, heir Michael Conway, b. 1895, 2 daur. Residence: Lippinghall Manor, Folwell, Bucks. Clubs: Snooks': Coffee House: Aeroplane: See Bidlicott."

"H'm!" he said. "Did you ever know a publisher?"

"Uncle Timothy," Winfred replied.

"Alive, I mean."

"Monty knew one at his Club. He brought him here to dinner once. Monty was always thinking of writing a book, you know, about how to make money on the turf. He tried to interest that man."

"Well?"

"He put him on to a horse—for the Two Thousand. We didn't see him again. He was rather smart if I remember."

"Did it win?"

"No; it ran last, I think."

"Can you see any connection between a sucking baronet and publishing?"

"People do all sorts of things nowadays. The great stunt seems not to be idle—so different from our time. To do nothing was the thing then. But I suppose it'll come again."

"This young Mont that I'm speaking of is very sweet on Fleur. If it would put an end to that other affair, I might encourage it."

"Has he got style" asked Winifred.

"He's no beauty; pleasant enough, with some scattered brains. There's a good deal of land, I believe. He seems genuinely attached. But I don't know."

"No," murmured Winifred, "it's very difficult." Then dismissing the subject she announced she was going to Hyde Park.

Soames took his leave. All the way down to Reading he debated whether he should tell Fleur of that boy's father's death. That boy would be independent now, and only have his mother's opposition to encounter. He would come into a lot of money, no doubt, and perhaps the house—the house built for Irene and himself—the house whose architect had wrought his domestic ruin. The thought then crossed his mind that this might not be such a bad thing: *his daughter—mistress of that house! That would be poetic justice!* Soames uttered a little mirthless laugh. He had designed that house to re-establish his failing union, meant it for the seat of his descendents, if he could have induced Irene to give him one! Her son and Fleur! Their children would be, in some sort, offspring of the union between himself and her.

It would be the easiest and wealthiest way out of the impasse, now that Jolyon was gone. The juncture of two Forsyte fortunes had a kind of conservative charm. And she—Irene—would be linked to him once more. Then, reality set in. *Nonsense! Absurd! He put the notion out of his head.*

On arriving home he heard the click of billiard-balls and through the window saw young Mont sprawling over the table. A title—land! There was little enough in land these days; perhaps less in a title. The old Forsytes had always had a kind of contempt for titles, rather remote and artificial things—not worth the money they cost, and having to do with the Court. Soames remembered how his own mother, Emily, *had wished to be presented* at court *because of the fashionable nature of the performance, and how his father had put his foot down with unwonted decision. What did she want with that peacocking—wasting time and money; there was nothing in it.*

The instinct which had made and kept the British Commons the chief power of the State, a feeling that their own world was good enough and a little better than any other because it was their world, had kept the old Forsytes singularly free from 'flummery'. The present generation, *as it seemed to him, laughed at everything.*

However, there was no harm in the young fellow's being heir to a title and estate—a thing one couldn't help. He noted the young man's eyes, fixed on Fleur bending over in her turn; and adoration in them almost touched him.

Then they saw him, and Soames said:

"I'll mark for you."

He sat down on the raised seat beneath the marker, trim and tired, furtively studying those two young faces. When the game was over, Mont came up to him.

"I've started in, sir. Rum game, business, isn't it? I suppose you saw a lot of human nature as a solicitor?"

"I did."

"Say we offer an author good terms—he naturally takes them. Then we go into it, find we can't publish at a decent profit and tell him so. He's got confidence in us because we've been generous to him, and he comes down like a lamb, and bears no malice. But if we offer him poor terms at the start, he doesn't take them, so we have to advance them to get him, and he thinks us damn screws into the bargain."

"Try buying pictures on that system," said Soames; *"an offer accepted is a contract—haven't you learned that?"*

Young Mont turned his head to where Fleur was standing in the window—a contract?

"No," he said, *"I wish I had. Then there's another thing. Always let a man off a bargain if he wants to be let off."*

"Does your firm work on those lines?"

"Not yet," said Mont, *"but it'll come."*

"And they will go."

"No, really sir. I'm making any number of observations, and they all confirm my theory. Human nature is consistently underrated in business, people do themselves out of an awful lot of pleasure and profit by that. The more human and generous you are the better chance you've got in business,"

Soames rose.

"Are you a partner?"

"Not for six months, yet."

"The rest of the firm had better make haste and retire."

Mont laughed.

"You'll see," he said. *"There's going to be a big change. The possessive principle has got its shutters up."*

"What?"

"The house is to let! Good-bye, sir; I'm off now."

After Mont was gone, Fleur approached her father:

"Have you done anything to stop Jon writing to me, Father?"

Soames shook his head.

"You haven't seen, then?" he said. *"His father died just a week ago to-day."*

"Oh!"

In her startled, frowning face he saw the instant struggle to apprehend what this would mean.

"Poor Jon! Why didn't you tell me, Father?"

"I never know!" said Soames slowly; *"you don't confide in me."*

"I would, if you'd help me, dear."

"Perhaps I shall."

Fleur clasped her hands. *"Oh! darling—when one wants a thing fearfully, one doesn't think of other people. Don't be angry with me."*

"I'm cogitating," he said. *"Has young Mont been bothering you again?"*

Fleur smiled. "Oh, Michael. He's always bothering; but he's such a good sort—I don't mind him."

"Well," said Soames, "I'm tired; I shall go and have a nap before dinner."

He went to his picture-gallery, lay down on the couch there, and closed his eyes. A terrible responsibility this girl of his—whose mother was—ah! what was she? A terrible responsibility! Help her—how could he help her? He could not alter the fact that he was her father. Or that Irene...! What was it young Mont had said—some nonsense about the possessive instinct—shutters up—To let? Silly!

CHAPTER FIVE

THE FIXED IDEA

*The fixed idea of love runs with eyes turned inward to its own light, oblivious of other stars. Those with the fixed ideas that human happiness depends on their art, on vivisecting dogs, on hating foreigners, on paying supertax, on remaining Ministers, on making wheels go round, on preventing their neighbours from being divorced, on conscientious objection, Greek roots, Church dogma, paradox and superiority to everybody else, with other forms of ego-mania—*the building blocks apart from birthright that make us 'Forsytes'—*all are unstable compared with him or her whose fixed idea is the possession of some her or him. And though, Fleur, those chilly summer days, pursued the scattered life of a little Forsyte whose frocks are paid for, and whose business is pleasure, she was 'honest to God' indifferent to it all. She even kept Jon's letters, covered with pink silk, on her heart, which in days when corsets were so low, sentiment so despised, and chests so out of fashion, could be no greater proof of the fixity of her idea.*

After hearing of his father's death, she wrote to Jon, and received his answer three days later on her return from a river picnic. It was his first letter since his meeting at June's. She opened it with misgiving, and read it with dismay.

"Since I saw you I've heard everything about the past. I won't tell it you—I think you knew when we met at June's. She says you did. If you did, Fleur, you ought to have told me. I expect you only heard your

father's side of it. I have heard my mother's. It's dreadful. Now that she's so sad I can't do anything to hurt her more. Of course, I long for you all day, but I don't believe now that we shall ever come together—there's something too strong pulling us apart."

Her first impulse was to reply—her second, not to reply. These impulses were constantly renewed in the days which followed, while desperation grew within her. She was not her father's child for nothing. The tenacity which had at once made and undone Soames was her backbone, too, frilled and embroidered by French grace and quickness. Instinctively she conjugated the verb 'to have' always with the pronoun 'I'. She concealed, however, all signs of her growing depression, and pursued such river pleasures as the winds and rain of a disagreeable July permitted, as if she had no care in the world; nor did any 'sucking baronet' ever neglect the business of a publisher more consistently than her attendant spirit, Michael Mont.

Soames was almost deceived by this careless gaiety.

Winifred invited them to lunch and to go afterward to 'a most amusing little play, "The Beggar's Opera",' and would they bring a man to make four? They motored up taking Michael Mont, who, being in his seventh heaven, was found by Winifred 'very amusing'. 'The Beggar's Opera' puzzled Soames. The people were very unpleasant, the whole thing very cynical. Winifred was 'intrigued'—by the dresses. The music, too, did not displease her. Michael Mont was enraptured by the whole thing. And all three wondered what Fleur was thinking of it. But Fleur was not thinking of it. Her fixed idea was all she heard and saw. *Her lips might smile, her hands applaud, but the comic old masterpiece made no more impression on her than if it had been pathetic, like a modern 'Revue'. When they embarked in the car to return, she ached because Jon was not sitting next to her instead of Michael Mont. When, at some jolt, the young man's arm touched hers as if by accident, she only thought: 'If that were Jon's arm!' When his cheerful voice, tempered by her proximity, murmured above the sound of the car's progress, she smiled and answered, thinking: 'If that were Jon's voice!' and once he said, "Fleur, you look a perfect angel in that dress!" she answered, "Oh, do you like it?" thinking, 'If only Jon could see it!'*

During this drive she took a resolution. She would go to Robin Hill and see him—alone; she would take the car, without word beforehand to him or to her father. It was nine days since his letter, and she could wait no longer. On Monday she would go! With something to look forward to she could afford to tolerate young Mont *and respond. He might stay to dinner; propose to her as usual; dance with her, press her hand, sigh—do what he liked. He was only a nuisance when he interfered with her fixed idea. She was even sorry for him so far as it was possible to be sorry for anybody but herself just now. At dinner he seemed to talk more wildly than usual about what he called "the death of the close borough"—she paid little attention, but her father seemed paying a good deal, with the smile on his face which meant opposition, if not anger.*

"The younger generation doesn't think as you do, sir; does it, Fleur?"

Fleur shrugged her shoulders—the younger generation was just Jon, and she did not know what he was thinking.

"Young people will think as I do when they're my age, Mr. Mont. Human nature doesn't change."

"I admit, that, sir; but the forms of thought change with the times. The pursuit of self-interest is a form of thought that's going out."

"Indeed! To mind one's own business is not a form of thought, Mr. Mont, it's an instinct."

Yes, when Jon was the business!

"But, what is one's business, sir? That's the point. Everybody's business is going to be one's business. Isn't it, Fleur?"

Fleur only smiled.

"If not," added young Mont, "there'll be blood."

"People have talked like that from time immemorial."

"But you'll admit, sir, that the sense of property is dying out?"

"I should say increasing among those who have none."

"Well, look at me! I'm heir to an entailed estate. I don't want the thing; I'd cut the entail tomorrow."

"You're not married, and you don't know what you're talking about."

Fleur saw the young man's eyes turn rather piteously upon her.

"Do you really mean that marriage...?" he began.

"Society is built on marriage," came from between her father's close lips; "marriage and its consequences. Do you want to do away with it?"

Silence brooded over the dinner table, covered with spoons bearing the Forsyte crest—a pheasant proper as Swithin had researched—under the electric light of an alabaster globe.

Here were the strange seeds of the conflict that faced 'Forsytes' in 1920. Ireland, the Great War, and the Russian Revolution—where was the world headed? At first, like with Soames, it would seem only natural that 'Forsytes' would fight off the new order—favor that trend that would lead to fascism; and yet in the end, for their country's survival, indeed for the survival of the British Empire, they would be forced to embrace the anti-fascist element—a strange mix of odd bedfellows, communist, socialist, and democratic. But that was far away...

    'Monday,' thought Fleur; 'Monday!'

CHAPTER SIX

DESPERATE

J olyon was cremated. By his special wish no one attended that
ceremony, or wore black for him.

Cremation finally became embraced by 'Forsytes' about 1920.
It was brave souls who selected this path earlier like Susan Hayman.
After all, historically, the idea of burning the body was to destroy
the resurrection in any physical form—hence the burning of heretics,
ironically both Protestant and Roman Catholic. During the first half
of 'Forsythia', too, so many witnessed the practice among native
heathens of the Empire. Although little had dogmatically changed in the
Christianity practiced by the Church of England in the early twentieth
century, much had changed in attitude toward it. The challenge of
Darwin, other scientific experiment, and the almost unrecorded, but
steady loss of the established church's lower-middle and working-class
members to non-conformist congregations, molded attitude. Many of
the non-conformists historically could trace origins in their churches to
founders who were burned at the stake—martyrs. Not being members
of the ruling class, they, too, could relate more to the heathen natives
in practice if not in faith. Finally, we come to growing practicality. The
original churchyards of London and other large cities had filled up.
Large suburban cemeteries were also filling up, in part compounded by
the huge loss of young lives during the Great War and the even more
dramatic loss of life through the outbreak of Spanish 'flu' in 1919. Large

monuments and vaults such as that used by the Forsyte family in the Highgate cemetery of North London took too much space, and it was seen to be more practical to bury ashes in small plots with a simpler marker. Some 'Forsytes' like my own grandmother, Granny Mabs, were practical people, and in the changing religious climate, began to see cremation as a neater, swifter and more economic final solution. The aristocracy and landed gentry were slower to embrace the idea; but this was because for the most part they chose to be buried in the country at the village church where many of them still owned the living, and which was situated on or close to their inherited country estates.

Even so, Jolyon's decision was 'avant-garde' for the times, along with his instructions for the family not to wear mourning dress. After all, only twenty years earlier the whole nation had worn mourning dress on the death of Queen Victoria, at least in 'Forsyte' circles.

The succession of his property, controlled to some extent by old Jolyon's Will, left Irene *in possession of Robin Hill, with two thousand five hundred pounds a year for life. Apart from this, the two Wills worked together in some complicated way to ensure that property in the future as in the present, save only that Jon, by virtue of his sex, would have control of his capital when he was twenty-one, while June and Holly would only have the spirit of theirs, in order that their children might have the body after them. If they had no children, it would all come to Jon if he outlived them; and since June was fifty, and Holly nearly forty, it was considered in Lincoln's Inn Fields but that for the cruelty of income tax, young Jon would be as warm a man as his grandfather when he died.*

June was the one who took charge, but after she left Irene and Jon *alone again in the great house, alone with death drawing them together, and love driving them apart, Jon passed painful days secretly disgusted and disappointed with himself. He did not judge or condemn* his mother; *that was all too remote—indeed, the idea of doing so had never come to him. No! he was grudging and unnatural because he couldn't have what he wanted because of her.*

Together, however, they came to an agreement that June should not take possession of Jolyon's art work—better to arrange a one-man exhibition themselves, away from the prying eyes and *icy blasts* of *Paul Post and other frequenters of* June's *studio.* They spent much time, therefore, in Jolyon's studio going through the work—a therapy against their bereavement and against their personal feelings and the *love that was driving them apart. Jon came to have a curiously increased respect for his father. The quiet tenacity with which he had converted a mediocre talent into something really individual was disclosed by these researches,* much as one day I still hope that my sister Diane's individuality and talent will be found. *There was a great mass of work with a rare continuity of growth in depth and reach of vision.*

The studio where they had been sorting and labelling, had once been Holly's schoolroom, devoted to her silkworms, dried lavender, music, and other forms of instruction. 'Forsytes' had a childhood fascination with silkworms. Diane kept silkworms, too, encouraged by our school. It was considered most important that they should be fed mulberry leaves, and mulberry trees were not that common in our suburban gardens. Through St. Christopher's, The Hall, expeditions were made to Lullingstone Castle in Kent, where there was a large supply of mulberry trees and the gathered leaves could supply the voracious little worms in our many Beckenham homes.

Now at the end of July, despite the studio's *north and eastern aspects, a warm and slumberous air came in between the long-faded lilac linen curtains. Jon, at the north window, sniffing air mysteriously scented with warm strawberries, heard a car drive up. The lawyers again about some nonsense!* He was composing a poem on the scents and sounds and *was still muttering it over to himself at the window, when he heard his name called, and, turning round, saw Fleur. At that amazing apparition, he made at first no movement and no sound, while her clear vivid glance ravaged his heart. Then he went forward to the table, saying: "How nice of you to come!" and saw her flinch as if he had thrown something at her.*

"I asked for you," she said, *"and they showed me up here. But I can go away again."*

Jon clutched the paint-stained table.

"I know I told you a lie, Jon. But I told it out of love."

"Yes, oh! yes! That's nothing!"

"I didn't answer your letter. What was the use—there wasn't anything to answer. I wanted to see you instead." She held out both her hands, and Jon grasped them across the table. His own felt so hard and hers so soft. She said almost defiantly:

"That old story—was it so very dreadful?"

"Yes." In his voice, too, there was a note of defiance.

She dragged her hands away. "I didn't think in these days boys were tied to their mother's apron-strings."

Jon's chin went up as if he had been struck.

I well remember at Newlands how cruel other boys could be if they felt a contemporary schoolboy was 'tied to his mother's apron strings.' One boy was harassed just because he got more than a once a week letter from his mother. It was instilled into us that we were 'men' from the moment we went to boarding school at eight. We had to leave behind, 'The Nursery', 'Nanny', 'Mother', 'Au Pairs', 'Ayah' and all those feminine influences of our formative years.

"Oh! I didn't mean it, Jon. What a horrible thing to say!" Swiftly she came close to him. "Jon, dear; I didn't mean it."

"All right."

But in a sort of paralysis, he made no response to her.

"Well, I'll go if you don't want me. But I never thought you'd have given me up."

"I haven't," cried Jon, coming suddenly to life. "I can't. I'll try again."

Her eyes gleamed, she swayed towards him. "Jon—I love you! Don't give me up! If you do, I don't know what—I feel so desperate. What does it matter—all that past—compared with this?"

She clung to him. He kissed her eyes, her cheeks, her lips. But while he kissed her he saw the sheets of that letter fallen down on the floor of his bedroom—his father's white dead face—his mother kneeling before it. Fleur's whisper, "Make her! Promise! Oh! Jon, try!" seemed childish in his ear. He felt curiously old.

"I promise!" he muttered. "Only you don't understand."

"She wants to spoil our lives just because..."

"Yes, of what?"

Again that challenge in his voice, and she did not answer. Her arms tightened round him, and he returned her kisses; but even while he yielded, the poison worked in him, the poison of the letter. Fleur did not know, she did not understand—she misjudged his mother; she came from the enemy's camp! So lovely, and he loved her so—yet, even in her embrace, he could not help the memory of Holly's words: "I think she has a having nature," and his mother's, "My darling boy, don't think of me—think of yourself!"

When she was gone like a passionate dream, leaving her image on his eyes, her kisses on his lips, such an ache in his heart, Jon leaned in the window, listening to the car bearing her away. If Fleur was desperate, so was he.

In the 1980s I had a wonderful relationship with my Japanese girlfriend, Kazumi Masuda. We met at sea on a Norwegian cruise and fell in love. Kazumi, however, was married and although as good as separated from her husband, was not legally divorced. In the fairy tale world of my cruising career we courted each other on all the continents— staying in the finest resorts and most romantic guesthouses, and sailing on the most luxurious cruise ships of the era. Then, on vacation, we had my own romantic get away—Sea Island and St. Simons Island on the Georgia coast. The move to divorce, however, never came. After twelve years, this extraordinary passion and idyll ended abruptly, as Bettine Clemen, a celebrated and amazing flutist fell into my life. The period of struggle in the last weeks of my relationship with Kazumi was excruciatingly painful for us both, even as the hopes for my future soared with Bettine. It is so hard to relinquish the true passion of real love, and despite it all, Kazumi and I have remained close friends.

Jon *would have given anything to be back again in the past—barely three months back; or away forward, years, in the future. The present with this dark cruelty of a decision, one way or the other, seemed impossible. If only Fleur and he had met on some desert island without a past—and Nature for their house! He shut the window, drew curtains over it, switched off the lighted sconce, and went upstairs.*

The door of his room was open, the light turned up, his mother, still in her evening gown, was standing at the window. She turned and said:

"Sit down, Jon; let's talk." She sat down on the window-seat, Jon on his bed.

"I know Fleur came to-day. I'm not surprised." It was as though she had added: 'She is her father's daughter!' And Jon's heart hardened. Irene went on quietly:

"I have Father's letter. I picked it up that night and kept it. Would you like it back, dear?"

Jon shook his head.

"I had read it, of course, before he gave it to you. It didn't quite do justice to my criminality."

"Mother!" burst from Jon's lips.

"He put it very sweetly, but I know that in marrying Fleur's father without love I did a dreadful thing. An unhappy marriage, Jon, can play

such havoc with our lives besides one's own. You are fearfully young, my darling, and fearfully loving. Do you think you can possibly be happy with this girl?"

Staring at her dark eyes, darker now from pain, Jon answered:

"Yes; oh! yes—if you could be."

Irene smiled.

"Admiration of beauty and longing for possession are not love. If yours were another case like mine, Jon—where the deepest things are stifled; the flesh joined, and the spirit at war!"

"Why should it, Mother? You think she must be like her father, but she's not. I've seen him."

"You are a giver, Jon; she is a taker."

That unworthy doubt, that haunting uncertainty again. He said with vehemence:

"She isn't—she isn't. It's only because I can't bear to make you unhappy, Mother, now that Father..." He thrust his fists against his forehead.

Irene got up.

"I told you that night, dear, not to mind me. I meant it. Think of yourself and your own happiness! I can stand what's left—I've brought it on myself."

Again the word "Mother!" burst from Jon's lips.

She came over to him and put her hands over his.

"I shall always love you just the same, Jon, whatever you do. You won't lose anything." She smoothed his hair gently, and walked away.

He heard the door shut; and, rolling over on the bed, lay, stifling his breath, with an awful held-up feeling within him.

CHAPTER SEVEN

EMBASSY

Enquiring for her at tea time Soames learned that Fleur had been out in the car since two. Three hours! Where had she gone? He had never become quite reconciled with cars. The things typified all that was fast, insecure and subcutaneously oily in modern life. Pace and progress pleased him less and less; there was an ostentation, too, about a car which he considered provocative in the prevailing mood of Labour. On one occasion that chauffeur fellow Sims had driven over the only vested interest of a working man—a dog. Not many people would have stopped to put up with it. He had been sorry for the dog, and quite prepared to take its part against the car, if that ruffian hadn't been so outrageous. With four hours fast becoming five, and still no Fleur all the old car-wise feelings he had experienced in person and by proxy balled within him, and shaking sensations troubled the pit of his stomach. At seven he telephoned to Winifred by trunk call—another of these new necessities.

I am reminded of a scene in the 2011 Masterpiece Theatre production of *Downton Abbey*. When telephones were first installed in 'Forsyte' homes they were placed in the butler's pantry, as most late Edwardian upper-class households were run by a butler. Carson in *Downton Abbey* is seen practicing answering the telephone in the privacy of his pantry. Here, was kept the china and silverware over which butlers had charge. The telephone also became the butler's responsibility. He would relay messages to the master or mistress as an intermediary. At first, it was not considered quite the thing for members of the family to have to speak into a machine. Later, when butlers were no longer universal among the three percent, the telephone was moved into its own small room off the hall where members of the family could answer the machine in privacy. This was how it was in Granny Mabs' house on Wickham Way. It was not really until after the Second World War that telephones found their way into bedrooms, and in my childhood they were rarely found in living rooms.

The telephone at Tullamaine Castle, when I lived in Ireland in my last years of 'Forsythia', was still in the butler's pantry, and the only one in the castle. When the butler or houseman was on duty, he was still expected to answer the phone and relay messages to the master or mistress. The telephone still came with a handle to turn that rang in the local post office. The postmistress in the village, then was alerted and connected your line to the party you wanted to reach or passed it down 'the trunk' to other towns or villages—and this was the 1960s! Needless to say, the telephone number at Tullamaine Castle was simply 'Fethard 2'. This meant Tullamaine Castle was the first house in the Fethard area apart from the Post Office to have a telephone.

The message came back to Soames from his sister Winifred. *No! Fleur had not been to Green Street. Then where was she? Visions of his beloved daughter rolled up in her pretty frills, all blood and dust-stained, in some hideous catastrophe, began to haunt him. He went to her room and spied among her things. She had taken nothing—no dressing-case, no jewellery. And this, a relief in one sense, increased his fears of an accident. Terrible to be helpless when his loved one was missing, especially when he couldn't bear fuss or publicity of any kind! What should he do if she were not back by night-fall?*

This was the same anguish and the same fear that passed from my mother to my father and back again as we waited for Sally that night at Hockeredge. Where was she? Had she met with an accident? Was she in hospital? Should we notify the police? When, in reality, she was at that extended party at one of her boyfriend's homes only streets away.

At a quarter to eight Soames heard the car. A great weight lifted from off his heart; he hurried down. She was getting out—pale and tired-looking, but nothing wrong. He met her in the hall.

"You've frightened me. Where have you been?"

"To Robin Hill, I'm sorry, dear. I had to go; I'll tell you afterwards," and with a flying kiss, she ran upstairs.

Soames waited in the drawing-room for her to join him for dinner.

It was not a subject they could discuss at dinner—consecrated to the susceptibilities of the butler. In the pocket of Soames' *dinner-jacket was a letter from Annette*—his other worry. *She was coming back in a fortnight. He knew nothing of what she had been doing out there. And he was glad that he did not. From the look on* Fleur's *face, he became certain that she wanted something from him, uncertain whether it would be wise of him to give it her. He pushed his savoury away uneaten, and even joined her in a cigarette.*

After dinner she set the electric piano-player going—worse than *that musical box of his nursery days. Here it was—the same thing, only larger, more expensive, and now it played 'The Wild, Wild Women'. He augured the worst when she sat down on a cushion footstool at his knee, and put her hand on his,* but he needed to know.

"Darling, be nice to me. I had to see Jon—he wrote to me. He's going to try what he can do with his mother. But I've been thinking. It's really in your hands, Father. If you'd persuade her that it doesn't mean renewing the past in any way! That I shall stay yours, and Jon will stay hers; that you need never see him or her, and she need never see you or me! Only you could persuade her, dear, because only you could promise. One can't promise for other people. Surely it wouldn't be too awkward for you to see her just this once—now that Jon's father is dead?"

"Too awkward?" Soames *repeated.* *"The whole thing's preposterous."*

"You know," said Fleur, *without looking up,* *"you wouldn't mind seeing her, really."*

Soames *was silent. Her words had expressed a truth too deep for him to admit.*

"What am I to do if you won't, Father?" she said very softly.

"I'll do anything for your happiness," said Soames; *"but this isn't for your happiness."*

"Oh! it is; It is!"

"It'll only stir things up," he said grimly.

"But they are stirred up. The thing is to quiet them. To make her feel that this is just our lives, and has nothing to do with yours or hers.

You can do it, Father, I know you can. If you will, Jon and I can wait a year—two years if you like."

"It seems to me," murmured Soames, "that you care nothing about what I feel."

Fleur pressed his hand against her cheek.

"I do, darling. But you wouldn't like me to be awfully miserable."

Why should he help her get this boy, who was killing her affection for himself? Why should he? By the laws of the Forsytes it was foolish! There was nothing to be had out of it—nothing! To give her to that boy! To pass her into the enemy's camp, under the influence of the woman who had injured him so deeply! And suddenly he was conscious that his hand was wet. Fleur was crying. *"Well, well," he said. "I'll think it over, and do what I can. Come, come!"*

He did not see Fleur again that night. But, at breakfast, her eyes followed him about with an appeal he could not escape—not that he intended to try. No! He had made up his mind to the nerve-racking business. He would go to Robin Hill—to that house of memories. He went up by train and down by train, and from the station walked by the long rising lane, still very much as he remembered it over thirty years ago. Funny—so near London! Someone evidently was holding on to land there, just as they were all around Beckenham in 1920. *After all was said and done there was something real about land, it didn't shift. Land, and good pictures! The values might fluctuate a bit, but on the whole they were always going up—worth holding on to, in a world where there was a lot of unreality, cheap building, changing fashions, such a 'Here to-day and gone to-morrow' spirit. As Aunt Juley might have said—quoting 'Superior Dosset'—*Soames' *nerves were 'in a proper fatigue'. He could see the house now among its trees, the house he had watched being built, intending it for himself and this woman, who, by such strange fate, had lived in it with another after all! Passing the poplars in front of the house, he thought: 'How they've grown; I had them planted!'*

A maid answered his ring.

"Will you say—Mr. Forsyte, on a very special matter."

The maid came back. "Would the gentleman state his business, please?"

"Say it concerns Mr. Jon," said Soames.

And once more he was alone in that hall with the pool of grey-white marble designed by her first lover. Ah! she had been a bad lot—had loved

two men, and not himself! Suddenly he saw her in the opening chink
between the long heavy purple curtains, swaying, as if in hesitation;
the old perfect poise and line, the old startled dark-eyed gravity, the old
calm defensive voice: "Will you come in, please?"

He passed through that opening. She seemed to him still beautiful.
And this was the first time—the very first—since he married her six-
and-thirty years ago, that he was speaking to her without the legal right
to call her his. She was not wearing black—one of that fellow's radical
notions, he supposed.

"I apologise for coming," he said glumly; but this business must be
settled one way or the other."

"Won't you sit down?"

"No, thank you. It's an infernal mischance: I've done my best to
discourage it. I consider my daughter crazy, but I've got into the habit of
indulging her; that's why I'm here. I suppose you're fond of your son."

"Devotedly."

"Well?"

"It rests with him."

"It's a mad notion," Soames said.

"It is."

"If you had only...! Well—they might have been..." he did not finish
the sentence 'brother and sister and all this saved,' but he saw her
shudder as if he had.

"So far as I'm concerned," he said, "you may make your mind easy.
I desire to see neither you nor your son if this marriage comes about.
Young people in these days are—are unaccountable. But I can't bear to
see my daughter unhappy. What am I to say to her when I go back?"

"Please say to her as I said to you, that it rests with Jon."

"You don't oppose it?"

"With all my heart; not with my lips."

Soames stood biting his finger. "Where is he, your son?"

"Up in his father's studio, I think."

"Perhaps you'd have him down."

He watched her ring the bell, he watched the maid come in.

"Please tell Mr. Jon that I want him."

"If it rests with him," said Soames hurriedly, when the maid was
gone, "I suppose I may take it for granted that this unnatural marriage
will take place; in that case there'll be formalities. Whom do I deal
with—Herring's"

Irene nodded.

"You don't propose to live with them?"

Irene shook her head.

"What happens to this house?"

"It will be as Jon wishes."

"This house," said Soames suddenly: "I had hopes when I began it. If they live in it—their children! They say there's such a thing as Nemesis. Do you believe in it?"

"Yes."

"Oh! You do!"

He came closer to her.

"I'm not likely to see you again," he said slowly. "Will you shake hands"—his lip quivered, the words came out jerkily—"and let the past die." He held out his hand. Her pale face grew paler, her eyes so dark, rested immovably on his, her hands remained clasped in front of her. He heard a sound and turned, That boy was standing in the opening of the curtains.

"Well, young man! I'm here for my daughter; it rests with you, it seems—this matter. Your mother leaves it in your hands."

The boy stared at his mother's face, and made no answer.

"For my daughter's sake I've brought myself to come," said Soames. "What am I to say to her when I go back?"

Still looking at his mother, the boy said quietly:

"Tell Fleur that it's no good, please; I must do as my father wished before he died."

"Jon!"

"It's all right, Mother."

In a kind of stupefaction Soames looked from one to the other, then, taking up hat and umbrella which he had put down on a chair, he walked towards the curtains. The boy stood aside for him to go by. He passed through and heard the grate of the rings as the curtains were drawn behind him—that sound so reminiscent of the inner and outer hall at Hockeredge. The sound liberated something in Soames' chest.

'So that's that!' he thought, and passed out of the door.

CHAPTER EIGHT

THE DARK TUNE

Soames' *embassy had come to naught. But he was rid of those people, had regained his daughter at the expense of—her happiness. What would Fleur say to him? Would she believe he had done his best? She would be terribly upset! He must appeal to her pride. That boy had given her up, declared part and lot with the woman who so long ago had given her father up! Soames clenched his hands. Given him up, and why? What had been wrong with him?*

He reached home at half-past nine. While the car was passing in at one drive gate he heard the grinding sputter of a motor cycle passing out by the other. Young Mont, no doubt, so Fleur had not been lonely. In the cream-panelled drawing-room, she was sitting with her elbows on her knees, and her chin on her clasped hands, in front of a white camellia plant which filled the fireplace.

In the summer months after the chimney sweep had done his spring clean, when my grandparents stopped having fires in the principal rooms, they used to make fans out of gold foil and put them in the grates of the empty fireplaces. In front of the fireplace they would then put a screen, usually embroidered like a tapestry. Granny Longley enjoyed embroidery and made several such screens for family members along with tea-tray cloths and teatime tablecloths. I imagine that such firescreens were commonly found in 'Forsyte' homes, as most 'Forsytes' in my childhood were still living in late Victorian, Edwardian, or early 1920's homes that all had Victorian-style grates designed for coal, somewhat smaller than the larger fire openings with end irons for logs that one found in eighteenth century and early nineteenth-century homes. The fireplaces at Tullamaine Castle in Ireland, however, had large, marble 'Adam' fireplaces, too large for these Victorian and Edwardian embroidered screens, and it was my practice when estate manager there, to fill their hearths with potted plants in the summer months, including white camellias.

"Well, Father!" exclaimed Fleur excitedly.

Soames shook his head. His tongue failed him. He saw her eyes dilate, her lips quivering.

"What? What? Quick, Father!"

"My dear," said Soames, "I—I did my best, but..." And again he shook his head.

Fleur ran to him, and put a hand on each of his shoulders.

"She?"

"No," muttered Soames; "he. I was to tell you that it was no use; he must do what his father wished before he died." He caught her by the waist. "Come, child, don't let them hurt you. They're not worth your little finger."

Fleur tore herself from his grasp.

"You didn't—you couldn't have tried. You—you betrayed me, Father! You didn't try—you didn't—I was a fool—I won't believe he could—he ever could! Only yesterday he...! Oh! why did I ask you?"

"Yes," said Soames quietly, "why did you? I swallowed my feelings; I did my best for you, against my judgment—and this is my reward. Good-night!"

Soames started to leave. *Fleur darted after him.*

"He gives me up? You mean that? Father!"

Soames turned and forced himself to answer:

"Yes."

"Oh!" cried Fleur. "What did you—what could you have done in those old days?"

The breathless sense of really monstrous injustice cut the power of speech in Soames's throat. What had he done!

Soames went out. He mounted, slow and icy, to his picture-gallery, and paced among his treasures. Looking out of a window, he heard a monstrous sound. *Why! That piano thing! A dark tune, with a thrum and a throb! She had set it going—what comfort could she get from that? His eyes caught movement down there beyond the lawn, under the trellis of rambler roses and young acacia trees, where the moonlight fell. There she was, roaming up and down. His heart gave a little sickening jump. What would she do under this blow? How could he tell? What did he know of her—he had only loved her all his life—looked on her as the apple of his eye! He knew nothing—had no notion. There she was—and that dark tune—and the river gleaming in the moonlight!*

'I must go out,' he thought.

The same sense of rescue had come to me on board ship when I became aware of the unhappiness of a teenager traveling with her grandmother, who I saw surreptitiously leave the captain's farewell reception on board the *Royal Viking Star*. I was the cruise director and I just had an intuition that 'I must go out' and follow this girl. On board ship we would have one or two suicides a year. I followed her. She was at the railing. I talked to her. Eventually, I coaxed her back inside to rejoin her grandmother just in time for me to announce the captain, and for him to make his farewell speech.

I learned on board ship that there were many for whom cruising was an escape. Every summer there were any number of well meaning grandparents who took troubled teenage grandchildren on the 'cure all' cruise. There were also sad lonely people who believed a cruise would be some sort of panacea. It often was not. There were unhappy crew members, too. I remember a musician who threw himself down a stairwell, and the captain's mother-in-law's nurse, who left only her red shoes on the promenade deck, her person never to be seen again. I even encountered murder at sea!

Some shared their misfortunes with me, as when I was a cruise director I was also an acting chaplain. It was known that I was a theologian, and traditionally, the cruise director conducted Sunday worship services on board, except on British ships where it remained the captain's prerogative. Because of my unusual qualifications for this role, I became a shoulder to cry on, both for my staff and for unhappy passengers. Among the younger passengers there were no small number, who had elected to take a cruise or had been forced to accompany a well meaning relative on a cruise to take their minds away from broken romance, or as often perceived by the relative—unsuitable romance.

My last job for the Albertini family, apart from selling up Tullamaine Castle, had been to arrange the interviews and possibilities for placing Mr. Albertini's daughter into Hollins College at Roanoke in Virginia. The young lady only attended for a year as she became involved in a perceived 'unsuitable romance.' The result was her father removing her from the college and taking her to Hawaii to get over the romance. This was much the same action as was taken by Jolyon Forsyte when he sent Jon to Spain with his mother.

In his fear that Fleur might contemplate suicide, Soames *hastened down to the drawing-room, lighted just as he had left it, with the piano drumming out that waltz, or foxtrot, or whatever they called it these days, and passed through onto the verandah.*

He stole down through the fruit garden to the boat-house. He could watch her from there—*he was between her and the river now, and his heart felt lighter. She was his daughter, and Annette's—she wouldn't do anything foolish; but there it was—he didn't know! From the boat-house window he could see the last acacia and the spin of her skirt when she turned in her restless march. How long was she going to roam about like this! That tune had run down at last, thank goodness. And suddenly* he *saw her coming down to the bank. She stood quite close, on the landing stage. And Soames watched, clenching his hands. She had everything in the world that he could give her except the one thing that she could not have because of him!*

Then, with an infinite relief he saw her turn back toward the house. She set that tune going again. Why—it was a mania! Dark, thrumming, travelling from the house. And mousing back through the fruit garden, he regained the verandah. Though he meant to go in and speak to her now, he still hesitated, not knowing what to say, trying hard to recall how it felt to be thwarted in love.

The tune died, and was renewed, and died again, and still Soames sat in the shadow, waiting for he knew not what.

Then, the lights in the drawing room went out. *All was silent and dark in there. Had she gone up? He rose, and, tiptoeing, peered in. It seemed so! He entered. The verandah kept the moonlight out; and at first he could see nothing but the outlines of furniture blacker than the darkness. He groped towards the further window to shut it. His foot struck a chair, and he heard a gasp. There she was, curled and crushed into the corner of the sofa! His hand lowered. Did she want his consolation? He stood, gazing at that ball of crushed frills and hair and graceful youth, trying to burrow its way out of sorrow. How leave her there? At last he touched her hair and said:*

"Come, darling, better go to bed. I'll make it up to you, somehow." How fatuous! But what could he have said?

Chapter Nine

Under the Oak

After Soames left Robin Hill, Jon returned to his father's studio. *The expression on his mother's face confronting the man she had once been married to, had sealed a resolution growing within him ever since she left him the night before. It had put the finishing touch of reality. To marry Fleur would be to hit his mother in the face; to betray his dead father! It was no good! Jon had the least resentful of natures. For one so young there was a rather strange power in him of seeing things in some sort of proportion. It was worse for Fleur, worse for his mother even, than it was for him.*

And in this vein, he considered the world. *He pictured the people who had nothing—the millions who had given up life in the War, the millions whom the War had left with life and little else; the hungry children he had read of, the shattered men; people in prison, every kind of unfortunate. He could not go on staying here, walled in and sheltered, with everything so slick and comfortable, and nothing to do but brood and think of what might have been. He could not go back to Wansdon, and the memories of Fleur. If he saw her again he could not trust himself; and if he stayed here or went back there, he would surely see her. To go far away and quickly was the only thing to do*—and without his mother. *Then, feeling that he was brutal, he made up his mind desperately to propose that they should go to Italy.*

He dressed solemnly for dinner.

His mother had done the same. They ate little, and at some length talked of his father's catalogue. The show was arranged for October, and beyond clerical detail, there was nothing more to do.

After dinner she put on a cloak and they went out; walked a little, talked a little, till they were standing silent at last beneath the oak tree. Jon put his arm through hers and said quite casually:

"Mother, let's go to Italy"

Irene pressed his arm, and said as casually:

"It would be very nice; but I've been thinking you ought to see and do more than you would if I were with you."

"But then you'd be alone."

"I was once alone for more than twelve years. Besides I should like to be here for the opening of Father's show."

Jon's grip tightened round her arm; he was not deceived.

"You couldn't stay here all by yourself; it's too big."

"Not here, perhaps. In London, and I might go to Paris, after the show opens. You ought to have a year at least, Jon, and see the world."

There developed in latter 'Forsythia', especially in that last decade, the idea that before a young 'Forsyte' went into business, or attended a college or university, he should spend a year traveling, getting some perspective on the world. This was common practice among Tonbridge students of my day, who left school at eighteen, but did not enter university, particularly Oxford or Cambridge, until nineteen. A popular choice was to take a position in a diplomatic family as a tutor for their children. The position took one away to some foreign part of the world and yet allowed for a safeguarding of lifestyle, time to travel during vacations, and in many cases the opportunity to dabble in a foreign language. This all was considered not only adventurous, but also practical preparation for university life or whatever was to follow.

It was my intention to apply for a position with a diplomatic family in Madrid, Spain, but my headmaster sidetracked me when he suggested my applying to that American Old Tonbridgian with whom he had spent Christmas in Vermont—William Diaz-Albertini. The thought of an Atlantic crossing on the *Queen Elizabeth* or the *Queen Mary* tipped the scales for me, and I wrote to America rather than Madrid and ended up a lot closer to home in County Waterford in Ireland where Mr. Albertini was then renting Ballyin, that dower house on the Duke of Devonshire's estate at Lismore Castle. Two years later, as a student at

Cambridge, I spread my travel wings as part of a student expedition to the Holy Land, traveling through eastern Europe, then behind the iron curtain, the Balkans, Turkey, Syria and Jordan. I worked the summer as a kibbutznik on Israeli community farms, mostly picking fruit. I also toured many biblical archeological sites, and then after a sea passage to Greece, enjoyed the drive back with the other members of this expedition through Europe on a different route. In particular, this journey opened my eyes to the beauty of Montenegro and Dalmatia and introduced me to Venice, which has remained one of my favorite places.

"Yes, I'd like to see the world and rough it," Jon said, *"but I don't want to leave you all alone."*

"My dear," said his mother, *"I owe you that at least. If it's for your good, it'll be for mine. Why not start tomorrow? You've got your passport."*

"Yes; if I'm going it had better be at once. Only—Mother—if—if I wanted to stay out somewhere—America or anywhere, would you mind coming presently?"

"Wherever and whenever you send for me. But don't send until you really want me."

Jon drew a deep breath.

"I feel England's choky."

They stood a few minutes longer under the oak tree. The branches kept the moonlight from them, so that it only fell everywhere else—over the fields and far away, and on the windows of the creepered house behind, which soon would be to let.

Chapter Ten

Fleur's Wedding

Fleur suddenly announced her engagement to Michael Mont on the rebound. Among the Forsytes there was wide speculation as to how long this would last. Soames, after a month or two of depression, saw it as possibly uplifting—a way forward from that awful sight so imprinted on him of his daughter crumpled up in the corner of that sofa after she returned from the brink of suicide. Besides, ever since that day at Winifred's when he had checked out the Mont family in Debretts, he could see the advantages this might bring to Fleur for her future.

In the union of the great-granddaughter of 'Superior Dosset' with the heir of a ninth baronet was the outward and visible sign of class in class which buttresses the political stability of a realm. The time had come when Forsytes might resign their natural resentment against a 'flummery' not theirs by birth, and accept it as the still more natural due of their possessive instincts. Besides, they had to mount to make room for all those so newly rich—the likes of Prosper Profond.

Michael Mont and Fleur Forsyte were married at St. George's, Hanover Square—a fashionable church then as now. My mother's cousin, Jeanne Cuthbertson, the 'chic' one who lived on Hanover Square, was also married at St. George's in the 1960s. We did not see Jeanne very often in my childhood, but when we did, as aforementioned, I always remember that she was very fashionable, usually dressed in smart, haute couture suits and had a tendency to wear rather fine hats. When she married Arthur Edney they moved from Hanover Square to the north of England and we rarely ever got to see them again, although they continued to send us splendid Christmas cards in keeping with her style.

At Fleur's wedding in Hanover Square in October of 1920, it was *impossible for those not in the know to distinguish the Forsyte troop from the Mont contingent—so far away was 'Superior Dosset' now. Was there in the crease of his trousers, the expression of his moustache, his accent, or the shine of his top hat, a pin to choose between Soames and the ninth baronet himself? Was not Fleur as self-possessed, quick, glancing, pretty, and hard as the likeliest Muskham, Mont, or Charwell filly present? If anything, the Forsytes had it in dress and looks and manners. They had become 'upper class' and now their name would be formally recorded in the Stud Book, their money joined to land.*

Whether this was a little late in the day, and those rewards of the possessive instinct, lands and money destined for the melting pot—was a question still so moot that it was not mooted. After all, Timothy had said Consols were goin' up. It was whispered, too, that this young Mont was a sort of socialist—strangely wise of him, and in the nature of insurance, considering the days they lived in. There was no uneasiness on that score. The landed classes produced that sort of amiable foolishness at times, turned to safe uses and confined to theory. There were members of this class on either end of the fascist and communist bandwagon, who in the 1930s supported both sides in the Spanish civil war—families like the famous Mitfords, who were split between two ideologies, but still living their lives within their privileged world. Ironically, I met three of the Mitford sisters. Deborah, the youngest, as the Duchess of Devonshire was the mistress of Lismore Castle in Ireland, and it was through her that Mr. Albertini heard about Tullamaine Castle being for sale. This was because Deborah's older sister, Pamela Mitford, had once been the mistress of Tullamaine Castle when married to Professor Derek Jackson. Pamela visited Tullamaine Castle while I was estate manager there as did Nancy Mitford, the famous author. The other three Mitford sisters, whom I did not meet, showed their political extremes, Jessica being a socialist and supporting the communists in the Spanish Civil War, Diana, who married the British fascist leader Sir Oswald Mosley, and Unity, a close female companion of Adolf Hitler.

In the church on Hanover Square, *George* Forsyte, the wag, *remarked to his sister Francie* before the marriage service started: *"They'll soon be having puppies—that'll give* young Mont *pause."*

Forsytes, Haymans, Tweetymans, sat in the left aisle; Monts, Charwells, Muskhams in the right, while a sprinkling of Fleur's fellow-sufferers at school, and of Mont's fellow-sufferers in the War, gaped indiscriminately from either side, and three maiden ladies brought up the rear together with two Mont retainers and Fleur's old nurse. In the unsettled state of the country as full a house as could be expected.

Holly sat with Val and inevitably thought of her half-brother, Jon. *'I wonder if Jon knows by instinct,' she thought—Jon, out in British Columbia. She had received a letter from him only that morning.*

"Jon's *bought some land and sent for his mother,"* she informed Val.

"What on earth will she do out there?"

"All she cares about is Jon. Do you still think it a happy release?"

Val's shrewd eyes narrowed.

"Fleur wouldn't have suited him a bit. She's not bred right."

"Poor little Fleur!" sighed Holly. Ah! It was strange—this marriage. The young man, Mont, had caught her on the rebound. She, who had made a love-match which had been successful, had a horror of unhappy marriages. This might not be one in the end—but it was clearly a toss-up; and to consecrate a toss-up in this fashion with manufactured unction before a crowd of fashionable free-thinkers—for who thought otherwise than freely, or not at all, when they were 'dolled' up—seemed to her as near a sin as one could find in an age that had abolished them.

The prelate, a member of the Charwell family, started the ceremony. *Val, beside Holly, was thinking—she was certain—of the Mayfly filly at fifteen to one for the Cambridgeshire. Holly's eyes caught the profile of the ninth baronet, in counterfeitment of the kneeling process. She could just see the neat ruck above his knees where he had pulled his trousers up, and thought: 'Val's forgotten to pull up his'*—just like my father, 'The Clown'.

Soames and Annette were kneeling side by side. A little smile came on Holly's *lips—Prosper Profond, back from the South Seas of the Channel, would be kneeling, too, about six rows behind. Yes! This was a funny 'small' business, however it turned out; still it was in a proper church and would be in the proper papers to-morrow morning.*

By 1920, nearly half the churches in England, particularly in the cities, were non-conformist churches—Methodist, Presbyterian, Congregationalist, and various chapels of Baptist leanings. These breakaway protestant churches had captured the souls of much of England's lower-middle class. The three percent, however, remained staunch supporters of the king's church, the established Church of England. In the country villages, too, the Church of England still held sway with its structures now seven or eight hundred years old. In 'Forsythia' the proper church was the Church of England, the Anglican Episcopal Church headed by the king and governed by one of the monarch's most senior ministers, His Grace, The Archbishop of Canterbury.

The Charwell Anglican prelate delivered his discourse. *He told them of the dangerous times they lived in, and the awful conduct of the House of Lords in connection with divorce. They were all soldiers—he said—in the trenches under the poisonous gas of the Prince of Darkness, and must be manful. The purpose of marriage was children, not mere sinful happiness*—something brought home to 'Forsythia' by His Grace, The Most Reverend Cosmo Lang, Archbishop of Canterbury during the abdication crisis of 1936. He said two days after King Edward VIII abdicated: "From God he received a high and sacred trust. Yet, by his own will he has surrendered the trust because of a craving for personal happiness which he sought in a manner inconsistent with the Christian principles of marriage."

When Forsytes and Monts were signing in the vestry, general relaxation set in.

A voice behind Holly *said:*

"Will she stay the course?"

"Who's that?" she whispered.

"Old George Forsyte!"

Holly demurely scrutinised one of whom she had often heard. Fresh from South Africa, and ignorant of her kith and kin, she never saw one without an almost childish curiosity.

"They're off!" she heard him say.

'Forsyte' weddings and other family gatherings, but particularly weddings, seemed to bring out playful cynicism among differing branches of the same tree. This was certainly so in my family, where weddings were almost a means of taking stock on how the other branches were doing. It used to amuse my father immensely. I can almost hear him saying, as he so often did on those occasions: "Oh dear, oh dear," shaking his head at some quirk of a cousin, or more likely their offspring. The 'its' had to prove themselves, and they rarely did.

Holly thought *Mont was spiritually intoxicated* when they came out from the vestry, *but Fleur! Ah! That was different. Outwardly she seemed all there. But inwardly, where was she? As those two passed* down the aisle, *Fleur raised her eyelids—the restless of those clear whites remained on Holly's vision as might the flutter of a caged bird's wings.*

The reception was at Winifred's in Green Street.

"They're always so amusing—weddings," Winifred murmured, finding Soames after a brief word with the baronet. *Soames was curiously still, and Winifred saw at once what was dictating his immobility. To his right was George Forsyte, to his left Annette and Prosper Profond. He could not move without either* the baronet or George *seeing those two together, or the reflection of them in George Forsyte's japing eyes. He was quite right not to be taking notice.*

"They say Timothy's sinking," he said glumly.

"Where will you put him, Soames?"

"Highgate." He counted on his fingers. "It will make twelve of them there, including wives. How do you think Fleur looks?"

"Remarkably well."

Soames nodded. He had never seen her look prettier, yet he still *could not rid himself of the impression that this business was unnatural—remembering still that crushed figure burrowing into the corner of the sofa. From that night to this day he had received from her no confidences. He knew from his chauffeur that she had made one more attempt on Robin Hill and drawn blank—an empty house, no one at home. He knew that she had received a letter, but not what was in it, except that it had made her hide herself and cry. Well, there it was!* Michael Mont *seemed quite delirious about her. Annette, too, had been in favor of it. "Let her marry this young man. He is a nice boy—not so highty-flighty as he seems,"* she had said. *His wife, whatever her conduct, had clear eyes and an almost depressing amount of common* sense. So, *he had settled fifty thousand on Fleur, taking care that there was no cross settlement in case it didn't turn out well. Could it turn out well? She had not got over that other boy—he knew.*

Winifred's voice broke on his reverie.

"Why? Of all wonders—June!"

She must not have been at the church.

There, in a djibbah—what things she wore!—with her hair straying from under a fillet, Soames saw his cousin, and Fleur going forward to greet her. The two passed from their view out on to the stairway.

"Really," said Winifred, "she does the most impossible things! Fancy her coming!"

These could have been the words of my own mother at one of these family gatherings, echoed almost immediately by my father with: "Who does she think she is?"

"What made you ask her?" muttered Soames.

"Because I thought she wouldn't accept of course," Winifred replied.

* * *

On receiving her invitation, June had first thought, 'I wouldn't go near them for all the world!' and then, one morning, had awakened from a dream of Fleur waving to her from a boat with a wild unhappy gesture. Fleur was now one of her 'lame ducks' *and she had changed her mind.*

When Fleur came forward and said to her, "Do come up while I'm changing my dress," she had followed up the stairs.

Fleur locked the door.

"I suppose you think me a fool," she said, with quivering lips, "when it was to have been Jon. But what does it matter? Michael wants me and I don't care. It'll get me away from home." Diving her hand into the frills on her breast, she brought out a letter. "Jon wrote me this."

June read: "Lake Okanagan, British Columbia. I'm not coming back to England. Bless you always.—Jon."

"She's made safe you see," said Fleur.

June handed back the letter.

"That's not fair to Irene," she said; "she always told Jon he could do as he wished."

Fleur smiled bitterly. "Tell me, didn't she spoil your life too?"

June looked up. "Nobody can spoil a life, my dear. That's nonsense. Things happen, but we bob up"—said with the confidence and practicality of my Aunt Daphne.

With a sort of terror she saw the girl sink on her knees and bury her face in the djibbah. A strangled sob mounted to June's ears.

"It's all right—all right," she murmured. "Don't! There, there!"

But the point of the girl's chin was pressed ever closer into her thigh, and the sound was dreadful of her sobbing.

Well, well! It had come. She would feel better afterward! June stroked the short hair of that shapely head; and all the scattered mother-sense in her focused itself and passed through the tips of her fingers into the girl's brain.

"Don't sit down under it, my dear," she said at last. "We can't control life, but we can fight it. Make the best of things. I've had to. I held on like you; and I cried, as you're crying now. And look at me!"

Fleur raised her head; a sob merged suddenly into a little choked laugh. In truth it was a thin and rather wild and wasted spirit she was looking at, but she had brave eyes.

"All right!" she said. "I'm sorry. I shall forget him, I suppose, if I fly fast and far enough."

June left her, sitting on the bed with a cigarette between her lips and her eyes half closed, and went downstairs. In the doorway of the drawing-room stood Soames as if unquiet at his daughter's tardiness. June tossed her head and passed down on the half-landing. Her cousin Francie was standing there.

"Look!" said June, pointing with her chin at Soames. "That man's fatal!"

"How do you mean," said Francie, "Fatal?"

June did not answer her. "I shan't wait to see them off," she said. "Good-bye!"

Soames, moving to the well of the staircase, saw June go, and drew a breath of satisfaction. Why didn't Fleur come? They would miss their train. That train would bear her away from him, yet he could not help fidgeting at the thought that they would lose it.

As noted earlier, my sister Sally was always late and used to cause similar anxiety to both my mother and my father every time she displayed this tardiness. My mother would work herself up. "It's too bad!" she would say, sometimes stamping her foot. My father, a little more philosophical would simply reply: "You know how she is." And then, Sally would arrive, making a glamorous entrance and with no apology. Father would laugh under his breath and shake his head.

And then Fleur came down, running in her tan-coloured frock and black velvet cap, and passed him into the drawing-room. He saw her kiss her mother, her aunt, Val's wife, Imogen, and then come forth, quick and pretty as ever. How would she treat him at that last moment of her girlhood? He couldn't hope for much!

Her lips pressed the middle of his cheek.

"Daddy!" she said, and was past and gone. Daddy! She hadn't called him that for years. He drew a long breath and followed slowly down. There was all the folly with that confetti stuff and the rest of it to go through with, yet. But he would like just to catch her smile, if she leaned out, though they would hit her in the eye with the shoe, if they didn't take care. Young Mont's voice said fervently in his ear:

"Good-bye, sir; and thank you! I'm so fearfully bucked."

"Good-bye," he said; "don't miss your train."

He stood on the bottom step but three. They were in the car now; and there was that stuff, showering, and there went the shoe. A flood of something welled up in Soames, and—he didn't know—he couldn't see!

CHAPTER ELEVEN

THE LAST OF THE OLD FORSYTES

Shortly after Fleur's wedding, Uncle Timothy died—*the only man who hadn't heard of the Great War—the end of the old Forsyte family on earth. For Smither and Cook poor Mr. Timothy must now take a harp and sing in the company of Miss Forsyte, Mrs. Julia, Miss Hester; with Mr. Jolyon, Mr. Swithin, Mr. James, Mr. Roger and Mr. Nicholas. Whether Mrs. Hayman would be there was more doubtful, seeing that she had been cremated.* As aforementioned, there was still that doubt among devout Christians, even Forsytes, whether the burned body allowed for a place in heaven.

Cook *cried while Timothy was being prepared, and they all had sherry afterward out of the yearly Christmas bottle, which would not be needed now. Ah! dear! She had been there five-and-forty years and Smither three-and-forty! And now they would be going to a tiny house in Tooting, to live on their savings and what Miss Hester had so kindly left them—for to take fresh service after the glorious past—No! But they would just like to see Mr. Soames again, and Mrs. Dartie, and Miss Francie, and Miss Euphemia. And even if they had to take their own cab, they felt they must go to the funeral. For six years Mr. Timothy had been their baby, getting younger and younger every day, till at last he had been too young to live.*

It fell to Soames to issue invitations for the funeral. He had them drawn up by Gradman in his office—only blood relations, and no

665

flowers. Six carriages were ordered. The Will would be read afterwards at the house.

He arrived at eleven o'clock to see that all was ready. At a quarter past old Gradman came in black gloves and crape on his hat. He and Soames stood in the drawing-room waiting. At half-past eleven the carriages drew up in a long row. But no one else appeared. Gradman said:

"It surprises me, Mr. Soames. I posted the notices myself."

"I don't know," said Soames; "he'd lost touch with the family."

The way they had flocked to Fleur's wedding and abstained from Timothy's funeral, seemed to show some vital change, or were they afraid of what might be in the old man's will?

At twelve o'clock the procession left the door; Timothy alone in the first carriage under glass. Then Soames alone; then Gradman alone; then Cook and Smither together.

At Highgate cemetery, they walked up two and two—Soames and Gradman, Cook and Smither—to the family vault. It was not very distinguished for the funeral of the last old Forsyte.

Soames took Gradman into his carriage on the way back to the Bayswater Road with a certain glow in his heart. He had a surprise in pickle for the old chap who had served the Forsytes four-and-fifty years—a treat that was entirely his doing. How well he remembered saying to Timothy the day after Aunt Hester's funeral: "Well, Uncle Timothy, there's Gradman. He's taken a lot of trouble for the family. What do you say to leaving him five thousand?" and his surprise, seeing the difficulty there had been in getting Timothy to leave anything, when Timothy had nodded. And now the old chap would be pleased as Punch, for Mrs. Gradman, he knew, had a weak heart, and their son had lost a leg in the War. It was extraordinarily gratifying to Soames to have left him five thousand pounds of Timothy's money. Back at the house, they sat down together in the little drawing-room. Soames faced Gradman; and crossing his legs began:

"This is the last Will and Testament of me Timothy Forsyte of The Bower Bayswater Road London...

Soames was the only person who knew the content of the will. There were only two immediate beneficiaries—himself, to whom Timothy had left one thousand pounds, and Gradman who was to receive that five thousand pounds. All other monies were to be set in a trust to hold until all living male descendents of 'Superior Dosset' at the time of Timothy's death had passed on, and some were only babies. Then, any male descendents born after Timothy's death, and after all the now living had deceased, would receive equal portions of the trust on attaining the age of twenty-one. Had this somehow leaked out to those living Forsytes, to the likes of George and young Nicholas who would now receive nothing?—Perhaps Smither or Cook?—maybe, for none of the family had chosen to pay their last respects.

Gradman made quick lawyers' calculations.

"Why, in a hundred years it'll be twenty million! And we shan't live to see it! It is a Will!"

Soames said dryly: "Anything may happen. The State might take the lot; they're capable of anything in these days."

"And carry five," said Gradman to himself. "I forgot—Mr. Timothy's in Consols; we shan't get more than two per cent. with this income tax. To be on the safe side, say eight million. Still, that's a pretty penny."

Soames rose and handed him the Will. "You're going into the City. Take care of that, and do what's necessary. Advertise; but there are no debts. When's the sale?"

"Tuesday week," said Gradman. "Life or lives in bein' and twenty-one years afterward—it's a long way off. But I'm glad he's left it in the family..."

The sale was more freely attended than the funeral, though not by Cook and Smither, for Soames had taken it on himself to give them their heart's desires. Winifred was present, Euphemia, and Francie, and Eustace had come in his car. The miniatures, Barbizons, and J.R. drawings had been bought in by Soames; and relics of no marketable value were set aside in an off-room for members of the family who cared to have momentoes.

I remember at The Breach after Granny Longley's funeral, the momentoes all laid out in the dining room for my father, Biddy, Gyles and Dennis to make their division, while we in the younger generation, along with cousins like Audrie, and the devoted and beloved retainer, Miss Coath, sat in the drawing room fortified by the wine that my grandmother had specifically left us for the occasion. There was something terribly sad about this moment—it was the end of an era— the pruning of a 'Forsyte' tree—the Longley tree.

At The Bower *not one piece of furniture, no picture or porcelain figure appealed to modern taste. It was painful to Soames to see the chairs his aunts had sat on, the little grand piano they had practically never played, the books whose outsides they had gazed at, the china they had dusted, the curtains they had drawn, the hearth-rug which had warmed their feet; above all, the beds they had lain and died in—sold to little dealers, and the housewives of Fulham. And yet—what could one do? Buy them and stick them in a lumber room.* My sister Sally, tried to do this when rescuing beautiful items of furniture from Granny and Grandpa Collings' home. She stored them at a friend's house, Beau Lodge in Beckenham, where many of them sat for half a century.

No; Soames thought in that sale room, *they had to go the way of all flesh and furniture, and be worn out. But when they put up Aunt Ann's sofa and were going to knock it down for thirty shillings, he cried out, suddenly: "Five pounds!" The sensation was considerable, and the sofa his.*

When that little sale was over in the fusty sale room, and those Victorian ashes scattered, Soames *went out into the misty October sunshine feeling as if cosiness had died out of the world, and the board 'To Let' was up, indeed.*

He made his way to *the Goupenor Gallery. That chap Jolyon's water-colours were on view there. He went in to look down his nose at them—it might give him some faint satisfaction. The news had trickled through from June to Val's wife, from Val to his mother, from her to Soames, that the house—the fatal house at Robin Hill—was for sale, and Irene going to join her boy out in British Columbia, or some such place. For one wild moment the thought had come to Soames; 'Why shouldn't I buy it back? I meant it for...!' No sooner come and gone. Too lugubrious a triumph; with too many humiliating memories for himself and Fleur. She would never live there after what had happened. No the place must go its way to some peer or profiteer. It had been a bone of contention from the first, the shell of the feud; and with the woman gone, it was an empty shell. 'For Sale or To Let'.*

He passed through the first of the two rooms in the Gallery. There was certainly a body of work! And now that the fellow was dead it did not seem so trivial. 'His father and my father; he and I; his child and mine!' thought Soames. So it had gone on! And all about that woman!

Soames made his way out from the exhibition without buying anything when to his surprise he saw *Irene, herself, coming in. So she had not gone yet, and was still paying farewell visits to that fellow's remains! But when he had gone by he could not for the life of him help looking back. This, then, was finality—the heat and stress of his life, the madness and the longing thereof, the only defeat he had known, would be over when she faded from his view this time. But, she too looked back. Suddenly she lifted her gloved hand, her lips smiled faintly, her dark eyes seemed to speak. It was the turn of Soames to make no answer to that smile and that little farewell wave; he went out into the fashionable street quivering from head to foot. He knew what she had meant to say: "Now that I am going for ever out of the reach of you and yours—forgive me; I wish you well." It hurt; yes—more than if she had kept her mask unmoved, her hand unlifted.*

Three days later, Soames visited Highgate Cemetery *and mounted through its white forest to the Forsyte vault. Close to the cedar, above catacombs of columbaria, tall, ugly, and individual, it looked like an apex of the competitive system. He could remember a discussion wherein Swithin had advocated the addition to its face of the pheasant proper. The proposal had been rejected in favour of a wreath in stone, above the stark words: 'The family vault of Jolyon Forsyte: 1850'. It was in good order. All trace of the recent internment had been removed, and its sober grey gloomed reposefully in the sunshine. The whole family lay there now, except old Jolyon's wife, who had gone back under a contract to her own family vault in Suffolk; old Jolyon himself lying at Robin Hill; and Susan Hayman, cremated so that none might know where she might be. Soames gazed at it with satisfaction—massive, needing little attention; and this was important, for he was well aware that no one would attend to it when he was gone.*

He reflected on his life as he considered how many people had been buried in Highgate since 1850—*a lot of English life crumbled to mould and dust!*

In April, 2009, my Uncle Dennis passed away after a brief fight with lung cancer. He died at his home, Manor House, the beautiful little village house in Sandhurst where he had lived so happily with my Aunt Pat after the bitterness of his divorce from our beloved Aunt Brigid. The day before his passing, he had sorted out his affairs with my cousin, his second son, Robert Longley. That night, Pat had read to him from the autobiography of a friend of theirs. The next morning she found Dennis gone. He had died peacefully in his own bed. Just the week before, he had discussed with his brother, my Uncle Gyles, who had called him from Paris, how he might install a stair lift to help him up the old stairs of Manor House. It was never to be installed. It was Eastertide, the time of both my mother's and father's passing a year or two before, a time when the apple orchards, pears, and plums, create a patchwork quilt of pink and white blossoms over the weald of Kent—the garden of England. The Friday after Easter, Uncle Dennis was buried in the churchyard of the ancient medieval parish church of St. Nicholas on a hilltop beside the village of Sandhurst with commanding views over this wealden scene. His last remaining brother, my Uncle Gyles will be buried in Paris, his sister in Scotland. I cannot help feeling like Soames as I think of Dennis atop that wealden hill overlooking the country that he so loved—our family's wealden roots. From Highgate, the spirits of the Forsytes look out from their hill top mausoleum over the London that made them what they were. From St. Nicholas' Churchyard in Sandhurst, Cranbrook, my Uncle Dennis, the youngest son of Oliver Longley's oldest son, looks out over the 'beloved acres' of my family, over the yeoman lands of Hocker Edge, Marden, Frame Farm, and ultimately of our beloved home, The Breach—the lands that made and became our experience of 'Forsythia'.

Soames sat at Highgate *for a long time dreaming his career, faithful to the scut of his possessive instinct, warming himself even with its failures.*

'To Let'—the Forsyte age and way of life, when a man owned his soul, his investments, and his woman, without check or question. And now the State had, or would have, his investments, his woman had herself, and God knew who had his soul. 'To Let'—that sane and simple creed!

POSTSCRIPT

I lost my four grandparents during the two years from 1968 to 1970—first Longley, then Hovenden, and finally Cuthbertson and Collings. From Granny Mabs' estate, my sisters and I were each left the sum of five hundred pounds. It was not really enough to make a substantial investment, but it was nonetheless a fair gift in 1969. As I flipped through an atlas, looking at the areas in the middle east that I had visited a few years before when on that expedition to Israel with my friends from Cambridge, I saw on the far right of the double page, a map of the subcontinent of India—once the crown jewel of the Empire—the purpose of 'Forsythia'. I looked at Diane.

"Let's go to India," I suggested.

Diane and I had been traveling companions together in Italy, and we enjoyed taking in the art, culture, and history of foreign lands.

"Why not?" she agreed.

We spent our inheritance from Granny Mabs traveling to India. We went out on the old Orient Express. We were on one of the last journeys of that once so famous 'Forsyte' train—the setting of Agatha Christie's classic mystery, *Murder on the Orient Express*. It possessed the fading glory of its past from Paris to Venice, but from Venice to Istanbul, our one old carriage was shunted on to a series of local trains taking us through the Balkans, passing some of the most spectacular scenery of Europe, but by 1970, all behind the 'Iron Curtain'. We could not leave our carriage at any time and our steward literally cooked for us on a potbelly stove at one end of our locked in sleeper car. This journey through the Balkans and subsequent journeys in India were, however, on the last trains we traveled in our lives that were pulled by steam locomotives. With a spectacular belching of black coal smoke and white steam, the train snaked its way through European Turkey to finally deliver us to Istanbul. It slowly skirted past the city's curtain walls beneath the spectacular domes and minarets of the Blue Mosque, Santa Sophia, and the Topkapi Palace beside the sparkling waters of the Bosphorus. Across this divide between Europe and Asia, we could see the long façade of Florence Nightingale's Scutari Hospital. Here, Turkish and English soldiers had recuperated during the Crimean War of the 1850s during the dawn of 'Forsythia'.

Istanbul was Diane's first encounter with Asia, although I had spent time in Turkey on my way out to Israel in 1965. It was exciting for her to experience the souks and bazaars with their gaudy mix of gold, gem stones, bronze, copper, and brass; sandalwood, ivory, and ebony; and the rich patterns of carpets, rugs, and genie-like gossamer muslin. Old men, with sunburned wrinkled faces, smoked hookahs that until then we had only known in the drawings by Sir John Tenniel of the caterpillar seated on his mushroom in *Alice in Wonderland*. It was exciting and we now knew we were on our way to India.

Perhaps we could now feel something of the curiosity and apprehension of the young subalterns and memsahibs on their way out to their first postings East. Those great P and O steamships stopped at Port Said, Egypt, before passing through the lifeline of the Empire, the Suez Canal. There, as they came down the gangplank, the new recruits for imperial service saw the 'gully gully' man on the dockside magically producing little chicks from his person; 'Muhammad' waiting with a flea-bitten horse to take them into town in a dusty carriage; and like Diane and me in Istanbul, they encountered the souks and bazaars of the East for the first time.

Diane and I had originally hoped that we could travel all the way to India by train, but unfortunately the route from Istanbul to India passes through territory that in 1970 was a part of the Soviet Union. It was too complicated to get the appropriate visas, and so we flew from Istanbul to Delhi.

At the end of *The Forsyte Saga* we saw Jon Forsyte traveling to Canada to make for himself a new life away from the complication of his impossible relationship with his cousin Fleur. Earlier, we had also seen him travel with his mother to Spain, again with the idea that the excitement of foreign sights and aromas would take his mind off Fleur. In a way, it was the same for me. I traveled to India with Diane just two months after I had unsuccessfully proposed to June Kennedy at that street café in Paris. This dangerous relationship that had threatened my position at Tullamaine Castle in Ireland and my future with the Albertini family had interesting parallels. June was now, officially out of my life, but was she? My heart still yearned for her and it was difficult not to see her when she returned to Ireland from Normandy. My journey to India, therefore, although not planned that way, was a chance for me to break from this dangerous liaison. The ghost of June followed me to India, however, much as the ghost of Fleur had lived with Jon Forsyte in Spain. In some ways, I regret this, as the experience of my first visit to India was very special and could have been enjoyed all the more if there had not been a part of me that was wanting to get back to Ireland. In 1970, India was just twenty-two years on from its independence. The trappings of 'Forsythia' were still very evident in the great subcontinent, and in a sense this journey shared with my sister was the swan song of our 'Forsythia' upbringing.

We arrived in Delhi at 4:30 a.m. By the time a taxi took us from the airport, dawn was breaking over the once imperial capital. In that mist of dawn, Diane and I first saw the Rajpath—the great wide boulevard leading up to the Vice-Regal Lodge, once the power of the king emperor's throne. By 1970, it was the President's Palace, but for Diane and me it was still the Vice-Regal mansion with its brown, be-domed, stone edifice behind imperial gates still mounted with the British royal arms. Guards of the Indian army stood at the sentry boxes as if they had been trained at Buckingham Palace.

Our taxi took us to the Imperial Hotel, a structure that still breathed its colonial magnificence in a decayed dress coat. What a thrill it was, however, to enter a lobby where parrots and parakeets flew freely in and out from large open louvered windows and screeched above the potted palms. Staff members were still dressed in elaborate Maharajah uniforms with colorful turbans and silk sashes. We were greeted with a refreshing fruit drink before signing the register—a register that had signed-in countless 'Forsytes' before us throughout two centuries of imperial rule. Cooling fans and even an occasional swaying punkah were the air-conditioning, and open windows brought the sounds of the waking streets to us, drifting up to our room—a mix of bicycle bells, motor horns like claxons, and the clip-clop of tonkas. The cost—five pounds a night! We had arrived.

In Delhi, we explored the India of our immediate forebears, but also the great past of the moguls and their architectural wonders at the Red Fort, Humayan's tomb, and the Jamma Mashid mosque. We wondered at the blend of Hindu and Moslem styles at Akbar's tomb celebrating that mogul emperor's lifelong desire to reconcile the two great faiths of his dominion. We saw the extreme contrast of rich and poor—the red sandstone, the inlaid marquetry of precious stones, and the white marble filigree, looking out onto a canvas and corrugated iron city of slums lit by swaying hurricane lamps and delivering the pungent odors of open sewers, spices, and cooking chapatis. Then, by train, we traveled to Agra.

Here was the Red Fort of Shah Jhan, set on the banks of the Jumna—the palace of cooling waterways—the Alhambra of the East, of which the great mogul wrote: 'If there is paradise, it is here, it is here, it is here...' But of course, even more impressive to the traveler is Shah Jhan's greatest edifice, the Taj Mahal, the tomb he built for his wife. The entrance gate is impressive, but once passed through, the sight of the great white marble tomb gleaming at the end of long reflecting pools is one of the wonders of the modern world. The sun catches its great dome at all angles throughout the day as does the pale luminosity of the moon by night, and both cast shadows through the arches of the twin mosques that flank the bejeweled structure where monkeys play. It is hard to know which is more impressive, the actual structure against the clear Indian sky, or its reflection in the pool. Our young Indian guide touched our post-imperial souls when he explained the complexity of the thousand fountains built into the fabric of these pools. They are fed by a very intricate system of wheels carrying the water up from the passing River Jumna, a tributary of the sacred River Ganges. In 1970, since the British left India in 1948, the fountains had only played twice. The first time was to honor the coronation tour of Her Majesty Queen Elizabeth II on her first visit to India as head of the British Commonwealth of Nations, India having retained membership in this ex-imperial club. The second time, was to honor the visit of the granddaughter of Lord Curzon, who was Viceroy of India in the Edwardian period and did more than any other representative of the King Emperor Edward VII to restore these great mogul monuments, witnesses to India's pre-imperialist past. In the immediate decade after independence, the Indian people still had such respect for Lord Curzon that they felt obligated to show this by allowing the fountains of the Taj Mahal to play for this visit of his granddaughter.

The other great monument outside Agra is the lost city of Fatepur Sikri. This was built by the mogul emperor, Akbar the Great, as his capital and in keeping with his lifelong belief that he could harmonize the Hindu and Moslem faiths. The city is an incredible mix of both architectural styles. It was only inhabited for a few years before the watercourse that fed it dried up. As a result we are left today with the ruins of Akbar's dream, but what incredibly romantic ruins they are with their great courts, tiers of cupolas, and intricate marble filigree. In 1970, there were few tourists visiting India other than us curious 'Brits' whose families had almost all been touched by the 'Crown Jewel of the British Empire' over a two-hundred-year period. Diane and I were able to visit these incredible mogul monuments virtually alone, although usually accompanied by a young Indian boy, whose main task was to tap on stones to check for snakes. We were very curious throughout our visit to India to feel out how the India of 'Forsythia' was looked on by this newly independent nation. We were surprised what respect and nostalgia we still found.

My uncle, Gyles Longley, was able to help us on our journey, as he was at that time still a managing director for Gestetner, the French duplicating company, then as significant as Xerox, and was able to provide us with a Gestetner chauffeur-bearer to drive us around vast areas of central India and Rajasthan. This enabled us to visit Udaipur, Jaipur, and Jodhpur. Rajahstan is such a colorful area, noted for its fabulous maharajahs with their palaces and past tiger hunts. In Udaipur, we stayed at the newly opened Lake Palace Hotel that originally was a summer residence built in the artificial lake that the maharajahs of Udaipur constructed in the heyday of their splendor. It compliments an island sanctuary that Shah Jhan also built in the lake—a sort of 'ivory tower' where the great mogul wrote poetry. From the Lake Palace, which was a very open building with internal courtyard gardens, there were magnificent views across to the vast, rambling, terraced palace that was then still the official residence of the maharajah. As we were served dinner by bearers in the flamboyant livery of His Highness, golden rays of sunset caught the ancient stones and domes across the water.

Udaipur impressed me greatly. Its streets were crowded, teaming with life, but so colorful. Rich and poor alike were dressed in the most elaborate saris in colors of red, gold, yellow, and green. Later, I captured a street scene in Udaipur on canvas. I believe it was the best oil I ever painted. It featured an Indian artisan copper-beater working outside the crumbling white walls of his open shop. A lady in a beautiful red and yellow sari was watching him, holding a ceramic jar on her head with one hand and clasping the hand of a little girl with her other. The girl was wearing a shiny shift in apricot, gold, and silver thread, and beside them stood an old battered leather suitcase. Within this painting, you could almost breathe the dust of this Udaipur street scene, smell the pungent odors, and feast on the brightness of the colors—quintessential India. I remember, too, as Diane and I watched this scene, all of a sudden an elephant came wandering down the street, its bells clanging. This scene in Udaipur became the inspiration for a description that I later incorporated into my novel *Two Thousand Years Later*—an elephant in the streets of Udaipur.

> *Tired, Jeremy went to bed. In his dreams that night he saw himself as a young Indian boy...*
> *The sun beat down and dust swirled in the streets that were filled with putrefied dung. The streets didn't look dramatically different from those with which he had become familiar. Painted elephants guarded the doorways into houses and stores. People mingled with sacred cows that had bells around their necks. But there were no bicycles, no motor scooters and no rusting cars. No overcrowded buses honked their horns to clear a passage. Bullock carts were more numerous, elephants were more in evidence, and camels abounded. Yet the people looked much the same. Their clothes were little different— great color mingled with dirty rags. Graceful women carried water pots and baskets on their heads. Men sat squatting in doorways watching the world go by while others drove their beasts onward with sticks and shouts. There were beggars with crippled limbs and monks with shaven heads. The monks wore long, yellow, brown, and red saffron robes. Artisans sat under colorful awnings, spinning and weaving, shaping clay and working wood. Boys like Jeremy seemed everywhere. Some were thieving, others just playing and laughing, running about without any apparent purpose. Jeremy sensed himself amongst them. He felt a compassion for these street companions. They seemed to respect him and called out to him by*

name. "Ravi! Ravi!" they shouted. They called to him because
he was their leader. He brought water to the beggars and had
a kind word for the cripples.
Then, as 'Ravi' in his dream, Jeremy turned from one of the
side streets into a more major thoroughfare that led down to
the river. The road was teeming with life. People were run-
ning, many were laughing and farther up Ravi could hear the
trumpeting of elephants. The elephants moved into the crowd,
clearing a path through 'the untouchables' as Ravi knew his
kind were called. Ravi watched as they passed. The giant
beasts were decorated with golden tassels and the mahara-
jah's coat of arms. Heavy bells hung from their sides clanging
with the elephants' ungainly motion. Royal guests, including
white rajahs in elaborate nineteenth-century uniforms, swayed
in their howdahs, while boys little older than Ravi sat behind
the elephants' ears. The boys wore fine clothes, and held their
heads up high as they swatted flies away from the elephants'
hides. Other boys held colorful umbrellas above the howdahs
to protect His Royal Highness' guests from the glaring sun.
After the elephants, there seemed to be a pause in the Royal
parade. People began to mingle in the street again, waiting
for the maharajah's carriage. Ravi joined them. Many hoped
that maybe a few silver annas might fall from the royal hand,
while others, who revered the maharajah as close to heaven,
just wanted to touch his carriage with its gilded frame.

In Udaipur in 1970, it was very easy to imagine this nineteenth-century scene. The maharajah's lakeside palace was right beside the small city of ancient streets and buildings through an elaborate gateway leading from the city into the decay amid past splendor that was still His Highness' home. It had been part of the success of the British structure in imperial India that the princely states of the subcontinent continued to be governed by their local rulers, and only the old areas originally governed by the British East India Company were under direct rule from Westminster. However, the whole subcontinent was under the suzerainty of the king emperor, of whom the last, in 1948 was King George VI. This came about after the Indian mutiny of 1858 when the mogul emperor, a gentle poet, was deposed, and Her Majesty Queen Victoria proclaimed Empress of India in his place. The maharajahs, therefore, were essential to the British government of India, holding princely purses of crown funds to rule their respectful states. After independence, these princely purses came to an end, and the elaborate wealth and prestige of the maharajahs waned. At Udaipur, however, His Highness' presence was still felt in 1970. The population of this Rajahstan city might still witness their prince out in the streets, although elephants and gilded carriages would be a less likely sight than His Highness' old Rolls Royce or Aston Martin sports car. The palace was not quite as glamorous as it had been, and the stables for three hundred horses, thoroughbreds and polo ponies, were much reduced, but Diane and I were touched by the English gardener we met attending the gardens of the Lake Palace Hotel. His name was Hugh Davenport and he spoke with the clipped British accent of 'Forsythia'. In 1948, after independence, it had been his decision to "stay on" and continue to tend His Highness' gardens where he served as head gardener for many years. Likewise, at least for a decade, Great-uncle Bert Cuthbertson 'stayed on' in Bombay, now Mumbai, building bridges and dams for Sturtevants.

Before we flew south to Bombay, Diane and I were driven by our Gestetner chauffeur to Jaipur and Jodphur. In 1970, there were no less than five palaces around Jaipur, named "the pink city" because of the extraordinary color and luminosity of the sandstone. Three of these palaces were still in use by the Singh family, the hereditary maharajahs. A member of this family, Prince Aran Singh, was up at Cambridge with me in the early '60s. I met him once, as at times, mostly through rowing circles, our social groups meshed. One of their palaces in Jaipur was, like the Lake Palace in Udaipur, a luxury hotel. We visited there one night, as the old palace hotel, the Ramburgh Palace, had been recommended to us by our Aunt Daphne, who had a year or two before visited India with her husband Gordon Noble. Many of these maharajahs' palaces are true luxury hotels today, but in truth, in 1970 they had only recently been converted to hostelry and showed themselves then as decayed gentility with ancient plumbing and peeling paint. However, with imagination it was not hard to conjure up the grandeur of the recent Raj. I found it interesting to see how the lawns were maintained by a fleet of dhoti-clad men seated on the grass cutting the blades with sickles—such I imagine had been the timeless method used throughout imperial 'Forsythia'.

When we flew, it was in small Dakota or Fokker twin-engine aircraft of Indian Airlines. It seemed that at every airport we passed through we were offered an English breakfast of fried eggs and bacon with toast and marmalade. Apparently, this British tradition had survived even in the tropics! What was even more incredible was that these breakfasts were free! It was considered part of the flight. As we finished our eggs and bacon at the Delhi airport before flying south to Bombay, a clipped 'Forsyte' voice called out my name. I looked up to see a young man who had rowed with me seven years before in the St. Catherine's College 3rd VIII, when in the Cambridge Lent Races we had won our oars.

"What are you doing in India?" fell from both our lips.

"Traveling…wanting to see what is left of the 'Crown Jewel'," we agreed.

For a moment, I thought back on the three percent. It was the three percent who had "gone out" to run all aspects of the subcontinent—its schools and universities, law courts, railways, and engineering projects; its missions, factories, and most of all its police and armed forces. The three percent were tied together by old school neckwear, whether it was Eton or Harrow, Rugby or Tonbridge, Oxford or Cambridge. We were the great white rajahs. Many of us knew each other or had acquaintances in common; we were 'Forsytes', but by 1970, we were back in India to see what had survived of our Empire "after the sun had set."

Bombay was of special interest to Diane and me as it was here that Great-uncle Bert and Aunt Ruby had lived, and it was here that just a decade before, our cousin John Cuthbertson had gone for his summer holidays, when he lived with his Auntie Mabel on Wickham Way—our Granny Mabs. As we were spending the money Granny had left us, it seemed only fitting we should visit the haunts where her brother had spent a substantial part of his adventurous life. We saw the famed Malabar Gardens on their hill beside the sea, where in young John's childhood I have no doubt his 'Ayah' took him out for walks. The gardens are noted for their animal topiary that fascinated young sahibs.

Other relics from Bombay's imperial past are the incredible façade of the busy railway station—a combination of all the great terminals of London dressed in an Indian veneer—and the Madan—a vast area of grass and trees between the main buildings of past commerce and the principal highway running up the peninsular. Here, as in the past, cricket is played—cricket the great glue of the Empire.

Everywhere the 'Forsytes' of the Empire roamed, they took England's sacred game with them—the game of their schooldays. The natives took to the game, and many imperial capitals had their equivalent of

Bombay's Madan. We find 'The Madan' in Kualur Lumpur, Malaysia, in Singapore, and in a more formalized form in the great cricket grounds of Australia, New Zealand, and South Africa. However, among the native peoples, it was the Indians who became the greatest cricketers. By late 'Forsythia', the MCC tie, standing for Marylebone Cricket Club, the governing force at Lords in London controlling the rules of the game, was almost as important a neck tie as the old school tie itself, and contributed just as keenly to the network that ran the Empire.

As we have noted, Tonbridge was a keen cricketing school. It's verdant field, 'The Head' was one of the finest of all the public school cricket grounds. It was famous as far back as the 1860s when a magnificent print was made of the school titled *The Cricket Match*. 'The Head' looked much the same then as now, with the school behind the Quad as its backdrop. In fact, I had an uncanny experience with this print that 'Forsythia' somehow had spread around the world, even to the United States. I was sitting in a restaurant in Springfield, Missouri, and looked up to see my old school peering down at me from across 'The Head'. There, in a gilded frame was the famous print: *The Cricket Match, Tonbridge School, Kent* complete with spectators in crinolines and curled dandy top hats.

In Bombay, Diane and I stayed at the venerable old Taj Mahal Hotel on the waterfront by the Gateway to India, the gray stone mogul-style arch that had been built to welcome Their Imperial Majesties King George V and Queen Mary in 1912 for the Delhi Durbar. Here, the first imperial British sovereigns to visit India stepped off their royal launch to set foot among their Indian subjects. While they were staying in Bombay, before taking the royal train to Delhi, they visited the racecourse at Poona. As a result, subsequent Poona race meetings became an Indian 'Royal Ascot' attended annually by the viceroy in an open carriage, and a royal enclosure well frequented by the racing maharajahs, who bred the finest horses. I have no doubt that at some time Great-uncle Bert attended the races at Poona, because I have photographs of the vice-regal carriage procession at the track, probably taken in about 1938 by Uncle 'Moley', as my mother always called him, and sent back to Granny Mabs.

Throughout our stay in India, Diane and I had eaten many versions of chicken curry. I have to say that the curries concocted at the Tandoori restaurant in the Taj Mahal Hotel were the best. In Rajastan, we had stayed in several rest houses, or state guest houses that had been set up along the road routes of imperial India to provide basic comfort for traveling subalterns, sahibs, memsahibs, and colonial administrators. Their uniform diet of scraggy chicken curry was adequate, but usually rather watery. In Bombay it was rich. Obviously this diet of curries agreed with us both, for in all our travels in India, where 'Delhi belly' was a long time music hall joke, Diane and I never had a day when we were sick. It is also interesting that curry has remained one of Diane's favorite foods, and to this day my other sister, Sally, always takes Diane out to a nice Indian restaurant on her birthday.

After visiting the Elephanta caves on an island across the bay from Bombay, we flew up the Ghats and back onto the Deccan to visit Aurangabad and the incredible Hindu and Buddhist cave temples carved out of the rockface at Ellora and Ajanta. The temples date back as far as the second century and must have taken many years to complete. The intricate carvings of elephant jousts, and flora and fauna, at Ellora are as breathtaking as the paintings within the stuppas of the Buddhist caves at Ajanta and Elephanta. I couldn't help thinking of Dr. Aziz, the sad victim of British misunderstanding in E. M. Forster's great interpretation of India in the 1920s: *A Passage to India*. In his attempt to impress the British memsahibs, poor Aziz arranges a wonderful excursion to ancient caves where he becomes framed on charges of rape. His innocence is obvious, but British administered justice sided with the alleged 'Forsyte' victim, who was suffering from hallucinations brought on in the caves. The whole story set in all the pomp and glory of imperial India, shows the deep division of caste, most notably the accepted division of the British Raj and its brown-skinned subjects. About the time Diane and I visited India, *A Passage to India* was made into an amazing film, but I was already familiar with E. M. Forster's work as he was himself a Tonbridgian and we wore the same old school tie. Like John Galsworthy, Forster saw the winds of change in the 1920s and illustrated that message within the depth of 'Forsythia'.

The Forsyte Saga was first published in 1922, and as I am sure John Galsworthy intended, it was to be the entirety of the Forsyte chronicles. In the aftermath of the Great War, Galsworthy, himself a 'Forsyte', like Soames, probably considered 'Forsythia' to be about to close—'To Let'. As the labor movement took hold, social unrest increased, and income tax took its bite, it seemed that 'Forsyte' survival was unlikely. It had died with old Timothy Forsyte in October, 1920.

However, 'Forsythia' did not die. In fact, in the spirit of the brave new world, it took on a new lease of life. During the 'General Strike' of 1926, it was 'Forsyte' volunteers who fired the steam locomotives keeping the railways running, ran canteens and drove the buses. They overcame socialism in their own way—possession. They put off the evil day.

Between the wars, 'Forsythia' actually reached its greatest heights, and Galsworthy continued the saga. The full 'Forsyte Chronicles', therefore, carry on the story of Fleur and Mont and the other Forsytes of their generation in *A Modern Comedy* and *End of the Chapter.*

Despite the agricultural depression, the Welsh miners' strikes, and even the abdication crisis, which took 'divorce', an important theme throughout the saga, to the highest level, 'Forsytes' lived on in great comfort, enjoying the advantages technology had brought them in that brave new world. They spoke to each other on their telephones, drove magnificent cars, and traveled to the outposts of their Empire and elsewhere in the most luxurious ocean liners that were ever built—the largest moving objects ever designed by man. Some even started to fly, first in great airships and ultimately in jet planes. Railways united every town in Great Britain and branch lines almost every village, and steam engines built in centers like Swindon, England, were exported to run an amazing network of railways in India, Africa, and Malaya, as well as the Dominions. 'Forsytes' continued to govern, manage, and build up the greatest empire the world had ever known, and in its outposts around the world—those colonial 'Clubs'—they dressed for dinner, sang their Gilbert and Sullivan operas, and planned their endeavors—building dams, improving agriculture, alleviating starvation, administering 'British' justice, and teaching millions of natives to read and write in the mother tongue. Others, like those in the 'Saga' were in business, the law, medicine, banking, publishing, and other 'City' activities, keeping the center intact. Just as they pulled together in the 'General Strike', so they pulled together again in the Second World War. They survived, not just the war, but even the new welfare state, and they signed up a new generation of 'Forsytes' to attend those public schools and carry on the endeavor. I belong to that generation.

Those of us born in the 1940s were the last generation of 'Forsytes'. We were teenagers before the dissolution of the British Empire, 'The Beatles', or the sexual revolution of the swinging sixties. Diane and I belonged to this last generation of 'Forsytes'; my younger sister

Sally, four years younger than me, barely knew it. She was a teenager in those changing sixties when 'Forsythia' collapsed—a part of the baby boomer generation that embraced those changes—civil rights, relaxation of dress codes, and sexual freedom encouraged by birth control. The swinging sixties almost passed me by as I lingered on in that continuation of 'Forsythia' that surrounded my unusual life in Ireland. For me, perhaps, 'Forsythia' ended with the sale of Tullamaine Castle in 1977. Nonetheless, all three of us were influenced by the struggles we observed in the manner in which our grandparents and our parents faced their changed world, and little snippets of the 'Forsythia' of their youths could be glimpsed to their graves. We were not alone. All the descendents of the three percent could make similar observations, which is why so many of us, both initially in the late 1960s and again in 2002, could look at ourselves in those two brilliant television productions of *The Forsyte Saga* and recognize so much.

Although a good part of what I have written is a direct precis of John Galsworthy's magnificent manuscript, it is retold for the purpose of showing the story of my own 'Forsyte' family. It is not intended as a substitute for reading Galsworthy's work. In the precis, there is little acknowledgement of one of Galsworthy's greatest achievements in writing the saga—his parallel between human lives, emotions and feelings and those observed in nature. To miss this subtle interplay and evocation found in those glorious descriptive passages is to miss Galsworthy. Nobody could have embalmed that great British upper-middle class in a more convincing way, partly because he himself was a product of that class, but also because he saw its foibles and weaknesses, along with its inevitable fall. 'Forsythia' and the British Empire came and went hand in hand.

Peter Longley
January 2012

Coming Soon

THE CEDARS OF BECKENHAM

A New Novel by Peter Longley

'The mystery of an antique German doll reveals a rich tapestry

of the Twentieth Century'

To be published by Austin Macauley

in January, 2023

CPSIA information can be obtained at www.ICGtesting.com
Printed in the USA
LVOW05s0146120913

351854LV00001B/4/P